ELIZABETHANS
AT HOME

Lord Cobham and his family

ELIZABETHANS

at Home

by

LU EMILY PEARSON

STANFORD UNIVERSITY PRESS
STANFORD, CALIFORNIA, 1957

STANFORD UNIVERSITY PRESS, STANFORD, CALIFORNIA
LONDON: OXFORD UNIVERSITY PRESS

Printed in the United States of America by
Stanford University Press

Library of Congress Catalog Card Number: 57-9305

Published with the assistance of
the Ford Foundation

To My Husband

Preface

This book attempts to make a synthesis for both the student and the general reader interested in the material which is available to us about Elizabethan domestic life. It does more than merely survey the homes which Elizabethans built, the gardens in which they spent their happiest hours, and the means they used for rearing their children and preserving harmony in domestic affairs. We shall rise with them in the morning, sometimes stand among those who assisted at the intricacies of putting together various parts of their daily attire, follow them through the multitudinous duties of the home, sit with them at table, and join them at evening for family prayers. Even for the worldly, life at home followed a more or less rhythmic beat of ritual, and this rhythm, in turn, affected their very speech, which was full and high-sounding in their conduct books, in their public utterances and sermons, and even in their most intimate letters. In the conflicting forces swirling with increasing intensity and confusion at the end of the century, the home was the chief steadying influence, saving the people from the dissipation of their faculties.

Elizabethan English has its charms for the student, but its eccentricities present impediments to rapid reading. For this reason modern spelling and paraphrasing have been used in reporting the writing of this period. Many of the primary sources for this work are in the Henry E. Huntington Library, to whose assistants, especially Mary Isabel Fry, Registrar, I am indebted for innumerable courtesies. The secondary sources have been consulted in libraries in America and England, but particularly in the library of Stanford University.

Years ago Hardin Craig persuaded me to begin research on the subject of Elizabethan family relationships, and that research has been supplemented by continuous teaching in Shakespeare and Elizabethan literature. Of late others have been of very great assistance to me. Levi Fox, Director of Shakespeare's Birthplace Trust at Stratford-upon-Avon, suggested where, in addition to the great country houses, might be found English cottages, farms, and almshouses that have been in continuous use for the last four hundred years. Through the unfailing courtesies of the English people themselves it was possible to visit these places and to examine them in detail. Mr. Fox also advised me about obtaining illustrations for the book, and Mr. Ronald Worrall of Welford-on-Avon, through his extensive knowledge of English rural life, introduced me to much of its lore.

Lu Emily Pearson

San Jose State College
San Jose, California

Contents

Illustrations

ELIZABETHANS
AT HOME

CHAPTER I

HOMES AND GARDENS

*For a man's house is his castle, and home is the
safest refuge for everyone.*

SIR EDWARD COKE (1552–1623)

SOME writers today insist that the home is no longer an integral part of our civilization, but mankind still dreams of it as a refuge or as a place of relaxation or recreation. This dream Elizabethans tried to make a reality. True, the rich Elizabethan's house might be used as a depository for some showy collections to tease the covetous or as a place in which to entertain influential friends who might assist him in his struggle for power. And for the poor, home was far too often a dubious shelter in which the family ate scanty meals at irregular intervals and slept, crowded, on hard straw mattresses or in crude beds. But the self-respecting man, rich or poor, sought to maintain the integralism of his home. In its well-managed beehive industry there was no room for the laggard, yet always time for merriment and repose and worship. From this center of life emerged whatever stability was present in political, social, or religious Elizabethan England.

This deep, abiding faith in home was developed not so much by the moralists (of which there was no dearth!) as by the conditions which drove man in upon himself for entertainment or quiet ease. It was an age of distrust and fear not unlike our own; yet at the same time it was an age of yearning hope and almost compelled faith, again not unlike our own. The wisest of the preachers and moralists, however, made of this faith something good and wholesome rather than a demon urging man on to greater effort that he might secure the salvation of his soul or more and more creature comforts of food, clothing, and shelter. Then, as perhaps at any time, music was the touchstone of their civilization. Though it might differ for Puritan, Catholic, or Anglican, most households, rich or poor, recognized it as the lodestone which drew people together. Whether singing psalms or gay ditties or devotional hymns, they yielded to the spell by which their music bound them.

Maids sang at their household duties, men sang in the fields, apprentices sang at their work, and when the mother stilled her fretting babe with song, she hummed to herself as much as to the child. Often the housewife spinning with her maids was entertained by the singing of one in the group. When Shakespeare's queen said, "Take thy lute, wench! my soul grows sad with troubles; Sing and disperse 'em, if thou canst" (*Henry VIII*, III:i:1–2), she made no unusual request of a lady among her maids. Often the citizen's wife who did not help her husband in the shop might lead her servants in the singing of psalms or ditties as she supervised the routine or special labors about the house. Any incident, trivial or grief-heavy, called for emotional release; then the household became unthinkingly vocal, for no solemn inhibitions restrained their volatile emotional life until the rootlets of stoicism began their exploratory creeping into thoughtful souls. Light chatter, gay or shrill scolding, snatches of song, free interchange of opinion or quick repartee—all somehow fitted into their work, which did not leave master or mistress or servants with frayed or sodden nerves at the end of the day.

In the planned way of living in well-ordered households, servants were free from tension. Not machines, but men and women served the families to whom they felt bound by ties of genuine responsibility. More often than not they were important members of the home; they belonged to it. Yet they were not slaves; they might break the ties that bound them if they chose. Of course, some masters and mistresses abused the power that was theirs. But society itself did not condone ill treatment of workers. On their side, well-trained servants regarded themselves as very necessary to the smooth and harmonious functioning of a respected household. And so they were. They took pride in their work; they had time in which to do it well, and often they were entrusted with duties which brought them into close intimacy with the family. When they were faithful to their trust, it was not unusual for them, like other members of the family, to be remembered in the master's will.

Elizabethans sought as much spaciousness as they could afford in their homes. They were also compelled to make compromises. What, in the construction and management of their houses, reveals Elizabethan shrewdness in bargaining with life's limitations? What was special in the pattern of their domestic life?

Whether in town or country, each home had its own garden. On a pleasant day, a visitor calling by appointment on the master of the household was almost sure to be told by the servant, "You will find him walking in the garden." Then he would be ushered to an orchard with paths of grass or gravel and with flowers or vines growing about the trees. If a lady came to "gossip" with the mistress and the weather permitted receiving guests out of doors, she would expect to be shown into the garden. When wind or rain drove them indoors, fortunate Elizabethans had great halls or long galleries where they might walk for exercise or pleasure. In the great hall flanked by its musicians' gallery, members of the household often made merry among themselves and with friends.

Common people naturally made what adaptations they could in order to acquire some of the luxuries of the upper classes. The lives of the poor did not alter much, but when chance smiled upon daring speculators of the middle class, the favored ones seized eagerly the comforts and graces of domestic living within their reach. For them especially home became the best means of expressing their creative instincts, and individual taste dictated many of the building projects. A spell of home building had been cast over the entire nation as it made the old search for beauty and comfort and change.

But it was a new beauty and a new comfort they sought. Those unable to construct new houses added what new rooms they could afford in order to achieve more privacy. Then they planned how chimneys might be added and the gardens enlarged. Open beams gave way to ceilings, glazed windows gradually replaced the dark lattices or thin, translucent horn, and fine stairs succeeded the narrow, twisted stone stairways of the old houses. When glass became less expensive, as many windows were built in as the owner could afford in order to make a fine showing with them as well as with the elaborate chimneys. Some owners had movable windows and firebacks or grates in order to store them when they were compelled to be absent from home for a time, or that they might will them separately from the house, like furniture or fine paneling of rooms. When side fireplaces supplanted the open hearths in the center of the rooms, some moralists insisted the more effective way of drawing off the smoke was not an improvement, for they argued that smoke was good for both people and the timbers of the house.

In all this building activity the new individualism of Elizabethan England was clearly and definitely reflected. Meanwhile those who were dispossessed of their homes by poverty or by the dissolution of the monasteries and by the enclosure movement made a sorry picture beside the new architectural wonders. No doubt the vagabonds who could still remember the homes once theirs passed on to their children a yearning for a roof of their own or a hopelessness about ever knowing such a refuge. All during Elizabeth's reign one of her most pressing problems was to provide food and shelter for the starving and at the same time to find some means of restoring to the homeless a bit of the self-respect lost in the bitter upheaval of economic change. Perhaps the almost fierce effort to make the home as secure and as fine as the owner knew how was one means of trying to push back the frightening forces of mutability.

The construction of Elizabethan houses, although varied, was also romantic when the best architectural talent was expended on it. When this was not within the owner's reach, he used his imagination and common sense, both of which he often possessed abundantly. What plans were used? What were the various rooms, and what were the employments of each? How were the gardens laid out, and what was grown in them? Long and careful research can enable us to answer these questions and actually see Elizabethans at home.

Yet one must expect to find almost inexplicable contrasts in the houses. There were mansions of stone with fronts over three hundred feet long and with large bay windows glazed in quaint patterns. These buildings were heated by scattered fireplaces only; they had no plumbing and no proper disposal of waste and garbage until late in the century, and they were lighted at night by torches and candles and rush lights, the latter simply rushes dipped in grease. In time comforts were more numerous, but as building became a special pursuit, some owners designed their own houses and left to their builders problems of comfort and construction. In their eagerness to establish themselves socially, wealthy new families often chose for their homes whatever embellishment was most elaborate and most recent in fashion. Meanwhile, householders of limited means with the same building fever made in their houses all the changes their hearts and purses could devise. Yet no matter how these structures grew, they were almost invariably planned as homes for parents and their children and their children's children.

While enterprising young men went abroad to study architecture in France and Italy, some at their own expense and some at the expense of their wealthy patrons, other householders secured what were called pattern books and studied them closely for ideas. These they adapted to their own uncertain taste and then explained them to steward and surveyor who superintended the work done by contracts with the various trades. At first Elizabethans were enamored with the decorative devices of arabesques, mermaids, dolphins, and the like. These were used on wainscoting, windowheads, plasterwork in ceilings, and tombs, and were combined with pilasters in Doric, Ionic, and Corinthian design with their own proper pedestals. Later, the householders' interest turned especially to Flemish and French designs, which they studied closely in their pattern books.

In James Lees-Milne's informative book, *Tudor Renaissance* (1951), we are told how Sir John Thynne sent directions to his steward about the building of Longleat. The walls from the first floor up were to be "but two bricks length in thickness." Carefully Sir John explained how the paving tiles were to be laid in the great hall, crests put on the rain-water heads, wood seasoned for doors and wainscoting, chimneys torn down and rebuilt of stone, the hall door enlarged and a special kind of hinge used on it, all the glass carefully cut in appropriate shapes and fitted into place, and so on. Just as specifically he directed the landscaping. Lanes must be made, harvests cared for, timber felled, lawns sown, vistas provided by clearing away underbrush and trees, and the new fruit trees (cherry, plum, and apricot) brought from France and watered with great care.

Foreign influence, with its curious romantic mingling of French or Italian and Old English medieval and classic characteristics, produced the so-called Elizabethan architecture, in which the Italian symmetry is reflected in the H and E styles of the great houses. Such residences provided a means of achieving an elaborate entrance and for this reason had a strong appeal to the ambitious builder. In these homes the hall made the crossbar of the H and the back of the E, with the central bar of the E forming a projecting porch leading to the hall. The upper and lower bars of the E and the two uprights of the H formed a perfect balance between the servants' and master's quarters, with the hall as the connecting link. In the servants' quarters were workrooms very important to the welfare of the family; they consisted of the principal kitchens, a buttery, a pantry and "a pastry" with at least two ovens to supplement those in the kitchen, a dry and wet larder, and a "surveying" (serving) room. In larger houses were other such rooms consisting of the scullery, a "meal house," a "bolting house," a spicery, a "trencher room," a pewter room, and a "brush." Both servants' quarters and family apartments were usually at least two stories high, each wing having its own staircase to the bedchambers above. Frequently the upper floor of the wings was separated by the high two-story hall. Thus the aim was not only stateliness but comfort and privacy for the family, these qualities being achieved not only by the physical features of the house but also by a careful decorum in living. Adaptations of the H and E designs continued for some time. For example, they may be traced in the ground floor plan of Doddington Hall (1595), Burton Agnes (1602–10), and Aston Hall (1618–35). During the forty years Lord Burghley was building Burghley House, he worked out an elaborate design and a magnificent symmetry in his entrance of French towers and triumphal arch. Towers were much favored in Elizabethan houses and sometimes were embellished with two or more superimposed orders of columns or pilasters, often with niches between them; they were very effective in the H and E plan.

Most ordinary houses were of two stories, except those in London which were three and sometimes four stories high. They were usually built of wood, though better ones were of brick, with roofs of tile and even lead. London roofs, because of fire hazard from thatch, were mostly red tile, and high-pitched. In the poorer sections, however, wooden houses might be thatched, and in case of fire they were a great menace; the only way of fighting fire was to pull down burning buildings with great iron hooks. Tradesmen planned their houses so that the entire front downstairs might be used for a shop. Porches with narrow sloping roofs invariably sheltered the entrance and sometimes extended along the entire front of the lower story, over both door and windows. Under this penthouse covering, the trader set up his stall. These penthouses of London and other towns had upper projecting stories. Naturally they darkened the streets, but they also enabled the gossips at the second- and third-story windows to discuss the news of the day as people passed by on the dirty cobbles below. So close were some of the houses thus facing each other that neighbors might have clasped hands from the windows of their upper stories. But the gardens at the rear of the houses, large enough at least for growing herbs and a few flowers, did not encourage such friendly contacts. In cities these gardens were separated from each other by walls of brick or stone or baked mud, according to the individual owner's means.

Homes in less crowded areas were set in gardens or parks and, in the country, in open or shaded fields.

The prosperous middle-class people in towns and cities built their houses of heavy timbers, lath, and plaster, the framework in front being elaborately carved. Grotesques, such as leering satyrs and fantastic combinations of medieval gargoyles, were often fashioned to look as if they supported the heavy timbers. These details, however, were usually provided by the workmen, especially if the owner left the general plan to the surveyor (responsible for supervision more than design) or to a master mason. Such buildings were frequently planned as they grew, and individual workmen were given much freedom with which to indulge their whims.

The plaster-filled squares and triangles formed by the wooden braces of the massive timbers made a pleasant setting for the many glass windows of pretentious homes. When foreign glass had to compete with that made in England, the cost of windows declined. Soon the two upper stories of the narrow fronts of crowded houses in London were filled with rows upon rows of windows that sparkled when the sun shone. Houses of rich merchants along the Cheapside-Holburn thoroughfare were especially notable for their many-windowed façades. The evolution of fine windows is a study in itself, but briefly one might say they started with the medieval oriels, which in turn were succeeded by semicircular bays, often one above another, square, angular, and even pointed. Then came the great expanse of crinkled glass panes or straight windows of latticed panes covering an entire wall; eventually this façade became more glass than wall.

The oft-described home of Paul Pindar (1556–1650) was an example of a many-windowed house. Though surrounded by a park and fine lodges, the house's chief distinction was its beautiful oriel two stories high, each story having a series of panels at its base. The central part of this great glass façade was semicircular, and on each side was an angular projection. All the panels were elaborately carved, with the owner's shield in the central panel. Then this variety and rhythm were intensified by the glazing patterns. This famous window became a museum treasure.

The humblest dwellings, of course, underwent little change. Built of wood and thatch, they were poor protection against wind and rain, and their single room provided no privacy. Here the family ate, slept, and performed all domestic duties. The yeoman's home in town or country had several rooms, but the poor laborer's cottage consisted of one room with clay walls on a thatched timber frame and one or possibly two crude windows with lattice shutters. Sometimes such a house might have an attic with a dormer window, latticed to keep out the worst of the wind and rain. Eventually oiled linen replaced the lattices, and finally thin, murky horn or small panes of cheap glass. Frequently this upper room was reached by ladder instead of crude stairs, and it served not only as a

bedchamber but in the country as a storehouse for winter herbs and vegetables. In such homes the term bedroom literally meant one's room in
a bed that might hold a dozen people.

Not far from Stratford-upon-Avon, in the village of Temple Grafton,
is a little timber and thatched house about four hundred years old. The
building is not over twenty-five feet square. Originally its ground floor
was entered through a heavy oak door at right angles to the fireplace,
which partially divided the interior into two unequal parts. The larger
area, twice the size of the other, contained this fireplace, at which the
roasting and cooking were carried on. Its great oven extended back like
an arm across one entire end of the smaller room, or kitchen, and there
the family bread was baked. Most of the housework except the fireplace
cooking was done in the kitchen, the other room serving as living quarters
and, if necessary, as bedroom also. At the left of the entrance door was
a narrow, twisted stair.

One climbed the stair warily and reached a bedroom where the roof
sloped sharply at two sides. In this "head" room slept the parents, and
the daughters in the room beyond. Still beyond that may have been a
boys' room or attic, but it is now sealed off. Since the roof slanted obliquely
on all four sides, the upper rooms were quite small, and making beds in
them was no easy task. Cottages with more than three rooms upstairs
usually had the "head" room at the center, with the menservants' room
beyond the boys' room, and the maids' room beyond that of the daughters.
Of course all members of the household were thus forced to pass through
the parents' room when they retired for the night, but by this arrangement
parents were able to maintain proper decorum.

In Boat Lane at Welford-on-Avon is a cottage very similar in construction. Here, however, the fireplace is on the outside wall of the living
room, and is separated from the entrance by a winding stair. There is a
"penthouse" over the door. On the upper floor, the "head" room leads
into a spacious bedchamber with a charming dormer window built almost
flush with the wall so that the outer ledge provides ample space for plants.
The two hinged windows, twelve by sixteen inches, have crinkled sixteenth-century glass, and are fastened with an iron latch of the same
period.

Better cottages in town or country differed from one another chiefly
in the location of their gardens and outbuildings. In the cities the gardens
at the rear of the house varied chiefly in size, with devices for pleasant
walks or restrictions in space permitting little more than herb and vegetable plots. In the country, houses were more or less surrounded by outbuildings, with their number and location, like the size of the house, being
determined by the taste and circumstances of the owner. There might
be a hall on the first floor with two or three bedrooms above, each opening
off the other. A parlor off the hall was converted into a bedchamber when
necessary. The buttery and kitchen were in a separate outbuilding or off

one end of the hall, and the front wall of the house usually had a pent-house. Outbuildings and house were constructed of like materials, mostly of thatch, timber, and lath and plaster. The exterior of these homes, especially when the cottage was set in a garden of flowers and shrubs, might be attractive to the eye, but the interiors were often cold and damp.

At Tredington, in the Avon country, is a farmhouse that in spite of some effort at modernization retains its original floors and walls and many other features revealing sixteenth-century life. Off the entrance hall, with its wide stair leading to the four bedchambers on the floor above, is a door opening into the family living room. Heavy dark oak timbers support the plastered ceiling and show through the white plastered walls, and small-paned windows look out onto the courtyard still almost surrounded by barns, shops, dovecote, stables and cowsheds.

There are two kitchens, one off the living room. Back of the small door which now closes off the inglenook of the large fireplace of the living room is another door opening into a "warm room." Here, with scarcely a break for over three hundred years, hams and sides of bacon have been hung, cured by letting in the smoke from the fireplace and then stored in this closed room till needed. The uneven stone floor of the kitchen to the right of the living room records the many, many steps of housewife and servant busy at tasks. The "warm room" is accessible to the kitchen, and when its door is opened, one drinks in the redolence of deliciously cured meat. The stone walls of the kitchen are supplied with niches holding utensils and receptacles for nonperishable ingredients needed in the day's brewing and baking. Adjoining is a stone buttery with more wall niches and also two large vats for making cheese. Cool and pleasant in summer, it still serves as a dairy room, with its crocks of milk covered with thick Jersey cream.

Across the living room and a passageway is the other stone kitchen, no longer in use. Adjoining it and down a few steps is the cellar with its slanted wall niches for wine and its arched vaults for casks of ale. Directly in front of this kitchen is a large room once used as parlor or bedchamber. Faintly showing in its plaster are fragments of a painted frieze, whose blurred, disconnected story is still warm with the breathing of the past.

Naturally the kind of building materials was more or less determined by the resources abounding in the region chosen for the new home. In Derbyshire, Yorkshire, and Lancashire, for example, the houses were plain, even severe-looking, with their hard gray stone walls and flattish roofs. An abundance of freestone and other building materials in the midlands enabled the wealthy homes of Somersetshire, Wiltshire, Oxfordshire, and Lincolnshire to achieve richness, delicacy, and charm. In the eastern counties brick and stone or brick and plaster were used, the brick offset by ornamental parapets, cornices, and pilasters. Fine large oaks in Cheshire, Worcestershire, and Hereford encouraged the use of timber and plaster in houses that became very ornamental, especially in comparison with those of plaster and half-timber in Kent, Surrey, and Sussex. Since established families lived for generations in the same house, the new families wished their homes to be built of lasting materials like brick and stone, and among the rich such materials became increasingly popular. Moreover, if they used fine old forests of oak that could not be replaced, even though the timber was on their own land, they were likely to be criticized severely for wasteful extravagance.

Well-to-do farmers and yeomen liked stout oak timbers in their homes, for they, too, wished to provide dwellings for generations sprung from their own loins. Furthermore, the appearance of stability in such wood appealed to the sturdy, thrifty householders. If they could afford it, they had ornately carved trimming for the bay windows, or if they could do the carving themselves, they made full use of the chance to exercise their ingenuity. Outbuildings of such homes were within easy reach and usually included a dairy (with churn, crocks, tubs, vats, cheese presses), a dovecote, a chicken house, a pigsty, and a stable. The barns, farmsheds, and dovecote surrounding the old farmyard of the Mary Arden home in Wilmcote suggest the arrangement of the sixteenth-century farmyard of some pretension. The house is made of local gray stone, oak timbers, red brick, and tile, and its back forms one side of the yard. Near its back door is the pump. The outbuildings are of gray stone, and they form the other three sides of the yard, a tall archway in the side opposite the house providing entrance to the yard. Adjoining the house is a dovecote containing over 650 nesting holes built inside the walls and an entrance for the birds through a louver in the roof. The difficulty of supplying fresh meat for the table made pigeons important to Elizabethan farmers. Beyond the dovecote is an open cowshed and next to it the cider mill. With only a little imagination one can see the ponderous stone wheel set in motion once more to crush out juice for hot cider on bone-chilling nights. Barns, shops, and other enclosed buildings complete the arrangement.

Larger estates had additional buildings, such as a slaughterhouse, a malthouse (where ale was made once or twice a month), possibly a mill, a smithy, and a carpenter's shop, a saw pit and woodyard, a bakehouse (with bread-making paraphernalia such as querns and molding board), a cheese-press house, a cellar, and barns and stables for horses, cattle, and sheep. That all repairing was done at such a home made of it a little village in itself. And if this was the case, the yeoman had moved up the social scale enough to become the owner of a small manor. Even so, all estates above the rank of a cottage usually provided most of their own food and other household necessities.

The arrangement of attaching the rural manor to a village provided advantages to both in the way of security and better communication with the outside world. Such communities had to be practically self-supporting, for they lived pretty much to themselves owing to the poor transportation over very bad roads. If additional supplies were needed by the villagers, the people were more or less dependent on the squire or lord of a great house. Long since, the fine old Roman roads had fallen into decay, but they were still used because there were no other main roads. Indeed, most of the roads to villages were mere tracks over which a noble's coach and heavily laden wagons had to be dragged through sheer force by many horses. If bridges were needed at rivers and streams, they had to be maintained by ecclesiastics or the private persons who made frequent use of them. The parish church or the great house, therefore, was likely to be the center of a community. The same was true of the manor house of a country squire of some consequence, and the stately avenue of trees leading to his house often connected it with the church. When a two-storied manor house was made of stout timber, covered with whitewashed plaster, roofed with tiles or slate, and supplied with many glass windows, it was usually a source of as much pride to the villagers as to the owner. With possessive admiration they would gaze at it set in its garden surrounded with high thatched walls, and they would have heard of its lofty, spacious rooms with their pattern of oak wainscoting.

In the town of Conway, Wales, is a rather modest house known as Plas Mawr (Great Mansion) that was once the great pride of a small village with but few inhabitants, as it is now the pride of a town with many people. When it was built, there were wide stretches of gardens about it instead of the cottages which now press close to its walls, and in the day of its pride it faced the Conway River, with landscaping extending far enough away to give vista and privacy. Although the first servants' quarters (later replaced by the Keeper's House at the new entrance) and stables and outbuildings have disappeared, the house itself has the warm, inviting appeal of a home once loved by those who lived in its charmingly arranged interior. The first owner, Robert Wynne, was born in 1520, and according to Norman Tucker, a former Curator of the Cambrian Academy of Art now established in the home, Wynne was an Elizabethan adventurer descended from an illustrious family. While his house was being constructed, Wynne made use of abandoned abbey buildings extending to the very site of his new home, for the tops of blocked-up arches show on either side of the door leading from the terrace of the present entrance to the banqueting hall, an imposing room added later to this "mansion." The house has two dates in its plasterwork—1577 and 1580.

If a guest of the sixteenth century rode to the original entrance of this house, he dismounted from his horse and gave it in charge of a servant, who led it down a cobbled passage (dividing into two almost equal parts the lower floor of the house) and into the upper courtyard and the stables beyond. Meanwhile, the guest could walk down this cobbled passage to the original entranceway at the left, where a servant would escort him past the "small" kitchen to one of the spiral stairs. If he was not led up the stairs to the reception room above, he was likely to proceed along the

Bread safe suspended from ceiling of the small
kitchen at Plas Mawr, Conway, Wales

passage and through a door into the banqueting room. Should the person be a member of the family, he might prefer to enter the living room, now called the Queen's sitting room because of the royal initials E and R over the mantel. In this case he would turn right off the cobbled passage into a hall leading past another spiral stair and past the "still" room to the sitting room situated on a corner of the house. If a servant was sent to the great "west" kitchen to give orders for the preparation of some special dainty, he turned left at the sitting room, passed the pantry, and entered the kitchen. So carefully was the first floor planned that one could also enter the upper courtyard easily and quickly from kitchen, sitting room, or banquet hall.

The banquet hall was thirty by twenty feet and thirteen feet high. On its dressed stone fireplace is the date 1580. The Wynne arms were in the center of the chimney breast and, when painted in correct heraldic colors, showed a green field with golden eaglets and silver fleurs-de-lis on black. On either side were Tudor roses—white superimposed on the red. Close to the ceiling were red shields with silver stags' heads and silver lions rampant at the base, but they have now long since lost their glowing colors. The outlines and the initials "R. W." are as clear, however, as the building date on this fine, dignified structure. Of almost equal interest in this room is the ceiling with its attractive symmetrical design culminating in several Tudor roses. Mullioned windows light the room pleasantly, for the lozenge-shaped panes include some of the original glass of soft green hue.

One may leave the banqueting room by way of a passage to the "small" kitchen, or through a door opening on the terrace of the lower court, or through still another door to the upper court. In the "small" kitchen the first thing to attract attention is the huge fireplace with its beautiful arch, making the room warm and cheerful. In front of it a large wooden cage is fastened close to the ceiling between stout oaken beams. Such a cage is known as a bread safe or bakestone safe, and is still used on farms far out in the Welsh hills. Since the kitchen fireplace backs up to that of the banqueting room and since it is so convenient to this great dining hall, it must have been a busy place indeed when a large company enjoyed the hospitality of the master's good food and wine.

Crossing the cobbled passage to the entrance at the right, one reaches what is now called the "still" room. The porter of the entrance gate may once have occupied this room. Later, when the main entrance was built opposite the banqueting room, this little "still" room adjoining the sitting room and close to the kitchen was most convenient for a lady who liked to spend much time concocting medicines and perfumes and sweet waters. The sitting room still retains the spirit of the welcoming host and hostess who talked away many pleasant hours with their guests made comfortable on stools and benches before its great fireplace. The royal coat of arms on the chimney breast flaunts the Tudor rose and portcullis, and is supported by a Welsh dragon. The low plaster ceiling, richly and freely ornamented, and the floor of stone flagging even now give the room an intimate quality. In the plaster wall at right angles to the fireplace is a great recessed window with Robert Wynne's initials and coat of arms very large at either side of it. The date of this room is shown below the heraldic emblems, "15" on the left and "77" on the right.

Around the corner from this sitting room was the bolting room for the sifting of flour; it also served as a pantry, and its twelve-by-twelve feet of space must have been crowded with activity. Adjoining it was the large "west" kitchen, opening on the upper courtyard. In this room was always much running to and fro, for the preparation of food was as important as the serving of it. Here bread was baked in ovens on either side of the great fireplace over nine feet wide, and here the "cradle" spit with its supporting irons held game and fowls as they were roasted for the master's table. In spite of its size, this kitchen was not large enough to serve the needs of the household when the banqueting room was added to the house; hence the "small" kitchen.

If one climbs the spiral stair off the passageway from the sitting room, one comes to another passageway connecting two bedrooms, and a locked storeroom directly opposite the head of the stairs. These three rooms are just above kitchen, pantry, and sitting room on the floor below. The bedroom over the "west" kitchen is called the Wynne room because of the shield, which is a quartering of four shields, over the fireplace. The date 1577 is also prominently displayed. On either side of the fireplace are closets with small windows. Perhaps the most debatable thing about the room is the use of the "bear and ragged staff" design in the plasterwork, since both the Earl of Leicester and the Earl of Warwick used such a device, and Wynne may have used the design to flatter one or the other of these prominent Elizabethans, just as he used the Queen's initials over the sitting room fireplace. The room is large and light and cheerful, and the master of the house must have found it warmer and more comfortable than any of the other chambers. The other bedroom is also large and cheerful, and with its outlook over the river and gardens it must have been considered fine enough to house the Queen. Indeed, it is now called Queen Elizabeth's bedroom. Its fine oak screen and low ceiling designed with heraldic devices are its outstanding features.

The other spiral stair leads to another wing of rooms very similar in size to those in the wing just described. Although one is now called the Council Room and the other large one the Lantern Room, with a small one between these called the House Keeper's Room, they must have been bedchambers, the small one being used by the housekeeper. Connecting these two wings with their four spacious chambers is a large room now called the Reception Room. It may very well have served as a withdrawing room or presence chamber. Directly over the "small" kitchen, cobbled passage, and "still" room, it looks out toward both the upper court and the river and is well lighted by large windows. Both stairs led to it by means of short passageways, and when guests filled the house, it may well have been crowded in spite of its commodious size. The ceiling is so designed as to set off the date 1580, and discerning guests sitting on the seats that are still around the wall could have studied the structure of the ceiling and the details of the chimney breast if they felt time heavy on their hands. A fine Tudor rose encircled by the Garter reveals the work of a craftsman who knew his flowers better than his alphabet when he decorated the open space above the fireplace.

The room might also have served for devout Catholics to gather in secret to hear a courageous priest as he presided at the mass services. Although the spiral stairs provided easy access to the room, they also permitted hasty departure, and the great windows looking out far over the landscape would make it difficult to be surprised in the daytime. Moreover, there were lookout windows in the high staircase tower extending well above the upper courtyard; these gave a fine view of the whole countryside. Between the end wall of this reception room and the end of the bedchamber now called the Lantern Room is a space that might have been used for a secret hiding place or priest's hole, and since this space was seemingly provided for in the actual building of the house, one can scarcely doubt that it was intended to serve such a purpose. The very name of the Lantern Room also may have some significance, for in the fine oriel window of this bedchamber, a light was once kept burning all night to light the terrace below. Examination of the priest's hole today shows how one of the joists could well have been movable, enabling a man to climb from a ladder through the entrance to the hiding place; then he could have replaced the floor covering to make the ceiling look intact. Though the owner, Robert Wynne, was presumably buried in the Protestant Church, there were strong rumors of his Catholic inclinations, and one feels that both the so-called Reception Room and the priest's hole may well have been carefully planned for religious purposes when this part of the house was built.

The country gentleman, like his rich city cousin, usually built his house symmetrically around three sides of a courtyard and divided the family living quarters from the kitchen and servants' quarters by a large hall. The best of such houses included a chapel. If after inheriting such an estate a gentleman wished to add new rooms, he would probably include a matted chamber, a study, more servants' quarters, and more bedchambers, some of them provided with sitting rooms. The number of servants would vary according to the owner's wealth or inclination, ranging from thirty to a hundred and thirty, but most of them would be women—ladies' maids, needlewomen, laundresses, dairy maids, poor relations such as widows, spinsters, or elderly women who would rather be waiting maids than go into service. It took many women to manage a country estate, whether it was a great house, a squire's manor house, or merely a large farmhouse, for only women took care of the food raised on the land, made the clothing and linens used by the household, and carried on the many activities necessary in maintaining a home.

If the new owner could afford it, he would replace the twisted Tudor chimneys of his inherited house with massive chimney groups, arranged to give the effect of rhythmic balance, and would add porches and a fine stairway leading to the upper chambers. Since a proud home must be symmetrical in all things, especially in the façade, he would have to correct any discrepancy even though he might have to balance the bay window off the hall by a similar one off the pantry. For the Elizabethan, symmetry in a house was achieved only when the ground plan and elevation provided perfect balance.

The farmer of moderate means who had had a year of prosperity also might plan some improvements for his home. If he could now afford a comfortable hall or living room, he would show his pride in it by adding as elaborate a chimney piece as possible. If he had open beams and could afford having them carved and a bit of carving done over the door, he might even aspire to paneling for the walls. When all these things were achieved, he would feel "honestly" housed.

Country palaces near London were built between the Strand and the Thames River. Here were located the houses of Bacon, Leicester, Raleigh, Essex, and the Cecils. West of their mansions extended the gardens and orchards of Queen Elizabeth's palace of Whitehall, and out beyond, the Thames curved toward Hampton Court and Richmond and Windsor. Wherever Elizabeth lodged, there the court was also, and when she came up to London, she stopped at Whitehall. Lord Burghley could easily go from Cecil House to Whitehall on the Thames by his own boat with its liveried watermen, or after a walk of a few minutes he could hire a boat at a public wharf at the foot of Ivy Lane. On the Thames at night were torch-lit wherries for ladies and their escorts making their way to Richmond or Westminster for the Queen's revels. They might also enjoy revels and plays at Hampton Court, for in its great hall Elizabeth was accustomed to receive foreign ambassadors. If on gala occasions there were not enough rooms to house all her courtiers after the ambassadors had been cared for, the courtiers pitched their tents in the square, and the colorful sight made the whole court gay. But Elizabeth felt most luxuriously housed at Windsor Castle, and here her sixty musicians provided soft or lively strains for a queen who loved dancing above all other pastimes. Here, too, she summoned her royal barge with its two large cabins embellished with much ornamentation and, with her lords and ladies, floated down the Thames on summer evenings to the music of flutes played by the courtiers. But she spent even more time at Richmond, which she loved for its park and walks and the hill she could climb.

Between Westminster and London were continuous green fields and beautiful gardens of proud establishments. Cecil House was set back from the river and, like many of the other mansions, fronted the Thames with its terraces and private tilt-boats (covered passenger boats) with their liveried watermen. Four turrets marked the four corners of the house, and in the study were stored some of Burghley's most precious books, especially those by Belleau, du Bartas, du Bellay, Ronsard, and Montaigne. But the gardens, like those of his famous house, Theobalds, were famous for their beauty. Both gardens were supervised by Gerard, the horticulturist, and for over twenty years they delighted the eye with their variety of colorful flowers, their fine shrubs and trees, and their pleached walks adorned with fountains, sundial, and statuary.

Indeed, the gardens of these fine homes made the north bank of the Thames an extended park of beauty and color, enhanced by the bright liveries of the watermen of private barges and those of the hired barges floating by. The mansions in this setting were usually as magnificent inside as out, spacious, and imposing in their stone or brick. Their great halls had open beams richly carved, for at the early part of the century nobles and retainers and men-at-arms numbered three and four hundred, and the homes must enable the owners to dine hundreds of people at one time in the hall. Besides this hall was a chapel for the family and household; family bedchambers were above the first floor, and guest chambers off the court. Later additions made as building plans matured consisted of a private parlor or dining room for the family, the great chamber, the withdrawing chamber, the breakfast room, the study, and the library. To the servants' quarters and offices was sometimes added a hall whose employment carefully followed that of the master's own.

When Sir Thomas More built his large, comfortable house in Chelsea about 1520, he surrounded it by spacious gardens filled with flowers and fruit trees. Near by were open fields and green meadows. Rosemary ran over his walks; he loved it because it was considered sacred to friendship and remembrance, and because the bees loved it too. Near the house but separated from it, he built a library, a gallery, and a chapel. In the mornings he worshiped in the chapel with his family, but in the evenings he assembled the entire household for psalms and prayer. Here he often retired for quiet meditation, reading, or prayer, particularly on Fridays when, if he was not compelled to be at court, he spent the entire day in worship.

Like both his contemporaries and his Elizabethan successors, Sir Thomas More filled his home with what he considered beautiful and captivating things. He collected ancient coins and precious books, pictures, furniture, and fine plate made by contemporary craftsmen and artists, and sought the advice of Erasmus and Holbein when he purchased his treasures. Interested in fine workmanship, he enjoyed discussing the arts and crafts with his children and his close friends. But he also exercised his own taste; for example, he was particularly fond of a heart of amber in which a fly had been imprisoned, for it was emblematic to him of the friendship of the man who gave it to him—a friendship that could not fly away or perish.

In his house and garden More kept many kinds of strange birds and animals, among which were dogs, rabbits, weasels, ferrets, and even a monkey. To illustrate for his children how they might withstand the temptations of the devil, he compared the devil to the monkey, which had to be watched all the time lest it take advantage of them. Thus he combined moral instruction with natural history. Most Elizabethans, like More, were interested in birds and animals. Many a country home had its caged thrushes or skylarks in little houses made of wicker and hung just outside the door on pleasant days. Among the nobility animals and birds were often kept for display, especially if the species was rare. Trained animals fascinated them. Women often led squirrels around on a chain and kept such pets as monkeys, parrots, and muskrats. But the toy dog was the favorite pet of all fine ladies; it was expensive. For most people dogs and cats were the chief pets.

There were certain features of the house that wealthy Elizabethans especially loved. In general they planned a home setting of intricate courts and wide gateways and, in the house, lofty halls, elaborate stairways with ornately carved newel posts and balusters, many and beautiful windows, and richly decorated walls and ceilings. All of these details were enhanced by colorful draperies and by the dancing flames from fireplaces upon which artists concentrated much of their attention.

Ordinary homes had wainscoted walls hung with painted cloths to take the place of expensive tapestries, but all had fireplaces, some very large, at each side of which were put high-backed settles. Most of the homes of the common people had heavy oak furniture, crudely made by hand, which was replaced, as their owners could afford better pieces, with furniture made by skilled craftsmen. Such treasures might become household gods indeed if they were embellished with intricately carved animals and flowers. The wealthy could afford furniture made of newly imported hardwoods, delicately inlaid with pearl and other hardwoods of different color, many of the pieces being especially designed and made for them by craftsmen among their own servants. From tables and chests and beds and stools were developed cabinets and dressing tables and chairs, besides other new pieces constructed to meet the needs of the new rooms added to the new or old dwellings.

Many sixteenth-century moralists complained that people were growing soft through their use of fireplaces and glass windows and upholstered stools. Even the gardens were criticized for no longer growing the good old herbs and fruits and vegetables or for being crowded with strange new imports or foolish grafts on old shrubs and trees.

Houses built for the entertainment of royalty and other distinguished company were necessarily more magnificent in their proportions and appointments than those designed primarily for homes. Such were the palaces of Theobalds and Holdenby, for example, as well as others such as Audley End, Knole, and Buckhurst. In general these establishments followed the E or H plan, or the so-called square or courtyard plan, all of which emphasized the main entrance at the front façade, the court façades, and the symmetry of the building. The E plan was not so well liked apparently as the H plan. Charlecote Hall near Stratford-on-Avon used the E design, but more builders seem to have adopted the H plan, one example being Montacute House in Somerset. The square plan usually broke its stiff lines with towers and porches, but even so it consisted mainly of open courts or solid masses of the building with symmetrical façades, those of front and back or front and one side exactly matching. The main entrance would not be through a courtyard, but through one of the outer fronts, as at Whitehall, near Shrewsbury. In the courtyard plan the lines of the cloister were followed, with the great hall resembling the monastery dining hall. But instead of the monastery entrance, this type of house used a gatehouse, which, when placed in the center of the front wall of the courtyard and directly opposite the screen opening into the great hall, could be very imposing; at the same time it also provided the much desired symmetry.

These great houses all had large kitchen departments and innumerable guest suites of two or three rooms each, for one important guest meant a retinue of at least a suitable if not an impressive following, and even though it was customary for guests to share bedrooms, both at inns and at private homes, still the accommodation of all members of a party might require considerable planning on the part of a host.

Among the designers of great Elizabethan homes was John Thorpe, and it may have been he who designed the greatest mansion of this period, Holdenby. This very extravagant house was built by Sir Christopher Hatton for the purpose of entertaining the Queen most sumptuously. Of course he also planned to accommodate other important guests, but the Queen was the inspiration for this fantastic dream of a home. The building began in 1578, and was frequently visited by its owner during the the five years before it was completed. In 1579, Lord Burghley visited it too and expressed his delight over its "magnificent front" and its "large, long, straight fairway," its "stately ascent" from the hall to the great chamber, and the "largeness and lightsomeness" of its bedchambers. When it was completed, Sir Thomas Heneage called it the best house of the age for showing the "good judgment and honour of the builder."

According to Eric St. John Brooks, there were 1,789 acres attached to Holdenby, with 606 acres in park, the house site and its gardens, and pastures. In his book, *Sir Christopher Hatton* (1946), Brooks gives an interesting account of the effort that went into the creation of this "home" for the Queen, and the plan of the establishment after its completion. One approached Holdenby over a road winding through a park until within a quarter of a mile from the lodge. Here the road became straight, passing through green meadows of nearly seventeen acres, called the Green, and flanked on the north by stables. This was the stretch Burghley called the "fairway"; it terminated at the beautiful gatehouse, which was separated from the main house by the base court with its surrounding wall. Such walls were likely to be high and solid, though they might be designed merely for appearance with pierced and ornamental patterns. When an Elizabethan gatehouse accommodated the porter and his family, it usually had two rooms downstairs and perhaps three above. Some impressive gatehouses had porters' rooms on three and even four floors, and others were merely ornamental entrances.

Holdenby's base court had two large gateway towers. Beyond the second was the house with its costly, rare chimneys and its many commodious chambers and withdrawing rooms. In the side walls of the base court were large archways through which one might walk into the pleasure gardens. As one passed through the far gateway of the base court, one mounted a short, broad stair leading to the terrace on which stood the house, only a few feet above ground level and built around two great courts. One of these was 128 by 104 feet, and the other was 140 by 110 feet. The first of these two courts, around which were arranged the principal rooms of the house, opened into a loggia or colonnade. At the four corners of this court were large, ornate towers, which no doubt provided extra stairs to the upper floors. The second, larger court was not so elaborate as the first, for one side of it was occupied by the kitchens, and its far entrance led into the kitchen gardens and like areas. The north gardens were walled and occupied about an acre each, and beyond them were the ash woods or thickets and the village with its inn.

South of the house was its "pleasant, spacious, and fair garden." Here the ground sloped away rather sharply and was laid out in a series of terraces, with a broad, straight path at the top, flanking the entire length of the base court, the house, and the orchard beyond. At the far end of this path was a cross-path, at each end of which was a prospect mount providing a good view of the surrounding country. As one of them wound its way up to the mount it led to a summer or banquet house at the top. It is possible both mounts had such houses to give the necessary protection from wind and rain and to permit the beauty of its surrounding undergrowth to frame the views seen from the mount. Below the terraces of this "fair garden" were fish ponds and orchard trees, and in its southeast corner was the chapel. But its most distinctive feature seems to have been the rose garden. In the middle of the terraces, graded to extend at right angles with the house and on a level with it, was the rose plot laid out in a simple, geometric design, probably with a wide path around its four sides and others bisecting the sides and converging at the center with its fountain or statue. In all the gardens were attractive benches or statuary or garden knots to provide both symmetry and variety. Since the house site and gardens occupied almost forty acres, we can well understand why Burghley said that such ambitious layouts caused men like him and Hatton in their entertainment of the Queen to "exceed their purses."

Owners of mansions usually preferred an approach to the entrance court of their establishment by a long drive through a park where deer grazed under spreading oaks. Frequently the three walls or ornamental battlements of the court would be completed on the fourth side by the front of the house, whose projecting wings came forth to meet the court's side walls. If the court walls formed open corridors, the gateway opposite the house might also be an open arcade, surmounted by a cupola. Sometimes the entrance through the archway was doubled, with one smaller than the other. In this case the smaller one was used by pedestrians and the larger by vehicles. With such an arrangement the entrance arch might be a square or octagonal tower with or without a porter's rooms. As a rule, however, when the tower housed the porter, it stood about fifty to a hundred yards from the house and was a unit in itself. When a projecting porch was built in the middle of the front of the house, it usually ran as high as the house, and its upper floor served as living or lookout apartments. Such a porch might become a magnificent entrance if ornamented with good taste by columns, friezes, and the owner's shield.

If there was a gateway house, it was likely to be on a straight line with the entrance to the mansion. Sometimes these porter's lodges took on a very military appearance, extending on rare occasions as high as eight stories. The porter stood on guard, however, not against strangers or possible enemies but against the beggars infesting the countryside after the suppression of the monasteries. If the porter's lodge stood opposite another tower leading from the base court into the inner or second court, with three of its sides formed by the front of the house and wings meeting the court's walls, this second tower entrance was likely to be matched in its ornamental details by the first entrance tower. At such a house, one who was admitted by the porter would have to pass through two large courts, one vast and somewhat open, and the other surrounded by the imposing building of the owner.

If one made a tour of the grounds surrounding a great house one would, on returning, enter the screen passage which connected with the great hall and which had other doors leading to the kitchens and perhaps to the gardens. This screen passage supposedly kept drafts out of the hall as people entered and left the house. But when the main entrance was placed in the middle of the hall, the room was no longer comfortable for living purposes and became eventually the modern vestibule. The pleasure gardens of a great home would be extensive, with long, broad walks, terraces, bowling alleys, orchards, and prospect mounts. Beyond the gardens would be lake or woods or meadows and, in the distance, the village and its church. Walking about these gardens and admiring the ornamental details of the imposing residence, the visitor would notice the large mullioned windows with columns between them, façades with great bays reaching perhaps as high as the parapet, gables terminated by a flat scroll, massive chimneys carefully spaced at regular intervals—a strange combination of periods and styles of architecture somehow blended into the picturesque.

Less pretentious establishments usually had short driveways leading straight to the front door, the lodge being supplanted by an attractive gateway only. If the owner carried out his desire for symmetry in house and gardens, the gateway, front entrance, and doorway leading to the back gardens might be in a straight line, with the house carefully balanced on each side of the hall. Such a plan influenced many early American homes, especially in the southern states; the adaptations of it are an interesting study.

The attention given to the design of the main entrance was reflected in the intricately recessed doorway and the elaborate projecting porch. Often several shallow steps led to the carefully designed door, and if the house belonged to a member of the gentry, the family coat of arms would be in evidence, perhaps in each corner of the arch. A typical doorway had several recesses, each a work of art with its paneling, carved moldings, and the design repeated in the lunette of heavy wood. If the doorway was divided by a central pier with a beautifully carved statue, the entrance was charmingly hospitable when the doors were thrown open to welcome guests. On formal occasions bowing servants would show the guests to dressing rooms on the first floor where they might remove outer garments and retouch powder and paint; then the usher would escort them to the host and hostess receiving in the presence chamber.

Internal doors and doorways became more and more important to Elizabethans as they learned the romantic possibilities of the recess design they used so often. They liked their doors flanked by pilasters and the doorways lavishly carved. The doors themselves were paneled, freely molded, carved, or inlaid with fancy embellishment. The very hinges must be ornamental, some taking the form of a cock's or dragon's head, and others resembling serpents, frogs, or lizards. Even the nuts of these hinges were engraved. Nor were the locks neglected; some of them were of great size in order to provide more room for beautiful detail, and their keys were correspondingly large and heavy.

In the early houses, one ascended a flight of easy stairs to the porch sheltering the main entrance and then entered the screen passage. Usually an usher stood at the door, but sometimes the door was open and one entered the screen passage to await the coming of the usher. This passage was usually a paneled room ten or twelve feet high, and it was situated at the end of the hall close to the servants' quarters, where there was most traffic. From this room a visitor was ushered into the great hall or led through another door into the buttery.

In ordinary homes the hall continued to serve many domestic purposes throughout the century, but in the fine houses the hall became more and more a room for special entertainment, and most of its space was kept clear for tables that could be hastily set up when needed. Its two long sides would be protected by courts which could be seen through its large windows, but since it was situated at the center of the house, it became more or less a thoroughfare. Here the usher was in charge and must be responsible for all who entered the house. He had to see that the hall was kept clean and free from dogs, but most of all he had to watch out for all comers so that he might announce the "better sort" to his master. The "meaner sort" he questioned about their business and dismissed as soon as possible, but not without some cheering drink, unless he served a parsimonious master.

Perhaps the H plan of house was favored so much and so long because it served admirably the needs of the usher as he discharged his duties. On the ground floor the kitchens and servants' quarters would be located in the back wings of the H uprights, and the hall and buttery on the cross bar of the H; thus there would be concentration of the work areas. The two front wings of the H uprights would consist of a dining room on one side, near the buttery with its hatch gate, and the study or solar on the other side, with an upper arcaded gallery connecting dining room and solar for those who did not care to cross the open court or great hall when going to and from these rooms. If the solar contained a suite of rooms for the family, it was in almost constant use. In serving the family in their dining room, the butler would have little difficulty coming from the near kitchen, but there would be much walking for a servant from the far kitchen, as he would have to traverse the entire length of the hall. Moreover, a servant in the far kitchen from the solar would also have a long distance to travel if he was summoned to the family rooms in the solar. But an usher's duties were much lessened by the H plan, for he could send a trusted messenger arriving at the hall to the hatch of the buttery for a drink or into the near kitchen for food. If a visiting master and his servant were admitted to the hall, the usher conducted the visitor to his master, and then escorted or directed the waiting servant to the buttery. In a household where many people came and went at all hours, this arrangement had its advantages.

Since the screen passage was cut off the lower end of the great hall, it was flanked on one side by this hall and on the other by the buttery and was usually merely a narrow lobby back of the main entrance. Its side seen from the great hall, however, was highly ornamented with pilasters, panels, fretwork, pinnacles, and heraldry. In fine homes the minstrels' gallery was built over the low screen passage, and the players

A formal garden with paths and knot gardens

Long gallery over the hall at Knole, Kent

Kitchen in a farmer's home, showing the inglenook
inside the fireplace

on formal occasions could provide music for the hall guests without being obtrusive when they took their places behind carved baluster and rail. Eventually the "screen" was movable like the paneling in the walls so that it might be willed to heirs who did not inherit the house. Movable screens could be utilitarian, artistic, and adaptable. Consequently they were rarely carried to the full height of the great hall. Most of the screen passages that were also used as waiting rooms had all their walls handsomely carved, the panels designed in various combinations of the reticuled pattern, with vine ornaments molded on a scroll or an adaptation made of the linenfold design, which was the most popular of all patterns for panels.

Great houses, of course, had very elaborate screens, and a visitor interested in design might be somewhat compensated for a long wait as he studied the intricate details of the ornamentation. The side of the screen passage opening into the great hall might have double doors separated by one or two carved columns, flanked on the outside by similar columns. If there was a third door in the screen, it would balance the other two in its design even though it might lead to serving chambers above, reached by a servants' stairway. It might also lead to a recessed main stair off the great hall. When closed, such a door would shut out drafts. The main stair, however, became one of the most attractive architectural features of the great hall when it was made an open, decorative ascent to the important chambers on the upper floors.

Always great care was taken in balancing the design of the screen wall on the side facing the hall. If the minstrels' gallery, for example, had a windowed wall instead of balusters and rail, the windows would be symmetrically placed, not only in relation to each other but also to the doors below. As the great hall grew smaller and was used more and more for a comfortable living room, the screen lost its importance in connection with a minstrels' gallery, but was still important for keeping out drafts by providing a private entrance to the living room. However, when the great hall so diminished in size as to be used no longer for a living room but as a vestibule instead, the screen disappeared altogether.

Some Elizabethans were loath to part with the great hall even when it was no longer fashionable, and continued to build it in their new homes. Besides the screen, other features in this room received their attention, among them being the fireplace and windows, decorated walls and friezes, richly carved open beams in the ceiling, and the great stair. Such was true of Theobalds Hall, which was one of the surprising architectural achievements of the age. Though Burghley said this mansion was designed to serve the Queen, it was also planned to serve his son, his successor in statecraft.

Before he built this great show place in Hertfordshire, Burghley had had considerable experience in working out plans for his two building programs at Burghley House in Northamptonshire. While he was Secretary to the Duke of Somerset he had watched the construction of Somerset House and had begun to dream of the home he might build for his posterity. In 1553, he fell heir to his father's estate and began making his dream come true, directing this project till 1564. After a few years of rest he began the second attempt at making this house into a magnificent establishment, and did not finish it till 1587, when he was already deeply involved in building Theobalds.

Burghley first studied pattern books published in France, and learned the mass grouping device which he employed in the arrangement of his tall cylindrical chimney columns at Burghley House. Elizabethan chimneys were of stone or brick, made straight or twisted in one single large stack or in clusters forming a square, octagon, or diamond. To add interest to their roof lines, Elizabethans depended much on tower-like chimney stacks or chimneys massively stacked in arcaded rows, with additional decorations like stone or brick or wood balusters and obelisks, heraldic beasts, vases, balls, etc. They also spent much time on designing gables, which they made corbie-stepped and curvilinear or rising from parapets of beautifully chiseled copings. Yet sometimes they preferred square gables with a blunt apex, or steeply pointed gables, or simply pointed gables of wood.

In his early building Burghley was carried away with his ideas about a stone vaulted stair, which consisted of two long flights connected by a shorter cross flight, and elaborate designs in the ceiling. Most Elizabethan great stairs were of wood that permitted endless opportunities for carving and lavish treatment of newels and balusters and vied with the ornamentation of the great chimney pieces. Now Burghley studied the Flemish pattern books which displayed pierced windows for relieving plain walls, ogee doorways, turrets and spires and weather vanes, arcaded balustrading, and other like flamboyant details. So keen was his interest in building matters that J. Alfred Gotch (*Early Renaissance Architecture in England*, 1901) believed Burghley might have become a very great architect if he had been born two centuries later. At any rate, he planned two impressive features for his new palace—its great bays and a gallery that ran 128 feet long.

When Hatton was building Holdenby he corresponded freely with Burghley because he had been so impressed by Theobalds; naturally Burghley basked in the sun of such lively appreciation of his building achievements.

Burghley's great hall at Theobalds was the center of the house; it was thirty feet wide and twice as long. For pillars it had trees, six to a side, provided with bark so artfully joined and with birds' nests and leaves and fruit so realistic in treatment that birds flew in at the open windows to enjoy them. In the ceiling were represented the twelve signs of the zodiac, the stars appropriate to each being visible at night.

During the day, the sun, by means of some ingenious mechanism designed for the purpose, ran through its course.

This house was not finished till 1588. It was set back from the road on a high hill with a splendid view toward the north and was approachable by a causeway running across the grass for some two hundred yards between avenues of ash and elm newly planted. The steepness of the site necessitated the building of two courts approached by imposing flights of steps leading to the terrace that extended to the front door. The great garden lay to the south. On the east was a small sunken garden for oranges.

The building was thus laid in three courts, with the sides unequal in height, and with walks along the east and west sides. Suites of three and four rooms were grouped around the courts, but there were few corridors, for the wings of Elizabethan houses were only one room wide. Thus guests wishing to enter the great hall or the long gallery or the great chamber had to leave their suites by means of side doors opening into their court, which in fair weather or foul had to be crossed in the open. Yet, inconvenient as these suites were to the great hall (which took up most of the side of the principal court and was thus closest at hand), they provided much more of the coveted privacy than the guest rooms which merely opened off one another.

By the end of the century the great halls were used chiefly for serving sumptuous meals to many guests or for merrymaking on annual feast days. They were also used as trophy rooms for weapons and articles of the hunt, especially in the country houses where they might serve on rainy days as a convenient place for mending arrows, cleaning guns, polishing armor, or setting broken hawks' wings. Early Elizabethan builders had included both the great hall and the long gallery in their house plans, but later Elizabethans were inclined to let the long gallery either supplant the hall or take precedence over it. For the employments of the hall were now being distributed among such rooms as the great chamber, the withdrawing room, the parlor, the breakfast room, the study room, day rooms, bedrooms, and lodgings. If the hall was retained in building plans, it was still designed to accommodate hundreds of guests on state occasions and to charm the appraising eyes of those who loved ornate fireplaces, great windows, and high, decorative ceilings, the latter with open beams in original designs or plastered with shadowy coffering and enhanced by the paneled walls and beautiful tapestries. At Kenilworth, the three-story windows of the open-beam hall were magnificent. The dais at the north end of the room had an octagonal bay. In the southwest corner was one fireplace, and two others were located in the side walls between the dais and the screen. A tower on the west side provided access to the family and state apartments.

The old, old custom of the family dining at the "high table" on the slightly raised (six inches) dais at the end of the hall opposite the screen was more or less discarded before the end of the sixteenth century. At formal dinners when guests might be entertained by short plays between courses, the raised platform of the dais could make an excellent temporary stage if family and guests were seated in the hall proper. When guests were not too numerous, they dined with the family in the private dining room off the upper end of the hall. Such a room was often called a parlor, which even modest homes liked to possess even though its furniture might consist of little more than table and joint stools and possibly a plain chair. In more comfortable homes, this parlor might be wainscoted and decorated with painted cloths. There might be a table that turned up after supper, another small square table, a chair, stools, a cupboard of pewter or silver, and two or three chests.

When the family dined in the great hall they observed much ceremony. All the household guests and servants were seated according to rank. Here the family and their most distinguished guests were seated on the dais at their own table or at the head of the long table; the rest of the household might be placed at tables as follows. In a noble's home providing a clerks' table would be seated the clerks of the kitchen, the master cook, and, at a distance, his assistants consisting of all or part of the following—usher of the great hall, grooms of the great chamber and wardrobe, the caterer and slaughterman, the brewer and underbrewer, the baker and underbaker, and the gardeners. At another table would sit the nursery staff. But at the envied long table were assigned seats for the personal servants of the family, the barber, the scrivener, the indoor servants of minor degree, such as footmen, and the outdoor servants, such as huntsmen, falconers, grooms, stablemen, postilions, the armorer and his men, the birdcatcher, and men to carry wood. At a fourth table might be the laundry maids, the porter, and a blackamoor, and at a fifth, the scullery maids and kitchen underlings. Strangers of less consequence than those dining with the family sat at tables appropriate to their rank, but those vouched for by a discreet retainer of the master might be admitted to the buttery or even served at one of the tables.

In most households the superior servants dined at the family table, among these being the chaplain, the steward, the gentleman of the horse, the gentleman usher, the auditor, the secretary, pages, and several women, among them probably the housekeeper. It is small wonder that the family of a large establishment was glad to give the hall over to their numerous servants at mealtime while they retired to their own dining room or parlor. Sometimes they had both a summer and a winter parlor, the latter as a rule quite close to the kitchen. If a wealthy family made much use of the great hall, they had a hall especially for the servants. But on feast days, certainly during the Christmas holidays, the family was expected to be democratic enough to share the long anticipated Christmas dinner with the household. Then the great hall came into its own glory once more.

When the family dined on the dais, not only were they elevated above the others but they were favored by the soft light from the great bay window at their end of the hall. Other windows in the room might be high on the walls and their light blurred by the roof timbers. Usually a fireplace came close to the dais and provided both warmth and cheer. Wall panels extended as far as the cornices or halfway to the high window sills, in which case the upper walls were often plastered, and the household armor, bows, pikes, spears, swords, and fowling pieces and trophies of the hunt were hung between the windows. Since colored glass helped to soften the light, the one or more great bays were made especially beautiful by it, and usually one of them afforded still another opportunity for displaying the heraldic emblems illustrating the owner's descent and his ancestors' notable marriages.

Perhaps the great hall was retained so long by certain families because of their romantic attachment to it for its connection with the old Christmas festivities when the Lord of Misrule was in charge of the entertainment. For a long time the hall continued to be used also for masques and plays when wandering minstrels might be invited in to entertain the entire household. Later, after the family had become accustomed to its own dining room, the usher no longer paraded the great length of the hall calling, "Give place, give place, my masters!" No longer did he daily head the impressive train of servitors advancing with the dishes and, walking up and down, see that sufficient silence reigned for conversation between members of the family and their guests. But when unusual entertainment was necessary, the hall came into prominence again, and its beautiful interior was resplendent with solemn servants in fresh liveries and with sparkling glass and gold and silver plate.

Of all interior features, the chimney piece was given most attention. This had been true since the time of the reredos, which served as a movable back to the fire built in a hole in the earth of the primitive hall. As the reredos gradually moved back to the wall, the chimney came into being and soon, because of its great size, formed a small cosy chamber with settles on each side and with dog irons or andirons in front to support the logs. Sometimes these chamber fireplaces were called "stoves" and were introduced into the halls of both modest and large buildings. In the homes of the wealthy, however, fireplaces were soon built in all important rooms, sometimes two of them in such rooms as the great hall and long gallery. Smaller than chimney pieces in the larger rooms, many lesser fireplaces were nevertheless works of art, and in them was centered a pride not unlike that reflected in great chimney stacks. As an increase in the number of fireplaces made havoc of the fine old forests, especially the oaks, coal was introduced. Those who could afford wood continued to burn it, however, and fastidious ladies often refused to enter rooms in which coal smoldered. When wood for fuel became a luxury, woodburning fireplaces became increasingly artistic and took on more and more elaboration of detail.

In wealthy homes columns and fantastic pilasters might support the heavy molding over the fire opening, and panels and pilasters, crowned by a cornice, would reach up as if to support the ceiling itself. The pillars and niches and carved decorations above the mantel made a background for the coat of arms at the center of the chimney breast or for the owner's initials at the right of the center and a device of trophies on the left. Such decorations were usually free or paneled floral designs and friezes. Stone was used more often than brick, and plaster instead of wood, though the whole structure, regardless of material, was often a network of carving. When classic columns and pilasters were used they were likely to be embellished by smaller columns of various designs. Carved scenes, both classical and allegorical or scriptural, included such subjects as Diana bathing, Job and his comforters, the Judgment of Solomon, and statuettes of Roman gods with suitable Latin inscriptions. At times the whole piece was severely classical, and again, regardless of the pattern, the mantel frieze might be carved with monkeys, birds, and fruits, and against the lintel, conventional designs in scroll or strapwork.

The rear openings of these expensive fireplaces were frequently of bricks laid herringbone-wise, and against them for safety and durability might be a cast-iron fireback, ornamented with designs. For such purpose the eight-point star was used with an elaborate wreath encircling the family coat of arms. In front of the fireback would stand a pair of andirons with carved faces or animal heads, each with a back leg to hold the burning logs.

There was one important use of the great fireplace that was full of dread and danger. Those who were persecuted for their religion knew it best, for the chimney piece might serve them as a hiding place. If enemies forced their way into the house, the master might escape up the great hall stair, thence to a small secret stair leading to the top of the house, where a concealed trap door opened into a blind passageway and stair in the middle of the house and connected with a dark chamber of the great chimney. Or he might flee immediately into the great hall chimney and into a secret chamber in which he could hide for hours while the house was being searched. Or, leading his pursuers up the great stair, he might descend quickly by a secret passage and make his escape through an inconspicuous side door the enemy had not troubled to have strictly guarded. Some of the central chimneys contained rooms that would enable several men to stand upright in them; these chimneys were called "priests' holes" or "conveyances." Such hiding places were known only to the owner of the house and his eldest son, and knowledge of them was handed down with solemn secrecy to the next generation.

After the Act of 1584, which made priests in England guilty of high treason, to harbor such a clergyman made the householder guilty of a felony. Catholic households, however, yearned for the rites of their faith to such an extent that in spite of the great danger of having a priest come to their home secretly to hold mass or to give the sacrament, they ran the risk of imprisonment or even death. Such services were conducted in upper rooms and at odd times, but so great was the fear of the informer that the greatest secrecy was observed about this worship. A sudden search might occur at any moment, with officers of the law tramping through the rooms, tearing up boards, ripping off paneling, and sounding the walls for secret rooms or priests' holes which they knew were in many houses. Though such rooms might hold several standing men, they were often so small they scarcely accommodated one, yet here a priest might be forced to stay for hours or days till it was safe for him to come out. Of course, there were many rumors concerning the "green man" and his assistants who made these hideouts, but the men were too wily and their workmanship too clever to be discovered by the law unless they were betrayed by a fellow workman.

Only great Elizabethan homes with their constant flow of guests could shelter such renowned men as Father John Gerard, to whose own account (*The Autobiography of an Elizabethan*, trans. 1951) we are indebted for many intimate details on this subject. A priest's success in serving his devout followers in England during this time depended on his host's willingness to face his risks and to share with him in his religious activities. Priests in such homes had to conduct themselves like gentlemen of fashion when in company with other gentlemen. They rode to the hunt with their host, who made up hunting parties of likely converts, and the host introduced the priest only when he was *sure* it was safe to do so. Often devoted Catholic hosts subordinated all their social life to the priest's labors, sacrificing even the privacy of their home, as Father Gerard admitted, to make certain of a safe hiding for the Lord's servant. In some cases the priests remained in remote corners of great homes and never ventured abroad unless called to a sick person. Since Father Gerard was able to open up a great mission field—later developed by Jesuits and secular priests—officers of the law were constantly trailing him from one refuge to another.

One of his most exciting accounts of hiding four days "squatting in a very confined place" deals with the search at Braddocks in April of 1594. During this time he was without food, and the mistress of the house would not eat either, because she wished to "find out by testing herself" how long the priest could go without nourishment. When the officers were finally gone and Father Gerard was released and saw the face of the lady, "it was so changed that she looked like a different person." Indeed, he would not have known her but "for her voice and her dress," so ravaged was her face by anxiety for his safety.

Only strong missionary zeal enabled men to run these great risks for themselves and their flocks, and reports of their success so infuriated the officers of the law that they did all they could to make the hazards of these people's lives as great as possible. Yet Father Gerard proceeded calmly with the details of his method of winning converts to Catholicism in districts where there were few Catholics. At first he must "bring the gentry over," he says, and after them their servants, "for Catholic gentle folk must have Catholic servants." He even believed he would have won Penelope Rich (sister of Essex) to the faith but for the "tactics of her lover, Charles Blount," who wrote her he would commit suicide if she turned Catholic. In the desolate days after his death, she often talked with Mistress Dean, one of her waiting women, about accepting the Catholic religion, "but," says the priest regretfully, "she died before I could bring her into the *fold*."

Elizabethan interest in windows continued throughout the age. When the hall had divided the house into two halves, domestic and service, it had run the depth of the house and had had high windows on both sides. But these had given way to oriels extending to eye level, then to the great bays, placed near the dais as a rule. If, however, a bay was centered on one side, it might be balanced by a porch and another window. Since the open beams of rich Gothic timbers with lavish carving on the braces and pendants gave way to the plaster ceiling, this ceiling was dropped to only one story, and the screen, also diminished in size, was made of stone. Now, with the family enjoying its summer and winter parlors and other living rooms downstairs, and the servants having their own range of offices, the great window displays of the hall were moved to other rooms of the house. For the Elizabethan, from the outside of the house, was not so impressed by any particular window (unless it extended to the parapet) as by fenestration. This was particularly true of the orderly array of windows in the whole front of fine houses in both country and city, for in such homes the second story also was framed by windows.

Such a house, for example, might have the lower-story windows large and balanced, with tiny jeweled square or diamond panes set in designs of ornamental lead. Since all the lead work was narrow, the glazed windows were made safe against intrusion by having the leaded panes attached at their edges to the outside of the casement. The transverse saddlebars were also attached to the casement at certain intervals on the inside by straps or wires. Openings, too, had iron bars. Pairs of windows balanced by other pairs and all set in ornamental window casings with delicate scrolls and designs would give the house a rich, sparkling appearance.

Many times the beauty of large windows in the great halls was increased by their heraldic designs. Mullioned windows were especially well adapted to the hall's impressive height of two or more stories, with ceiling open-beamed, but later in the century somewhat the same effect of height was achieved with ornate plaster ceilings. Windows for rooms with plaster ceilings were either of the Tudor square-headed or arched type with crystal panes, or they were a carry-over of the earlier Gothic type, having piers between the pointed openings made of elaborately carved columns or colonnettes. Though these Gothic windows were usually intricately glazed, it was not unusual to see clear panes contrasting with panes of stained glass or with panes of armorial designs. Early bays were square, but later ones were splayed or semicircular.

Since the north was the favorite exposure for large windows, the glass had to be of such quality as to soften the light. When the great size of windows did not make drapery feasible, the small glass panes might be the wrinkled, speckled, greenish type of early days. Deep window seats, used with leaded glass and wood carving or plaster designs, also helped to subdue the light by causing it to enter at an angle. Great shallow bays, their openings divided by stone crosspieces, might be very illuminating. But if their light was softened by side drapery and valances of rich material, they gave beauty and dignity to the rooms of expensively furnished homes. Besides ornamental panes of glass and costly drapery, there were paneled walls and ceilings for softening the light.

People of modest means were not likely to suffer from too much light in their homes. The dormer windows which were commonly used in cottages never permitted excessive light to enter a room, yet such windows were further darkened by protective shutters. The farther one lived from the city, the greater the difficulty of procuring glass, regardless of how cheap it might be. Modest homes, therefore, suffered from too little light. City dwellers, however, especially in London, crowded their houses close together in rows upon rows, and were only too glad of the light afforded by their many-paned crystal windows. In ordinary homes, the lack of window drapery was not felt, perhaps, except by the housewife who yearned for the beauty they might provide in framing the windows. Thus "pretty faces" at London windows were easily seen by those passing by, and undoubtedly gave as much satisfaction to those without as to admirers within.

The walls of their homes were the source of much pride to Elizabethans when they could afford to line them with panels. In the great halls panels were frequently plain, and rarely exceeded two feet at most in size. When they were nine to ten inches wide and fifteen to eighteen inches high, they made a perfect background for small or large pictures and for tapestry and furniture. When they were of hardwood artistically molded and then rubbed till they shone, they were a very rich decoration.

The linenfold pattern was favored most for panels because it showed well the contrast of light and shadow on its rigid surface; the austerity of its straight vertical lines provided an excellent foil to the richness of delicate carving above and below its folds. Often the same design for panels was used in many houses, and sometimes an entire house might use but one panel design throughout. In the great halls rich paneling extending to the cornices set off the armor hung against it, and in other rooms it might frame a Holbein or Dutch painting for those who could afford such treasures. Since there were not many of these pictures except in royal palaces or the homes of great personages, the panels in most wealthy homes were small and decorated with painted designs in brilliant greens and vermilion, or were intricately carved with arabesques of small animal or human heads. If one had a coat of arms, it would occur in at least one of the panels. Occasionally paneling was inlaid, especially if it took the place of tapestry. Paneling might cover ceiling as well as walls or it might reach only as high as the frieze, with tapestries covering the plastered space between frieze and ceiling.

The finest tapestries had elaborate handwork, and some were woven with gold or silver threads. Most of these were imported from Flanders, and their designs were chiefly in flowers and figures, though some had scenes of hunting and hawking. Others were of an armorial character, the arms surrounded by floral designs in low tone. Such work was very different in subject matter from that of painted cloths which later competed with tapesteries through their lively "histories" of the Prodigal Son, Holofernes, David, Saul, Tobit, Abraham, Jacob, and of Greek and Roman heroes such as Hercules, Alexander the Great, Hippolytus, and Julius Caesar.

When rooms of great houses were lined with tapestries, they made an impressive appearance, and so highly were they valued that the family took them all down and packed them away with their plate and other precious things when they moved from house to house. Since tapestries helped to keep out drafts, they also served a very useful purpose. The treasured ones were never hung close to the walls because of dampness; instead, they were suspended from light wooden frames or hung on iron hooks about a foot from the wall. Thus they were protected from mildew, but often they served thereby to conceal mischievous eavesdroppers.

Paneling supplanted much of the tapestry when painting developed sufficiently to encourage the importing of small, inexpensive pictures from the Netherlands. Bought at fairs or popular festivals, these pictures were hung by their proud owners in the panels of best rooms, and soon French and Low Country artists in London began to prosper by painting pictures of wealthy merchants and their wives. Those who could afford it often had pictures painted directly on the panels or had them firmly built into the walls as part of the paneling. Later, when English artists began their imitation of foreign paintings, their work was done on cloth or canvas. By this time the collecting of foreign pictures had begun. Since this expensive pastime occurred late in the century, some of the purchases were promoted by the advice of men like Inigo Jones.

Though some painted cloths might be found in paneled rooms, they usually decorated the plain walls of tradespeople who could afford neither tapestries nor panels. Such pictures were carried out in water staining and tempera on canvas, and were especially popular in bedrooms, though they were also placed in formal rooms. Often they were direct but crude copies from tapestries. The love of lively scenes, however, frequently resulted in their being painted on plaster friezes above fine paneled walls. In the Savoy House at Denham, plaster paintings consisted not only of the scenes of Moses and his followers but even of their speeches printed on scrolls.

In both painted cloths and plaster painting, the subject matter was according to the taste of the owner. Most of the common people chose biblical subjects, but the more cultivated mind ranged further afield, often preferring classical stories. Seldom was there any merit in either type of decoration. Those who chose the classical subjects were often pleased if dainty verses accompanied the gods and nymphs that sported on flowery meads. The important thing was for the design to tell a story and for its coloring to harmonize with the furnishings of the room. Some of the more favored scenes for friezes would show Venus pursuing Adonis, the battle of Lepanto, Antony meeting Cleopatra, or even such ambitious efforts as maps or plans of earth and sea. The presence chamber of Hardwick House was sixty-five feet long, thirty-three wide, and twenty-six high. Here the walls were decorated with pictures and tapestries, but its deep frieze was in colored plaster relief representing the Court of Diana. Over its door was Koheleth's popular advice—"The conclusion of all things is to feare God and keepe His commaundments." If neither tapestry nor painted plaster adorned a frieze, it might be covered with embossed leather or carved wood, carefully designed to harmonize with the ceiling. But all the decorative detail of walls must be a prelude to the massed harmony sought in the ceiling, perhaps because Elizabethan stuccoists were superior to all others in the field.

Until the middle of the century most ceilings were of wood, with two or more massive, molded beams supporting lesser timbers, the spaces between filled with plastered lath. When plastered ceilings came into use, they were designed with carved or angular plain panels that had ribs covered at the intersections with rosettes or fleurs-de-lis. Later the ribs were made wider and shallower, with deep pendants at the panel intersections. The flat panels were then decorated with foliage designs. When the important rooms above the ground floor were plastered, their ceilings were vaulted, raised to the roof, coved, and entirely covered with lively detail. By the end of the century the ceilings were enriched with elaborate designs that included pendants as part of the composition of foliage and fruit. Most of the ceilings were white, but some were gilded or touched with gilt.

Ceilings of such formal rooms as the presence chamber were likely to be elaborately ribbed and patterned in heavy relief, though some of them had merely a simple geometric design of free-flowing curves. Yet when such curves repeated no pattern at all, they somehow managed to give the effect of studied rhythm. On the high ceilings the family coat of arms was usually combined ingeniously in the geometric or floral pattern. In less lofty rooms the plaster relief was delicate and the detail less formal.

Lord Burghley's ceiling with its twelve signs of the zodiac included also in its plasterwork a high rock, painted in several colors and studded with semiprecious stones to reflect the light from burning tapers. But perhaps the most elaborate of all these ceilings was in the long gallery at Blickling Hall, with its twenty-one pictorial panels shown in the 1612 edition of Henry Peacham's emblem book, probably derived from the Flemish emblem books. Such literature, like that of the ancients, especially in the Bible, contained wise sayings and old proverbs that Elizabethans liked to see worked into the designs of their chimney pieces and ceilings.

As a rule, the houses in the south of England had high ceilings with deeply undercut modelings that absorbed much of the light from the great windows. In the north the attempt was made to diffuse the light and to irradiate it with soft and delicate patterns in low relief, their shallow concaves and melting outlines forming interwoven geometric designs that permitted the play of lights and cross-lights. For lofty rooms, the plaster ceiling usually emphasized its pendants because they broke the possible monotony of design and added to the richness of the studied effect.

In spite of the wealth of detail in such ceilings, they could hardly be as impressive as those with open beams, even when space permitted them to carry the design up to form a cove, and the pattern was enhanced by pendants and by decorated walls. Crosby Hall in Bishopsgate Street, for example, had a majestic vaulted roof with the family coat of arms in the center. Its three longitudinal beams and nine transverse beams at their intersection formed twenty small, flat-pointed arches with richly carved pendants. The whole effect was a challenge to any plaster ceiling in this riotous age of building.

Ordinary homes had plain plaster or wood ceilings. Humble homes, unable to provide themselves with the warmth of ceilings, continued to use open beams, even for their very low rooms. These, of course, were soon blackened by smoke from the fireplace. Such homes could not afford the cheapest painted cloths for their walls to shield the family from damp and drafts. Nor even, if they could afford plaster, could these people do much more than dream of wallpaper, which began to appear at the end of the century, especially in the bedrooms, to which this covering gave an air of cosiness. Wallpaper was printed from wooden blocks, and, like all innovations, was dear. The rough-hewn wood of the interiors in humble homes and the dim light from strictly limited window space made these houses dreary enough in the country and almost intolerable in crowded cities. In the country they were likely to be close to the crude shelter provided for the animals and fowls, or divided from such shelters by frail partitions or none at all, and in cities they were wedged in close to the noisy, smelly habitations of others as poor as themselves. Ceilings, then, as we think of them in Elizabethan homes, bordered close onto luxury.

When dinner was over in the hall of the better homes, the women with leisure retired to a withdrawing room at first situated on the floor above. Here they gossiped or entertained one another with song or with the music they were able to produce on instruments designed especially for women. If they could look out on the street, they were likely to watch the passersby and to exchange comments about them. Or they might take out their embroidery and compare their work as they followed or originated designs for their busy hands. Of course, if the weather was pleasant, they might retire for at least part of the afternoon to the garden to wander about the paths or to sit chatting in some bower. Those who desired solitude were likely to go to their rooms or to seek a secluded nook in the garden; there they might busy themselves at sewing or reading. Meanwhile the men whose employments did not call them away remained at table drinking, telling stories, or attending to some business transaction.

If the men sat long at table and the light began to grow dim, candles furnished them with light. These were in holders or chandeliers of wood or iron suspended from the ceiling, some of which could be raised or lowered at will. Torches stuck in iron wall brackets were outmoded in later Elizabethan homes. Oil lamps and wax candles were dear, for they were imported from France or Italy, though candles of wax or white tallow, with cotton wicks, might be purchased from candlemakers or made by journeymen who traveled from house to house, working for fourpence a day. Thrifty people used homemade candles, and the poor used rushes dipped in the dark fat accumulated from cooking. In houses that could afford good candles, surplus fats were given away to women who came to the kitchen door. Few candlesticks were used on the average table, for they were expensive enough to prohibit common use till near the end of the century. If made of silver they were suitable gifts even for the wealthy; these had a spreading base, and were baluster-shaped. Cheaper ones were made of latten or pewter. Thus wax or tallow candles which had to be used in candlesticks were more or less a luxury for all but those in lavishly furnished homes.

Furniture in the great halls was for use, many of the treasured pieces being removed to the long gallery or presence chamber. What remained consisted of tables, a few chairs, sideboards, and benches, and, if the hall was used for dining, a good many stools and benches. When not in use, these latter pieces might be pushed back out of the way. Just as benches and stools served for chairs, so did chests often take the place of sideboards. At feasts or great dinners trestles or forms were set up and boards laid over them for the table top. If the dais was used, the master sat at the shovel board. Later this table gave way to one with an extension top, known as the draw table. Here the honored guests sat on stools or possibly chairs. Benches and joint stools were used at the long table, the benches mostly for the lowest in rank. Sometimes additional seating was provided by chests, of which there were usually a great many in a household. Most of the tables were narrow, and it was customary for the diners to sit on one side and to be served from the other. In this way heavy dishes could be placed on the table with very little difficulty.

Early furniture, made of oak, was massive and put together with wooden pins instead of nails. Legs were straight from top to bottom, although bulbous legs, especially for tables, came later. In a home that did not change its floor rushes very often, the footrails of tables and chairs served a practical purpose. As cleanliness increased, however, this rail was raised till it formed a stretcher, but even then it served children and short people for a footrail. Rushes were too expensive for poor homes, and among the rich, they were gradually replaced at the end of the century by mats of woven rushes or by straw matting or even by rugs. In large halls the table rails were used to hold the joint stools when they were pushed out of the way under the table with their legs turned inward. Joint stools were so named because they were joined together. They served for tables quite as often as for seats. About two feet high, this stool was sometimes used by the carver (hence the supposition it got its name from the joints carved on it), but it was most in demand as an extra table, not only in formal rooms but also in private chambers.

Chairs were a luxury introduced slowly into the homes of the common people. During the middle of the century the square oak chairs became popular, their solid and paneled backs and arm rests made comfortable by cushions. Crimson satin, velvet, silk, and damask were used for this purpose, as only the wealthy could afford such chairs, and the wife and her maids embroidered the material in conventional designs of birds, insects, and flowers. Backs and portions of the frame were also covered. Later, the seats of chairs were carved and covered with cushions, and still later, both chairs and stools in homes that could afford them were covered with leather and studded with nails. By the end of the century high and low X-shaped chairs and stools were popular. They were studded and made comfortable with quilted upholstery of velvet and had legs and frames of birch covered with gilded gesso. The seats, upholstered in velvet or damask, were trimmed with fringed galloon. Finally even windowseats were padded, by this time feathers being used for the purpose, and the covers were made of silk or cloth of silver or gold, and frequently embroidered.

Chests, chairs, and benches reflected the Elizabethan love of panels. The wall or wainscot bench was found in homes of almost all classes. It had grown out of the chest, and was in reality little more than a long chest with a paneled back about three feet high, and finished at both ends with arms. In most comfortable homes of the middle class, two of these wall benches would be put by the fireplace of the hall or living room, one at each side. Their high backs kept out the drafts.

Some furniture was made to fold into chests, and thus could be easily moved from place to place. Such pieces were likely to be found in the homes of people who wished to take many of their belongings with them as they moved about. A secretary designed in this fashion had a fall-down front, and when open displayed one large and twelve smaller drawers, each with a central iron handle. The inlay ornamentation on front and drawers was in a simple floral design, and the whole piece was mounted on trestle legs joined by stretchers. Another ingenious adaptation of the chest was for a chair or table. It consisted of a bench fitted with a flap or top that moved on a pivot and folded back for a bench or settle or a table top; its lower portion served as a chest. This piece of furniture was known as a table bench or a monk's bench.

Until the turning lathe made possible the beautifully modeled arms and legs of furniture, most chairs and stools were boxed or paneled. When chairs became more comfortable, the backs were no longer extended to meet the seats, but the tops were extended till they spread to side ears. The folding X-type chair or stool became popular because it was portable and adapted to the needs of all classes. Three-legged chairs and stools were also popular, but chiefly because of the possibilities their turned legs gave for carving. Indeed, carving and the rich materials— woods for frames, and fabrics for cushions and upholstering—were often the chief differences between chairs of modest and showy homes. When farthingales came in, chairs had to be made without arms, but the backs and seats were upholstered and often adorned with rich lace and embroidery.

Frequently covered and carved chairs were enumerated in wills or inventories that included such examples as the following: a green velvet or tuft taffeta chair from the great chamber, a yellow chair from a bedroom, a green cloth chair from the dining room or parlor, and another chair with black wrought velvet, laid with silver and gold lace. Stools with the same upholstery would accompany these chairs, their number in bedroom and parlor-dining room running from two to a dozen or more. Leather stools might also be mentioned in connection with dining room furniture. Though chairs supplanted stools as time went on, the stool was not easily dispensed with in the intimate rooms of the house.

The family dining room or parlor just off the hall was often elaborately paneled and richly decorated and furnished, for aside from its use at mealtime it often served as a gathering place in which to chat com-

fortably. Here were certain modifications of the great hall. The roof
might be fairly low and ceiled, yet with fully exposed rafters, or it might
be high with ornate plaster work. In the chimney piece, windows, and
walls, every effort would be made to give the room a feeling of warmth.
It might be paneled in the linenfold design and made cosy by a fireplace
of stone with carved pilasters and panels and semi-raised work. The
leaded windows were likely to be enriched with the family coat of arms
in colored glass and with embroidered drapery. One or two cabinets of
oak or walnut with beautiful inlay would add a graceful touch. In such
a room the family would dine at a draw-top table about two and a half feet
high and capable of being extended to over seven feet when the ends
were pulled out. Its bulbous or melon-ball legs would be joined at the
base by a footrail. The chairs most likely would be panel-backed, and the
joint stools, used for little extra tables, would have their stretchers near
the top and curiously carved. On the floor would be broad-leaved rushes
plaited coarsely into mats.

The sideboards or court cupboards of the great hall were massive,
richly carved pieces of furniture for displaying the family plate. Smaller
cupboards held wine and table linens and servants' livery allowances. A
somewhat simple adaptation of the court cupboard was a buffet or table
with a widened footrail that could exhibit showy plate. Baluster columns, turned from solid squares of hardwood and carved with acorns,
flowers, etc., supported the front of the shelves. The back supports were
usually plain, though the stretchers between front and back to hold up
the shelves were covered with carving. When inlay was used on the flat
surfaces, the designs were not elaborate, the contrast between woods serving for embellishment. Holly, bog oak, and ebony were commonly used
for inlays. The fastidious lover of fine furniture was attracted to small
pieces in which the gloss of flat surfaces was heightened by varnish and
beeswax to reveal the grain of the wood or the beauty of the marquetry.
Nevertheless, large, strong pieces were needed to hold the heavy plate,
and for this purpose nothing could take the place of the court cupboards.

Late designs of court cupboards made them not unlike two chests,
the narrower one on top of the larger. The smooth surfaces of the sunken
panels at the sides and the rich carving of the baluster columns were in
direct contrast. Sometimes the upper cupboard would be polygonal, and
the lower one open, supported by carved columns, or closed with paneled
doors. In either case the lower shelf must be wide enough to hold plate
or glasses and cups. If the top portion of the cupboard was closed, a door
in the middle might open upon some secretly locked cabinet, but the two
doors on each side of it would open on shelves for holding plate. Below,
two wide paneled doors would indicate that the interior was to be used
for linens; if open, it was to hold containers for wine, cordials, etc., or
cups and glasses.

Sideboards and court cupboards were so massive and richly ornamented that only the very rich were likely to possess them. In the late sixteenth century, they were frequently made of rosewood or walnut and inlaid with marquetry, as was customary with display pieces. Occasionally court cupboards were used in long galleries with cabinets holding treasures, but the customary place for them was in the great hall in which large assemblies of guests dined. In private dining rooms, adaptations like the buffet took their place.

One of the most decorative features of the great hall and of the entire house was the great stairway leading to the upper chambers. Previously the staircase had been a tower-corkscrew type or a straight flight set in a thick wall. Although this latter staircase was used till late in the period, the central stairway was one of the new, popular architectural features. Its width was greatly increased during this expansive age, and many new details were added to give it magnificence and charm and utility.

Perhaps Burghley's great vaulted stair with its long flights of stone steps was one of the earliest to be built for show as well as for use. At first the rectangular treads of stone or wood were placed against the wall of the great hall, and then within a spacious stairwell with tiers of balustered panels. Later came the elaborate continuous newel stair with plaster panels, and still later the open-well type with free newel posts at the corners of the balustrades. Some of the stairs were entered through a door leading from the screen passage, and some through a carved gate that kept the dogs in the hall from the upper rooms. The spiral stair in a tower usually wound to the right, perhaps to make use of the sword arm less awkard when the master or a servant of the house must turn on the stone steps to face an enemy pressing close upon him. Now, with their feeling of greater security, Elizabethans felt the main stair should be located at the center of the house. Moreover, they made its ascent easy by means of low treads and many landings, for steps in the short, straight flights seldom numbered more than eight. When the stair was well located in the great hall and was wide and open, turning in graceful angles, it made a very impressive appearance.

In an open stair the handrail was no longer neglected. It became massive, and was filled with turned or flat or square carved balusters arcaded to follow the incline of the ascent. Although commonly the oak newels and sometimes the balusters were provided with finial figures like the obelisk, ball, and urn, the more elaborate designs carried the newels well above the handrail. In such a stair the tops of newels were wrought into striking shapes and figures, human, animal, and fantastic. Some were heraldic, like the leopards sitting on top the newels at Knole House. Some were simply odd, as in the case of a design using garden tools. Arabesques were much favored, and sometimes allegorical figures were used, or even pretty little boys playing musical instruments. Typical of the Elizabethan love of extremes was one series crowned by the figure of a divine holding book and spectacles, another series with a playful mendicant friar, and another with genii playing pipes. Fantastic animals distinguished the newels of the great stair of Crewe Hall in Cheshire and provided a charming touch to the carving. In sharp contrast to such figures were the classical statues of women surmounting the newels of the Aldermaston staircase in Berkshire. This wide stair with its many landings wound gracefully around its great well, and its massive newels framed and held together in an artistic manner the entire structure. In simple designs the turned balusters and square newels often terminated in a ball or acorn, or were divided horizontally to make two triangles. For geometrical divisions frequently accentuated the symmetry in the great stair as in other features of Elizabethan building.

Mounting their fine stairways, Elizabethans usually faced a great tapestry suspended from the ornate frieze of the paneled wall. Sometimes beautiful windows cast their soft light on a stair located at the side of a great hall or revealed a garden beautiful with flowers and shrubbery. Prosperous householders built at least two kinds of stairways, a handsome one for family and guests and one or more plain ones for servants. The latter stairs were never ornamented even in the great houses. When servants were quartered in retainers' galleries at the top of the house, however, they might well be out of the way of the family, but unless they were closely supervised they might also engage in no little mischief among themselves. Despite the fact that great houses had many stairways, most of them placed in the projecting turrets of the four angles of courts, only the great stair, like the great hall, was a feature about which the whole house was planned.

Though the standards of the wealthy in one generation frequently set the standards of the lower class in the next generation, the changes in the Elizabethan period were often too sudden for such an evolution. Rich ecclesiastics, for example, sometimes furnished their homes as sumptuously as if they were lords, particularly if they were of lowly origin. Thomas Cromwell, mentor of Cardinal Wolsey, supplied his hall with the following pieces of furniture: a gilt cupboard, a large paneled shovelboard table, a pair of trestles and six stools and footstools, a large gilt chair, one chair upholstered in leather and another in Flanders work, three little gilt chairs for women, three long settles or benches, six handsome cushions embroidered with the Cardinal's red roses, two scarfs, a rich red and green silk hanging, a paneled screen, a gilt mirror with Flanders work, a painted cloth bearing the Cardinal's prized arms in gilt, another with the "history" of Lucrece, a canvas picture of Charles the Emperor, and for the fireplace, andirons, tongs, and bellows. For his time he was comfortably established, but an Elizabethan hall in which the owner carried out the details according to Elizabethan rules of good taste and ostentation was far more elaborate.

Many Elizabethan halls were brilliant with color. Instead of wall panels that in Henry VIII's time might display large medallion heads of helmeted warriors, dolphins and other animals, or family portraits, biblical characters, etc., the light oak panels of the Queen's time might be left untouched except by wax or varnish, and the window rails and stiles painted a rich red. Again, the panels might be tastefully decorated with green or red or blue to harmonize with the color of window rails and stiles, painted cloths or tapestries, and window draperies embroidered by the housewife and her maids. The material of the draperies would range from velvet and silk to linen, according to the householder's purse. The show pieces of furniture would be in the hall unless the house included a long gallery. If there was no gallery, a late Elizabethan hall might be refurbished by cabinets, court cupboards, chairs, and, after the 1590's, tables with marble tops. Until then, fine tables were inlaid with ivory, silver, tortoise shell, colored woods, and even semiprecious stones. An effort to harmonize upholstery of chairs and stools in both color and quality would add to the charm of the hall's appearance and reveal the interest in beauty that was pursued in one form or another by all owners of comfortable homes.

In ordinary homes, simple wainscoting substituted for fine paneling. If the housewife loved her living room and had leisure for adorning it, she spent long hours embroidering window curtains in bright colors. Certain adaptations would be necessary for windows, fireplace, and other architectural features by which a home was given individuality. Instead of a coat of arms on the chimney breast, a motto might be carved such as "Hast thou a friend as heart may wish at will? Then use him so as to have his friendship still." The mantel might be of carved oak or stone or artfully laid brick, but the fireplace would have to be useful.

If the hall served as kitchen also, as in the humble cottage, the whole chimney piece would be designed for use. The uprights of the andirons would be fitted with hooks to hold the spits in position before the fire. There would be no carved faces or animal heads here, though the spit rack might be quaintly shaped of wood and simply carved if the owner or a friend could do such work. The ample spit rack, as a rule, extended from the ceiling down to the mantel piece and held all the spits. Well-equipped kitchens of farmhouses or the better inns sometimes had very ingenious chimney cranes with levers working on a ratchet, the whole mechanism being capable of sliding back and forth by means of a wheel at the top.

The kitchens of poor working people would be cluttered with such tools as looms, rakes, pails, bushel measures, shovels, axes, and spades. Then there would be trestles and boards and stools, and perhaps a bolting hutch. No matter how hard the good housewife might try to keep things in place, she would achieve little order in such a crowded room.

In the kitchen of a noble's house the adjoining rooms devoted to culinary purposes as well as those used for storing provisions increased the bedlam of activity. Commands would be called out to servants in the kitchen, pantry, spicery, and wet and dry larders. In the latter were stored liquors, meats, and other foods. Bread was kept in the pantry, where the pastry ovens were also located. Spiceries were special departments only in wealthy homes, and in the wet larder were butts or casks of liquor. Later this room was called the buttery and was used for all kinds of provisions.

Some of the kitchens were vaulted and were so large that, with their subsidiary rooms, they required a whole wing of the mansion. Such kitchens might be provided with more than one huge fireplace, each with a pastry or pantry near at hand, containing a large oven. The walls would be almost covered with shelves containing wooden platters, jugs, and tankards, all sorts and shapes and sizes of cooking pots and skillets of brass or earthenware or pewter, and cleavers and skewers hanging by their leather thongs. Cleaning pots and pans in the scullery was the most disagreeable task even in the best of these kitchens, and such labor was usually performed by a sorry lot of workers.

The great fireplace was the chief feature in any fine kitchen. It would project yards into the room, and beneath it, on either side of the hearth, might be benches. Back in the vast chimney sides would hang hams and dried tongues and sides of bacon. When two or three fireplaces were in use they would be the center of activity, and the kitchen scullions would be called forth to turn the spits. Some of the roasts would reach clear across in front of the fire as they revolved and would take the strength and skill of a strong man, for they had to be expertly browned. In a farmhouse a small spit might be turned by a dog caged in a revolving wheel fastened at the side or above the fireplace, but in one of the great kitchens the spits demanded the strong muscles and quick eye of the trained helper. Meanwhile, at a large table running across the room the master cook would superintend the preparing of fish and fowls that must be ready for dinner when the roasts were done.

When meals were served in the great hall, the master's family and guests were seated first, and then all the servants took their proper places, each in his own "office," the chief servant having inspected the tables, especially the upper table and the sideboards to see that dishes, glassware, silver, and napery were in order. During the meals there was need for continued supervision lest among members of a numerous household the noise of conversation and the rattling of dishes interfere with the comfort of master and guests. No wonder the private dining room became one of the most prized comforts of the age.

Between meals snacks might be set out on the ledge of the buttery hatch, and also tankards of ale or beer or some other refreshment for male members of the family coming in from the hunt. Here, also, the

butler might serve strangers or guests between meals if they were vouched
for by the head usher. Lest servants take advantage of these privileges,
it was necessary for strict rules to be made concerning the buttery—when
it might be open, how late the butler was to remain in his office, and even
how much refreshment might be allowed servants. On festive occasions
these rules were likely to be suspended. The butler was usually a very
busy man, for he must see that fresh water was brought in twice a day
to wash the plates and cups after dinner and supper, he must prevent
servants from tippling at the hatch, and he must keep out strangers who
might try to take advantage of his master's hospitality. In more modest
homes the butler's position was of even more importance, for upon his
honesty depended much of the household thrift and the cleanliness of
the kitchen.

Naturally it was difficult to keep kitchens clean, and often they were
indescribably filthy. Henry VIII had to enact a law against such conditions in his own establishment, though at table he grew beastly in his
eating habits as he felt old age creeping near. Good housewives made
frequent inspections of their kitchens, and were expected to do so, especially in middle-class homes. Such kitchens were often provided with
double fireplaces also, which, with their spits and large pots hanging from
a series of rods and chains fastened to the andirons, were like a lord's
establishment on a limited scale. The tops of many pots were like brazier
baskets and could be filled with coals to cook sauces in pans. Large, three-
legged kettles were used by rich and poor when they cooked food over
hot coals. Since custard pies were served at nearly all feasts, the common
housewife who had a brick oven could also serve this delicacy. After the
firecoals had been raked out of the oven, the day's supply of little bread
loaves would be put in, and then the pies, which took less time than the
bread for baking. Poor people eventually used public ovens at the town
or city bake houses, but housewives with their own ovens were very proud
of the convenience. Families with such kitchens, of course, did not dine
in the kitchen but in their hall or parlor.

When Cardinal Wolsey introduced the long gallery at Hampton
Court, he provided a means by which the wealthy might indulge their
love of display. In mansions, the long gallery and presence chamber
might occupy most of the first floor above the great hall. Though not
fashionable in country palatial homes or in the Italian type of house, it
was added to many of the new town or city homes. It was lofty and wide
and long, the longer the better, and much more impressive for size than
the retainers' gallery, a room that, extending halfway into the roof of the
house, was called an attic in later years . The long gallery in moderately
sized houses of lords might be a hundred feet long; in their large houses
it often extended twice as far, with windows along one whole side to command a fine view. The width was not important, varying as it did from

fifteen to twenty-five feet; when this room lost favor, it too became known as the lumber room or attic if it was located at the top of the house.

When built into the lower floor of the mansion, the long gallery might supplant the hall and serve as a place in which to wait for an audience with the master of the house, but in smaller establishments it frequently served as a place for exercise or as a music room. If it became the center of the house as the hall had been, the family and guests came to it to listen to music, to dance stately measures, and sometimes to romp through their leaping dances. Should inclement weather forbid walking in the garden, especially in the case of women, they might take their exercise in the gallery and enjoy it if one side afforded a fine view.

Since the gallery denoted a home of some pretension, it was used for the choicest displays of the owner's wealth. Many families stripped their halls of their treasured pictures and tapestries and ordered for a display of smaller objects the finest cabinets and court cupboards obtainable. Burghley covered the walls of his gallery with genealogical trees showing the pedigrees of the Tudors and their predecessors and with the heraldic devices of many English nobles, knights, and squires. The Haddon gallery was made beautiful by its great bay windows looking onto lovely gardens. Its walls were ornately paneled from floor to ceiling, the circular-headed panels divided by pilasters, and the plaster ceiling ornamented in a geometric ribbed design. The long gallery of Hatfield House was twenty by one hundred sixty feet, and its ceiling was sixteen feet high. A series of windows on one side provided the much desired view. Its impressive chimney piece was of marble, and fluted square columns divided the wall panels. Similar small columns divided the molded panels of the deep frieze, which was supported by heavy molding where it joined the paneling of the walls.

Such a room was in keeping with the grandiose architecture of Burghley's Theobalds with its Elizabethan windows, its little towers and cupolas, its fancy chimneys that looked like Greek columns, and its ornamental parapet along the roof. The long gallery was also in keeping in Montacute House. Here the gallery extended the full length of the house, which had statues in its niches, great bays and chimneys, curved Dutch gables, a parapet along its roof, and miniature obelisks mounted on the garden walls. At Hampton Court the long gallery held valuable furniture and treasures. Between high windows stood handsome court cupboards filled with shining plate and cabinets of ebony and tortoise shell with treasures of gold and silver and precious stones. There was a long table carved in mother-of-pearl, and there were virginals made of polished wood inlaid with precious stones. On the walls hung tapestries and pictures, and at the windows velvet curtains. For distinguished guests there were two chairs of state and, for guests of lesser rank, piles of gaily colored cushions.

With such a display room, the owner was encouraged to collect treasures, and he often began with portraits of the family. Leicester's gallery at Kenilworth contained portraits, face and full length, displaying rich costumes, which Holbein's paintings had made fashionable at Henry VIII's court. Lord Lumley of Nonesuch Palace collected historical portraits for his gallery as well as books and manuscripts. Often the owners covered their pictures with protective drapery. Shakespeare puns on this custom in *Twelfth Night* (I:v:250) when Olivia, before unveiling to Viola, says ". . . we will draw the curtain and show you the picture." Deloney's prosperous clothier in *Jack of Newberry* has fifteen "fair" pictures, each covered with a green silk curtain, fringed with gold. No doubt miniatures became so popular, not because they could be worn on watches, pins, and in pomander boxes, but because collectors desired them for display in beautiful cabinets in their galleries.

Accordingly, against the rich paneling of these rooms were placed cabinets about four feet high, with two shelves of drawers for holding rare collections. Smaller cabinets on tables would stand out in the room, for they were decorated on all sides, were exquisitely made, and were often full of tantalizing "secret" drawers. Like the buffets, they had checkerboard marquetry or were inlaid with precious stones and other rich contrasting materials. A chiming clock might be placed on a wall bracket, or a table clock, made of metal or wood and with a dial and one hand set on its circular or square top, would be an interesting exhibit. Elizabethan travelers were always on the alert for treasured curios, and whatever seemed new and strange to them frequently found its way into a cabinet at home or was housed in a cabinet designed especially for it.

Since the long gallery was not planned for quiet conversation, its furniture did not include many easy chairs; however, what were there were usually the best in the house. Bay windows provided comfortable seats with cushions and there were richly upholstered stools and some benches. In Hardwick long gallery, however, there was a day bed made of oak, painted a chocolate red, and ornamented with floral arabesques and the family coat of arms. Its two paneled ends inclined outward from its bed or sofa, which was over seven feet long, and its loose mattresses were covered with red damask, embroidered with colored silks and gold thread. Shakespeare's "love beds" of *Twelfth Night* and *Richard III* probably refer to such a piece. Though popular for their novelty at the end of the period, these day beds were far from comfortable because of their stiff angularity. At Knole House, where many original pieces of furniture were designed by resident skilled craftsmen, was built a similar day bed that is proudly shown present-day visitors. (Today at one of London's fine furniture stores a modern expensive adaptation of it is offered for sale.)

Because of their length, the long galleries frequently had two fireplaces. By the end of the century they were very fashionable. Here children played at skittles and blindman's buff; the young engaged in love-making, and the older people walked for exercise while listening, perhaps, to a chaplain or attendant read to them from the Scriptures or from literature pleasing to their taste. And here men engaged in talk, serious or light, as they entertained important visitors. As they strolled back and forth, talking, the master might refer unobtrusively to details seen from the windows that indicated the magnificence of his home.

Floors of important rooms like the long gallery might be covered with rushes, but the tendency was to use matting; an estimate of "twelve score yards" for the purpose was not unusual. The increased demand for rushes in the late 1590's made them expensive, a load costing seven or eight dollars or more of our money today. If a household could not afford rushes, its stone or wooden floors were left bare, though in small towns and the country, hay, when cheap, might be substituted for rushes during the cold, damp months of winter. Thrifty owners floored the rooms that would have hard wear with the boards set edgewise, thus providing greater rigidity and durability. Houses that cultivated cleanliness often sanded the floors. In the humblest homes, the floors were hard-packed clay or earth. Homes using rushes might become infested with fleas and other vermin if the rushes were not changed often. As pride in the home increased, however, cleanliness increased. It was customary, therefore, in well-ordered homes to change the rushes once a month, or oftener, and always to renew them in unoccupied chambers when preparing for important guests.

In the new homes, the parlor often became the withdrawing room and, for formal receptions in mansions, the great presence chamber. The indefatigable Bess of Hardwick, with eight establishments to her credit, was still satisfying her creative building instincts with great zest when she was over seventy years of age. In all her plans she considered the drawing room important. Her love of both comfort and grandeur was expressed best at Hardwick House, where she lived with her notable granddaughter, Arabella Stuart. Much eager planning and many years of building finally brought this home to completion in 1598. Set high on a hill in the center of a park, it looked out over rolling countryside, and from afar its four elaborately scrolled towers proclaimed the magnificence of the house. A flagged path led from the gatehouse to the entrance hall, which was two stories high and embellished with paneling and tapestry. Off the great stair on the left and shut off by an openwork oak screen was the curious little chapel. Close by was the state bedroom with its adjoining dining room, from which the minstrels' gallery led to a wainscoted, tapestried drawing room.

A beautifully dressed bed in parlor or presence chamber could make these rooms serve two purposes. This bed was the most comfortable seat in the house and was so used by day. A richly appointed bed in a lord's great chamber might enable him or his lady when recovering from an illness to hold an elaborate reception there for friends and guests. Shortly before time to give birth to a child, the mother had this room prepared carefully for the day when her friends might visit her to present gifts and to wish her well. The bed hangings, exquisitely made of silk or satin in rich homes, might be embroidered with mother-of-pearl. Before the reception, rose petals were strewn on the floor, and precious cabinets with chased silverware and tinted china, and beautiful small tables, chairs, stools, and cushions would be brought in to dazzle the eyes of the guests. This chamber, usually facing the east, was also used for christenings, marriages, betrothals, and funerals. Of course, if used for a death chamber, it was draped in black.

Often the presence chamber was provided with a recess in which at formal receptions the chair of state (or throne) was placed. Here sat host and hostess under a canopy, attired in their richest raiment, receiving their guests. Such a room was frequently called a throne room. Its draperies were very rich, and all the appointments were meant to proclaim wealth and rank and power. As furnishings grew better, the rushes on the floor were replaced with matting, but if the room was to be used for balls as well as receptions, the floor was laid with hardwood, rubbed smooth. Most homes, however, used the long gallery for entertainment of guests at formal social gatherings.

Carpets were not used in any but the richest homes. Most of the carpets referred to in literature of the time were used on tables and window seats—on the floor only when one knelt in prayer. To walk on carpets was a privilege of royalty and important nobles only. Carpets were costly imports from the East; but Elizabethan ladies often made what they called carpets by embroidering canvas with "turkey work," which consisted of a treble cross-stitch done in wool and cut open to a close pile. This imitation in needlework of fine Eastern rugs was beheld with pride by its owners and was usually made in gay colors. Such pieces might well adorn the furniture in a parlor, but only Eastern carpets would be fine enough for a great presence room, a splendid long gallery, or a proud state chamber.

In these rooms of the privileged class, windows, walls, ceilings, and fireplaces were elaborate and often individually impressive. Deep, colorful friezes were frequently used to make the walls outstanding. Sometimes they were designed with human figures in various poses against a background of delicately colored plasterwork. Sometimes they depicted idyllic woodland scenes, abounding with animal life in which most often the deer and the leopard were shown in graceful action. At Hardwick House, the presence chamber was perhaps the most beautiful of all the carefully planned rooms. There was little paneling, for the walls were plastered and covered with tapestries. The frieze, also of plaster, was eleven feet in height, with glowing scenes of the hunt against a strange floral background carefully harmonizing with the rich, decorative hangings. When such a house had no long gallery, the choicest treasures were placed in the presence chamber, unless, of course, they went into the great hall.

In following the example of the rich, the common people made their parlors as attractive as possible, the good housewife especially adding to the comfort and appearance by means of needlework for curtains, cushions, and "carpet" work. In early days the family rooms were situated beyond the parlor, but Elizabethans preferred their bedchambers on the first floor above the hall, and the guest chambers above these or in wings. A somewhat confusing but nevertheless informative description of an English house occurs in Juan Luis Vives' *Tudor School-Boy Life: Dialogues* (1539) (Dialogue XII). One of the noticeable points in this textbook conversation is the interest boys were supposed to have in the arrangement and functions of rooms in a Tudor house. Since the device of using familiar material with which to introduce new Latin terms determined much of the matter in the dialogue, one must not expect exactness in the descriptions. At the same time Vives could not have succeeded in his purpose had he strayed too far from the facts about how people lived or should live when he wrote his little book.

Vives begins the dialogue with a visitor entering a house through a magnificent door which stands open all day without guard, but is closed at night. In the screen passage he is met by the chief usher who directs him into a spacious hall where there are numerous pictures. One represents the plan of the earth and the sea, another shows Spain discovering America, and another portrays Lucrece killing herself. Now the usher comes to escort the visitor up the great stairway to the master of the house on the first floor. A less pretentious stair leads to rooms above this floor.

The visitor is announced, and as the master comes forth to greet him, the usher takes his departure. As he is led into the private sitting room or "closet" of the master, the caller notices over the doorway the carved inscription, "Withdraw from your troubles and enter the haven of peace," and just inside the doorpost another inscription, "Bring into this haven no tempest." The "closet" is furnished with tapestry covering much of the wainscoting and it has rush mats on the floor. Pictures in this room are of Mary and Jesus and such classical characters as Narcissus, Euryale, Adonis, and Polyxena. Since this is a new home, the master offers graciously to show it to his friend. The winter parlor has darker and better furniture than that in the "closet," and it also has a fireplace, still called a "sweating chamber." An interesting convenience in the inner bedroom is a steam pipe for a heating device. The bedroom is furnished with the usual pieces, besides basins, pans, and chamber crockery.

From these family rooms can be seen the chapel with its beautiful little towers and pyramids, its columns and weathercocks. The master is proud of his chapel and draws his guest's attention to its architectural embellishments. Talking of building and such problems, they descend the great stair to the family dining room just off the great hall. Here the beautiful transparent windows are artistically painted in shaded outlines, their subject being Griselda's suffering and reward. Along the walls in niches are statues of Paul, of the courageous Scaevola, of Helen of Troy, and of Homer pointing his finger scornfully at Helen. The gilded wainscoting is decorated here and there with pearls of small worth.

The visitor is next taken to the kitchen with its buttery, wine cellar, and larder. He is shown also the back door of the house and told how it is always fastened with iron bars, and when the master is away, it is bolted and locked. The windows at the back open onto a narrow street, and they are also barred, but with wood instead of iron. The welcoming front door and the carefully locked back door are features that tell much of the Elizabethan way of life.

When it came to comfort, Elizabethans were most concerned with the bedchambers. The chief articles of furniture besides the bed were various types of chests and plain or embroidered hangings for windows and bed. Here, what were luxuries were to become necessities for the next generation. The walls were given considerable attention with storied pictures on plaster or stained cloths or worked into tapestries or embroidered hangings. Shakespeare suggests the common taste in subject matter through Falstaff's remark about the hangings at the inn, which, he says, are "a pretty drollery," but the Prodigal Son or a German hunting scene on painted cloths would be worth a thousand such tapestries. Homes that could afford it imported artists from Italy to paint stories on their walls, but in most Elizabethan homes the nimble-fingered housewife was the artist, and her tools were the needle and wool or silk. The fireplace and its andirons also provided both the rich and the comfortable middle class with opportunities to show their love of comfort and beauty, but most of all they concerned themselves with the soft and luxurious bed.

Queen Elizabeth's father and brother used a bed eleven feet square, with hangings of silk, glistening with gold and silver. Elizabeth's own bed was made of many different colored woods and inlays and had curious designs on coverings and cushions, many of which she embroidered herself. Among these patterns were two horses, one with a rider, embroidered on velvet; another was of popinjays embroidered on sarcenet, and still another was of dolphins embroidered on purple silk. Her wall tapestries came from a French king, and her chairs were carved or upholstered in rich silks and velvets. Purple velvet, fringed with purple silk, was used on one chair; another had a cloth of gold background with a raised pattern of crimson velvet; a third had a cloth of gold background raised with black velvet, and another had a cloth of silver background with a crimson velvet pattern of leaves and flowers.

The Queen's love of glitter and jewels was reflected in her gilded ceiling and her jeweled furniture. One of her writing tables had two pedestal cabinets of exquisite silversmith's work; another was of ebony inlaid with silver, its two boxes containing ink and sand. Its writing board lifted up and formed the lid of a receptacle for papers, with a mirror inside. Elizabeth kept her jewelry in a chest ornamented all over with pearls, and her clock was an elaborate ornament in itself, consisting of an Ethiopian riding a rhinoceros, his four attendants making obeisance at the striking of every hour. Clocks were prized, especially when they struck the hour musically. An expensive clock for expensive taste might be about twelve inches high with gilt or gold filigree ornamentation of its bronze or gold and black surface. The internal works would be gilt and bronze, and its bells would strike every quarter hour.

Adjoining Elizabeth's bedroom with its single window—to prevent drafts, in spite of the silken hangings—were two bathrooms, luxury indeed! Bathrooms were not built in even the best of houses till late in the 1590's, and they were so expensive then that when the Countess of Northumberland had one put in her home, her irate husband protested loudly against such extravagance. Most baths were taken in wooden tubs before the fireplace, and the soap, scented with sweet herbs, was round like a ball and frequently homemade. Large households, however, usually bought their soap by the barrel. Tudors had more pride than their successors in personal cleanliness; they even had public baths at which people spent much time, till fear of the plague kept them away. The Queen, therefore, able to bathe in comparative safety as well as in luxury, enjoyed her bathrooms, whose ceilings and walls were covered with glass mirrors at a time when few ladies could afford more than one small glass table mirror. She also kept a plentiful supply of mouth washes and tooth soap and linen cloths used commonly for cleansing the teeth. The contents of the washes varied, but in general they consisted of vinegar, rosemary, myrrh, dragon's herb, boll ammoniac, and spring water, with flavoring such as cinnamon, honey, or mint.

Because Elizabethans entertained lavishly and their guests were likely to stay for long periods of time, they had to plan for many bedchambers in their homes. At first some of these were little more than thoroughfares for the rooms opening off them, but when corridors were added to provide individual entrances, much privacy was achieved. Homes entertaining large companies of people still retained the old arrangement, however, and added corridors to enable guests with retinues of servants to be accommodated in as many adjoining rooms as they needed. If guests expected to stay very long, they brought their own servants and furniture. In great houses, all the guest chambers were handsomely supplied with chimney pieces, paneled walls, and patterned ceilings. In smaller houses, the bedrooms were necessarily plainer. Fireplaces were considered important, although, when provided, they were often lighted in the morning merely to freshen the atmosphere.

Modest homes could not afford fireplaces in their bedrooms; in fact, they could afford little more than the bed and a chest and a stool, with perhaps an old table. Usually the chest had to serve as a dressing table and washstand, the towels being hung on a roller attached to the wall above. Floors were often bare, accentuating the heavy, forbidding aspect of the sparse furniture. Most of the poor, unable to afford beds, slept in the one room of their huts on straw pallets with thin, coarse coverings. If they were able to make a stout frame of pieces of wood, they placed their pallet on it and were the proud possessors of a bed. Then, if they were ambitious, they looked forward to the time when a mattress of feathers might be added to the pallet, for such a mattress with its pillows meant comfort indeed.

Some beds had paneled heads, sometimes with painted pictures on the panels. More elaborate beds had testers and hangings, down mattresses and pillows, fine linen for sheets and pillow covers, and silken coverings. The common man had to be satisfied, however, with straw mattresses, later covered with feather pallets, and sheets and coverlets made by his good wife. She, in turn, might gossip with her friends at times about soft beds with velvet and silken coverlets or even fur rugs, with two or three or four silken or velvet pillows and fur head sheets or pillow covers made of ermine. If for brief moments she ever yearned for these things herself, she never told anyone of such stark foolishness.

Yet it was a room with such a bed Shakespeare described for his appreciative audience as they listened to Iachimo make his report of the sleeping Imogen (*Cymbeline*, III:iii:69–91). Though he put rushes on the floor, Shakespeare made the silver silken tapestries tell the story of Cleopatra meeting Antony, and the carving on the chimney piece show the "chaste Dian bathing." The andirons were two winking cupids, and the ceiling was "fretted" with "golden cherubims." The one window, tight closed against the drafts and night airs with their fairies and other "tempters," caused the room to be so still that the taper left burning by the attendant scarcely made a movement in its shadow on the wall.

All important beds were canopied. Their four great posts were connected at the top by rails called cornices, from which hung the bed curtains. The foot of the bed frame might be detached from these four posts, the head and foot being formed of panels of elaborately carved wood. Behind the panel at the head might be a high panel of tapestry or embroidery or more carved wood, sometimes called the tester, and over the top, reaching from the two posts at the back to those at the foot, was the real tester or "ceiling" or "sparver," that was made of either carved wood or some rich woven material. Sometimes the top valances of the tester were finished with a fringe or plumes of feathers. The four great posts of these standing beds might be deeply fluted columns, quasi-Ionic columns, or massive oak with flat carving. A bed of this type had posts about five inches in diameter, set in square blocks at top and bottom and inlaid with bone designs of flowers and fruit and birds. At the base of each, a word such as hope, faith, love, and truth might be carved. Curtains around these beds were carefully drawn at night, and the sleeper had them pinned if there was any draft from ill-fitting doors or lead glass.

By the end of the century such heavy beds were supplanted by lighter ones, with the posts being a part of the bed frame itself, and the tester and hangings consisting of silks, velvets, heavy woolen cloth, or linen. Beds were treasured because of their appointments, which might often cost thousands of pounds. A bed prepared for James I when he was visiting the Earl of Dorset had embroidered cloth of gold hangings said to have cost the owner £8,000.

The framework of beds was much the same in all homes. In farmhouses the trestle beds for children or servants were put together with pegs, but the same kind of criss-cross ropes held the straw pallet and chaff pillows of the poor and the better mattresses and pillows of the rich. Late in the century a family of any means had two or three feather beds and many homespun sheets and pillow covers. The more fortunate had finer sheets, warm blankets, and pretty coverlets. Sometimes a thin feather bed was used by both rich and poor as a coverlet, but the difference in them ranged from coarse homespun to satin linings, and from coarse feathers to softest down.

Among the middle class the average bed was joined, stood about four feet high at the back, was carved, and ended in short, knobby posts rising about three feet above the rail. If the owner could afford it, the bed was curtained with both upper and lower valances, for when drawn they gave privacy. Children and servants slept in the low trundle beds which, in the daytime, could be pushed out of sight under the low valances or "basses." Small households might own one four-poster bed. In common households the canopied beds and valances were retained long after they were discarded by the upper classes.

Embroidery, which made such a showing in bed hangings and window drapery, was used in all rooms that made any pretense to comfort. Rich embroidery often showed much black silk, enhanced by gold or silver thread, and was used on white linen. Petit point was used for large pieces of furniture or for heavy hangings. Chair embroidery was made on canvas first and then cut out and applied to a velvet ground. For stools, the blue borage and the poppy were favorite designs, but for chairs, many flowers such as roses, daisies, and strawberry blossoms were used, supplemented by fruits and leaves and even caterpillars worked cunningly into the design. A good housewife was never idle; if she had any spare time she and her daughters or maids took up their embroidery. Hence both rich and middle-class homes had embroidery, not only on hangings and pillows, on bedspreads and furniture, but even on book bindings and table covers, on women's caps and other wearing apparel, on men's clothing, and, for the clever needlewomen, in pictured scenes, such as hunting the wild boar, milkmaids wandering through a pretty wood, huntsmen shooting the water fowl or rabbit, fishermen with their catch, and ladies and gentlemen strolling on the green.

One of the best storing places for finished or unfinished work of this kind was the chest, but there were other important uses for this necessary piece of furniture. The young girl had her hope chest in which she stored her carefully stitched linens for the day she was to become a bride; only the very poor brides lacked this essential part of a dowry. Every household had chests. Even in the most scantily furnished bedrooms there must be one or two chests to serve as washstand, dressing table, or, most important of all, as a clothes press or chest of drawers. The chest might also be used as a locker or trunk for storage or travel. Covered with cushions, it might even serve as a bed. Mounted on legs, it could hold silver or brass ewers, basins, or other toilet articles. Real dressing tables were rare and expensive, and were used only by the wealthy. Important households, indeed, often had more chests than chairs, for two or three in a bedchamber could serve many purposes.

Originally chests were designed to hold clothes or linen, especially the linens, hangings, napery, etc., of the bride, and were often supplied with a little hanging box for candles to keep away moths. Later, these small boxes were covered and used to hold jewelry, money, and all kinds of trinkets, dress details, and small dresses. Fine chests were beautifully carved and often inlaid with marquetry. If there was no table in the lady's bedchamber, she might arrange on a chest her small standing mirror and silver boxes and jars for essences, cosmetics, and paints.

The early chests were without panels, the one slab of the front giving the piece of furniture the name of the coffer chest. When paneled chests became common, carving was introduced, which became very elaborate. Next, legs were introduced to lift the chest off the ground and out of the floor dampness; then a drawer was added below the chest compartment. Gradually, the number of drawers was increased, the side panels becoming a recessed frame for carrying these drawers, and with the discarding of the flap lid, the piece became a tall chest or tall-boy. As long as the lids were kept smooth, they were suitable as a seat or table top, but when paneling came into fashion, the lid was made with a small flap at the center, backed by a mirror, and raised above a shallow drawer for containing toilet preparations. If other drawers were not added below the shallow one, the space was used as a large receptacle for bedroom articles. Dresses, however, were stored away or hung in wardrobes (called fripperies) that were supplied with handsomely carved doors. Dresses that must be readily accessible were hung in closets or small dressing rooms furnished with shelves and wooden pegs.

In their private sitting rooms or "closets," Elizabethans enjoyed a retreat. When Shakespeare shows Ophelia alarmed by Hamlet's unceremonious entrance into her "closet," he indicates she has cause for fear, but when his mother desires to speak with him in her "closet," she wishes her son to believe they are speaking together alone. Henry V indicates to the French princess that he knows well the ways of women when he asks her to speak "mercifully" of him to her serving women in her "closet," for he is slyly referring to the gossip women indulged in while in the privacy of their own rooms. The term was not always used with this meaning, however, for sometimes it referred to a small cabinet or writing desk. For example, Lady Macbeth unlocks her "closet" and takes from it a paper which she folds and writes on; Antony tells of finding Caesar's will in a "closet," and Gloucester tells Edmund of a letter safe locked in his "closet."

The privacy of his closet was a great luxury to the Elizabethan. Here it was customary to burn perfume in a censer, not only to clear the room of mustiness from being closed against the cold outside air, but also because an individual's personality was supposedly reflected by his choice of a perfume. Usually rose leaves or musk or little rose cakes sold at the apothecary's shop were used for this purpose. Before any important social event in the home, the entire house was given a general cleaning, and little bouquets of sweet-smelling herbs were placed in the various rooms, especially in the bedchambers and rooms in which people would gather for music or conversation.

Of course, perfume was also valued as a deodorizer in the home. Perhaps the use of flowers and sweet herbs for this purpose may seem crude to those who take modern plumbing and deodorants for granted. In 1594 Sir John Harington invented a type of water closet that in principle was not unlike those in use today. Since Elizabethans believed that melancholy was induced by bad odors, Sir John wrote a treatise on sanitation in the home to prevent melancholy, and described his invention. His book, however, was Rabelaisian in character, and in order to make it still more popular, he used Ajax as an example of a victim of melancholy, and entitled his work *The Metamorphosis of Ajax*. Since he facetiously referred to his rather crude invention of the water closet as an "Ajax" or very foul-smelling convenience, it was not long before a privy was being called an Ajax or *A Jax* or *A Jakes* or *A Jaques*. The ridiculous affectation of the melancholy Jaques in *As You Like It* was amusingly indicated by his name, therefore. In all this laughter, the Queen had an Ajax installed at Richmond Palace.

Nevertheless, in even great houses sanitation made little advance in this respect. In the early part of the century, garderobes or latrines were moved closer to apartments for the sake of convenience. Those who lived in the old castles continued to use garderobes located in large projections on the face of walls, with drains that discharged into deep-walled pits or moats or streams running near the walls. Some castles had two garderobes on each floor; some had them placed in a corner of the courtyard or in cellars or even on the leads. Two seats were often provided to accommodate more than one person at a time. The one for the master's use was frequently furnished with cushion and blanket to keep him warm on cold days. Most lovers of comfort, however, continued to use chamber crockery that, like the pails used by ordinary people, was emptied into large containers likewise emptied at need, or the pails were taken to a window and the contents tossed outside. The inhabitants of cities who did not have their barrels collected and emptied regularly took it as a matter of course that all such debris would be taken care of by "dustmen" hired for sweeping narrow, filthy, evil-smelling streets.

The need of garderobes near the sleeping apartments and the common practice of using chamber crockery made it necessary to air and scent bedrooms frequently. Growing flowers and herbs, therefore, was not entirely to satisfy the love of beauty only. Foreigners frequently commented on the English use of fresh nosegays and sweet herbs in their bedchambers, sweet-smelling rushes on the floors, and even sweet wood at times burning in the fireplaces. As they sank into slumber on English beds, these foreigners must have slept better, not only for the warm blankets and the soft mattresses but also for the clean, lavendered sheets, fresh from the clothes press.

The library was a late addition to Elizabethan homes. Most of the books lay on tables or chests in private apartments, unless they were beautifully bound volumes put on display with other treasures. Toward the end of the century, however, fine houses added the library as a matter of course, and in homes where books and learning were appreciated, it was soon a necessity. Here the master kept his rapidly accumulating books, and here he retired to read or write. Naturally there were some books in all libraries that were peculiar to the social class to which the householder belonged. The gentry, for example, were likely to include one or more books on hawking, and the middle class at least one "good" book on manners. The pious of both classes kept the Bible, in or out of its Bible box, in a prominent place on a library table, for this holy book was sure to catch the attention of one whose glance wandered idly over ornamental candlestick, hourglass, writing materials, and handsome sand shakers.

The libraries of the wealthy might be very sumptuously furnished with rows of books beautifully bound in velvet of different colors, especially red, some studded with pearls and other precious stones, and all shelved to show their jeweled or otherwise ornamented clasps of gold or silver. Reading chairs with high paneled backs had their seats made comfortable with embroidered cushions. The window seats would be cushioned and the windows softened with beautifully embroidered hangings. Romances and satires, sometimes moralized and sometimes translated with care from the original, would find their way into the homes of the rich and worldly and even into serious libraries if their ribald contents were artfully pointed toward some "good" purpose. Those interested in conduct and even in new fads of behavior would read Castiglione's *Courtier* and Sidney's *Arcadia* and Lyly's *Euphues*, and when dramas were printed, they would eagerly buy plays dealing with gay rascals or "reformed" men and women. The learned might well read their many books in Greek and Latin and French and Italian, but they were also likely to read clever burlesques or controversial discussions on sex and the eternal wisdom and foolishness of men and women.

In the homes of the middle class, books were added in greater numbers as cheaper editions were turned out by the presses. Suitable translations of Castiglione's *Courtier* and Guazzo's *The Civil Conversation* were adapted to their needs as increasing emphasis on morals and manners occurred in the schools. Besides these were countless others at low prices. If the household was pious, it would have the Bible and its concordances flanked by sermons printed about religious matters under general discussion. Foxe's *Book of Martyrs* and St. Augustine's *City of God* continued in favor and shared space on the shelves with serious histories of England and other countries, especially Greece and Rome, and North's extremely popular translation of Plutarch's *Lives*. Those who could afford gardening for pleasure and could purchase some of the newly imported plants would own one or more herbals, and women interested in fine needlework would buy books with new patterns in embroidery and lace making. Women in the middle class were encouraged to read and write whenever it was believed such effort would make better housewives of them.

Indeed, there was every reason for an Elizabethan to justify the addition of a library to his new home. In the stalls were books on every subject, in English, including translations, as well as in the original French or Italian. Every taste could be satisfied, whether it reveled in travel, naughty or clever ballads and songs, gardening, serious thoughtful discussion, or even cookery as a fine art.

But Elizabethans did not spend any more time indoors than necessary, for they were lovers of gardens if they loved their homes. In fact, the general arrangement of their homes was carefully considered in their correct relation to the scale and magnificence of their gardens—from the external courtyards for privacy or pleasure on fine estates, to the walled garden in front with a terrace and steps and a small, simple archway in the wall of a small manor, to the still other modifications of these features determined by the owner's means. Though they might plan an eastern exposure for early sun in bedrooms, a western light for winter living chambers, and a northern light for studies and cellars, still they integrated all the home so closely with the gardens that they made ornamental features in the grounds about as important as the house attractions. They walked in their gardens for exercise or even rode if the paths were extensive enough, and here they raised fruits and herbs and flowers for their comfort in sickness and in health.

Gardens of the rich were usually formal with their terraces, arbors, and fountains, and as their owners strolled along the green shady walks or through the pleached alleys or along smooth, graveled paths, they took pleasure in whatever added to the landscape symmetry. Both house and garden might be set off when the house was enclosed in a formal garden with stone walls, relieved by artistic balustrades. To break the straight lines in such walls, Elizabethans frequently had domes or towers or piers or statues built into the stone. If the garden was pretentious, it might have little garden houses at all the wall angles, and the gateways might resemble little lodges with their turrets and other ornamentation. They might also combine hedges and piers, especially if the hedges were tall enough and thick enough to combine harmoniously with piers ten to twelve feet high and surmounted by obelisks; certainly such a wall would make an effective barrier. Regardless of the number of individual gardens on an estate, they were frequently referred to as the garden unless one of the features was special enough to be spoken of as in the north or south garden.

At Wimbledon, the garden for Lord Exeter's house was planned with roses growing among the orchard trees, lime trees for scent and shade, and a walk in one orchard extending over six hundred feet. The Whitehall gardens had broad paths, lawns with trim flower beds, fantastically trimmed bushes, and tall gilded columns surmounted by grotesquely carved beasts. In the middle gardens were ingenious sundials and a fountain with a concealed hose that a prankster might use to give unwary guests a shower. Queen Elizabeth laughed heartily when this joke did not please the victim.

Another type of garden might achieve distinction by its arrangement of terraces and steps, for every change of level provided an opportunity to display flowers, trees, or garden ornamentation. For instance, a stroller might climb a flight of easy steps immediately after entering the pillared gateway. Then, as he walked along a broad path in the base or outer court, he would notice the hedge with pillars surrounding the court, and the green grass with bright flower "knots" divided geometrically by paths on both sides of him as he advanced. He might then ascend another flight of easy, circular steps leading to another court set with more flower beds, paths, and statuary placed at intersections of its paths. From this second court a third flight of steps might lead to a terrace extending across the entire front of the house, flanked by its ornamental balustrade, with a flight of steps at each end, one leading to the inner garden and the other to the kitchen gardens. Both rich and poor often cared more for the herbs and fruits than for merely ornamental lawns and flowers. This inner garden of a fine estate might have stone walls with hedged paths, a fountain at the center, and a banquet or summer house with a porch on its upper floor to serve as a "prospect mount." This summer house would match the home in architecture.

The gardens might be a home's chief attraction; some felt this was true of Theobalds, where throughout the year, even in his absence, Burghley kept many people at work. Besides his regular household he fed twenty to thirty people at his gates each day, and then set them to work weeding or performing other tasks directed by his gardeners. Many different kinds of shrubs and trees were planted in careful design and augmented by numerous curious columns and pyramids of purely decorative purpose. The maze was one of the fashions he particularly indulged in for the entertainment of his guests; the puzzling paths truly tested any person's ability to "thread the maze." So extensive were Burghley's garden walks that in two miles of walking or riding one would not repeat any of his tour.

Beside the banquet house with its twelve marble figures of Roman emperors set in a semicircle was a beautiful fountain, and within the house was an arresting table. Fourteen spans long, seven wide, and one thick, it was made of a solid piece of black touchstone that left a streak when rubbed by gold or silver. The noted Gerard had framed vistas marked by sundial and silver fountains and, to offset the charm of pleached alleys and bowers, had planted banks with violets and covered arbors with honeysuckle and rose vines, and scented the air with beds of lilies. Leaden tanks held water in which fish swam about, and a moat surrounding the south garden would carry a boat; it was a romantic reminder of days when a man had to defend his castle, and thereby made the comparative peace of the Queen's reign doubly precious. On the north side was another extensive garden.

Fish ponds were ornamental or utilitarian, supplying households with various kinds of fish. Gervase Markham, in *The Pleasures of Princes, or Good Mens Recreations* (1614), gave full directions for cleaning the ponds, which must be done every third autumn to remove "weeds and filth" by means of a "small boat and a sharp hook." Ponds subject to mud should be fully drained every seventh spring, the "spaded out filth" to be used as compost on the land. When the sides and bottom had been "sodded with green sods" fixed "hard into the earth with small stakes," the fresh water could be put in and the fish returned. Ponds easily drained he would "renew" often. Markham also gave directions for feeding the fish with brewer's grain, bread chippings, curds, and fresh grain every morning. The larger fish, however, might enjoy the "small fry" and "minnows of such species as roach, dace, and miller's thumbs, and, for sudden fattening, food like garbage, or the blood of sheep, cattle, and even hogs.

Like Sir Thomas More, Cardinal Wolsey loved rosemary and planted the gardens at Hampton Court with it. But two other features distinguished these gardens: the topiary art of the remarkably trimmed trees and shrubs, and the amazing "high and massy" fountain. The rich cardinal could afford to indulge in such fancies, for human labor was cheap

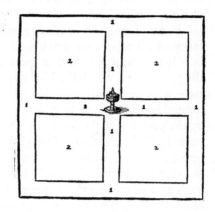

Examples of a maze and of flower knots, from
*Certain excellent and new invented Knots and
Mazes*, by Gervase Markham, 1623

and water for his fountain required that "only a man" keep turning a wheel by hand; an ingenious mechanism forced the water through a lead pipe that fed the spray. But Raleigh surpassed this spectacle when he had a river drawn into his garden through the rocks. His orchard or garden and grove were so delightful as to be scarcely paralleled during the reign of Queen Elizabeth.

In the famous Nonesuch gardens was a fountain that attracted the fancy of all who were privileged to see it. Here the water was carried by a lead pipe to a bird that spouted it into a marble basin at the foot of the pyramid on which the bird perched. On the principle that if one spectacle was good, two were better, these gardens had an exciting retreat located in a lilac grove in which Actaeon, turned into a stag, was sprinkled by the goddess of the fountain, Diana, and her nymphs. On the statuary were Latin inscriptions. Delighted visitors referred to this place as the grove of Diana. Nonesuch gardens, like all show places, possessed a bowling green and a "wilderness" of considerable acreage given over to nature itself and providing the romantic feeling of wild spaciousness opposed to careful order. The display features followed the usual pattern of being located in the inner garden, in which the walls were fourteen feet high, like the walls of the kitchen gardens adjoining it.

Here were pleached alleys with their vines carefully trained on trellises to provide a shady walk, thorny hedges, and paths following geometrical designs. One of the show features was a spiral pyramid, and another the banqueting house. This imposing structure was of wood, three stories high and enclosed by a brick wall. The main room on the ground floor was its hall, where guests in pleasant weather might be served drinks and cakes and various other kinds of delicate sweetmeats. On the two upper floors were three and five rooms, paneled in oak. The top floor served also for prospect mounts by having its corners provided with balconies that afforded fine views of the surrounding countryside. Foreigners as well as the English took great pleasure in the amount of space English houses gave over to gardens and hunting parks and orchards designed mostly for pleasure. Nonesuch gardens, from the deer parks bordering the approach to the house to the prospect mounts in the banqueting house, seem to have included all the features of the garden plan—the bowling green, the walks and paths with flower beds, fountains, obelisks and statuary, the summer house and prospects, and the wilderness.

Nonesuch Palace had been begun by Henry VIII in 1538 but was not finished till the Earl of Arundel purchased it. During the reign of Mary he kept more than two hundred men constantly at work on it up to the time of completion. The lower part was of stone, the upper of half-timber with the studding covered with gilded lead scales. Pictorial scenes in highest relief adorned the panels of this upper part, and decorative towers and pinnacles concluded the work done by English artificers. Then foreigners were called in to add further details. When Elizabeth was able to bring this house back to the Crown, it became one of her favorite residences; in keeping with its magnificence she had elaborately sumptuous gardens laid out for it.

James Lees-Milne (*Tudor Renaissance*, 1951) feels that Nonesuch started among the English the bad taste of applying a mass of extraneous ornamentation to the outside surfaces of their houses. Yet on the whole he admits that their "extraordinary medley of traditions and styles" from Italy, France, and Flanders somehow did produce a "pervasive individuality" glorified by "its youthfulness." He particularizes this type of beauty in the "silvery façades" of classical Longleat, the elegant "filigree cresting of cypher and coronet over the bays of Hardwick," the dignified "packed masses of red brick and dressed stone" comprising the symmetry at Hatfield, and the startling, romantic "first dramatic spectacle of the pinnacled towers at the end of the straight drive of yew" leading to the rose-brick wings of Blickling. He continues with his comments on the importance of the setting for the house, a matter of harmony which is essential to fine homes, but especially to houses restricted in ground space. Not only must man work with nature in locating his house artistically, but sometimes on large or small sites he must seem to anticipate the magic touch of nature's own hand. Two gardens, one at New Place in Stratford-on-Avon and the other at Compton Wynyates, a neighboring country house, present interesting replicas of the sixteenth-century features of flower "knots" and of topiary art. At New Place are the broad avenue and intersecting paths along which one strolls to examine the different patterns of colorful flower beds symmetrically arranged in knots. The hedges along the avenue and surrounding the garden have been clipped to represent decorative birds and geometrical figures, especially the cube and the sphere. At Compton Wynyates, the extensive gardens illustrate topiary art at its best. Here all the shrubs and trees and hedges have been carefully trimmed to represent many different geometrical forms and animals and birds; among the latter the elephant and the peacock are especially notable.

The Earl of Leicester at his Kenilworth gardens seems to have engaged in a long contest with nature as he beautified the extensive setting for his castle. The inner garden itself comprised at least an acre. Along the castle wall ran a terraced path about ten feet high and twelve feet wide, with fine green grass underfoot. The side of the avenue facing the garden was plentifully supplied with obelisks, spheres, and sculptured animals, especially with the bear of Leicester's crest. There were two fine arbors of sweet scented trees and intertwined flowers, and at each end of them gardens of geometric paths with grass in one and sand in the other for easy walking. At each path intersection was a square pilaster fifteen feet high, resting on a base two feet square. About a foot from their base and about two feet from their ten-inch orb at the top, these pilasters were pierced ornamentally, and the whole was painted to look like one piece of porphyry. Both of these gardens had wild strawberries as ground cover; in fact, this was the only way Elizabethans grew the strawberries they loved so much. Along the sides of the gardens were fragrant herbs and flowers and fruit trees—apple, cherry, and pear. It is probable that the flowers bordering the fruit trees harmonized in color with the trees' spring blossoms.

Between the gardens and the terraced path was the magnificent summer house, joined to the north wall of the castle. About thirty feet long and fourteen wide, its one story reached up twenty feet at least and provided a suitable retreat in which to serve the last course of a sumptuous banquet. For this course Elizabethans liked to retire from the great hall in pleasant weather and enjoy the delicious concoctions served in an attractive summer house in its garden setting. The walls of Leicester's banquet house were wainscoted about breast high, and above the paneling were four windows in the front wall and two on each side. These windows were ten feet high and five feet wide; they were arched at the top and were separated by flat, projecting columns so designed as to seem to support the roof. The columns were painted to look as if covered with diamonds, rubies, and sapphires garnished with gold.

Another feature of Leicester's show garden was its "caves," evenly spaced for heat and coolness, and filled with birds of brilliant plumage. A good caretaker kept their water vessels and grain dishes clean. These birds were much prized, for they had been imported from France, Africa, and the Canary Islands; they also included some favorite English songsters.

The show piece was a white marble fountain eight feet square and four feet high. It was surmounted by a column consisting of two atlantes, back to back, facing east and west, their hands holding up a basin about three feet wide. Small pipes conveyed water to the basin. In the pool, which held two feet of water, at the base of the fountain swam many fish. One side of the marble square was carved to show Neptune with his trident, seated majestically on his throne while sea horses sported in the waves. On the second side was Thetis in a chariot drawn by dolphins, on the third, Prometheus herding his sea bulls, and on the fourth, Doris reclining on the sand with her daughters. The whole design was given movement and restless energy by its waves whipped to froth by whales and various kinds of fish swimming in its stone engraved pools. So strong was the spray from the fountain that visitors took care not to approach too close lest they be dampened by a shower.

To view this garden from the terraced path was a delight. The fountain spray cooled the winds above and made the path pleasant on hot summer days. This whole path was also like a prospect mount, from which one caught glimpses of the fruit and flowers in the geometrical plots below and heard the songs of birds of modest plumage or the cries of those of exotically brilliant color. From here one's eyes could also rest on the woods, beyond which roamed the red deer. So Robert Laneham saw the house and gardens when he was in attendance on Leicester during the festivities of 1575 as the great Earl entertained the Queen.

Such an estate was beautifully arranged for lavish hospitality. The deer parks themselves comprised over seven hundred acres, and the distant pool or lake, over a hundred. The hunting, says Laneham in the letter to which we are indebted for much of this description, was excellent, especially when the deer were driven from the woodside into the lake and became an excellent target for the excited party. The boundaries ran about twenty miles, and the portion within the castle walls consisted of about seven acres. Though the castle was magnificently appointed with comfortable lodgings for the guests, it would not have been complete without its jewel, the inner or privy garden.

Modest householders, hearing of such wonders, followed the examples of these displays in their own way. If they could afford them, they had garden knots, and they trimmed their hedges according to the prevailing taste in the topiary art. Fragrant flowers were placed at intervening spaces, but most often about fruit trees. Though they might envy the gardens of the well-to-do, who imported rare plants and medicinal herbs and experimented with coloring, doubling, and enlarging of flowers with "incredible" results, they clung to their old favorites and did what they could to make them decorative. Meanwhile, expert gardeners did more than improve annuals; they converted some of them into perennials. They also learned much from the plants imported from the Indies, the Americas, the Canary Islands, and other parts of the world. Many Elizabethans, however, regretted seeing the old herbs or "simples" crowded out by the new ones from abroad, for they had been proud of their own herbs. Moreover, the common people were not so willing as the rich to part with the remedies made from familiar herbs, for they could not so easily call in a physician when home treatment failed.

Among the many new fruits grown in the gardens of the rich were apricots, almonds, peaches, figs, oranges, lemons, and olives. Roses were also the object of intensive culture, and everyone knew about the Antwerp rose, which, in 1585, was said to have one hundred eighty petals. A slip from it sold for £10, a sum that would be somewhat comparable to five hundred dollars today. Grafting became such an engrossing art that trees were made to bear many varieties and colors of the same fruit, and roses of several varieties were grown on the same bush. By 1620, some imports that graced English tables were improved pippin apples, melons, and musk melons. Other popular imports were licorice, tobacco, olives, carp, and turkeys.

In the kitchen gardens of the rich the so-called Irish potato was grown to supply an exotic dish, the tubers not being much larger than a walnut. The sweet potato flourished, having been cultivated since 1565. So eager were people to make their gardens grow that the very dish water was used, even in the finest gardens, to nourish the plants. The prosperous common man also brought to his garden any new plants and shrubs and trees he could acquire, thus carrying out, in miniature at least, what he had heard of in the privy gardens of the rich.

With all their love of display, Elizabethans had a strong feeling for utility. In modest gardens utility and beauty were combined by planting flowers between rows of vegetables, but such flowers must be useful. True, these gardens were not impressive like those located near the great kitchen offices, or the privy gardens which were used only for decorative and recreational purposes; still they satisfied the owner's instinct to use to best advantage what little of the good earth he possessed. As in the great garden, the small garden had its gate, sometimes locked, but capable of giving direct access to the garden from the street. Here were grown many herbs that were carefully gathered by the good housewife.

Gardens with gates were convenient for all kinds of assignations, and many plots were undoubtedly hatched there and many secrets unfolded. Phillip Stubbes spoke contemptuously of the secret use of gardens "walled very high, with their arbors and bowers fit for the purpose" of evil-doing and supplied with banquet houses to make "sumptuous" the evil person's designs. He also referred bitterly to the locks on the gates with their three and four keys, the lady keeping one and her paramours the others. Good mothers, therefore, had their daughters as carefully attended in the garden as in the house with its visitors and servants. The modest garden might have fewer opportunities for concealment, but even here the careful mother watched over her daughters.

Elizabethans felt free to talk without being overheard in their gardens, though they frequently did have eavesdroppers. In private chambers conversation might be interrupted, especially if doors opened off them into other rooms, and always there was the danger of eavesdroppers concealed behind hangings. But in the garden they felt so much less restraint that Shakespeare could delight his audience with plots showing lovers and secret agents and businessmen betrayed while they made plans revealed to ears not intended to hear them. In no play, perhaps, occur so many hilarious examples of overheard intrigue as in *Twelfth Night*. In spite of their feeling of security in their gardens, Elizabethans knew their secret talk might be overheard by servants or other people walking quietly on the other side of a tall hedge, especially if they walked on grass. However, those who walked in gardens with comparatively low hedges, across which they could see, felt reasonably secure. The danger of being overheard in the banquet house or in bowers was greatest, of course, for here what might conceal one person or two might also conceal another. This occurs amusingly in *Much Ado*.

Its quiet and comparative freedom from intrusion made the garden an especially favored place for receiving guests. It was also used for walking in before and after meals, for sleep in the drowsy hours of the day, for reading and soft music, and for gentle sports. All these uses Shakespeare illustrates, sometimes for dramatic contrast. In *Twelfth Night*, Olivia in the garden is so impressed by the charm of the Duke's messenger that she violates all decorum and orders the gate shut, all servants dismissed, even her maid Maria, and awaits impatiently her "hearing" of the "beauteous youth." Later she brings a priest to the garden to hear her plight her troth, and in haste retires with the priest and her lover to be married in the chantry near by. In *II Henry VI*, when Richard, Duke of York, seeks the throne, he invites to his garden the two lords he hopes to bind to him (II::1:1 ff.). There they walk in covered alleys, weaving their plot. Hotspur's father (*II Henry IV*) walks in the garden awaiting news of the son he has failed to support in his revolt against the king. Anxiously pacing the flower-bordered walks, he hears the beat of hoofs on the road approaching the house. When the porter inquires of the messenger, "Who shall I say you are?" and receives a satisfactory answer, the Earl hears him say, "His lordship is walk'd forth into the orchard; please it your honor knock but at the gate, and he himself will answer." Even as this messenger is seeking to reassure the troubled father, another horseman and still another arrive with news of the son's death (I:1 ff.). The pleasant garden now lies in the shadows of death and an unquiet conscience seeking revenge.

Part of the horror in the ghost's revelation to Hamlet is due to the setting for the father's infamous murder. In Elizabethan minds, a king's garden would have many beautiful retreats near its arbored paths, and always its banquet house would provide a cushioned bench or chair on which one might take his ease. To heighten the horror of the deed Shakespeare has the king slain while peacefully asleep, as was his custom, in the shade of an orchard tree, thus contrasting sharply the feeling of perfect security and the creeping danger.

Walking over grassy paths was calming to the nerves; it also put one in the right mood to entertain ideas a persuasive soul might wish to suggest. When Kate's father (*The Taming of the Shrew*, II:1:112–13) says to his guests, "We will walk a little in the orchard, and then to dinner," he is merely being the gracious host. The high-strung Petruchio, however, seizes upon this offer as an opportunity for a quiet walk in the garden where he may talk privately with the father about a generous dowry for the daughter he has despaired of every getting off his hands. At the same time, grief as well as nerves might be quieted in a garden. The queen of Richard II retires to the garden to ease her troubled heart. As she and her ladies walk along considering what games they might play to "drive away the heavy thought of care," they name bowling, dancing, telling tales, and singing. The queen will have none of them, and as a gardener and servants approach, she retires with her maids. Returning alone, quietly, she surprises these men who are discussing the deposing of her husband, and when she presses the gardener for proof of his "ill tidings," he tells her sadly what "everyone doth know." As the brokenhearted woman retires once more, the gardener vows he will set a bank of rue where the good queen wept bitter tears (*Richard II*, III:iv:1 ff.). With the right setting for such emotional scenes, Shakespeare unerringly drove straight to the hearts of his bewitched audience.

Elizabethans, though much concerned about their wills and the right and proper disposal of their property to heirs and friends, seldom if ever bestowed their gardens by deed of gift. The English house was too closely bound to its setting to disrupt the property in such manner. It must have impressed them, therefore, when Shakespeare, to exalt the generosity of Caesar's character, describes how this great Roman had willed his gardens "this side Tiber" with all their walks and private arbors and new-planted orchards to the people and their heirs forever as "common pleasures" in which to "walk abroad" and "recreate" themselves (*Julius Caesar*, III:ii:252–56). To Elizabethans, a home without its garden was like a precious stone torn from its setting, or perhaps one should say the two were like twin pearls, and to separate them would be an act of desecration.

Music in the garden occurs again and again in Shakespeare's plays, not only because of the romantic setting it provides but also because Elizabethans liked to go into their gardens after supper to enjoy music on soft summer nights. Lorenzo and Jessica (*The Merchant of Venice*) sit in the garden enjoying the moonlight, and are told that Portia is coming home. They call forth the musicians to welcome her. As they await her arrival, Lorenzo, to the accompaniment of music, entertains his bride with a dreamy but Elizabethan interpretation of the relation music has to mood and character. In this way the poet joins to the treasured setting a poetic statement of an idea deeply significant to his listeners.

When the Elizabethan family and guests retired to the garden for the last course of supper, the sweets were likely to be varied and elaborate. At table there might be much pleasant conversation. The weather permitting this use of the garden, there would probably be masques performed by hired minstrels or by those of the household. Then the gentlemen would ask the ladies to dance, and the close-cut lawn would make a romantic outdoor dancing floor. Torches would be used if the moon was not bright enough. Meanwhile, in the lighted banquet house, other members of the company would play cards, smoke, or engage in talk. Still others would wander about the shadowy paths. On bright nights they often climbed to the prospect mounts to gaze at the view spread before them in the magic silver of the moon. An early supper on clear nights with the moonlight metamorphosing the gardens into fairyland justified the existence of the banquet house even if it was not used more than a few times a year.

Whether rich or poor, elderly people of most households liked to spend pleasant evenings in the garden. Here they wandered along the paths, enjoying the fruits that were in season, or they sat on benches and watched the young play games and dance. It was at this time that Burghley loved to ride his little mule through his magnificent gardens. He seldom or never played any game, for he could not do so on his gouty legs; instead, he looked on while shooters or bowlers enjoyed themselves as he ambled by on his gentle beast.

The common man often used this time for work about his garden if he could not afford servants to labor for him, or, if he did none of the hard work, he liked to take this time to inspect his fruits and flowers. Usually he himself attended to the grafting and pruning, or closely supervised it. His garden was his love, and here he spent most of his free time, unless he made his living by tilling the soil. When the shadows grew too heavy for him to see well, he enjoyed his evening smoke, for tobacco, after its introduction in 1565, had become very popular by 1600.

If he was to enjoy his garden in such a way, however, it was necessary to wall it in; the higher the walls, the greater the satisfaction of those who could afford them. No doubt such high walls quieted the anxiety of fathers who had daughters to marry, and gave husbands a certain feeling of assurance about their wives. Shakespeare's Juliet describes such walls when she asks Romeo, "How camest thou hither . . . ? The orchard walls are high and hard to climb" (II:ii:62–63). Even country gardens had high walls. Shakespeare describes them for us when he has Iden, the country squire (*II Henry VI*), enjoying his "little inheritance" in Kent, free from the turmoil of court, and taking quiet walks along the paths. But Cade, driven by starvation, climbs the wall, though with great effort, and seeks food in the garden to give him strength by which to elude his enemies. Ironically, the squire, startled from his peaceful reverie, accosts the intruder and in the struggle that follows exults over killing the weakened Cade (IV:x:18–90).

A more detailed garden description occurs in *Measure for Measure* (IV:i:28–33). This rather ordinary garden is walled with brick. On its west side is a vineyard, and a plank gate that is kept locked gives entrance from the street. Entering this gate, one walked through the vineyard, and then through a small door in the brick wall of the inner or privy garden. When they could not afford such walls, Elizabethans had to use walls of baked mud or clay, thatched on top. Such walls, of course, were in need of constant repair and, being so easily broken, were of little real protection. Their chief purpose was to mark boundaries and to give the feeling of privacy.

The chief need for walls about house and garden was due to the thieves and robbers in town, city, and country. During the time of the Tudors, the economic changes kept the whole of society in a state of flux. Advanced standards of living put the emphasis upon enlarging or rebuilding the home, adding more and better furnishings, and using more elaborate food and clothing. With so much attention fixed on possessions, there was great concern about safeguarding one's valuables, especially when anxiety over inflation made worldly goods increasingly desirable. In addition to the towered gatehouse, therefore, the new home barred its windows and increased the height of its garden walls. More modest homes followed as they could with modifications of these measures for their safety.

Thus, although there was no longer constant fear of an enemy's army of soldiers bearing weapons of war, there was always the fear of starved unemployed laborers. Evicted from their homes by the high fines on new leases as the old ones expired or by the enclosure movement that turned the tilled soil into pastures, many people from the country had no place to go to earn a living. Hence they took to the open road, there to swell the hordes of roving beggars, whose numbers had also been increased by confiscation of the monasteries. In summer they infested farmers' outbuildings at night; in winter they swarmed the dark narrow streets of town and city so that few people left their homes at night unless upon urgent business. This was another reason why the garden became more and more important as a place for evening recreation and gentle exercise.

The privy garden of a merchant in comfortable circumstances would probably have brick walls and tidy paths, sanded or graveled. Rushes might grow along the cool wall if the garden was large enough to grow them for practical purposes. There would also be sweet-smelling herbs to be mixed with the rushes when they were laid on the floors. A path down the center of the garden would have smaller ones leading from it to carefully planted hedges and around little beds of fragrant flowers to be used by the housewife for making sweet waters and essences. In a corner with the most desirable exposure would be a tiny garden house, covered with flowering woodbine and honeysuckle, and along the warm, sunny wall with its southern exposure would be some apricot and peach trees, their laden branches carefully espaliered. At their base might be narrow borders of flowers contrasting pleasantly with the fruit blossoms in spring.

In the little beds of flowers would probably grow French marigolds and gilly flowers, which at blooming time would make the air heavy with spicy fragrance. The hedges about these beds would be low and at regular intervals shaped into pillars or square posts with balls at the top. Symmetrically placed in relation to the flower beds would be little shrubs, some flowering and some a glossy green. The green ones would be likely to have fancy shapes made by a skilled gardener who could copy the work of a topiary artist. One shrub, for example, might resemble a basket with a high handle, another, an urn, and another would be shaped like a bird or animal, but all would be trimmed with the idea of symmetry in their relation to each other. Among the flowers might also be a few imports—say a lily from America, a rose from the Lowlands, and possibly some larkspurs, white lilac, or laburnum, and they would be placed to advantage for their display purpose. Most of the flowers would be of use for their scent or, like the fashionable passion flowers and Christmas roses, as gifts for friends.

Surrounded by a well-trimmed hedge and located for easy access to the kitchen would be the merchant's herb and vegetable garden. If space permitted, there might be separate gardens for these, however. For most middle-class householders, the herbs might be far more important than the vegetables and could well be included in a part of the flower and fruit plantings. One would be impressed when looking over such a merchant's garden retreat because of its orderly paths, its clipped greenery, and its bright flowers. Most of all one would be delighted by walking in the paths carefully planned for just such exercise.

In the garden of the humble city householder the chief purpose would be utility. If space was greatly restricted, the flowers, grown more for use than for beauty, might be planted between rows of vegetables. Medicinal herbs would be important unless the housewife was careless and indifferent to the precious knowledge of caring for the sick by tonics and teas, plasters, ointments, and salves. Vegetables grown would probably be beans, carrots, peas, parsnips, pumpkins, onions, and salad greens. If there was space for fruit, it would include such trees as apple or plum, or both, for these were commonly grown in all gardens. Other fruits likely to be grown here would be gooseberries, cherries, quinces, pears, mulberries, and perhaps peaches, though fruit was eaten raw with discretion lest it bring on a fever.

Gardens of the great houses along the Thames were full of lovely exotic flowers and fruit trees, grottoes and fountains, groves and avenues, benches in secluded arbors, smooth lawns, and attractive banquet houses— all delighting the eye or exciting wonder and admiration. On pleasant evenings, a host might suggest that his guests play cards; if for money, they would choose primero, but if only to relax, they would decide on trump or tables or some variation of backgammon. If they preferred exercise, he might suggest bowls or tennis, but if they wished merely to watch the traffic on the river, they would sit at ease on the porch and chat idly or to some purpose on business or affairs of state, or test their wit at merry guessing games of jesting and questions and answers. In such games ladies would be invited to take part.

Thinking of these gardens, Francis Bacon dreamed of one he would like to design for his own establishment, and just as in his studies he would take all knowledge to be his province, so with gardens he would include all ornamentation he had seen. He planned how one might stroll along the wide center path of the green-lawned outer court, walking abreast with one or two friends without crowding. He laid out the other paths in geometric design, leading past little figures cut out in juniper and yew, past other greenery placed at the angles of their intersections, and past flower beds covering the carefully spaced hillocks dotting the lawn. He gave the stiff symmetry of the knotted flower beds a graceful touch by the variety of shrubs, both evergreen and flowering, used at the center of each plot; sometimes colored sand instead of growing things was used on these plots. Elizabethans delighted in this use of sand. Shrubs in Bacon's garden would also include holly, roses, red currant, gooseberry, bay, sweetbriar, and rosemary. The flowers would be showy or fragrant, and his list grew till it included wild thyme, pinks, the pungent germander, the vining periwinkle, violets, gilly flowers, cowslips, musk roses, monkshoods, strawberries, daisies, lilies, sweet williams, columbines, primroses, marigolds, and daffodils.

Had Bacon been concerned with flowers for use instead of chiefly for display, his list would have included kitchen herbs and flowers like the medicinal lily for bile trouble, goat's rue for its tang in ale, camomile for headaches, and even dog fennel for a lotion applied to weak eyes. In addition to the flowers like violets, marigolds, primroses, and cowslips used for fancy salads at banquets, he would have named the common ones for everyday salads—the longwort, liverwort, and purslane. In food Bacon's taste was rather delicate, and it was natural for him to skip the pungent flowers and leaves of the well-supplied kitchen garden—harefoot, seablite, pennyroyal, bloodwort, salad burnet, cat-mint, tansy, and saffron. The last of these was important for coloring, especially for certain dishes at great feasts and for the housewife's concoctions in the distillery. Since most great ladies loved to experiment with essences in the distillery, Bacon's list might well have included sea holly, blessed thistle, valerian, wormwood, and plantains. Of course, Bacon was interested in the strawberry as a ground cover, for it was a favorite with many owners of fine homes. Since he also listed the periwinkle, he might have included as well the deep and light blue lupin and the white and yellow, all of which made showy carpets on hillsides. Like all Englishmen, Bacon liked the sweet william. Favorite flowers he omitted, however, were the larkspur, single and double, and the hollyhock, very showy against walls.

Bacon's discerning eye saw the beauty of a controlled bramble. Instead of ths usual blackberries, dewberries, billberries, and hazelnuts grown for this purpose by those who had a brook near the house, he substituted smooth-stemmed vines. He referred to nut trees he would have planted, probably having in mind walnuts, chestnuts, filberts, and the almond loved for its spring blossoms as well as its sweet nutmeats. Why he omitted medlars and quinces commonly used for their strong flavors in preserves is understandable, but one wonders why he did not mention the pomegranate with its brilliant red flowers, which also colored fancy dishes at great feasts. His garden plan wisely ruled out the deep shade of the purple fig in spite of its fruit, for Bacon must have light and sun to illumine his displays.

Since his garden was planned to comprise about thirty acres, Bacon divided it into three parts: the green-lawned entrance or base court, a main court, and a far garden. The outside surrounding hedge was to run as high as ten feet, with gilded figures placed between the shrubbery arches. On these figures were to be hung broad plates made up of round colored glass to reflect the sunlight. In the outer court the five main features were its lawn, its wide central path, its knots of flowers or vari-colored sand, its covered alleys along the sides, and its stately side hedges. In the main garden the hedges would be low enough to show the heads of those walking along the paths that intersected at the center. Adjacent to the outside hedge would be wide arbored alleys leading to other diagonal paths connecting with a banquet house. Fragrant vines like honey-suckle, jasmine, roses, or clematis were to form the covering for the alleys that they might delight by their perfume and protect one walking in the alleys from wind and rain. This plan was to provide much walking exercise, and also much variety, for the paths led past features Bacon described in detail.

Instead of one fountain in this main garden, Bacon would have two. One would send its spray into a basin with a floor of stones arranged in colorful mosaics, kept clean by fresh running water. The sides of the basin would be of thick colored glass, embellished above with a narrow railing and supported by statues. The other fountain would have a basin of "lapis blue stone," and its supporting statues would be decorated with gilt. Could he place this garden near the Thames, Bacon would have the overflow from the fountains join to form a brook, which, by a series of terraces and miniature waterfalls, might flow down to the river. Paths crossing this brook would be bridged with graceful structures, and their ingenious beauty would add much pleasure to walking in the garden. Near the brook would be planted violets, wild strawberries, and primroses, and farther up the bank, honeysuckle, sweetbrier, and woodbine, forming a bramble that could be controlled at will.

If the banquet house at the middle of this main garden was too far from the house to enable servants to provide the guests with refreshments from the house kitchens, then it must have its own kitchen. Since the main purpose of the summer or banquet house was to provide a retreat from the household confusion, Bacon would enhance the charm of his garden by having the banquet house so cunningly placed as to give one the impression of coming upon it unawares. All of it, therefore, except its neatly cast chimneys and bright panes of glass would be covered with vines. Yet this "woodland cottage" might be open on one or two or three sides, but if it was near the Thames, its porch must extend along the river side. Here would be placed carved wooden benches where one might sit at ease while watching the colorful procession of boats passing and repassing in their journeys east and west.

Two other features in the main garden would be the maze, so complicated that it would test the best mind to discover its exit (for both entrance and exit would be one), and the rose garden with its grassy paths edged by colored stones or sand. The important features of the main garden, therefore, would be the fountains, the banquet house, the maze, the rose garden, and the interesting walks provided by the paths with their little bridges over the winding brook. Bacon comes back to the plan of the banquet house to enumerate the uses for it, his practical mind demanding that he justify this expensive attraction. He points out that from it as well as from various parts of the garden one might watch those taking part in sports like tennis, bowling, and wrestling. Inside the house would be tables and benches and a rustic type of comfort—cozy nooks where one might engage in close talk with a friend or spend a quiet hour with a book. To some, of course, its greatest appeal would be in the seclusion it offered by its nearness to things growing out of doors as well as by its stout walls and roof.

In the far garden would be many fruit and nut trees placed at convenient spots for sun and accessibility, some of the trees being espaliered and some growing in the center of flowered borders. Recessed alcoves along the paths would be supplied with benches for private conversation or for observing the view. If the lay of the land was right, a spiral path would lead to a prospect mount, from which might be seen a long stretch of the river and surrounding country. Bacon must have thought a great deal about his dream of the perfect garden. True, he crowded into its thirty acres about all the features that embellished the most showy gardens of his time, but by means of symmetry and devices for increasing the comfort and pleasure of one following its walks, he succeeded in giving to his plan charm as well as ostentatious display.

This love of display affected owners of modest gardens as well as lords and ladies of fashion and great wealth. But the Elizabethans were able to adapt themselves as well as the things they coveted to their own station in life. All the effort spent on home and garden was for the purpose of providing a setting for living. The house and garden might be rich or poor, but for the householders the jewel of domestic life was in the pattern set by the family. Such a jewel, like no other, was achieved only by the willingness of parents to accept the responsibility of instilling into their children the desire to conform to the demands of the home regime. Thus marriage and the establishment of a household without children was unthinkable. The patterned life so evolved, therefore, was not only at the center of all their interests—it was the *summum bonum* of their very existence.

CHAPTER II

FATHERS AND MOTHERS

Care is heavy, therefore sleep you,
You are care, and care must keep you;
Sleep, pretty wantons, do not cry,
And I will sing a lullaby,
Rock them, rock them, lullaby.
DEKKER (?), *PATIENT GRISSEL*, 1600

OME Elizabethans planned the care of their children at their very conception. Children, they believed, were entrusted to them to bring up in the Lord's service and to be trained as good subjects of an earthly sovereign. Children, then, were the basic unit in the home just as the family was the basic unit in society. This is why they believed the whole structure of the family must be as well ordered as that of the hierarchical organization in Church or State. To Puritans, especially, marriage and children alone justified love, at least in theory, about which they said a good deal. Consequently they as parents or guardians were inclined to regard children as grave responsibilities. Perhaps this is why the relationship between wards and guardians was closer sometimes than that between parents and children.

There was much use of the ward system among Elizabethans of high birth or great wealth; there was also abuse of it. The profits to the guardians, however, even when some family heads disposed of their children in this manner much as they would speculate in their worldly possessions, did not minimize the gravity of the duties to be discharged, as their very wills indicated. For example, the notorious friend of Henry VIII, Charles Brandon who became Duke of Suffolk, willed a ward, who was the heir of the deceased Anthony Woodhall, to his son with the warning that he not only provide for her "custody" but also a suitable marriage. Brandon, keen in bargaining, had "bought" this ward (for whose care £20 was paid annually) from another guardian, but he always treated her very kindly, and she and his other wards were fond of him.[1]

The anxiety of a noble who feared he might not live to rear his children is seen in the notes written by Sir Walter Devereux, father of Essex. He declared to the Queen that his oldest son would lead a life "far unworthy of his calling" if she did not assume his wardship. He wrote Burghley, who discharged the duties to wards whom Elizabeth accepted, begging him to let his son's education be in the Burghley household, where he might learn "wisdom and gravity" from the great

---

[1] Lady Cecilie Goff, *A Woman of the Tudor Age* (1930), p. 161.

statesman, and "lay up" his "counsels and advice in the treasury of his heart."[2]

Convention if not affection demanded for children a careful religious training. Members of important families, even though they might not be religiously inclined, knew their heirs must be so trained if they were to take their proper place in both church and civil society. The family discipline, therefore, was the very nurse of this life, for by means of it the child was trained to assume the responsibilities as well as the rights to which he was born. Accordingly, loving but conscientious parents often sent their children as wards to homes of friends who could provide them with advantages not to be gained in their own homes. Such parents were quick to admit the importance of heredity, but they also were practical enough to insist upon the best possible environment for their children—it was their right. Many of them believed children were evil only through their rearing, and such children, denied a special right of proper environment would "render a straight reckoning to God for their evil bringing up."

The chapel, therefore, was an important part of the great house, for here the family worship was conducted, as a rule, and devout members of the household went to commune with their Lord. Families without chapels gathered in the great hall or the family living room for their devotions, and even the humblest family generally observed grace at meals. Harmful results from the decline of ecclesiastical discipline had to be offset by some corrective influence, and in a great measure the home assumed this duty, using much of the old church regimen in the daily lives of parents, children, and servants. Early morning services might be attended at home, in the chapel, or at church, but since daily family worship was the rule rather than the exception, evening services for the entire household came after supper and were usually held in the home.

When the Bible was put into the hands of the people, its teaching became compulsory, especially among the Puritans, who were particularly susceptible to conventional and devotional discipline. In all homes, however, inculcating doctrine or moral living was the father's duty, for to Elizabethans religion was primarily a matter of authorized right living. Thus the father became the instructor, not only of his children, but also of his wife and servants, reading the Bible to them with or without his interpretation, and catechizing them whenever he had time or inclination. For this duty he was likely to seize upon any device that might aid him, and when the domestic conduct books were printed in large numbers, he was quick to be one of the many who helped to make them phenomenally popular.

Although these books gained such popularity that some of them eventually ran into more than thirty editions by 1625, still they fol-

---

[2] Sir Walter Bourchier Devereux, *Lives and Letters of the Devereux, Earls of Essex* (1853), I: 141–42.

lowed the old pattern so popular with Elizabethans. Based on Paul's
Epistles, they were bound around with commentaries of Church
Fathers, Xenophon's Treatise of Households translated by Gentian
Hervet in 1534, and borrowings from other writers on domestic life from
Aristotle and Plutarch to modern French or Italian books of manners
and polite speech. Many translations of these latter books were made,
either by those who actually felt they should be adapted to English use
or by those who wished to gain by bringing out conduct books based on
material not yet borrowed from foreign literature of this nature.

Miles Coverdale's translation of Henry Bullinger's *The Christian
State of Matrimony* in 1546 was one of the early books giving Protestant
parents advice about the management of their households. Such advice
became almost as binding as biblical law. Bullinger believed all mothers
should nurse their children unless too frail to do so, and if a wet nurse
was necessary, she must be virtuous that the child might "drink in with
its milk" only virtue. Yet mothers of rank scarcely ever nursed their
own children. Middle-class women, however, faithfully followed Bullinger's advice, and when he frowned on baby talk, insisting plain and
distinct words should be spoken to the child, they tried to observe this
command also. Had not the good man declared that a child as it was
"first formed to speak" would so continue all its days? When he further
objected to all "light or vain" stories told children, they meekly bowed
their heads and replaced such amusement with what was "godly, grave,
and fruitful."

As soon as the Elizabethan child was able to commit to memory wise
sayings or "sentences," he was burdened daily with some of Bullinger's
favorites:

> There is one invisible God, creating Himself and all creatures.
> He is of the highest good; without Him nothing is good.
> He needs nothing to aid Him in His work.
> To lie is the most shameful vice of all.
> Backbite nor curse no man.
> All men are brethren.

After the little tongues had twisted themselves around such mountainous
words, they were taught to say the Lord's Prayer, the articles of faith,
the Ten Commandments, the Proverbs of Solomon, and the Book of the
Preacher. Recited "distinctly and perfectly" though imperfectly com-
prehended, in time the child would "understand all."

Their parents, meanwhile, actually tried to use only "godly and
honest conversation" in their children's presence and tried to teach more
by example than even by words of "virtue and goodness." They heeded
Bullinger's warning to try to keep their children from light company
and "sinful sights," and to "act before their little ones as they would act
before God." Servants were cautioned to do likewise, for parents tried

to prevent any "corrupt person" from ever entering the home "lest he sow evil among children and servants." Truly, they said with their mentor, unless virtue only is planted in the hearts of children, there can be no virtuous harvest.

As the sixteenth century grew older, the social side of life was developed in the general households as well as at court. Even so, in well-disciplined homes stress was still laid on "godly, grave, and fruitful instruction" that would prepare children for a life of accomplishment. Always the important thing in this teaching was its insistence on form, order, and discipline.

In the Elizabethan plan, idleness was unthinkable, and each member of the middle-class family and of many noble families must perform some labor. Had not Bullinger urged that every child be taught a trade or craft? Almost everywhere this admonition was taken to heart, for parents thought of their children as belonging to the State, and the State as founded on the home; ergo, a healthy State was shaped by faithful, conscientious parents and obedient children. Even the smallest children were taught to say grace at table and, when old enough to set the table at mealtime, to serve the food to their parents in "a clean, mannerly way." All their moments were carefully planned to be filled with useful activity. Wards in fine homes, learning to perform these same services but according to the pattern of wealth and perhaps luxury, grew in charm and self-control as they were taught that each must some day become the head of a household demanding efficient and gracious performance of the duties in that position.

Bullinger spoke also of the need of keeping children well fed, well clothed, and carefully supervised during play hours. Never must they be pampered with rich food or fine dress. Had not Daniel's clear skin and fine disposition been due to his diet of bread and water? Excess of "meat [food] and dress in youth" would lead to gluttony, drunkenness, lechery, and pride, vices that could not be removed as the child grew older. No child should be permitted "to run out of doors day or night without parental consent, and even when he had cause to absent himself he must recount all he did in his absence lest without such surveillance he learn to play "unlawful games," or acquire bad or vicious habits. If to maintain such discipline a parent was forced to use the rod, he must do so "with love and not in a way that would cause fear." The father must always keep in mind, however, that the "foolishness of young hearts" can be "driven forth with the rod of correction" and that it is better "that children weep than old men."

Critics have often condemned the dull repetition of Elizabethan conduct books, but not the enthusiasm of the writers. Each usually felt that his point of view enabled him to see family relationships in new and better perspective, and it was his duty to share what he knew. In the early 1560's Thomas Becon's *The Book of Matrimony* and

Catechisme set forth their rules for domestic conduct. Children should be their parents' "chief joy, felicity, and, next to God, their staff in old age," he says, if the father will observe four things—godly training of his sons in character, preparing them for practical careers, preventing their association with evil companions, and providing them with suitable marriages. About two decades later Bartholomew Batty's *The Christian mans Closet* stressed more careful education of children in the knowledge of God, in an understanding of the arts, and in better manners. To achieve this end, the father himself must cultivate certain important virtues—justice and courage in defending his possessions, liberal assistance to the good and the chaste, hatred of filthiness, honesty in word and deed, gentleness, avoidance of suspicion, diligent provision for his family's needs, more love for his children than for his own life, and finally, careful government of his household. Then he makes some practical suggestions. The mother, immediately upon realizing she is pregnant, must commit her child to God "with fervent prayers" and, until its birth, avoid any disquiet or anger, all dancing and intemperate eating or drinking, and all "immoderate stirring or striving or lifting." The father, when finding his children do not study their lessons diligently, should encourage them with praise and small gifts and enticements before threatening them with "stripes," but if compelled to use the rod, he must exercise moderation. Each writer, then, set forth much of what had been said before, adding what he insisted he had learned from observation or experience. For example, William Gouge in *Domesticall Duties* (3d ed., 1634), after repeating what Batty and others had said about expectant mothers, charged such women to take great care to "gratify" their "cravings" for food.

Since the father was the head of the household, at least in theory, he was responsible for his family even when he could not be with them. Lodowick Bryskett (*A Discourse of Civill Life*, 1606) urged the father, therefore, to appoint an honest and virtuous man to care for his children and to provide suitable companions for his sons when he was called from home on business or affairs of state. Such companions must be of equal age and rank. To ease the weight of the many obligations by making them easier to remember and thereby to perform, William Perkins in his 1590 *Christian Oeconomie* placed them in two categories—those concerned with the household's private worship and those demanding honest and profitable labor from each of the members. The first, he said, was recommended by all holy men as well as by reason because it enabled the family to discuss "eternal life and to give prayers and thanksgiving" for this life as they assembled for worship at morning and evening and said grace at meals. The second duty made parents responsible for their children till they were able to establish homes of their own, and required training of each in some useful occupation. Perkins insisted, however, that before training began, the natural gifts of the child must be studied. He also emphasized the need of play, which he believed should "solace them in recreation fitting for their years." Then, when they returned to work, if the children needed discipline, words should be used first and the rod only when words did not prevail.

Vives, the protégé of Henry VIII's first wife, Catherine, declared solemnly in *The Instruction of a Christian Woman*[3] that parents should not have children at all unless they were entirely willing to take full responsibility for the lives entrusted to their care. This strong statement was probably due to the writer's effort to defend Catherine when court gossip about Henry's plan to divorce the queen became more and more difficult for Catherine to bear. Nevertheless, it so impressed its readers that many Elizabethans frequently quoted it. "If the cares and sorrows that children cause their mothers" were known, he said in referring to childbirth, "women would be sore afraid of them as death . . . and hate them like cruel, wild beasts or venomous serpents." They gave but little joy. When young they were "nothing but tediousness," and when older they caused "perpetual fear." If they were ill they brought sorrow; if they were good the mother constantly feared they might suffer harm or die. Yet barren women, he noted, practiced every means they heard of "except prayer" to take away the "dishonor" of sterility. Children, he continued, had to be watched always lest they be idle, and if the mother did not keep them from this danger, she might better "bear a snake or wolf."

Next to idleness Elizabethans feared deformity in their children, some even advocating the death of such unfortunates. Bryskett was so moved by the argument over this matter that he called the "black hearts" of those who would slay "children born imperfect" monstrous beings who were themselves, "crooked and misshapen." They "should be buried quick," he said. Simple babes "have no election" and can "yield no tokens either of good or evil." To condemn them to death before they had even offended was "exceeding cruelty." Yet fear of giving birth to a monster preyed on many a pregnant woman's mind, for most Elizabethans believed a crooked body meant a crooked heart. Idleness was worse because it made a willing tool for the devil to employ. Idlers, however, could be cured by the alert parent, but twisted bodies could not be made straight.

A practical woman might dismiss her fears about her child's possible deformity, but she could not contemplate childbirth with any degree of assurance. Its grave dangers and the usual morbid attitude toward death probably had much to do with the convention of preparing for an impressive "lying in" bedchamber. If one survived the ordeal of birth, then it was fitting to celebrate the occasion in an appropriate manner. If

[3] Juan Luis Vives wrote his book in 1523. It was translated by Richard Hyrde in 1540 and republished in 1541. The 1541 edition is the source used in this study.

one did not survive, then such a person at least performed her last duty on earth with the magnificent gesture it merited. Among the rich the extravagance of upholstery in the great bedchamber at the time of child-birth was almost incredible. When the Countess of Salisbury, for example, was "brought to bed of a daughter" in 1612, she gave the gossips a chance to describe with much detail her rich bed hanging of white satin, embroidered with silver and pearls and valued at £14,000.

At such a time all classes of society observed some form of celebration. Those who could afford it held receptions and card parties in the mother's room on the theory that all this excitement was good for her and hastened her recovery. Visiting the mother and making presents to her and the child was of no little benefit to the poor when their friends came full-handed.

Rejoicing over a child's birth took most elaborate form at the baptizing and naming. Conduct books gave very specific directions for proper christenings. They urged fathers, if at all possible, to attend the ceremony and to note diligently all that was promised there in order that the child might be brought up according to the vows and promises. The baptizing must be performed suitably, some insisting that the child's face be sprinkled and others that the form of ceremony was not so essential as the spirit of the biblical command (Matt. 28:19). Christenings were usually performed in a public place "where God's people were accustomed to meet for service," and the ceremony was held on the first Sunday after the child's birth, or as near then as possible.

The naming of the child gave Elizabethans much serious thought, the father being chiefly responsible for the final choice. He must find a name with a "good significance," such as one from the Scriptures, and must also consider a name in the family or at least one commonly used in England, such as Henry, Edward, William, Richard, or Anne, Bridget, etc. Dorothy Leigh's *The Mothers Blessing* (1618) naïvely discusses the subject. She preferred saints' names to those of good meaning like Susanna, exemplifying chastity. Saints' names would better fortify women against "men who lay in wait to deceive them." Though Mary was the loveliest name of all because of its associations, she also liked Michal because David's wife by that name had saved his life, and Abigail was also good because this wife was noted for her wisdom. Rachel was associated with amiability, Judith was beautiful for the bravery shown by the heroine of this name in the Apocrypha, and Anna was a proper name because of biblical Anna's patience and zeal in prayer. All writers agreed on one point—whether named for hero or heroine in English or biblical history, the child must be encouraged always in living up to its good name.

During the christening, the child was borne upon a cushion as costly and as beautifully embroidered as the parents could provide, and covered with a handsome bearing cloth. On the child's face, the priest laid a face-cloth or chrisom cloth of white linen, emblematic of purity; it was used till after the churching of the mother about a month later. An infant who died during the wearing of the chrisom was called a "chrisom" or "chrisom child." Robert Herrick's "Upon a Child that Died" describes a chrisom.

> Here she lies, a pretty bud,
> Lately made of flesh and blood:
> Who, as soon, fell fast asleep
> As her little eyes did peep.
> Give her strewings, but not stir
> The earth that lightly covers her.

Following the christening, especially among the middle class, was the gossips' feast, at which occurred much fraternal drinking and exchange of sentiment. Sugar, biscuits, comfits, marchpane, sweet suckets, etc., were passed around, and often the good gossips ate more than they had brought or returned home with a goodly store of little cakes in their capacious skirt pockets. As each guest was expected to bring the child a gift, there might be a good deal of rivalry while the presents were examined at the feast. With interest in material possessions mounting in proportion to the increasing extravagance of the time, the christening gifts also became a matter of ostentatious display.

In early times the godparents had presented the child with simple gifts, such as little shirts with narrow bands and cuffs edged with blue silk thread or, in the case of a noble child, edged with fine lace of black silk or gold. The little shirts seldom cost over a noble and usually sold at two or three shillings. As the presents grew richer, they might include a candle cup, a silver mounted coral with bells (supposed to indicate illness if the coral changed color, and to aid in teething as well as to avert the evil eye and all witchcraft), an expensive gilt cup, a porringer, knives with ivory handles, and apostle spoons with thin handles and big bowls. These spoons with the engraved figures on the handles became so popular as "first" gifts that wealthy godparents sometimes presented a complete set of them, including the master spoon engraved with the face of Jesus. Shakespeare refers to such spoons in *Henry VIII* when the king, partly to spite his enemies who have sought Cranmer's life, chooses the archbishop to be a godfather to the child Elizabeth. As Cranmer gratefully and obsequiously accepts the honor and asks how he may deserve it since he is such a "poor humble subject," the king says with a kindly ironic smile, "Come, come, my lord, you'd spare your spoons" (IV:iii:168–69). When these spoons were given singly they represented the saint of the month in which the child was born. Among the lower classes, who also liked to present apostle spoons, base metal served in place of silver and gilt. A mother who was poor might be given money to help with the lying-in expenses, and her guests would bring their own contributions to the feast. At such a time the husband was not forgotten. For example, in Oxfordshire particularly, the new father might be presented with a rocking-cake that added much to the spirit of festivity. For the first child a cradle was most acceptable. Sometimes oak cradles, carved with appropriate verses, were presented. Cradles of the rich, however, were covered with velvet and trimmed with gold fringe.

Among the nobility christenings, like weddings, were formal ceremonies. A formal invitation to act as godfather or godmother was a social honor as well as a social responsibility. It was written with great care and accepted with the same concern for correct form. Soon christenings were a means of asking and conferring honors among the socially conscious people. Robert Sidney's secretary, for example, in his letter to his lord about plans for christening a newly arrived daughter, reveals the satisfaction of his master's household in the arrangements. Since the anxious father could not leave his post at Flushing to return home at this important time, the secretary comforted him with "My Lord Southampton did take it exceedingly kindly that he was desired to be a godfather, and will most willingly do it. My Lady Sussex sware that she longed to be a godmother, and is proud that she is chosen to be one."[4]

A week later the secretary wrote another letter to describe the event. The child had been named Bridget. Lady Bedford, unable to attend, had sent her "deepest protestations" by her father and mother, saying that nothing but illness kept her away, and her absence grieved her more than her illness. She sent a bowl, desiring it to be accepted "as from a third godmother." Countesses, lords, and captains of Flushing were there, and all things were "prepared for their calling."

When Robert's little son was born, the child's mother was ill with the measles, and this delayed the christening. As soon as she was sufficiently recovered, an invitation was sent to Lady Penelope Rich to serve as godmother, and she graciously accepted. Then she too broke out in a "tether," and the christening had to be delayed again. Meanwhile the anxious father had been permitted to return home from Flushing to attend the funeral of his aunt's husband, the Earl of Huntingdon. The impatient parents, however, had to wait for Lady Rich to recover, for as the first godmother, she had the right to set the date for the christening. When after a delay of five or six days she announced the date, they were greatly relieved.

By this time the child was a month old, a very late christening in times so precarious for infants. But all came off well. The gifts were rich and fashionable, each of the godparents presenting a standing bowl,

---

[4] This letter by Roland White is dated February 22, 1590, and is among the *Letters and Memorials of State: The Sydney Letters* (1746) compiled by Arthur Collins.

and at the reception the guests seemed especially happy as, smiling graciously, they conducted themselves with perfect Elizabethan decorum. The child was named for his father.

When unable to accept the honor of being a godparent, an Elizabethan noble was careful to write the correct note of regret and to secure a substitute that would honor both himself and the infant's parents. Sir Christopher Hatton's letters, edited by Sir Nicholas Harris Nicolas, include such a note sent to the person he wishes to act for him at the ceremony. Hatton begins by saying he has been asked by Sir Richard Knightly of Fawsley in Northamptonshire to christen a child it has "pleased God to send him," and he would be glad to perform in person an office so "full of piety in itself" but that state affairs "dispose" of him otherwise. He therefore makes "so bold" as to ask the Earl of Hertford to take his place, there being no noble at court at the time "fit to accompany" the earl's mother who is also to take part in the "holy action"—"to be a witness in baptism, of God's goodness participated through that holy Sacrament" to the young infant, "of whom" Hatton hopes "an other day" the Earl of Hertford will receive "both thanks and comfort." Meanwhile he will himself make as "grateful acknowledgment" of Hertford's courtesy to him for taking his place as lies in his power to "requite with all faithful goodness." Knowing the earl will not refuse his diplomatic demands of him, Hatton concludes his note by saying he will send to Hertford on the next day at "one of the clock" a gentleman to wait on the earl "with such duty as is fit and belonging to the ceremony." And so he closes with the usual Elizabethan expressions in which he wishes him the "gracious favor of the Almighty," and remains his "very loving assured friend" to whom he can write with such confidence from his present residence with the Queen, "the Court of Nonsuch, the 7th of August, 1584."

Children of close kin to royalty had elaborate christenings, as was the case with Jane Grey, for whom the ceremony took place forty-eight hours after her birth. At this time (1537), it was customary for the whole family, godfathers and godmothers, and guests to walk in procession from home to church, there to be met by the clergy. After a short prayer the child was named and baptized at a font covered by a richly carved and painted canopy that could be pulled up or down to keep the holy water clean. Here, in the middle of the church, the back of the child's head and her heels were immersed in water. Then she was anointed with the chrism oil on back and breast.

After the ceremony came the presentation of gifts from the various sponsors and friends. Ironically enough, among the presents was a rich bowl with a chiseled cover from Mary Tudor, the cousin who was in time to order little Jane's execution. The abundant refreshments provided for the crowd gathered outside were the usual wafers, comfits, and hippocras (spiced wine), served from the church porch. Now the procession made its way back home, the child carried in great state, carefully wrapped in a robe of rich brocade. At home an elaborate dinner concluded the celebration.[5]

Royal christenings were often the occasion for tediously detailed ceremonies. Before and after the christening of Prince Henry (son of James I) at Stirling, Scotland, on September 5, 1594, there were court revels, and the ceremony itself was intended to be very impressive. It has been suggested by G. B. Harrison[6] that the play on the lion in Shakespeare's *Midsummer Night's Dream* may have been due to the pageant master's idea for surprising the guests with a red lion drawing a triumphal chariot at the banquet following the ceremony; at the last moment, however, there was apprehension lest the lion, being unused to courtly entertainments, might forget himself or frighten the ladies. Today a guide at Stirling Castle points out to favored visitors the "very courtyard" in which James I kept his lions, and "the very door" from which people in the castle looked down upon the restless cats. If sufficient interest is manifested by the credulous visitor, he will have pointed out to him the distant grounds where James I hunted with his lions. In spite of the grandiosity of Prince Henry's christening, it probably did not exceed that of his little sister Elizabeth, for when she was born James was hopeful of becoming King of England. The font for this rite was of silver, and was worked with all kinds of imagery, yet it was only one of the many details in the elaborate preparations for this event.

The nobles were quick to follow the example set by ostentatious royal christenings, and the lower classes, in turn, made of the occasion what they could. As far back as 1559, the church had been hung with arras for the christening of Sir Thomas Chamberlain's son, and the ceremony had been followed with banqueting dainties and hippocras. Eventually both service and refreshments became so extended that the feasting was often preceded by a sermon or an address to parents and godparents. Since the mother was rarely able to be present, the father was expected to listen carefully to the advice given him and the sponsors. Puritan preachers were quite likely to make a long tiresome sermon of this discourse, but sometimes the advice given was so well expressed that it was discussed at length by the congregation afterward. Fees for baptism varied according to the social position of the family. In 1560, a ruling provided that the curate was to be paid no less than four pence, but among the people of means, the fee was as generous as the ambitious father cared to make it.

Because christenings took place so soon after the child's birth, the mother seldom attended to any of the details of the ceremony; conse-

---

[5] Richard Davey, *The Nine Days Queen, Lady Jane Grey and her Times* (1909), p. 15.

[6] See *Shakespeare under Elizabeth* (1933) or *The Elizabethan Journals* (1939).

quently the father was often a little nervous about the event coming off , properly. A letter[7] to Henry VIII's secretary, Cromwell, was written under such strain that it reveals much of a parent's emotions at such a time. Timidly the writer, Ralph Sadler, apologizes for interrupting a man engaged in "weighty affairs" when his own are such "trifles." Then he plunges into the purpose for his writing. His wife, "after long travail, and as painful labor as any woman could have, hath, at the last, brought forth a fair boy," and he desires the secretary to "be gossip unto so poor a man" as himself. He says that the child will bear the secretary's name, and he hopes the secretary will have more cause to rejoice than in the other child he had honored by his presence since it died so soon after the christening. He assures the secretary that he knows it "died innocent, and enjoyeth the joys of heaven." Then he approaches a delicate matter that troubles him. He wishes the godmother to be either Mr. Richard's wife or Lady Weston, both of whom live near by, but he dares not choose Mr. Richard's wife. Women, he is told, have a certain superstition about pregnant women serving as godmothers, and he does not know whether Mr. Richard's wife "goeth with child." He is sure of Lady Weston, and therefore names her. Apparently he is also sure the secretary will do him the honor he craves, for he concludes with the details of time, "tomorrow in the afternoon . . . at three of the clock," and place, "the holy Trinity." Again he apologizes, this time for writing with so "rude and hasty hand," but he is Cromwell's "most assured and faithful servant during his life."

Many Elizabethan mothers nursed their children only because they believed an infant could absorb evil as well as good with the milk it took from the breast. Shakespeare refers to this superstition in *The Winter's Tale* (II:i:56–58) when the jealous Leontes says to his wife whom he accuses of infidelity, "Give me the boy. I am glad you did not nurse him . . . you have too much blood in him." Vives was quoted again and again by writers of conduct books, saying a chaste mother might have a dissolute child if its wet nurse was dissolute, and whatever infants learned in their "rude and ignorant" age they "ever sought to counterfeit and follow cunningly" when they grew older. Such writers declared God intended mothers to nurse their children because an angelic command urged mothers to carry themselves in such a way as to be able to produce milk.

If wet nurses had to be provided, they were chosen by careful parents according to the merit of character. They should also be "well conditioned," of good complexion, clean, and able to speak "plainly with apt words" so that the little ones from their cradles might learn good speech

---

[7] Letter CCII of *Original Letters Illustrative of English History* (1825), edited by Sir Henry Ellis, II: 225–26.

and good manners. It was suggested also that the mother keep the wet nurse near her always; in this way the child would know its mother and father and the rest of the family from its infancy. Such knowledge was important because "whatever behavior" a child first learned he was sure to retain.

Disapproval of those who refused to nurse their children was shown in the common charge that these mothers feared they might "change the form of their hard round paps." One writer threatened that punishment was sure to come to them when they would hear their children say what another child told its mother: "You bore me but nine months in your womb, but my nurse kept me with her teats the space of two years; that which I hold of you is my body, which you gave me scarce honestly, but that which I have of her proceedeth of pure affection. And moreover as soon as I was born, you deprived me of your company, and banished me your presence; but she graciously received me . . . between her arms and used me so well, that she hath brought me to this you see." Various adaptations of this story from Stefano Guazzo's *The Civil Conversation* (1581) appeared from time to time in the conduct books, and it made a strong impression upon many women.

Weaning the child was observed with due solemnity in homes making the most of opportunities that might provide ceremonious occasions. A child was often two years old or more before being weaned. Royalty, of course, attached much importance to the event, as was shown in the case of Jane Grey. When she was eighteen months old, suitable preparations marked the day, for mass was said at the chapel in the presence of the whole family, including the wet nurse and Jane, and the baby was blessed with holy water. Then the family returned from the chapel to the great hall of their home and sat down to a sumptuous banquet. Though not a royal babe at this time, Jane was cared for as if she were by her ambitious parents. Was she not the grandchild of Henry VIII's favorite sister? Nor were her parents' ambitions unfounded, for Henry included her among his heirs.

Cradles for Elizabethan babies were of solid wood with deep rockers. Often they were handsomely carved and filled with feather pillows and blankets and soft robes. Some were even upholstered. Of course the cradle was kept near the fireplace, and the child must have been almost suffocated in the clothes and bedding piled about it by anxious mother or nurse. As the mother or other attendant rocked the cradle, she sewed long seams with beautiful tiny stitches, plain or fancy, and sang lullabies to still the child. Some of the charming old songs have been handed down to us. Occasionally old lullabies are sung on the concert stage, but more often, if they are heard at all, their tinkling notes sound when a lady raises the lid of her powder jar and releases the spring that starts the music box concealed below. Or there is the doll cradle with such a box placed in it that a child rocking her doll might be amused by such old melodies as Elizabethan mothers loved to sing: "Rock-a-by Baby on the Tree Top," "Bye, Baby Bunting, Father's Gone a-Hunting." Lovers of this type of song know well the lullaby in Dekker's play, *Patient Grissel*, and Greene's "Sephestia's Song to her Child." Another, perhaps not so well known but still quite typical of the lullaby, was composed about 1566 by John Phillips.

> Lulla by baby, lulla by baby,
> Thy nurse will tend thee, as duly as may be.
>
> Be still, my sweet sweeting, no longer do cry,
>   Sing lulla by baby, lulla by baby.
> Let dolors be fleeting, I fancy thee, I,
>   To rock and to lull thee, I will not delay me.
> Lulla by baby, etc.
>
> What creatures now living would hasten thy woe?
>   Sing lulla by baby, lulla by, lulla by baby.
> See for thy relieving, the time I bestow,
>   To dance, and to prance thee, as prett'ly as may be.
> Lulla by baby, etc.
>
> The gods be thy shield and comfort in need,
>   Sing lulla by baby, lulla by, lulla by baby;
> They give thee good fortune and well for to speed,
>   And this to desire, I will not delay me.
> Lulla by baby, etc.

It is noticeable that this nursery song alludes to dancing the baby on one's knee, and the conduct books show that such practice was not unusual. Indeed, many authors warned Elizabethan parents against spoiling their children by too much pampering. There was not nearly so much show of affection in the Tudor times as when James I reigned as king and set an example of fondling children that strictly disciplined homes not only frowned upon but feared. In the middle-class families especially, the old austerities of discipline were clung to as a necessary part of the ideal of decorum. Those parents who manifested too much affection for the child's own good were frequently criticized for laxity. When James I persisted in addressing his son Charles as Baby Charles even after he was grown and ready to marry, he set an example that those used to Elizabethan ideals abhorred.

In many Elizabethan nurseries the child was gradually introduced to the strict discipline of the age. At first, then, he was taught simple rhymes and games. Mothers and nurses recited to him the old jingles "This little pig went to market" and "Shoe the horse, shoe the mare." The toes were playfully tickled as they were named Harry Whistle,

Thommy Thistle, Harry Thible, Tommy Thible, and Little O Kerbell. The fingers were also named Tom Thumbkin, Bess Bumpkin, Bill Winkin, Long Linkin, and Little Dick. Many of the children were taught to amuse themselves by reciting "Little Boy Blue" and "Little Bo-peep" as they played with their toys.

For in spite of being dressed like little men and women, Elizabethan children had their toys. Most of them came from Holland or France. For girls they consisted of wooden dolls with painted faces and rather crudely jointed limbs, but they were loved for all that. For little boys there were hobby horses and toy soldiers mounted on movable slides, and toy ships and drums. Both little boys and girls played with hoops and balls.

Perhaps some of the seventeenth-century reaction against the severity of Elizabethan parents was due to a feeling in the new generation of having been denied sufficient attention when children. But most of the overindulgence of children was in keeping with the general disorder of the age under the Stuarts. Parents who had been brought up under the Tudor regime more often than not refrained from coddling their children. This was true of the capable Elizabeth Tanfield, who, an heiress at fifteen, married the first Lord Falkland.

As a child, this Elizabeth had been obliged on special occasions to ask a blessing of her mother on her knees and, like all Elizabethan children of good manners, to address her parents as Sir and Madame. With all her own eleven children, however, she was less formally firm but tender. She nursed at the breast all but the first, who was taken at an early age and put in the home of his grandfather for the careful rearing fitting to the heir of the family. Although this young mother had never been particularly interested in dress, she took much pleasure in that of her children. Yet she trained them all carefully in religion if not in any "distinctive tenets," and she herself gave them their first school lessons. When necessary for her to punish a child, she made it kiss the rod with which she whipped it in order to show penitence and submission. Shakespeare refers to this common practice in *Two Gentlemen of Verona* (I:ii:58–59) when Julia compares the moods of love to a "testy babe" that "will scratch the nurse and presently all humbled kiss the rod."[8]

That some parents were inclined to be too severe is indicated by the admonition in some of the conduct books against making the break between play and study too abrupt. It was argued that unless children were brought gently from the stage of childish prattle to learning they would not be likely to love knowledge. Most of these writers felt that three was late enough, however, for a child to be entrusted to the tutor. They

[8] An excellent discussion of the contrast between Elizabethan and Stuart home discipline occurs in Elizabeth Godfrey's *Home Life under the Stuarts, 1603–1649* (1903).

suggested, nevertheless, that this person be not too different from the nurse lest the child be shocked: "to take a child from the breast and from his nurse's bosom, and to put him suddenly under the hard government of a cursed master, would be too violent a change, and force the tender nature overmuch." The mother was deemed best to fill this gap; in most places she was expected to do so, beginning with moral teaching in which the child was encouraged to commit to memory moral and religious "sentences" about God, country, family, social relationships, courtesy toward elders and equals and inferiors, temperance in food and drink, honesty and open dealing, and avoidance of evil companions.

During a child's tender years, this instruction was interrupted by play, and his parents were concerned that his playfellows be the right kind for such periods of relaxation. In middle-class homes the mother, of course, was expected to be fully responsible for the selection of play-mates. First, she must assure herself that they had no speech difficulty; next, she must supervise the play lest it get too rough; and finally, she must see that the children were clean and honest in their conduct. Puritan mothers were especially warned against letting their children play with others that were likely to swear or babble. They must also try to find companions for their children that had a certain gravity and modesty even when merriest "so that gravity and sobriety and modesty might grow with them from the very cradle." Thomas Becon, in his *Worckes* (1564), was one of those who insisted on a child's "gravity," and Becon was a "guiding light."

Games at which little boys might become rough were sham fights, running, leaping, wrestling, stone-casting, flinging bucklers, sliding, skating on bones, and whatever in these simple tests of skill developed or challenged the competitive spirit. Games that both boys and girls played, sometimes with much hilarity, were Drop the Cap (like Drop the Handkerchief) and Barley Bridge (like London Bridge). The singing and excitement of Drop the Cap culminated in the chase as the child behind whom the cap was dropped pursued the one who had dropped it. Sometimes when the caught person was kissed as penalty for being caught, there was a sharp contest that might become quite rough. Barley Bridge ended in a tug-of-war that strained muscles in the effort of the two sides to outtug each other and often was extremely rough. Drop the Cap was quite a different game when played by men and women on the village green, for they could engage in much pretty dalliance, but with children it was almost always an exciting game that might end in tears or squabbles.

If a child did not care to play with his fellows, he might take one of his storybooks and go into a corner to enjoy it by himself. The elaborate and varied children's books of today had strange predecessors in the Elizabethan chapbooks and peddlers' tales sold for children. Some of the stories were illustrated by coarsely colored woodcuts, and some were merely in black and white on cheap paper. Often the gruesome tales printed on broadsheets for their elders fell into the hands of the young who read them with shivering delight if they could comprehend them at all. In some households stories enjoyed by both young and old for their romantic adventures were those of Guy of Warwick, the Danish Havelock, Chevy Chase, the tales of King Arthur, nursery tales like Babes in the Wood, and moral stories like Aesop's fables. Strict Catholics and Puritans, of course, would substitute for much of this reading graver stories from the Bible, especially from the Apocrypha, and long moral tales.

Dorothy Leigh, for example, taught her children to read the Bible in English instead of foolish stories because it prepared them for death. She must have lived much in the dread shadow after she lost her husband, for she actually believed that children should be prepared to endure its frightful presence by learning to know how unavoidable it is. This melancholy picture of life she attempted to brighten by stories of Jesus, for she felt they were best to help purge children of their "savage and wild nature." In discussing Jesus as an example of the virtues she wished to instill into her sons, she said, "If all the sea were ink and all the iron in the world were pens, and all the creatures were writers, they could never declare the benefits, the great blessings, and the great mercies . . . of Christ." Yet so slight was her faith in human nature and so great her fear of evil that she insisted her children be taught to pray constantly that they might learn to recognize Satan, "who was always baiting his hooks so cunningly that only God" could save them from him.

At the opposite extreme from this solemn mother was the careless type, who was criticized severely by the conduct books as overindulgent. A lively translator of Plutarch, who called his work *A President for Parentes*,[9] blamed mothers for their unconcern about bad habits formed by their children. He complained that almost all children had learned to "dash out loud lies," that not one in a hundred could tell the truth; the others invented "so handsomely" and so "cunningly" that their lies were a "wonder to behold." At five years of age they were "as perfect in their art" as if they had gone to school for twenty years to learn how to conceal the truth. Parents, he said, *must* teach their children long before they go to school how to tell the truth. For the most part, lying was punished by the rod, though this type of chastisement was under fire in the conduct books.

As far back as 1530, Sir Thomas Elyot had objected to "strypes," which, he said, were for villeins and slaves and not for those of gentle

---

[9] Plutarch, *A President for Parentes*, Teaching the vertuous training up of Children and holesome information of yongmen. Translated and partly augmented by Ed. Grant, 1571.

blood or for children of gentle nature. His account, repeated by Roger Ascham, of how Jane Grey's parents slapped and even kicked her when she gave offense was told to make his point: that a child, even an excellent one like Jane, learned better by praise and light rebuke than by stripes. Both Elyot and Ascham would probably have been amazed if they had been told their story was to give succeeding generations an impression of unloving parents among the early Tudors and Elizabethans. Such an impression could not be further from the truth. Even Elyot admitted that some parents were too indulgent as some were too harsh, and then added, "too much love is not love at all."

Stern fathers were nearly always loving fathers who were very much concerned about their children's welfare. Like Walter Devereux as he lay dying in Ireland, they too might well say, "My only care for any 'worldly matter' is for my children" and, again like him, bestow on their children all their "love and blessing," praying devoutly to God that "He would bless them and give them grace to fear [obey] Him." Fathers compelled to be absent from their families while they were at the wars or abroad on ambassadorial duties often suffered keenly about the welfare of their children. A typical letter sent by a father who had gone as Henry's ambassador to meet Anne of Cleves tells of his anxiety over Anne's delayed arrival because it kept him from home. He quaintly addresses his wife as his "right loving bedfellow," and tells her he is, "thanks to God, in health, trusting shortly to hear like news" from her and his "little boys, of whose increase and towardness" he is "not a little desirous to be advertised."[10]

Sternness in parents had been supported in large measure by the *Bishop's Book* (1537), a handbook of moral instruction and doctrine. In its preface was an admonition to parents "to imploy their diligence and busy care to educate and instruct their children by all means in virtue and goodness, and to restrain them from vices by convenient discipline and castigation." The humanists, following the teaching of Erasmus in *De Civilitate*, had tried to let their children "drink the seeds of love" before they disciplined them. Becon accepted this ideal also, and his followers agreed with him that if parents would use stripes moderately, together with words that proceeded from the heart, they would not dull the wits of their offspring or drive the child away from a "home of tyrants." But a wise kindness is much more difficult to achieve than discipline that is ruled by harshness or fondness, and exceptional parents among Elizabethans were not so numerous as could be wished. Each generation thinks it is more enlightened than the age immediately preceding it. Moderate use of the rod, therefore, was urged by Elizabethan moralists as a means of impressing upon the child's mind instruction

---

[10] Letter CCCLIV of *Original Letters*, III, 253–54.

about conduct, for they truly believed that minds too young to reason could learn by a little pain. It was too cruel to leave all punishment to life itself, which always meted out to the ignorant and willfully disobedient the same harsh treatment.

Parents who went from one extreme to another, being too exacting at one time and too indulgent at another, were severely criticized in conduct books. Batty, for example, quoted from Seneca, Cicero, Socrates, and St. Augustine to prove his contention that discipline in the home was a primary duty. He repeated the old story of a wise father who, while congratulating his son upon the birth of an heir, urged him when necessary to chastise him suitably, but without "contumely, check, or taunt," and, when occasion permitted him to praise, to show approval without "flattery or adulation." Only on an even level of training could his son learn due regard for the "gravity of life" and the "pleasantness of manners." As he taught his child, he must also keep ever in mind that one day this heir might be a man and a father like himself, and his life would be built upon the moral teaching and living of not one human being but many forebears.

In the flurry of words over discipline too severely administered, one author in what he entitled *Tell-Trothes New-yeares Gift* (1593) said the very devil in hell boasted he peopled his domain with victims of severe and indiscreet judgment, and William Vaughan's *The Golden Grove* (1599) insisted parents could "reap joy" of their children only if they were strict. So great was his horror of disobedient children that Vaughan believed mothers might do well to frighten wayward children when they were small by telling them of "the horned and hairy monster being in hell to catch bad children, and how the good ones go to paradise, dancing with the angels." He was sure very few children were inclined to virtue. "Suffer the son to have his will for a time," he said, "and he will become rude, inflexible, and wantonly disposed to all manner of vices; chastise the child and imprint discipline in his heart while he is young" that he may bow to parental instruction. Like roses, children would wither if overcome by the briers of too much affection; if it was necessary to "whip the devil" out of them, the rod must be applied unsparingly.

John Davies summed up such writing in verses which advised the widow of Sir Thomas Overbury how to select a husband who might aid her in bringing up her children:

> The parcels of thyself (thy children) strike
> When they misdo; yet, not so oft as then:
> Sometimes to wink at what we do mislike,
> Is well to see to do like prudent men:
> That is, when sweetness, more than sharpness, will
> Their proper good, keep from improper ill.

As such an hand still bear thou on the reins,
As bridle may, with ease, their coltish will;
With ease to either; for, to neither, pains
Are pleasing; so that kindness do not kill.
As fond apes do their young: Thy children so,
Thy will, with ease, shall still both do and know.

So much has been said of the severity of Elizabethan parents that the high death rate of their children has been at least partly attributed to harsh discipline. But if such was true, why did some of them become, as Mrs. Godfrey describes them (*Home Life under the Stuarts*), "an incomparable race of valiant men and heroic, much enduring women" when they were still in their tender years? She has suggested that the extreme youth of many Elizabethan parents may have caused the weak children to be especially feeble and immature in constitution so that they quickly dropped blighted into an early grave; the strong ones, on the other hand, may have been especially robust, and thus able to endure the rigors of the age. It is much more likely, however, that the high rate of infant mortality was due to contagious diseases and the unsanitary conditions of the sixteenth century. As for the remarkable character of the children who survived, why should one hesitate to attribute much of their precocity and self-assurance and stout ability to endure to a discipline begun in the nursery and continued as long as they were under the parental roof? The children in Shakespeare's drama are regarded as unnaturally idealistic or mature. Yet letters and private records usually bear out the truth implied by his details of intimate family life and in his portrayal of extraordinary children.

It might be well to compare some of the theory of conduct books with some of the facts in Elizabethan domestic life. In many respects, Lord Burghley was a typical father of the upper class, though he was not born to his position among aristocrats. He had almost dashed his hopeful parents' dreams of their son becoming a noble of great wealth and influence, surrounded by friends, occupied with the details of large estates, and happy in studious pursuits. For his first marriage was sudden and ill advised from their point of view, and the child of that union was to call forth all Burghley's forbearance as he lay awake at night trying to devise a way of setting the boy on some path of accomplishment. The wife's early death enabled him to follow the wise advice of his parents, and this time Burghley made a very successful social alliance. Now his father-in-law was the learned Sir Anthony Cooke, and among his friends were congenial minds that both he and his second wife could enjoy. They became the center of an intellectual group as Burghley's ability and power increased.

The son of the first marriage was a wastrel in his youth, and he brought Burghley untold grief and humiliation. Probably Burghley was partly responsible for the boy's rebellious love of pleasure, for Burghley tried to train him for an ambitious career unsuited to the youth's inclinations. Yet it must be noted that in time the boy did find a satisfactory place in life through his father's unflagging effort. The son by his second wife, however, followed in Burghley's footsteps, maintaining the family tradition of skill and clever management.

By temperament, Burghley was able to conform easily to the state religions set up by Mary, Edward VI, and Elizabeth. Through his own ability to make the right compromise, he moderated his views sufficiently to maintain an intellectual interest and a private attachment to Elizabeth's religious compromise. Thus he became known for his wisdom and good judgment at a time when survival sometimes depended on these very qualities. More important still, he learned how to wield power without abusing it, in his home as well as in state affairs. This is the chief reason why his large house was always crowded with children besides his own and many servants and guests.

In his home Burghley probably enjoyed the challenge to his powers even as his conscientious heart responded to the burden of domestic problems. Though his son by his second wife was his special care, he willingly assumed the responsibilities of the wards in his household also. For Robert, therefore, he set down the twelve tenets a youth should make his by study and practice if he would take his place with dignity and ease in a world beset with snares yet rich in rewards. There is nothing new in these rules except in the arrangement and emphasis given by Burghley. Like the advice given by Polonius to Laertes, it was culled from conduct books and precepts from the Bible and classical literature that schoolboys and adult readers searched for in their reading. When thoroughly assimilated into the individual's own philosophy, it might become a very practical type of wisdom, whose object, according to Ascham, was to know all that was fitting and to be able to apply what he knew as he served with love the country in which he was born. Such a man was supposedly above the lure of money and the love of power for its own sake.

Burghley maintained his early habits of reading all during his life, encouraged, no doubt, by the serious nature of his wife Mildred, famed for her piety, her domestic virtue, and her unobtrusive benevolence. To such a wife and mother Burghley could well trust little Robert's religious education, in which she emphasized plain teaching of the Scriptures. By the following tenets (abridged for our purpose), Burghley could round out and complete his son's training, especially in prudence.

1. When come to man's estate, a person must use "great providence and circumspection" in choosing a wife. From her a man's good fortune or evil would spring. Like a stratagem of war, matrimony could be entered erroneously but once. If in good circumstances, he should "match" near home; if not, he should marry far from home, and quickly. First, however, he must inquire diligently of the wife's disposition and youthful training. If poor, he should not choose a wife for her wealth alone

lest others condemn her and her husband learn to loathe her. She must not be too talkative, and she must not be a fool, for nothing was worse than a she-fool. And she must not be a dwarf lest she beget pigmies.

2. As to hospitality, it should be moderate and according to his estate, but plentiful rather than sparing or costly. No man would grow poor by keeping an orderly table.

3. He should not spend more than three-fourths of his income, and not over a third of that on his house. He should not sell his land, for an acre of it was like an ounce of credit. Gentility was no more than ancient riches.

4. Children should be brought up in learning and obedience, yet without austerity. They should be praised openly and reprehended secretly. They should be maintained according to the parents' means lest they make life a bondage and long for the inheritance to be derived from their parents' death. Daughters should be married in due time lest they marry themselves. Sons should not be permitted to travel "beyond the Alps" lest they learn nothing but "pride, blasphemy, and atheism." Sons trained to be soldiers became in time of peace like "chimneys in summer."

5. He should not have kinsmen as servants: they expected too much and worked too little, and it was best "to keep two too few than one too many" of them. Those he must keep should be fed well and paid with the most and boldly required to perform good service.

6. It was well to have kindred allies at table, and to uphold them in all their honest actions.

7. He should beware of acting as security to the best of friends. To pay another's debts was to seek his own decay. He should not borrow from neighbor or friend, but from a stranger. Even then he should be "precious" of his word, for one who kept days of payment was lord of another man's purse.

8. He should never sue a poor man. It was a base conquest. If he did sue, he should be sure he was right and then press his suit hard.

9. He should always keep some great man for his friend, but never trouble him with trifles. He should compliment him often with small gifts, but if he bestowed a gift of value, it should be of such a nature as to be daily in sight.

10. He should be both humble and generous toward his superiors and, with his equals, "respective." Toward his inferiors, he must show much humility and enough familiarity to bow and shake hands and uncover the head. The first would achieve advancement, the second would make one known as well-bred, and the third would gain favor with the populace. He could not afford to neglect, or too much affect, popularity.

11. He should trust no man with his life, his credit, or his estate.

12. He should never be scurrilous in conversation or satirical in jests.

Sometimes such moral and religious instruction was delayed till the child was mature, and sometimes it was given early that it might be com-

mitted to memory for future understanding and application. It is doubtful whether Burghley ever let sons or wards lose sight of such precepts
from the time they learned them in tender years.

When fathers were separated from their sons, they often included
such advice in long letters, especially if these sons were heirs. When
Philip Sidney was a boy of twelve attending school at Shrewsbury, he
wrote his father dutiful letters, and received in return much parental
counsel. "I have received two letters from you, one written in Latin and
the other in French," wrote Sir Henry. He was pleased and asked Philip
to exercise his learning often in this manner, for it would stand him in
good stead later in the "profession of life" he was "born to live in." Since
this was his first letter to his son, the father said he would not fill it with
the advice he felt inclined to give to one so dear to him, but let it come
later. Then he proceeded to fill pages with fatherly admonitions.

First, he wished his son to make a habit of prayer as soon as he rose
in the morning, not just mouthing words but meditating on them. Next,
he concerned himself with his boy's study hours. He was sure the master
would limit them according to a youth's learning and health, and he hoped
his son would keep them carefully, marking the meaning of important
words as he read. "So shall you enrich your tongue with words and your
wit with matter, and judgment will grow as years groweth in you." He
urged "humble obedience" to the master, "for unless you frame yourself to obey others, yea, and feel in yourself what obedience is, you shall
never be able to teach others how to obey you." He would have his son
courteous and affable to all, for nothing like courtesy "winneth so much
with so little lost," yet he would also have him "frame his manners"
according to the "dignity of the person" whom he addressed.

A boy of twelve is likely to have a good appetite, and Sir Henry hoped
his son would not eat too much at table lest he dull his wit and make his
body feel heavy. Nor must he drink enough to become "inflamed."
Exercise was another thing he must not overdo, for he must be careful
of his bones and joints while seeking to increase his force and "enlarge his
breath." Cleanliness in dress was important, also cleanliness in body so
that he might be "delightful" company instead of loathsome. When with
others he must try to be "merry," and always remember that a wound
given by a word was harder to cure than one from a sword. If he did not
learn to control himself in "wit and body and biting words," he would
be no credit to his father.

At school his son would have many companions, and Sir Henry hoped
his boy would learn to be a hearer and a "bearer away of other men's
talk" instead of a "beginner" of speech; he did not wish him to be accused
of delighting to hear himself talk. If he listened well he might commit
to memory wise sentences and apt phrases for effective use later. To keep
his speech habitually good, he must never let "oath be heard" to come out
of his mouth "nor word of ribaldry," things he should detest in others.

And in all assemblies he must be modest, not "pert" or "bold," even though he be accused of "maidenlike shamefastness" by "light fellows" among his companions. He knew such habits would not be easy "to be come by," but they could be acquired if Sidney could remember before uttering a word that nature had "ramped" his tongue with "teeth, lips, yea and hair without the lips," as "betokening reins or bridles for the loose use of that member." Above all, he must tell no untruth, not even a trifling one, for the custom "is naughty," and after a falsehood is known, it is for the teller's shame. "There cannot be a greater reproach to a gentleman than to be accounted a liar." If he will "study," therefore, and "endeavor" to be occupied virtuously, he will "not know how to do evil" even if he would. Finally, he must not forget the "noble blood" on his mother's side so that he may be an "ornament" to her illustrious family.

After all these admonitions, the father ended his letter in a more natural manner, for he adored this son: "Well, my little Philip, this is enough for me, and too much I fear for you. But if I shall find that this light meal of suggestion nourish anything the weak stomach of your young capacity, I will, as I find the same grow stronger, feed it with tougher food." Then piously he concluded, "Your loving father so long as you live in the fear of God."

Older Elizabethans sometimes wrote fatherly letters of advice to younger men, as Bacon prepared some of the advice in his essays for the young Essex. In turn, Essex wrote little "essays" in his letters to younger men, as exemplified in a letter sent to Rutland about "active" minds.[11] The first way to attain experience in forms of behavior, he says, is to "make the mind expert, for behavior is but a garment," easily made for a comely body that is well-proportioned, but not for a deformed body that even a tailor's art fails to adorn. Yet a man "may mend his faults with as little labor as cover them." Next is to "imitate," for which one must make good choice of companions with whom to converse. Mental health, like physical health, comes from observation of "what diseases we are aptest to fall into, and to provide against them, for physic hath not more medicines for diseases of the body, than reason hath preservations against the passions of the mind." He finds it harder to tell how a man may acquire strength of mind than to urge upon him good temper or good behavior, for "behaviour or good forms, may be gotten by education, and health, or even temper of the mind, by observation." But if a man does not have in his nature "some procurer" for strength of mind, "it can never be obtained by industry." The virtues proper to the "activity" of a strong mind are "liberality or magnificence, and fortitude or magnanimity," and some men are "by nature so covetous or cowardly" that it is as useless to try to "enlarge" their minds as to "plough the rock." In such letters

---

[11] Devereux, *Lives and Letters of the Devereux*, I, 322–23.

an Elizabethan might feel he had used to advantage some of his memorized good sentences. In this letter Essex may also reveal why he was at times prodigal of his liberality.

When their children grew older, parents felt that more than the good sentences of youth were needed. Childish faults might be light and easily corrected, but those of maturity were likely to be "grievous and full of danger." Now the mother usually took charge of the daughter's further education, and the father the son's. This was a time when the son must be ruled by a strong hand if he was not to form habits of "riotous living" that would "consume his inheritance" by "inordinate and chargeable gaming, surfeits, deflowering of maids, and corrupting good women."

Elyot, following Plutarch's teaching, advised fathers to be "sometimes exhorting, another time menacing, other while desiring," and again consoling by "promises and allurements" or by declaring what dangers they themselves had sustained in youth before attaining honor.[12] He believed virtue might be instilled by two principal means: fear of pain and hope of reward. Correcting, therefore, should be merciful, but also prompt and rigorous. He would marry off lecherous sons to wives who, in the father's judgment, would make their sons happy, useful citizens. The more stable and gentle sons he would prepare against evil companions, especially flatterers, who might try to entice them into reveling and idleness. Similar advice was carried on by Thomas Fuller about a century later in his *Holy State*[13] as he stressed the importance of the father's example of worthy conduct to his sons. "Though the words of the wise be as nails fastened by the masters of the assemblies," he said, referring to a verse in Ecclesiastes, "sure, their examples are the hammer to drive them in, to take the deeper hold."

When their sons were away from home traveling with a tutor, fathers kept in very close touch with them by correspondence with both son and tutor. Many were the letters Sir Henry Sidney wrote to his sons at this time in their lives, but to Robert he wrote more freely than to Philip, whose judgment he seemed to trust. No doubt he, like everyone else, felt the older son would make the family illustrious, and perhaps, with the others at home, he was a little in awe of Philip's superior mind. The younger son's charm was like sunshine, and Philip himself delighted in it, but the father warmed his heart in it.

"Robin," began Sir Henry in one of his chatty letters, "I hear well of you and the company you keep, which is of great comfort to me." Then he reminds him of the need noble families have of setting a good example to others. He speaks of his continuing the friendships Philip has estab-

---

[12] Sir Thomas Elyot, *The Education or bringinge up of Children* (trans. from Plutarch, 1530?).

[13] *The Holy State and the Profane State* (1642), Bk. I, Ch. V.

lished. Yet, since Robin seems to win the hearts of all he meets, Sir Henry warns him against taking too much honor upon himself among both his own countrymen and strangers, for he must always conduct himself according to his "degree and birthright." In this respect he can do no better than follow his "discreet and virtuous brother's rule," whereby he won love and "plied ceremony with ceremony."

Then Sir Henry refers to matter-of-fact affairs connected with the tour. He is glad Robin has "the Dutch tongue sufficiently," and asks him to discharge his Dutch tutor and send home for Mr. White, "an honest young man" recommended by friends of the family as "good and sound." Since the father had to watch his expenditures and yet keep up the appearances so necessary for the ambitions he entertained for his sons, he tells Robert he is sending him £30 by a servant, not as "arrearages," but out of which he is to reserve £20 for Mr. White; the rest he must make out with for some months. As he writes, however, his heart warms to his son, and he hastens to reassure him. "I will send you at or before Frankfort Mart £60, either to bring you home or to find you abroad, as you and your brother shall agree, for half a year ending Michaelmas . . ." Perhaps he was also thinking of impressing the tutor, for he adds, ". . . how I intend to deal with him you may see by the letter I send him. He shall have his £20 yearly, and you your £100, and so be as merry as you may."

Like all inexperienced travelers, Robert does not always spend his money wisely. Instead of accusing him of wasting his allowance, his father writes with a sly twinkle, "I thank you, my dear boy, for the marten skins you write of . . . and I will thank you more if they come, for yet I hear not of them nor ever saw Cassmyre's picture. The messenger (of the picture, I mean) played the knave with you, and me, and after that sort you may write to him; but if your tokens come, I will send you such a suit of apparel as shall become your father's son to wear in any Court in Germany." He concludes this letter with the customary formality but with the usual Elizabethan affection for such a son. "I love thee, boy, well. I have no more, but God bless you, my sweet child, in this world forever, as I in this world find myself happy in my children. From Ludlow Castle this 28th of October, 1578. To my very loving son, Robert Sidney, give these. Your very loving father."[14]

Conduct books accused fathers of being unable to instruct their sons well or, if they had the wit for such a task, of giving too much time to their own affairs. Sir Henry's happy touch was not easily approximated. Still, writers thought it was a pity fathers could not realize their children would learn more from a wise father than ever from a master. One author taunted them with having become too vain to be masters to their sons and, worse still, with being too indifferent to provide hired masters, the rich

[14] Collins, *Letters and Memorials of State*, I:271–72.

beginning to scorn study as the poor were driven to it.[15] What could be more shortsighted on their part when they who had dealings with the world knew that "riches are so brittle and frail" it takes wit (trained minds) to keep them. If some of their sons were foolish and without wit they could at least be kept busy at tasks that would keep them out of harm, and no inheritance should ever be passed on to them. Their other children with normal minds should be provided with capable and virtuous teachers.

Though all the schoolmasters in the world, continued this writer, could never take the place of a good father's influence, all fathers and sons were under constant scrutiny. If children grew up wise and good in spite of bad fathers, no one would believe them good but would constantly "throw it in their teeth" that they had a wicked father. If a good father had a bad son, then the father's own honesty would be questioned, for people would say no son would go astray "unless he were by a father led thereto." Like father, like son. But worse still was for a son to treat even a bad father with contempt and to refuse to care for him in his old age or at death. The interdependence of father and son was so close that whether it was a relationship of confidence or of distrust, it could lead to good or evil for all members of the family.

For the well-being of the entire family, therefore, parents should not fail to see a son's faults, and to correct them early. On the other hand, parents must not expect of him or of their other children as much as they expected of themselves, having them "old in youth." Parents like this would always have the rod in their hands and permit no natural, youthful liberties. They would be incapable of judging what sort of life their sons were inclined to, and would so dull their wit that they would not know how to conduct themselves socially. Entering a room with guests present, such children would not know which way to look, but would stand about like simple idiots. Wise parents, on the other hand, would "keep with their children in awe with only shaking their heads at them or using some such sign," and would be able to correct them with only a word. Such children grew up gentle and courteous instead of rough and desperately wanton in their conduct.

Perhaps the worst failure in parents, this author continued, was not to know when their children had grown up. He considered this fault very grave in an age when children seemed to be "born wise, and have gray hairs in their youth." Fathers should allow their sons certain liberties at home, such as permitting them to welcome companions and make good cheer and sometimes even entertain strangers. They should be taught also how to use "the goods of the house" that they might be good husbands, augmenting their estate. A son knowing and trusting a good father would wish him to live long, but when he did have to take

[15] *The Court of Good Councell*, an anonymous version (1607) of Stefano Guazzo's *The Civil Conversation* (1607).

over the management of the estate, he would know how to care for it. Moreover, a father with a son so trained could afford to retire early enough to enjoy his old age. Seeing a son managing the lands well, ordering the household discreetly, and rightly disposing of his living would enable a good father to "arrive at a haven of happiness" and to "die contentedly." True, the Bible counseled against fathers ever giving any member of the family authority over them, still this writer knew of fathers who had done so without bringing themselves "in subjection to their children." Their sons, before coming of age, had been given reasonable stipends to live on and proper duties to perform, and had been both able and willing to assume responsibility when it came. This was the crown of a father's duty well performed.

It was with such hopes for his heir that Sir Walter Raleigh looked to the future. His own life at court was that of ups and downs, fears, and disillusionments. He would have his son profit by his mistakes and, concurring with the educational theory of such men as Ascham, have his son learn to live according to reason instead of through the heart-break of experience. Thus he set down in ten chapters his worldly-wise instructions—what to avoid in the bitter experience of others, and what to emulate in the lives of successful men. Though he, like Burghley and Shakespeare, repeats the "wisdom" of the age, he also reveals the special prudence he acquired by his contact with many kinds of people. His instructions are to conduct books what Bacon's essays were to six-teenth-century attempts at this new kind of literature. If slightly con-densed and somewhat changed in their order, these instructions can still be carried in a man's wallet.[16]

1. The choice of friends should include the wise and virtuous. Since a person is judged by his friends, he should choose his betters and shun the poor and needy, for if one service fails a poor friend, he forgets all former benefits and becomes a mortal enemy; a person's betters are more likely to esteem him for his own worth, and will keep his counsel carefully because they have more to lose. A man's folly should be his greatest secret. He should never trust friend or servant with anything dangerous to himself or to his estate lest he be put at such a person's mercy. "Great ones" especially might be tempted to do unlawful things or labor for themselves. To venture a true estate in hope of a better in future is madness.

2. In the choice of a wife, beauty is the chief danger to his honor, credit, and safety. Beauty will not last, and when possessed, it kills de-sire. A fair woman is bound to become dishonest, and lewd women be-come a man's enemies. A wise man marries while he is young and strong, at best toward his thirties. If too young he is not fit to choose or govern, and if too old he will not live to educate his children. It is better for

---

[16] *Sir Walter Raleigh's Instructions to his Son and to Posterity* (reprinted 1927).

children to be unborn than to be ill-bred lest they be a shame to a man's name and family. A man marrying late wastes himself on harlots who destroy his health, impoverish his estate, and endanger his life. Youth should be used as the "springtime which soon departeth, and wherein thou oughtest to plant, and sow all provisions for a long and happy life." Before he marries, a man should be experienced enough to be sure of his taste and to know love abideth not want.

A wise man is more sure of his wife's love than of his own for her. He knows she loves him if she industriously cares for his estate, tries to please him, and is sweet to him in conversation. He is not sour or stern with his wife, and lets her have an equal part of his estate while he lives. At his death his wife will remarry one who will naturally hate his memory and his children and who will spend his estate if he can. Therefore he will leave his wife property enough to live on according to her custom, but none to will to another. Thus a wise man provides for his children and does not leave his estate to his wife, for wives were ordained to continue the generation of man, not to transfer a man's house and estate —these should live in his son, not in his wife.

3. Even wise men are abused by flatterers, the worst kind of traitors. They are base, creeping, cowardly persons that bite smiling. They strengthen one's imperfections and encourage one in all evils. They are often hard to know from one's friends, but a friend will endanger a person's love for him by telling him his faults in private, and flatterers are obsequious and full of protestations. Like wolves, they pretend to be friends; like apes, they play tricks and provoke laughter. Few men can endure criticism, but they delight in praise and become the victims of flattery—one of the "universal follies which bewitcheth mankind."

4. A man should avoid public disputations at feasts or tables. Ruffians and brawlers are more dangerous than a battle; in a battle a man may get honor and protect his Prince and country, but men's fortunes are oftener marred by their tongues than by their vices. ". . . the heart of a fool is in his mouth, and the mouth of a wise man is in his heart." Disputation, if at all, must be among wise and sober men from whom a person may learn reasoning. He should defame no woman publicly. He should accuse no man of crime unless to save the Prince or the country. He should not lose reputation. Better not to live than to live a coward. A liar is commonly a coward, is trusted by no one, has no credit, and his vice is proper to Satan. He is odious and contrary to God.

5. A man should not spend before he has his substance. Borrowing is the canker and death of every man's estate. He should know what he has and not waste it by servants and officers. He should not be surety for another. If necessary, he might give part of his estate, however. No friend would ask for more. If he lent to a person who was mightier, he should count the money lost.

Poverty is often the curse of God and a chain among men; it is an imprisonment of mind and a vexation of every worthy spirit. A poor man cannot help himself or others, has no way of showing his virtues, is a burden and eyesore to his friends, is scorned by all men, and is made to make dishonest shifts. A rich man has pleasure in health, comfort in sickness, freedom of mind and body, safety from perils, relief from the distresses of old age, can aid poor and honest friends, and has a means of providing for his posterity.

6. Servants should be such as can be commanded. Servants without hire cost too much; a man should pay all, and have only yeomen who can be paid. If he trusts a servant with his purse, he should take account ere he sleep, for if he puts it off he will find it tedious afterward and neglect it. "I myself have lost thereby more than I am worth." A servant gaining by this means will only laugh at his master's simplicity. Such carelessness also makes servants thieves.

7. Clothes should not exceed in the "humor of rags and bravery," for these will soon wear out of fashion. Money in the purse, however, will ever be in fashion. No man is esteemed for gay garments except by fools and women.

8. Riches wrested from the poor will never prosper one . . . the complaint and cry thereof piercing the heavens. It is most detestable to God and most dishonorable before worthy men. A man who pities another man's sorrow will be free from it himself, but he who delights in that sorrow will fall into it himself. The Lord will recompense those who are merciful to hard workers. A man must aid those who labor to live, those too old to work, fatherless children, and poor tenants who "travail to pay their rents and fall into poverty by mischance and not by careless expense." He should not deny the needy or curse another in the bitterness of his soul, for such a prayer will be heard by Him that made him.

9. No man loving wine ever came to honor or preferment, for wine transforms man into a beast: it deforms his face, rots his teeth, ages him, and makes him despised of men. It is better to be subject to any vice rather than drink. Drunkenness is a cureless canker of youth, a beastly infection of old age, and a shameful infamy to posterity. The first draft of wine is for health, the second for pleasure, the third for shame, and the fourth for madness. The sooner he begins to help nature, the sooner she forsakes him. A drinker is without honor, for he is trusted by no man, forgets his wife and children, his friends and comeliness, commits disorders, and offends virtue and honest company.

10. No man is wise or safe from the temptations of the world but that he is honest, standing upon his own guard against all that tempts him . . . or may practice upon him in his conscience, reputation, or his purse. "Serve God, let Him be the Author of all your actions, commend all your endeavors to Him that must either wither or prosper them;

please Him with prayer, lest if He frown, He confound all your fortunes and labors like drops of rain on the sandy ground; let my experienced advice and fatherly instructions sink deep into your heart; so God direct you in all His ways and fill your heart with His grace."

A comparison of Lord Burghley's and Sir Walter Raleigh's instructions to their favorite sons reveals the similarity and difference in each man's approach. Both were greatly concerned about continuing their family line with honor, but Burghley, well established at court, was more impressed with the position in life his son might take and the material advantages to be gained from that position. Raleigh, whose long imprisonment came at the prime of life, turned his thoughts more and more to man's uncertain relations with his fellow men. Each sought to save his son from the errors he had made. Together, the two sets of rules form a representative picture of the type of worldly advice given by important Elizabethans to their sons. Men in more modest circumstances naturally adapted their advice to their experience also, but worldly goods and worldly relations, with or without thought of the future life, were the basis of most fathers' anxiety. What would be the result to the family welfare when it was dependent upon the wit or good will of their heirs?

If fathers found it hard to know when their sons had grown up, how much more difficult was it for mothers to treat their sons like men. Even the learned mother of Sir Francis Bacon was guilty of this feminine weakness. She was a woman of such "tenderness and anxious affection"[17] that in spite of her "fervid piety" she had the tendency to suspect everyone near her son of "preying upon him and abusing his simplicity and inexperience." Her Puritan upbringing did not lessen at all her natural inclinations along this line. Still greater was her concern for her older son Anthony, about whom she possessed an "irritable jealousy with regard to her maternal authority, curiously mixed with little solicitudes about his physic, his diet, his hours of sleeping, waking, and going abroad, and all his smaller household arrangements." She was indeed an "affectionate, vehement, grave, and religious soul."

Anthony had left Trinity College at nineteen for the tour abroad, and did not return till 1574, when he was thirty-five. During this time his mother had just cause for excessive worry about his physical and moral welfare. Often she wrote him to be "constant in profession" of his faith, and that from his heart, for she feared he might turn Catholic during some sudden illness when he could secure aid by no other means. Later she feared his interest in atheism and urged him to guard his speech and never "talk suddenly," but only where "discretion requireth, and that soberly." When she reminded him about good manners in speech, she

[17] James A. Spedding, *The Letters and the Life of Francis Bacon* (1861–74), I, 115.

may have feared her letters would be read by spies, and she may have cloaked her concern about his rumored loss of faith under her advice to him never to use "too common familiarity in talking," as "unprofitable" words were never without some "hurt-taking."

Part of her distress was undoubtedly due to her widowhood. "Remember," she writes, "you have no father, and you have little enough, if not too little, regarded your kind and so simple mother's wholesome advice from time to time." She entreats him to pray twice a day without fail, for "it will be to your best credit to serve the Lord duly and reverently." She is disturbed that Francis is also negligent about his prayers, but she is sure Anthony will perform this duty "well and zealously." She says Francis' weak stomach is due to his "untimely going to bed" and his late rising, causing even his servants to become slothful as he grows more sickly. So she laments her sons' "haste not to hearken to their mother's good counsel in time," perhaps not believing they could possibly consider it trivial. At Anthony's return to England, she could not even send to him the strawberries he was so fond of without reminding him that the boy bringing them was so "shrewd-witted" and "untoward crafty" that he must not ask him to stay to rest and must not reward him with more than a sixpence, which was really too much. Besides, she expected him to return immediately as he could easily make the journey in a day, "God willing."

But this lady was concerned about others besides her sons, especially if these men were friends of her children. When, therefore, she heard that Essex was unfaithful to his wife, she wrote him a letter of protest over his "backsliding" and his "dishonorable and dangerous-to-yourself coursetaking," which was "an infamy" to his wife and also to the Queen. She hoped Essex would "speedily, by his grace," end his relations with the woman before "some hidden mischief" occurred. Already the lady's husband, ancient and noble, had sold his house "as one out of comfort." She feared he would "revenge . . . his provoked and most intolerable injury even more desperately" because of his love for his wife whom he still "greatly, as with grief, laboreth" to win. It is a pity the court is not "cleaned by sending away such an unchaste gaze and common byword . . ."

The pious woman writes on, criticizing Essex for not having "learned Christ and heard his holy word." She refers to Paul's first letter to the Thessalonians (4:3–5), saying, "This is the will of God that ye should be holy and abstain from fornication, and everyone know how to keep his own vessel in holiness and honor, and not in the lust of concupiscence . . ." "There is more heavy threat," she says, "if it please you to read and mark well . . . Good, my Lord," she pleads, "remember and consider the danger hereby of soul and body. Grieve not the Holy Spirit of God that honoured you, and reward him not with such evil for his kindness toward you. . . . Sin not against your soul."

Still she had not finished. She calls attention to his wife's expected confinement, urging him to be good for his child's sake. This he can do if he will be "strong in the Lord, your and our patient God." For Christ will assist all such men and look favorably upon them and their heirs. She herself calls upon God to grant his holy mercy and grace to "my dear Lord and worthy Lord in Christ Jesus," upon whom "with my very inward have I presumed thus ill-favoredly to scribble."[18]

Essex had made himself liable to such criticism, for he had set the gossips to chattering about his affairs with women. It is now known that he had a son by Elizabeth Southwell, and that his attentions to Lady Mary Howard, Mistress Russell, and the "fairest Brydges" excited the jealousy of the Queen and caused his wife unbearable heartache. The letter from Bacon's mother, however, struck Essex deeply, and he did not delay even one day in answering it. The tone of his reply indicates not only the tact and courtesy of this great Elizabethan, but also the spirit in which a man in his position should face reproach for immoral conduct or, if innocent, defend himself. He says he takes it as a "great argument of love" that this mother has written to him so freely about the "worst" she has heard of him and that she should be sent as "an angel to admonish" him with her "no small care" for his "well-doing." He knows how "needful" such "summons" are to all men, but especially to one in his place, and he "had rather, with the poor publican," knock his breast "and lie prostrate, and confess" when he had done all he could, that he was an "unprofitable servant, than pharisaically to justify" himself. But he is writing now "for the truth's sake" and not his own to "protest, before the majesty of God," voluntarily and unadvised, that "this charge . . . newly laid" upon him is "false and unjust." Since his departure "from England towards Spain," he has been "free from taxation and incontinency with any woman that lives." He declares he "never saw or spoke" with the lady under discussion "but in public places," and if "other seers and hearers" would do him right, they "could justify" his behavior. But he lives in a place where he is "hourly conspired against, and practised upon," and though the worthy lady may think him a "weak man, full of imperfections," he wishes her to be assured he endeavors "to be good," and had rather mend his faults "than cover them." He concludes: "I wish your Ladyship all true happiness, and rest at your Ladyship's commandment. Burn, I pray you. 1st December, 1596."[19]

Essex knew that even though it was usual for mothers to assume the responsibilities of the household when their husbands were deceased or away from home, still it had taken no little courage for Bacon's mother to write him. Such a letter should have come from a man, if written at all, and in his heart Essex must have acknowledged her mettle. The age

---

[18] *Ibid.*, I, 407–10.
[19] *Ibid.*

demanded that a woman be modest and retiring at all times, and a letter
of this nature took real moral courage.

Yet even the mildest of women might forego all such restrictions of
modesty when driven by necessity. At such a crisis, Southampton's mother
"took up her pen in her shaking hand" to write Robert Cecil about her
son's imprisonment for his entanglement in the plot that was to cost
Essex his life. She asked the secretary to let the "bitter passion of a per-
plexed mother" move him to pity, for if her son had "led the dance of
this disloyalty" she would not think of begging that mercy be shown
him. She actually believed her son had been bewitched, that in his despair
over failing to achieve preferment at court he had become a victim of
those who would use him for their purposes. "I rather fear it than know
certainly what bewitched him that he should not know of . . . conspiracy
before the execution of it," she said, and this fact alone had induced her
to plead for him. She had "examined" him and found "he had not forty
shillings about him nor in his store," even though he had sold land
recently. That he paid his money to his creditors rather than to the conspirators was proof, she believed, of his innocence. She concluded with:
"O Good Mr. Secretary, as God hath placed you near a Prince, so help to
move her Majesty to do like a God whose mercy is infinite, which I hope
may be with her safety, when the head of this confusion is taken away,"
and signed herself "the most sorrowful and afflicted mother."[20]

Most Elizabethan mothers were so careful of their "modesty" that
they carried on all their public actions with due regard to their position
as homekeepers or helpmates of their lord in the home. Thus they were
usually much closer to their daughters than was the father. Except for
the daughter's intellectual training, which was in the hands of the father
or masters chosen by him, the mother was responsible for all the details
connected with a girl's training, including her preparation for marriage.
The influence of Vives at this point of home management can scarcely
be overestimated. All Elizabethan conduct books defer to him, and any
changes or additions they made in their instruction are usually insignificant, especially for middle-class daughters.

According to Vives' *The Instruction of a Christian Woman*, the baby
girl's training should begin in the cradle. Of course the mother should
nurse the child to strengthen the tie between them, and if possible she
should supervise the play in the nursery and choose playmates for her
little girl when she grew older. If another had to perform any of these
tasks, the mother must find for the purpose an honest or "sad" (serious)
woman with some knowledge of life. All little daughters should be care-

[20] Charlotte Carmichael Stopes, *The Life of Henry, Third Earl of Southampton,
Shakespeare's Patron* (1922), p. 218, quoted by Mrs. Stopes from *Salisbury Papers*,
XI, 71–72.

fully kept from men lest they learn at an early age to delight in their company. Love "continueth longest toward them with whom we have passed our time in youth," he said, and women were especially susceptible to this influence because they were "most disposed to pleasure and dalliance."

When too young to distinguish between good and evil, maids should not be taught to flee from vice, he urged, for "it is much more surety and more profitable . . . not only to do none evil but not once to know it." This ideal many parents cherished along with Vives, and when daughters were led to the marriage altar, it was hoped they were chaste in thought and speech as well as in deed. Vives would have mothers begin early with a training in which every step was to fit carefully into the plan of chastity's culmination in the blushing bride. He urged mothers, therefore, to begin with their daughter's first smiles and baby prattle, teaching them to speak plainly and innocently and allowing "no uncomely deed, neither by words, laughing, nor countenance, neither kiss nor embrace . . ."

As soon as the little Elizabethan girl was able to learn, the mother was expected to begin instructing her in whatever might pertain to her "soul's ornament" and her ability to keep and order a home. Some domestic books would have this teaching begin at four, others at seven, but Vives would leave it to the mother's judgment of her child's abilities. He cautioned mothers not to let their love make weaklings of their daughters, who would be controlled best by fear or respect for their mothers, no matter when they began their training. Later writers would temper parental austerity somewhat. Thomas Salter's *The Mirrhor of Modestie*[21] suggested that the mother proceed like a good physician, "who, to cure young children . . . do give them wormwood or such like bitter thing, anointed over with honey, to the end that they, deceived by the upper sweetness, may swallow down the wholesome bitterness and thereby receive help of their disease." He would leave "bitter stripes" for the last remedy. If, then, a maid had been so carefully reared that she trembled at her mother's frown, the mother could carry on most of the advanced training with a "sweet and gentle smiling."

Among her daily tasks, whether she was princess or maid, should be skilled performance at work "done by hand," as, for example, the handling of wool and flax. When her household duties were finished, she might read and, when tired of that, again dress wool, card it, and spin it.

When taught "cookery," it was not so important for the daughter to learn how to provide for many, but how to "dress meat pleasantly" for her own family. In times of sickness such skill was most necessary. No maid, says Vives, should loathe the name of kitchen, for here are the means by which "sick folks can mend" and "whole folks live." Further-

[21] *A Mirrhor mete for all Mothers, Matrones, and Maidens, intituled the Mirrhor of Modestie* (1579).

more, mistresses and daughters supervising the kitchen would make the servants more honest. He had in mind chiefly the morals between the sexes, though waste in the kitchen was supposed to be controlled by the thrifty housewife whether she was rich or poor. Vives solemnly declared, therefore, that the first duty of the mistress in the kitchen was to teach the maids that if they laid their hands on any man but their husbands they blackened them "more than soot." He would also have the housewife so proud of her cookery that she would feel less shamed to be seen in a kitchen than at a dance, or at playing cards. Indeed, it was better for a woman to taste a "supping" that she or the maids were brewing if her husband gave her the cup, than for her to drink at a banquet from a cup handed her by a guest who was showing how gallant he could be. Without kitchen training, how could a young wife know how to please her friends with meat "come cleanly unto the table"? Daughters-in-law without this skill would be hated, but with it, whether rich or poor, would be honored.

Elizabethan girls might be seen but not heard, though the ideal rearing prevented a maid from even being seen by the opposite sex till she was ready for matching in marriage. Among the upper and wealthy middle classes, she was usually surrounded by servants or waiting women, and among the respectable classes of even limited means, she was always under the watchful eye of a trusted servant or relative. In every home, therefore, that could afford to bring up its daughters "honestly," the maid was allowed little if any privacy and was kept busy with tasks, heavy or light, or with learning graceful deportment. She must be protected from any possible contact with worldly or unchaste experiences, and her father must keep men from seeing her till he was ready to receive suitors for her hand in marriage.

During this brief interval between childhood and marriage, the maid was put through the most intensive part of her training in self-control. Vives gives what was generally believed to be her nature at this time when he said that a maid's tendency to "lust of the body" must be strictly prevented from development by keeping her from hearing or seeing or even thinking any foul thing. He would require fasting to "quench the heat of youth," and forbade anything in her diet but the plainest food. "It should be mean [not rich] and easy to get," he said, "neither hot of itself, nor spiced . . . nor delicate." Her drink should be water or some ale or small wine, and only enough of this to digest her meat without inflaming her body. If her stomach was strong enough, her meat might be served cold, and cold water mixed with her wine. When, however, Vives said "Neither the burning of Etna nor the country of Vulcan nor Vesuvius nor yet Olympus boileth with such heat as the bodies of young folks inflamed with wine and delicate meats," he also referred to exercises that heated the body, ointments, silks, and expensive clothing, loose talk, and "the very sight of men." Queen Catherine, whether thinking of this advice by Vives or of the general attitude toward maids in her time or of her own unhappy marriage, or possibly all three, advised Princess Mary during this period of her training, ". . . use your virginals, or lute, if unto me, to keep your heart with a chaste mind, and your body from all ill and wanton company, not thinking nor desiring any husband, for Christ's passion . . ."

The emphasis upon diet was common to all domestic literature. The "fortune teller" in "W. M.'s" *The Man in the Moon* (1609) blamed the maiden's diet for five "blemishes" in her reputation which deformed her more than "fifteen wheals or pimples would disgrace her face"—scurrility of speech, talkativeness or "much babbling," a foolish joy or petulant kind of gesture, vomiting, belching, or such like, and drowsiness of body and dullness of mind. These defects might be marked in anyone, but sooner in a maiden. He considered wine as bad as poison for a virgin; it was "a two-fold brand to kindle lust." Overdelicate clothing should never be worn by maids, but plain, coarse, yet comely materials, for "garish and fantastical clothes" were "speechless reporters of wanton minds."

Vives objected to women going "abroad" on the streets; there was enough at home to keep any honest woman's mind from thinking of the allurements and foolish prattle in the homes of gossips. If the maid did go abroad, however, she should not follow the custom of virgins "letting their breasts and neck go bare" lest she "set on fire" wanton men she might meet by the way. She should even hide her face and go "with scarcely an eye open to see her way withal." Any modest maid would desire neither to see nor to be seen and, if necessary for her to go forth, would not cast unstable eyes hither and thither or "be busy to know who dwelleth in this place or that" when she "ought scarcely to know her neighbors."

Richard Whitford's *A werke for householders* (1533) preceded Vives' book and had less of the Spanish and more of the English attitude toward women. Consequently it found its way into middle-class homes with the Vives book. When he said he knew fathers who did not allow their daughters to go out of doors more than once or twice a year, and others who permitted them to visit their friends at their homes and to be abroad at other places, even banquets, he gives a fairly accurate account of the situation. He believed that keeping daughters too close at home might make them foolish and fearful and very embarrassed in company, but to permit them to go to banquets frequently took away their modesty and tended to make them wanton in manner and less prized in good society.

In general, however, writers were not so liberal as Whitford, chiefly because of the general danger to women on the streets. They agreed, therefore, that women should be kept so busy at home there would be no chance to go abroad. Like Vives, they urged mothers to order their daughters immediately after prayer in the morning to set to work with wool and weaving. Their minds should be further occupied by holy study and prayer instead of cards and dice. Vives declared that these pleasures were worse for women than men because at games women grew greedy for money, and if men were present, the women might hear "uncomely" things. Nothing could be worse, therefore, than for a woman to exchange her basket of wool for a table board, her spindle for dice, or her prayer book for cards even though her companions were all women.

When the maid was introduced to society she was expected, according to Vives, to have little speech with men or maids. Man's speech was especially skillful in its double meanings, and thus injurious to maids. She, on her part, could not be too circumspect in her choice of words, for she was always open to suspicion. Certainly she must never withdraw from others to talk with a man even though he might be her own brother. Vives wondered why any chaste maid could wish to go off in a corner to talk with anyone when she was sure to invite the censure of all who saw her. Her words at all times should be "full of soberness, honesty, and wisdom," but if she could think of nothing to say in this manner, she should remain silent. In the choice between two evils, it was better for her to "seem rude than naughty."

It may seem strange that Vives declared a woman might better lose her possessions than her good name for honesty and shamefastness when she scolded or chided abroad, but at this time women frequently suffered criticism for their loud speech and disagreeable "clacking of tongues." Their running shrill voices continued to be the point of attack all through the century. The "fortune teller," for example, typed women in 1609 according to their speech: "a proud woman, rapping, arrogant words; a foolish woman, fond words; a wanton woman, lascivious words; but a chaste woman, modest words and few." He would therefore have a maid's words "wise, civil, slow, and sparing" that she might be "accounted as excellent for her speech as for her chastity."

With so much written on a low, sweet voice, it was natural that Vives objected to laughter in women, calling it a "sign of a very light and dissolute mind" and being in itself bad manners. "If a woman laughs back at a young man who laughs at her," he said, "she is naught, or else a fool . . . a woman that giveth a gift giveth herself; a woman that taketh a gift selleth herself. In laughter, there is a giving and taking no honest woman can be guilty of."

Daughters of the common people were first taught by their mothers that they were to be housewives in homes of their own. Next, they were told they must always respect their elders and never be scornful of young or old. When a man came a-wooing and was honest, they must be courteous, but never sit or stand alone near him. If a man should speak to a maid on the street, she should answer him curtly, but she must never answer a stranger lest he tempt her heart. If she accepted any fine gifts, she bound herself to the man who gave them to her. Of course she must not forget that "all fair talkers were not necessarily true," and she must be careful in giving her trust, remembering she could never trust anyone so much as herself. All maids were told it was dangerous to roam the streets—to do so made them the prey of every roving man or boy. They were also told never to go near taverns or to do anything that might attract attention to themselves. When on holy days they put on their best dresses to go to church, or when on holidays they went to sing and dance on the village green, they knew they must not hang their kirtles too high or too low, and in the dances, they must refrain from wild leaping lest they show their stockings.

These daughters were also told there were some things virtuous maids simply did not do: they did not tap with their feet; they did not sit alone with a man, for fire and tow would be sure to kindle; they did not talk too much, for a fool's bolt was soon shot; they did not change friends too often or give pledges too hastily; they did not spend more than they earned if they worked for wages, and they did not drink too much or gorge their food or indulge in light looks or laughter.

When a girl was ready to marry, she knew how to conduct herself as a good housewife. All day long she would be busy at her tasks, and at dinner and supper look neat and clean as she greeted her husband at table. In church, whither she would go, rain or shine, she would not gossip with friends, but worship God. Since she must love her husband better than anything on earth, she would show her love by proper wifely deportment. This required meek answers to all he said to her, mild moods, fair speech, a good conscience, and the avoiding of even the suspicion of evil. Should her husband become angry, she would never answer him in kind, but remain cheerful. Yet this did not mean she could be light and giddy, for she would no sooner give way to loud laughter than toss her head as she walked or yawn widely or lower herself by swearing. Instead, her laughter would be soft and sweet, and as she walked, she would carry herself without shrugging her shoulders or making other awkward movements of her body. This was the ideal deportment to which she aspired as she dreamed of marriage.

Such a girl would be taught that a housewife did not go to town except to trade, for she would not have time to run hither and yon. At home she would have all she could do to accomplish her work well and quickly. In her husband's absence she would have to assign the servants to their tasks and see that they were performed well. When her husband was home, ale would be served, but she would take very little of it. Though he, like other men, might go to taverns or markets or even cock fights, she would stay home willingly, preparing the kind of food her husband liked best.

There might be many things she would not be expected to do in her home, but she would have to know how to perform all the work of the household from baking to spinning so that she might supervise it correctly. Early to bed and early to rise would be a daily occurrence; no more lying a-bed till called. Should she marry well, she must help the poor, welcome guests with meat and drink, and still not make her husband poor with her generosity and hospitality. If she had rich neighbors and but little wealth herself, she must not begrudge the good fortune of others. When she herself became a guest at the homes of friends or acquaintances, she must not upset their household arrangements, but adapt herself and be pleasant.

A girl expected marriage to bring her children, and she was reminded that as soon as a daughter was born to her, she, like her own mother, must begin preparing for the child's marriage, gathering linens for the girl's dowry, and watching over her carefully that she might be matched well at the proper time. She must never forget that maidens were usually unstable in love, and must guard her daughter vigilantly that she might be married a maid. If her children disobeyed, she must not curse them or scold them, but use the rod wisely.

Whenever a girl was sent from the middle class to learn a trade, she was warned against improper manners. If she was to become a female barber, she must not flirt with the customers, but must busy herself with washing the razors and such work. If she was sent into service in the home of a lady, her mother would start her out with much practical advice and training, but the mistress of the new household would be expected to be more or less responsible for the girl's further training. Here as in all homes, however, a girl must be kept busy to keep her chaste—every minute of the day would be filled with such labors as spinning, carding, weaving, sewing, baking, brewing, sweeping, and scouring.

Middle-class homes that did not send their daughters to school might give them instruction at home in writing as well as in reading. Vives disapproved of the romances so popular with many people and recommended good history or the Bible for a girl's reading pleasure. If a girl wished to sing ballads she would be told in religious homes to sing psalms instead, for Vives had severely criticized "the foul and ribald" songs of London that were "written to corrupt the manners of young folks." He compared the composers of these ballads and songs to evil ones who infected common wells with poison. Strangely enough, however, he listed classical literature as suitable reading for girls.

Some authors of conduct books took issue with Vives on this last point, because they felt the moral and natural philosophy of the classics was unsuitable for maids. Salter, for example, said the classics would teach them too much about "the evils imminent to human life . . . which knowledge is not requisite to young women." Classical literature, he felt, was too mixed with the good and bad, for the examples in it of evil men and details of corrupt lives and pastimes and deceits were an enemy to the good life and religion of a maid. In a virtuous and modest girl such information was bound to be more dangerous and hurtful than praiseworthy. He could not see how any man of reason and understanding "but had rather love a maiden unlearned and chaste than one suspected of dishonest life, though never so famous and well learned in philosophy."

The only objection Vives found in formal learning for maids was that it made some of them dislike work in the kitchen, and such women were likely to send "a husband's house into decay." At the same time he admitted a woman who could only spin and sew was like a country wench or milk maid among court ladies. Thus parents must train their daughters according to the marriage they were to make for them. If they were to marry prominent gentlemen, they must be put into service to some great lady at court, where they might become learned in reading, writing, discourse, singing, playing on instruments, and dancing. For proper instruction in all these things the great lady would be responsible. Yet Vives believed that marriages were made in heaven, and thus no father could be sure of his son-in-law. Nevertheless, this did not excuse any father from presenting his son-in-law with a daughter chaste in mind and body. Of course, Vives warned fathers that if they had beautiful daughters they must be even more careful of them, for they were subject to more temptations than plain maidens.

Vives addressed fathers seriously because they were responsible for matching their daughters in marriage. Following his advice, the later conduct books had much to say about planning a girl's marriage according to her rank, but they also advised parents to consider individual disposition and temperament. Actually, the training of daughters varied from close restriction to considerable freedom. For example, reading and writing for some girls was a cultural attainment from which they received much pleasure and individual satisfaction; for others, especially in middle-class homes, it was chiefly a means by which to learn how to keep household accounts. In all classes, however, chastity was given about equal stress, but if favorable matching was important to parents, chastity was that part of the girl's qualities which weighed most on their minds, particularly when they felt death approaching. For this reason the father of Penelope and Dorothy Devereux prayed constantly in his last days that "God would defend" his daughters and "make them fear His name . . . and give them grace to lead a virtuous life."[22]

John Fletcher's play *The Elder Brother* used a popular appeal— popular in somewhat the same way as a present-day moving picture—in the plot of the father's attempt to match his daughter well. The father will not have his daughter wasting her youth like girls in rich families. Those pampered damsels, upon waking in the morning, are served breakfast in bed, then sleep again. Finally, when they rise, they are dressed by servants, led in to dinner, and then play cards or lie down again. After supper they go to bed once more, and so spend their lives in such idleness

[22] Devereux, *Lives and Letters of the Devereux*, I, 134.

that they develop diseases of both mind and body. His daughter will have wholesome exercise. Rising with the sun, she will walk and dance or hunt, visiting groves and springs to learn "the virtues of plants and simples" so that she will not fall into the green sickness by eating "coals, leather, and oatmeal." The portrayal of decadent life appealed to the unthinking mind bent on mere diversion and was popular in its fantastic exaggeration.

So much has been said of the Elizabethan father making the best bargain possible for himself through the marriage of his daughters that it is only fair to say these parents more often than not were honestly concerned about the happiness of the daughters they sought to marry well. Financial arrangements took up so much of their attention in this matter chiefly because they realized how much of a child's happiness depended upon the legal details in the marriage settlement. Attachment and compatibility might be cultivated or taken for granted, but the law was full of snares for the unwary. Consequently, plays dealing with chastity and dowries were likely to be popular.

Middleton's *A Fair Quarrel* made its chief appeal to the risibilities of the audience through its treatment of the dowry and chastity themes. A miserly father laments he is left with a daughter instead of a son. A son might shift for himself, but he cannot be too "careful" or "tender" with his daughter. Like a cupboard of glasses, she will be broken or cracked if given the "least shake." When he secures for her a suitor with "thousands," he is delighted. He admits the man has more wealth than wit, but that will "advantage" his daughter because she will "keep the keys to all." Besides, "for generation, man does seldom stamp 'em from the brain." Hadn't wise men fathered fools, and fools wise children? So he adds a "thousand pieces" to his daughter's dowry to seal the bargain with the rich suitor, only, of course, to discover she has already married a poor man. In *The Changeling* Middleton laughs chiefly at the chastity theme, and bitterly. The heroine is told that her lover, whom she had engaged to murder her betrothed, has been successful. When the lover asks as payment for his crime that she give herself to him, the girl is horrified at losing her chastity.

> Why, 'tis impossible thou canst be so wicked,
> Or shelter such a cunning cruelty,
> To make his death the murderer of my honor!
> Thy language is so bold and vicious,
> I cannot see which way I can forgive it
> With any modesty.
>
> III:iv:121–26

If for any reason the father could not arrange a marriage for the daughter, the mother took over this responsibility. If such a mother had a daughter serving at court, she was likely to feel the necessity of exercising all her wit to marry the girl before the pearl of chastity had been tarnished. The Queen's objection to marriage for any of her waiting women added to such a mother's difficulties. Lady Bridget Manners was one of Elizabeth's favorites, but her mother would not let that discourage her. On August 20, 1594, the mother married her daughter at her home in the country to a young man of her own choosing and without the Queen's knowledge. Two months earlier, this mother, the Countess of Rutland, had written the Queen, asking that her daughter be allowed to visit her, for she had been separated from her child five long years. The Queen gave her consent for the visit. Meanwhile, the mother had concluded arrangements for the wardship of Mr. Robert Tyrrwhit, whose grandmother had been a governess to Elizabeth. When the two young people learned of the mother's plan to marry them, they were pleased, for they had known and liked each other at court. Moreover, the girl was tired of being away from her beloved country home, and the boy was delighted with the girl's beauty and charm.

As soon as the Queen heard of the marriage, she was enraged, especially with the Countess, who professed ignorance of the marriage even though it had been performed in her own home by her own chaplain. The Queen would not believe the girl would marry without her mother's consent, for such would be a serious breach of duty. Therefore she blamed the mother and took steps to show her displeasure. She imprisoned Mr. Tyrrwhit in London and put the girl in the custody of a lady, where she stayed till she melted the Queen's heart by taking upon herself full blame for the marriage. By November she was free, and friends were able to plead the husband's illness so well that he was released from prison. The mother, of course, continued to bear the reproaches of the Queen,[23] but probably with quiet exultation.

Lady Russell, who found her daughters too heavy a financial responsibility, made her nephew, Robert Cecil, exercise his wits to free her from the burden. She complained that the father of her deceased husband had not made adequate provision for them, and she was forced to bring them up on slender widow's means. Now they were ready for marriage, and what was she to do? Must she make nuns of them? Immediately to this "threat" came an answer: her daughters were chosen as maids of honor to the Queen. Later, when she felt she must give the Queen a New Year's gift for taking her daughters in service, she wrote her nephew again, saying she would give the Queen £20 in a purse, even though she had not above £600 *de claro* left to live on, and signed herself as his aunt "that liveth in disdain, malice, and rancour, fearing, serving, and depending only upon God and my Sovereign, & Dowager."[24] Did she smile grimly with satisfaction over the release from caring for her daughters?

[23] Violet A. Wilson, *Queen Elizabeth's Maids of Honour and Ladies of the Privy Chamber* (1922), pp. 194–97.
[24] *Calendars of State Papers, Domestic Series, 1595–1597*, edited by Mary Anne Everett Green, CCLV, No. 29.

The charge that Venetian parents sent their daughters to nunneries when they could not afford dowries was common talk in England, as indicated in Lady Russell's letter to Robert Cecil. Stories of the loose life following this Venetian disposal of daughters filled English parents' hearts with horror. In 1608, Sir Henry Wotton wrote home a letter about Venetians that added fuel to the fire. "Unwilling nuns," he said, "were not likely to be chaste," and "the immediate cause" for "filling cloisters with such . . . wanton creatures" was their parents. If they had five daughters, they would "impose commonly that life upon three" of them, and so with other numbers "in proportion." The fathers excused themselves for this practice by saying they could not afford the "excessive rate" of the "marriage portions" demanded of them, that a gentleman's daughter must have no less than "twenty-five or thirty thousand crowns" for bestowing her honorably. Such a sum two hundred years ago would have been a "good provision in the public treasury!" The causes for such extravagant demands were two: "the opening of the Indies and increase of money" (inflation), and the old practice of "purchasing some credit and strength in the State" or at least of "saving themselves from injuries" by buying "at a great rate" a son-in-law from the nobility, "which induced the corruption of giving so much with daughters."[25] The second cause must have struck home to the heart of certain ambitious Elizabethans among the merchant class. Not to protect themselves from injury, but to climb into a higher social class, they sometimes married their girls to poor nobles by providing their daughters with handsome dowries. Nor must the fathers take all the blame here; often the girls themselves begged for such "fine" marriages.

English marriage portions also indicate the increase in living costs. To keep a daughter indefinitely at home was almost unthinkable, for a woman's destiny was marriage. But not all women did marry, and the care of them, despite their services in the household that accepted them, was often as not burdensome. This fact, as well as the perils of widowhood, hastened the remarriage of women who lost their husbands. Members of families responsible for widows set their own estimate on the cost of keeping them, and this did not help the lot of women left to the mercy of grasping kinsmen. A letter by Henry Lok to Secretary Cecil on July 12, 1598, says his aunt's estate has been estimated at £68 a year during her life. He considers this a competent pension for a lone woman and desires to be allotted that sum for keeping her.[26] To be "found" with board and room was enough, apparently, for such a dependent. A middle-class woman, however, would get along on one-third that pension, and wards were frequently kept for less. A joiner of London who had presumably

[25] Logan Pearsall Smith, *The Life and Letters of Sir Henry Wotton, 1568–1639* (1907), I, 439.

[26] *Calendars of State Papers . . . 1591–1594*, CCLXVIII, No. 3.

taken upon himself the care of such a child named all his goods and chattels as security for her wardship, according to the "assignment by Thomas Robinson, joiner of London, to John Lacy, yeoman of the guard, of the . . . issue of his goods and chattels, etc. within the realm of England, on condition that the said Lacy shall support and educate Elizabeth, daughter of William Howell, and pay her £20 on her marriage or coming of age."[27]

Elizabethan daughters entering nunneries probably did so from choice rather than by command of Catholic parents or relatives, who would have to keep such a disposal of their daughters most secret. It was reported that an English nunnery was established in Brussels on November 20, 1589, and here English women might take the veil. By 1606, the increased number of Catholic converts caused by the work of Jesuit missionaries and the lenient Stuart attitude toward Catholicism sent more English girls into nunneries. The five Jesuits of England in 1588 had become forty-five by 1606, and two decades later there were a hundred. In 1606, there were about twenty English nuns in the Flemish convent on "Half Street" of Louvain, where Margaret Clement, daughter of John Clement and Margaret Giggs, was the Mother. It would have pleased Sir Thomas More to know that his beloved adopted daughter, Margaret Giggs, was to have a child who would become so distinguished in the faith. In the same year of 1606, Jane Wiseman, daughter of a neighbor of Penelope Rich, at Northend, Essex, entered this nunnery, and three years later, with the aid of Father Gerard, she founded the English convent of the order of the Sisters of Saint Monica in Louvain. Here she was to preside for twenty-four years. Now the convent might be used as a home for dowerless daughters, but it was more than likely the home of those devoted to the religious life.

However, so much emphasis continued to be placed on the dowry in England that divines felt it necessary to remind fathers and mothers that there were other important duties for them to perform for marriageable children. Wedding sermons were the occasion for many of these promptings. Thomas Gataker, in such a sermon, after commending parents for their concern about dowries, urged them not to forget to instruct their sons on how to be kind to their wives and how to live with them in concord and content. Children must be educated for happy marriages, he said, by instruction in household management, housewifery, and habits of industry. They should be told the need of wisdom and discretion and fear of God in the marriage relationship. Just as the sons should be taught the value of good wives, so daughters should be taught that unless wives are good their children cannot be good. Indeed, the wife is the root and vine, and her children the fruit (*A Good Wife Gods Gift: A Marriage Sermon*, 1620).

[27] *Ibid.*, CCLXII, No. 12.

A convenient way for imparting much parental counsel was by means of the wise sentence. Should a son, for example, observe a girl he had known growing into idle habits and mention it to his father, the answer might be, "Ay, she hath broken her elbow at the church door." If she was too often seen on the streets, he might add, "Women and hens, through too much gadding, are lost." To which the son might say,

A woman oft seen, a gown oft worn
Are disesteemed and held in scorn.

If the son approached his father about making preparations for his marriage and the two, amiably and seriously, sat down to talk over the plans for this step, the father might say, "A good Jack makes a good Jill, my son." If at the same time he wished to impress upon the lad the value of thrift, he might add: "Be a good husband, and you'll get a penny to spend, a penny to lend, and penny for a friend." Should a son be too indifferent in the presence of women, the father might find a suitable moment for saying in his ear, "Women commend a modest man, but like him not." During a time in which father and son might be exchanging ideas about the remarkable nature of some women's intuitions, the father might nod his head wisely and with a twinkle in his eye say, "Take your wife's first advice, not her second, lad." Of course when a son decided it was time for him to marry, he would be likely to grow impatient over delay. If the father felt he was too young or for some other reason not ready to marry, he would probably say, "Who weds ere he be wise, shall die ere he thrive." If he was not pleased with the lad's somewhat flighty attitude, he might discourage the idea of marriage for a time by asking him to remember, "The married man must turn his staff into a stake." Shy but capable sons often needed prodding, and at the right time a father might call the attention of one of them to a likely lass, adding, "He that's needy when he's married shall be rich when he's buried." By such sentences a child was expected to learn a good deal of the common sense stored away in the average householder's attitude toward the duties expected of all the family members. These maxims were so much a part of the school texts and daily comments at home that a large part of their advice was absorbed unconsciously by young minds. This was exactly what the parents desired.

When parents let children make their own choice in marriage, they were likely, if very religious, to encourage them to seek divine guidance rather than to trust their own judgment. Dorothy Leigh took this attitude toward her sons, saying she believed that with prayer they would find godly mates, for divine guidance would not fail them. In *The Mothers Blessing* (1618), written for them, she asked that they marry only through love and, after making a choice, let nothing remove that love. "If a man hasn't enough wit to choose a woman he can love always, he should have wit enough to conceal his folly; if not, he is not fit to

Son of Sir John Thynne

XV MAII·M·D·LXXII   ÆTAT MENS·X

Daughter of Sir John Thynne

marry." Nothing could hurt her quite so much as "to have a son marry a woman he could not love to the end." She insists that if he "served God, he would obey God, and then he would choose a godly wife, and live with her in a godly manner." This meant not making her a servant and a drudge—"a woman fit to be a man's wife is too good to be his servant."

Amusingly feminine is her advice about the eternal mother-in-law relationship. She expects her sons to be patterns of virtue for their wives, especially in patience, that they may bear with them as a weaker vessel. The wives, on their part, will love and honor her superior sons who will make them realize their imperfections. Although she admits that the Bible commands a husband to leave father and mother for a wife, she is sure that command applies only to sons with ungodly wives and that it is but a test of such a husband's love for his wife. The command, therefore, does not disturb her, for she knows her sons would sooner desert their wives than their mother. Then she hastens to add piously that she hopes her sons will ever have in them the grace to love their wives always and always.

Quite at the other extreme from this woman's attitude was that of the disillusioned Earl of Northumberland in his worldly counsel to his son, written while he languished in prison on suspicion of being connected with the Gunpowder Plot. He had eagerly awaited this son and heir finally born to him by Dorothy, sister of Essex. Because his wife and daughters, he felt, had made his life almost intolerable, he was well qualified to advise his son on the management of women. First, then, he would have the boy choose a wife who knew but little, for she would be likely to show him due respect. If she bore him daughters, he should seek to "fashion them modest, neat, graceful, and obedient to draw on the likings of husbands." This would enable him to marry them off while they were still young and pretty and would relieve him from the strain of finding husbands who would be interested in their learning and virtue. If they showed any ability at needlework, he should encourage them "to begin great works that will ever be in the beginning and never ended." A little waste of sleeve silk on such articles as pillow slips, a pair of hangers or belts for rapiers, or for beautifying purses would keep them too busy to try to interfere in men's affairs.[28]

Many husbands, the earl wrote, gave in to their wives for the sake of peace and quiet, but he hoped his son would pluck up his courage by remembering "women's only weapon is the sharpness of their tongues, for they can neither strike nor bite to any purpose." If they get their way, however, they "will be froward and perverse"; but his son must remember that pain from such conduct is "very small" if it is without cause even though they "do talk preposterously enough" to madden their

[28] Violet A. Wilson, *Society Women of Shakespeare's Time* (1925), pp. 172–75.

long-suffering husbands. Arguing with a woman is sheer waste of breath, he said. For example, she will wear what is in fashion and nothing else, and when she gives a present, she selects the same gift other people choose, regardless of its suitability.

The earl warns his son that children always make trouble, for the mother will have her will about them, always believing her way is better than the father's. He says he has heard of their being so violent when crossed that they have threatened "to act many mischiefs upon their own persons," but at such times skillful men "have remedied by offering furtherance to their threats: as, if they would needs kill themselves, to give them a knife; if to hang themselves, to lend them garters; if to cast themselves headlong out of windows, to open the casements; if to swoon and die, to let them lie till they come to themselves again . . ." Yet he has never heard of any that "perished by such mournful deaths." As he writes, the earl shakes his head sadly and continues with a picture of how the world has changed. "A passionate woman will pride herself on being a lady of good spirit," but he remembers the time when, before the education of women, such creatures were called plain scolds. He hopes, therefore, that his son will assert his authority and in public will carry "a graver and commanding fashion" toward his wife and daughters than most men show in their "present dalliances and attendances and ridiculous obsequies" to their wives.

Possibly the most tragic theme in literature or life is unaccountable friction between parents and children. Even the best of training and discipline fails so miserably at times that it seems nothing can make right what is so hopelessly wrong between a mother or father and the offspring. Some Elizabethans, when cut to the heart by ungrateful or indifferent children, were inclined to attribute their grief to fate; others put the blame on improper training in the home or on heredity; still others left it all in God's hand. In theory, at least, most of them believed a disobedient child transgressed against the laws of God more than against parental authority. Like the Greeks, they felt that disobedience struck at the very roots of the family organization and, if not checked by severe punishment, might even endanger the welfare of the very State. Indeed, they regarded with terror the ingratitude of rebellious children, for they saw in their conduct a sin so unnatural as to upset by its treachery the harmony of nature itself. To them disobedience was ingratitude, and ingratitude was moral decay that led to monstrous acts. In all the range of human iniquity there was nothing comparable to it, for it rejected reason by which God had raised man above the beast. Since beasts were capable of gratitude, a human being who was incapable of it was an unspeakable horror, and might be guilty of the worst crime.

Lear, gazing into the eyes of Cordelia as he questions her frantically, "But goes thy heart with this?" can scarcely believe he hears aright when she answers, "Ay, good my lord." Seeing what he believed in her level glance was a suddenly ungrateful, rebellious daughter, he felt his soul rise to the overwhelming shock of it. In one moment all the ties of family affection were seemingly dissolved, and she had become an enemy that might disrupt not only his own kingdom but the well-being of the whole universe. As she stood before him, seemingly defying her own father, the king, so she defied her Father in heaven, the King of the whole world, and she was, therefore, a lost soul. It is ironic but fitting to the dramatic action that her seeming ingratitude, which Lear looked upon as treason to the state, should lead ultimately to her death. Heading the French army of invasion for the purpose of restoring her father to the throne, Cordelia in her great effort to prove—too late, alas—her devotion and gratitude to King Lear, actually becomes guilty of treason. This point in the Lear plot would have been intensely interesting to Shakespeare's audience; indeed, it is doubtful whether any of the other tragedies could have touched them so deeply.

In his way, Batty was trying to present his exposition of the mystery involved in unhappy relations between parents and children as he wrote *The Christian mans Closet* (1581). He would have parents count their successes in rearing children as worthy of hearty thanks to God for prospering their labors, but when their efforts fell out contrary to their expectation, they should bear patiently this test of their souls. He also blamed nature itself for the child's failure to respond to parental love: human frailty inherited from Adam made children desire love rather than give it, and they looked upon parents as in the descendant while they themselves were in the ascendant. How foolish, then, for parents old and poor to depend on their children! But worse than foolish parents were those "too fond through affection," who while still alive yielded "into the hands of their children their goods, coin, and all their inheritance, wholly persuading themselves to live more easily off the benevolence of their children whom often times they found foolish, negligent, and careless, to their great loss, hindrance, and utter nothing, with intolerable sorrow and grief all the days of their living."

Most authors, however, attributed faulty relationships in the family to parents' overindulgence and selfishness. Some of them could not bear to see their children suffer the hardships they had themselves endured and, being rich, pampered them "delicately and wantonly" until by idleness "their natural forces" decayed. The author of *The Court of Good Councell* (1607) compared the children of the poor with those of the rich by saying both might be born with a quick wit, but rich children often "waxed poor" because through "idleness or gluttony or some misgovernment" they became "slow and bull headed." Poor children, on the other hand, often became rich by their own labor and industry; hence the proverb, "Riches breed pride, pride breeds poverty, poverty breeds humility, humility breeds riches, and riches again breed pride." A wise father, therefore, would never trust too much to his own blood but would seek rather to better his children's own nature.

Stuart influence caused writers of conduct books to look back to the strong parents of Elizabeth's time and admire them increasingly as they saw with alarm the evil effects caused by weak, indulgent parents. "Doth not the child call his own mother *drab* and *queen*," exclaimed Thomas Carter in *Carters Christian Commonwealth or Domesticall Dutyes deciphered* (1627), "and his own father *fool* and *knave* and the like" while the foolish parents "rejoice to hear their chat!" He accused parents of even teaching them such things themselves, "hereof it cometh as a just plague for their follies, that before they can well go from their hands, they hear them curse them to their faces!" Some parents even winked at their children's pilfering and stealing. And almost anywhere children could be heard "blaspheming the holy name of God with great oaths, and singing most lewd and filthy songs, full of most odious speeches to the grief of the good heart or chaste ear . . ." He can excuse no parent from teaching his children the laws of God, for even though he may not be able to read them himself in the Bible, he can hear them at every parish church.

Such reproaches had also occurred during the Queen's reign. In 1581, Batty had criticized mothers severely for letting their daughters "roam abroad," and had declared they would be visited by "horrible punishment" for neglecting their children in this manner. If they continued as they were, they could kill the very souls of their children and overthrow the foundation of the Christian religion, which depended for its life on the "succession of our posterities." Children neglected in their tender years became "like unto a garden, which in the spring time . . . where there is nothing sowen, there is like to be nothing reaped but weeds." He said parents were as Erasmus had warned they would be— keeping their grounds well husbanded, the house decent, the vessel as bright as silver, their garments fine and trim, and all the whole house in very good order. The horses were well broken, the family well instructed, only the nature and the wit of their child was neglected, and it had become "stained, filthy, unfruitful, and out of culture."

The culmination of these deplorable evils in family discipline was apparently reached in the life of Frances Howard, daughter of the Countess of Suffolk. She became a horrible example to which parents of both gentry and middle class alluded as they sought to impress upon their children the results of evil-doing. Her father, a bluff, cheery, honest man, was so fond of his pretty child that he spoiled her shamefully, and her mother adorned her with Elizabethan finery. Among the many others who petted and spoiled her was her uncle, Henry Howard, who made her his chief care whenever he could have her with him. Yet at thirteen she was married with perhaps no effort to consult her feelings. Her fifteen-year-old husband was the son of Elizabeth's favorite, Essex, but he had none of the father's charm. Carefully and religiously educated by the strict and very moral Sir Henry Savile, young Essex could not understand the pretty spoiled darling who had become his wife. Nor was he given any opportunity to do so, for he was sent abroad on the tour immediately after his marriage, and Frances was returned to her mother till the young husband had finished his education.

While abroad, Essex came down with smallpox, which so disfigured him that when he came home six years later, he disgusted Frances, who, meanwhile, had been spending most of her gay young life at her uncle's fine mansion. From there she had attended every masque and tournament at the court of James I, and was celebrated in both London and Whitehall as the brightest star among all the beautiful ladies. Her husband, at his return, immediately took her away from all this gaiety to his house in the country, there to become the mother of his children. Outraged, she rebelled and secured an annulment of the marriage in 1613.

Now she married Somerset, the king's dissolute favorite, who returned her to life at court. Men fought to kiss the hem of her gown, and poets deluged her with sonnets. All along Somerset's adviser, Sir Thomas Overbury, had objected to her regime and especially to her second marriage. When, therefore, she became involved in his murder, everyone turned from her with loathing, and she became the object of ribald rhymes and ballads from all who knew how to dip their pens in ink. Her very name was twisted into a foul epigram by one who was crowned a wit for his pains. Then came her sensational trial, conviction, and imprisonment. Now, especially among the Puritans, her very name was a horror. Parents, terrified lest they overindulge their children, plied the rod with cruel severity.[29]

Partiality to one or more of their children had always been condemned as an indication of foolish fondness in parents. Now it was argued that such favoritism might lead to suspicion of the legitimacy of children less loved, as well as to envy, malice, and contention among the children themselves; it might even lead to punishment inflicted by God on the pampered child. Some writers, therefore, objected to second marriages simply because they were likely to cause partiality toward children. Fathers might prefer those of the favorite wife or might promise the second wife before marriage to disinherit the heir of the first marriage for the sake of the son to be born of the second alliance. Such a practice was not legal, however, unless the first heir could be proved illegitimate or notoriously wicked.

Some writers argued that favoritism should be avoided if any peace was to reign in the family. They admitted it was not man's nature to love all his children alike, no matter how hard he might try to do so. If one child proved incorrigible after the father had tried to be fair to all, that

[29] Edward Abbot Parry, *The Overbury Mystery* (1925), p. 32 and *passim*.

child might be cast out of favor. Unjust partiality, however, was sure to breed discontent in the family; if it did not, the children less loved were likely to triumph over their disadvantage and later "heap coals of fire" when they were needed to assist their parents and the parents' darlings in time of trouble. At critical times the pampered child nearly always proved a dullard, as such children usually turned out the worst. For his own sake, then, a parent might well try to avoid partiality.

Guazzo was frequently quoted in this discussion, for he did not spare those in the family guilty of favoritism. The abused child, he said, not only lost affection for its parents but was likely to carry on war with the favored one. This trouble was most likely to occur between brothers, and might become serious. Since it was a father's duty to maintain peace and quiet in his home, he defeated this aim if he favored any child, and sowed the seeds of discord. Furthermore, the innocent were made to bear the punishment of the father's imperfections. Guazzo's followers actually believed that when parents found it hard to be fair to unattractive children, they knew that at the time "they did beget them" they themselves had been "possessed with some infirmity of mind or body." So firm a hold did this idea have in man's mind that it persisted till well into the nineteenth century.

Perpetuity of the family, of course, was the aim that motivated most parents in the instruction of their children. At the same time the conduct books would instruct these very parents not to live up to the extent of their estate or run into debt by riotous living till they bound their very children to pay their debts long after they had quit this world. Nor must parents be too miserly in giving of their store to their children or make drudges of themselves to amass wealth for their children to dissipate. Again and again were they warned not to deplete their land of its timber except when the lawful advancement of their children necessitated parting with some of their valued worldly goods. But they must use discretion at such times lest they give away their loaf and have to come later to their children for bread.

To ensure peace in the family after the death of the head of the household, there must be a will. For this matter parents must secure good advice, making their wills while still in good memory for recalling debts and assets, and engaging lawyers who would use "distinct words and phrases" to express the meaning, which in itself must be free from exceptions at important parts of the will. In their care about declaring the uses for the family resources, parents usually considered the dowry most important. For pious parents, seeking mates for their children must be performed "in God." By this they meant their children should be married according to the following rules: marriage must not be with one too near in blood or too far in religious beliefs, and the son must woo, and the daughter accept attentions from suitors, as if in the presence of God. Only by this means did they feel that mutual respect for each other and concord after marriage would be likely to follow. If, then, older sons must follow instructions in wills about the marriage of their brothers and sisters "in God," these responsibilities were likely to weigh as heavily on the minds of dutiful sons as on the hearts of parents.

Marriage, however, did not necessarily take children away from home or parental authority. The pattern established by Sir Thomas More was still the pattern in many Elizabethan homes loving peace and order and close family relationships. In his *Utopia*, More had recommended eighteen as the lowest age for a bride, and twenty-two for the groom, yet he married his own children early. His favorite, Margaret, was scarcely sixteen when she was married to William Roper, and then she continued her education at home in "More's school." John, his only son, was married early to a young heiress, Ann Cresacre, a ward of the Crown. More had "bought" her of Henry VIII, but since he did not get the ward he expected, he was especially strict about her training in his home. Pretty little Ann did not care for religious exercises; she laughed one day at discovering her father-in-law in a hair shirt. When asked what she would like as a gift after More returned from one of his official trips abroad, she told her father-in-law a "Biliment of pearls." When he came home he was received with the usual demonstrations of delight, and as he passed out the little gifts, he presented Ann with a box. Opening it joyfully, she could hardly keep from weeping when she beheld an ornament set with white peas. But she was quick to see the intended lesson and in time was able to adapt herself to the More household and to become one of his "loving daughters." In spite of his strictness, More's children, his own and those by marriage, loved him.

The patriarchal family so successfully maintained by More was preserved with little change through the sixteenth and well on into the seventeenth century. Here the authority rested chiefly on the father, as it had in ancient biblical times and especially in ancient Rome, when a daughter, married without *conventio in manum*, remained in the power of her father or tutor or guardian even after marriage. The consent of the paterfamilias was so indispensable to sons and daughters alike, and this rule was so strict (even down to the time of Marcus Aurelius) that the children of a *mente captus* could not contract a legal marriage as long as the father was unable to give his consent. Elizabethans, of course, would transfer authority from a household head *mente captus* to one able to assume the duties of that position, but they preserved the spirit of the Roman family law with little other change.[30] More, with his admiration for domestic customs in the golden age of Rome, took over those customs he deemed best, but not all his followers had his good judgment in choosing the best.

[30] Edward Westermarck, *A Short History of Marriage* (1926).

Consequently, grown children trained under this system deferred to their father as meekly after marriage as before, and they required like obedience of their children to their grandfather. When Margaret Denton, for example, was married at the age of eighteen to Sir Edmund Verney in 1612, she was not taken from her father's home. It was agreed that she remain under her parents' roof for four years, and her husband was to be allowed his board while with her. Eight of her twelve children were born at her parents' home, for her husband's duties kept him much of the time at his house in Drury Lane or in his chamber at the court of Prince Charles. During all this time she and her children were responsible to her parents as she had been before her marriage. Later, at her husband's home, she and her children observed the same decorum in their relations to the head of their household. Margaret's dowry, £2,300, was also given into the hands of her husband for him to use as he deemed best for his family.

Children's obedience in regard to marriage contracts was essential lest they not only harm their own interests but embarrass their parents. If their conduct offended the Queen, then the matter was truly serious, for they made their parents as well as themselves liable to public chastisement. Such was the case when Thomas Shirley, son of Sir Thomas Shirley, the Queen's Treasurer for the wars in the Low Countries, secretly married Mistress Vavasour, a lady-in-waiting to the Queen. As in the secret marriage of Lady Bridget Manners, the Queen was furious. This time she took the young man's father to task, and while the son was being committed to the Marshalsea, Robert Cecil was told to write to the father that he was to make it publicly known he could not "digest such an act of contempt of her Court, as well as wilful perjury and disobedience to himself, nor do for a son that has so highly offended her who always furthers honorable marriages."

Even grandfathers retired from active life were still liable for the conduct of grown children, especially when it affected any alliance between families. Again Robert Cecil was forced to write a letter of warning, this time to Lord Henry Norris. He begins by saying he is loath to trouble one who is retired, but he must speak for Her Majesty who has given him his title of honor, which he is sure Lord Henry would not wish diminished by any blemish to the honor of his house. Then he tells him bluntly there is "an intention to cut down the woods" about his house. The act, he is sure, is not due to Lord Henry's orders, but to those of one "who cannot be contented" with this aged man's "extraordinary goodness, but must seek to tread upon him whom God and Nature hath appointed to be head of the house." Now that Sir Robert has brought his attention to this act, he hopes that Lord Henry "will not execute what can never be repaired" or make the Secretary "repent having bestowed" his niece on Lord Henry's son. He adds that he is alarmed over the grandfather's position in his own house, for his son Edward "gives it out" that no one shall ever speak with Lord Henry but by "his own favor." Cecil assures the father of this son, however, that he has the Secretary's confidence in his ability to assert his authority and not to permit "the seat of his posterity" to be defaced. Although Lord Henry was seventy-five at the date of this letter (September 21, 1591), Cecil was playing a clever hand by appealing to him. Only in this way could he save the fine old oaks of the estate to be inherited by the man his niece had married and at the same time circumvent the plans of one he detested.[31]

The relationship of parents with newly married couples presented new duties and problems. The mother-in-law, of course, was put in the most delicate position, and in conduct books, as probably in real life, she took the brunt of criticism. The finger of scorn might be pointed at her if she visited her daughter while her son-in-law was away, for she was likely to be suspected of trying to "stir up strife" by suggesting the wife was "kept short." If this was true, she might even persuade her daughter to "purloin from her husband." In any quarrel between husband and wife, such mothers were sure to take the part of their own blood, "regardless of the right." If necessary to live with their children, their lot was almost always difficult and uneasy, for they were inevitably regarded with suspicion.

Vives had given explicit advice to women forced to live with their married children, and his opinions were quoted, if not strictly followed, during the entire age of the Tudors. The wise woman, he said, would never pursue her daughter-in-law. She would love her enough to give her good counsel when asked for it and always would serve as a good example of chastity and gravity. She would avoid any discord between husband and wife, but if it should arise, she would with all her might try to reconcile the two children. Loving both of them, she would lightly bind them to her, increasing her son's love for her and her daughter-in-law's respect for her. So wise an "instructress to his wife" would mean greater happiness in the son's home, and his wife would respond naturally to a woman who tried to be a real mother to her.

If the daughter left home at marriage, Vives reminded the mother she must ever keep in mind the fact that her daughter had entered another household to increase its family. She would give only such counsel to her daughter, therefore, as she was sure her son-in-law would approve. She would not take her daughter to church or bring her home or even so much as speak to her against her son-in-law's will. At her daughter's marriage she gave up all right to her, and she must never disregard this fact. Thus she would always exhort her child to obey her husband in every point; to do otherwise was to make of her an adulteress or thief. Her own love for this son-in-law would be reverence, in no way like the love she would bear her own son. She would desire his welfare, nevertheless, as much

[31] *Calendars of State Papers* . . . *1595–1597*, CCLXXV, No. 36.

as that of her own son, and she would give him good counsel, yet always in the manner of advising, never of commanding. The whole purpose Vives has in mind here is to avoid friction between the two households allied by marriage, for no matter how close their interests or even their regard, their way of managing their affairs would have just enough difference to make even the slightest critical appraisal irritating. If one will but keep in mind the fact that there was little privacy in even the wealthiest Elizabethan homes, one will better understand why so much precaution was necessary to avoid discord.

To prove, apparently, that there actually existed the Vives type of mother-in-law, Lucy Apsley Hutchinson wrote of her husband's mother as having such "a generous virtue" with such "attractive sweetness that she captivated the hearts of all who knew her." It would have pleased Vives beyond measure to read this glowing tribute. She is described as "pious, liberal, courteous, patient" and extraordinarily kind. At the same time she was ingenious in "all things she applied herself to." In spite of her education at court she loved the country and managed all the household affairs "better than any of the homespun wives" brought up to nothing else. As a wife she was most affectionate; her love of her father's house was great, showing that her leading virtue was honoring her parents. In her own family she was a "wise and beautiful mistress, a blessing to her tenants and neighborhood," and, to her own infants, indulgently tender.

Even in dying, this lady was an example of Christian virtue, for she sang a psalm with more than her usual sweetness; it was "as if her soul had already ascended into the celestial choir." Apparently singing at death was the "good death" all pious souls hoped to achieve. In an age when death was looked on as a momentous occasion, the watcher might well believe he caught a fleeting glimpse of paradise opened to receive the blessed soul. This moment of transition was anxiously awaited and eagerly, intensely observed. The daughter-in-law's account in this instance, therefore, should be accepted as a genuine revelation of her sincerity and awe.

Regardless of the Elizabethan conventions about family affection, the members of a household could be most practical. The daughter-in-law's account continues with a brief description of how her father-in-law mourned his wife. "Though never was a deeper nor truer mourning than his," still the "long drooping grief did but soften his heart for the impression of a second love." And so he married "a very honorable and beautiful lady," Katherine, the youngest daughter of Sir John Stanhope of Elvanston. With all their sentiment and song, these sixteenth-century families, ancient and honorable, rich or poor, must not stop the flow of life.

The chief obstacle to remarriage seems to have been primarily the presence of two sets of children in a household. Advice to stepmothers was given in most conduct books, and authors were very critical of women called to fill so difficult a position. Second wives more than second husbands were regarded with suspicion till they proved themselves worthy of trust. In his words to stepmothers, Vives again set the pattern for authors of domestic literature.

Since widowers with children usually married widows, these stepmothers, said Vives, must beware of talking too much about their first husbands lest they make their new husbands unhappy and they themselves become jealous of the mothers whose children they must now care for as their own. He reminded them that human nature was likely to forget past unhappiness and to place more value on past joys than they deserved, but wise women would not let the past color the present too much. They must not forget either that all happiness, past or present, includes some bitterness.

Because jealous stepmothers were tempted to mistreat a first wife's children, Vives urged them and their husbands to share the children as if they were born to them. If second wives came to their husbands with no children of their own, they must especially try to regard the stepchildren as their own. He assured them that if they would but think how they would like their children treated by a stepmother, they would find it easy to be kind to the lives entrusted to their care. Then, when the day came that a stepmother heard the children call her mother, and fondly, she would lose all fear of the real mother's vengeance, which was believed to haunt stepmothers. Vives believed stepfathers could be good without much effort, but stepmothers had to strive to be so. Still, the gratitude of stepchildren was reward enough for the struggle to be kind.

Shakespeare interweaves closely the cunning villainy of King Claudius with a stepfather's speeches of perfect decorum in the early part of the play of *Hamlet*. Tenderly and appropriately he addresses Hamlet, the grieving son, and even when Hamlet answers his mother sharply because she objects to his continued mourning, the king carefully masks his own irritation. He says it is "sweet and commendable" for a son to mourn so dutifully, but he must remember his own father lost a father, "and that father lost, lost his." He admits a son is bound by "filial obligation" to show "obsequious sorrow" for a while, but not so long as to seem unmanly or to be guilty of "a will most incorrect to heaven." Feeling safe in his use of such two-edged phrases, he goes even farther, in fact far enough to betray himself to the soul of Hamlet, for he says grief must not make him show a "heart unfortified" or a "mind impatient" or "an understanding simple and unschool'd"; instead, he must face life courageously. Then the king plays out to the end the stock of decorous phrases for this occasion. He declares that his fatherly interest in Hamlet is so great because Hamlet is *his* heir to the throne, and that he has for him "no less nobility of love" than that which a "dearest father bears his son." A daring speech this! On the surface it is strictly conventional but, to Hamlet's acute perceptions, a revelation of the dangerous man before him. For this reason he can only "consent" meekly as the king joins

Hamlet's mother in urging him to stay with her. The king's response that Hamlet's obedience is a "gentle and unforc'd accord" which "sits smiling" to his "heart" is a climax scarcely appreciated if one fails to note the irony in the perfection of his acting in the role of a stepfather (I:ii:87–125).

This scene, combined with those of Hamlet brooding over his mother's remarriage, would have powerful appeal to the Elizabethan. The queen had "doted" on his father, and that father had taught his son to love and cherish his mother. The Elizabethan, watching Hamlet discover his mother's incestuous love for his father's smilingly deceitful brother, would not react to a plot that was merely sensational. He would see instead the appeal to the passions of the strong helplessly intertwined with the overstrung emotions of the neurotically weak. It was these chaotic forces in society that the home must combat by careful guidance of the lives for which it was responsible.

Two households exemplify the effort made by the home to keep serene and stable during joy and grief in spite of the disordered world pressing hard against it. One, early in the age, helped to shape the Elizabethan home, and the other, coming late, reflects Elizabethan influences still potent in domestic life. Both households were religious, one Catholic and the other Anglican, and both took over the best ancient and English domestic customs of family discipline to combine with the parents' common sense in teaching children moral and ethical principles of behavior. Perhaps not many fathers so nearly approximated the ideal as did Sir Thomas More and Sir Edmund Verney, according to reports that have come down to us from relatives and close members of these men's families, but most fathers in their own way struggled toward a similar goal.

More's own children and those bound to him by marriage were devoted to him. His son-in-law, William Roper, tells how More's training of his children began in their infancy, and how from the very beginning he admonished them to take virtue and learning for their "meat" and play for their "sauce." When he was at home, he took his whole family to the chapel of an evening, and upon their knees they repeated certain litanies, psalms, and collects. After he had dismissed them to their night's rest, he still remained long in the chapel at his devotions. He had built the chapel chiefly for his own periods of retirement from the world, and he loved it as a precious retreat from the world, which, he felt, made many demands upon his daily hours. Here, no doubt, he received the grace with which to knit firmly together in love his whole household.

The circle was close, for he and his children and their eleven children and his second wife were a harmonious, busy group. More ruled by kindness and love, preserving his strict discipline with apparently no effort, and his wife was of great help in managing the many details of the household. She was a very practical woman who tried to carry out her husband's ideals, but she lacked his touch, for she had no sense of humor and no intellectual interests. She might argue with him over the plans he made for her and the children, but at the same time she wouldn't dream of changing one detail without his consent. His commands were gentle, but they were the law by which all of them lived.

In More's time few men sought genuine companionship in women, especially in their own family, but for most of the Elizabethan period, thanks to More, such was no longer the case. In Margaret, More was blessed with a daughter who by inclination and ability was delightfully responsive to him. When the blow of Henry VIII's disfavor fell upon More, this daughter became his chief solace. He let her wash and mend his clothes while he was imprisoned in the Tower. In stature, manner, appearance, and even voice, she resembled her father more than any of the other children, and in mind she seemed to think like More, as, for example, when father and daughter made a Latin translation of a passage and, upon comparing the result, found similar graceful expressions. Like her father, Margaret was able to write in both Latin and Greek and, again like him, excelled in Latin. It was to her More sent his hair shirt just before his death, for this symbol of his religious life would be doubly precious to her whose "daughterly love and charity" did so much to lighten his last hours.

Though Margaret was more congenial than all his children and is usually referred to as More's favorite child, he never was guilty of showing her a partiality that would wound the feelings of the others. He tried to give his time and effort equally to all of them in helping them to acquire the new learning so important to men like him. Erasmus, who was attached to both More and his family, tells, in a letter he wrote to a friend, how More trained his daughters in Latin.[32] With no help from the father on choice of theme or correction of the writing, each was told to write to Erasmus, and then to make a neat copy of her work, which More sent on exactly as it was. Erasmus "was never so surprised," for he found in them "nothing whatever silly or girlish" and the style showed "they were making daily progress." His close acquaintance with them is shown when he tells how the girls could read Titus Livius without translation except for an occasional word that would perplex even himself. And he also tells how More's second wife instructed the girls in housewifery that they might be as proficient in "womanly duties" as in learning. He says that the wife "excels in good sense and experience rather than in learning," for she directs the "whole company with wonderful skill, assigning to each a task and requiring its performance, allowing no one to be idle, or occupied with trifles. To Margaret, Erasmus writes of his

---

[32] Roper and Stapleton have provided many interesting details of the intimate life of More's household. A biography by More's nephew, William Rastell, has disappeared, a great loss to students of this period.

loving admiration for the family when he is sent Holbein's picture of them, and he says he recognizes each one, but none more than Margaret, in whom he sees a "soul shining through the most beautiful household even more beautiful . . ." He asks her to give his compliments to her mother Louise, whose picture he has kissed as he could "kiss herself," and sends his best wishes to her brother and his family.[33]

While away from home, More kept in as close touch with his family as the poor roads and uncertain delivery of letters permitted. Stapleton reports his concern in a letter More wrote Margaret, telling her he "would be still more delighted" had she told him of the studies she and her brother "were engaged in," of their "daily reading . . . pleasant discussions . . . essays," and whatever made the days pass swiftly and joyously in their "literary pursuits." Though anything she writes gives him pleasure, the most "exquisite delight" comes from her writing what only she and her brother could tell him. He concludes earnestly: "I assure you that, rather than allow my children to be idle and slothful, I would make a sacrifice of wealth, and bid adieu to other cares and business, to attend to my children and family, amongst whom none is more dear to me than yourself, my beloved daughter."

In another letter Stapleton provides, More addresses all the girls, his "dearest daughters" and "Margaret Giggs as dear as though she were my daughter." He tells them of the "very deep pleasure" their "eloquent letters" have given him, especially when he sees that in spite of their "traveling and frequently changing" their abode they let nothing interfere with their "customary studies" as they continue in their exercises in "logic, rhetoric, and poetry." This convinces him that they love him as they should, even though he is absent, for they "do with the greatest eagerness" what they know would cause him pleasure were he present. When he returns they will see that he is not ungrateful for the delight their loving affection has given him. Again he assures them he has "no greater solace in all the vexatious business" in which he is "immersed" than to read their letters.

Not all the father's letters were weighed down with concern about his children's intellectual life, for More could write with pretty playfulness and simple compliment. Stapleton has preserved an example of such badinage in a letter to Margaret, who has asked her father for money with, as he says, "too much bashfulness and timidity," for she is asking of one "eager to give." If he had the means he would not be like Alexander who paid Cherilos a golden philippine for each line of verse, but rather he would show his love for her by rewarding each of her syllables

---

[33] State Papers: *Letters and Papers, Foreign and Domestic, of the Reign of Henry VIII, 1524–30* (arranged and catalogued by J. S. Brewer, 1876), No. 5924. The letter is dated September 6, 1529.

"with two gold ounces." As it is, he will send her only what she asks, and would send more but that he is "desirous to be asked and coaxed" by this daughter whose virtue and learning have made her so dear to his soul. Then he concludes: "So the sooner you spend this money well, as you are wont to do, and the sooner you ask for more, the more you will be sure of pleasing your father."

So precious were his children's letters that More carried them about with him while he was away from home. Once, by accident, he pulled out one of Margaret's letters with some other papers while he was talking with the learned bishop of Exeter. When the bishop asked permission to read the letter, the father's heart must have been filled with joy to hear this scholarly man praise Margaret's writing for its pure Latinity, its correctness, its erudition, and its expressions of tender affection. Yet in spite of all her intellectual training, she was in no way devoid of feminine charm. As mother and wife, as well as daughter, she was beloved and admired.

By example as well as by teaching, More impressed upon his family the importance he attached to preparation for life after death. He frequently referred to ways and means of discarding the vanities of this earth that might interfere with the riches of life here and to come. Often at table the family engaged in serious conversation about the good life or in witty and delightful talk about the "little" affairs of the world in which they lived. When a learned guest like Erasmus was present, he would naturally take part in the friendly controversies. Occasionally, no doubt, More would discourse on the vanities of life in comparison with the Christian way of living in pretty much the way he wrote of such things.[34] The devil's damsel would consider herself fair, "weening herself well liked for her broad forehead" while "the young man beholdeth her," marking her crooked nose. Men are proud of glistening stones, "of which the very brightness, though it cost these twenty pounds, shall never shine half so bright nor show half so much light, as shall a poor halfpenny candle!" A man may scorn his neighbor because his own gown is made of finer wool, and yet, "fine as it is, a poor sheep wore it on her back before it came upon his . . ." All man has he receives from God—"riches, royalty, lordship, beauty, strength, learning, wit, body, soul, and all." Almost all these things, however, have only been "lent us." From all of them man must depart, except the soul alone, which in time he must "give God again also."

More's disapproval of the divorce of Henry VIII from his first wife and his refusal to take the oath of Henry's supremacy over the Pope's authority brought him in time to his execution, an event that threw his

[34] E. M. G. Routh, *Sir Thomas More and His Friends* (1934), p. 129 (quoted from Allen's *Selections of More's English Works*).

family into almost unbearable grief. But for his own moral courage and faith in the future life, More would surely have weakened when he saw his children's anguish as he was led to the Tower after his sentence of death. Stapleton tells us how his son John threw himself at his father's feet as he passed by and, on his knees, with tears running down his cheeks, begged his father's blessing. Though it was customary for a son to ask a blessing in public or private when he felt the need of this assurance, such a demonstration as John's was most touching. In the Tower, More wrote that his son's filial affection shown at such a time and place had given him "no little consolation."

When Margaret approached her father, she fell upon his neck speechless with agony. Walking away a few steps, she returned and "clung about his neck" but uttered no word. More's own speech was choked with tears, but when he could command himself, he asked her to pray for his soul. One can imagine with what fervor she obeyed his request. According to one legend, she risked her life after More's execution to have his head removed from its place of disgrace on the bridge, and to keep it safe from his enemies, she carried it about with her, preserved in alcohol. At her own death, the head was buried with her.

The high seriousness of the More household was observed, with a difference, in the life of the Verney family. This diversity was not due to religion so much as to other influences. In the time of More, the love of learning was at the upswing of the pendulum; in the time of the Verneys, it was swinging back. The softening effect of greater ease and comfort in life, caused by better houses and furnishings and many imported luxuries, had added to the list of wants by which men tried to widen the horizon of their daily existence. And the general lowering of moral character at court had inclined society to a more indulgent attitude toward life and its pleasures. Greater fortunes and greater poverty had helped to increase the average man's respect for material possessions, and though a family might seriously think of life after death, it looked with appreciation or envy on the good things to be enjoyed on earth. As always, however, society brought forth its highly moral individuals to prove, as it were, that fundamentally man undergoes little change from age to age except, perhaps, in degree.

The Verney family was strictly Anglican in faith, and capable, therefore, of genuine enjoyment of the "legitimate pleasures of life." Sir Edmund Verney and his beloved son Ralph were not so religious as to exclude from their individual philosophies a large geniality as well as a strict conscience. Their respect for women, for example, was genuine and pleasing, and it added grace and tenderness to the family life. This they enhanced by their delight in wit and mirth and such pastimes as dancing, fencing, hawking, and pursuit of all the liberal arts. They were never guilty of the grossness prevalent at the time of James I or the narrowness of the Commonwealth, and their wives were as graciously high-minded as they were themselves.

Sir Edmund's loving and courteous treatment of even his poorest dependents was typical of the best elements in the tradition of the Elizabethan gentleman. For example, when his steward's father asked him for some wood to burn, Sir Edmund wrote to the son that the "poor old man" had offered to pay him for some ashwood, but he was to see that the father always had that "wood or any other wood to keep him from the cold," and freely. Sir Edmund never spoke of his cottagers and farmers with anything but good will and friendly interest, showing them the kindness he would give a neighbor.[35] His letters reveal this generous concern in spite of his heavy duties at court. One tells how he was asked for a buck from Whaddon Chase; another requires him to decide a matter in the interest of his niece, Doll Leeke, whom he had taken into his home at Claydon, and another shows his concern about an old lady in London needing his aid. A lord might ask him to get a kinsman out of some difficulty, friends appealed to him to find wives for their sons or husbands for their daughters, and others wrote to thank him for the gift of a hog or a recipe for a cake. His wife's relatives were devoted to him; even his caustic mother-in-law had nothing but praise for him.

Sir Edmund's wife, Margaret Verney, loved people. The oldest of eleven children and the mother of twelve, she knew the meaning of crowded days, yet she always managed to maintain her intimacy with her family of brothers and sisters and nephews and nieces. Her last child was born when she had a granddaughter a year old. Besides her own six daughters and her daughters-in-law, her household included her mother and her mother-in-law, the latter living to a good old age and assisting her in rearing her children.

Margaret's own mother was never hesitant in giving her daughter or son-in-law the advice she felt they needed even as grandparents. When Margaret's grandson was sent up to London in 1639, and was so shy that his father and grandfather complained of his manners, Lady Denton was upset. She excused the three-year-old by saying that he could not be blamed for being shy when he was not even acquainted, and she begged that "nobody whip him but Mr. Parrye" who knew and understood the child's nature. "If you do go a violent way with him," she wrote, "you will be the first to rue it, for I verily believe he will reserve injury by it." He was too young to be "strudgeled in any forcing way." Then, like the typical mother-in-law of all times, she gave her opinion of the child's grandfather as she wrote to Sir Edmund's son Ralph: "I thought he had more wit than to think a child of his age would be acquainted presently. He knows the child was fellow good enough in my

[35] Frances Parthenope Verney and Margaret M. Verney, *Memoirs of the Verney Family during the 17th Century* (1925), pp. 65–66.

house." She even begs Ralph to show his father what she has written of him, for she wants to make sure the little boy will not be frightened, as he is "of a gentle sweet nature, soon corrected."

A year later the child, greatly improved, is back home, and this time Ralph's mother writes him. She asks him to tell his wife how much she thinks the little fellow has grown in grace. In time he will be "a complete courtier," for she can get nothing from him but "Bless me, Lady," and "Good morrow, Lady." He is just as courteous to his aunts, "and he is as much reformed of his wilful way in this short time as ever I see, and it is all done with love and fear." She is worried, however, about his health. For his diet peas seem to be "satisfying," but she finds "hard cheese is the fittest thing for him." Although she had reared all twelve of her children to vigorous adulthood, it was another matter to be responsible for a grandchild that was so apparently delicate, as the usual treatment for ailing children was still vomiting, purging, sweating, and bloodletting.

Meanwhile at court, Margaret's husband, Sir Edmund, continued to be devoted to his wife and his children and grandchildren in spite of his other duties. Perhaps he achieved so much because he could lean heavily on Ralph who he knew in his absence would keep the home intact. This trust led to a very close bond between father and son, and Ralph's children were as much Sir Edmund's concern as if he had been with them constantly. He was devoted to his little granddaughter Marie, and yet, ironically, when she lay dying, he was at home and the father was away. Now it was Sir Edmund's difficult duty to break the news to his son. As he sat writing at one o'clock in the morning, his gentle heart found a way to soften the blow.

"Ralph," he began, "your sweet child is going apace to a better world; she has but a short time to stay with us. I hope you have such a sense of God's blessings to you as you will not repine at his decrees." Then he gave the best possible antidote to such grief—anxiety for another who struggled under the same pain. "Make all convenient haste to your good wife who wants your comfort." Then he is practical. "Yet come not too fast, for that may heat your blood; and that may give end to all our comforts; as ever I shall entreat anything from you, take care of yourself, for this is a dangerous year for heats and colds. The God of Heaven bless you."

Most Elizabethan parents, as long as they were able to bear burdens at all, carried in their hearts the problems of their children. This is why, even when children left the family rooftree to try their fortune in the world, they still wrote home for advice at critical times. As long as their parents lived, they felt the ties of home. True, this durance sweet was altered by individual temperaments, but in theory at least, only death cut the bonds. The family loyalty caused definite sacrifice but made the Elizabethan family a strong unit in the social order. The government counted on it, and the Church looked to it for its very means of existence in a world of changing beliefs and disruptive acts. Knowing this, parents sought earnestly for whatever means might ensure the perpetuation of family relationships in all their strength and beauty and cohesive power. On this foundation depended society's best chance for purposive living and for man's collective happiness.

As the tip of death's wing brushed across the heartstrings of these two notable fathers, Sir Thomas More and Sir Edmund Verney, each gave the right comfort to the anguished soul dearest to him—one by begging his daughter to pray for his soul, and the other by urging his son to take care of himself for "all their comforts." Yet as both stood in the shadow of death, they also faced life. One saw in life the light of the hereafter; the other saw life in the light of both worlds, but in that of the hereafter a culmination not so near as to be intrusive. These two homes, one ushering in the ideal home life which many Elizabethans were to try to achieve, and the other maintaining much of the decorum and tenderness of the late sixteenth-century family, frame for us the picture of domestic life in the age of Elizabeth.

CHAPTER III

EDUCATION OF CHILDREN

*Education is the bringing up of one, not
to live alone, but amongst others . . .*

RICHARD MULCASTER, 1561

INCE the avowed purpose of education was to teach individuals how to take their destined place in life, each class in society must have its own particular type of formal instruction. True, all types pointed to one road, and some of them used one or another sign to indicate the goal toward which the road led. However, Elizabethans in general saw at the end of this road of education health and riches and the approval of God, friends, neighbors, and the family. The stress on such approval may have been due to their uncertainty about shifting standards of behavior, but one standard did not suffer much change in theory—that good manners indicated good morals, and so manners proclaimed the man, his character, his place in life, and his worth to society.

Shortly before Elizabeth ascended the throne, an unknown writer quaintly described the gentle class in his *Institution of a Gentleman* and insisted that "gentlehood" had its origin in gentle deeds, which could be taught young people by education and practical training. He spoke of the "gentle-gentle" as one born to gentle living and gentle manners, of the "gentle-ungentle" as one born gentle but corrupted by bad manners, and of the "ungentle-gentle" as one born in modest circumstances but grown into a state of virtue and knowledge and good works through education and the acquisition of good manners. Gentlemen, he declared, must serve the Commonwealth by means of their ability and virtue, but they must also dress like gentlemen and even in their sports follow only the gentleman's pastimes. This book expressed what the ambitious parents of modest birth hoped education might do for their children.

All classes, however, acknowledged the importance of good manners. The upper class, after the children were out of the nursery, usually put them in charge of the family tutor, who began teaching his charges proper decorum. In the middle class, the boys were sent to the local schools, and the girls, until later in the century when they also attended school with their brothers, were given to their mothers to train. The ideal that infected nearly all this teaching, however, was that of the gentleman or lady. As a husband could elevate his wife to his own social position, the ambitious maid dreamed of marrying a gentleman. A common man by distinguished service of some kind might also rise above the class in which he had been born. From the time of Henry VIII, men of low birth began to realize dreams of social advancement, and the gentleman's position was no longer limited to those intended for only court or civil service.

This state of affairs resulted in many attempts to define the gentleman, but all more or less followed a pattern such as that, for example, in the work of the Puritan reformer, Laurence Humphrey, Regius Professor of Divinity at Magdalen College, Oxford. In 1563, Humphrey wrote his book *Of Nobilitye* to define the rights and duties of the aristocracy and to distinguish carefully between the old and the new nobles. He criticized the faults of both, especially of the latter, and expanded upon their duties as noblemen and teachers, dividing their virtues into public and private ones as Spenser intended to do about three decades later in his *Faerie Queene*. Among the public duties, Humphrey listed religion, liberality, justice, and equality; among the private virtues, temperance, continence, and moderation in diet, dress, sports, managing estates, maintaining a modest train, and devoting time to reading and study.

Meanwhile Humphrey had been influenced, no doubt, by Elyot's *The Boke named the Governour*, written in 1530 to win Henry VIII's favor. Besides defining the nature and duties of the commonwealth and the nobility, Elyot discussed polite conduct and set forth a type of education for youths who were to become servants of the state; for these youths he enumerated suitable sports and the necessary public and private virtues. Then when Sir Thomas Hoby translated Castiglione's *The Courtier* for men and women at the English court to read and emulate, he gave them a book that was to become the sixteenth-century ideal of the lady and the gentleman, reflecting the very spirit of Renaissance courtesy.

With so much said about the "gentle" conduct of the nobility, it was natural for the ideal of gentility to penetrate to the soldier, the yeoman, the physician, and the rich of any class. True, the title of gentleman could be borne only by those awarded a coat of arms, but now that a title could be acquired by anyone performing some distinguished service for the state, hope for social advancement ran high. Money, of course, could perform many "services"; however, lest a title degenerate into a mere commodity, an elaborate system of heraldry was established. Although this provision did not always succeed in its purpose, it became necessary in a gentleman's education to give him an adequate knowledge of heraldry in order that he be able to recognize a gentleman's social position by the coat of arms he displayed. Another part of his education required him to know how to give each man his due courtesy, not too much and not too little.

By the 1590's the common people were so eager for admission into the fashionable "gentle" class that the *nouveaux riches* believed a careful reading of conduct books would enable them to master the rules by which they might at least deport themselves like their "betters." Moreover, since the wheel of fortune might turn favorably for their children whom they wished to make "gentlemen," they insisted that children's textbooks provide exercises in etiquette as a part of their formal scholastic education. For this purpose adaptations from translations of foreign manuals were used, foremost being such books as Giovanni della Casa's *Galateo*, which taught what to do and what not to do in polite society, as pleasing others was important for personal success; an anonymous dialogue of *Cyvile and Uncyvile Life*, which evaluated life in city and country both for individuals and the state they served; Stephano Guazzo's *The Civile Conversation*, which by examples and tales covered pretty much the whole field of proper conduct, and eventually even adaptations from Castiglione's *The Courtier*, which had been designed only for court society. Such translations increased rapidly in popularity from the time of their introduction in the mid-1570's, and were commonly read by adults who longed for social success.

Along with *The Courtier* and its stress on the physical, ethical, and cultural development of the gentleman at court serving his state, was, of course, the Bible and its moral teachings. The ideals advanced by these two books were expected to balance perfectly the development of the person educated by their precepts, and, as was natural, the influence of the ideals so presented depended as much upon the family's instruction, colored deeply by its cultural background, as upon the schools. Consequently, *The Courtier* was never quite understood or absorbed by the common man, but the Bible's moral teaching was pretty much the same in all classes, though its cultural elements were a matter of individual appreciation. For the Elizabethan gentleman, however, the three-part program of physical, ethical, and intellectual instruction advised by *The Courtier* was expected to produce a perfect expansion of the individual, and, with its emphasis upon decorum in speech, apparel, and hospitality, it hoped to achieve a perfect harmony in the being who was to serve his state with distinction. When this ideal was further fused with the principles of the Bible's moral teachings, it was likely to temper the graceful and perhaps careless manners of the gentleman with a seriousness and stability that made him unique as an exponent of English statesmanship. So far as we can tell today, there was no gentleman in England who more perfectly represented the ideal courtier than Sir Philip Sidney. Though his early death may have caused our knowledge of him to be somewhat etherealized, still the influences for which his name stands did much to shape the Elizabethan program of education.

Richard Mulcaster, when ready to declare his program of education for middle-class children, took as practical a view of the individual's moral, intellectual, and physical training as his situation would warrant. When, therefore, he stated that the purpose of education was to teach a man to live with others, he explained he must be trained to "execute those doings in life which the state of his calling shall employ him unto, whether public . . . or private . . . according unto the direction of his country whereunto he is born and oweth his service." Education for this purpose must be physical as well as mental in order to help "nature achieve perfection in the individual." Thus he would have English schools provide vocational education to enable the child to make use of innate abilities, and parents should work with the schools in helping their children discover their talents. To make this teaching more natural and more helpful, he advocated the use of English rather than Latin in and out of school.

Richard Mulcaster's ideas, published in *Positions* about 1581, opened a controversy as to what minds were capable of being trained. He admitted minds "too bare" or too difficult to train could not profit from mental preparation, though all children should be taught to read and write lest in time they become "seditious." Minds fit for state duties should be selected "not in haste for need, but at leisure for choice." Bullinger had also insisted on this deliberation. Careful training for state affairs, said Mulcaster, would require "intolerable labor" and for so long a period of time that poor people could not afford to spare their children for this purpose no matter how gifted they might be. Ordinary children should learn any "just and true" occupation that would bring them God's blessing. Mulcaster reminded ambitious parents that their children might be capable of no other training. It was true that education was a thing no misfortune could take from a person, but in some cases an education must be training in a craft. In fact, grammar schools had to weed out by various devices those who might retard the "fit" minds. At St. Paul's the unfit were dismissed; at Harrow they were given a year's grace.

Since a child in his tender years was likely to be obedient to school order, neither offending nor suffering punishment easily, being gentle, courteous, and helpful, yet also able to defend himself in time of need, still he must not be considered a genius by his parents or teachers. Not every bright child was destined for a great career or "specially chosen of God." Mulcaster knew from experience as headmaster at Merchant Taylors' School in London that children's mental ability was not likely to "make any evident show" until they were in grammar school. In the elementary grades they might well profit from having the competitive spirit appealed to, but in grammar school all such devices should be dropped lest the children become "malapert." If, in grammar school, they showed any inclination toward a special career "without any either great fear or much heartening," then an effort should be made to find their natural gifts, and in this matter parents should cooperate with teachers. That Mulcaster was highly respected by the middle class may be indicated by the fact that in the schools where he taught he received support from the parents as they worked together to achieve "complete development" of the child.

At about fifty-five, Mulcaster retired to teach privately for a few years, but in 1596 he became master at St. Paul's, where he stayed till 1608. Three years later he died in poverty and was buried in a nameless grave. Yet this man was recognized in his time, as he is in ours, for his advanced ideas on education. For example, he believed that in the first three years the foundation of education is laid; he would have girls for the most part taught by women; he knew that the memory must be put to work while the analytical powers are developing; he insisted that what was learned must be learned well, and he actually stated that a child learned best by doing, by putting into practice what he was taught. Not only did he advocate taking time from foreign languages to study English, but he believed grammar was important as an aid in writing and speaking and not for its own sake. In supporting the use of English, he pointed out its value in disputation, saying it was "better able" than any other language "to utter all arguments." Like Ascham, he also disapproved of too much beating in the schools. Colleges, he said, should specialize in particular subjects with definite programs of study; universities should train teachers, and the government should control endowments even of private schools "according to the needs" of the time and its people.

Before the Tudor age, advancement among the lower classes was possible only by entering the Church or by serving in the house of some sponsoring lord. Elizabethans permitted greater ease in moving up and down the social ladder. But Elizabethans, like their forebears, continued to believe in the importance of degree, priority, and great place. This insistence on a social hierarchy was taught people in school and church, on the stage and in the literature of poets and prose writers, and even in the speeches of the Queen, the ministers, and the members of Parliament. At the same time possible advancement in the social scale was dangled like a prize before ambitious eyes. In the country, prosperous yeomen made prudent marriages that added to their holdings until they might dower their daughters well enough to marry them to gentlemen or, in some cases, marry into the gentry themselves. Without ambition and ability they might also lose whatever they had inherited and become mere laborers for others. In towns and cities, laborers and artificers might improve their position, but the greatest gains were made by those in trade.

Ambitious, capable Elizabethans, then, sought to direct their creative energy along channels of self-control which would set free this energy but give it bounds and form and stimulating goals. The similar restraints of order and degree would intensify their spirit of emulation and deepen their personalities, resulting in the possibility of receiving recognition. The means by which this self-controlled drive and its benefits were to

be achieved was education. They could will the energy, but all the energy ←
in the world was of value only when directed, guided, and controlled
by the magic of education. When this hope flowered in the hearts of
the middle class, opportunities for schooling rose rapidly to stretch still
further the soaring plans of parents for their children. Among the Puritans, especially, the dream of education was to enable their sons to rise,
not only from low to high estate, but, by means of reading the Word
of God, even to heaven itself. Happiness, wealth, wisdom, godliness—
these were the prizes that dazzled their eyes as they beheld the panacea
of education.

Devoutly ambitious parents still hoped to send at least one of their
children to the university to become preacher or scholar, and they were
supported in their hopes by such men as Archbishop Cranmer, who had
insisted that only the "apt in learning" were to be admitted to the Canterbury Cathedral School, that gentleborn dullards were to be replaced by
brilliant youths from the poor. Eventually, as the middle class began
to grow wealthy, universities and inns became crowded with students
from such families, and they, as time went by, brought the wheel full
circle by becoming the drones who attended school because it was the
thing to do.

Meanwhile, as attendance at the universities increased, grammar
schools were added to the towns, the school exercises seeking to cultivate
the memory and understanding and to provide systematic training in
the all-important morals and manners. Finally, Puritans in the late sixteenth and early seventeenth century were strong enough to demand both
a learned ministry and grammar schools free from all social or financial
barriers. Of course they themselves largely supported these schools, but
this fact also enabled them to send the promising grammar school students on to the universities. By this time not only boys but girls were ←
attending public grammar schools, for there were few schools for girls
only. Now Mulcaster's hope that the same education be given girls and
boys was realized. Even the poor laboring classes might have their children taught to read and write enough to get some instruction from their
Bibles and to write wills and ordinary letters or to record market prices
and birth and death dates. Formerly they had had to depend on the
schoolmaster or clergyman to perform such services for them. Their
poor cousins in the country, however, still had to rely on this assistance.

Confiscation of the monasteries by Henry VIII and suppression of
the chantries or singing elementary schools by Edward VI was a great
blow to education among the lower classes till the movement began for
the establishment by the Crown of secularized monastic schools. Henry
had intended to do a great deal for education, but the financial situation
was such that he accomplished very little. His new cathedral schools,
however, were much stronger than the old chantries and guilds of the
monasteries. Still, their number was alarmingly decreased, especially in

the case of the chantries. These schools had been of two kinds: one in which a priest, paid by some rich person, said daily masses for the dead and instructed boys and girls in his free hours; the other in which choir-boys were trained in connection with the church; here elementary school instruction was also provided. Over twoscore such schools were abolished, though if the people were energetic enough to demand their re-establishment, they sometimes were provided with new schools. Henry and his son did begin establishing secular schools for the people, and they were joined by the laity and others who contributed money for grammar schools. But Elizabeth did not believe it was the Crown's responsibility to provide such education, though she would restore a school if the people of the district insisted long enough and hard enough.

When the laity became interested in schools, however, the wealthy middle class were especially sympathetic to the situation, and soon towns-men, trade guilds, and rich burghers began founding and administering grammar schools for boys and girls. This, of course, pleased the Queen, and she smiled on their activities. Then it became fashionable for the rich to support poor but brilliant scholars at the universities; and among the religious, this charity became an obligation. By 1600, there were some three hundred sixty grammar schools teaching written and spoken Latin, for it was necessary to all those who would better their lot by entering one of the professions, such as diplomacy, law, medicine, or civil service. It was also deemed necessary for those wishing to advance in such fields as trade, music, building supervision, serving as bailiff of an estate, seeking office as town or guild clerk, or applying for the command of an army or a ship sent to explore the New World.

Thus wealthy merchants or tradesmen, for the sake of their salvation or to show their loyalty to their birthplace or to be part of the fashionable group of founders, would endow a school or contribute generously to one already established. So began Uppingham, Rugby, Harrow, and the famous Merchant Taylors' School, but the largest and most important of London grammar schools was St. Paul's, founded by John Colet. Being the first and only child of his father's eleven sons and eleven daughters to reach maturity, John felt he had been set apart to perform some mission. His father encouraged him to take orders and to travel in Italy, where he studied law, politics, and Greek. Upon his return he was so persuasive in his sermons that he is said to be chiefly responsible for the Pauline cult, which was to touch the very heart of domestic life. Such a man naturally had ideas and reforms to advocate, and with the courage of another Tyndale, he also urged the need of a vernacular Bible. More-over, he objected openly to relics, he suggested that the fall of man was biblical poetry, and in his will he asked that no masses be said for his soul. No wonder that Colet, when founding a school for boys, began a type of modern education and planned it for intelligent middle-class youths. Entrants, therefore, must be able to read and write Latin, and they must prove themselves capable of making progress according to the school's high standards.

Merchant Taylors' boys were naturally more mixed as to class than those of St. Paul's. Among its two hundred fifty boys were one hundred well-to-do free students who paid fees, one hundred who were poor, and fifty without petty school preparation, which they had to obtain at Merchant Taylors'. There were four masters, and here Mulcaster, as headmaster till 1586, had set his seal on the hearts of boys studying literature and good manners. The school was founded in 1561 to prepare its gifted students to enter St. John's College at Oxford to study divinity, for Merchant Taylors' Guild had founded this college in 1555.

By the end of the sixteenth century, each "corporate" town had a grammar school. For the boys of north Wales and northwest England as well as the children of the town there was the grammar school of Shrewsbury. This school was famous for its combination of town and Cambridge University government, perhaps set up to prevent the university's choosing and dismissing the teachers at will. Among the school's four hundred boys were sons of the nobility, the gentry, and the burgesses. Those of the gentry from near-by towns lived in the town, as did Philip Sidney. Classes were begun at 7:00 in the morning, were recessed at noon for an hour for dinner, and were dismissed at 5:30 in the afternoon. Though the boys engaged in none of the popular sports of today, they did take part in Latin and English plays that provided no little excitement and pleasure. Boys from prominent grammar schools frequently gave plays at court or in the Middle Temple Hall. On Candlemas night in 1574 and Shrove Tuesday of 1575, they played before the Queen at Hampton Court. In fact, boys from Shrewsbury, St. Paul's, and Westminster were still playing before the Queen by 1583. One reason these boys were so pleasing in their entertainments was that their school instruction included, besides Latin and Greek and Hebrew, daily lessons in music, singing, and the playing of musical instruments.

Many familiar names from the nobility occur among the donors to grammar schools, and among the middle class rich gifts were made for founding or assisting the schools of Rugby, Aldenham, Tonbridge, Tiverton, and Charterhouse School and Hospital by a brewer, a skinner, and a clothier. When the grammar school of Sutton Valens in Kent was founded, the stipulation was made that its poor children be educated "in fear of God, in good manners, and in knowledge and understanding," and the founder of Harrow insisted on the teaching of archery in addition to the usual subjects, though he believed the boys should supply their books, pens, ink, paper, bowshafts, and winter candles.

In general, secularization of the cathedral schools, in spite of the immediate evils resulting from the change, tended to make English schools more efficient. At Worcester, for example, the number of boys was increased from fifty-four to two hundred fifty-four, and the educators from eighteen to sixty-five. No limit was set on the town boys except in age, nine to fifteen years, though choristers with broken voices might be older. The headmaster's salary was £15/2 per year, and he was provided with liveries of cloth. When the school at Westminster Abbey was secularized, it came to rank with those of St. Paul's, Shrewsbury, and Merchant Taylors. Before the change it had been conducted by an abbot and twenty-four monks.

Mulcaster's suggestion of English in the grammar schools was never accepted. Latin was used even on the school ground, and Lyly's Latin grammar was studied by one generation after another for over two hundred years. At schools like Eton, Harrow, Westminster, and Shrewsbury, Greek was also taught, but works by Renaissance scholars were studied in all the schools side by side with those of classical authors. Such works were the *Colloquies* of Erasmus, the *Latin Language Exercises* of Vives—general favorites everywhere—Battista Spagnuoli's (Mantuan's) *Eclogues*, and Palingenius' very long *Zodiac of Life*. As a rule no modern language was taught, and no history as we know it today.[1]

One of the first problems parents had to solve about their children's schooling was when it should begin and what kind of instruction should be chosen. The conduct books advised them about this matter too. Most of these writers had read Elyot's translation of Plutarch's work on educating children and had absorbed a good deal of Elyot's own philosophy introduced with the work. Thus all of them stressed teaching a child to honor its parents, to reverence its betters, and to obey the laws of the state. An educated child, they agreed with Elyot, would naturally give place to those in authority, favor his friends, and when he had children of his own, treasure them, but love them with reason. He would also know the folly of being servile or of rejoicing too much in prosperity or of suffering too much in adversity. The weakness of active life was its lack of philosophy; education would teach how to unite the active life with the contemplative lest it lose its effectiveness and profit. Such ideas, of course, were reserved for the youths expected to become the leaders of their generation, but in a measure they were also fitted into the very heart of all teaching in which the classics predominated in the curriculum.

Some domestic books advised letting parents themselves decide when a child's formal education should begin, though they suggested that the age of four was usually best. Teaching at home in the ordinary man's family continued till the child was ready for grammar school or for learning a trade. Most of these parents, however, sent their small children to a dame's school, where they learned to read and perhaps to write. Since good grammar schools made heavy demands of their boys,

---

[1] Louis B. Wright, *Middle-Class Culture in Elizabethan England* (1935), pp. 47–59; and especially A. L. Rowse, *The England of Elizabeth* (1951), pp. 491–99.

men like Mulcaster believed parents should not send their children to these schools till they were sure the bodies had caught up with the minds. Nor must they delay till the bodies had outstripped the minds; that would be deplorable. But before the children began this part of their training, their parents must know their inclinations well enough to choose the right master or the right school for their offspring.

Bullinger, whose suggestions were so agreeable to Puritans, objected to any set age for beginning formal instruction, but believed that in most cases a child was ready for it between the ages of five and seven. Of course he stressed moral training in the study of the Bible, that a child might become discreet, learned, and godly. Much of this could be given during the writing lessons, he said, with hours devoted to both printing and writing moral precepts. He also advised the teaching of ciphering, with casting up accounts, adding, and subtraction. And he emphasized the learning of a trade. At the end of a school day, the child would return home expecting to serve his parents at table in a clean, mannerly way. After that he would be occupied with long lesson hours and short play hours lest he fall into ungodly idleness.

Batty (*The Christian mans Closet*, 1581) named as the most dangerous kind of idleness a child's indulgence in improper reading. Becon's *Catechisme* (1581) expressed the same opinion. The fear of light reading was very strong in Puritan homes, where the value of Ovid, Plautus, Terence, etc., even when expurgated, was questioned. Up to 1570, the average man's reading was chiefly romances, popular tales, jest books, riddles, ballads, treatises on health, almanacs, and conduct books. By 1590, the Puritans were making great changes in these reading habits, though their efforts were often defeated, too, by sanctimonious dedications and forewords which introduced works of a very ribald character. That strict measures were taken may have been due in part to the Puritan agreement with Becon's opinion that nothing could be more learned than the writing of the New Testament and the parables of Solomon.

Becon had also insisted that a child should hear psalms at school as well as at home, and prayers and biblical readings. He would even have church sermons correlated with school instruction. When a child was properly catechized about sermons he was compelled to attend, and answered well, he must be praised, but if not well, he must be rebuked gently and encouraged to do better. Some children actually took notes at these sermons, and many of their elders took mental notes for later discussion at home or among themselves. Becon would have a child kept at school till almost suppertime. This would require him to hurry home and not idle along the way. At table he might be asked to say grace or to read a chapter from the Bible. After supper, if he was able, he might take part in the discussion about a selection read from the Scriptures.

Some children were started to school without any previous training in reading and writing, for general schools taught beginners also. Mothers who could teach their young ones to read and write tried to find time for such instruction lest the children have to sit through the weary hours with little attention from the master's assistant. An alert mind might learn something from the recitations of older children, but most of the little children suffered through a long day.

When children were sent to school for the first day, the father usually tried to accompany them. As a rule he paid for the instruction according to the demands of the individual teacher or according to the per capita sum agreed upon in the community, which in turn paid the teacher. If the parent took his child to a school where he paid directly, he could choose the teacher he thought best. Sometimes the parents' desire to secure the "best" instruction led unscrupulous teachers to demand high sums to attract the unwary. The conduct books soon began warning their readers about such practices, and they also discussed advantages and disadvantages of public and private schools.

In principle and practice there was not much difference between the two except, as Mulcaster said, that the private were best limited to a number for a private end, and the public schools were best when the number was limited to what was best for the public service. In fact, gentlemen's private schools were not supposed to vary much from the public schools except in providing leisure to continue where the poor had to stop. Nevertheless, Vaughan (*The Golden Grove*) considered it a misfortune to be sent to a private school like Eton, Westminster, or Winchester, where board and tuition were high and where the child was so far removed from the home influence. If a child was too delicate or too susceptible to infectious diseases to attend a public school near home, he would have him taught at home. Indeed, he preferred home instruction, for there the teaching could be more diligent and the child could be given more attention than in a public school. He admitted, however, that most wise men preferred public schools because of the contacts provided there with other minds. Accordingly, he suggested as a compromise that a child attend a private school till he was thirteen and a public school for two or three years before entering the university.

When beginners started to school, they carried a hornbook attached to their girdle or swinging from a cord about their neck. This paddle-shaped piece of wood or metal had a hole in the handle for the cord, and if a child got into a squabble on his way to or from school, he might use the hornbook as a weapon of defense. The front of it was protected by a thin piece of transparent horn, bound round with brass, and completed by a long pin or quill called a fescue, which was used as a pointer. Fine hornbooks had the back of embossed or colored leather with the Queen's picture.

In the sixteenth century the sheet of instruction under the horn was no longer vellum, as in the old days, but paper. On it was a large cross, followed by the first line of the alphabet; this was called the crisscross

The family at church, from *Chronicles*, by Raphael Holinshed, 1578

row or cross row or Christ row. The alphabet was first in large and then in small letters, and sometimes in both black letter and roman type. It was followed by another cross. The next line was composed of vowels and their combinations with consonants to form short syllables, although sometimes the syllables were tabulated. Usually a benediction or the exorcism "In the name of the Father and of the Son and of the Holy Ghost, Amen" followed the syllables. Then came the Lord's Prayer, and finally the Roman numerals. Such was the child's first primer, and if he came from a humble home which was purchasing a hornbook for its first child, he might have watched his mother buy it for threepence from a chapman, who also sold almanacs, books of news, ballads, etc., to those he called on. The child might also have watched his mother examine several hornbooks, hesitating whether to get one with just the first page or also the second, on which were sentences of one syllable—"Ah, it is so; he is my foe." Usually the hornbook was light and easy for childish fingers to hold.

If the child had been instructed at home before starting to school, he might have learned a simple Accidence at a very early age. The teaching would consist of learning to read the alphabet and the syllables and simple sentences of words with one syllable, as "Boy, go thy way to the top of the hill where the big tree is." If his parents had tried to give him the instruction of the beginners' form, they would have taught him the rules of pronunciation with such words as "mill, mile, bid, bide," etc., and a little grammar. The school method taught grammar by means of dialogue, and parents might use this form in home teaching. They might also teach him some very simple rules of numbers, and how to write and commit to memory some simple texts. At school, beginners were taught their catechism by means of metrical psalms learned by heart from a book with a glossary of hard words and a specimen of black letter. If a child had been taught all these things at home, as often occurred in the middle-class family, he would be ready to start in the first class of the lower form in the public school.

In this form, beginning instruction in grammar was intimately related to the child's reading and to the idea of training or disciplining the young mind. If girls were sent to grammar school, they were seldom expected to finish the school's work before being placed under their mothers for instruction in housewifery. If they attended inferior schools in which writing and arithmetic were not taught, their formal education was indeed slight. Robert Recorde's arithmetic book of 1558 seems to have been the first of its kind printed in English; it was used in different editions for over a hundred years. It made use of the dialogue form with questions and answers and included moral instruction in the explanation of its problems. For writing, Beau Chesney's book of 1570 was used, the children copying texts from it as writing exercises.

Among the five schools of London, social distinctions manifested themselves early. Eton, partly because it was founded by royalty and partly because it was attended by rich men's sons, became very fashionable. St. Paul's was noted for its fine instruction in Latin and Greek, suitable for the brilliant mind. Its first headmaster was William Lyly, Latin scholar and grammarian, whose Latin text was popular for so long. Merchant Taylors', Westminster, and Winchester appealed to parents, especially of the middle class, who wished their sons to make a solid place for themselves in the world. Schools planned for boys who could not return home at night but must "board out" in the town were distinguished from the day schools by being called colleges. Only about a dozen boys could board at the ordinary school. Winchester, with its warden and schoolmaster, its fellows and officers, its chaplains and bursars, its clerks and sacristan, its usher and singing master, was in most respects typical of the "college." It had its "quiristers," children from poor families who must make the fellows' beds and wait on the students in the hall. The senior boys disciplined the younger ones, and the servants for household matters were similar to those in any large home.

At most boarding schools the religious training was even more important than the instruction in Latin or Greek. For some parents this was very reassuring. Prayers were said every morning and evening, and on Sundays the boys were required to attend the regular services and to take notes in shorthand on the sermons. They were carefully taught the catechism and examined in it every week, or oftener. At Winchester, after the boys were in bed at night, a chapter from the Bible was read aloud in every chamber. At Westminster, the dean sometimes kept the advanced boys up till eleven o'clock teaching them Greek or Hebrew. Yet all had to be up early the next morning for lessons that began regularly at six o'clock and lasted till 5:30 in the afternoon, though at nine o'clock they might have fifteen minutes for breakfast and at noon they all took two hours for dinner. They had half-holidays on Thursdays, holy days, and special days.

Whether the boy was educated at home or at day school or at boarding school, he must become proficient in Latin if he was to take his place in the society of educated people who used it for all formal occasions. The increase in foreign trade necessitated the mastery of modern foreign languages by those whose careers would bring them in close contact with foreigners, but few grammar school boys in England were taught any language besides Latin. Those who studied foreign languages did so chiefly as a matter of discipline. It was foreigners in England who took the initiative by trying to speak English, and later by teaching their languages to English boys. At first, the English were amused by the foreign accents of these people, and when dramatists reported the laughable awkwardness of their speech, they were trying to be merrily realistic. Pure Latin, free from what the Renaissance mind termed "medieval corruption," was insisted on in all good schools. English boys, if they did not study the plays of Terence and the Epistles of Cicero thoroughly, were at least drilled in phrases from these authors, that they might use them in their conversation, and they were made familiar with such letters as Cicero wrote to his wife, and to his servant Tiro.[2]

When foreigners became teachers of boys who must speak foreign tongues correctly, they followed the dialogue form introduced by Vives to teach Latin easily and "merrily." In fact, some English teachers taught Latin by dialogues which they wrote for their boys according to the Vives type. By this method the boys started at once reading interesting material they were required to pronounce correctly, and then learned the rules of grammar illustrated by the dialogues. The pattern of material consisted chiefly of chit-chat about getting up in the morning, dining (usually at dinner), buying and selling, arriving at an inn, and sometimes "wise sentences" from catechisms on good manners and morals. Always the details illustrated commonly known material out of the boys' daily living or from old books as familiar as nursery rhymes. Some of it dealt with serving a meal as in medieval times or with manners expected from dutiful children in the "good old days."

Hollyband and Florio were very popular for their language-dialogue lessons for boys. Hollyband's *French Schoolemaister* (1573) and *The French Littleton* (1576) were designed for young middle-class boys, and Florio's *First Fruits* and *Second Fruits* were designed for aristocratic young men. As in the Vives dialogues, Hollyband has the child in *The French Schoolemaister* rise in the morning and figure in scenes that deal with the wayside, a tavern, and serving a meal; in *The French Littleton*, Hollyband shows a man taking his son to school, discussing the school fees of a shilling a week, and entering the child as a pupil. The boy comes in contact with the schoolground peccadilloes and learns "wise sayings" and proverbs. Incidentally, Hollyband also introduces many actual details of Elizabethan home and school life. So much did he admire the Vives method of dialogue instruction that he even translated these dialogues into French and English and arranged them side by side with the Vives Latin. He brought this text out in 1583 as *Campo di Fior*. Florio's books were more literary than Hollyband's, though he too used the early morning rising scene, meals, and games.

Boys left home to start school usually at the age of six or seven and continued their studies for about seven years before they were ready for the university. Much of the work was designed to cultivate the memory by means of writing compositions suggested by quotations, by analysis of sentences for their rhetorical elements, and by reading from Latin authors who supplied suitable material for conversing in Latin and for

---

[2] George Arthur Plimpton, *The Education of Shakespeare* (1933), and David Brown, *What Shakespeare Learned at School* (1940).

recitations at all hours of the day. The reading selections were made for their moral teaching and for their qualities of rationalizing. As the work advanced, analysis became quite strenuous. Taxing the memory to retain by rote long speeches or sermons was universally observed as one of the most important pedagogic devices for sharpening the wits and for serving as a foundation for analysis. As soon as a boy was out of the beginners' class he began to feel the pressure of the mental discipline. Sometimes the strain during grammar school training caused a mental breakdown. Such a severe course of study was more likely to occur in the home, however, than out of it, and once the race for distinction began, parents as well as children became the victims.

Whether boys went away to grammar school or not, they found themselves in a group taught by a master or a master and usher, according to the size and needs of the school. If the master had a helper, he himself was on duty only from 7:00 to 10:00 in the morning and from 1:00 to 4:30 in the afternoon. His usher was in the schoolroom all day, however, from 6:00 to 11:00 and 1:00 to 5:00. In larger schools, there might be several teachers, variously assigned; hence the term of headmaster to distinguish him from assistants. Sometimes the master and usher achieved a certain privacy for their classes by arranging them so that a curtain could separate the forms, the usher teaching the lower forms and the master the upper ones. There were usually five forms, though there might be eight. In a way the schools had an organized curriculum that was "standardized" into essential uniformity by the middle of the sixteenth century, and the same material was covered, whether there were five or eight forms. This was due to the fact that schoolmasters themselves had pretty much the same education. Daily attendance was carefully noted, often by "prepositors" who reported morning and afternoon to the master.

The usher had to give a good deal of individual instruction before the beginners were ready for the first lower form. Since most boys, however, usually entered school with training that prepared them to read and write, the usher began their teaching by proceeding directly to the Accidence, with its short introduction to the declensions and conjugations of grammar. As the boys were drilled in grammar, they learned a vocabulary by way of illustrative words for drill, and they were taught not to parrot the teacher but to speak well in modulated voices of their own. Now that very detailed studies of certain Elizabethan grammar schools are available,[3] this account is concerned with no more than a general picture of the school's activities. For if the child was taught at home, his tutors more or less approximated the work of public schools.

For all forms there was almost constant review, the Elizabethans

[3] T. W. Baldwin, *William Shakespeare's Small Latine & Lesse Greek* (1944), I and II.

believing that one must be sure of foundational knowledge before passing on to the new. Thus Friday and Saturday afternoons were usually set aside for recital of what the boys had learned in the other four days of the week through lectures, speeches by other boys, their own compositions and daily memorizing, and the explanations by teacher or boys from the upper forms.

The usual method of instruction began with the master's reading from a text or merely improvising material of his own, then explaining carefully any points that might be obscure. If a text was used, the boys in studying must memorize all the details connected with grammatical drill, note important precepts and wise sentences, and in following the presentation of the subject, be prepared to recite its points in their own order of arrangement. They must be able to construe every word and passage, with particular attention paid to the hard ones they or the teacher would discover, parse all the words as they construed, giving rules and examples, and finally, know the etymology and syntax of all the words.

When the boys wrote their compositions, they imitated the rhetorical examples they were studying, and then proceeded to inventions of their own. A great deal of preparation was necessary before they could undertake this work. Their first extended composition was usually an epistle, copied, probably, from Erasmus' *Epistolae*. Then would follow a type of composition consisting of wise sentences, etc., learned by heart or jotted down in their notebooks from reading assignments. These they would string together in the best order they were capable of, but the first quotation of their exercise was expected to give the beads on the string some sort of unity and coherence. As they improved in this type of writing, they were required to illustrate by examples the most significant quotations they used and always to end with a conclusion that, if they were clever enough, would give a climactic touch.

The method as thus developed became a sort of art achieved by imitation and exercise. Grammar was always the first point of interest, rhetoric the second, and there must be enough logic to justify the whole. At first the boys wrote in prose, but later they turned prose themes into verse, and if they were able, they turned verse into oratorical composition, for oral expression was the crowning achievement. If the boys had made good progress, they might be rewarded by the opportunity of putting on a play at Christmas or Easter or Shrove Tuesday, for by acting they were expected to learn better how to speak with expression of voice and gesture, how to modulate their voices, and how to use their whole bodies with grace and eloquence.

This method of teaching kept to prose in the boys' compositions in the lower forms. It began with the usual colloquies and "vulgars," or English translations, the boys memorizing the grammar and learning to speak and compose correctly. In their reading they were introduced to Cicero and Virgil especially, and sometimes Terence, Cato's and Aesop's moral precepts, and Erasmus' *Apothegms*. From easy selections in Cicero's letters, they advanced to Virgil's *Eclogues*, then to Cicero's *Amicitia* and *De Senectute* and Virgil's *Aeneid*. From the study of different types of verse, they proceeded to a carefully expurgated Catullus and selections from Tibullus and Horace. Meanwhile, they were drilled in various kinds of compositional exercises, dealing with subjects found in their reading and elaborated by their growing vocabulary and poetic figures and *sententiae* collected in their notebooks. Now, with most of their grammatical study completed, they were ready for a study of prosody and perhaps a serious study of music. All this time they memorized precepts from the Sunday sermons, which they listened to as carefully as any of their assigned schoolwork, for they expected to be examined on the sermons, and to be catechized regularly.

In the upper forms the boys usually began the study of versification and poetry, though prose must balance the poetry. They usually started with Ovid's *De Tristibus* and epigrams from Martial, Catullus, and even Sir Thomas More. In *De Tristibus* they memorized, construed, parsed, picked out figures and tropes, and applied verse rules in detail. They followed the same procedure as they went on to Ovid's *Metamorphoses*, adding to their analysis such story details as proper names and mythological matter. Various kinds of versification would now be introduced from Horace, Juvenal, Persius, etc. In this study, music was not neglected, but history was also added that its moral material might be used in compositions. History and orations were thus woven into all their reading, for the boys must learn how to dispute *ex tempore* on any ordinary moral questions presented to them.

The Bible, of course, was now a very important part of the school program, especially when the boy had mastered his Greek grammar well enough to read Greek. All along he had been turning much of the English biblical translations into Latin, the most popular for this purpose being Proverbs, Ecclesiastes, the Wisdom of Solomon, Psalms, the Gospels, and Paul's Epistles. Often these translations were versified, especially in the case of Psalms. The Bishops Bible, with its Apocrypha, was the text used for this purpose.

Gradually the boys' compositions took on rhetorical polish as they memorized trope schemes to use in their writing and enlarged their compositions by methods of "varifying" according to the rules in Cicero's *Topica* and Erasmus' *Copia*. These rules taught the use of synonyms, paraphrasing, various tricks of turning verse skillfully into prose and prose into verse, and gave advice concerning translating into Greek and Latin. Most important of all, however, from the Elizabethan point of view, were rules for emulating the most copious classical authors.

While studying Greek, the boys continued with Cicero and Virgil. Now their notebooks would be full of precepts and examples of fine oratory and fine writing taken from Cicero's *De Officiis*, *De Oratore*, *Elo-*

cutio, *Inventio*, and *Partitiones*. From Virgil's *Aeneid*, at least the first six books, they would learn what imitation could do: as Virgil had imitated Homer, so might some of them imitate the great classics! Other reading in the upper forms included Caesar, Sallust, and Livy; Plato's *Dialogues*, Aristotle's criticism and dialectic, and excerpts from theologians, and philosophers.

If Ovid was read, which was unlikely in Puritanical schools, he was ranked next to Virgil for his technical range. If his *Heroides* were studied, these verse epistles took the place of studying Horace, but in religious schools Paul's Epistles supplanted the works of both Ovid and Horace. As a rule Greek and Hebrew were taught to enable special students to read the Scriptures in the "original," but only serious scholars could add these studies to their program. While learning Greek, the boys used Latin grammars and English translations with carefully indexed vocabularies for each word to prevent their making any errors when they translated the holy text. Only conscientious students would profit from such a method of study. Most boys were supposed to be drilled in the Bible till it became common knowledge among them. However, though it was still the commonest and most discussed book of the late years in the Queen's reign, it was not read ardently in the schools except, possibly, by Puritan children; by this time many of its religious ideas had become merely conventional subject matter for the Elizabethan intelligentsia.

Latin for conversation was taught in the upper forms, and boys who were to learn this means of communication began early to acquire the necessary vocabulary. There were many colloquies representing boys' conversations in nearly all phases of life. Besides Erasmus, whose dialogues were in constant use, partly because of their literary qualities, there were Vives, a master of easy dialogue, Gallus, the Roman elegiac poet, and Castalio, to name a few of the authors acceptable to teachers. Castalio, who was especially famous for his Latin and French translations of the Bible, had his place in the religious homes and schools. Books like Udall's *Floures*, written in impeccable Latin, supplied the boys with many expressions to ease their use of the language in their speech and writing. But Erasmus, with his use of witty and useful information and his quips and puns and keen eye for life itself, was read in practically every grammar school and home school in England.

Since Elizabethan grammar schools provided the only formal literary training in the country's school system, boys attending them were about as well informed in the classics as university graduates. The universities themselves were professional schools. Boys from good grammar schools could pass on to university training in logic and rhetoric. Those who could not complete the grammar school work but could go only as far as the upper forms at least learned grammar and grammatical Latin, but those who completed the work of the upper forms learned poetics besides rhetoric and logic. In both lower and upper forms, moreover, the boys came in contact with great classic writers, and in taking part in plays, they became acquainted with still more of them. But first, last, and always, Elizabethan schools were planned to teach morals and to emphasize the importance of analysis of the old in order to create something new out of it by the process of imitative adaptation.

Whether public or private, the grammar schools were closely integrated with university ideals of education, and the same relationship was sought in training boys by tutors in the home. Many of the teachers in all three situations were university men who achieved a certain uniformity in English schools because they based their course of study on the old system involving the trivium (grammar, logic, rhetoric) and the quadrivium (arithmetic, geometry, music, and astronomy). Such a teacher, with his Master's degree from Cambridge in 1586, wrote a book on how a child should be prepared for entering the university at the age of fifteen years. This strict Puritan, John Brinsley, sought to make his work (*Grammar Schoole*) pleasurable, however, and cast it in the form of a dialogue between two teachers.

Brinsley would have a child's education begin at five years lest he learn hurtful things, like play, that might interfere with his schooling or prolong his grammar school years. Started early, he would form good habits of orderly industry. In the first year he would be taught to pronounce every letter plainly, fully, and distinctly, memorizing the alphabet forward and backward, and learning the letters well enough to pick them out at random. Next, the child would be drilled in spelling syllables, first of two letters and then of more, repeating again and again those he misspelled, and taking great care to pronounce them right. For reading, he would use the Primer, to be read through twice. At the same time he would learn psalms in meter to make the task pleasant and easy, and verses from the New Testament, *The School of Virtue*, and other manuals of good manners.[4]

Evidently this teacher had struggled with youngsters slow in writing and arithmetic, and he had strong feelings about what to do with them. If the child did not learn to read numbers readily, both the Roman and Arabic, he would have him sent to a ciphering school. In order that he might learn to write well, he would have to make his own pens; there was no need, said Brinsley, for the careless writing of children in his time. He would agree that all children should have penknives that they might keep their quills sharp and clean. Fine writing and how to teach it was the subject of more than one Elizabethan treatise.

Because children did not study any language besides Latin in the

---

[4] Plimpton (*The Education of Shakespeare*) says this teacher may have instructed William Shakespeare.

schools, parents complained that their children forgot their own tongue. Brinsley, therefore, would have the child learn to use his own language correctly by daily translating Lyly's Latin rules into English. In addition to this he would have daily practice in translating familiar letters to friends, of reading fables in English, and of taking notes in English on sermons every child must attend. Biblical history in the English translation of the Bible should also be studied to help ground the child in English speech. However, this history would need to be supplemented by "teaching in all grounds of religion," by sermons on substance, doctrine, proofs, and uses—all of these to be rehearsed at school in English.

The general stress on Latin rather than English in the schools had caused Sir Humphrey Gilbert, the explorer, to propose a plan for a good practical school which he called an academy. His plan was worked out in 1564 when any opposition to the classical ideal was hopeless. Sir Humphrey outlines a careful study of English at his school, with practice given in making orations in English, learning choice English words and figures of speech and oratorical beauties, and in building good sentences. He would have English learned like the speaking and writing of ancient and modern languages of French, Spanish, Italian, and German, with the same devices for acquiring correctness in pronunciation and use. Of course his academy would have lectures given on civil policy, peace and war, and the importance of the commonwealth, but especially in mathematics dealing with fortification, cosmography, and astronomy. Boys at his school would be taught shooting, riding, marching, navigation, and the elements of medicine and surgery. There would be a school library, and to it every publisher would be required to send a copy of every book he had printed. All in all, his school would prepare boys for the kind of active life Sir Humphrey believed in, and not a carefully integrated program of languages and ideas to be adopted from the ancients.

Brinsley's interest in the moral side of teaching, which Sir Humphrey Gilbert is not concerned with, far overshadowed the rest of this Puritan's argument. He would have even the little children in the lowest forms at school taught to answer questions on sermons. Every Saturday, for half an hour or more, he would have the child work at his catechism, with the teacher or parent to help him understand all the words. As soon as children could take notes on sermons or take down the very words in shorthand, Brinsley would have monitors see that the boys were diligently setting down the text and every point of doctrine. Those in the highest forms would outline the Sunday sermons and translate them into good Latin or read an *ex tempore* Latin version of them.

To such religious training, he would add prayers for every morning and evening and every day and night, prayers of thanksgiving, to be supplemented by reading from M. Paget's *History of the Bible.* He believed that religion would not only care for their souls but also teach them as good manners as would the works of Cato, Cicero, *The School of Virtue*, or *The School of Good Manners*, all of which were approved by good parents.

Elizabethan teachers were quite free and often quite human in expressing their ideas about methods and subject matter to be used in the schools. Besides the works of such well-known writers as Elyot and Ascham we have those of Florio, the learned grammarian and professional translator and resident professor of Southampton. In a moment of irritation he expressed himself in a way that would have delighted Montaigne whom he admired so much, saying he would like to "cut off the heads" of parents who let their children be badly educated.

In small towns the schoolmaster's lodgings were in the simple thatched school where he taught. The building was usually on land adjoining the chapel, and statutes concerning the school were read in church from time to time, especially in regard to holidays at Easter and Christmas. The teacher of such a school had to be thirty years of age as a rule, and unmarried and approved by the clergy. Besides his stipulated salary, he might receive small admission fees from the children and penny payments from them at Christmas. His annual vacation was seldom over a month in length, and he had to give notice in the church six months before leaving his post. He was also notified some time in advance if he was required to leave. When he was away on vacation, the children were not supposed to be idle; instead, they were expected to "exercise in their books" at home.

Possibly the rather frequent half-holidays on Thursdays and Saturdays made such a strenuous program bearable. As far as the schoolmaster was concerned, his full authority over the children (when the school's overseers did not think him unreasonable in the use of his powers) may have been sufficient reward in itself for so exacting a profession. If he was seriously bent on improving young minds, he had ample opportunity to do so, but if he enjoyed the authority he exercised, particularly in matters of discipline, he might play the tyrant. As towns and villages were the center for the surrounding country life, their schools were important to aspiring parents. Poor roads made communication between villages difficult, and often in small villages one person served as schoolmaster and church official, teaching the children chiefly catechism. For this reason many yeoman could not read or write, nor could their wives and daughters. If the men were not able to sign legal documents, they might have to make their "mark." In such a locality, therefore, the teacher was not in the same category at all with the schoolmasters who were carefully chosen for the town school.

The Elizabethan village, however, might be prosperous enough to afford a fair teacher, especially if it had a thriving yeoman. The "husbandman" farmed less than a hundred acres, but the yeoman a hundred or more. When he became prosperous, he ate yeoman's bread made of wheat, and with the profits from his land he might buy his way into the gentry. Should this occur and he find himself handicapped by his lack of education, he would try to prevent his heir from suffering any like disadvantage. If, then, he did not wish to send his son away to grammar school, he might try to secure a teacher for his village.

He might also plan to make his son the squire or rector or vicar or curate of his village. Sometimes villages were visited by ecclesiastics when a crisis occurred there, and such an official might impress a yeoman enough to wish a son of his to fill such a position in the church. Were not all the villagers compelled to attend a parish church on specified days, to be married in the parish church, to have children and wife baptized in the church, and to receive communion there? All families must contribute to the maintenance of the church and churchyard, and to the purchase of ornaments and utensils used in the services. The yeomen might make his gifts so "handsome" as to gain a good "living" for a son thereby. But first he would have to send him up to the university to be educated for the church.

Still, educating and dowering his children were expensive. He must acquire more than the dozen milk cows and five or six work horses, besides sheep and smaller stock, owned by the average man in his class. True, such a man might have £500 or more in sheep alone, but he must be better off than the seventy or eighty thousand yeomen who, with such possessions, were themselves content to serve as mere church warden or give gratis their services as constable. Though he might wear homely russet, he would be a shrewd farmer, making shrewd deals in buying and selling land. As a yeoman he could not legally own over 500 acres, but he would make those acres yield enough to make him a gentleman. Then, indeed, he might have servants like any gentleman, dress in fine clothes and play the lavish host on Christmas and other holidays, send his sons to the university or Inns of Court, and marry his daughters well. But to be *this* shrewd in business he had to be a better farmer than most yeomen, and he must know how to read and write, for he must read books on animal husbandry as well as learn by the slow process of experience, and perhaps he might have to read enough about the law to manage his own affairs without paying out his profits on expensive fees. So this yeoman might dream his dreams, and he *might* set the feet of his educated sons on the same road as that traveled by the gentry.

It was the yeoman, perhaps, who by his choice of teachers often caused the small town schools to follow as much as possible the same program as that in the London schools, making whatever modifications were needed by their communities or required by the father's ideas about the needs of the family. The differences in Elizabethan schools were very slight in comparison with the similarity of details in their organization and management, for they made their main effort the combined teaching of good authors of Roman eloquence and wisdom with Christian wisdom

in "clean, chaste Latin, either in verse or prose." And always their purpose was to increase knowledge for advancement in worldly life and to
insist upon worship of God and Christian living with its emphasis upon
good morals and good manners.

Part of this emphasis may have been due to the sudden increase in
foreign travel and the consequent interchange of ideas and customs; part
of it may have resulted from the competitive spirit under the stimulus
of a growing nationalism that *must* somehow be reconciled with the principles of Christianity. For example, when George Pettie made his translation of Guazzo's *The Civil Conversation* in 1581, he blamed English
travelers for not practicing abroad the good manners learned at home,
and he objected to their giving foreigners the wrong impression of English people. He complained of the English when in Paris so foolishly
aping Parisian manners as to make their conduct ridiculous, "yea, bar-
barous." He was particularly disturbed by their behavior because "at
home it is well known that we live in laws as orderly, in manners as decently, in apparel as comely, in diet as delicately, in lodging as curiously
and sumptuously, in all things as abundantly, and every way as civilly,
as any nation under heaven."

The stress on proper speech as vitally connected with conduct was
not new, for monastic education had used this emphasis in the pattern
for training its pupils. In monastic schools the youths, mostly sons of
gentlemen, had been taught riding and jousting, courtesy in words, deeds,
and degrees, and the graces of harping, piping, singing, dancing, and
table etiquette.[5] Their masters had sat at table with them to see that they
ate and drank properly and conversed according to the rules in a book
such as *Urbanity*. This program was followed, with additions, in the time
of Henry VIII, for though he as king might in his careless old age violate all rules of etiquette at table or elsewhere, he believed in strict
decorum for others. Among the nobility, especially those recently elevated to rank, the old ways of chivalry were cherished, and its decorum
little changed. Thus the chivalric ideal profoundly affected the education of the upper classes even in the time of Queen Elizabeth. This may
be seen at a glance if one compares the education of two nobles, one in
Henry's reign and the other in the reign of his daughter.

In the time of Henry VIII the son of the Earl of Essex studied
French, writing, fencing, casting accounts, instrumental music, etc. He
was also required to read English aloud for correct pronunciation and
was taught the etymology of Latin and French words. After mass in
the morning, he read from Erasmus' *De Civilitate Morum Puerilium*
that he might learn to practice its precepts of conduct. Then he wrote
for an hour or two and read from Fabyan's *Chronicles*, which gave "a

[5] Edith Rickert (ed.), Introduction to *The Babees Book: Medieval Manners for
the Young*, from the texts of Frederick J. Furnivall (1923), p. xxiv.

lively history" of England from its beginning to 1485 and the battle of Bosworth Field. The rest of the day he devoted to the lute and the virginals and riding. But while riding he was required to listen to his masters tell stories of Greeks and Romans, which he had to repeat to them. When he did have time for recreation, he engaged in hunting, hawking, and shooting with the longbow.

His descendant Robert in the Devereux line, who was to become Elizabeth's favorite, was educated at Burghley's house with other wards of the Crown. Among these wards was the youth, later the Earl of Oxford, who was to be the Queen's favorite for a brief time. The program Oxford followed in his education under Burghley was representative of the care with which nobles destined for important duties were trained in the early part of Elizabeth's reign. At 7:00 he was ready for breakfast, though it was popular for most Elizabethans not engaged in strenuous labor to omit this meal. From 8:00 to 9:00 he studied Latin, and in the next hour he had dancing lessons and exercise in walking. At 10:00 he occupied himself with writing and drawing, reading the Gospel, especially Paul's Epistles, and at 11:00 he had dinner. In the afternoon he studied cosmography from 1:00 to 2:00, French from 2:00 till 3:00, and then Latin for another hour or two. Between then and supper, which came at 6:00, he spent the time in walking, writing, and prayers; after supper he was free for "honest" recreation. Burghley's son Robert, whom he trained to follow in his footsteps, was given pretty much the same education though his exercise, because of his curved spine, had to be adapted to his infirmity.

Most of the walking done by Burghley's wards was in the extensive gardens of the Secretary's estate, though on unpleasant days they could find ample room in the great gallery for this exercise. At all times the youths' tutors would take advantage of every opportunity to teach proper conduct, though the Erasmus *Civilitate* was by this time the text of boys in the great middle class rather than in the nobility. However, Burghley's instructors would not hesitate to use Erasmus when needed, for they all would know his treatise by heart. The boys, then, would learn courteous speech and the lesson of being affable to all, especially their inferiors, and they would be told to enter only just quarrels, to be merciful and forgiving to friends and servants, to stretch their purses to give liberally to the needy, and not to be too much concerned over what the common people might say of them. Like most Elizabethans, Burghley believed that although the extent of "youthful fooleries" was infinite, they could be rooted out by due correction and diligent exhortation; he also accepted the general belief in the importance of environment: that only by being well nurtured (educated) would a gentleman realize the full extent of his powers or learn how to conquer his unlawful affections.

Burghley's training was admirably adapted to harmonize the teaching of upper- and middle-class ideals, for he was close enough to the latter's concern about moral teaching to cherish its values, and he was shrewd enough to see the necessity for training in conduct that would adhere to the mores of the group in which the upper-class individual was bound by inheritance and the accidents of life. This wisdom, his position at court, and particularly his conscientious, even punctilious, care made Burghley trusted by Queen and nobles as unmatched in his training of wards. Not even his worst enemies could doubt he gave his wards the same care as his own children.

The most notable change in this program of education during the Queen's reign was the greater formality practiced as time went on. Eventually, her wards went to church at 6:00 in the morning, studied Latin afterward till 11:00, dined from 11:00 to 12:00, had music from 12:00 till 2:00, French from 2:00 till 3:00, and Latin till 5:00. Then came prayers and supper, after which they might indulge in "honest" recreation till 8:00. Finally, there was an hour of music before they retired for the night. Latin was at the heart of the day's study, and prayers and music had a set place in the day's planned activities. Latin included disputation, which was used in all the grammar school forms, not only to sharpen the students' wits but to further their knowledge of language. Here, too, disputation was constantly practiced, but noble youths must learn how to carry on an argument in *pure* Latin and with a wide vocabulary without any chance at preparation beforehand. The Quintilian ideal, so admirably adapted to Christian morals, had been pretty universally adopted, at least conventionally, by the upper classes in training for oratory. Quintilian had insisted that without oratory no man could be a good citizen; therefore noble youths should be trained to bring to their treatment of human affairs minds eminent in natural endowments and these better than in men of any previous age, perfect in every respect, but most important of all, "thinking the best thoughts and expressing them in the best language."[6]

Gifted sons of wealthy men were given an education somewhat approximating that of nobles if these sons intended to prepare for important careers. Their highest ambition, of course, was to be trained to serve the Queen brilliantly in peace and war. For all classes, however, there were certain general theories just as there are today. Individuals must be studied by parents and teachers in order to discover the strength of individual capacity; the rod must be used only in moderation and only when necessary, though Puritans were inclined to use it frequently under the impression that slow progress was due to original sin and must therefore be castigated; correct apparel must be taught, for one should dress according to rank and good taste, which in itself required much instruc-

---

[6] Quintilian's *Oratorical Education* was very popular among teachers of this period. His beliefs in the need of training the memory and of a system of competition and rewards were often discussed, and favorably, but his belief in play as a means of education had to wait till practically the present century for adoption.

tion; and when possible, travel was encouraged even for boys expecting to go no higher than the crafts, that they might learn new developments. For the privileged, travel was urged for recreation as well as for further training in statesmanship, though most parents demurred at the idea of sending their sons from home to seek recreation. Then as now, theories were hedged around with many objections by the practical minds.

The desire for more and more of the privileges of the upper class and the hope of achieving them through education can be better understood if one remembers what William Vaughan said on the matter in *The Golden Grove* in 1599. A gentleman, he writes, could not be challenged by an inferior man to combat or to appear in the lists; he would be preferred in the Commonwealth to bear office, to sit in commissions, and to arbitrate between parties; his testimony would sooner be approved than that of the common man, and he might absent himself from criminal cases if he provided a substitute; he was to be judged by his peers if he committed a heinous offense and, if found guilty, was to be beheaded instead of hanged like a common man; and finally, he and his wife might wear cloth of gold.

By Vaughan's time writing as a tool for advancement had a significance no one would have dreamed of attaching to it when Elizabeth ascended the throne. Now it was taken for granted that children in respectable homes would learn writing before they even started to school, and one reason for the assumption was that paper was no longer dear. In 1585, a half ream of paper and a half pound of sealing wax had cost two shillings. But a German immigrant by the name of John Spilman had set up a paper mill in England and was manufacturing white paper, which was far better for writing than the coarse brown paper still being made in England. Now writing became a fad, and housewives began making their own ink. Eightpence would buy two ounces of gum, two of copperas, and four of gall, which they made into ink that the whole household might use. When James I came to the throne, he knighted Spilman for his service to the realm in setting up a mill that put white writing paper into so many homes.

The interest in writing had been growing for some time, however. In 1570 a book was published in London on penmanship, its subject matter derived from a French book with thirty-seven styles of writing. Almost immediately the schools found the teaching of writing made easier by the new emphasis on composing letters. In 1576, Abraham Fleming's examples of letters from classical sources on all sorts of subjects provided as much instruction in moral conduct as letter writing. Consequently, his *Panoply of Letters* was very popular. About a decade later came Angel Day's *The English Secretary*, which discussed tone in writing, methods of argumentation, and rhetorical figures. But the sober common people probably preferred Nicholas Breton's *A Post with a Mad Packet of Letters* (1602) to anything yet prepared for beginners in the

Above: Instruction in the home

Left: Boys at school

fine art of writing, for with moral instruction, he combined many comments on industry, thrift, and sobriety. Meanwhile, there were countless other books for the eager public wishing to write or to teach their children how to write. There were books of proverbs, similes, precepts, and interesting bits of biographical material to use for examples of parents' own inherited store of wise sentences. Many of these books might well serve as school texts.

In homes where parents wished to teach more than reading and writing, they could find help in the new histories and geographies sold now at "reasonable" prices. Those who could not afford to travel but wished to be well informed also bought these books. Possibly the most helpful book for middle-class parents was Coote's *The English Schoolmaster* (1598). It contained instruction on reading, spelling, grammar, arithmetic, the catechism, and moral precepts, and was much in demand for over a hundred years. Its point of view was that of parents in the rapidly developing class of trade, and it emphasized the moral principles they constantly preached in the home: serving God, obeying parents, and showing courtesy to all men. If parents could teach their children something about the arts and crafts, they might supplement their practical training with books. In spite of the many aids in bookstalls, however, most parents found it necessary to let the schools give formal instruction to their children, and they supported the teacher's efforts by moral training at all hours of the day.

The value of music in the school curriculum, both at home and in the public school, was urged by most writers. Their reasons were gravely heard because of the feeling that original sin had closed the ear to heavenly harmonies and education might possibly correct the deficiency. In 1585, William Byrd of the Chapel Royal published a treatise on why all people should learn to sing, though from the time of Henry VIII and even before, England had been noted for her sweet singers. A good pupil and a good scholar "enabled singing to be learned quickly and easily," he said, and was a delightful exercise that aided in preserving health. It helped to open the "pipes" and to strengthen the breast; it was a good remedy for stuttering and stammering; and it was the best means of procuring a perfect pronunciation and of making a good orator. Though the gift of a good voice was so rare only one in a thousand had it, the only way of knowing whether nature had bestowed this gift was by singing. He felt no music was comparable to that made by the voices of men when they were good singers and their voices "well sorted and ordered." The better the voice, he concluded, "the meeter to honor and serve God," and the more necessary that it be employed to that end. That so many men were carefully trained in music when they were being prepared for state service, however, was probably due to the belief that music was a powerful aid for developing their oratorical powers. This treatise may well be another example of how the educational program made its strenuous effort at reconciling moral principles in the State religion with practical training in State service.

Though in music and dancing the English were never so light and airy as the French, they were recognized for a while as superior in church music, and very fine in the descant. The Reformation, however, almost killed English church music, its place being taken over largely by psalm singing. In the last forty years of Elizabeth's reign, over ninety editions of metrical psalms were produced with music. Fortunately, at this time secular music developed also, and in this field England, in some respects, surpassed even Continental composers. Most of these talented men were among household companies of musicians or were sponsored in their artistic work by nobles. Their madrigals and instrumental pieces for virginals and particularly lutes were often very fine. Thus, in spite of the psalm singing, love of good music did not die out in England or in English homes. Some parents, no doubt, hoped their sons who were gifted in music might find a career at court, especially if they had fine singing voices.

The descant, with its combining two or more musical phrases or melodies, did much to develop English song. At this time the art of accompanying music to the main song or plain song was also developed, usually in the lower part, instead of depending on only polyphonic singing with its parts of composition so fitted in that each was important for its own sake. Perhaps polyphonic singing had gone as far as it could go, and was therefore put aside for a new development along the lines of our present-day homophonic singing, in which the main melody is carried in the highest part, with the other parts merely enriching it. At any rate, music was an art that was used by many writers as a theme for personal discussion, but for the people at large it was a joy that could wing its way along in one form or another just for the delight it gave.

Nevertheless, some serious souls must apologize for love of joy, and some people must have ready an apology for their love of music's joy. Lodowick Bryskett satisfied both types in *A Discourse of Civil Life* (1606) as he recommended music in connection with physical exercise. This combination, he said, produced modesty and temperance and even fortitude. Had not the Greeks believed music tempered the passions and prevented discord and disharmony? He believed that if young men gave themselves over to exercise of the body only, they would become fierce in their hardihood, and be "hurtful" to the Commonwealth. Music alone would make them soft-minded. Together, music and bodily exercise would produce good habits and a noble temper that would enable young men to defend their country with valor and wisdom.

In spite of the stress on mental and moral training, Elizabethans did not neglect the problem of when and where and how to train their youth in bodily exercise. Mulcaster was so much interested in this phase of education that he even included such things as spontaneous laughter and shouting—of course in moderation if they were to be wholesome and good. He also agreed to running, dancing, and riding. Loud speaking he believed could be very beneficial because it exercised the vocal cords, opened the lungs, and scoured the body by increasing the peristaltic action and rapid disposal of superfluous humors. Though weeping purged the body of certain humors also, he believed that on the whole it did more harm than good.

Mulcaster agreed with the Greeks that dancing helped to preserve the health and morals; if used "in time, by order, and with measure," as in formal Elizabethan dancing, it could have this good effect, but if it did not avoid the "lewdness and lightness" of the popular, lively dances, it could be very harmful. Wrestling, a more violent exercise, required a master "both cunning to judge of the thing: and himself present" to prevent harm. Weapons in exercise with an adversary met with his approval because they quickly betrayed the coward, especially in fencing. He was opposed to exercise that required the use of only one hand and arm, however, for he believed children and men should be ambidextrous, if possible. Walking was good because it opened the head and prepared for sleep. Running must be done with little clothing, and leaping should be done only naturally and cheerfully if it was to be beneficial. Because of the harm swimming caused to the head, he insisted this exercise be taken under the supervision of a master. He was a bit dubious about riding and found it difficult to account for the general enthusiasm for it, especially among physicians. If one must ride, then he should choose the easiest gait, ambling. Of all sports Mulcaster favored hunting because it exercised the body, delighted the mind, and seemed to appeal to man's natural instinct to assert his mastery over animals and birds.

For children, he preferred handball and tennis, for if accidents occurred, the children themselves were to blame. Tennis was too expensive for any but the rich, however, and most children would have to be denied its pleasure. For handball, Mulcaster probably had in mind the type played without a racket and with a soft ball; this sport permitted much exercise with the bare hands. The other type required a racket and a fairly hard ball. Mulcaster preferred a child to play ball alone against a wall; in tennis he might strive to win and strain himself against his adversary, but in playing by himself he exercised both hands and used "every kind of motion that concerneth any or all exercises."

In spite of the general objection of writers to football, Mulcaster argued in favor of it because any faults were the players' and not the game's; he believed football was "a help, strength, and comfort of nature." He deplored the abuse of the game with its "thronging of a rude multitude, with bursting of shins, and breaking of legs" until it was "neither worthy the name of any training to health." Another rough game, invented by the king of Naples, was armball. It was played with the arms as football was played with the feet, each arm being protected by a wooden brace. In football the shin was so protected, but never adequately, for the game became a violent contest as it ran its course.

Mulcaster judged the value of exercise by whether it helped one to regain health or preserve it. He advised that for either purpose it be taken in the morning, both summer and winter, after purging the body, when the body was light and free from food but strong from sleep. Thus he required his schoolboys to rise in the morning at a given hour, purge the body, comb the hair, wash hands and face, dress, and walk before breakfast. He objected to exercise after a meal, before purging the body, or when one was hungry. Exercise was most needed between the ages of seven and twenty, and more of it in winter than in summer. He recommended that all masters of this subject be well read in books on it, that they be discreet in training children, and most of all, that they believe in the thing they were doing.

It is notable that Mulcaster approved of fencing, but the sport was so abused by duels that the Crown and moralists frowned heavily on it. Still, most nobles included fencing (a shortened form of *defencing*, both terms being used interchangeably) in their sons' training. Because only men of dignity and importance were permitted to carry a sword, this weapon was as much a part of a gentleman's attire as his ruff. With the means always at hand to avenge an insult, the temptation to resent real or fancied slights by dueling was very great. Thus it was not uncommon for a gentleman to receive a challenge he must answer by weapon or by wit; if by wit, he must be very able indeed.

A challenge[7] sent to the eldest son of Sir Nicholas Bacon, Elizabeth's Lord Keeper, in July of 1600, takes him to task as "a lying knight" for reporting that the writer causes his tenants "in their examinations, to set down what I like." He will justify his "dealings" before the Privy Council and Justices of the Assize, and if the slanderer is not the coward the writer thinks him to be, he will agree to a meeting in the last of August "either at Flushing or Middlebury, there to run three courses with the sharp lance"; if the challenger is defeated, he expects his throat to be cut "without mercy." If, however, the Lord Keeper's son is defeated, his life will be pardoned only if he serves the writer "in three sundry services." But if the writer dies in the combat, he will charge his children and friends not to let his death be revenged. If this knightly contest does not appeal to his enemy, the writer will deal with him "with the rapier and the dagger." If "filthy fear" makes him refuse, then he must serve the writer on "horseback or foot, in three services," and "who first and most honorably assaults and damages the enemy, let the other be accounted a recreant and a discredited person in all honorable company." If any of these offers is accepted the writer will "repute" the

---

[7] *Calendars of State Papers, Domestic Series, 1598–1601*, ed. Mary Anne Everett Green, CCLXXV, No. 22.

challenged man a gentleman, but if refused, he will "secretly report and openly blaze" him as a "dunghill-spirited man, participating in nothing with the silver mould of his honorable father."

News about challenges of this nature often reached the Queen's ears before anything serious occurred, and she immediately took the necessary steps to end the matter promptly. But since every gentleman felt it was necessary for him and for his son to defend his honor, training of youths in the art of fencing made due progress.

Wards in great houses might be exposed to gossip about honor and duels, but unless they were nobles' sons, they were kept busy preparing for a career of importance. Few had the opportunity of being educated according to the ideals of More's *Utopia*, but many Elizabethans had dreams of such an education for their sons. In More's popular fantasy, the teacher was described as "not more honorable for his authority, than for his prudence and virtue . . . though stricken in age, yet he bare his body upright. In his face did shine such an amiable reverence as was pleasant to behold, gentle in communication, yet earnest and sage . . ." The teacher's speech was "fine, eloquent, and pithy." He had "profound knowledge, in wit he was incomparable, and in memory wonderful excellent. These qualities which in him were made by nature singular, he by learning and use had made perfect."

When More was a ward in Cardinal Morton's household, he and the other quiet lads served the guests who came to their master's table— men of letters, nobles, statesmen, lawyers, representatives of the Church, and travelers from the Continent. Their host directed the conversation, but encouraged the others to talk freely. While the boys handed the dishes and poured wine, and ate as they stood whatever might be given them by those at table or waited patiently for their own table afterward, they often heard very impressive conversation. On festive occasions, as at Christmas, they were frequently asked to entertain their master. If they presented him with an interlude, they must have wits quick enough to improvise whenever their parts demanded it. Of course youths at important households like this came from the best families in England, either noble or middle-class. At lords' houses the youths were usually sons of lords, though some lords made a practice of serving as patrons to specially gifted boys like More. These they might bring up in their own homes till it was time to send them to the university, or they might have them educated at public schools.

More was so delighted with the cultivated minds at the Cardinal's that he planned to acquire the same graces himself. Thus, besides Latin and Greek, he studied French, partly, according to Stapleton, by his own private study, and partly through meeting and talking with those who spoke French. He became skilled in music, arithmetic, and geometry, and read all the history he could find. Loving Plato, he studied him and his followers at every opportunity to strengthen him in his dream of some day serving the state. He thus mapped out for himself a course of study that served as a model for educators of Elizabethan wards. More's distinguished career at Oxford is well known. When he married and had his own family, his career took on more significance, for the burdens of his parental responsibility rested lovingly on his shoulders. More's training of his children and children's children was often closely imitated by devout Elizabethans accountable for both children and wards.

For him and his pious followers, religious training preceded the secular training of the children. More believed they should be started at learning with great care, but as soon as they were old enough, he turned them over to the best of tutors, whom he had selected with great solicitude and whose work he supervised tactfully but with close attention to detail. The first tutor for More's children was John Clement, who became a doctor of medicine and a Greek scholar, his later lectures on Greek and rhetoric at Oxford winning the praise of Linacre. Previous to his employment as tutor, he attended More on his journeys for the king, seeing to his comfort, caring for the horses, carrying messages, listening to his conversation, writing letters from dictation, copying manuscripts, and picking up knowledge of the world and becoming acquainted with good letters. By means of such close association, More was assured of the man's fitness for the important task of teaching his children. In the same way he could approve of Clement as husband for his adopted daughter, Margaret Giggs, and Clement likewise assured himself of Margaret's fitness to be his wife. She helped her husband a great deal in his extensive Greek translations.

More's second tutor, William Gunnell, was a friend of Erasmus while at Cambridge. Before he became a tutor he had also had previous experience as a teacher in his own school, assisted by his brother. Gunnell, too, became a great man, lecturing at Cambridge and holding many positions of authority. Other tutors had charge of More's grandchildren, for whose education he felt as responsible as for his own. At his "school" the children were taught Latin and Greek literature, logic and philosophy with formal disputation, mathematics, astronomy and arithmetic, music, writings of the Fathers, and the almost daily translating of English into Latin and Latin into English. During his lifetime, eleven of More's grandchildren received this instruction.

More felt compelled to defend the education of women because he had four daughters and only one son, and also because he felt men's and women's minds were "equally suited for those studies by which reason is cultivated, and become fruitful like a ploughed land on which the seed of good lessons has been sown." He had heard woman's brain called bad and "apter to bear bracken than corn," but he knew that if a woman's wit was poor it must "all the more diligently be cultivated," that nature's defect might be "dressed by industry." He rewarded his children when they applied themselves well by gifts of cake or fruit or a piece of silk and many, many kisses. If ever he had to give blows, it was always with a peacock's feather. Whenever he wrote them he always urged them to progress in goodness and learning that he might love them even more. That he also encouraged them to open their hearts to him is indicated by his statement, "a man doesn't merit the name of father who does not weep at the tears of his children."

His letters to his children were written in careful Latin but with such pleasantry that they were read almost to pieces. Their own free replies were written with the knowledge they would be closely criticized, but also with loving appreciation and encouragement. For example, after telling them what he thinks of their logic and composition, More says he is bringing home a young scholar who hopes he will not find them too far advanced for him to join them in their "witty and acute discussions." In another letter, More slyly suggests he may find them able to overcome their tutor "if not by force of argument," at least by not having to confess themselves beaten. At still another time he tells how John's letter has pleased him best, "both because it was longer than the others, and because he seems to have given it more labor and study." He has not only "put his matter prettily and composed it in fairly polished language, but he plays with" his father "both pleasantly and cleverly," and turns his jokes back on him "wittily enough." Yet this he "does not merrily, but with due moderation, showing that he does not forget he is joking with his father, and he is cautious not to give offense at the same time he is eager to give delight."

Apparently More's messenger was normally expected to return shortly with letters from his children. Therefore the father asks them to have their letters all written before the man's arrival and not keep him waiting. If they need a subject, thinking there is nothing at all to write about, then they must write "that nothing at great length." For the girls this will be easy since they are "loquacious by nature." Yet as they write nonsense, he would have them put their mind to it. Then he advises writing first in English so they will have less trouble turning it into Latin; "not having to look for the matter," their mind "will be intent only on the language." After this he "strictly enjoins" them to examine carefully what they have composed, first the whole sentence and then "every part of it" to detect "any solecisms" that have escaped them. Having made their corrections, they must "write out the whole letter again, and even examine it once more, for sometimes, in re-writing, faults slip in again that one has expunged." He assures them that by this "diligence" their little nonsensical trifles will become "serious matters," for there is "nothing so neat and witty that will not be made insipid by silly and inconsiderate loquacity," nor is there anything "itself so insipid" that it cannot be seasoned with "grace and wit" if they will but give it a little thought.

By such instructions More anticipated the theory of Ascham (for a while the Queen's teacher) about accurate grounding in Latin composition through combining accidence and syntax. First, as in all good schools, Ascham would familiarize the child with the parts of speech, joining nouns with adjectives, nouns with verbs, and relatives with their antecedents. Then he would take a simple passage from Cicero's epistles, and after explaining the occasion for it and its purpose, or requiring the child to do this, he would have the passage translated into English, and every word parsed. Then he would have the passage translated, without any assistance from the teacher, and an hour later turned back into English without consulting Cicero. Now the teacher would look over the child's work, comparing it with Cicero's, pointing out errors, discussing reasons for Cicero's turns of expression, and asking questions in grammar, discussing case, gender, etc. This sounds very tedious, but Ascham urged tutors to be patient during this part of their work and, whenever opportunity for praise arose, to encourage and commend the pupil.

In advocating gentleness in the teacher, Ascham said the master must study the child to prevent his favoring the quick-witted and punishing the slow-witted; always he must judge the child not by its present work but by what it might accomplish in the future. Perhaps the most Elizabethan of all his utterances, however, was that education was better than experience. He actually believed education might save individuals from the extravagant waste involved in experience, that one might learn more from books in one year than from experience in twenty years, and the process was not only less costly but far safer. This was the basic idea of education for the Elizabethan, but in the home, parental advice was expected to supplement the books. Together, they provided the *real* and *only* road to wisdom.

This is why Ascham, as well as parents who dreaded sending their sons abroad to finish their education, felt a close study of such a book as Castiglione's *The Courtier* was worth more than three years of travel in Italy. Since the same belief in the efficacy of learning from books penetrated to the middle class, it was possible to adapt such books as *The Courtier* to their needs also. For this book, though its suggested course of exercise was part of the program for every gentleman's son, made clear the fact that physical training was as significant as an exacting study of classical literature when it taught children how to live.

Instruction in the home, then, varied according to the training desired by the parents and the kind of teachers they chose to train the minds of their children. Instruction in the public schools reflected the attempt of schoolmasters and ministers and public-spirited men to evolve a systematic organization of methods and subject matter that would prepare children to become good citizens. In the general uniformity, new ideas were not unwelcome, though the middle-class demand for a more and more "practical" education was very much like the present-day clamor for more and more vocational education. With all their desire to become "gentle," the ambitious common people recognized the necessity of worldly goods even for the wellborn. Furthermore, the old tendency to favor the rich man's sons over those of the poor man, even in schools originally founded for the poor, may have increased the demand of the common man for a practical curriculum. At the same time, those who wished to be "gentle" in the Lord's eyes insisted on a strong religious training, and at home they exerted themselves to make up for whatever the public school lacked in godliness.

Both Stubbes and Harrison complained that places in free schools were more often "sold for money and friendship than given gratis" to the deserving. And yet Stubbes was very proud of the training given children in Elizabethan grammar schools. He felt it was a pity, therefore, when so many parents withdrew their children from schools in city, town, and country as soon as they could read and write and put them out to trade or learning some craft. He also admitted that children who loved learning and became teachers, even the best of teachers, could "hardly live by their learning." This was true in the country far too often if here they were paid a mere pittance which would scarcely maintain them in decency. Yet most parents did want their children to attend a good school so that the new generation might reach a better position in life than they had themselves. And since good schools meant good teachers, the towns and cities were justified in such pride as Stubbes showed in the grammar schools of his time.

As with all things worth while, the children's education took concerted effort—on the part of parents, teachers, and children. A typical school day required the children to leave home early enough to begin the day's work at 6:00 o'clock and to stay as late as 5:00 in the evening. In winter, therefore, they often made their way to and from school carrying lanterns to light their way. Those who arrived first got the best places, and here they studied till the first recess at 9:00 o'clock. Fifteen minutes later they were back at their studies for another two hours, some schools even requiring them to make up time lost in recess. One and sometimes two hours were allowed for dinner, and if a child was not too far from home, he had dinner there; otherwise, he took his dinner with him when he left in the morning. After dinner came two more hours of study and recitation, followed by a recess and work till 5:00. Usually, before they went home, part of a chapter from the Bible was read by the master, then a psalm was sung, especially in Puritan schools, led by the master, and finally came the prayer for dismissal. These long hours of study were observed in many of the homes educating their own children, but the work was provided with changes to prevent excessive fatigue.

The time spent for catechism must have been wearisome for both teachers and children, but the task must be performed conscientiously to meet the requirements of the law. Elizabethan law insisted that children under twenty years of age were to be catechized and instructed every Sunday and holy day before and after evening prayers. In many public as well as home schools the instruction for catechism was offered. Parents, masters, and mistresses who did not send their children to the catechizing were reported to the Ordinary to be censured and punished.

The long school hours raised objection among thoughtful people, in particular to schools that did not vary the program sufficiently. By 1622, Henry Peacham was recommending that the hours be revised to meet the more humane principles adopted in the Low Countries. There, he said, the teacher, after an hour's lecture, walked in the fields for an hour or two with his fellows, or to the ramparts, where they conferred, and then back to school, where the same process was repeated throughout the day. The children were free to do as they liked during the rest periods, though under supervision. Peacham was convinced the long hours of English schools dulled rather than sharpened the wits. He regretted that parents in general did not read to their children and take the interest in their moral and intellectual development that Sir Thomas More had taken in his children.

Vives' dialogues of *Tudor School-Boy Life*,[8] written about 1539 as easy *Latin Language Exercises*, were used many years for beginners in Latin in home and public schools. Their popularity was largely due to the appeal of old, familiar things in a child's life. With due allowance for textbook material, we may find in them suggestions about how children of school age were expected to conduct themselves. The first dialogue shows the maid opening the shutters and the glass windows to air the room, and then calling the little schoolboy, who is a slugabed. While she helps him to dress, she lectures him on the need of early rising, but he listens sleepily till she accuses him of playing dice. Roused at this, he stoutly denies doing such a thing, for it is forbidden, but she playfully teases him about its being true, saying she saw him at a game as she watched through a chink in the door. Then he confesses his guilt, but begs her not to tell his parents.

After he is dressed, the child combs his hair and dons his cap. As the maid pours water into a bowl, he washes his face and hands, cleans his mouth, washes his eyelids and eyebrows, and his neck and ears. Then he gargles his throat. This done, the maid asks him for a kiss, and then she bids him kneel and say the Lord's Prayer and other customary prayers. The speech between maid and child, though of childish things, is as

[8] Juan Luis Vives, *Tudor School-Boy Life: Dialogues*, Foster Watson's English translation, published in 1908.

formal as that of adults. Such speeches must be turned into good English by the students using this storied text, and then again into Latin without consulting the text.

The next dialogue begins with the little boy greeting his family. "Hail, my father! Hail, my mother dear! I wish that this may be a happy day for you, my little brothers. May Christ be propitious to you, my little sisters!" Then as he kneels dutifully before his parents, the father says, "My son, may God guard you and lead you to great goodness," and the mother adds, "May Christ preserve you, my light." As the little boy rises from his knees, the mother asks, "How are you, my darling? How did you rest last night?" Told that he is "very well, and slept peacefully," the mother exclaims, "Thanks be to Christ; may He grant that this may be constantly so." This reminds the child that "in the middle of the night" he was "roused up" with a pain in his head. "In what part of the head?" asks the mother, "and how long did it last?" "Scarcely the eighth of an hour," he answers. "Afterwards I fell asleep again, nor did I feel anything further from it." To this the mother says, "Now I breathe again."

After a moment the child turns to his dog. "Ruscio! Come here, jolly little dog. How are you?" Holding out his hand to the animal, he cries with pleasure, "See how he fawns with his tail, and how he raises himself on his hind legs." Now he calls to a servant, "Hullo, bring a bit or two of bread which we may give him; then you will see some clever sport." When the dog refuses to eat the bread, the child says, "Won't you eat? Have you had anything today?" Then he observes sagely, "Clearly, there is more intelligence in that dog than in a crass muledriver."

At this point the father indicates he wishes to have a talk with his son, who answers: "Why, my father? For nothing more delightful could happen to me than to listen to you." The father questions the lad about the dog; is it animal or man? When told it is an animal, the father continues, "What have you that he has not? You eat, drink, sleep, run, play. So does he all these things." The child replies, "Yes, but he is not a man." The father persists, "How do you know all this? What have you now, more than a dog?" Since the boy cannot answer, the father says simply, "There is this difference: he cannot become a man; you can if you will." The child begs his father to bring this about as soon as possible, and is told, "It will be done if you go where all animals go to come back men." The child will go "with all the pleasure in the world," and wants to know where that place may be. "In the school," is the answer.

Now some food—bread and butter and fruit—is prepared for the little boy to take with him to school. The child starts off happily with his father to learn how to become a man. As they walk along, they meet a relative, and the father inquires about the best teacher for his son. Two are recommended; both are learned, but one has in addition to learning a most upright character. This second teacher has a smaller school, for not all parents are willing to pay more for better instruction. The father decides on the second teacher and, as he proceeds with his son, remarks, "Son, this is, as it were, the laboratory for the formation of man, and he [the teacher] is the artist-educator." As they approach the schoolmaster's house, the father instructs his son how to act, saying he must uncover his head and bend his right knee, and then rise. The son satisfies the father and the teacher by his manners, and is enrolled in the school, the father paying in advance the required fee, as was customary at the time of Vives.

A child at such a school would be expected to learn what his parents did not have time to teach him, and yet as he reported from day to day what he had learned, they would usually manifest close interest. True, some parents would shunt all responsibility for both their children's good manners and their formal education onto a school with a good reputation. Others, as among middle-class families in which both parents worked in the shop, would send their children as boarders to grammar schools. Vives pictures boys at such schools receiving the care and training they would be expected to have in good homes.

First was the simple diet, which after the time of Vives, however, included more meat and fewer vegetables. Breakfast was served about an hour and a half after the boys had been called from their beds, and consisted of coarse bread and butter, and fruit in season. The chief dish at dinner would often be a pottage of cooked turnips or cabbage with wheat meal or rice added. There might be mutton at times, with a broth and sauce, and root vegetables and herbs. On special occasions meat pie would delight the boys, and sometimes there would be veal or kid, especially in the spring. On fish days, in addition to the daily individual cakes of bread, salt fish with peas or lentils or beans, and buttermilk would be served. Dinner usually began with a salad of finely chopped greens, sprinkled with salt and moistened with vinegar and oil. Following it was the meat or main dish, and then cheese and pears or peaches, quinces, etc., or dried raisins or figs. The dinner was really a three-course meal.

The boys were always warned to eat moderately, never to become sated. At supper the diet was light, with water or light beer or diluted wine, some bread and almonds or other nuts, and fruit. Of course, the diet was also determined by the locality. For example, in the country the dinner might consist of fresh cheese, cream, horse beans soaked in lye before cooking, salad, bread and butter, etc. Boys were privileged to have guests at dinner or supper, but only with the master's permission. Since supper was the last meal of the day, it was usually observed in these schools, as at home, with much ceremony, one of the children saying grace and all taking part in the table discussion of religion or morals or light, witty entertainment.

Vives describes the preparations for supper, with the boys setting the tables, putting the stools in place at the trestle tables, laying the napkins carefully at each place, and arranging the dishes. For each boy there must be a trencher, a drinking glass, and a little loaf of bread. Ale was drawn, water was brought from a cistern, and the glasses were polished carefully. After all were seated, the master would say, "Let each one draw his knife, and everyone chip his bread if there be either ashes or cinders in the crust," for when bread came straight to table from the floors of the great brick ovens, each was expected to clean his own loaf. This done, the boy chosen to say grace might recite as follows: "Feed our hearts with love, O Christ, who through thy goodness nourishest the lives of all living beings. Blessed be these thy gifts to us who partake of them so that Thou who providest them may be blessed."

If hungry boys had waited impatiently for grace to end, the master would say to those crowding their neighbors, "Sit as far asunder as possible, and do not thrust one another." If one of them, tired and hot, started to remove his cap, the boy appointed as usher for the week would tell him to replace it lest "hair fall into the dishes." While they dined, the master would watch closely to see they observed good manners, for he must set straight whatever was wrong in their conduct and admonish against crudities of any sort.

During supper, therefore, the master might have to tell them not to wipe their hands on their sleeves or the tablecloth, but on their napkins, or he might remind them not to touch any part of the meat except that they cut off for themselves. If they wore sleeves that hung long and open, he might have to warn the boys not to get them in the food, and might suggest that they "cast" their "hanging sleeves" back over their shoulders or turn them up at the elbow and pin them there securely. If some of them leaned on the table, they would be quickly reminded they must sit up straight on their stools no matter how tired their backs.

Supper over, the boys would sit primly while the usher took away the "leavings" to the buttery. Next he removed the salt, then the bread, and then in proper order the rest of the food and dishes. This accomplished with as much grace and dexterity as possible, he would stand at attention while the master asked the boys to clean their knives before putting them back in their sheaths. If any of the boys were picking their teeth with their knives, he would shake his head and tell them to make a sharp quill of wood for the purpose and to use it carefully lest they injure their gums. When they were ready to rise from the table, one of the boys would say grace somewhat as follows: "For this timely meal, we render Thee thanks, Lord Christ. Grant we may for eternity render immortal thanks. Amen."

Now water would be brought in one or more ewers, and the usher would pour some into a basin that the master might wash his hands and dry them on the fresh napkin handed to him. One by one, the boys would be served in the same manner, except that two or three would use the same water. When all hands were clean, the master would rise and the boys would be expected to rise like gentlemen, not jump up hastily for enjoyment of the precious evening before them. First they must put away the stools and trestles and boards so that a maid could sweep the floor. Now they played games inside or, if it was pleasant out of doors, they went for a walk till bedtime.

The Hollyband dialogues, written some forty years later to teach French to boys from the homes of well-to-do tradesmen, are far less formal than the Vives dialogues, and the pupils are like mischievous schoolboys. Since they are threatened with beatings which are seldom or never given, one sees here a lightening of the discipline in both home and school, and does not feel that the difference between the Vives and Hollyband dialogues is due entirely to the difference in personality of the authors.[9]

The boy of the Hollyband text rises early, but knows he is going to school, and proceeds to get his "gear" ready. He objects to washing in water from the muddy Thames, and asks for well water instead. He is chided by his father for being late and is threatened with a whipping at school. He has to be commanded to kneel for a blessing, and then his father, to keep him from a beating for his tardy arrival at school, says he may invite the schoolmaster home to dinner. However, the son is admonished to learn his lesson well so he can repeat it when he returns.

When en route to school with his child, the father stops a friend to discuss schoolmasters, especially the one who teaches Latin till 11:00 and French in the afternoon. They talk of fees, and the friend disapproves of paying any teacher in advance lest he become too sluggish to earn his money. They finally decide a shilling a week, a crown a month, a real a quarter, and forty shillings a year ample reward for teaching one boy. They like the preferred master's method of reading from Latin authors to his pupils according to their capacity.

After this leisurely discussion, the father proceeds with his small son, and at school he hands him over to the master, saying, "Master Hollyband, take a little pains with my son: he is somewhat hard of wit, understanding, and memory: he is shamefast, wanton, wicked, a liar, stubborn under his father and his mother: correct, chasten, amend these faults, and I will recompense you: hold, I will pay you the quarter beforehand." After this easygoing father takes his leave, the master questions the child as to his age. The boy does not know, but he says his father "hath put in writing the day" of his birth, and it is in their Bible, "which is at home." Now the schoolmaster dismisses his new pupil with the admonition that he learn thoroughly what he is taught so he can do well by his sovereign, his country, his parents, and himself.

If Hollyband laughs at the English, he can also laugh at himself,

---

[9] M. St. Clare Byrne, *The Elizabethan Home Discovered in Two Dialogues by Claudius Hollyband and Peter Erondell* (1949), Introduction, pp. ix–xvi.

for his schoolmaster listens patiently to whatever complaints the boys make of one another, even when the black sheep is accused of all the sins in the schoolboys' calendar: fighting with his fists, "casting snow and balls of snow," playing with points, pins, cherry stones, counters, dice, and cards, besides being a little bully on his way to and from school. Though one tittle-tattle is struck on the hand for reporting misconduct, he is carefully heard to the end of his account of how William spits on his paper, tears his book, breaks his girdle, mars his copy, but, worst of all, speaks English instead of Latin on the school ground.

The boys are shown very realistically struggling with their writing "gear" (penknife, goose quills, ink, ink horn). They are taught how to soften their pens with spit and to rub them against the inside instead of the outside of their coats. As they write the text, they are admonished, "As much as you can, write with your head upright: for if one stand with his head downward, humors fall down to his forehead, and into his eyes; whereof many infirmities do arise, and weakness of sight." All their lessons are learned by heart, though the laborious copying of the text in the writing lesson must have planted it firmly in their minds.

When the dinner hour approaches at 11:00 o'clock, the boys are eager to be dismissed, but first they must kneel and say their prayers. Still they are detained till the master has reminded them to take off their caps to all their betters on the way home, and they are warned that if they are not back promptly at 12:00, they will be whipped.

On arriving at school in the afternoon, the boys are told to "turn" their lessons first out of French into English, then out of English into French, and to decline a noun and a verb in French. Since Latin, French, and writing are the master's subjects, he means for the boys to do him credit. Thus he cautions them to read over their lessons at home six or seven times after supper and again after prayers just before they go to sleep. By 5:00 o'clock it is dark, but still the children must wait for prayers. Dismissed at last, and armed with lanterns and torches, they make their way through the cold, dank streets.

By 1610, Philip Stubbes' *A Perfect Pathway to Felicity* gave the Puritan plan of middle-class boys' school training. As if to offset the indulgence attendant upon the new reign, he ignores the parental affection in the Vives dialogues, the tenderness of Sir Thomas More, and the human attitude of Hollyband. As soon as the child enters the presence of his parents in the morning, he should not only salute them, but also fall down upon his knees "and desire them to pray God to bless him." At table he must be obedient and courteous, modest, humble, and sober as if in the presence of God, eating only "so much as nature requireth, not how much insatiable appetite desireth." He must be amiable and pleasant to all but "spare as well of hands as of tongue." All his speech he must try to season with salt in order to "give grace to the hearers," remembering that "at the day of judgment" he must "give accounts" for every "idle word." Some Puritans really seemed to believe that a child could achieve such speech if he would "use not to laugh much, jest, scoff, to flout or mock, to deride, backbite, or detract from any man behind his back, but in all things demeanor" himself so that he would "not dishonor God" or give "offence or evil example unto any at the table." At meals, the child would say grace.

Following supper, the child must not run and play, but spend his time with his family, singing psalms and other spiritual songs, or "conferring, reasoning, disputing, reading, expounding, and interpreting the Bible." Before retiring for the night, he, like every other member of the household, must make public confession of the day's sins, and crave God's pardon. To ensure the child's offering suitable prayers, this Puritan plan provided models for him to use before and after meals.

Parents in any social class who failed in this stress on morals and manners or who neglected to send their children to teachers who would give this instruction were a disgrace. Each class had its own proper speech and its own proper apparel and its own ideal of hospitality, but most of all, its own proper manners. Not to know the code of living according to one's own class was unthinkable for a self-respecting person, and not to have children properly taught in this respect was more than a disgrace: it was a sin against God and society.

To put into mere words a feeling and a principle which Elizabethans had evolved through a long, slow, difficult process of trial and error and chance circumstance was not easy for them. Yet this they tried to do again and again. Nor were they satisfied with their own ideas and expressions of them, but searched the conduct books of other nations, especially of France and Italy, taking here and rejecting there, but always building toward a very English way of life. A most necessary part of their educational system, however, was to teach each person how to adjust himself to new conditions in his own little world of class. With religion and government and the economic state of life like quicksand under their feet, their homes must help them to hold fast to their faith in this planned life. They must do even more—they must not only give the plan a significance that would combat and outlast the disorder of their age, but they must also make their way of life serve future generations.

There were several books which parents and schoolmasters consulted for hints and helps in teaching good manners, such as Rickert's *The Babees Book, Urbanitatis, The Lytylle Childrenes Boke*, Hugh Rhodes' *Boke of Nurture*, Seager's *School of Virtue*, Garland's *Liber Faceti*, Sloane's *Boke of Curtesye*, and Erasmus' *De Civilitate Morum Libellus*. The last of these was most popular of all after Robert Whitington translated it into English in 1532. Many, like Garland's *Faceti*, illustrated their rules by moral maxims from the oft quoted Dionysius Cato, and some, like Seager's *School of Virtue*, gave examples of good speech or proper prayers for children to commit to memory for certain occasions. But *De Civilitate* belonged to everyone—parents, teachers, and the children themselves.

Erasmus might be read and understood by the superior child who could learn good manners by this method. Most children, however, had to be drilled in good manners by their parents and teachers, who found Erasmus an invaluable aid for this purpose. Vives and Hollyband, concerned in their texts with the teaching of languages, made decorum incidental to their main objective, Stubbes made good manners and morals the foundation upon which rested his argument of training children for eternity, but Erasmus taught by clever and witty examples of behavior exactly what good manners were. Since Erasmus was able to help tutor or parent intent on teaching a child how to deport himself correctly at all times and under all ordinary conditions, his *De Civilitate* was used in all schools whether at home or under the supervision of those outside the home.

Like all other texts of this nature, *De Civilitate* dealt with much that is taken for granted today as purely personal in the care of the body or in one's relations with other members of the family. But Elizabethans were too wise to take such things for granted—they *knew* that good manners (and morals) must be repeated from day to day and even hour to hour to make them a part of one's life at home or elsewhere. Most of all, they believed this instruction must prepare the social classes to walk separately or together as time and circumstance required, but with remarkable freedom from ill will or hostility. When clashes did occur, they were more often due to abuse of economic privilege than to resentment over class social barriers. Belief in the rights of each class and belief in the chance to climb the ladder of social classes by means of personal effort and good character and intellectual preparation gave hope to an age that had suffered much from the disillusionment wrought by change.

Elizabethans were deeply aware of the fact that once good manners become intrinsically a part of gentle behavior, they cannot change. Erasmus' little treatise was based on this principle, and because he knew how to make its importance clear to parents and, by his charmingly familiar examples, to present good manners attractively, no child escaped its precepts, and no home of well-mannered children deviated much from its standards. The little book was also thorough, for it gave rules of conduct for every waking hour of the day. As soon as the child's eyes were open early in the morning, he must rise, say his prayers, and, if he had no personal servant, sponge and clean any spots from shoes or clothing before he dressed. Neat appearance was essential, and the child must smooth down his hose lest they wrinkle, tie the collar of his shirt carefully at the throat, fasten his girdle securely, and attach to it his knife and purse. After combing his hair, putting on his cap, paring nails that needed attention, washing hands and face and teeth and ears, the child must "cast up his bed" unless he had a servant to perform the task for him. Elizabethans were apparently disturbed by unmade beds, possibly because such rooms served so many purposes and so many people.

His room in order, the child was ready to go forth to meet parents or guardian, greeting everyone most affably, whether servant or superior. To his superior he doffed his cap, speaking most courteously, but when he approached his parents, he must kneel for their blessing. If he was a ward, he approached his lord quietly, never rushing into his presence, and with his head up, bowed with one knee bent. Both knees were bent only to God and to parents, who were the agents on earth of the Heavenly Father's authority. While bowing to a person of importance, the child kept his cap removed till asked to replace it.

No child must rush off to school (Erasmus objected to the lack of control in such haste), but prepare for his departure by assembling his gear and placing it neatly in his satchel. While going along the street he must doff his cap to all good men and women he met and bid them Godspeed. If asked to stop at a neighbor's house on an errand, he must say on entering, "God be here," and then without fidgeting speak courteously to those of the household. As he delivered his message, he must look straight into his listener's face and not talk too much or too eagerly.

Continuing on his way to school, he must not throw clods or stones at "dogs or horses or hogs," he must not climb walls to steal fruit or birds' nests or to recover a ball, he must not fling stones at glass windows, and he must not quarrel with other children or lose cap, gloves, or satchel. As he joined his companions, he must be careful to speak to them gently, and not play tricks on them or be party to any escapades of stealing. Although no Elizabethan expected his child to remember to obey these instructions all the time, he did expect him by hearing them repeated constantly at home and at school to acquire a reasonable control over wrong impulses.

Arriving at school, the child must greet his master with reverence, doffing his cap most courteously, and walk quietly to a seat instead of making the usual rush for the best place. Erasmus would have the child take out his books and begin studying as soon as he was seated, but this would require considerable control if the other children were inclined to play or talk before the master appeared and called them to order.

During morning recess children engaged in various activities. Those who had left home without breakfast might eat a light lunch, but most boys looked on these lunches as the coddling of small children. Delicate children never left home in the morning without some hot milk and porridge, and perhaps some butter and eggs. Since infant mortality was so high, only the strongest were likely to survive, and most of them were able to adapt themselves readily to the Elizabethan custom of only two meals a day. Play on the school ground, according to Erasmus and later educators, must observe social class restrictions. In this way possible frictions might be avoided. With the increase in schools, each more or less designed for a certain class, the child's concern about such matters was probably lessened, but he was, nevertheless, encouraged to be class-conscious.

Erasmus set forth rather difficult rules for a child to observe at play. For example, a little boy must be slow to anger and quick to forgive, and he must strive with all his might to keep out of arguments, especially as third to a dispute. He must also remember that too much laughter or even loud laughter indicated an empty head or a wicked soul, and too much smiling proclaimed deceit. Above all things he must be straightforward and honest and not carry tales about his companions. Erasmus believed that a child must establish harmonious relations with his fellows by speaking to them cordially and freely and by always trying to conduct himself in such a way as not to be misjudged.

The composure during class hours that every child must achieve was discussed in detail by Erasmus. When reciting or talking to companions or to his betters, he must not let his eyes wander and he must not lean against anything for support. Nor must he stand blushing and confused. If his master had occasion to speak to him sternly, he must answer courteously and not shuffle his feet or wiggle fingers or toes. If teased by an older child, he must not blush and stammer, and he himself must never harm a smaller child or beast. Always he must avoid deceitful and treacherous companions, and he must never mock or speak ill of anyone. Yet in telling the truth, he must ever be bold and generous.

When school was dismissed, the boy must walk with a companion of his own rank and station and moral upbringing, and not join a noisy group, running "in heaps like a swarm of bees." He must never jangle with his companion as he walked, but go gravely, humbly, and using few words, and those "with grace." Should he meet a friend of his father and be asked to walk with him, he should join him but not walk at his side unless invited. He must remember the man's sword hand should be kept free for any emergency that might arise, and hence keep his position carefully, a little back and to the left, as he walked. With his own companions he should remind himself it was better to be too courteous than not courteous enough, though he must not overdo good manners.

At home once more, the child must greet his parents reverently, but speak little unless requested to tell about his schoolwork or some occurrence of the day. In his report he must watch his words and try to speak as wisely and briefly and pointedly as possible. Of course he must not sit till invited to do so. If, on his return, he should find his parents in serious conference, he must not listen or interfere in any manner, but leave them quietly. Even as he left them, however, he should think of some useful occupation to keep him busy, remembering that his arms, like a bird's wings, must perform some useful task.

If his parents called him to them and commended him for his work at school, he should thank them; if they entrusted him with any secrets, he must keep them with all his might. Erasmus, however, felt parents were very unwise to exact any promise from a child except that he would try to be good. Should the boy's parents ask him to sit with them and chat, he must try to choose suitable subjects for conversation. If asked to talk to a guest, he must choose his subject according to the tastes of the guest. For example, the clergy should be approached by matters relating to God, doctors on health, and painters on design. He must never speak, however, unless invited to take part in the conversation. If he knew nothing about the subject under discussion, he must listen as the others talked. And always he must be sure what the subject of conversation was before he responded to any invitation to express his opinion; if necessary, he should ask what the topic was.

Erasmus believed little boys should be taught as soon as possible to uphold the honor of women, and in speech about them to utter nothing but praise. Only a churl or a dishonest man, he said, would belittle them. He believed small boys should say little to ladies, but bow to them and be very courteous, treating even female relatives formally as if they were not relatives, but always providing them with pleasure and showing them every reverence.

When ready to retire for the night, the elders should precede the child as they went to their rooms. If another person was to sleep with the little boy, he should be permitted the right to choose when to go to bed and on which side he wished to lie. When in bed, the child should lie straight and, after a little chat with his bedfellow, say goodnight. In the morning he should greet his bedfellow as soon as he awakened. If the sleeping companion was an older person or the child's master, the boy should sleep as far from him as possible to avoid disturbing his slumbers.

It may be a little difficult for the present age to grasp the importance of Elizabethan insistence on training in manners and morals, without which no child of that time could be prepared for the exigencies of everyday problems. Self-control was not only the supreme achievement of man over his lower nature; it was also the key to worldly honors and to the future salvation of his soul. Along with the effort to acquire this control was constant instruction in whatever would make a person acutely aware of his individual place in the social and spiritual scheme of life as determined by State and Church.

In England Richard Whitford's *A werk for householders* (1530) was also a favorite during the Tudor period, and in early America it was in use a long time, partly because its instructions were so explicit. According to this book, a child retiring at night was expected to say, "Father, I beseech of you your blessing for charity," or "Mother, I beseech you of charity give me your blessing." Then the father or mother should hold up both hands, joined, and say, "Our Lord bless you, child." Should the child be "stiff hearted, stubborn, and froward," and unwilling to ask a blessing, he should be whipped with the rod until he was obedient. If too old for such punishment, he should be required to have his meals alone, sitting on a stool in the middle of the hall, eating only brown bread and water, with every person in the household rebuking him as if he were a thief or traitor. Was not the disobedient child likely to become a traitor? they would say in awed and perhaps faltering tones. For a penitent child, Whitford suggested he recite the following verses:

> If I lie, backbite, or steal,
> If I curse, scorn, mock, or swear,
> If I chide, fight, strive, or threat,
> Then am I worthy to be beat,
> Good mother, or mistress mine;
> If any of these nine
> I trespass to your knowing,
> With a new rod and a fine
> Early, naked, before I dine
> Amend me with a scourging.

It was this kind of disobedience and its punishment that the Queen probably had in mind when the proud sister of Essex dared to "flout" her Majesty's judgment. If Penelope was to act like a "stubborn, wilful" child, so must she be punished like a child, and she was made to approach the Queen across the long hall on her knees, there to beg pardon under the critical eyes of the Queen's companions. Elizabeth herself had been subjected to such treatment as a little girl, possibly because her father wished to show his authority over Anne Boleyn's child, but more than likely to prevent her from developing that in her nature which had brought her mother to ruin. Stern parents frequently required their children to approach them on their knees when they had a request to make. The purpose, usually, was to prevent the child from developing any tendency to willfulness. Indeed, the value set on obedience was so high that a man's most precious jewel was wife or child who was immediately responsive to this duty, and a father often looked on an obedient, respectful child as his chief accomplishment in the education of his own flesh and blood.

It was all very well for most manuals to use the word obedience as a blanket term to cover the many parental commands during a child's training in proper decorum, but it took Erasmus to give the Tudor age a picture of natural daily conduct in its children. His little book was not content, therefore, with telling a child he must take a clean napkin (handkerchief) to school with him. Erasmus went into particulars, warning the little fellow against drying his nose on his coat sleeve or his cap or his hands. Good manners, he said, required the use of a handkerchief, with the head turned aside. If he spat on the ground, the child must tread the phlegm under foot.

It was bad enough, he continued, to snuff with the nose, but worse to snort. Wrinkling the nose was like a scoffer or a natural fool, and no child would choose to be a fool. Apparently sneezing annoyed Erasmus. If it had to be done in the presence of others, the child should turn aside, and then bless his mouth with the sign of the cross, and take off his cap and thank those about him who asked Christ's mercy on him. One reason for asking Christ's help, he said, was that sneezing and yawning were bad for the hearing. A polite child, therefore, would remove his cap and say "Christ help you" if one of his elders sneezed. Erasmus frowned on those who made a shrill noise when sneezing, but to stop a sneeze was dangerous to the health. He referred to those who needlessly coughed and spat at every third word, and reminded them that liars did the same thing out of custom. It was very bad manners to cough in another's face, and one should never clear his throat in the presence of company unless compelled to do it. When yawning, one should cover his mouth with his handkerchief or the palm of his hand.

The child who showed fright in the presence of others might best overcome his timidity by learning to play in interludes or comedies, said Erasmus. He deplored seeing a child stopping its mouth as if afraid to take another breath, or gaping like an idiot. He should be taught to press his lips softly together and not to pout them. Pursed lips reminded him of old pictures, in which the lips were pouted as if for kissing just to make one look genteel. The child must not bite its underlip, either; that was a sign of malice. Licking the lips with the tongue indicated folly, and only a knave would put out his tongue to mock another.

Erasmus expressed the general disapproval of too much smiling and laughter, especially in a child. Those who laughed like a neighing horse and those who showed all their teeth when they smiled or laughed were like a snarling dog and were not to be trusted at all. Proper laughter should not disfigure the mouth, but even so, it was best to cover the mouth with a handkerchief when one laughed. As excessive smiling betrayed malice and deceit, so loud laughter indicated an unsteady mind or downright madness. Yet no one loved a fine wit better than this Dutch scholar who has given the world so much laughter.

Care of the teeth and hair were problems in the time of Erasmus. He suggested that boys use salt for the teeth and alum for the gums; tooth powder seemed girlish to him. Toothpicks were best made of an ash splinter or the small, sharp bone in the leg of a fowl. Each morning the hair must be carefully combed to keep it clean from lice; yet a boy should not try to make his hair look glorious like a maid's by frequent combing of it. Instead, he should part it neatly and keep it from growing long enough to cover his brows or to lie upon his shoulders. He must never shake his hair, like a colt, or scratch his head. Any scratching at all, of the head or body, showed very bad breeding.

The straight carriage of head and body should be natural and easy.

Yet Erasmus warned that a child would have to be watched to keep him from walking with the head turned to left or right and with one shoulder humped. If bent in youth, the tender bodies could never become straight. Hands should be carried at ease, not held stiffly at the sides like a warrior at arms. When sitting or standing, the child should keep his legs together. Italians stood around like storks; in children this would be even worse. He also objected to crossing the right leg over the left as kings did in old times.

Every child must be taught how to enter a room and how to bow. He must not stride in like a warrior, nor hesitate and play with his toes or fingers like a fool. He must enter naturally with good poise. Bowing must also be according to the customs of the country in which a child happened to be living. For example, in France, the right knee was bent with "a pleasant return of the body." Though some curtsied with both knees bent and some with an upright body and others with body bent, Erasmus noticed that in England it was correct to bend the right knee first and then the left. Knowing such customs, the child would become tolerant of the manners of foreigners.

Erasmus was particular about neatness in clothing. Bad fitting and much color were indicative of light minds. Just as bright feathers belonged to parrots, so a child in gorgeous apparel would desire to be seen by others, like a peacock or ape. No child should ever praise its own apparel, but let others do so if they were pleased. Rich men who showed their glory by their fine clothes won only grudge and envy; for this reason, the greater one's fortune, the more gentle and amiable and the more modestly appareled he should be.

As children were accustomed to dine with their elders, Erasmus observed how often they were fed too much or too little. He believed too little food made children weak and dulled their wit. He had also seen parents permit their children to eat till they were ready to burst or till they had to vomit. He could think of nothing more disgusting. Parents should remember a child's stomach must be supplied with food more often than a mature person's, but never filled to capacity. They should also remember a feast was far too long for a child, and the conversation, over its head, was exhausting. Therefore, little children should be permitted to leave the table as soon as they had had enough to eat. Nor should parents let their children sit too long at supper, for they should go early to bed.

If a child must rise from a long supper or feast, let him take his trencher with its fragments and make a bow. But he must return by and by to show he did not depart for play or some other light cause. At his return, he should ask whether there was anything lacking at table, or note it with his own eyes, and he should engage in some "honest" serving at table. He must learn as early as possible how to set down a dish or take it up without spilling anything. Whether pouring or reaching for something, at table or while serving, he must use his right hand. If asked to snuff a candle, he must first take it off the table, and after putting out its light, dust it or "tread it under foot" lest the odor be unpleasant to anyone.

Erasmus believed a child should say little at table. He might ask grace if he could do it "with good behavior" and readily, but otherwise he should keep silent till invited to speak. His attitude at table should always be respectful, especially toward great men or guests. He must find no fault with the food, and must not gossip about absent people, or try to renew or settle "scores of any sort" while dining. The child must learn that if anything ill-mannered occurred through ignorance, it should be ignored, for nothing must give displeasure to the feast makers. Under the influence of meat and drink certain things might "slip out unadvisedly," but the child must never rehearse anything that happened at table. He must learn, too, that one giving a feast never tells the cost of it and never praises it, and above all, he must never repeat at table anything his elders might have discussed "beforehand."

Although the church manners which Erasmus taught applied to Catholics in particular, they were taught to Protestant children later in the century. For example, if a child happened to pass through a church when divine service was in session, he should stop and worship "with all his body, thinking Christ as there with thousands of angels." Erasmus condemned the practice of walking up and down the great aisles of the church for exercise, as Elizabethans were to use their long galleries later or, as he said, "like Aristotle and his followers in the market place." Thus he would have the child in the distance listen "with all his heart turned toward the altar." And at service he would have the child "kneel with both knees," keeping his mind strictly on the service.

As Erasmus believed the eye was "the seat of the soul," he had much to say of the child's proper way of using his. To look down was to give the appearance of folly or evil, to look aside, a token of disdain, and to turn the eyes this way and that was to seem foolish, "light-witted." Frowning eyes indicated cruelty; rolling eyes, madness; spying eyes, suspicion or deceit; twinkling eyes, instability; too sharp eyes, malice. A child, therefore, should keep his eyes stable, honest, and amiable. In Spain, he said, men posed as if half-blind in order to look "fair and amiable, and their mouths kept narrow and straight to indicate virtue." He did not believe in these affectations, which diminished natural charms. Wrinkling the nose, crooking the mouth or narrowing it, moving the brow up and down like a hedgehog or wrinkling it like an old person's or making it crooked like a bull's—all these grimaces were signs of inconstancy. A child should keep his forehead merry and his eyes stable. Did his and Elizabethan insistence on the straightforward stare give to Elizabethan portraits the peculiar intensity of the eyes that look out from mature and childish faces?

To impress upon children what not to do, Erasmus drew their attention to some bad manners of the untaught carter, who, like Shakespeare's ignorant clowns, broke all the rules of decorum. The carter shook his head and hair, coughed without cause, hemmed and retched, scratched his head, picked his ears and nose, struck his face like a man weeping or ashamed, rubbed his neck, and shrugged his shoulders.

During this age good manners were so closely associated with good birth that a noble child was taught he must live up to his family's best traditions and not dishonor his ancestors. It was truly his duty as well as his family's to set the standards for other classes to follow. If, however, said Erasmus, fortune willed a child to be of common or low stock and "uplandish" behavior, he must "labor the more" to achieve good manners. Though no one could choose father, mother, or country, he could acquire wit and good manners. For example, the chief part of proper conduct was to pardon other men's faults gently, and not to be less compassionate to the less deserving. If one's companion was of good character, but offended unintentionally, he should be reproved, if at all, gently. When necessary to listen to an old man tell a long story, a gentle child would not interrupt but hear him out to the end. Always the soft voice was itself a condition of good manners. This was why, he said, children should early acquire a good speaking voice. Moreover, they must use their voice without gestures; they were never to beckon or shake the head in denial as their elders often rightly did with them.

There were times, of course, when the child might have to say unpleasant things. For example, he might have to correct another or disagree with him. In such case, he should never say, "You lie," but first beg his pardon and then say, "By your favor, it was otherwise told me," etc. He must not contend with the other person, however. If the two could not come to an agreement, the matter should be settled by an arbitrator.

Living harmoniously with others was complicated by sleeping with others. Erasmus would have the child avoid loud and clattering speech in bed and when dressing or undressing. Knowing the temptation to tell secrets to one's bedfellow, he cautioned the child against trusting any bedfellow or even one he believed to be a friend when it came to a matter of secrets. In no case should he take part in a secret council unless invited to do so. If he heard from other sleepers in his room things not intended for his ears, he should act as if he knew nothing of the matter and dismiss it from his mind. When the master or friend or companion opened his casket of letters, the child must go apart, and never, under any condition, open letters not belonging to him. At a time when privacy was either impossible or a great luxury, such instructions were drilled into children.

Erasmus knew that a child's unpleasant traits might be shown in gaming and sports. Thus he advised him to learn how to overcome strife and deceit and lies that so often crept into the playing of crafty people. If he conquered little faults of this nature, he might expect to be victorious over great ones when he became a man. Should he find himself playing with one who was ignorant enough to lose all games, then he should let his unskilled opponent win occasionally to keep the game merry. He must always keep in mind the fact that play was for recreation and not gain; thus in playing with persons "meaner" than himself, he would do well to show his good breeding by losing now and then gracefully.

The self-control which Elizabethans wished for their children was promoted by whatever device seemed feasible. Though Erasmus would not encourage childish prattle, for example, stern Elizabethans were even quicker than he would have been to discourage parental indulgence in such childish foibles. In all associations with their elders, children were taught to profit in whatever way they could, but especially in speech, choosing their words with the care and precision expected of mature minds. No wonder the children's voices that have come down to us in literature of this period sound like the speech of little men and women from a very far-off land, bewitching, haunting, sweet, and perhaps pathetic.

The insistence on speaking "with reason and advisedly" was duly impressed upon parents by Stefano Guazzo, whose knowledge of polite speech had been deepened by his ambassadorial duties with king and pope, by his founding the Academy *degli Illustrati*, and by his writing, especially his *Civile Conversazione*. In George Pettie's popular translation of this work, as *The Civile Conversation*, Elizabethans found readily available a whole table of precepts which they could recite to their children at opportune moments:

Don't speak till another has finished, and never interrupt.

Report the truth slowly and plainly.

Don't be too hasty in replying; answer slowly even about things you know perfectly.

Be chary of discussing matters not easily believed.

Never speak of yourself in praise or dispraise; one is arrogance, the other, folly.

Never stoop from your own dignity.

Do not mock or scorn others; it is dangerous to scorn what is done ignorantly and even more dangerous to scorn physical defects.

Avoid too great brevity in speech or too much diffuseness or too many subjects or too much repetition.

Ceremony may be dispensed with among friends, but friends are rare. Perfect friendship is found in one person alone: "I know not who is your assured friend, but I am sure that I have not yet found mine with whom I might use such open, simple, and free behavior . . ."

In the country a child would be denied the many contacts Guazzo took for granted, but if the parents were well-to-do and had sufficient education themselves to wish more for their offspring, they tried to overcome the deficiencies of isolation. If they could afford private instruction even remotely comparable to that provided by Sir Thomas More for his children, they might feel they had brought up their children well. Those who were not able to afford private teachers might not have to watch their children grow up without any intellectual training if they lived close to a parson willing and able to take over the duties of the parish schoolmaster. If, however, they had to depend on such a person as the sexton or bell ringer, their children would do well to learn their ABC's. But if the parents had the usual feeling of responsibility for children, they would teach them all they knew themselves of morals and manners, drilling these things into the childish minds until they were practically second nature.

The Elizabethan effort to produce an educated citizenry and an intellectual aristocracy was integrated by the idea of training the young minds which were unable to serve in Church or State to take a responsible place in the trades or crafts. Though the service of the lower classes was very limited in capacity in comparison with the duties assumed by the aristocracy, still their young were definitely trained, each in his own social class with its own decorum in speech and dress and correct behavior. Many were put out to work in the fields or sent into domestic service in the homes of the rich or great, but they were trained for these services also. True, many of the common people could not read or write, but even today illiteracy is still existent. Moreover, education in the sixteenth century was not compulsory except when parental authority made it so. Schools were provided for poor boys, where with parental consent they might be taught to read and write and cipher, and if they remained in school till fourteen, they could be apprenticed to some useful trade. It was the duty of parents to find for each of their children a place in society in which they could be useful and harmoniously adjusted. Some parents failed in their duty, of course, but not without mortification or grief when the accusing finger of scorn was pointed at them by members of their own social class.

Among the poor boys there was usually a chance for those with brilliant minds to receive scholarships at the university, where they too might learn how to serve the State as preacher or teacher or in some other capacity. It was not difficult to find these brilliant poor students, for sons of squires, tenants, and yeomen attended the same local school or were coached by the village priest for entrance to the university. If clever poor boys did not wish to become grammar school teachers or to train for the ministry, they might aspire to university careers. It was no social disgrace for them to work their way through this training, for in the university sons of nobles, commoners, and servitors sat side by side. And sizars did often become Fellows.

A youth's education as well as his birth, therefore, was intended to prepare him for his place in a complex society keenly sensitive to class and class distinctions, but insistent on harmony in the diversity. Many merchants who were well educated consorted with the nobility, and many a gentleman's younger son was apprenticed to a promising or rich merchant. True, after such training this son might become a rich merchant and enjoy certain privileges by means of his birth that otherwise would be denied him, but his education in this instance would also fit him for trade and the decorum of a gentleman in trade. This overlapping of classes and class privileges as the century drew to a close had a profound effect on the educational program. It was in its way as profound as the effect of the Puritans upon the national religion by their insistence that ritual must be simplified and communication with God become direct by means of learning to read and understand His Word. Thus, as the middle class became more conscious of manners, the upper class grew more concerned about vocational education. The university training, however, continued to make its appeal to the professional student or to the leisured class through its conservative retention of professional subjects or of a purely intellectual program.

For this reason the university education remained a privilege enjoyed by a comparative few. In spite of this exclusiveness, however, serious parents of either class dreaded the time when they must send their children away from the home influence into that of the university. Fathers feared their sons might fall into evil habits of idleness, drinking, swearing, frequent attendance at plays, for example, and forget the moral training of their youth. Mothers, of course, were most solicitous about the health of their sons. Would they suffer from lack of proper food or the favors they had enjoyed at the home table? They often sent them dainties by special messenger or for special occasions, as at holiday times when for one reason or another the student could not return home. They also sent extra money to pay for extra care when they needed it. In *The Compleat Gentleman* (1622), Henry Peacham objected strongly to the overindulgence of such mothers, as had other writers before him, saying that their sons learned at the university and Inns of Court only how to spend money lavishly, and returned home after four or five years quite "untaught." Poor judgment in this case harmed sons as much, he said, as when other parents sent their incorrigible sons to court to become pages or to France or Italy to see fashions and to mend their manners, only to have them return ten times worse than if they had stayed home.

In fact, Peacham believed parents who were not concerned enough about their sons' welfare or who did not know how to be concerned were the cause of much harm to boys at the university. For example, he complained of parents who, motivated by ambition, sent "young things of twelve, thirteen, and fourteen" to the university when they scarcely knew where to sup on Friday, and had to have illustrated texts to be able to understand the contents, yet even then scarcely ever opened a book. Many such boys were quite unable to cope with life away from home, and when they were supplied with extra funds by indulgent parents, they used their "too much liberty" by associating with varied companions in "too many recreations in town and fields abroad." Other parents, he said, determined upon their child's career when he was still in his ABC's, and then forced him to follow the choice they had made for him. This kind of parental selfishness caused many evils and much heartbreak when boys went up to the university. Those incapable of intellectual training were driven from the university or, unprepared, they turned to marriage or went out into the world as failures. Then with little or no money in their purses, they became beggars or thieves. This was why the extreme youth of boys who were unfit for university life drew the fire of critics.

The impractical nature of the university training also received its share of criticism. When Sir Humphrey Gilbert planned his academy in 1564, he wished it to circumvent the weaknesses of both grammar school and university, and although he included in his curriculum many subjects commonly taught in both levels of instruction, he emphasized the practical purpose such studies would serve. For example, horsemanship should prepare for more than riding at the tourney; it should teach a youth to ride like a soldier. Modern languages should enable a youth when traveling to win the respect of the foreigners he met by speaking their language with ability. Fencing was of no value if it did not enable a youth to defend his honor. And the languages of Greek, Latin, and Hebrew, as well as logic and rhetoric which he would have taught at his academy on somewhat the same level as they were taught in the university, would be included, not for their own sake but to illuminate political and social matters. Finally, Sir Humphrey, believing caste would ever pervade English society, would have the education at his academy teach a harmonious way of life by training the boys to be leaders with responsibilities to the common people.

Boys of the common people, if they finished grammar school, had their future pretty clearly mapped out for them. When their parents could not afford to send them to the university, or when they were not brilliant enough to warrant a scholarship or a patron's interest, they were bound over to a master to learn a trade just as were boys who did not finish grammar school. Not infrequently such apprentices succeeded to their master's business, particularly if they could win a master's daughter in marriage. Boys who did not attend grammar school at all but were made apprentices at an early age often were protected somewhat by their parents who had a clause inserted in the indenture or contract to ensure their sons being taught reading and writing and "a little figuring."

The apprentice was bound to his master as to his father, and the master was expected to be as responsible for him as for a son. He must feed and clothe his "boys," and he had the right to use his discretion about punishing them when they were disobedient. He took the boys into his home and taught them to be useful serving at table, running errands, and, if he kept a shop, carrying bundles, and step by step learning the business. When large enough, one of them would accompany the mistress on her errands "abroad," and when the master was forced to go out in the dark streets at night, his boys would serve as bodyguard, carrying lanterns and clubs.

After seven years of instruction with the master, the youths were ready to be journeymen with the right to wages, though they still lived with their master till they could prove their skill to take over the management of some part of the trade or to go into service for wages in another man's shop or business. All this time they were also taught the manners belonging to the trade or skill they were learning, as well as the proper decorum of the society in which they were to remain so long as they followed the kind of service in which they had received their training.

Puritans, if they could possibly afford it, sent their sons to the university instead of making them apprentices. Frequently their ambitions for the early acquisition of such training caused them to send their sons away when "too tender" in years. William Vaughan (*The Golden Grove*) felt that the danger in this practice could be avoided, however, if parents were careful to provide their sons with good tutors at the university. The discipline of these tutors was very strict during the Queen's reign, and the boys had to work very hard. It was customary for them to sleep in trundle beds in the tutor's room so that he could be sure they did not slip out to visit taverns or fairs or to play dice or cards or stay out later than 9:00 o'clock at night. He had to be strict with his charges because he knew broken rules meant fines, beating, or expulsion from school. He also roused them at 5:00 in the morning if they did not hear the chapel bell, and supervised their work till supper at 5:00 or 6:00 in the evening.

The tutor had a full day if he was like a father to his "company" of boys, seeing that they attended lectures and disputations, helping them with their studies, keeping their money and paying their expenses, and being responsible for them during their hours of recreation. If the boys had horses, they might ride, practicing tilting, hawking, etc.; otherwise, their free hours were supposed to be occupied with wrestling, swimming, and the like. When a tutor received £20 or £25 for supervising a student, he received a nominal sum thereby. For a "company" of boys who paid him at this rate, he would thus make a fair living, but he also earned it if he performed the duties expected of him.

Vaughan deplored the practice of unprincipled tutors who, instead of reading to their boys, secured the substitute services of young "bachelors" at a very low sum. These immature young men could neither read well nor exercise proper care in the selection of books to read. Worst of all, they could not compel obedience from the sluggards. Vaughan advised parents, therefore, to engage tutors with the Master's degree, which would ensure maturity and learning, and above all, with integrity of character. Such men would range in years from twenty-seven to forty, and be able to handle young boys at the university. They should be "sober" in words and deeds, preventing idleness and willfulness, dicing, swearing, fighting, etc. When the boys should be in their rooms, such tutors would keep them there, thus eliminating the parents' fears of their sons being injured in quarrels or "students' battles," or wasting their money in undue extravagance so dear to youth. All in all, they would keep their charges in awe and obedience without too much severity or too much familiarity.

It had been customary among the upper class for a family tutor to accompany the youth to the university, but in the latter part of the century, many of the middle class depended on securing tutors at the university. Thus there was cause for advice like Vaughan's. Of course, among the nobility, tutors were usually chosen with great care, especially for the heirs. Then parents could be easier in their minds about their sons' diet and morals and manners as well as about their intellectual progress. In the middle of the sixteenth century, however, the Duchess of Suffolk had not fully trusted tutors even of her own choosing, but went to Cambridge with her boys. There she secured a cottage close to the university that she might supervise the diet of her sons, and see that they had the proper physical care. Part of her anxiety had been caused by the publicity given the sad plight of poor boys at the universities of Europe. Up at 5:00 or 6:00 in the morning to attend common prayer and an exhortation on private studies or common lectures, they had no food till 10:00. That had consisted of "a penny piece of beef amongst four, having a few pottage made of the broth of the same beef, with salt and oatmeal and nothing else," according to a preacher's account given at St. Paul's Cross. After this "slender dinner" they studied till 5:00, after which they had a supper no better than the dinner had been, and then came disputation till 9:00 or 10:00 at night. On cold days, they kept warm, if at all, by running up and down an hour before going to bed.

The picture was not exaggerated, for the suffering of poor boys at universities at this time is well known. The Duchess, therefore, would trust her boys' physical well-being to no one. In manners and morals and intellectual training she relied a great deal on the tutor, but she had her sons with her for dinner and at night. At table her instruction under the tutor was strict, one of them reading from the Bible a "chapter of the Greek Testament," which he translated into English, and each of them taking turns in saying grace. During the meal the two boys propounded and expounded questions in philosophy or divinity, "and so spent all the time at meat in Latin disputation." The older boy was fourteen and the other "some years younger," yet both attended public disputations, and every morning read and translated from Plato in Greek and at supper "presented their labors." All their time not occupied during the day with private lectures or disputation was accounted for to mother and tutor. The tutor tells of the older boy's learning as exhibited in so "notable an oration in Latin" while he was in France at thirteen and of "such comely riding" in "charging the staff" that he astonished the French.[10] It is possible the boy accompanied an embassy to France before he entered the university, but it is more likely that the tutor got his facts a bit mixed. Even so, the Duchess had cause to supervise most carefully the diet of her precious boys at school when it was possible for her to take this means of keeping them in good health.

Vives describes a wealthy student of the university at about the same time. His room is comfortable, and so well equipped that the bed even has a mosquito netting. But the boy suffers the discomforts of a bed infested with lice, fleas, and bedbugs. The "ghastly odor" of the bedbugs is especially offensive to him. Vives explains that this pest came from Paris, where it was known to breed in a kind of wood, or from Lyons, where it was found in potter's earth. The student, meanwhile, has a lamp instead of a flickering candle to read by, and he keeps at the side of his bed an alarm clock with the pointer set at 4:00 A.M. His dressing gown is lined with fur, and he reclines on a soft bed, curtained with rich hangings. On the floor of his room are rugs, and near the bed is the chamber crockery on a footstool. Besides his "Minerva or Christ's table," on which rests the crucifix, he has a book case, pens, and a sand case. He uses a scribe. In sharp contrast with this fanciful picture is the actual one of Burghley's university days just prior to the middle of the century.

Instead of being awakened by an alarm clock, Burghley was roused at 4:00 in the morning by a hired bell ringer. Though he did not matriculate till fifteen, he was so studious that, according to one of his contemporaries, with his "early rising and late watching, and continual sitting, there fell abundance of humors into his legs . . . which was thought the original cause of his gout." He took time from his books, nevertheless, to meet secretly at the White Horse Tavern with other young men of brilliant minds to discuss the new learning and the works of Luther. And at these times his eyes lingered too long on a pretty girl. But he was wise enough not to neglect his studies, and in scarcely four years was given the honor of reading the Greek lecture at his college of St. John's. In health he paid dearly for his long hours of study, for when he should have been in the prime of life and able to take long walks in his fine pleasure gardens, he was forced to take his exercise on a gentle-stepping

[10] Lady Cecilie Goff, *A Woman of the Tudor Age* (1930), pp. 181–87.

mule. Moreover, the pain he suffered from his poor, knotty legs must have been almost unbearable at times.

When Burghley's wards went to the university, how differently some of them won their degrees in comparison with the plodding hours of the brilliant young Cecil. Essex, for instance, entered Cambridge in 1577 and three years later, at thirteen years of age, left with his Master's degree, presumably *per gratiam*, of course. As a rule, the university course required seven years. After the first degree of sophisters came four years of study for the A.B. degree, then three more for the A.M. degree. Sons of nobles were sometimes granted degrees they could not possibly have earned in the short time they remained at the university. Though Elizabethans matured early, few of them were ready for the university at the age of twelve, when so many commonly matriculated.

Such young boys, of course, were susceptible to evil influences, as conduct books so frequently warned they would be. Since in the late 1590's boys could choose their own lodgings, they frequently wasted most of their time unless closely supervised by a good tutor. During Elizabeth's reign, Oxford and Cambridge forbade any residents at the university who did not belong to a college and in this way somewhat tightened the control over boys in comparison to that of medieval times when boys lived in hostels or lodgings. But like all other controls, these lessened as the Queen's reign drew to a close and her indulgent successor took the reins in his unsteady hands. A good tutor, therefore, became almost priceless in a boy's university training. Yet to all his other requirements, William Gouge (*Of Domesticall Duties*, 1634) would add another—repairing the negligence and defects of grammar school teaching. This duty was often necessary for those in charge of squires' sons who had been taught by the village parson. Because good tutors were hard to find, bad tutors were severely criticized. Gouge felt that tutors with an evil influence could do more damage than could ever be repaired. Life with them might be cruel and hard. The boys might be given frequent beatings, or permitted too much horseplay, or indulgently granted trips to the country, or allowed substitutions of too much music or play-acting for hard study. Bad tutors left boys so much to themselves that they easily fell a prey to idle companions. Even though boys did not enter the university till thirteen or sixteen, poor tutors could ruin them as easily as they could lads of twelve years.

From the university, boys needing further practical training were often sent to the four Inns of Court in London and the nine smaller Inns of Chancery, which were a sort of third university giving instruction in common law. Such boys were nobles' sons or sons of the wealthy middle class who wished to learn enough law to enable them to look after their own property or, if they had to earn their own living as stewards or officials, to receive the necessary training here. Those planning to be professional lawyers stayed six to nine years as students and then five years as barristers, after which time they could practice law in the courts of Westminster. For ten years after they were called to the bar, they were admitted as "ancients" of their society. Long years of preparation, these, but not devoid of pleasure unless one was inclined to serious effort only. If they could avoid too much of this effort, many youths enjoyed the last years of their formal education. There were readings and exercises in the mornings and moots in the evenings, and frequently plays in the afternoons. Here they could form many friendships; here occurred feasts, revels, much merrymaking, some play-acting, and the social activities that were surpassed only by those at court.

Young men who needed to speak French or Spanish or Italian or German fluently expected to go abroad with a tutor who would be responsible to the parents for securing the best foreign masters obtainable in these tongues. By the end of the century, the need for foreign languages had greatly increased among those planning careers with the government or those expecting to enter fashionable society. In the lower classes the demand for these languages caused some of the grammar schools to offer limited instruction in modern tongues. But even among the crafts and trades, any sons wishing a practical use of these languages felt the need of a tour abroad. The fever to travel was infecting all Elizabethan youths.

Fathers who wished to uphold or to advance the family honor sought in every way possible to prepare their heirs for distinguished service. Soon wealthy men's pampered heirs were begging their parents to let them finish their education at foreign universities. Even some younger sons asked their indulgent fathers to set them up in foreign trade or to help them see the world, declaring "home-keeping youths" were likely to have "homely wits." Had not Bullinger declared that as soon as a son learned his craft he should travel in "other countries" to get further experience and practice? Of course he had also added that young men so privileged should keep modest and sober and mind their own business while away from home. Abroad they could still be gentle, friendly, courteous, and able to conform to honest fashions and manners. One of Shakespeare's servants boldly criticizes his master in *Two Gentlemen of Verona* (I:iii:8–10) for not sending his son abroad. Young men of "slender reputation" (or lower social position) are leaving home,

> Some to the wars, to try their fortune there;
> Some to discover islands far away;
> Some to the studious universities.

It is a great "impeachment to his age," says this persistent man, for his master's heir to know "no travel in his youth." Yet parents who granted the "tour" with reluctance could do nothing but rely upon the tutors accompanying their sons, hoping to read good news in the reports to be sent them regularly about their sons' activities. Shakespeare's Polonius in the play of *Hamlet* (II:i:1–75) is pathetically suspicious in the scene with his servant Reynaldo as he instructs him to spy on his son Laertes studying abroad. In this two-edged comic scene, the father has no more illusions about youth than he has about any man not under surveillance, and he fears his son may take advantage of his freedom from parental supervision. Indeed, he is concerned not only about the son's welfare but also about his own honor as a parent. Fearing the worst, hoping for the best, and certain of nothing at all, he is driven to ascertain the truth in whatever way he can. Meanwhile Laertes welcomes unknown experiences with gay expectancy. But not all young men went abroad to seek adventure.

Some young men took the tour to gain military experience in foreign wars or to study with foreign scholars. Others went for additional training in ecclesiastical or civil law. But young Englishmen of gentle birth usually had as their main object some political purpose. They were expected to observe different forms of government, to penetrate into the secrets of foreign courts, to procure information that might be of value to their government, and to take by means of the tour their first steps in practical training for service in the Commonwealth at their return.

Often such young men were but informal spies on foreign princes or on English exiles, and often they tried to fathom plots and discover warlike preparations against their own country. Actually many of them were sent abroad at England's expense to give them the necessary training for subsequent public service. They were never free, but were restricted by the licenses they were required to have as they went to certain countries at certain periods of time. On their return they were expected to make public whatever observations might benefit the people at large, but their report of secret affairs which was given to the Crown they made from carefully kept journals. These records were very detailed and, of course, dangerous if discovered by foreign spies sent to spy on the spies. In general, these reports compared foreign economic and military organizations with those of their own country in order to show how England might improve her courts and schools and churches and armies. But there was in them much material about domestic matters also—the vices and virtues of the people in the countries they visited, how the subjects obeyed the laws, how nobles kept their wives, children, and estates, how they provided for their younger children, and how they kept their households as to diet, etc.[11]

In fact, the chief justification sons could advance for permission of their fathers and sovereign to travel abroad was that they might become well-informed servants for their government. They were expected to study cosmography, policy, economy, and languages. Lest they be en-

---

[11] Clare Howard, *English Travellers of the Renaissance* (1914).

ticed away from England by flattering offers from foreign countries hoping to use their services or to make willful traitors of them, they were
also kept under surveillance by Lord Burghley's spies and, later, by the
spies of his son Robert. The chief fear, of course, was that Catholicism
might exert its power and charm to make converts of England's gifted
young travelers in order to use them in plots against England. Another
fear, especially of the parents, was that youths might waste their substance in travel and neglect their studies; another was that they might
become involved in duels abroad. After James I came to the throne,
there were no more expert Italian fencing masters in London, and young
men had to go abroad to learn fencing. English ambassadors in Paris
had cause for their bitter complaints of the English brawls and duels
fought there. "The affront, giving the lie, the challenge, involving both
principals and their seconds who also fought: these things might easily
come the way of the Englishmen traveling abroad, and occasionally they
travelled abroad for the sake of these things."[12]

If a young man was not chosen by some influential Elizabethan as
worthy of foreign travel and education, the youth might hope to make an
English ambassador his patron. Many nobles enrolled their sons in the
trains of ambassadors with this purpose in mind. And, in turn, some
ambassadors seeking promotion might pay special attention to sons of
great nobles on tour. The tutors of such sons also had their hopes of
advancement, most of them aspiring to become secretaries later. Besides
tutors and companions and personal servants, young travelers had mes-
sengers and servants to carry letters and to provide fresh horses for travel.
As a result, a son's expenses might be of no little concern to a parent
whose resources were not unlimited.

A youth's education while abroad consisted of further practice in horsemanship, perfecting his skill with weapons, drawing, and elementary
geometry "as a decent prelude to the science of fortification and the practice of seige warfare." In order to improve his manners, he continued
his lessons in dancing and lute playing, though most of his tutors, no
doubt, laid greater stress on Latin, French, and history. According to
J. W. Stoye, a youth's day while studying abroad would consist of two
hours, beginning at seven, on horseback, two hours in language—one in
reading French, and one in "rendering to his tutor some part of a Latin
author by word of mouth"—one hour learning to handle a weapon, two
hours for dinner and discourse or some "honest recreation pertaining to
arms," one hour in dancing, and two hours, till five, in his chamber, reading some Latin author and translating it into French, his faults to be
corrected by the teacher on the morrow. Then came supper, and after
that, "a brief survey of all."

Although some travelers went by foot, an English youth of gentle

[12] John Walter Stoye, *English Travellers Abroad, 1604–1667* (1952), p. 62.

blood nearly always rode horseback, and for safety he and his followers joined other gentlemen he met casually or by arrangement while on tour. From Calais the traveler usually followed the coast to Dunkirk, Ostende, and Bruges or south to Abbeville, up the Somme to Amiens, and on to Paris. Some took their horses across with them, but since this was expensive, most hired post horses unless they could secure a seat in a public coach. English youths of high rank customarily visited the Low Countries on their way to France and, after a time at the French court, proceeded to Italy. Not until James I came to the throne did they visit Spain. Although many of the followers in the train consisted of tutors with a knowledge of foreign languages and affairs, the youths themselves were expected to observe carefully what they saw as they went from city to city and country to country. Their notes, therefore, ranged from comments on military fortifications which they visited to information about city and national government, commerce, agriculture, and business affairs. If this was to be their only tour, it was like a last year or two of freedom, for at their return they must be ready to marry, assume the responsibility of their estates, take part in the political matters of their country, and in general become loyal, capable members of the realm.

During Elizabeth's reign the English treaties with France made that country safe for Protestant travelers, many Huguenots serving as landlords, riding masters, and even preachers of sermons which the young Englishmen "might safely hear." Mothers and fathers, therefore, did not fear so much for their sons' safety till they learned they were to depart for Italy. As England was at war with Spain till the treaties of 1598 and 1604, and as Spain during this time controlled much of Italy, young Englishmen traveling to Milan, Rome, and Naples had to pass as Catholics or "go very warily." If possible they put on some disguise, avoided "dangerous" cities, and especially shunned their fellow countrymen who were Catholics in exile. Possibly Italy held such a strong attraction for some because of its "romantic" dangers, especially if they were Protestants seeking "diplomatic intelligence." To such, Florence was the scene of immoral politics, Venice of licentiousness, and Rome a "blurred image of the Papal city, Jesuits, assassins, Machiavelli's politics, Venetian harlotry," overshadowed by the "menacing power of Spanish overlords."[13] Those who found in Italy the delight of being close to the art and literature of classical antiquity did not dare to stay long lest they be regarded with suspicion at their return home.

That travel was a maturing experience for their children parents were told in enthusiastic accounts published by travelers. These writers described how rude and arrogant English youths leaving their country for the first time met "salutary opposition and contempt from strangers, and thereby gained modesty." Observing the refinements of older

[13] *Ibid.*, p. 110.

nations, rough "barbarian cubs were gradually mollified into civil courtiers." Travel was also proclaimed the best mentor for giving them prudence and patience. The tender and effeminate and the cowardly were hardened by contention, "by unwonted cold or rain or sun, and by hard seats, stony pillows, thieves, and highwaymen." Simple, improvident, foolish youths would be stirred up to vigilancy by a few experiments with "the subtlety of spies, the wonderful cunning of inn-keepers and bawds and the great dangers" to their lives. The perils and discomforts of travel were a "wild prelude" to life itself and taught youths how to be "cunning, wary, and bold" so that they might hold their own "at court, at sea, or even among Elizabethan adventurers."[14]

Serious youths on tour without political or social connections usually tried to live with scholars or eminent booksellers. Consequently these places were often overcrowded with guests. If an English Protestant youth took ill while living at a Catholic home in some foreign country, he would not be likely to get any care unless he turned Catholic, and the physician, apothecary, and kitchen servants would also be forbidden to serve him. If he died, his body was not buried in sacred ground, but in the highway like a dog's. Hence there was good cause for Protestant parents with a son unaccompanied by trusted servant or tutor to fear that their child might be converted to Catholicism while abroad. If this occurred, he would be regarded by his country as a traitor, and at any anti-Catholic disturbance after his return home, he might be cast into prison. Socially, he would be ostracized.

Under the laws of James I, such a person was denied any share in the government and could hold no public office and practice no profession. Neither law nor medicine nor parliament nor army nor university was open to him. Banished from London and the court, he was shunned by his former companions, and lived out a miserable, lonely existence in some country house, plagued from time to time by officers in search of priests. Finally he was likely to go abroad, where he would wander out his life in exile and, if met by one of his countrymen at some foreign court, treated with contempt. Or he might enter a monastery, where eventually he would die and be buried in the cemetery of the brotherhood.

In spite of the dangers of foreign travel, most conduct books urged sending English sons abroad to finish their education. If they were well "grounded in the fear of God" and if they were accompanied by an honest tutor, there was no reason, they argued, why these sons should not return "adorned and garnished with excellent learning." Bartholomew Batty (*The Christian mans Closet*, 1581) agreed to the English idea of an early marriage for heirs, but called parents' attention to the custom of Jews who did not permit their sons to travel abroad till they were mar-

---

[14] Clare Howard's summary of Herman Kirchener's causes given Elizabethans for travel, in *English Travellers of the Renaissance*.

ried and had "lived in wedlock" for at least three years and had "begot children." This bond, he felt, would steady the son and heir sufficiently to make him proof against any temptation during the tour.

Naturally, with the perils of foreign travel so great, most parents did make every effort to provide a good companion or tutor for their sons on tour. If possible, arrangements were made to house the youths with a relative or friend engaged in some diplomatic service abroad. The English ambassador in France, burdened with such men under his care, had these burdens made heavier by the many letters he felt obliged to write parents about their sons. The children of recusants, of course, had no protection from the State, and were invariably accompanied by a tutor who would prevent their being housed at the home of a Protestant relative. If the son's inheritance could descend to a Protestant member of the family, however, such precaution was not taken. Still, in spite of all the provisions they might make, the travelers were likely to encounter many perils on the tour, and parents never felt safe about their sons till they were once more in the homeland. Part of this anxiety had been so intensified by the massacre on St. Bartholomew's Day that for years mothers and fathers dreaded even to think of the tour.

When Fynes Moryson traveled in Europe (*An Itinerary*, 1617), he made his way mostly on horseback, except in Germany and the Low Countries, where he rode in rude lumbering carts, called coaches by courtesy, and holding about six people. On his way to Italy, he pretended to be a Frenchman lest he be liable as an Englishman to imprisonment in Spanish territory in Italy. In Rome he felt safe only when he could prove he was not a spy. Shortly before, Henry Wotton had been sent abroad to complete his education and to report to the English Crown. He had followed about the same route taken by Moryson, and had reached Italy in 1591. Since he would have been imprisoned as a spy if discovered, Wotton traveled to Italy as a young Roman Catholic German and spoke the German language so fluently he deceived a young German traveling with him. He remained two years in Italy, learning the language and studying in the libraries of Padua, Siena, and Florence, and visiting Rome and Naples. Later, in government service, this training served him well, for when he was sent to warn James in Scotland of a plot against his life, Wotton assumed the disguise of an Italian, and performed his mission so successfully that James made use of him later for diplomatic missions.[15]

Wotton served Essex as his secretary, and was exiled to Italy between 1601 and 1603 because of his compromising relationship with the Essex plot. Part of this time he studied at the Laurentian Library and part of the time he sought the favor of Cosimo, Duke of Tuscany, whose service

[15] Logan Pearsall Smith (ed.), *The Life and Letters of Sir Henry Wotton, 1568–1639* (1907).

he tried to enter. It was the Duke of Tuscany who had sent him to Scotland to warn James of the assassination plot. In 1604, Robert Cecil, Secretary of State under James I, made Wotton ambassador to Venice, a position he held till 1610. So well did Wotton please the king by his efforts to form a Protestant league with James as its patron that he might have become Secretary of State at Cecil's death if only he had been in England at the time. Instead, James gave the honor to his favorite, Rochester, and Wotton became an ambassador to the Low Countries, and twice again to Venice. His career does indicate, however, the possibilities of advancement that might fall to the sons whose education abroad was a carefully planned program of training to enter the service of their country.

From such prospects to those of boys with merely a grammar school education may seem to be a long road of disparity, yet the common school education with its stress on Latin was just as seriously considered in relation to the purpose for which it was intended as the last part of the rich young lord's tour abroad. Even though such boys might never go away from home to school, and even though they might be trained for nothing more than trade or the arts and crafts through the apprentice system, all of them while in school were expected to be instructed in the manners (and morals) that would enable them not only to fit contentedly into the life of their class but, if fortune was kind, to climb the social ladder. This was no small undertaking, and how well Elizabethans succeeded in their flexible plan of education for *all* classes may be determined in part by the influence of their ideas on succeeding generations.

For example, the table manners they insisted on as so important an indication of a person's social training still apply in well-regulated homes if, of course, one considers slight differences caused by changes in home life in general. The earliest French books on table manners came at about the close of the fourteenth century and the English not till one hundred and fifty years later. Italians, however, had such books by 1265, though many of them consisted of little more than tables of rules. The pointed details of Erasmus' discussion soon made his little book on table etiquette the chief one in English homes. As the child was taught to behave like an adult, the basic principles of his training make an illuminating picture of the age. Briefly, they consisted of a person's coming to the table well groomed and in a merry but not ribald mood. He must, therefore, put aside all grief or unpleasant thoughts. His hands must not rest on trencher or table or be folded over the stomach. He placed his napkin over his right shoulder and did not lean on his elbows unless he was weak or feeble. His cup was kept on the right, and when not using his knife, he cleaned it and put it at the left of his bread.

Breaking bread was a ceremony. Erasmus preferred having it cut, though he admitted that most men at court (where good manners were obligatory) held the bread in one hand and broke it with the fingertips of the other hand. Bread must always be handled with respect, and the crust must never be plucked off top or bottom of the little loaf. He refers to the custom of his time in which men picked up fallen bread and kissed it to show their respect for the staff of life.

Drinking was a matter of much formality. To begin a meal with drinking was very ill-mannered and harmful. A child should not drink more than two or three times during a meal, though he might drink afterward. He must never bolt his food or wash it down with copious drinks of wine or ale. Though water was best for a child, he might not be harmed by wine diluted with water. Before drinking, the child must wipe his lips with his napkin, especially if a common drinking cup was used, and he must never look aside while drinking or drain the cup to the dregs. If anyone at table saluted the child with a drink, he must curtsy to the person and, if asked to drink, just touch his lips to the cup, tasting a little, then wiping his lips as if he had drunk. If still urged to drink, he should answer he would when older, for a courteous person would never compel a child to drink.

At the time Erasmus wrote, only the spoon and knife were used during a meal; indeed, the fork was never in general use during the entire age. Since it was also customary to use the fingers to take food from dishes as they were passed, it was very bad manners to touch food not taken from the dish, to choose the choice morsels, or to be greedy in helping oneself. If a child or lady was given a dainty morsel by a neighbor at table, the food should first be refused, but if pressed, then divided with the giver. What could not be conveniently taken in the hand must be placed on the trencher. A custard pie or anything served with a spoon should be disposed of in the same manner. If one was given a liquid or thin sauce to taste, the spoon must be wiped clean on a napkin before it was returned. Greasy fingers must never be licked, but wiped on the napkin. When meat was cut for child or lady by a neighbor, it must not be touched till offered by the person performing the little service.

If anything was offered that did not agree with his stomach, the child must not say as much, but rather, gently, "I thank you." If this courteous refusal was not sufficient, then the child must say the food did not agree with him, or that he could eat no more. As soon as possible the child was taught to cut his own meat correctly, whether beef, fish, or fowl. Bones and all unwanted food must be laid on a corner of the trencher till the fragments were removed by a servant. No animals must be fed at table. No bones should ever be gnawed, but picked with a knife. Salt was taken with the knife and never with the fingers. Indeed, the knife was deftly handled by a well-disciplined child, whether he used it to cut food or to lift food to his lips, or to remove an egg from its shell.

The English habit of eating without pause (to which Erasmus objected) was deplored by foreigners, for they urged that good table talk was a matter of good health as well as good manners. Eventually table conversation became very important to proper decorum during meals. Erasmus felt a child should listen carefully to the conversation of his elders that he might learn what subjects were suitable for table talk and what might be said about them. It was very ill-bred, he said, to sit at meals in a stupor or ecstasy, hearing nothing and perceiving nothing but food. It was just as bad, however, to be too quick to talk. In the sixteenth century such progress was made in table etiquette that English travelers back from France and Italy tried to introduce foreign dining customs and manners they had observed. Unfortunately many were so self-conscious in their own use of these refinements that their manners were considered affectations. However, as travel increased and travel literature became popular, table manners began to bridge the gap between old crudities and new fads, though they still followed the pattern set by Erasmus—considerate treatment of others at table, courtesy to the host, and respect for one's own status as a person helping to make the gathering of family and guests a pleasant occasion.

Except among the daughters of nobles or, at the end of the century, among the Puritans, formal schooling for girls was not encouraged. Instead, girls in well-to-do homes were expected to study little more than music and the means of acquiring a dignified and gracious deportment in relation to the home. Such training included, besides the ordering of a household, dancing the stately pavan and lively courant, skill in the art of fine needlework and embroidery, and knowledge in the use of medicinal herbs and various healing arts. Of course there was instruction in the Bible and prayer book and very careful training in morals and manners for every act in their daily routine.

Children brought up and educated at home by a resident tutor might be better taught, as at the home of Sir Thomas More, but sometimes in the homes of nobles the family chaplain acted as tutor for a while. By the time the sons in such homes were ready for the university, the daughters, who had been given the same education as that of their brothers, were turned over to their mother or a trusted woman relative who "earned" her way acting as a governess for the girls of the family. If girls grew in wisdom as they learned household management and good discourse and how to be excellent musicians, they were expected to entertain their husbands and to bring up their families so that their husbands would be both proud and grateful for their services.

Daughters in modest middle-class homes, however, were usually taught that cookery was more important than singing, and laundry a better accomplishment than fine sewing. On the farm, girls were not always taught to read and write, but if their fathers were prosperous, they must become skillful at fine needlework. If they were to inherit wealth, their education must fit them for the marriage their wealth would make possible. Even so, all girls must have some training in needlecraft, for all women must learn to sew for their family, since all of the clothing was made and mended by hand.

They began with the sampler, on which they learned to make many kinds of stitches—cross-stitch, tent-stitch, long and short stitch, crewel and feather stitch, and after these, as many of the complicated ones as their family permitted or they themselves had the skill and patience to learn. This advanced work consisted of the Spanish stitch, tent on finger, tent on the frame, and Irish, fore, gold, twist, fern, rosemary, or chip stitch. Then came raised work consisting of Geneva work, cut or laid work, and the fancy stitches including backstitch, queen's stitch, satin stitch, finny, chain, fisher's, bow, needlework-purl, virgin's device, open cutwork, thorough stitch, rockwork, network, and tentwork. Those who had the time might embroider proverbs, moral sentences, or scraps of verse on sampler and wall hangings, etc. Sometimes the sampler combined a drawn-thread pattern with the usual alphabet and cross-stitch pattern. When, in the 1590's, oriental workmanship became popular, girls learned to embroider flowers and birds in conventionalized patterns or in realistic forms. Those with time and skill and patience often engaged in decorative embroidery. Shakespeare romantically describes Marina in the play of *Pericles* (Gower's prologues to Acts IV and V) embroidering cambric with her fingers "long, small, white as milk." Her designs challenge nature's own "shape of bud, bird, branch, or berry." As she works she sings, making "the night bird mute." If a girl wished to make a gay coverlet, she might embroider vines and roses entwined in a conventional pattern with a border of carnations, pansies, and sunflowers, all harmoniously blended by her skillful mind and fingers.

Girls sent to public schools with their brothers remained little longer than to learn how to read and write. Always the chief part of their education was housewifery taught at home. If a middle-class father had several daughters, he might have to resort to various devices to educate them for advantageous marriages. One might be sent to a friend who was a merchant or servant of a civil or religious institution in his town or city, and another might be sent to the home of a judge or lawyer. Another might remain at home. Whoever accepted the responsibility of educating the daughters would be expected to give them in their new environment the training necessary for the marriage their father was arranging for them.

The future of these daughters would depend largely on the father's position and the dowry he could bestow on each. If he was but an ordinary merchant in a small town, his daughter at home might marry only a yeoman, the one with the merchant friend might marry a foreman of a weaving "factory," and the one with the lawyer might marry a young lawyer-son. If the father was a rich merchant, his daughters might hope for a good deal through marriage, especially if a young noble or two were serving as apprentices in his shop or shops. In any case, the dowry would be an all-important factor in each arrangement, and the parents, knowing what sort of marriage they had reason to expect for the girls, would train them accordingly under their own rooftree.

Among noble families, it was common practice to put the daughters out to households of the minor gentry. Here they were expected to learn to read, write, keep accounts, manage a household and estate, make salves and practice surgery, besides learning the graceful accomplishments of dancing and singing. Their marriages would also depend on the dowries their father could provide, but their training would be adequate for any husband of gentle birth. However, since such marriages were often planned years in advance, the training of the girls might be adapted to the particular households they were to enter and to the particular kind of home each would be expected to establish with her husband. Of course, this ideal was but a goal, for Elizabethans were too practical to count too much on the future.

Among all classes, then, a girl's training was colored by the belief that she must know first how to manage a home and next how to conduct herself according to the manners of the social class in which she would find herself after marriage. In another respect all classes were of one accord— that a "diligent eye" must follow every girl's "virtuous education" that she might come to the marriage altar in a state of "sweet and modest virginity." So much emphasis on the woman's virginity naturally raised the question of a single or double standard of morals for the sexes. Most Elizabethans would condone the follies of youthful sons if they did not go too far or last too long. A few writers of conduct books advised parents to let their sons learn something of the "light women infesting" social life in order to make them more fully appreciative of a virtuous wife. Needless to say, the Puritans did not take this point of view, though they did advocate more study of the Scriptures for the "frail daughter" than for the weak son.

Becon, who insisted that girls be kept ever busy with household tasks, also outlined in his *Catechisme* the kind of training that should be given girls in public schools. Before the time of Henry VIII, girls were educated as wards in homes of friends or at nunneries. In the latter part of Elizabeth's reign, thanks to Puritans especially, they could attend co-educational schools. But this was not enough. Becon wished girls to be instructed by schoolmistresses in schools just for girls, and he would have the teachers paid "honest and liberal stipends" so that they would "more gladly and willingly take pains" in teaching maids. He would not require the girls to wear uniforms; rather, they should be permitted "what apparel they would so as it were honest and seemly." Their prayers, too, must be free from compulsion, and not in a language like Latin which they could not understand. He regretted at his time that the rules of England did not consider how to re-establish schools for women after disposing of the nunneries. If wise women conducted schools for girls, they could be trusted to teach the "future nurses and mothers and house-keepers" of the nation how to be "discreet, chaste, housewifely, good, and obedient." When, however, the future prospects of any girls warranted instruction in social graces, such maidens should be taught discreetly how to dance, to do fancy needlework, and even to entertain young men on proper occasions.

Mulcaster's interest in the education of girls caused him to favor co-education up to a point. Some subjects he felt were particularly adapted to girls—drawing, writing, logic, rhetoric, philosophy, language, and housewifery. By the end of the century girls were not receiving instruction in all these subjects at the co-educational schools, but they were often staying in school as late as time for marriage at thirteen or fourteen years of age. There were some educators who did not favor co-education at all. Perhaps the nunneries established abroad for exiles and daughters of Catholics may have had some influence in bringing back to England boarding schools for girls. A stronger influence was probably Protestant parents who wished their daughters to attend such schools. At any rate, girls were again taught in private schools established for them. At Putney and Hackney, for instance, were such schools, and at Hackney the girls received instruction in French, Italian, bookkeeping, and verse making. Of course only daughters of the well-to-do class could have such advantages.

Becon, on the other hand, was interested in the education of girls who would have to support themselves, through choice or necessity. Although he firmly believed woman's chief occupation should be "woman's work," he admitted that certain girls might, perhaps, become not only teachers but also practitioners in some type of medicine pursued by midwives, surgeons, barbers, etc. In this case their preparation should include careful instruction about the care of their bodies and the need of a temperate diet. He preferred them to work at housewifery, however, waiting patiently and hopefully for marriage. But they must never seek to contract an alliance without the consent of parents or tutors or friends or guardians. Rather grudgingly, then, he gave his consent that they might learn to dance, adding, however, that it must always be done "trimly."

According to Puritans, the Elizabethan girls of the prosperous middle class were frequently given far too much freedom. The pious Batty urged mothers to keep their daughters indoors and under close watch and not let them go running about the streets. They must be taught to hate idleness, "the fountain of follies and the mother of all mischief." For this reason mothers must refrain from "decking them out in trimming and niceness," for they were most suitably dressed when "beautified with wisdom, modesty, silence, and chastity," the best endowments for marriage. He would have them unable to understand the "filthy words, merry ballads, jests, and rhymes" of the age. Instead of mothers loading their daughters with jewels and letting them dye their hair in an unnatural color or drinking wine or dining openly at their parents' banquets, he would have the daughters modestly removed from all social groups engaged in light entertainments. He would not have them even know of zithers, lutes, harps, etc., but when they wished music, let them entertain themselves with psalms. The books their governess might read from must not be "gaudily garnished with gold, but inwardly perfected and learnedly distinguished for the better increase" of the girls' faith in God.

The practical Elizabethan often put the daughters of the household in charge of a governess or poor relative who was chaste, wise, and religious. They hoped she might have a good knowledge of business affairs which a woman should know, such as keeping accounts, and would be able to teach writing, physic, surgery, and, during the lessons in good housewifery, somehow instill into the minds of her charges a degree of wit and humor. She would not permit the girls to indulge in idle or wanton talk, and she would guard against dalliance of all kinds. In large households, this type of governess would have to be capable of keeping daughters away from serving men and their ribald talk, and when the daily lessons were finished, she must find a way of occupying their time with sewing, reading in herbals or pious books, writing letters, or perhaps singing psalms.

The education of many daughters after they reached the age of thirteen or fourteen years was simply specialization in housewifery. If, however, they were to become dame teachers, they were often prepared in guild schools to teach little children. When a woman failed to marry or was widowed, this was a means of making a living that did not require much knowledge. Besides teaching young boys and girls how to read and write, the dame teacher showed little girls how to do simple sewing. In the home, more interesting prospects opened up for the girl expecting to marry. Her mother or governess taught her about special dishes connected with cookery, special formulas for making salves and lotions, how to care for the injured as well as the sick, and how to concoct medicines or what medicines to order from the apothecary for certain diseases. Valuable information of this kind was handed down from generation to generation, but not until the girl was ready to be trusted with careful preparation of the ingredients designated in recipe and formula. Should a girl of the middle class prove to be gifted in caring for the sick, she might wish to enter a guild school teaching her how to become a practitioner in some branch of medicine. Then if she did not marry and had to make her own living, she might enjoy a certain independence.

Near the end of the century, the religious-classical education of noble women declined. No longer was the Vives program followed in which women had been accustomed to read Plato, Homer, Hesiod, Propertius, Anacreon, Sappho, Callimachus, Cato, Plutarch, Lucan, Horace (expurgated), the Bible of St. Jerome or later translations, St. Augustine, and

St. Ambrose. Now they turned to modern writers who would help them become good conversationalists. If women were born to beauty and rank, they might be trained according to their wit, but they could do no better than marry men of honor and rank. Now, men were insisting that women were by nature best fitted for marriage and subservience to the masculine will, and their sisters or mothers or wives agreed with them as the wars lessened the number of marriageable men. Thus the women of the last years of the Queen's reign were trained especially to become good companions to their lords. Yet as the classical education for noble women declined, the education of middle-class women advanced far beyond the rudimentary type advocated by writers of conduct books. This gain, however, came about largely through the ambitions of parents who desired to advance the honor of the family.

At first, however, the decline of classical learning among noble women did not result in any neglect of their education. Instead of long hours poring over Latin and Greek and translating classical languages came lighter and perhaps gayer hours of study in foreign languages that might be of more practical use as they conversed with visitors from Italy and France and Spain. True, the wife of Master Parker of Corpus Christi College, Cambridge, had found her classical training invaluable as she entertained her husband's distinguished friends and official visitors and occasional scholars from the Continent. A man in Parker's position and with his accomplishments must play host to many learned guests. In addition to her Latin and Greek, his wife could rule her household with dignity or, on occasion, with magnificence, for she kept prudent account of her expenditures and carefully supervised all her servants. She also had time to write a cookbook that is still in the college library. But Lucy Apsley, in spite of her religious and agile mind, is somewhat representative of the change taking place in the formal education of privileged girls: at seven years she was provided with eight tutors in languages, music, dancing, writing, and needlework. At about the same time the cultivated and more sophisticated Anne Clifford, daughter of a lady at court, was learning to read and write before she was twelve, and then was taught dancing and singing; for her own pleasure she read poetry, history, the classics, Montaigne, and the Bible.

The shift by women at court from classical languages, philosophy, and mathematics to lighter subects was but natural at the time, for the Bible and such romances as Lyly's *Euphues* and Greene's Susanna story in his *The Mirror of Modesty* provided literature more in keeping with the later Renaissance period. Just how instrumental the Queen was in causing the change cannot be determined. Some writers like Gamaliel Bradford[16] suggest that before Elizabeth was sure of her position as England's sovereign she may have found much solace in the study of

[16] *Elizabethan Women* (1936).

Greek and Latin authors, and that later she found genuine pleasure in merely Renaissance literature. As the tendency to choose the easier authors in preference to the classical grew among the people at court, Elizabeth alone or with the aid of a learned group could not have turned the tide even if she had wished to do so. Early in the next century the drift of the tide was clear, and a letter by Ralph Verney to his uncle, Dr. Denton, describes it for us: "Let not your young girl learn Latin, nor shorthand: the difficulty of the first may keep her from vice, for so I must esteem it in women; but the easiness of the other may be a prejudice to her; the pride of taking sermon notes hath made multitudes of women unfortunate . . ." that is, unfortunate for marriage. Men were insisting on special training for the women they were to marry in order that they might be entertained by their singing and dancing and graceful conversation. Others with more serious minds, especially among the Puritans, wished companions capable of singing psalms and discussing the Bible and its moral lessons.

Women's interest in the Scriptures showed clearly the cleavage in the two kinds of minds at this time. Increasing skepticism in religion among cultivated women led them to find sincere pleasure in romantic and realistic stories of the Bible. Here were portrayed for them, as in good classical literature, genuine qualities of human interest that would appeal to one experienced in the ways of the world. Since Puritans made the stern moral teachings of Paul and the Old Testament prophets their special concern, Puritan men did not lose many opportunities for stressing the Pauline insistence on woman's place in the home. The reaction now in motion against the extraordinary privileges (chief of which was formal education) accorded the "weaker" sex rapidly gained momentum. There were still a few men who did not fear feminine advancement along intellectual lines, and even encouraged it. Gradually, however, the old war of the sexes, precipitated by sixteenth-century interpretation of the Pauline Epistles, flared again. More and more often men expressed the belief that it was dangerous to give women too much education, and then began to believe their own words: the more a woman knows the harder she is to manage, or "the wiser, the waywarder."

As the Queen's reign neared its close, it had become fashionable to cultivate women of beauty and not too much wit, even to gibe a little at learned ladies. By the next century learned ladies were even scorned. Most fathers with daughters who were difficult to marry because of their brilliant minds or natural intelligence read the writing on the wall soon enough to avoid being burdened with learned daughters they could not marry at all. Their obedient wives were made to understand the situation and to take the necessary steps to bring up their daughters according to the new requirements for marriage.

Meanwhile, Puritans did not minimize the hours of formal education determined upon for their daughters; they merely controlled them more carefully. Those likely to marry were given every opportunity within a father's means and a girl's wit to train her to perform the intellectual and domestic duties demanded of a Puritan wife. Others not likely to marry were trained to earn their own living honestly at domestic service, teaching, or practicing some form of medicine among the sick and injured. All of them, however, were drilled in biblical moral laws and the manners of their own social class, and few if any of them even dreamed of disregarding this part of their training in any way.

Less religious middle-class parents who tried to realize through their daughters their own desire for worldly achievement educated them as a rule for advantageous marriages. Since in all social classes a woman's chastity was her chief dowry, they caused her training to support that virtue in every way possible. At the same time they tried to prepare her for the kind of life which the suitable husband they had in mind might demand in a wife. Girls whose parents were more indulgent than wise often relied on the attraction a pretty face and pretty manners might have for a suitor, but if the girls themselves had any wit at all, they would not be indifferent to the morals as well as manners of their own class while they heard them defined at school, found them in the literature that warned even as it invited to evil, and heard them again in their enforced attendance at church and catechism.

In the time that had to intervene before the about-face toward education could be accomplished, however, some Elizabethan girls were caught in the whirlpool of pedantry or were given the old classical type of education in spite of their own inclinations. As a result, the age of Elizabeth was more divided in its opinion about the proper education of women than of men, except, of course, in the matter of a virtuous upbringing and the importance of learning housewifery. Even among the women themselves there were conflicting ideas about the importance and purpose of educating their sex. In spite of this confusion many Elizabethan women achieved a broad and deep cultivation, lightened with simplicity and graced by patience as they performed their daily tasks in the home. Sincere and intelligent and ready to make necessary sacrifices, they were capable of exercising remarkably good common sense in forming their decisions. These qualities they tried to instill into their daughters.

On the other hand there were some who were so steeped in classical moralities as to become self-suppressed in behavior and expression. It is quite possible that such an education caused in some of them the peculiar quality of their greed and ambition and also the excesses they sometimes indulged in after reaching maturity. Since the cramming caused early decline and even imbecility in some of the boys, why should it not have had an evil influence on the girls?

Dressed like their mothers from the time they reached the age of three, some of them, especially among the nobility, never knew the freedom of childhood. Mary, the sister of Jane Grey, was given an education similar to Jane's, with long hours of difficult study. When she was thirty she was no larger than a child of ten. Princess Mary, half-sister of Elizabeth, was educated according to the ideals of Vives and her mother. When she reached a "marriageable age," she was reported as "very handsome and admirable by reason of her great and uncommon endowments," but so "thin and spare and small as to render it impossible for her to be married for the next three years."[17]

Besides the social graces of her time, Mary was trained in the practical affairs of the housewife. She learned to dance and play on the virginal and to play cards. She had her own minstrels and listened to interludes presented by the children of the Chapel under Heywood's direction. She even acted in the court masques and in some comedies of Terence. Among her pets were greyhounds and a parrot, which may have stimulated her interest in the flora and fauna of the New World. As Queen Mary she had many foreign plants and trees imported to England. She was also interested in clock making, to which she gave many hours of her time. Always lavish in her gifts at births and christenings and weddings and in tips for those who served her, she still kept a keen eye on her accounts and always closely supervised her household. She was never idle. When not translating or paraphrasing the classics, she was engaged in religious worship or household tasks or sewing, which seemed to fascinate her. So went the days of this strangely conscientious little being, and so would she have ordered the days of her daughter had the God to whom she prayed so ardently for children answered her prayers.

Such a mother as she might have been found her counterpart in the daughters of Sir Anthony Cooke. Mildred, the second wife of Lord Burghley, was famous at twenty for her translations of Greek. As a wife she was so efficient, aiding her husband in his many duties to Elizabeth, that at her death in 1589 he was desolate. Ann, the mother of Sir Francis Bacon, was exquisitely skilled in Greek, Latin, and Italian, translating Italian sermons into English and translating Bishop Jewel's *Apology of the Church of England* into English. Archbishop Parker was so impressed with the translation of the *Apology* that he had it published for use by the common people. She taught her sons Anthony and Francis from their earliest years, and they never quite outgrew the influence of their religious upbringing. Indeed she never gave them a chance to forget her precepts as long as she could wield a pen. Elizabeth, the third of these remarkable daughters, was twice widowed. Her first

---

[17] *Letters and Papers, Foreign and Domestic, of the Reign of Henry VIII, 1524–30* (catalogued by J. S. Brewer, 1876), Introduction for the year 1527, p. ccviii.

husband was Sir Thomas Hoby, who is famous for his version of Castiglione's *The Courtier*; her second husband was John Russell. She erected handsome monuments to both husbands and composed their Greek and Latin epitaphs. All learned men of her day consulted her on matters of science and languages, and she made many notable translations. She carefully educated her own children and never hesitated to give sound advice to them or to other people's children as long as she lived. Katherine was learned in Hebrew as well as Latin and Greek, and she composed poetry with skill.

The father of these four remarkable women had been their teacher; he had also taught Edward VI. From infancy he impressed upon them the seriousness of the Protestant faith, instilled into them lessons of obedience and modesty, and in spite of their sharp wit, taught them how to be good wives. From him they no doubt learned to love study until it was as delightful to them as play. Yet with all this intellectual training he saw that they became proficient in cooking, sewing, distilling, and all the household tasks they would be called upon to supervise when they were married.

The Countess of Cumberland belonged to the group that was deviating from the classical learning, yet in her way she was as notable a parent as the daughters of Sir Anthony Cooke. She saw that her little Anne spent much time "in reading the Scriptures and other good books, and in heavenly meditations, prayers, fastings, and deeds of charity." This daughter grew up to admire her mother for her "graceful behavior, which she increased the more by being civil and courteous to all sorts of people," and for her "discerning spirit both in the dispositions of human creatures and natural causes, and into the affairs of the world." Since the countess had been unhappily married to a man who spent much time at sports, especially horse races, tiltings, shooting, and boating matches, and who was also the Queen's "champion explorer," the daughter was more dependent on her mother's society than was usually the case.

She believed that her "dear and blessed" mother's wit was so "great, sharp, and natural" that there were few things worth knowing but she "had some insight into them." Though the countess knew no language but English, she read practically all the "worthy" translations by means of which she "enriched" an already "excellent mind" that nature had endowed with prudence, justice, fortitude, and temperance. This mother liked "distilling waters and other chemical extractions" that gave her and others much pleasure. She also practiced "alchemy" to find out "excellent medicines" to help others in need of them. Indeed, she had some knowledge of "most kinds of minerals, herbs, flowers, and plants."[18]

With this temperament and training, the countess naturally inclined

[18] Violet A. Wilson, *Society Women of Shakespeare's Time* (1925), pp. 141–42.

toward the new Elizabethan ideal of a noble lady's education. This ideal of classical and Renaissance literature had been partly influenced by Ludovico Dolce's course of reading for girls in which he advocated a literary education for young, unmarried women but advised the omission of Greek because it was too difficult. He suggested many Latin poets, though only selections from Virgil, and only the "chaster, moral parts" from such poets as Horace. His list included Sannazaro's *Christiad* and *Arcadia*, all of Cicero, Livy, and Sallust, as well as other historians, and all of Dante, Petrarch, and Bembo, besides the dialogues of Sperone and Castiglione's *The Courtier*. Like earlier study lists for girls, this one included much history as a means of disciplining the mind, but its poetry and instruction in court manners are definitely Renaissance in character.[19]

After her early training in the "grounds of true religion and moral virtue," Anne was provided with the renowned Samuel Daniel as tutor. He taught her history, how to read old archives, the significance of armorial bearings, and the laws of inheritance. Since her father had forbidden her any foreign language, she had to forego this important part of education for most girls in her class and be more strictly limited to "other knowledge benefit for her sex." However, she learned to enjoy Montaigne's *Essays*, Gerard's *Herbal*, Sir Philip Sidney's *Arcadia*, the poetry of Spenser and of her tutor, Daniel, the adventures of *Don Quixote*, and eventually she became an omnivorous reader. Like her mother, she was quick-witted and interested in "all things worth knowing." She became so accomplished that she was able to discourse "with virtuosos, travelers, scholars, merchants, divines, statesmen, and with good housewives, in any kind." Even John Donne paid her the compliment of knowing how to discourse "of all things, from predestination down to sleasilk."

When it became time for the countess to supervise her daughter's social and domestic training for the marriage she was expected to make, she provided Anne with a good dancing master to teach her the latest steps and with a musician to teach her to play the virginal. Often the girl accompanied her mother to private parties at some great house, where the guests were entertained by plays, masques, jugglers, etc. In spite of the friction between her parents, she was taught to "reverence" her father, and when they accidentally met, he would speak to her in "slight fashion" and bestow his blessing on her. Eventually she grew to be a very capable woman in the management of her land estate and manifested much interest in architecture and chemistry. Her love of life and its joys and her enthusiasm for legitimate pleasures made her a delightful companion to all who knew her.

[19] Ludovico Dolce, *Della Institutione Donna* (1547).

Further indication of the changes in the education of privileged women may be shown by a comparison of the studies of the Queen herself with those of the little Princess Elizabeth, daughter of James I. Before she was twelve, Elizabeth Tudor had advanced far in history and geography, understood many of the principles of architecture, mathematics, and astronomy, and was fond of poetry and the study of politics. She spoke French, Italian, Spanish, and Flemish. Before she was sixteen, she had read all of Cicero, most of Livy, some of the Church Fathers, especially St. Cyprian on *The Training of a Maiden,* and she had made translations from Isocrates, Sophocles, and Demosthenes. With her brother Edward, she had read from the Scriptures and had translated much from the Latin. In addition to these studies she had acquired considerable training in rhetoric, philosophy, and divinity. History was her favorite study.

The little Stuart Princess Elizabeth had for her governess the renowned Arabella Stuart, whose claims to the throne were as good as those of James himself, and whose education had been as extensive as that of an heir to the throne. She was dearly loved by her pupil. After James became king of England, he sent his daughter to Lord Harington at Coombe Abbey, Warwickshire, where she was surrounded by cultured companions who helped her still further in her education. Her writing master was Mr. Beauchamp, her teacher of music the famous composer, Dr. Bull, and Lord Harington taught her history, literature, and geography. Since the princess was very fond of animals, she was given a fairylike farm with the smallest cattle that could be found. She herself designed a little cottage, which was built for a widow and children who took care of the animals on the farm. Moreover, the princess studied insects through a microscope, a new invention that was fascinating to those interested in science, now accepted as a suitable study for good minds. When the poets Daniel and Donne called her "the pearl of England," they were paying her a genuine tribute of admiration.[20]

As the Queen's control grew less firm over the court decorum which she had kept so strict and formal, pleasures and indulgence crept into the lives of those who resented stern demands of mental and moral effort. Now the decline in education of the feminine mind spread rapidly through court society and penetrated the middle-class social groups that modeled their life closely upon that of the court. Even the Puritans who had eagerly sought the practical and spiritual advantages of education for their daughters developed two minds about their formal training: for one group there was still belief in the necessity of continuing in the cultivation of women's minds, but for the other group there was fear

[20] Charlotte Carmichael Stopes, *Shakespeare's Environment* (1918), "Sixteenth Century Women Students," pp. 295–330.

that possibly too much learning might make women less amenable to the Pauline ideas about a wife's obedience to her husband. There was still a third group, which tried to reconcile the other two points of view, and they found much support in conduct books stressing the need of serious moral training for women because of their mental inferiority to men.

In 1579, Salter's *Mirrhor of Modestie* had been dedicated to the wife of Sir Thomas Lodge, and this book was adaptable to the beliefs of the third group. The book itself was designed for daughters of the growing middle class, and it dealt especially with the type of reading they should engage in. First in importance, said Salter, was Plutarch's *Lives* of renowned and virtuous women, and "those of Boccaccio tending to the same," and side by side with these accounts he placed Foxe's *Book of Martyrs* and the "golden book of Erasmus dealing with the vices and virtues of the tongue." He deplored the "babble and chatter" of silly girls who had not been taught to listen carefully to the wise grave women about them. Part of their silliness, he felt, was due to improper reading, to ballads, songs, sonnets, "ditties of dalliance," and the like. Instead they should read about virtuous women of ancient and recent times. Salter also condemned the habit in some homes of letting daughters associate with young gossips who, under cover of gentility or gallant attire and costly ornaments or feigned religion, might hide corrupt or wicked manners. "Great ladies" of this character he considered especially dangerous, though daughters might also be subject to almost as much danger in their association with sinful children of their own years or with kitchen servants or idle housewives. He objected strongly to women teachers, for he felt a woman's modesty would not permit her to become a "professor" of science or a teacher of law or philosophy in schools or in other people's homes. Women, he said, should be "restrained to the care and government of a family," and should not be encouraged to read, but merely be guided in reading if they insisted on having books.

With the combination of their own love of pleasure and the masculine objection to the cultivating of female minds, women found themselves in an environment not conducive to intellectual development. It did not take long for idle girls of the rich middle class to center their interests almost exclusively in social accomplishments, among which dancing and music were most important. They were almost too easily persuaded that they must accept such a one-sided training because by it they would learn how to entertain their husbands, if not by psalms, then by songs. Ambitious parents, seeking to make "ladies" of their daughters after the father had won a fortune in trade and could thereby afford a handsome dowry, used such accomplishments to lure fashionable young nobles into a marriage or to entice rich young men of their own class into their net. Dramatists, of course, delighted in an exaggerated exposure of such "baiting." Middleton's *Women Beware Women* has a vain father who enumerates the qualities of his daughter and the pains he has taken to rear her gently; if, therefore, the duke is pleased with her, he will find her a satisfactory wife:

> Sh'as the full qualities of a gentlewoman;
> I've brought her up to music, dancing, and what not,
> That may commend her sex, and stir her husband.
>
> III: ii: 1–8

Of her singing he says proudly that she uses the prick song, not what she has learned by ear or committed to memory. Then he tries a swaggering jest:

> She took her pricksong earlier, my lord,
> Than any of her kindred ever did;
> A rare child, though I say't; but I'd not have
> The baggage hear so much, 'twould make her swell straight,
> And maids of all things must not be puff'd up.

Serious fathers, of course, still married their daughters with the expectation of their becoming wives and mothers praised most for their chastity and obedience and second for their knowledge and practice of home management. Such men still looked to these qualities as the basis of female education. Actually, praise of these traits in women persisted in English homes long after the conduct books and sermons which did so much to propagate them were relegated to dusty shelves in libraries of rare books.

The sixteenth-century conduct books, plays, private correspondence, and even its laws indicate that the aim of the educators was not merely to produce an intellectual aristocracy but to develop a citizenry trained to live according to the mores of the groups of which it was made. This was the practical side of the program. The aristocracy must also serve a practical purpose, at least in theory, for included in its many privileges was firmly imbedded the responsibility of securing a smooth functioning of Church and State and all classes of society. Each person, then, had his own niche to fill and definite duties to discharge in his own little domain. Some might perform duties of greater extent than those required of others, but each was made to feel that he must not fail in his own tasks lest the whole structure fail too. This in itself was the key to an age that still amazes the world for its remarkable achievements over so short a period of time.

Side by side with this practical effort to live in the present was the effort made by parents who would prepare their children for a better life than their own or to live this life in preparation for the one to come after death. Whether a person believed in the immortality of the soul (which he could not hope for unless he performed his duties to himself and his family and the State) or whether he believed he could become immortal only through his children, he was convinced that either guerdon was achieved through the education of his children. In either case, the father must be sure his children were *his* children; hence the value placed on the chaste wife. This is why chastity was the foundation upon which the education of daughters was planned. Though the cynic might call this virtue a fragile glass, the serious mind called it a pearl without price. To keep it unblemished, the son's education must be based upon the principle that he was to be the provider of his home and the protector of this virtue in his wife and daughters. Thus morals and manners became a part of the educational program which, regardless of the social group it served, had at its core the cultivation of chastity and reverence for women.

At the same time worldly-wise Elizabethans knew only too well that experience would teach morals and manners better than all the precepts crammed into young minds. They also knew that experience could not teach moral living unless the principles of moral teaching were existent in actual life. That is why parents took to heart the constant admonition that they serve as worthy examples for their children. When belief and effort thus coincided, they had cause to hope they might develop a society that would grow even more cultivated by contact with principles *and* examples of the perfect gentleman and the perfect lady. This was their idea of social progress, and back of the idea was something still more important to them—the value to be derived from good manners by those who practiced them.

To be able to recognize a person for what he actually was and then to give him his due according to principles of proper conduct was the Elizabethan way of saying an educated person would know human nature and how to deal with it. But Elizabethans required more than the knowledge of what group they belonged to. They insisted that children learn how to live with others placed by birth or accident in groups outside their own. Furthermore, Elizabethans at home did not shirk carrying the heavier end of the teaching for this way of life. This emphasis upon the home in the whole program of educating their children is perhaps the most important contribution made by Elizabethans to their successors.

CHAPTER IV

SONS AND DAUGHTERS

To you I am bound for life and education;
My life and education both do learn me
How to respect you; you are the lord of duty . . .
                    OTHELLO, I:iii:181–85

You have begot me, bred me, lov'd me: I
Return those duties back as are right fit;
Obey you, love you, and most honor you
                    KING LEAR, I:i:188–90

N these speeches by Desdemona and Cordelia are mere statements of fact in answer to a father's frantic appeal to the
natural tie which Elizabethans felt must bind a child to its
parents. In both instances the playwright makes the father
stagger under the impact of the blow his child inflicts upon him. For both
daughters flout the basic law of family life and its delicately balanced
relationships whose stability rested upon respect for the rights and feelings of all the members. Today's readers of the lines are likely to forget
the father's actual position in these plays and to let their emotions interest
them chiefly in the fair daughters, but no Elizabethan would have reacted
in this manner. To them a child's first duty to its parents was loving
obedience, not mere compliance or passive duteousness. The words of
cold subservience from the lips of Desdemona freeze her father's heart,
and those of Cordelia shake Lear into hot passion.

Gently reared according to carefully laid plans for a suitable marriage,
apparently submissive in both thought and deed to these plans, Desdemona by her marriage to the Moor utterly disregards every principle of
filial affection. As she mouths the word *respect*, her father can but falter
"God be with you! I have done." Then, recovering his fortitude, he
turns to affairs of state. Even so, he is human, and cannot stop the broken
cry, "I had rather adopt a child than get it!" With another effort he
summons what grace he can to give his daughter to the Moor. Then as
he looks upon the bride's fair face, he utters what any Elizabethan parent
would burn to say under such conditions: "For your sake, jewel, I am
glad at soul I have no other child; / For thy escape would teach me
tyranny . . ." (I: iii: 195–96). The Duke's efforts at comforting him
with wise sayings are, as the father laments, but words that can never
touch the "bruised heart," and again he urges the Duke to proceed with
the urgent affairs of state. The stoic energy with which Elizabethans
met the storms and stress of life could not heal this father's heart, for,
as Gratiano reports later, Desdemona's marriage was "mortal to him,"

and "*pure grief*/Shore his old thread in twain." Had the father lived to see his daughter's shameful death, the sight would have made "him do a desperate turn,/Yea, curse his better angel from his side," and in his great grief damn his own soul to perdition (V:ii:204–9). Elizabethans would recall how the tortured Brabantio had warned the Moor his daughter would deceive her husband as she had her father. Now she had paid for his rash prophecy with her life.

The conduct books, written for children as well as for parents, had much to say about filial love and duty. Becon named honor and obedience as the chief filial obligations, explaining in his *Catechisme* that by such means children were able to show "a fair and just reverence" for the wisdom and prudence of parents given them by God, not by chance. Therefore he commanded children to love their parents "from the bottom of their hearts," and to show their reverence by bowing the knee when asking a blessing. Boys would remove their caps in the presence of their parents, and girls would always "give place" to their parents and reply with a gentle and reverent gesture when father or mother addressed them. The debt of gratitude each child owed its parents for the gift of life and care should be requited by a *like* loving care that could be expressed only in "perfect" obedience. Herein Cordelia failed.

Becon continues by concrete examples of dutiful conduct in children. When their parents grew old and infirm, the children should "labor for them and let them lack no good thing," and if their parents seemed to be guilty of little faults or even of vices, they should do all in their power to conceal these shortcomings, and never, even privately, upbraid them for such frailties. "Make much of thy father in his age," said Becon, "and grieve him not as long as he liveth. And if his understanding fail, have patience with him and despise him not in thy strength. For the good deed that showeth in thy father, shall not be forgotten, and when thou thyself wantest, it shall be rewarded thee . . ." In the same way the mother's "little offences" when "recompensed with good" would bring reward to the child in his "day of trouble." Little sins of dutiful children would melt away like ice in fair weather, but "he that forsaketh his father shall come to shame, and he that despiseth his mother shall be cursed of God."

These writers recognized how a child's devotion and obedience could be tested when parents became garrulous, and infirm in mind and body. But disrespect at this time was severely condemned. To hear the counsel of the aged, said Batty, was wholesome, profitable, and necessary, and to "contemn" it was a "most pestilent thing and extreme madness." Life is so short youth must learn as much as it can from its elders. "Wherefore, let us hearken unto old men and give all reverence and honor unto them, neither let us depart from their sides, whose steps let us follow for their great experience in things . . ." This must be true especially of young, unmarried men. William Gouge asked children to try not to notice parents' infirmities in old age, and also to conceal them from others. When they had assisted their father and mother in need, they should bury them at death "according to the practice of their country and church." Finally, they should pay all their parents' debts, suppress all evil reports of them, and in every way possible imitate and exalt the good in their lives.

William Perkins, in his work *Christian Oeconomie: Or, a Short Survey of the Right Manner of erecting and ordering a Familie, according to the Scriptures* (1609), pointed to what he considered still more practical ways for a child to show "obedience and recompense for parental love." First came obedience in a boy's choice of a career and next in his choice of a mate. For a daughter there must be obedient performance of domestic tasks and learning how to be skillful in the management of a household. In marriage she should acknowledge her parents as "principal agent and disposer." Neither son nor daughter should be compelled by parents to marry their choice, "yet the reverent and dutiful respect" of a child would be sufficient inducement to obedience except in cases of "some great and weighty cause." With the eldest son particularly obedient, all the other children were more likely to deal kindly with their parents, like the brood of a stork which feeds its mother when she is old. Should this eldest son neglect his duties by word or deed, Perkins considered him worthy of death. William Gouge (*Of Domesticall Duties*, 1622) was less adamant. He believed children might object mildly when parents reproved them without cause, still they must listen respectfully and readily, and if their parents recommended wise acts, they must try to follow them. Perkins, of course, was more concerned about the privileges and responsibilities of primogeniture, which would admit "of no exceptions except in case of notorious wickedness." The eldest son being permitted "government and royalty, priesthood, and a double portion," was bound by his privileges to care for his parents in old age and to set an example for the other children to follow. Gouge was concerned about children in general.

So, too, was Dorothy Leigh (*The Mothers Blessing*, 1618) in her pious advice to her sons to pray often and zealously if they were to be faithful in their obligations to their parents. She believed in their praying in groups of two and three, but more often alone the first thing in the morning when the rest of the world was still asleep. Next they should read a chapter from the New Testament to "stir" them to further prayer, confessing their sins and asking God's grace to do His will. This practice, she said, would weed out sin and let the soul grow in obedience toward both the earthly and the heavenly father. Queen Catherine had had this thought in mind when, though she disagreed profoundly with Henry VIII's commands to his children, particularly to her own child by him, she wrote Princess Mary to pray for strength to obey her father in everything "save only that" which would "offend God" her heavenly father.

Gouge repeated the same advice, saying children could refuse to obey their parents only when asked to do something they were sure, after prayer to the heavenly father, might be contrary to His will. He would also have them show the same respectful obedience to parents-in-law.

Disobedient children caused parents genuine grief if they believed their offspring broke God's laws when they disregarded parental commands. Such grief may have been felt by Burghley when his son Thomas by his first wife, Mary Cheke, frustrated his father's plans for the boy's welfare. It is not unlikely that Burghley also felt this son was due punishment for his own hasty marriage, which had dashed his parents' high hopes for him. By the time this boy was twenty, Burghley had a son and daughter by his second wife, Mildred Cooke, but in justice to his firstborn, he felt Thomas should be given the training abroad to prepare him to succeed him as his heir. Burghley had intended to send Thomas to the household of Coligny, the Admiral of France and leader of the French Protestant party, but was advised against this plan by Nicholas Throgmorton, English Ambassador in Paris. Because of the danger of civil war, Throgmorton suggested that Thomas and his tutor take lodgings near the embassy and share his table while the youth trained to become a courtier by riding, playing the lute, dancing, playing tennis, and engaging in other appropriate exercise. Thomas Windebank, tutor of the boy, was asked for his advice, and told the anxious father he thought it would be wise to accept Throgmorton's offer of his table, for then Thomas might "learn to behave himself, not only at table, but otherwise, according to his estate."[1]

In 1561, Burghley sent Thomas abroad, accompanied by his tutor and two servants. Throgmorton was to keep the boy under general supervision. Two years previously, Throgmorton had been favorably impressed by Thomas, who was then visiting in Paris and seemed to be a youth of considerable promise, but now he was disappointed. Burghley, meanwhile, became increasingly anxious as both son and tutor failed to follow the plans so carefully worked out before the journey began. As soon as the boy was on foreign soil, his tutor lost control of him, and the journey which was to give Thomas a year in Paris and travel in Italy went wrong almost from the beginning. Time and time again Burghley tried to get Windebank and Thomas to give an account of their expenses, but in vain.

Instead of going directly to Paris as they had promised, they went to Rye, Dieppe, and Rouen. When they finally arrived in Paris, the troubled father wrote his son, wishing him God's blessing, though he did not know whether Thomas deserved it. He asked him to begin at once to translate French and to write "somewhat" to his stepmother. He wrote Windebank, asking him how the two of them were spending their

[1] Martin S. Hume, *The Great Lord Burghley* (1898), pp. 120–21.

time, and hoped Thomas was serving God "with fear and reverence."
In his answer, Windebank urged the father to repeat to Thomas his in-
junctions about prayer. Thomas paid no heed to such advice, and wrote
nothing to his stepmother.

They had taken three horses with them, and sold them on their arrival in Paris, Thomas keeping the money for himself. "Of study there
is little or nothing yet," he wrote Burghley a month later, but he was
excited about a fight between a lion and three dogs, in which the dogs
won. Such a responsibility as Thomas soon proved too much for the ambassador, who wrote Burghley, advising him to send the boy away from
the distractions of Paris. The tutor, in the meantime, had taken lodgings
for the two of them at the house of a gentleman, "a courtier and learned
but of indifferent religion," to whom he was paying 300 crowns a month.
Thomas had needed extra winter clothes, costing £20, and now he wrote
his father to send money to pay for horses. When Burghley objected
to paying so much for horses, the tutor explained that all gentlemen of
"estimation" rode, and it was not meet for Thomas to go afoot.

During the autumn of this year Burghley was required to accompany
the Queen on one of her progresses, but he wrote regularly to his son
and Windebank from the various country houses where Elizabeth was
entertained. Always he urged Thomas "to study, to pray, to avoid ill
company, to take heed of surfeits, late suppers, prodigality, etc." But
to no avail till Thomas fell seriously ill, when he became repentant. As
soon as he recovered, however, he fell back into his old ways. Finally
he lapsed to such an extent that his father wrote angrily in March of 1562
how all who came from Paris gave Thomas the character of "a dissolute,
slothful, negligent, and careless young man," and he signed his letter
"your father of an unworthy son."

Burghley wrote Windebank during this time, hoping he was instructing Thomas in "genealogy and alliances of French families, and especially in those matters important to men of high birth or to those recently
promoted to noble estate." He frequently commissioned him to send new
plants and gardeners, and continued his own study of heraldry and the
reading of good books. Gardening was his love, and may have eased a
little the pain Thomas was causing him.

Finally, in desperation, he wrote Windebank: "I am here used to
pain and troubles, but none creep so near my heart as doth this of my
lewd son." He admitted he did not know what to think of him, and he
feared the shame he would receive from so "unruled a son" would grieve
him more than if he "had lost him in honest death." He told Windebank
to consult with the Ambassador to whom he had "referred the whole,"
and said he "would be best content" if Throgmorton "would vomit him
secretly to some sharp prison." If that seemed unwise, he still would
prefer having Thomas sent away to Strasbourg if possible or to Lorraine,
for his grief would "grow double to see him before some sort of amends."
If such measures were not effective, he must be brought home, and he

would receive that which it pleased God to lay on his shoulders, "a daily torment" in the midst of his business cares.

Yet pride forced him to caution Windebank that if he brought Thomas home to "let it appear to be" by reason of the religious war in progress there. Naturally, Burghley, himself "promoted to noble estate," was most sensitive about the good opinion of the world. Who can say what he suffered when he received word from Windebank three weeks later that the tutor was "clean out of hope" about Thomas, who showed "utterly no mind nor disposition to apply any learning," but was carried away by such other affectations" that he forgot his "duty in all things." Windebank, therefore, resigned his charge and refused to accompany Thomas any farther.

Though eventually Thomas did mend his ways, his conduct had touched Burghley to the quick, for any reproach on the heir to Burghley's house and name was agony after all his effort to trace his ancestry back to ancient times and to become the head of a noble line. He must have put in many a desolate hour in contemplative thought over his own youthful disregard of parents when he married the daughter of the widow Cheke. Chance had caused this marriage to be a brief one, but its fruit, Thomas, must now have seemed to Burghley, as he recalled the disappointed hopes of his own ambitious father, at last a just as well as a daily torment. That Thomas did mend his ways was due to the good example or teaching or discipline of his father, though his interests were never political or intellectual like those of his gifted half-brother, Robert Cecil. Truly the "sour grapes" the father had eaten "had set on edge" the son's teeth.

The realism of Ben Jonson's satiric characters and situations must have come close to parents with sons like young Thomas. An old father in *Every Man in his Humour* (C. H. Herford and Percy Simpson, eds., 1927; I: ii: 122–36) muses on his heir's seeming wayward conduct:

> I am resolved, I will not stop his journey;
> Nor practice any violent means, to stay
> The unbridled course of youth in him; for that,
> Restrain'd, grows impatient; and, in kind,
> Like to the eager, but the generous grey-hound,
> Who ne'er so little from his game with-held,
> Turns head, and leaps up at his holder's throat.

He determines, therefore, to use gentle means of correction:

> There is a way of winning, more by love,
> And urging modesty, than fear.
> Force works on servile natures, not the free.
> He, that's compell'd to goodness, may be good;
> But 'tis but for that fit: where others drawn
> By softness, and example, get a habit.
> Then, if they stray, but warn 'hem; and, the same
> They should for virtu' have done, they'll do for shame.

Later (II: v: 5–15), the father is shocked by the disrespect of youths, and contrasts them to the young men reared with the strict discipline of his day:

When I was young, he liv'd not in the stews,
Durst have conceiv'd a scorn, and utter'd it,
On a grey head; age was authority
Against a buffoon: and a man had, then,
A certain reverence paid unto his hairs,
That had none due unto his life. So much
The sanctity of some prevail'd, for others.

The fault, he concludes, is due to lack of good examples in parents:

But now, we are fall'n; youth, from their fear:
And age, from that, which bred it, good example.
Nay, would ourselves were not the first, even parents,
That did destroy the hopes, in our own children:

Youthful licentiousness, then, springs from the failure in parents to set a good example, and in a long, railing speech, the cozened father, called Kno'well by the dramatist, takes parents to task. He is thankful no one can accuse him of showing his son "Venetian courtesans" or of urging him to get money by fair means or foul. He speaks contemptuously of foreign affectations: he has never "dressed snails or mushrooms curiously" or "perfumed his sauces" and taught his son such foppish "arts." This extreme pursuit of "gentle manners" Jonson satirized in other characters: the country cousin studying hawking in a book, a coward boasting of his fencing as he "elegantly" takes tobacco, mouthing his big oaths, and a city lad pretending to be a poet. Such things were often criticized by writers of conduct books as well as by vigilant fathers with sons to be launched successfully into society and life.

The reader of Elizabethan literature and letters and state papers is constantly impressed by the efforts of parents who, knowing that their own youthful indiscretions were not likely to be overcome entirely in their children in spite of good environment and careful instruction, still did not lessen their efforts to provide good training.

Not all Elizabethan parents, however, were wise or patient, and gossiping letters report the weakness of fathers and mothers and children who reacted emotionally to situations without due analysis of them, or who found themselves confronted with disappointments too great for them to bear with any tolerance. Such was the affair between Tobias Matthew, Archbishop of York, and his son Tobie.[2] It was for this son

---

[2] *Calendars of State Papers, Domestic Series, 1598–1601*, ed. Mary Anne Everett Green, CCLVI, Nos. 29, 30; CCLXVI, Nos. 13, 19; CCLXVII, Nos. 15, 24; CCLXVIII, No. 61; CCLXXXII, Nos. 25, 48; CCLXXXIV, No. 7. The father's argument with Edmund Campion, the Jesuit, in 1581 was considered important enough to publish after his death.

Sir Francis Bacon is said to have written his essay on friendship. Tobie was educated at Christ Church and was early attached to the court, serving on an embassy at Paris and sitting in Parliament. Yet he was eventually driven abroad because of his suspected activities as an agent of the Pope. Since his father was very active in forcing recusants to attend the Church of England, he suffered keenly from the disgrace he felt his son had brought upon him.

But Tobie's mother suffered also and, according to her way of looking at things, with good reason. Her father had been William Barlow, Bishop of Chichester, and her first marriage had been to the second son of the celebrated Parker, Archbishop of Canterbury. When as a widow she became the wife of the Dean of Christ Church and, in 1577, the happy mother of their son Tobie, she made plans for a brilliant future for both her son and her husband. She was not disappointed in the latter, who advanced in the Church till he became Archbishop of York, but she was bitterly resentful that Tobie frustrated her cherished ambitions for his career. By maintaining control of his fortune, the parents kept Tobie in a state of domination that prevented him from declaring his position openly as long as they lived. He was fifty-one when his mother died, and fifty-two when his father's death left him free, but so long had he been subjected to the stronger wills of his parents that Buckingham, the favorite of James I, still referred to him as "little pretty Tobie Matthew" when he was forty-six years old.

Tobie was never strong, was constantly running into debt, and yet was possessed of a charm that won him many friends.[3] When gossip began to bandy his name about, he lost whatever affection his mother seemed to have for him. Always suspicious of his religious inclinations, she grew increasingly distrustful of him. There was a bond, however, between him and his father that was never broken: both believed heart and soul in the English monarchy. Moreover, the father's great learning, eloquence, wit, and sweet conversation attracted Tobie's keen mind. The father had come from a Catholic family, but out of loyalty to his country had turned Anglican, and possibly this change in his life enabled him to understand his son's emotional upheaval.

By 1601, both Tobie and Bacon had been abroad, but the latter was never attracted to Catholicism, partly because of his unemotional temperament and his natural obedience to his Protestant mother, and partly because of his ambition to serve England and Elizabeth's religious compromise which he believed was made for the good of the State. Though Bacon must have been repelled by Tobie's religious nature, he may have excused his apostasy as due to his need for care during the severe illness abroad when his recovery necessitated dependence on the Catholic house-

[3] David Matthew, *Sir Tobie Matthew* (1950), and A. H. Matthew and A. Calthrop, *A Life of Sir Tobie Matthew, Bacon's Alter Ego* (1907).

hold in which he lodged. He was also much impressed by Tobie's wit and smooth charm; more than this, he must have been convinced that Tobie's love for the English State was as loyal as his own. Could Tobie's father have regarded with Bacon's detachment his son's religious experience, both would have been spared much grief. But under the conditions, such detachment in a father could hardly be expected.

The quarrel between Tobie and his archbishop-father, therefore, was far greater than the difference between the son and members of the Crown, and gossip reported avidly whatever it could find out about the "family scandal." His friend Carleton may have been as helpful as he dared to be to Tobie and still keep his position of trust in the diplomatic service, but he also relished whatever bits of gossip came to his notice about the quarrel between father and son. Wotton, also in diplomatic service, had no confidence in Tobie, and, according to Clare Howard,[4] called him the principal member of "a certain knot of bastard Catholics . . . who . . . did much harm" to English travelers in Tuscany. However, when Tobie came forward to show the delights of Italy to sons from good English families, he may have been motivated in offering his services by his yearning for contact with home as well as by an intention of winning them to the Catholic faith. His exile tortured him.

Nor did his father in England suffer much less. As a prosecutor of stubborn recusants and as a solid official of the Church of England, which had finally taken a firm stand against Catholicism, he was bound to denounce passionately a son who had entered the camp of the foe. Both were in a cruel dilemma.

In spite of the seeming indifference to religion as a personal force in the lives of many cultivated Elizabethans, one who turned Catholic under such stress as Tobie suffered would hardly dare break the vows he made to the faith which he embraced while desperately ill. To commit such an act would ostracize him from both parties. Though religion itself might be for many a matter of form or social necessity, it was also a strong habit inculcated by careful training at home. Indeed, so strong were these bonds of religious form and ceremony in the mind of even such an intellectual as Sir Francis Bacon that this man's most intricate and speculative thought and speech were held tight and bound together by its restrictive phases.

Still the fear of most Elizabethan children for their parents was really reverence. William Gouge had this meaning in mind when he called a child's fear of his parents "an honorable esteem" that made him desire to please rather than offend. Such an attitude was mixed with love and was not slavish, giving the child forbearance, causing him to speak only when spoken to, using modest and sober gestures, and making him wish

[4] *English Travellers of the Renaissance* (1914).

to give his parents "upper place" always. No honor, said Gouge, was equal to the dignity of fatherhood, for even when a child advanced to a higher position in the world than that held by his father, and even when in the eyes of the world he was held in such high esteem that out in society he might take the "upper place," nevertheless at home he must never put himself above his father. If his father should stand uncovered before strangers, the son must stand uncovered too. Moreover, the son must never under any circumstances be too conceited to ask his father's blessing with reverent obedience, bending the knee with love in his heart to both father and mother. If the father should die and leave the son's training and education to the mother, the son must be especially dutiful to her for his father's sake.

When writing from Germany to his mother, Henry Wotton followed this ideal of a well-bred son, expressed in the conventional Elizabethan phrases of fulsome compliment and courteous speech to show respect. Yet with all his formality, he retained a tone of sincere and warm affection. He addresses her as his "Most Dearly Esteemed Mother" who, he hopes, is as well as he finds himself. It would "comfort" him to hear such news of those he "reckons" his friends but to hear "the like" of his mother would be the greatest comfort of all. Though "all the world went well" with him, nothing could bring him such contentment as to hear well of his "dear mother," and he asks her to "persuade" herself that to hear otherwise would be "the deep grief" of his soul. He prays daily that "God will draw forth the sweet time" of her life "with ceaseless mercy," and he begs his "good and kind mother" to "let no cares" taken for her sons cause her "less comfortable thoughts." He reminds her of the "promise of Him which never fails them that live in His fear," and he begs her not to worry over his "not well-bestowing" his time or his falling into the "danger of sorting" with ill company or his indulging in the "too much pleasure taken in the manners of the people," for he assures her his "child's years are fully out, which were wont so regardlessly to look upon themselves." He believes it is now "high time" to draw his mind "to the certain course" he means to follow. "If (my dear mother) you ask my opinion what it is that I have unchangeably set down with myself to make myself happy with, I must in the faithfullest troth I owe you answer this: it is knowledge I seek, and to live in the seeking of that is my only pleasure. The God of Heaven lead me the true way to it." The letter closes with his "regardful duty and most entire love" to his "dear mother," and he remains her "most faithful obedient son."[5]

A courteous stepson would adopt the same respectful and affectionate manner toward his new mother or toward his wife's mother even though

---

[5] Logan Pearsall Smith (ed.), *The Life and Letters of Sir Henry Wotton, 1568–1639* (1907), I, 239–40.

she was not gracious enough to call forth such a response. However, in 1578, a letter to Sir Christopher Hatton[6] asks his powerful aid for a man's mother-in-law who deserves both "justice and consideration" from the Crown. Tremayne begins his letter by saying no man could be more "unwilling to trouble his friend with suits" than he is, but the state of his "poor mother-in-law" is such that it "differeth not so much from the state of a widow or an orphan" and can be "remedied" only by "a worthy gentleman" that will be moved by "his benevolence." He relies on Hatton's knowing "what a noble mind there is within that little body," and he feels sure Hatton will "use all means to keep her from calamity." If this "little lady" had the means to "bestow upon her Majesty . . . a present as great as this she now desireth" she would do so on the instant, but hard days have fallen to her lot. Tremayne is bound to her as to the mother of his wife, but also by "her rare disposition" which adversity does not alter. He asks Hatton to persuade the Queen, therefore, to "pardon the debt [or] at the least to respite it, without any danger to incur further forfeiture." If the little lady cannot be so favored, he hopes the Queen will not refuse to send her "good favor," for without it his mother-in-law's days will be shortened and her death hastened. Tremayne had good cause to hope for some gracious act on Elizabeth's part, for he had been sent with Elizabeth to the Tower during the Wyatt rebellion, and even when put to the rack had refused to admit her guilt in the uprising. Her gratitude to him had already been shown by her making him Clerk of the Privy Council as soon as she became Queen, and he knew that the plea in this letter would not fall on deaf ears. Elizabeth did not forget her old friends.

Obedient children were always willing to perform any service asked of them by considerate parents by blood or marriage. If any of their acts might affect the welfare of their parents, children would first consult with them before endangering their interests in any way whatsoever. In the selling of property, for example, no children would enter into negotiations without parental consent unless they were willing to face severe condemnation by society for their disobedience. There were times, though, when the care and disposal of property did prove to be a stumbling block in the harmonious relations between fathers and children. If deprived of his goods by his own flesh and blood, an Elizabethan father might become frantic in his feeling of outrage. In such a state on March 3, 1600, Sir Walter Leveson wrote a letter from the Fleet Prison to Robert Cecil that must have given the Secretary very mixed feelings. He tells of writing seven years ago to express his affection for Cecil, who he wishes "had better considered of it," for he and his son have no heirs and the letters have caused him "hard persecutions" from his son

---

[6] Sir Nicholas Harris Nicolas (ed.), *Memoirs of the Life and Times of Sir Christopher Hatton* (1847), pp. 95–96.

and "confederates." He swears "this surmise" against him "touching" the Secretary has brought him "heavy displeasure" he never deserved, "for they all know I ever loved and honored you, and was much bound to your father, and was never subject to that vile vice, ingratitude." He asks the Secretary to make trial of his love and faith, and says that he has been "ever free" from even the intent of hurting anyone except his son, who has caused his own father's imprisonment, and whose servant was the first man ever to lay hands on him. Since his imprisonment his son has "bought" all the executions he lies in prison for, and entered upon all his lands and goods. He has had from him not one penny for maintaining himself and wife and family for the past fourteen months. Then he concludes: "These extreme dealings of his forced me to forget myself, which I am now heartily sorry for, as my son and I are now reconciled since last term. I have freely forgiven him, and he has done the like by me."[7] This letter does not explain clearly the State's part in the "domestic affair," but it does indicate the feelings between father and heir and the possibility of quick, unexpected settlement.

The conduct books sought to cure such quarrels before they could ever begin. So great was the value placed upon material possessions and so uncertain was man's economic status in this time of swift change that moralists urged every means to preserve the family against occasions for actual disruption. Meanwhile responsible members of the family were deeply concerned about the very real problem of how sons and daughters might be made secure against want or privation, and parents were urged not to give of their substance till they lost their independence and became a burden to their children. If the daughters could be dowered, they might be reasonably sure of attaining some measure of security through marriage, and if they had good husbands, they found the best security possible for themselves. If unwilling or unable to marry or to become ladies' companions or tutors of children, they might have to join the servant dependents in a large household. In middle-class families and even among the gentry, such women often supported themselves by the spindle or by needlework both practical and ornamental. Shakespeare's duke in *Twelfth Night* (II:iv:45) refers to these "spinsters and the knitters in the sun" as chanting old songs. Unmarried women, however, had little cause to sing sentimental love songs. Frequently heads of families were sought by poor widows to place their daughters as waiting women in homes of their own station in life, and they were most gratified when such disposal could be made of them even though they became dependents. There was nothing for such daughters to do but accept their lot with resignation. Among the middle class they had more chance to be independent, though dame school teaching, nursing,

[7] *Calendars of State Papers . . . 1598–1601*, CCLXXIV, No. 67.

etc., were poor substitutes for marriage. If women were left widows with possessions, their families must protect them till they married again lest they lose their fortunes and become sad dependents like their unfortunate sisters. This "protection" could start quarrels, and conduct books had much to say about preventing them.

Younger sons of the gentry were the cause of many real problems for their parents or for the heir of the family, as convention frowned on gentlemen engaging in any kind of "traffic." Fynes Moryson in *An Itinerary* (1617; Part III, Book III, Chap. III) scoffed at this English attitude and contrasted it with the practice of Italians whose sons freely entered trade. He described Elizabethans as "perhaps thinking it unjust" to leave the vulgar people no means "to be enriched by their industry, judging it equal that gentlemen live off their revenue, citizens by traffic, and the common sort by the plough and manual arts," and yet all "members of one body . . ." The result, however, was harmful to the gentry itself, for heirs to estates sold "their patrimonies, and the buyers (excepting the lawyers) were citizens and vulgar men." Such a "mischief" made the prodigality of the English gentry "greater than in any other nation or age." He could but "marvel" how such "rashness or slothfulness" caused the English gentry to "neglect" and "despise traffic," since in England traffic surpassed "all other commodities" and was even "the very sinew of the kingdom."

Yet so strong was the English adherence to the social classes that the sharp-tongued Harrison,[8] who severely criticized whatever abuses came to his eye, set down in orderly array and with no little complacency the four orders of the English people during the years 1577–87. In the first order he placed the gentlemen—princes, dukes, marquises, earls, barons, lords, nobles, knights, squires; in the second, all free citizens within the cities and of sufficient substance to bear some office; in the third, the yeomen or freemen who were worth £6 a year in revenue from their land, and in the fourth, laborers consisting of artificers, tailors, shoemakers, carpenters, bricklayers, poor husbandmen, etc. All who could afford to live without hard work and could buy a coat of arms might be called gentlemen, but he would define a gentleman as one "born gentle," except in case of knights and squires who "became gentle through valor," and were then "called sir." He admitted that yeomen who were usually farmers on gentlemen's estates might, by thrifty management, succeed to those very estates, buying them and prospering enough to send their sons to the university and Inns of Court "to make gentlemen of them." However, he added quickly that yeomen could never be called masters; only gentlemen were so called, and the yeoman's son could never be idle like the gentleman's son. Harrison's and the prevailing English prejudice against

[8] William Harrison, *Description of England in Shakspere's Youth*, ed. Frederick J. Furnivall (1877), pp. 105–33.

the gentleman engaged in traffic was to outlast the Elizabethan period and to continue till England became involved in the First World War.

The pious Becon divided occupations into classes in order to encourage citizens to use this means for rising in the social scale. In the first, he placed the ministry, including pastors and preachers; in the second, ministers, including magistrates and those serving the Commonwealth; in the third, schoolmasters, and in the fourth, laborers in the honest and virtuous crafts. Actually, into these divisions were fitted the younger sons of the gentry far more often than the patriotic Englishman liked to admit. If the father of such sons could "lay up portions for them" or settle upon them other estates besides the main one, or could secure for them competent portions of the estate of the eldest son, only then could they remain outside some division of the middle class, and some middle-class occupation.

In theory, the eldest son fell heir to all the land of the family, and his brothers were trained in callings that would enable them to serve the Commonwealth. If the younger brothers were not put into the house of some great man to become pages or esquires or courtiers, they might be trained for some diplomatic employment or secretaryship or the like, or sent abroad on some mission. The adaptability of Elizabethans to sudden change probably grew out of the fact that they expected life to be difficult, to challenge their very right to existence, and they went forth to meet life with sharpened senses that quickened their wit and understanding. This is why so many of them succeeded, at least as long as the courage of youth lasted, in facing situations full of painful, exciting, dangerous intrigue. This was especially true of life at court, which was itself an education in culture and manners, but also an introduction to the treachery that bereft them of all their illusions or made them into smooth, worldly sophisticates.

When younger sons could be fitted into life in the army or navy or law or Church, they offered their family little concern; otherwise they might have to pocket their pride and enter trade, though in such cases the proud family suffered more, perhaps, than the sons. Sons looking forward to high careers, however, expected to enter one of the Inns of Court, where they would be taught courtly, diplomatic language, and a refinement of behavior influenced by dancing, fencing, and acting in masques and plays. If they had literary talent, they might even pass some of their idle moments writing plays for others to act in before great lords. To certain temperaments, the glamour of life at one of the Inns had tremendous appeal.

But there was more than glamour; there was hard study for the youths who would make a fortune at law or who looked to the career of a lawyer as a means of gaining political power. If sudden riches were their ambition, they hoped to learn how to invest their income from practicing law by shrewd buying and selling of land, especially country estates. Their very fees they expected to come from their clever handling of suits over land, and if they were very keen, they might build a fortune by this means alone. Such ambitions increased greatly the attendance at the Inns and, incidentally, the publication of books for the students.

Careers for younger sons in the Low Countries made an ironic chapter in Elizabethan history. England held Flushing and Brill from 1585 to 1616 as pledges for loans made to the Dutch states, and many young English sons found a military career at these garrisons and elsewhere when the Dutch employed them for the wars against Spain. At the same time young English Catholic sons were serving the governors in the Spanish Netherlands. It has been estimated that there were more permanent residents from England in the Low Countries at this time than in all the rest of Europe. Robert Sidney's career, which required him to stay at Flushing, has become common knowledge not only for his ability at his post but also for his distress over separation from his family while his children were growing up. At critical moments in his domestic affairs he could, perhaps, gain permission to hurry home to his wife and children, but such privileges were denied most of the younger sons stationed abroad.

A gentle family of limited means and many sons would have to find them careers in trade. They might apprentice them to drapers, silk mercers, or goldsmiths, for example. In time this necessity of gentle families was to provide material for drama. Then the younger sons retained their callings as citizens and ranked as such, but they also retained their position of being nobly born. When such men married daughters of wealthy tradesmen, they were wise to avoid any show of patronizing the citizens, for tradesmen were quick to resent any such quality in the seeming friendliness of the nobility for the lower classes. When the line between a rich merchant or tradesman and the gentleman was hard to draw, then the least touch of a patronizing friendliness was especially irksome.

It is not at all likely, therefore, that Antonio in Shakespeare's *Merchant of Venice* was meant to appeal to the middle class. Rather, such plays as Dekker's *The Shoemakers' Holiday* would serve this purpose, for here the lord's son willingly stoops to the manners and the trade of the shoemaker to win his beloved. Antonio, on the other hand, consorts with lords and maintains consistently the decorum of the lord. Dekker's young lord might also please the middle-class members of his audience by forsaking his position in the army to carry out his romantic plan, though in life he would be more likely to buy the service of another to take his place as soldier. When the shoemaker–Lord Mayor of London objects to his daughter's marriage to a lord because her station is too "mean," his act appeals to both nobles and citizens in the audience: the nobles because he bows to their social superiority, and the middle class because he admits the risk of marriage between a well-dowered daughter and an extravagant young lord. In this play Dekker exemplifies his adept handling of social problems as he uses them for purposes of entertainment.

If a younger son had the rank of birth behind him, he might do best for himself at law, but to those outside this privileged class the profession might not be very lucrative, for most fees were small in comparison with the work they required. Furthermore, up to a certain point every man was his own lawyer, as all men of any education at all were acquainted with technical forms of legal procedure. For this reason the counsel must have close relations with his somewhat exacting clients, whose lawyer as often as not acted as agent for the general conduct of cases. Since most litigation about real property was carried on in the Court of Common Pleas, or by anticipation or appeal in the Chancery, the lawyer's skill did not rest in oratory or rhetoric but in drawing pleadings, interrogatories, bills, and answers, and in collecting precedents and taking down reports.

But when the young lawyer was connected with the land by birth, and when he was ambitious and had high interests, he might well become very successful provided he directed the aim of his life toward the acquisition of more and more landed property and the foundation of a county family. Full use of his advantages made him a confidential agent, sometimes a usurer, a grantee of the Crown through the influence of its advisers, or even an enlightened speculator. To his prosperity he might well add political influence; then he was indeed a man with a career.[9]

Earnest young men, whether of the noble or middle class, chose their professions after considerable deliberation alone and with their parents. Of this type was Sir Thomas More, whose business and political career up to the point of his success was not unlike that of any very talented man in law in the age of the Tudors. Still he hesitated a long time before making his choice as he loved the monastic life. For many Elizabethans he set the example of choosing a layman after whom to model his life. In More's case the man was Giovanni Pico della Mirandola, renowned throughout Europe for both his encyclopedic knowledge and the sanctity of his life. More had made a translation of a Latin life of Pico and his letters, besides his twelve rules for leading a good life. During this period of doubt he attended sermons faithfully, particularly those by Colet at St. Paul's about the Lord's Prayer and the Creed, and hereby set an example for Puritans in the late part of the century.

More's choice of law was largely determined by his father's wishes. It has been said that his father deprived him of financial assistance in his study of literature at the university, but if More's patron, Cardinal Morton, financed the young man's education, the father's interference probably consisted only of his objections to More's inclinations. In More's case such an attitude on the part of his parent would lie heavy on his conscience. Moreover, More felt he must marry, and he could best serve

9 Hubert Hall, *Society in the Elizabethan Age* (1902), p. 141.

his country and maintain a family by the legal profession. Once he had made his decision, More applied himself diligently to his studies and became so clever in his knowledge of law that he was given the highest honor reserved for the best and most experienced lawyers—to lecture on law during the vacation from the feast of St. John the Baptist till Michaelmas. He had very practically studied English municipal law, and when he began practicing law, he was wise enough to take only such cases as he felt were in the right. At thirty-two he was elected by the people to be their Under-Sheriff, and now his feet were treading the highway of success.

Disagreement over a son's career was a very serious matter. It was long believed that More left his father's house after his university training because of his father's objections to More's love of literature and philosophy. Now it is known that More always remained on very cordial terms with all his family. He did take lodging with William Lyly, the grammarian, however, and delivered a series of lectures on St. Augustine's *The City of God*, setting forth his ideal that all things should be used for the common good and all rulers should be the servants of their people. At this time he also followed his ideal of Pico by choosing friends who might shape his career—Colet and Grocyn for a guide in conduct, Linacre as a "master in letters," and Lyly as his "confidant and most intimate friend." Later he chose still another friend, Cuthbert Tunstall, who became a bishop, first of London and then of Durham. At his father's house More would never have met and enjoyed the companionship of such friends, and when he chose to live with Lyly he made one of the wisest decisions of his life. It is quite likely that he made this decision because of his earnest desire to follow a pattern of life he had mapped out for himself.

Few young men at this time would have had the tact to leave home and still remain on good terms with a family that could not provide the companionship an aspiring, brilliant mind needed. It took fine intelligence as well as tact for More to make this break without the excuse of marriage. Most parents would have looked upon his departure as downright disobedience and suffered no little grief over it, especially since they would have missed their son's winning charm and delightful companionship. Had his mother been living, he might not have been able to leave so easily. He also maintained very pleasant relations with his three stepmothers, to whom he adapted his manners and speech with gentle, cheerful courtesy.

Elizabethan conduct books would not agree to a child's taking any step without the full approval of the family. Batty spoke for most of them when he urged children contemplating such an act to remember the mother's pangs at childbirth and the self-denial required of both parents in rearing a family. He would have them never forget that just as parents had nothing in this life wherein they were more affected and delighted than in the love of their children, so were they most offended when their children displeased them. That is why, he said, "many honest and virtuous parents are bitterly consumed and pine away with sorrow and grief of heart" over the heedlessness of their children, though unfortunately "careless youth" could not understand their distress.

"A Treatise of the Vocations," a series of sermons by William Perkins, summarized the Puritan argument about a young man's diligent pursuit of his chosen career. He must meet both spiritual and temporal obligations in a calling that would serve the Church, the Commonwealth, the family, his God, and himself. Now that public service was looked on as more acceptable to God than retirement from the world and now that the clergy no longer forbade a just accumulation of wealth, the individual calling required grave consideration, indeed. It must fit the man and the man must fit it, but if the man was gifted in many lines, he must choose that in which he had most aptitude. He might thus practice in more than one field, but always his labor must be honest, profitable, and necessary. To abuse one's calling for personal gain was a grave sin, and he listed those likely to be guilty of this evil—magistrates, lawyers, doctors, shopkeepers, rent catchers, corn hoarders, printers, and sellers of heretical books. He looked upon idleness as so sinful that he would forbid all beggary and would provide relief only when man worked for his bread. Therefore he looked upon indiscriminate alms as a menace to society. Beggary had become such an evil in Perkins' time that ballads and pamphlets took up the battle against it, and much of the advice to young men on choosing a vocation was meant to offset the evils of mendicancy.

In the reign of James I as well as of Elizabeth the climax in disobedience was reached when a son entered some religious order without parental consent. Fear of such a course was due to the powerful appeal the Jesuits made to the emotions of many young Englishmen when away from home, especially on tour. Pierre Ayrault's *A Discourse for Parents Honour and Authoritie* (1599) gave the complaint of a distraught father whose son chose of his own accord to become a Jesuit. He hoped he might even reclaim his son who was but a "counterfeit Jesuit." He believed the vow of the monk to be "justifiable and good," but such a vow without a father's consent was a denial of the honor due all parents when children needed advice about serious steps in life. By this publication he wished to let it be known he would forgive his son if he would make amends; that he would withdraw his action against him even though his act had "offended and despised" his father. He felt his own attitude was charitable, for he sued "unto the scorner" and thereby offered to make amends himself unto one who should first seek him. Though Jesuits held that a son of twenty-five might exercise his own will and not be condemned for disobedience, he maintained that "natural duty can neither be dayed nor yeared, nor be determined by age or eldership, nay the more years the more duty . . ." He was sure from the bottom of his heart that "neither God nor good man were he in his wits" would ever inveigle any man's child into undutiful conduct to his parents.

Just as a young man planning to be a lawyer could hope for a better career if he was of gentle birth, so it was for one choosing to enter the Church. During the Queen's reign, the position of humble pastors was a very inferior one, as the destruction of the monastic houses had left the poor students at Oxford and Cambridge without support and thereby decreased their numbers. Others, wearied by the disputes over religion, had taken to trade or mercantile pursuits, and rectors, vicars, and curates were no longer well-trained university men till the Puritans grew strong enough to begin the task of educating their ministers. Livings had become so poor they were worth only £10 to £30 a year, not enough to maintain a poor scholar, much less a learned man. Furthermore, out of such stipends must be paid tithes and first fruits, and subsidies and taxes for armor and munitions till £20 rapidly dwindled to £13. Then came the expenses from visitation of the archbishop, bishop, and archdeacon, and double inquisition fees to the sovereign. A vicar could preach only if he had permission from his bishop or the bishop's deputies, and all sermons had to be submitted in writing to the archdeacon for approval. In lieu of his own sermons a vicar must read from a book of homilies provided him, and consequently an ordained clergyman was frequently replaced by a lay reader assisting the parson. The younger son of a wealthy or powerful noble, however, might find in his career in the Church advantages that were both inherent and obtainable by purchase.

Hubert Hall[10] pictures the Church at this time in a most unflattering light. He says the bishops were but starveling pedants, creatures of a court faction, whose fingers itched after filthy lucre; or they were good, plodding, domesticated men, with "quiverfuls to provide for"; or worse still, they were but graziers or land jobbers who had mistaken their vocation and fallen into the lap of the Church. Narrow, harsh, grasping, servile, unjust, such men were despised as much by their masters as they were hated by their flocks, who longed for the dispossessed parson or parish priest of former times. Half the parishes in many dioceses had no proper curate. Many were provided with a trembling conformist, or a lewd and insolent bigot. In the best of cases the curate was at the mercy of either the Crown or amateur theologians among the parishioners. This is a sorry picture, indeed, and but for the Queen's compromise, would have lengthened its shadow over the land.

Into this field were sent younger sons of wealthy men or poor middle-class sons to make for themselves whatever careers they could. In the later years of Elizabeth's reign competent men were often found among the well-placed bishops and their superiors. This fact, combined with

[10] *Ibid.*, pp. 104–5.

the generally increasing skepticism of the age, tended to turn many of them who had no strong urge toward reform or religion to the field of ecclesiastical law, where they might serve both Queen and God, but perhaps more definitely the Queen. A younger son of the privileged class, wishing to take a degree in canon law, studied theology as a minor subject, and made law his major subject at the university. Here was a field opening up many opportunities for the right type of person.

At Trinity Hall, founded as a college for law students, the young men now made less study of English or common law and more and more study of civil and canon law—the former for its law of the Roman Empire and the latter for its law of the Church with its decrees of councils and rescripts of popes. For long after Henry VIII became head of the Church it was on the defensive, and canon law continued to claim jurisdiction over the clergy in questions of doctrine and practice and in all cases and suits criminal and civil that involved the clergy or Church property. Canon law also continued to control or at least to influence the beliefs and morals of the laity. Heresy, marriage, wills, contracts, oaths—all were in its sphere. Ecclesiastical judges and advocates, therefore, had to be trained, and bishops, chancellors, vicars general, commissaries, archdeacons and their officials, scribes, and registrars had to be lawyers. Well-born sons who could afford to study civil law might prepare for diplomatic service, as civil law was now becoming the foundation for international law. But the study of canon and civil law was of immediate value, for the decisions of the Court of Chancery depended on the law of both the Church and civil law. In the foundation charter of Trinity Hall one clause had read "for the advantage, rule, and direction of the Commonwealth."[11] Now, indeed, the Church secured a hold upon the morals and religious beliefs of the laity that enabled it to continue that hold upon the State, thereby uniting morals and religion and law in one cohesive bond in the minds of the people. Today this bond still has its roots firmly imbedded in the Church, which, on occasion, may draw heavily on its authority to keep the bond intact. In the Queen's time, therefore, those who did not prepare themselves for diplomatic service might turn to the Church for a career of worldly opportunity, especially if they received the blessing of their parents and natural gifts from God.

Because to parents obedience in choosing a career was so important, they began very early to instill into their sons the seriousness of their duty of making a living. When the apprentice system provided for the placing of children before they had much occasion to discover their aptitudes, if they did awaken to a realization of being trained for the wrong vocation, they saw too late the need of slipping out of the pattern into which they were being molded. For the sons of the privileged classes,

[11] James Arthur Muller, *Stephen Gardiner and the Tudor Reaction* (1926), pp. 7–8.

however, the training might be changed or deflected if parental consent was forthcoming. As opportunities for developing individual taste and inclination increased in proportion to the dignity and importance of a career, sons of the upper classes were not so likely to rebel against their means of making a living as were the less fortunate sons of the middle class. Instead, most of these sons were willing to agree to any means, honorable or according to their moral training, if only they could find some way to economic security.

Occasionally an Elizabethan son was a problem child, as was young Thomas, son of Lord Burghley. This was also true of Tom, the son of Edmund Verney who had been so carefully reared according to Elizabethan standards. Tom Verney was the one child in this large family to prove there were grounds for the fear of unpredictability in the results from heredity or environment of children. Indeed, Tom was so irresponsible and happy-go-lucky that at eighteen he had to be rebuked for proposing marriage to a girl without his father's consent. He merely shrugged off the matter by saying, "The thing was commonly spread about the house, and verily I thought it came to my father's ears." His father decided he should send his son to America, as it was becoming a land of opportunity for enterprising young men, and perhaps his Tom might find himself in the New World since he did not seem to fit in any corner of the Old. Accordingly he procured a cabin for Tom on a stout vessel and outfitted him with £117 worth of supplies. But in nine months Tom was home again. Now he was sent as a volunteer on a ship patrolling the Channel, and likely to go to war. Tom tired of this life and went to Flanders and elsewhere, spending the money sent to him, and when it was exhausted, he returned home again. Next he was sent to London to a keeper of the Marshalsea, and the keeper was warned not to buy anything for Tom without the father's permission. Of course, Tom wrote home for money, promising to spend it with fine results. Soon he was writing for more money for clothes and like necessities. Then he took service with the army in France and drew bills on his older brother for equipment, promising to pay after the "next fight." This time he would really show his family what he could do, and until then they would never see him again. But he was soon home again. Once more he was sent to France, where he quickly spent the £60 given him to defray his expenses, and again he was begging money for equipment and promising to repay it soon.

Now he returned to London, and almost immediately got into debt and quarrels. Finally, his desperate family outfitted him for another voyage to the New World, this time to the Barbadoes, where he was expected to settle permanently. As soon as he could write home he was asking for plate, pewter, brass, spoons, linens, and household stuff that made his relatives almost hope he was in his proper niche at last. But in little over a year he was home again, penniless and with debts and trouble dogging his name in the colony. When, eventually, his death in a battle ended his unhappy career, his family must have sighed with great relief that this unstable soul had actually come to rest.[12]

In middle-class families of ordinary means such a career as Tom's would be most difficult to understand. Why were his parents so long-suffering and why was he given so many chances? It is possible that the limits imposed on chances in careers in the middle class by economic and moral pressure closely woven into *one* pressure may have kept the "moral middle class" on the road of steady effort and often of certain accomplishment. Their sons were constantly reminded of their debt of gratitude to parents for their education and training for a career of useful living. From their cradles they heard again and again the words from Becon's *The booke of Matrimony* (1564): "Next to God do children owe their parents their education and bringing up, their trade or living, their wisdom, learning, science, riches, honors, and such like benefits," for which they must return to these parents "high honor and humble obedience." Elizabethans had learned a lesson they gravely taught their children, who, in turn, impressed that lesson upon their own children—that gratitude is a virtue which must be *taught* before it can flow from the heart of man or beast, and the foundation for the virtue of gratitude is always obedience to moral law.

It was possible for these people, therefore, to command obedience even in choice of a mate, although parents with any wisdom at all did not overlook the emotional factor involved in this duty. Becon, again, was frequently quoted by Puritans, who learned by heart the evils he said were in the souls of children disobeying parents who arranged marriages for them: first, an utter rejection of God's command that they honor and obey their parents in all things; second, scorn of the godly persons in the Scriptures who "enterprised" matrimony only by the appointment of parents; third, disregard of honor and obedience due parents; fourth, providing cause for enemies of Christianity to speak evil of it, and fifth, causing their parents great sorrow by casting themselves away from them. Becon believed the chief cause for a child's guilt in this succession of evils was influence from other people. In this way he pointed the finger of heavy scorn at the disobedient child's loved one. In itself, this criticism caused great agony to one naturally loving and obedient.

Some conduct books dealt with this matter in passionate terms. William Vaughan's *The Golden Grove* (1599) called the son who was disobedient about marriage as infamous as a Turk. He believed his parents should lead him to a magistrate to have imposed upon him "what pun-

---

[12] Frances Parthenope Verney and Margaret M. Verney (compilers), *Memoirs of the Verney Family during the 17th Century* (1925).

ishment the father demandeth." But such punishment could not be compared to that after death when his soul "in hot scalding lead" would endure the "horrible pains of hell." *The Court of Good Councell* (1607) was somewhat similar in tone. Its author said that whatever son strove with his father provoked the wrath of God, who would never let him live or die in peace. He would also suffer from his father's curse, and God would cause him to be utterly forsaken. Like Thomas Becon, Batty (*The Christian mans Closet*, 1581) gave five reasons for obeying parents—children owed to their parents both body and soul; they owed their rearing to parents; the Ten Commandments required children to obey parents; by having their children baptized in Christ, the parents made them heirs to God's kingdom, and finally, parents had their children taught certain handicrafts: science, trade, or some occupation by which to make an honest living. To disobey their parents, therefore, brought down on children plagues and punishments. Batty called a disobedient son "a cruel murderer of his parents," for they could suffer no sorrow in life "greater than that which ariseth of the calamity and wickedness of children." He gave four ways by which a child could show his parents due honor—by loving them with all his heart and mind and giving them high reverence; by showing them good manners, never murmuring against them, but suffering them patiently even when they seemed unreasonably wayward; by labor, relieving them in poverty and never letting them suffer the misery of neglect in old age, and finally, by performing all their services to them with a lowliness of mind as if to God himself.

Shakespeare puts into the mouth of Egeus in *A Midsummer Night's Dream* the words that describe the conventional father's idea of a child's obedience to parental authority. Like William Vaughan, who would lead a disobedient child to a magistrate to have imposed the punishment demanded by the father, Egeus drags Hermia before Theseus, Duke of Athens. She has apparently been bewitched by her lover's gifts, he says, for she would never otherwise have shown such a "stubborn harshness." The Duke, on the father's side, reprimands Hermia:

> To you, your father should be as a god;
> One that composed your beauties, yea, and one
> To whom you are but as a form in wax
> By him imprinted, and within his power
> To leave the figure or disfigure it.

I: i: 47–51

Modern interpretation likes to make a mere fantasy of this comedy, but it is not so simple as that. To resolve the difficulties of this child's disobedience and this father's harshness required a magic beyond the powers of human beings to use or to understand. Shakespeare's fairies have this magic.

In spite of all their rhetoric about a child's obedience, conduct books and sermons objected to forcing children into unwelcome marriages. Yet some of them when exemplifying the proper decorum with which a child approached a parent about marriage are more than "passing strange" to us. Of course, to ask for marriage was to ask for parental aid, and in some cases that meant establishment in one's own home. Batty, therefore, advised sons and daughters to "humble themselves" by going "most lowly and gently" to their parents, saying, " 'My good father and mother, let me have I pray you an honest and godly young person in marriage whom I love in the fear of the Lord.' " A son old enough for marriage would "not be afraid or ashamed to reveal his secrets and open his mind unto his parents" about this matter. A good son would "shun and abhor" any marriage without parental consent as "a very great madness." Without experience to guide him his choice might be not only unwise but full of peril. For a maid such guidance was even more imperative.

Batty was sure that if children approached their parents in the manner he advised there would be no objection raised to their choice unless the law of affinity was involved. Instead, an honest and wise father or mother would grant the request, though the dowry, goods, or sums of money might not be as much as they would wish for their child. But such dutiful children should have no fears, for God with his "unmeasurable and exceeding goodness" would bless and favor them in their "veil of wedlock." He warns children, however, against "exceeding fervency" lest it defeat the very purpose of marriage, the "pious begetting of children." But in a marriage blessed by God was pardoned man's "filthiness and miserable lust" wherein he was "conceived and born." A God-blessed marriage adorned and made man "more honorable by and through lawful matrimony." It was a time of groping for some means besides love for ensuring a happy marriage. It was not that Batty or any Puritan would deny love; it was simply a question of what was involved besides love, a question unanswered by religion or science or philosophy.

Pierre Ayrault, who in *A Discourse for Parents Honour and Authoritie* had insisted on the right of parents to direct children in the choice of their careers, naturally demanded the right to arrange marriages for them. In spite of all his excitement, however, he did not go so far as Batty in his statements. He began by quoting Scripture to show that God commanded parents to bestow children in marriage, and children to accept the marriages made for them. Besides civil and canon law, he said the laws of nature and of nations upheld this custom. Children might be guided by carnal desires when making a choice, but parents would be guided by experience and understanding and concern for their offspring. For anyone to lure children away to marry against their parents' wishes was to him "a worse kind of felony than stealing away the goods of man." Children were much more properly a man's own than his goods and far dearer to him, "yea, and so much more highly to be esteemed by how much more reasonable creatures are to be preferred before senseless and sensual things." Ministers, therefore, who married children against parental consent especially sinned, for they highly dishonored God's command while they bore "the person of God."

Ayrault calls to mind how long after Christ's passion parents were able to pass sentence of life and death on their children, but now civil law will permit a child to marry or to become a monk, though he believes in time civil law may change. God's laws and God's commands for children to honor their parents, however, will be perpetual, and this gives him comfort. A daughter, he continues, is subject by her very sex to her father who as the stronger must guide her, but a son owes his father a double duty—"the one in respect of disparity of years between them, the other in respect of his father's goodness towards him." He closes his discourse with the quotation from St. Jerome used so often by Elizabethans: "You that will be fathers hereafter, you must honor your fathers and love your mothers with a tender affection, that your wives after you be married may deserve to be mothers also."

When Ayrault referred to the daughter's weakness of sex, he meant her "frailty," of course. To preserve chastity in their daughters parents resorted most frequently to such writers as Vives, whom they quoted or gave their daughters to read. Again and again they used his statement of the old superstition that a woman's virginity had so much "marvelous honor in it that wild lions" regarded it with reverence. To lose it would make a girl find "everything sorrowful and heavy, wailing and mourning, and angry and displeasureful." So graceless a creature brought sorrow to her kinsfolk, cursing to her acquaintances, talk among the neighbors, friends, and companions, babbling and mocking among those who had before envied her, and loathing and abhorring among those who had loved her. All who knew her would desert her lest she contaminate them. Mothers would keep away not only their daughters but also their sons, and those who had seemed to love her would now openly hate her, even with words casting "the abominable deed in her teeth" till it would be a wonder that such a young woman could "either have joy of her life or live at all, and not pine away for sorrow."

Vives says he has known "many fathers to cut the throats of their daughters, brethren of their sisters, and kinsmen of their kinswomen" for the evil of being unchaste. Women possessed of unlawful love were dangerously untrustworthy, for they might suddenly hate love and charity, hate their parents, brothers, sisters, friends, acquaintances, and finally, themselves. Take from a woman her beauty, her kindred, her riches, her eloquence, her sharpness of wit, her cunning in craft (domestic duties), and then give her but chastity "and thou hast given her all things." Being more susceptible to love than a man, a woman, he said, might far better

Detail from the Bradford table cover; silk on
canvas, tent stitch (late sixteenth century)

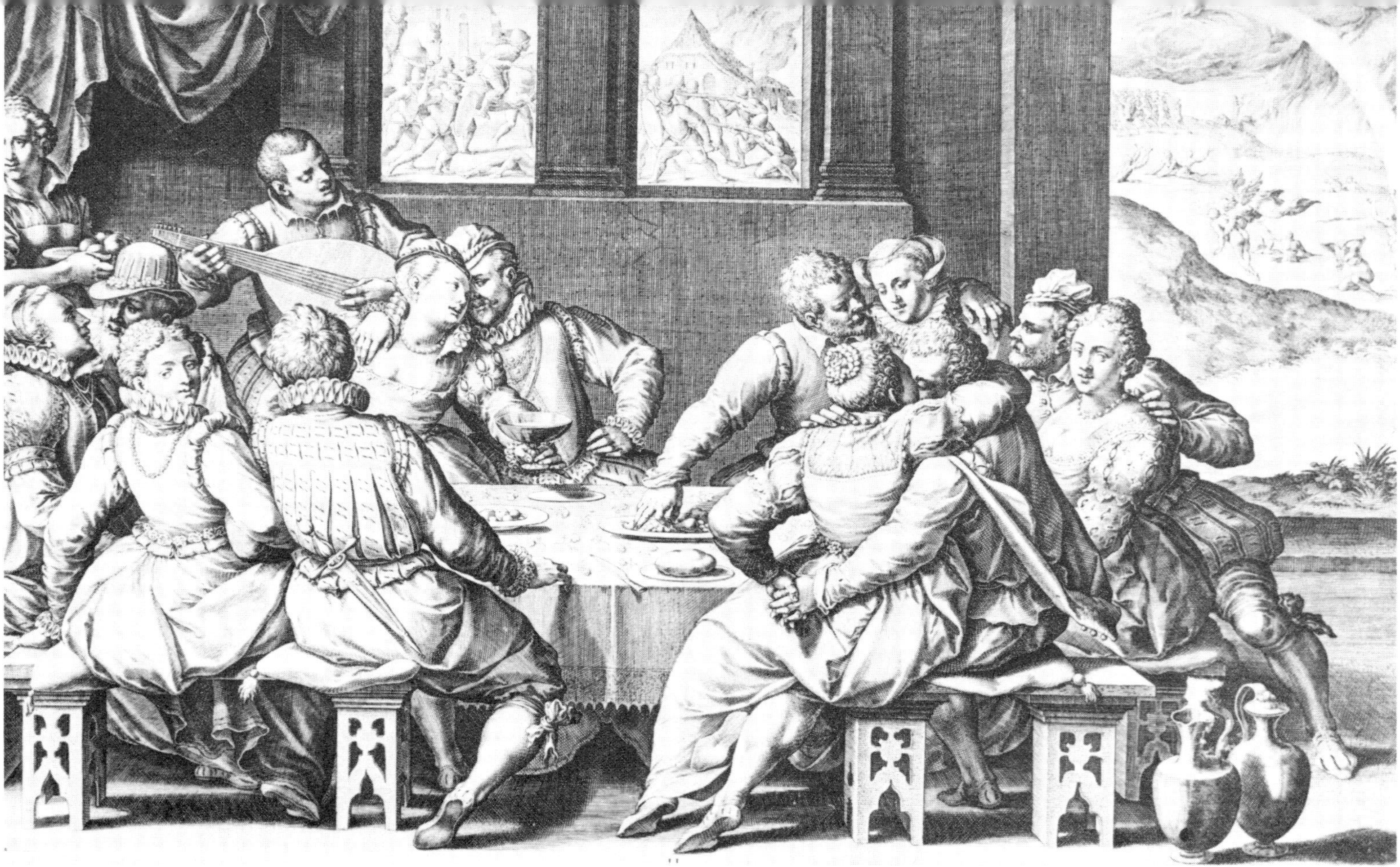

Picture Post Library

break "a leg of her body than a leg of her mind." To cure her of love he analyzed its qualities for her, though he used the term loosely.

To love, he began, was to forget all reason; it was the "next thing unto a frenzy, a foul vice, and an unmannerly one," for it troubled all the wits and broke "high and noble stomachs" and drew down "from the study and thinking of high and excellent things unto low and vile," causing those in love to be "full of groaning and complaining, to be angry, hasty, foolhardy, distraught in ruling, full of vile and servile flattery, unmeet for everything, and at the last, unmeet for love itself." If women sought desire, they spent most of their time in "suspicion, mourning, weeping, wailing, sighing, and complaining" till they not only made others hate them but they hated themselves, their kin, and their parents. Many "had even poisoned their own mothers that they might run away with their lovers."

But Vives did not leave the matter at this point. If a maid spurned "this inordinate and cruel affection" in time, she could reject it. Once in love, however, she was powerless to stop it, "for love first of all troubleth and tosseth all things upside down at his lust that himself may bear the more outrageous rule, and confoundeth and blindeth the wit and reason that it shall not see and know what is done with it but suffereth itself to be wholly led and drawn at love's pleasure." Though it comes as a sweet and pleasant thing, the maid must pay no more heed to it than to an enchanter or sorcerer. Usually a lover's hate instead of affection made him praise a maid's beauty or wit or birth or manners until he caused her to believe it all true. At such a time a maid should ask her lover whether he called her wise or honest; if not, he himself was not honest in his intentions.

Some lovers, Vives warned the maids, declared they would die if not accepted, but he asked how many among the thousands and thousands of lovers had ever died of love. Even if it did kill one of them, far better to do so than make the maid perish or cause both to die. Most love-making was deceitful, he continued, since once the appetite was satisfied, the man was done. Yet love of virtue and the mind was never satisfied. Then he described how many men, having abused young women for a season, "cast them into stews." Some of the maids, however, having loved fervently, learned to hate fervently, and killed their lovers. The results of such love could be seen in women still young who were "scabbed, in spitals, or went begging, pale and sick."

To overcome love, maids should firmly resolve always to keep from their sight or hearing the person loved and, if he did come into the mind, to put him out by turning to reading or praying or to some communication or to song or study or to some merry matter. If the loved one had a fault, maids should try to think of that rather than his virtue, for everyone had something in him to be despised. One did not always conceal his vices and magnify his virtues; when love was gone, the order was reversed. If he was of noble birth, he might also be haughty; if rich, also intolerant; if strong in body, also cruel. Let her search for these faults.

Vives would not have the maid devoid of love, for then she would be unnatural; indeed, mankind seemed made for love. He would have the maid, therefore, love God, Christ, Mary, the Church, all holy virgins, her parents, and her own virtuous soul. Since her parents had brought her into the world and nourished her with great labor and care, she must love them and worship them and help them with all her power. This she could do if she would regard their commandments and meekly obey them, showing in neither her mind nor her countenance any gesture or stubbornness, but always reckoning them as though they were the very image of God. With this attitude she would never be tempted to forsake her parents for a lover to whom she would serve for short pleasure only and cause her parents endless sorrow.

It was not comely, said Vives, for maids to desire marriage, much less show a longing for it. That is why, he explained, in the old honest days of Rome when a maid was brought to the groom's house she was carried in at the door to show "she came hither not of her own good will, where she would lose her virginity." When a maid's parents discussed plans for her marriage in her presence, she should do naught but weep and blush, just as in the picture which Virgil the poet showed of the King Latinus and his wife Amata talking before their daughter about her future husband. The maid could only weep and blush because it was not becoming for her to talk when her parents were debating such matters; she knew she must leave it all to them who loved her as well as she loved herself, and who, because of their greater experience and wisdom, would provide for her much better than she could plan for herself.

While a maid's parents were engaged in getting her a husband, she should pray to Christ and Mary to aid them in choosing for her one who would assist her in virtuous living. She must keep in mind the fact that her parents would take their responsibility seriously, for they would know they were preparing for her eternal misery or eternal felicity. And she must also think of how good marriages for their children would give parents good sons-in-law and daughters-in-law that would succor them in their old age. People like her parents would know only too well that if they secured "naughty" or irreligious mates for their children, they were providing themselves with enemies.

Vives considered a daughter's chance for a good marriage far better if she was seldom seen and if she was not too richly dressed. A maid in very rich apparel would frighten away men who might fear she would waste their wealth. A maid too talkative might be praised to her face, might be told she was a jolly dancer and was full of merry conceits and play and pleasance, and might even be called well-mannered and well brought up, but all these words would mean nothing at all. Men would never marry one with whom they might have easy talk, for they would not trust her. He said it was a pity maids could not hear young men discuss them, calling them babblers and chatterers: when they called them lusty tigers, they meant they were light-minded; and when they called them well-nurtured, they meant they were wanton.

Vives also objected to maids talking too much to their women companions lest their conversation be made light of or misconstrued. Elizabethans would support this criticism by Guazzo's remark to the effect that much of women's conversation was vain or unprofitable or dangerous or hurtful. Thomas Salter (*Mirrhor of Modestie*, 1579) spoke for many of them when he declared daughters should never listen to light gossip, for the conversation of such tattlers was ever ready to deal with that which "they ought never to hearken to," but rather to fear greatly. Juliet's nurse in Shakespeare's *Romeo and Juliet* is an excellent example of everything Elizabethans feared in the guardians of their daughters; they would see in her a corrupter of maidens just as Falstaff was a corrupter of youths. Each was doubly dangerous because each knew how to be irresistible to young minds.

Vives disapproved of maids at feasts because of the freedoms practiced there. Unless closely watched by her parents the daughter could not keep "pure and holy and not spotted with lust," for at table occurred many opportunities for "talking and touching and groping and plucking." Indeed, he called feasts "the springs of great and many vices, be they never so sober and moderated," and at them an innocent girl would see "many uncomely things and learn much naughtiness, even among men thought to be right wise." This was why, he said, a maid should live a retired life away from the chatter of the world. Then she would not hear women talking of how to get a husband by wiles and craft; in fact, she would not even know of such evil things. He could think of nothing worse in a maid than for her to try to catch and deceive by subtlety him that should be her "inseparable fellow."

Vives could not understand why parents had their daughters taught how to dance. He associated this pleasure with the "bawdy houses," and said it made Christians worse than pagans in their conduct. He referred to the new dancing in particular, with its "shaking, unclean handling, kissing, bragging, groping," and "a very kind of lechery." He recalls the time when kissing was not used except among kinsfolk, but now it was common in both England and France. To him it was "foul and rude," and it seemed that women danced chiefly for the pleasure of kissing. They could not go to church, he said severely, unless carried on horseback no matter how near the church might be, but at a dance they could stand "shaking unto midnight and never weary." In spite of the teachings of Vives, however, dancing became increasingly popular in Elizabeth's reign, for she delighted in all the latest "romps," and was merrily swung high off the floor in dances that required of her courtiers the skill of professionals.

Part of the moralists' objection to dancing was that it was likely to take maids out of the home for entertainment. Like Vives, they opposed the meeting of the sexes except under the closest supervision of their elders, and that would be difficult in any house but their own. If a girl was beautiful, she was in great danger if given any freedom in mixed company; no matter how honest or demure or virtuous she might be in her shamefastness, some would always suspect her of evil as soon as she stepped into the street. Moreover, away from home she could not avoid engaging in conversation. Vives had felt no girl could know how to avoid being slandered by those who would watch everything she said and did. If she talked too much, she would be called "light," and if too little, she would be called stupid. If she did not talk "cunningly," she would be called "dull-witted," and if cunningly, she would be called a shrew. Slow speech showed bad upbringing, and quick speech indicated poor training. Women sitting demurely would be suspected of dissembling, and if gay, were called foolish. If they did not look about them at the gay company, they would be accused, as Vives said, of "not being all there," and if they laughed as they talked they would be thought "easily won." From the point of view of moralists, therefore, it was unthinkable that a good woman would object to staying home or ever wish to go where she might meet many people or hear her beauty praised in songs. At times any woman might have to go from home, but never without the company of a "grave" woman known for her "virtuous lineage." On such little journeys, good women would look for good things to "treasure in their hearts," but if they saw evil, they would hate it for love of Christ.

Vives realized the wife must accompany her husband at times when he went to marriages or feasts. He admitted husbands wished their wives to meet men who might be impressed by their beauty and chastity. But if such a wife had to leave her daughter at home, she must be sure the woman left in charge of her had no wanton sons or brothers she might favor, and she must by a good disciplinarian. If a woman so trusted could be hired by a lover to provoke or move the daughter with speech or fair words, she was not a "reasonable creature," but a "devilish thing which a maid should flee" as she would "an adder or serpent." The mischief such a woman was capable of could not be described, for she could catch a maid with a look, without words, and by using enchantments and charms that could ruin her forever. Naturally such women favored light pastimes, where, if maids were present, they might be caught off guard by the female monsters.

Thomas Salter, though writing over half a century later, was still impressed by all Vives had said. In his *Mirrhor of Modestie* he tells how he would not permit a girl to indulge even in music lest it bear "a sweet bait to a sorrow and sharp evil," and open the door "to many vices." He admitted "true singing and delicate playing" had their use, but only for those "that be overworn with grief, sorrow, trouble, cares, or other vexation." It was most abused at banquets, he said, in order to promote evil and to kindle in men's hearts "lewd affections." Such objection to music was undoubtedly due to the effort to combat the growing middle-class custom among ambitious parents to have their daughters instructed in playing the lute and virginal and in dancing and fine needlework in order to use these accomplishments as lures for making matches that would benefit them socially. When by this means girls were taught to look for marriage above their class, some moralists felt the practice might cause an unwholesome attitude toward marriage and perhaps upset the old teaching that insisted on each class marrying within its own group. Most moralists writing plays or ballads or just conduct books insisted, therefore, that harmony and happiness in marriage could never be expected by those who violated this social custom. When fathers of the middle class attained special privileges through their own effort, they sometimes resented sharing them with those who had lost such privileges by sloth or mismanagement. Hence some fathers of the middle class frowned at their daughters wishing to marry impecunious heirs or younger sons of the gentry. If their wives wished such matches for their daughters, the fathers were doubly resentful, and they welcomed books like the *Mirrhor* for their "womenfolk" to read.

But there was another element in the emphasis upon the "pure maid" and the temptations that surrounded her. Elizabethans were moving steadily toward a refinement in manners as well as in morals, and they wished to hasten the movement. Women of the time were not only accustomed to jests that still shock a conservative society, but they indulged in such talk themselves. Some of the "young virgins" had become so worldly-wise that the exaggerated pictures of maidenly modesty may have been part of a deliberate effort by a self-conscious older generation to improve its new generation. Moreover, the English insistence on perfection in everything English during the period when nationalism was at white heat also demanded that English women be shown as surpassing the women of all other nations in the domestic virtues dear to English sentiment. The Queen, of course, loved this game and required all those near her to obey its rules. Her unspeakable anger with maids of honor who did not live the game instead of merely playing it was understandable, therefore. As Queen she could do no wrong, but maids of honor could set examples that might undermine the cult of virginity and make her own position untenable. Although her behavior might not always adhere to the pattern she required others to follow, she helped immeasurably to refine manners that needed the strict decorum she established at her court.

Salter's picture of a daughter that was supposed to delight her father's heart is probably allied to this trend in social improvement. He admitted a girl might be so shamefast and fearful as to approach "a point of folly fitter for babes" than maids. Still, when necessary for her to show her virtue, he would have her "ready but not bold, and by a sudden blushing,"—which immediately would overspread "her lily cheeks with roseate red"—show that she bore in her breast "a reverent heart, far separated from infamous and reproachful shame." With a cheerful countenance and well-tempered gravity, but with eyes cast down, she would show her humility and confidence, and when asked to recite a psalm or other spiritual song or godly sentence, "set herself forth to do it with a mild refusal, yet altogether void of undecent affecting, which thing the most of people" could hardly eschew. She would look on what she disliked with a mild and courteous countenance, politely veiling her true feelings. When praised, she would not dislike it too much, but bear herself modestly. Finally, she would be found, not at feasts or banquets, but "at convenient time and due leisure" walking in her father's garden.

This type of daughter became a dream of pious fathers and lovers and of husbands who hoped to find immortality in the children she might bring as a chaste wife. The type stimulated poets as well as moralists and also very human men. It was also the proper theme for an exercise by which a writer might test his rhetorical powers. Nicholas Breton tried his hand at piling up nouns and adjectives to describe this paragon. She was the beauty of nature whose spirit gracious made her the creature glorious. She was the love of virtue, the honor of reason, the grace of youth, and the comfort of age. She made holiness her study, goodness her exercise, humility her grace, and charity her love. Her countenance was modesty, her speech truth, her wealth grace, and her fame modesty. In conversation she was heavenly, in her meditations angel-like, in her prayers devout, and in her hopes divine. Her parents found her a joy, her kindred, an honor, and she was to her own self a felicity. Blessed by the highest, praised by the worthiest, loved by the noblest, she moved among the best. Of all creatures she was the rarest, of all women the chiefest, in nature the purest, and in wisdom the choicest. All her life was one pilgrimage, and when she died she but passed on to heaven, leaving a name that made all honor her and wonder at her loveliness. And so Breton brings to a conclusion his tribute to one who was "the daughter of glory, the mother of grace, the sister of love, and the beloved of life."

Yet even such fantastic performances pleased and had their effect. With models of this kind of behavior set before her, Lady Anne Halkett, though not born till early in the next century, had a girlhood according to pious Elizabethan training. Of course she may have idealized her training as she looked back at it, but she does mention some interesting facts about it. Her mother was left a widow with full responsibility for the education and rearing of her children, and she "spared no expense" in her effort to "improve them." If they did not make the most of their opportunities it was their fault, not hers. She paid "masters" to teach her daughters to write, to speak French, to play on the lute and virginal, and to dance, and she kept a "gentlewoman" to teach them all kinds of needlework. From their infancy they were instructed "never to neglect to begin and end the day with prayers" and to read the Bible every morning and to "keep the church as often as there was occasion to meet there, either for prayers or preaching." For years they were "seldom or never absent from divine service, at five o'clock in the morning in summer, and six o'clock in the winter . . ."[13]

Another such pious daughter was born in the Tower, but in spite of this inauspicious beginning, Mrs. Lucy Apsley Hutchinson tells us she had a very happy girlhood. "As soon as I was weaned," she writes in *Memoirs of the Life of Colonel Hutchinson* (ed. Rev. Julius Hutchinson, 1906), "a French woman was taken to be my dry nurse, and I was taught to speak French and English together." By the time she was four, she read English "perfectly," and because she had a good memory, was carried to sermons. When she was very young she could remember them exactly, and when praised for her efforts, she was "tickled," and attended "more heedfully" to every word that was said. When about seven she had eight tutors for languages, music, dancing, writing, and needlework. Her "genius" was averse to all but books, and her mother, fearing she would injure her health, tried to moderate her study. This "animated" her still more, and when she could "steal from play" she would "employ" herself in any book she could find if her own were locked up from her. In the hour allowed her for play after dinner and after supper she would "steal into some hole or other to read." Her father wished her to learn Latin, and she was "so apt" she "outstripped" her brothers who were away at school. She says her own teacher was only the "pitiful dull" family chaplain. Her brothers, however, were possessed of so much wit that they tried to "emulate" her progress, and that pleased her father. Her mother was not so pleased, for she would "have been more contented" to have a daughter not "so wholly addicted" to Latin that she neglected her "other qualities."

As a daughter, therefore, she must study music and dancing, from which she "profited very little." She would never practice the lute or harpsichord except when her masters were with her, and she "absolutely hated" needlework. She must have been very trying at other times also, especially when asked to play with visiting children. She despised these commands, and tired the children with "more grave instructions than their mothers'" and plucked all their [doll] babies to pieces." Indeed,

---

[13] Sybil Wragge (ed.), *The Age Revealed* (1929).

she kept them in such awe they were glad when she left them for "elder company," to whom she was very "acceptable." Living in a house "with many persons that had a great deal of wit, and very profitable serious discourses" at her father's table and in her mother's drawing room, she was "very attentive to all, and gathered up things" she would repeat "to the great admiration of many" that took her memory for wit. Her father must have been inordinately proud of his little prodigy, for she was the child of his third wife, who was quite young at her marriage.

The mother's instructions to this pious little girl and the sermons to which she was carried "convinced" her when she was still a child that the "knowledge of God was the most excellent study." Accordingly she applied herself to it, and practiced what she was taught. She would even "exhort" her mother's maids until she turned their "idle discourse to good subjects," especially on the Lord's day, when she also performed her "due tasks of reading and praying." Yet looking back on those days when she was only seven, she wondered how she could have thought that the rest of the Lord's day was hers for enjoyment in so far as "she did not sin." At that time she "was not convinced of the vanity of conversation which was not scandalously wicked," and "thought it no sin to hear witty songs and amorous sonnets or poems and twenty things of that kind" wherein she was so apt that she became the "confidante in all the loves that were managed" among her mother's young women. None of them, she says, but had "many loves, and some particular friends beloved above the rest." For so young a girl to undergo such mixed experiences and to emerge from them with a triumphant confidence in her judgment of right and wrong seems not to have surprised her parents or herself. When she married Colonel Hutchinson, she served him, she believed, as a perfect wife.

Piety like this was offset in Elizabeth's court by a kind of sentimental nostalgia in the new fad of pastoralism among the literary ladies. The Queen herself wished she was a milkmaid "all the month of May," because such maids were not "troubled with fears and cares" but "sang sweetly all the day" and "slept securely all the night." The pastoral ideals that Sidney and Spenser did so much to spread during the latter part of the sixteenth century swept on even to the next century with its stress on the blessings of bucolic life as a sweet escape from the harsh realism of the age. Overbury's character of "The Milkmaid" describes a country wench "so far from making herself beautiful by art" that her looks are a "dumb orator to commend her virtue." All her "excellencies stand in her so silently" it would seem they "had stolen upon her without her knowledge." Instead of being arrayed "in the spoil of the silk worm," she is "decked in innocency." Nature having taught her "immoderate sleep is rust to the soul," she rises with "chanticlere, her dame's cock," and at night "makes the lamb her curfew."

She is never idle, and her hands are as hard with labor as her heart is soft with pity. No perfume of "almond glove or aromatic ointment" has ever tainted her hands. As she milks the cow, straining the teats through her fingers, she makes the milk "whiter and sweeter," for her hands are so sweet from labor that the very "golden ears of corn fall and kiss her feet when she reaps them, bound and led prisoners by the hand that fell'd them." Her breath is as fresh as the new-mown haycock in June. When on winter evenings she sits at her merry wheel, spinning, she sings "a defiance to the giddy wheel of fortune." All things she does with such grace "it seems ignorance will not suffer her to do ill." At night she can go alone to "unfold the sheep" without fear of ill because she herself "means none." Good thoughts and prayers, though "short ones," keep her from ever being alone, and old songs keep her heart merry and free from "idle cogitations." So "chaste" are her dreams she "dare tell them," except Friday's which she conceals for fear of the old superstition. So she lives her blameless life, her only care being that if she die young the time may be April or May so that "a store of flowers" may be "stuck on her winding sheet." Thus Overbury records the details of the Elizabethan pastoral about country maids—the early rising, industry, and simple, pure, innocent thoughts which would prepare any maid to meet life or death without harm, and when she was shrouded at last, her friends covered her with the "untouched flowers" of spring.

Too much stress on what might be, but seldom is, roughens the temper of objective minds. Some Elizabethans, therefore, scoffed at these descriptions with about as much impatience as one feels today when youth is hailed as "the frankest, freest, and most intelligent" ever to "walk the face of the world." Francis Lenton's satiric character of "A Country Girl or Darling" tells of "a raw, young, and green maid, newly arrived at the haven of discretion and yet far from the port thereof." She "thinks more than she speaks, speaks more than she understands, and understands more than she dares express." Her "doting parents" have pranked her up like a peacock, for she is "the precious pearl of her mother's pride," and as each crow thinks his own bird the fairest, so her parents "think their goose a swan." Consequently they "trim her up" for every feast or fair where the rough plow drag salutes her with kisses and wins her heart with two pennies' worth of pears and two pennies' worth of red ribbon. Though she is the coarsest damsel in the country, she is her father's hope and her mother's happiness, but her father fears this "paragon of progeny" will elope with his "horse-keeper."

Nor is Lenton any kinder to the city cousin in his character of "The Alderman's Daughter." This vain thing struts her way along the noisy streets, pretending to be a queen. Her father has recently descended from "some lubberly farmer," and his vanity is displeased if his title of

Alderman is omitted. His daughter, therefore, is one of the "painted pagans of the city," and she cannot look "upon her splay foot for fear of crushing the set of her ruff with her chin." She wears her coat long to conceal her feet, yet is so proud of her silk stockings she cannot help raising her skirts to show them. She fancies her father's gold will disguise all her imperfections, and spurns a cockney of her class because she "aspires to the Court," thinking "a lord little enough" for her. She and her doting mother "pace with much pomp and equipage to the Spittle, to the Rehearsal Sermons, where she retains only two of her senses, a wandering eye and a lickerish palate; seeing of objects and tasting of sweetmeats with which her purl'd handkerchief is replete." Having set her mind on court masques, she neglects the city. Her greatest ambition is to be married, and her chief idols, her attire and her title. Down under the layers of this literary fashion lay many of the petty vices and vanities of the age, and women were made the victims of sharp pens and sharper tongues concerned with their little absurdities.

Just as daughters in the normal course were expected to become wives, so sons were regarded as potential heads of families. In the case of the eldest son and heir, this position of honor was often heavy with responsibility. Nevertheless, younger sons were inclined to see only the advantages in store for the heir, and sometimes they made his lot most difficult. On the other hand, heirs were likely to take advantage of their position and to deal unjustly with younger sisters and brothers. Truly, the law of primogeniture raised so many problems in the home that at times filial obedience was almost overwhelmed by it. Lest younger sons rebel against the misfortune of their position, wise parents made every effort to augment the love between brothers instead of building toward its destruction by carelessness or indifferences to the ties of brotherhood.

Conduct books had much to say of brotherly love, which they regarded as one of the most solemn duties by which children might show reverent obedience to parents. William Vaughan felt the affection of brother for brother one of the most acceptable services sons could perform for their Lord. This was why they should love each other above all friends and never let anger or any spirit of fault-finding possess their souls. One can easily make friends, he said, but one is no more likely to get a new brother than to get an eye which is drawn out or a hand which is chopped off. He objected to the common practice, especially in literary works, of placing love of friend above love of brother, for he believed man was commanded of God to follow nature, which would place love of brother first. Such a love was also more inclusive than love of friends, for if friends disagreed, their relations ended, but a man "forsaken of all his parasitical friends" was, by natural instinct, "received and comforted" by his brother.

Thomas Gataker's *A Good Wife Gods Gift: A Marriage Sermon*

(1620) called the tie between friend and friend only a civil knot in comparison with the natural bond between brothers. It was easier to glue together boards that came unglued than to heal flesh gashed and divided by quarrels. That was why it was harder to win back an offended brother than to take a strong city, for the contentions between the two were as bars of brass. Essex felt the strength of the bond of love for his brother Walter, and at his death laid aside the popular, flamboyant style of writing when he reported his loss to Robert Cecil in September of 1594: "Since the writing of my last, I lost my brother in an unfortunate skirmish before Rouen. I call it unfortunate that robbed me of him who was dearer to me than ever I was to myself. We killed divers of them and lost but two, whereof he was one."

A close tie also joined the two brothers, Sir Henry and Sir Charles Danvers, who were neighbors of the Earl of Southampton. According to one report, Sir Henry shot a man by the name of Long who was giving his brother Charles the worst of a fight. In another description of the affair Sir Henry is said to have thrust himself between his brother and Long just as Long raised his sword arm to kill Charles. Striking with his dagger, Sir Henry accidentally killed Long pretty much as Tybalt killed Mercutio in Shakespeare's play of Romeo and Juliet. G. B. Harrison says the mannerisms and tones of the Long and Danvers families were similar to those of the Capulets and Montagues. At any rate, Southampton gave the brothers shelter at his home and organized a series of hunting parties, under cover of which the two brothers were able to reach the port of Southampton. Here, armed with letters to the King of France, they boarded a ship chartered by Southampton. They were none too soon, for a sheriff appeared with a search warrant, but Southampton's barber and his friend John Florio threatened to drown the sheriff if he interfered with the Earl. In France, the two brothers were received most cordially and, after brilliant service in the French army at Rouen, were pardoned by Queen Elizabeth through the intercession of the French king.

Discord between brothers, said Guazzo, diminished the family's good name, particularly when caused by the father's partiality. He agreed that the eldest brother should be honored and obeyed by the younger ones, but he also insisted that the elder brother make every effort to keep the relations with his brothers on a friendly and respectful basis. There must be no taint of familiarity, but when he corrected faults he should do it gently, remembering that what stained one brother stained the other also. For the honor of their house, brothers should support one another; when one fell, the others ought to help him up again. An older brother who had no care for a younger brother's honor had no care for his own. These sentiments Elizabethan parents repeated over and over to their children.

Shakespeare's plays often represent the relations between brothers. King Henry IV, motivated by love of peace and opportunism, advises his son Thomas to take advantage of the preference which his elder brother, the prince, has for him:

> Thou hast a better place in his affection
> Than all thy brothers: cherish it, my boy,
> And noble offices thou mayst affect
> Of mediation, after I am dead,
> Between his greatness and thy other brethren:
> Therefore omit him not; blunt not his love,
> Nor lose the good advantage of his grace
> By seeming cold or careless of his will;
>
> *II Henry IV*, IV: iv: 22–29

Then the king describes the heart of the prince with its "tear for pity" and its "melting charity" but, when incensed, its flint hardness. He may be cruel like winter or kind like spring.

> His temper, therefore, must be well observed:
> Chide him for his faults, and do it reverently,
> When you perceive his blood inclined to mirth;
> But, being moody, give him line and scope,
> Till that his passions, like a whale on ground,
> Confound themselves with working.
>
> *Ibid.*, ll. 36–41

Having made this younger son proud of his seeming influence over the heir, the father makes the point he has had in mind, that this power must be used to good purpose. Though Thomas may learn how to manage his older brother and thereby "prove a shelter to his friends," those friends must be his brothers.

> Learn this, Thomas
> And thou shalt prove a shelter to thy friends,
> A hoop of gold to bind thy brothers in,
> That the united vessel of their blood,
> Mingled with venom of suggestion—
> As, force perforce, the age will pour it in—
> Shall never leak, though it do work as strong
> As aconitum or rash gunpowder.
>
> *Ibid.*, ll. 41–48

The literary source for the quarrel in Shakespeare's *As You Like It* is so long drawn out and so full of elements of family feuds that it reveals how the dramatist pruned Lodge's romance, taking for granted the audience's familiarity with this popular tale and the dissension shown in its family relationships. Instead of educating his younger brother with the portion his father had set aside from the family estate for this purpose, the older brother proceeds to violate the father's will. The younger brother stands up to his oppressor and claims his just dues:

I know you are my eldest brother; and, in the gentle
condition of blood, you should so know me. The courtesy of nations allows you my better, in that you are
the first-born; but the same tradition takes not away
my blood, were there twenty brothers betwixt us: I
have as much of my father in me as you; albeit, I confess, your coming before me is nearer to his reverence.

I: i: 46–54

The two brothers fight and the old servant tries to part them, but the
younger brother has not yet unburdened his mind:

My father charged you in his will to give me good
education: you have trained me like a peasant, ob-
scuring and hiding from me all gentleman-like qualities. The spirit of my father grows strong in me,
and I will no longer endure it: therefore allow me
such exercises as may become a gentleman, or give
me the poor allottery my father left me by testament; with that I will go buy my fortunes.

Ibid., ll. 69–77

To this the elder answers contemptuously, "And what wilt thou do? beg,
when that is spent?" But frightened by the gleam in the younger man's
eyes, he promises him "some part" of his inheritance.

Shakespeare's other brothers in this play deal with a still greater evil
of dispossession, for Duke Frederick has stolen his older brother's title
and position. So the duke expresses sympathy for the elder of the quarreling brothers and advises him to seize the younger one's lands and bring
the rebellious young man to court on a charge of treason. Delighted, the
brother confesses how he hates his younger brother. To this the duke
exclaims, "More villain thou!" As a younger brother, the duke is thus
neatly trapped into an amusing condemnation of himself. He also illustrates ironically the biblical teaching that the higher a man's position, the
greater his moral mouthings if he and one of his subjects are guilty of
the same evil act. Later in the play, when the younger of the quarreling
brothers saves his oppressor from the jaws of a lioness, he can explain
his humanity only by saying nature in him was stronger than his "just
occasion" to return evil for evil. Overwhelmed by such humanity, his
elder brother comes to his senses and wonders how he could be so "unnatural" in his injustice to a brother. It takes even more than returning
good for evil to bring the greater villain, Duke Frederick, to his senses.
Only the magic of the Forest of Arden can melt the hardness of his heart,
after which his remorse is so great he can but retire from the world to a
monastery after he has restored to his elder brother, the real duke, the
stolen title and position. Without doubt the sudden change of heart in
the brothers of this comedy, aside from following the borrowed plot and

providing the desired happy ending, delighted an audience used to sudden change in life and fully aware of the fact that human nature is not very predictable even where it should be most trusted.

It seldom happens that the ideal relation between brothers is lived out, but in the Sidney household it was very closely approximated according to the letters and records that have come down to us. Sir Philip's interest in his younger brother Robert shows a concern that is deep and tender in spite of its formality. "My dear Brother," he began one of his long letters of gentle advice, "for the money you have received, assure yourself (for it is true) there is nothing pleaseth me, as that which is for you. If ever I have the ability [to increase the allowance] you will find it, if not, yet shall not any brother living be better loved of me." Then he asks Robert to be patient with some of his father's whims by bearing them "with reverence."

Next he advises Robert about his journey through Germany and Italy, where he must spend most of his money "upon worthy men, and not upon householding," though he adds quickly, "Look to your diet (Sweet Robin) and hold up your heart in courage and virtue, truly a great part of my comfort is in you." If Robert follows this advice, Sidney says he will "never more have cares" about him. At the same time he wishes him to take advantage of every opportunity to improve his mind while traveling.

Naturally this leads to a discussion of Robin's study under his tutor, "an excellent man." Study of the Greeks and Romans will enable him to understand the events of his own age, even its virtues and vices and causes for ruins of great estates as well as warfare and the need for the soldier's discipline. He reminds his brother that history can teach him much about oratory and rhetoric and poetry and their effects as heard in "the whisperings of the people." But most of all it is important for its divine and moral teachings, as it sets forth sometimes like a Solon the virtues and the passions of a people.

Of course Sidney repeats advice he heard so often from his own tutors—to study in order to get at the heart of the author's presentation, and to memorize witty and wise sentences in order to store his mind with knowledge useful for the future. Nor must he neglect arithmetic and geometry that will give him a "feeling of active judgment." As an afterthought, and an important one, he adds that his brother must learn to speak Latin well but not be addicted to "Ciceronianism" as students were at Oxford. All this advice, he assures his brother, is for one who is of as much, if not more concern, to him than his own self, for *he* has "given over the delight in the world."

With God's help, says Sidney, returning to the pressing discussion of financial matters, he will see that Robert has the sum of £200 a year if the estates of England remain, but he asks him to use this money to his "best profit." Lord Leicester is sending £40, and promises at least that much each year, and so Robert should write this uncle "largely and diligently" if he wishes him to continue being "very good" to him. If Robin doesn't receive an odd £30 with the hundred he is expecting from home soon, Sidney promises affectionately to "jarl" with his father about it. Meanwhile he is sending his brother some of his own "toyful books" that may be of some assistance to him. At this time Sidney was living with Leicester and meeting many stimulating minds.

He wishes Robert not to neglect his music while he pursues his more serious studies. He himself says no one could believe "what a want" he himself "finds of it in his melancholy times." He also recommends books on horsemanship which will profit more in a month than others in a year, and asks his brother to note the directions about "bitting, saddling, and curing" horses. A good horseman must handle his weapons well, and Robin must have his "thick caps and bracers" also in order to "play lustily, for indeed ticks and dalliances are nothing in earnest . . ." He advises using "the blow as the thrust," as it is good in itself and also "exercises the breath and strength," and will make him a strong man at the tourney and barriers. First he must practice the sword and then the dagger, and let no day pass without an hour or two of diligent exercise. Then he can devote the rest of the day to study "and sedulous conversation" so that he may come home to be his family's comfort and credit.

Sidney looks back over his long letter, written at Leicester House in October of 1580, and is reminded to ask his brother to write a better hand. His own is bad enough, but Robin's is worse. Once more he urges careful attention to the diet. Then he asks God to bless this "sweet boy," and to help him accomplish the "joyful hope" he conceives of him. Suddenly he closes with "Lord, how I have blabbed, once again farewell, dearest brother, your most loving and careful brother."

Though Sidney's feeling of responsibility for Robert may have been due in part to affection and his own fine character, it was also due to his father's fine training. When quotations and examples of concord from such writers as Guazzo did not knit together the hearts of their children, Elizabethan parents might even use their authority to achieve harmony. Discord, they believed, not only offended God, but ruined their own "credit." Consequently, they urged older brothers to recompense the younger ones' humility with good will and liberality, even to show more consideration and respect than these sons could expect from other children in the family. Parents pointed out that if the younger brothers failed in their duty to the heir it would require all the older son's tact and good will to enable him to show his brothers their duty without causing them to harbor ill feeling. When he corrected their faults, therefore, he must be gentle and make them realize the good wishes that accompanied his admonitions. Above all things he must take great care against his younger brothers' becoming too bold or too familiar in word or deed. And if ever he had to tell them of their faults, he must do it privately in order to spare them the "mocks and scoffs" of others.

With so much responsible power in his hands, it is not strange that the heir to a rich estate, even with the best intentions in the world, should often seem unjust to his younger brothers. Lest he be so intentionally, fathers were urged to make provision for their younger sons, not only to ensure harmony in the home but to enable the family to continue its place in society as a united group. With proper provision for the younger children and careful training of the eldest son in regard to his obligations to the family, the hope of brotherly love under the system of primogeniture was not incapable of realization.

Abuses and carelessness make up a sad story, however, and the character of "The Younger Brother" as set forth by John Earle had more truth in it than an Elizabethan parent would like to admit. The father, says this sketch, "tasks" his younger son to be a gentleman and "leaves him nothing to maintain it." The elder son's knighthood must sustain the family, and the younger son's knighthood is beggary. Unable to "descend to the means of getting wealth" by traffic, the younger son "stands at the mercy of the world, and which is worse, his brother." He is a bit better off than the serving men, "yet they are more saucy with him than he bold with the master," for the older brother can look at him "with a countenance of stern awe," and reprimand him oftener than the servants. Like his brother's old suits, he is cast off, and even nature shows him more wit than compassion. Should his slender annuity enable him to attend the university, he must "with great heart-burning" enter the ministry because of his ill-fortune.

Then Earle considers the possibilities of escape from these intolerable conditions. Some younger sons take to the highway, and are saved from imprisonment only by the older brother's pride. Finally, as a last resort they go to the Low Countries, "where rags and lice are no scandal." Here they live like poor gentlemen, but die "without a shirt." Their only escape from their sorry lot is to "bait" some rich widow "that is hungry" for noble blood. Since the younger son is so discontented, he commonly refers to his more fortunate brother as a churl, and but for his love of the one little portion of his native land where he was born, he would long since have "revolted to the Spaniard."

In spite of his privileges, however, the older son was often sorely oppressed, particularly if the family left in his care numbered many children and dependents. Indebtedness might make his lot still harder. Lenton's satirical sketch of him reveals some of the thorns in his supposedly fortunate life. Often, he says, the eldest son inherits both folly and fortune when he becomes executor of his father's ill-husbandry. This causes him to grind his estate into smaller quantity to the diminishing of the manor and its appurtenances, or he is so encumbered with legacies to the younger heirs that his shallow brain is confused. His lady's extravagance often causes him to mortgage his estate till he finally sells his land, then leases it at the rate of purchase. If he has wit enough to become a justice of the peace he betrays his lack of learning in his books. Lenton leaves him then, "studying his pedigree."

Unless the father performed the duties expected of him, he made both heir and younger sons unhappy, and this could happen in the best of families. Sir Francis Bacon, for example, was the victim of unfulfilled promises when his father failed to keep his pledge to provide for him in his will. Again, when his older brother Anthony died, he received nothing, though he had good cause to hope for some financial aid from him. As John Chamberlain wrote to Dudley Carleton, Anthony died so deeply in debt that Francis was "little the better by him."[14]

Bad feeling between brothers could hardly be avoided if one of them was a bastard. So few rights were accorded bastards that they were almost sure to express their resentment at the injustice done them. Shakespeare frequently takes it for granted that his bastards do ill because they are illegitimate. When Don John in *Much Ado About Nothing* is advised to mend his manners if he will stand in the good graces of his legitimate brother, he retorts bitterly:

> I had rather be a canker in a hedge than a rose in his
> grace . . . though I cannot be said to be a flattering honest
> man, it must not be denied but I am a plain-dealing vil-
> lain. I am trusted with a muzzle and enfranchised with a
> clog; therefore I have decreed not to sing in my cage. If
> I had my mouth, I would bite; if I had my liberty, I would
> do my liking . . .
>
> I: iii: 28–38

These words proclaim him a somewhat romantic villain, but he had cause for his railing. He could not conceal his disgrace as a bastard, and his sadness was as he said "without limit." To listen to reason about his condition gave only "patient sufferance." He could expect nothing from life. Since he could not hide what he was, he determined to smile at no man's jest, eat only when he had the stomach, wait for no man's leisure, sleep when he was drowsy, tend on no man's business, laugh when he was merry, and "claw" no man in his humor. Cut off from friendly contact with the nobility, he was maddened by the injustice of his lot.

Commonly, legitimate children looked askance at the bastard blot on their family name. It took a most exceptional soul to treat a bastard like a human being. Henry Cornelius Agrippa stated the bastards' position, and showed why they might be inclined to take by force whatever they could obtain from their family, for the general feeling was that bastards were born bad. "All children are the fruits of matrimony," he said, and of God, not nature; hence "the bastard children be called natural," and

---

[14] *Calendars of State Papers* . . . *1601–1603*, CCLXXIX, No. 91.

"those that come of matrimony be only lawful." Therefore he would not have a bastard enter "into the church of God," for which reason he could not be "heir of temporal lands and goods." Then he repeats unequivocally, "only matrimony maketh children to be certain, and giveth undoubtful heirs."[15] Even after the Reformation this attitude persisted in the hearts of the people. Becon expressed the feeling of this time when he said that bastards were the gifts of God, but "contrary to the word of God" because their "generation, conception, and bringing forth" was "unlawful." God had "ordained the state of matrimony" for the propagation of the human race, and did not, therefore, bless whoredom but did "bless and glorify the fruit of matrimony." If he blessed both, the state of matrimony would be "in vain."

In *The booke of Matrimony* (1581), Becon was quite explicit about the subject of bastardy. He declared a bastard was "straightly prohibited both by human laws and the constitutions of wise men to be heirs of temporal lands and goods." It was impossible for those who were guilty of "neglecting and despising matrimony at the wanton and enticing lust of the flesh" to have lawful heirs. Moreover, it was "the common sentence and judgment of lawyers" that the bastard had "uncertain father and a naughty mother," that he was "base born," that he was the "son of the people, yea the son of no man." He also denied the bastard the right to enter a church, though he felt that since his father and not the bastard had sinned, "the father and not the child" should "bear the pain of wickedness . . ." He was ahead of his time, however, when he admitted that if a bastard who had been denied the comfort of companionship at church left "the wicked and ungodly ways of his father," he could not be hindered from embracing "true godliness" for "all the days of his life."

Sensitive to this general feeling toward illegitimate children, Shakespeare's bastards commonly hate their legitimate brothers and express their emotion very much like Don John, who says of his "lawful" brother's best friend, "That young startup hath all the glory of my overthrow. If I can cross him any way, I bless myself every way." Royal bastards, of course, both in life and in plays, did not suffer the blighting stigma of common bastards, possibly because the pope had proclaimed Elizabeth a bastard, and particularly because Henry VIII's promising bastard son until his lamented death had been made to take precedence over his half-sister Mary.

As a rule, bastards "legitimized" by their parents' subsequent marriage might be denied inheritance.[16] This cruel law could be circumvented only by an act of Parliament, which would make bastards both legitimate and capable of inheritance, as in the case of John of Gaunt's bastard chil-

---

[15] *The Commendation of Matrimony*, translated into English by David Clapham in 1540.

[16] Hardinge Stanley Giffard, Earl of Halsbury, *Laws of England* (London: Bellyard Temple Bar, Butterworth and Co., Ltd., 1931), II, 576.

dren.[17] Henry VIII was descended from one of these bastards. The usual practice among families of the upper class when troubled by both legitimate and illegitimate children of the same parents was for the bastards to inherit the mother's property settled on her in her own name and for the legitimate children to inherit the father's property. So confused were the civil and canonical laws in the matter, however, that the bastard's inheritance was never secure, unless there was cause for wealth or power to enforce his claims. Even then the outcome was not always assured if enemies of greater wealth or power opposed him. This is why only royal bastards might be assured of any rights in Tudor England.

When Catherine was generally admitted unable to have more children, Henry VIII's "entirely beloved [natural] son," the lord Henry Fitzroy, at the age of five, was made Duke of Richmond on June 16, 1525. The ceremony was attended with "extraordinary pomp and ceremony," and all the great lords of the state took part, with the Cardinal at their head. Sir Thomas More read the patent, and Henry's son was given a royal title and made Lord High Admiral of England; he was also granted princely revenues besides his precedence over Mary. Even when Henry VIII was most under the influence of Anne Boleyn, he never wavered in his attitude of devotion toward his son. This particular case after England's withdrawal from the influence of the pope may have had something to do with the mixed feelings about bastardy in England as well as the legal confusion over the inheritance of bastards. In one case the pope had condoned the king's bastard; later the pope was to declare Elizabeth a bastard.

Henry's bastard son had been born to Elizabeth Blount in 1519. She had been one of Catherine's ladies in waiting, and had excelled in all the court pastimes of singing, dancing, etc. Her son resembled both parents. In about 1522, the mother was married to Sir Gilbert Talboys, who, with his father, was presented great sums of money and many benefits. The mother was assured certain manors[18] "for her life time." It is not known when she had to part from her child, whether before or after he became Duke of Richmond. Of course, his father engaged the finest instructors obtainable for his son. One of these, Palgrave (author of the first French grammar in English), wrote the mother of her child's progress, saying, ". . . on my conscience, my Lord of Richmond is of as good nature, as much inclined to all manner virtuous and honorable inclinations as any babes living." He tells her the king says of him: "I deliver unto thee my worldly jewel; you twain (Master Parr and Master Page) to have the guiding of his body, and thou, Palgrave, to bring him up in virtue and learning."

[17] Sir William Blackstone, *Commentaries on the Laws of England* (1765–69; San Francisco, Calif.: Bancroft-Whitney Co., 1916), I, 656.
[18] *Letters and Papers, Foreign and Domestic, of the Reign of Henry VIII, 1524–30* (1876); Introduction by J. S. Brewer, cxlii–cxlvi.

For Henry VIII to untangle the law to make it favor his bastard meant only to cut knots, but after Elizabeth was able to withstand the onslaught of slander against her birth, she eased the legal difficulties of bastards if it pleased her to do so; if not, as in the case of the Earl of Hertford who secretly married Lady Catherine Grey, she imposed the onus of bastardy upon children. She could rely on the fact that feeling and custom lag after any law, and though the public attitude toward bastardy in her case had been deflected, she could make it turn in the direction she desired, carrying with it all the grief and dishonor she wished to impose upon a "rebellious" subject. James I was to follow this same course also.

The tie between brothers and sisters was not so likely to be severed by greed or envy as in the case of brothers. There are many accounts of a beautiful relationship between brothers and sisters, but few so close as that pictured in the old romances or advocated by the conduct books. One, nevertheless, has been preserved for us in the devotion of one of Elizabeth's maids of honor, Margaret, Mistress of Ratcliffe, for her brother. It is possible this attachment suggested to Shakespeare his Olivia of *Twelfth Night*, who has vowed to veil her face from the "ample view" for seven years that she may honor a "brother's dead love" (I: i: 27–32). Margaret, at the death of her brother, pined away. It was said she actually starved herself, and this, combined with her extreme grief, caused her death. When the body was opened at the Queen's command, it was reported well and sound "saving certain strings striped all over her heart." All the maids went into mourning for her, and she was buried as befitted a noble's daughter.

One of the best bits of realism in Shakespeare's characterization of Ophelia is in connection with her brother and father, who seek to protect her innocence. Laertes, ready to depart for France, must first give sound advice to his sister. In the play he begins as if continuing a conversation about Hamlet's attentions to Ophelia.

> For Hamlet, and the trifling of his favor,
> Hold it a fashion and a toy in blood,
> A violet in the youth of primy nature,
> Forward, not permanent, sweet, not lasting,
> The perfume and suppliance of a minute;
> No more.
>
> I: iii: 5–9

She loves Laertes well, and prompts him into larger talk, for she is sure of Hamlet's vows. She also knows Laertes delights in playing the "worldly-wise brother."

He rises to her bait, "No more but so?" He admits Hamlet may even love her now, but since he is a prince, his will is not his own and his words cannot carry weight till they are the voice of Denmark. This sobers her, of course, and he plunges on, warning her against her lover's songs and importunities against her chastity. "The chariest maid," he says, "is prodigal enough if she unmask her beauty to the moon," and as the buds of spring cannot withstand the canker galls, so she must remember that in the "morn and liquid dew of youth" her virtue is subject to the "most imminent" and "contagious blastments." Pleased with his figures, he rounds out his argument with a couplet that brings laughter to his sister's eyes:

> Be wary then; best safety lies in fear;
> Youth to itself rebels, though none else near.
>
> *Ibid.* ll. 43–44

With mock humility Ophelia answers that she will keep his "good lesson as a watchman" to her heart. But seeing Laertes' smile of satisfaction, she adds roguishly,

> . . . good my brother,
> Do not, as some ungracious pastors do,
> Show me the steep and thorny way to heaven;
> Whiles, like a puff'd and reckless libertine,
> Himself the primrose path of dalliance treads,
> And recks not his own rede.
>
> *Ibid.*, ll. 46–51

Her brother's stout "O! fear me not" is cut short by his father's entrance, and now he in turn must listen to repeated precepts and tthe paternal blessing before he can take his leave. His last word to Ophelia, however, is that she "remember well" what he has told her. Her arch response, " 'Tis in my memory lock'd, and you yourself shall keep the key of it," causes her departing father to turn back and look at her closely as he questions the meaning of her words. Laertes leaves quickly.

Ophelia's "So please you, something touching the Lord Hamlet" opens again the flood gates of fatherly advice. Polonius recalls he has heard too often of late that Hamlet has "given private time" to her and that she has been "most free and bounteous" in her audience; he fears she does not understand herself clearly enough to preserve her "honor" against the gossip her conduct will occasion. Bluntly he asks her to tell him truthfully what is between her and the prince.

Frightened, Ophelia says timidly that Hamlet has "of late made many tenders of his affection" to her. The father scoffs at her words, saying she talks like "a green girl, unsifted in such perilous circumstance." Gazing at her with hard, contemptuous eyes, he asks, "Do you believe his tenders, as you call them?" More frightened, she says dutifully, "I do not know, my lord, what I should think." Her father tells her brusquely he will teach her what to think if like a "baby" she has taken Hamlet's "tenders for true pay." Then, roughly, he demands that she "tender" herself "more dearly" lest she "tender" him the fool she is. Dismayed, Ophelia tries to defend herself: "My lord, he hath importun'd me with love in an honorable fashion." Scornfully he answers, "Ay, fashion you may call it: go to, go to." But Ophelia plunges on, "And hath given countenance to his speech, my lord, with almost all the holy vows of heaven."

This is too much for Polonius the Lord Chamberlain. The affair has gone farther than he thought, and he stands before his shrinking daughter, explaining what any "babe" should know: how the "burning blood" lends the "prodigal" tongue vows, how such "blazes" give more light than heat, and she must not "take fire" from such promises. As she falters before his logic, he gives commands: she must henceforth be "scanter" of her "maidenly presence" and set her "entreatments at a higher rate than a command to parley." She must not believe Lord Hamlet: he is young and expects "larger tether" than she may enjoy. She must consider his vows but "mere implorators of unholy saints, breathing like sanctified and pious bawds the better to beguile." Plainly, he will no longer have her "slander any moment's leisure as to give words or talk with the Lord Hamlet." Fixing her with a stern, parental eye, he says, "Look to't, I charge you; come your ways." Brokenly, submissively, Ophelia promises, "I shall obey, my lord."

For the Elizabethan audience this scene would have strong emotional appeal. The father would see the difficulties of a parent responsible for a daughter's chastity which was endangered by her love for one socially above her: he would be keenly aware of the fact that a man in the higher station had every advantage. The mother would tremble for her daughter's virtue. A brother with a loved sister would see the cruelty in the circumstances and perhaps ponder the unkindness of inscrutable fate. The maid, if allowed at the theater at all, would tremble for the hapless girl, knowing the strength of the cords which held the heroine fast in the net of decorum.

Seldom is the part of Ophelia played on the stage with the strength it demands: for this heroine is swayed powerfully by a passion which she represses so carefully that it reveals itself at last only in her mad songs. Though maidenly pride and the grief-laden situations in which she is placed are partly responsible for her eventual madness, it may be questioned whether the repression imposed by decorum was not its most contributory cause. As Herford declares, Ophelia's surrender of her love to Hamlet was most piteous, for it not only broke her heart and overthrew her reason, but it took away Hamlet's last trust in what was good.[19] Worse still, all this misery follows a father's conventional demands. In her obedience, Ophelia submits to situations which clash with

---

[19] Charles Harold Herford, *The Normality of Shakespeare Illustrated in His Treatment of Love and Marriage* (1920), p. 12.

her fine moral and intelligent nature, and is left with nothing but precepts for a guide to conduct. Her consequent repression, plus her brooding over Hamlet's madness, makes her unable to stand the shock of her father's death, for by it she loses her last prop of decorum upon which she has been made to lean too heavily. Living in the presence of Hamlet's disordered mind and bent by the strain of her love for him, she finally gives way to the "imitative tendencies of nerve diseases" from which she might have been spared had her attachment to lover and father been less strong. In most Elizabethan homes there was not likely to be any great danger from such inhibitions or too much curtailment of self-expression in the busy household, but there would be enough awareness of frustration to make this romantic play appeal to the sensibilities of the age.

Among the ladies at Elizabeth's court, there was probably no more loyal sister than Penelope Rich to her brother, the Earl of Essex. She was also beautiful and vain, yet so charming she appealed to both men and women. At her brother's disgrace upon his return from Ireland, both she and her sister Dorothy dressed in deepest mourning and sought permission to see Essex. They were refused. Now Penelope wrote the Queen, accompanying her letters by jewels and other presents. Still failing in her efforts, she applied to Sir Robert Cecil, and failed again. Again she tried the Queen, writing what she considered a little masterpiece of flattery in clever, impertinent, euphuistic phrases. She made the mistake, however, of showing it to some of her friends before she sent it on its way. Accordingly, Elizabeth heard of it before it reached her, and she ordered the Lord Treasurer to examine Penelope's loyalty to the Crown. Penelope passed the examination charmingly, and was set free with the stipulation that she approach Elizabeth the full length of the throne room on her knees to ask for pardon. Whether or not Penelope thought her little laugh at the "old Queen" was worth this humiliation, she did succeed in helping Essex to secure his release from prison.

But these were trying days, and there was much concern over Elizabeth's refusal to declare her successor to the throne. It is possible that Penelope's impatience caused her to urge her brother and his friends Mountjoy and Southampton to continue their plotting for the naming of King James of Scotland as the successor. At any rate Essex opened his house to others who favored James, and once more he was put under arrest. Now he "betrayed" Penelope to the Privy Council by saying she had a "proud spirit" that must be "looked into." Did he utter these words under the stress of mental and physical torture, or were they wrung from him in agonized fear of death? When she was told of her brother's accusation she showed amazement, but she was not crushed. She stoutly declared she had been "more like a slave than a sister" to her brother, and that her attitude had been due to love, not to her brother's authority. "What I have suffered," she said, "besides her Majesty's displeasure, I will not mention; yet so strangely have I been wronged, as may well be an argument to make one despise the world, finding the smoke of envy where affection should be clearest."[20]

Her well-considered answer to the Council shows that Penelope was not to be ensnared into sudden madness by her loved brother's strange confession of her guilt. She was, indeed, well prepared to live in an age demanding all a woman's wit and skill and warmth of heart. When put to the rack, as it were, she reacted humanly and naturally, as well as wisely, and in her way won a victory quite different from, say, that of Shakespeare's Isabella in *Measure for Measure*. With Penelope it was quick, passionate intelligence and absolute control of emotions; with Isabella it was instant refusal to sacrifice her chastity to save her brother. The execution of her brother must have grieved Penelope sorely, but the loss of her faith in him must have grieved her infinitely more, for all their lives they had been closely united by a community of friends and interests. Was there any greater irony, therefore, than her powerlessness to aid him because he had cast doubt on her loyalty? As for Essex, the terrors he felt at judgment's bar must have been somewhat like the fears that shook Claudio when told at what price he must save his life.

At first Claudio, like his sister or any Elizabethan, had felt nothing could compensate for the loss of his sister Isabella's honor, not even his own life. But suddenly realizing his life *was* at stake, and seeing the yawning pit of death looming before him, he was overwhelmed by the fearful spectacle. As his sister looked into his face and saw there the pleading of a desperate soul, she told him sternly a shamed life was worse than death. But her brother could only cry out against the unknown, "to go we know not where . . ." And worse than this, "to lie in cold obstruction and to rot . . ." No! the "weariest and most loathed life" of age or ache or penury or even imprisonment was a paradise to what he feared in death. Was this the terror that racked the soul of Essex as he made his last, and alas his most unmanly, effort to free himself from the coils of unrelenting punishment?

Affection between brothers and sisters-in-law was also a duty by which Elizabethans strove in every way possible to cement family ties. Indeed, children were taught that filial duty required harmony among even the most remote members of the family. A graceful letter by Sir Henry Wotton to his half-brother's wife reveals the attachment of this agreeable family. "My dearest Dear Sister," he writes from Heidelberg on December 14, 1589, "all your desires be unto you e'en as your own heart wishes them." Knowing her desires to be "all good," he wishes no addition to them except that "when they get a little leisure from their better cares," they will make "a poor traveler part of their thought." He knows his "most unfeignedly dear brother" will upon her entreaty tell his address. "The distance of that place to you, my sweetest sister, is very

---

[20] Violet A. Wilson, *Society Women of Shakespeare's Time* (1925), p. 125.

great; the love you have ever, with the free consent of your friendly heart, showed towards me is as great, and so there is nothing in this world that can make your faith towards me little." To live in that opinion of him does him no wrong in her thoughts, he adds playfully.

And so he wishes she will write him. "If," he says, "in some odd, happy hour, when your pen lies silently by you, you will take it up and bestow six lines towards Germany, I will preserve them from all hazards of fortune, and command all my pens to wait upon you with faithful service." In the meantime he commends her to "the full accomplishment of her good heart's requests which God of all happiness make good in haste," and signs himself her "most loving faithful brother."[21]

Three years later this beloved sister had died, and Wotton writes to Lord Touche of the changes such a loss will make in his brother's life: "God has taken away to his mercy his wife, who died on the 8th of May, a gentle woman in my opinion of most rare virtues. This will make him . . . resolve to enter the State, both for certain private respects . . . and besides, to wear away the sorrow with negotiation, a frequent custom of the ancients." Like his forebears, Wotton loved wisdom and quiet and retirement from public life, but he knew his brother at this time needed to escape for a while at least into the engrossing details of public life.

Wotton was almost as fond of his half-brother's child Philippa as he had been of her mother; he indicates this affection in letters to her husband, Sir Edmund Bacon. "I hear a little voice that you are come to London," he writes in one of his notes, "which to me is the voice of the nightingale, for since I cannot enjoy your presence, I make myself happy with your nearness; and yet now, methinks, I have a kind of rebellion against it, that we should be separated with such a contemptible distance. For how much I love you my own heart doth know, and God knows my heart." He must have paused a moment to think of how he had enjoyed sweet years of peace as provost of Eton College, for he continues, ". . . let me not fall into a passion: for what sin, in the name of Christ, was I sent hither among soldiers, being by my profession academical, and by my charge pacifical?" Then he briefly states the point of his letter. "I am within a day or two to send Cuthbert my servant home, by whom I shall tell you divers things." He concludes lightly, "In the meantime, I have adventured these few lines, to break the ice of silence; for in truth, it is a cold fault. Our sweet Savior bless you." And in typical Elizabethan manner, he adds a postscript to send his love to this Philippa, the "best niece in the world."[22]

But it was to be Wotton's misfortune to suffer the death of this young woman, too, yet he tried to console her husband. Among "those who

---

[21] Smith, *The Life and Letters of Sir Henry Wotton*, I, 236–37.
[22] Paul Elmer More, *Shelburne Essays* (1908), p. 231.

have deep interest in all that can befall" him, Wotton believes he may
be the best "witness" of the husband's "unexpressible affections" to his
"most dear niece, whom God hath taken . . . into his Eternal light and
rest . . ." He would consider himself "unworthy forever of that love
she bare" him if he could feel himself fit to comfort her husband, but he
will try to say something of help. ". . . only God can reconsolate" them
both when He "will unclasp the final book of His decrees, and dissolve
the whole; for which" Wotton hopes the Lord will "rather teach" them
how "to thirst and languish than to repine at particular dissolutions." He
reminds the husband how he himself "in a peculiar affliction . . . all
within the compass of little time" had been given much consolation; now
he hopes he may return that comfort back to him, and feels he can since
he is so "well acquainted with the strength" of this kind man's "Christian
mind."[23]

Besides his mother and his brother's wife and daughter, Wotton could
take into his heart no other woman except James I's delicate little Princess
Elizabeth whom everybody loved. Perhaps Wotton distrusted married
life, especially for himself with his many missions abroad. He is credited
with saying, "Next to no wife and children, your own wife and children
are best pastimes; another's wife and your children are worse; your wife
and another's children are worst." This was probably only an objective
summary, however, of the harried man's domestic complications as seen
from the bachelor's point of view. The affection shown in Wotton's own
dutiful letters strikes gently on the note played most often by moralists of
conduct books and sermons, and one wonders how far training and intelligence carried him along the way by which he learned to command the
felicitous utterances of his heart.

When Wotton and Lord Herbert were visiting the courts of France
and Italy in the early part of the seventeenth century, Sir Edmund Verney
was a youth traveling with them to finish his education that was to make
him a servant of the Crown. Sir Edmund finished his tour in 1610, and
soon married Margaret Denton, with whom he established a household
that was to continue the best Elizabethan domestic traditions. Their eldest son Ralph, whether by birth or training or temperament, was to become the type of son extolled by conduct books and grave moralists of
the reigns of both Elizabeth and James I. Forced at an early age to take
charge of the family during his father's absence from home on affairs of
state, Ralph was to learn how to carry on his shoulders the perplexing
and trying domestic problems that ranged all the way from tedious to
dramatic.

Always cautious and prudent in his management of his father's

---

[23] Smith, *The Life and Letters of Sir Henry Wotton*, II, 289.

estates, Ralph spared no pains for those he loved and who loved him, and even for those who were not always considerate of him. On him his family and friends laid their burdens, without mercy or very much gratitude, and always, in time of trouble, he gave them aid to the best of his ability. Old before his time, like many Elizabethan youths, he was a capable and loving husband and father before he was out of his teens. Moreover, he soon demonstrated a great love for business and the practical way of undertaking all transactions connected with it. His father affectionately called him his right hand, but the rest of the family freely used him or criticized him or asked him to share his means and influence which had been enhanced by his marriage to a rich wife.

Though this marriage occurred in 1629, it was involved in many of the difficulties that so frequently beset Elizabethan marriages. Ralph was fifteen at the time, and his bride was two years younger. She had been orphaned at the age of nine, though her father, the mayor of Abingdon, had left her his wealth and kindly, gentle ways. Since she was an orphan of considerable property, she was placed under the jurisdiction of the Court of Wards and became the object of much bickering among four of her relatives who had procured from the court a lease of her lands and her custody with the privilege of bestowing her in marriage when she was fourteen. They had promised to give the Crown altogether £2000 for this privilege.

One of the four, when Mary was only eleven, had arranged a marriage with his own son, got the license, bought the child's wedding apparel, hired a priest, and all but accomplished his purpose of securing the little girl's fortune for his family when one of her guardians appealed to the court to prevent this breach of trust. Then an order was drawn up that "the ward unmarried, unaffianced, and uncontracted" should, under a penalty of £5000 for breach of trust, be sent to Lady Denham in Bucks, to be brought up with her own sons and daughters. Meanwhile the other three guardians offered the child to Sir Edmund Verney for his eldest son Ralph. Sir Edmund agreed to take her and to pay the £1000 still due the Crown, though her uncles stipulated little Mary was not to be forced into marriage, and was to be well-bred and allowed to make her choice "at years competent." When Sir Edmund procured a decree from the court in his own favor, Mary was made the wife of Ralph.

Of course the two years decreed by all Elizabethans for children so young were allowed to elapse before the marriage was consummated, and during this time Mary lived with an aunt. When she was fifteen, she came to live with the Verneys, though her husband was still at Oxford, twenty miles away, studying. He used to ride home faithfully to see his wife, even in the rain. Their marriage was very happy, for the wife loved not only her husband but all his family of brothers, sisters, and parents, and was loved by them in turn. Shortly before she was to become a mother she had her portrait painted to make apparent her pregnant state, and was delighted when she bore a son, who, as heir, was appropriately named for Sir Edmund.

In spite of the Elizabethan type of formality retained in the Verney home, Ralph and his father were very close to each other. Frequently Sir Edmund praised Ralph's good judgment and good sense, his indefatigable industry, and his kindness. Although he often laughed at Ralph's bad horsemanship and lack of interest in sports, and although he was amused at Ralph's formalities and close attention to even minute details, he probably loved his son all the better for these traits. Until he lost his wife, Sir Edmund indeed seemed younger in heart than Ralph and was possessed of a more articulate grace. Never, on the other hand, was there a more devoted son. Sir Edmund writes Mary during their absence at the baths that he can't without a quarrel prevail upon Ralph to leave him and says, ". . . therefore, good heart, forgive us both since his absence is against both our wills." Ralph is "every day in the bath," and the father prays God it may do him good, for it certainly does himself no good. However, since he is there he will "try the uttermost of it" that he may not be reproached at his return for doing things by halves. At their arrival the town was empty, but now it is very full of good company, and the two of them pass their time "as merrily as pain will give . . . leave." He signs himself "Your loving father and faithful friend," and such he was, for he made as little mention as possible of the pain causing their delayed return home. The comfort this father took from his son is one of the pleasantest records we have of home life during this age, partly because of the father's quick acknowledgment of his appreciation of his son's devotion, and partly because of the son's willing obedience and loving care of both parents.[24]

In training and in practice, possibly the most distinctive quality in the filial attitude of sons and daughters was their unquestioning or unresisting obedience to parental law. This service was brightened by devotion in many homes, but when the children were merely dutiful, the family relationships were likely to be cold and formal. The insistence in conduct books and public sermons upon *loving* obedience suggests the difficulty almost always present when impatient youth questions the experience of the older generation. Yet upon the Elizabethan child's cooperation with responsible parents advising them in marriage and career depended the entire structure of a happy or auspicious family life.

In the Elizabethan way of life, the family was the very foundation of society and yet, at the same time, they tried to achieve a marked individualism of its members. From the parents' point of view the service

---

[24] Verney, *Memoirs of the Verney Family*, I, *passim*. Also, for an interesting account, see Elizabeth Godfrey, *Home Life under the Stuarts, 1603–1649* (1903).

of the family to society was the very thing that made life capable of significance. Individualism was precious, but if necessary, it might have to be sacrificed for the larger good. The position of the family in their scheme of things was, therefore, a source of great emotional intensity for parents: dutiful children meant a moving forward to better things, but disobedient children might put in jeopardy their most worthy ambitions and their dearest dreams and hopes for the future.

Of course religious parents regarded obedience as necessary for the salvation of their children's souls. But those who had lost hope in the conventional religious concept of a future life substituted for it the idea of the preservation of the family. For them the family was indeed the most important thing in the world. Whatever their children might do to cement together family ties and augment family prestige and family wealth by wise conservation or enlargement of material possessions depended, they believed, on the training they received in their own home. Consequently, any failure of the children to conform to the plans made so carefully for them meant the negation of the home's very reason for being. With both home and religion discarded there would remain only the immediate present. For the Elizabethan this was not enough.

From the Elizabethan children's point of view filial obedience was, in general, not only a bounden duty but an inescapable one. The high value placed on chastity by society did confine many intelligent daughters to a repetitious round of daily duties in their homes till the time came for matching them in marriage. If such daughters were taught from the cradle that the core of their activities and interests must be domestic, their lives might not be outstanding for independent thinking or very much initiative. In spite of all the emphasis upon demure maidens, few Elizabethan homes followed slavishly the theory of immuring their daughters till their wedding. In fact, the spirit of independent thinking, then as now, was smothered not so much by tradition or custom as by the individual laziness of mind. Women's achievements today depend a great deal, however, upon freedom from the restrictions of domestic duties; Elizabethan women's achievements were colored and made fruitful by their domestic accomplishments.

It is true that the law of primogeniture snared the eldest son before he was born; it is also true that younger sons learned at an early age the importance of their father's friends and connections in relation to any hope they might have for a successful career unless, of course, they were willing to try their luck on the capricious wheel of fortune. But the most significant thing in the practical side of life for Elizabethan sons and daughters of both the privileged and underprivileged classes was that if they were to find any economic or social security in the world, the surest way to it lay through the efforts of their own parents on their behalf. And many Elizabethan parents could actually come very close to the point of making secure the future of their offspring. Thus the old-new law of love and need applied to filial love and obedience as well as to other human relationships.

There are those, of course, who declare emphatically that obedience and love bought on such terms have no more value than any other purchasable thing. But obedience and love that spring from a realization of one's dependence upon another do have their value. Regardless of his resourcefulness, man must acknowledge his dependence upon some person or some force or some influence in his life. And such dependence need not rob life of its sweetness or its abundance. What, then, did Elizabethan sons and daughters attain besides material gain from their dependence upon their parents? They themselves would have been quick to recognize the enrichment of their lives through the spiritual inheritance that derived from family discipline. Under the best conditions love tempered this ordered pattern of their existence, and under the worst conditions they were still prepared in a measure for the harsher discipline of a chaotic world.

At home and at school the old training in the classical idea of obedience involved not only parents but all children's superiors in age and wisdom and experience. Thus children grew up with the idea that intelligent minds *might* bring order to their own little world in spite of the disorder prevailing without. They were hopeful; they believed they could build somewhat, at least, according to plan, and that their endeavors would not be altogether lost. In their own little groups and in their own little society, traditions and customs and manners could be perpetuated through the children from generation to generation. The amazing thing is not that their system lasted so long but that even modern instability and modern insecurity cannot destroy altogether the impulses still flowing from it.

CHAPTER V

PREPARATION FOR MARRIAGE

For this is the marriage ring: it
ties two hearts by an eternal bond.

JEREMY TAYLOR (1613–1667)

EREMY TAYLOR, silver-tongued preacher of the famous sermon *The Marriage Ring*, though not born till 1613 was
nevertheless Elizabethan to the core in all his thoughts about
the marriage bond. To him the circlet of cheap or precious
metal, plain or jeweled, when slipped on the finger of the bride altered
forever the destinies of two or more people. This simple conventional
ornament, without beginning or end, held within its narrow compass the
complex history of all racial marriage rites. As such it was an emblem of
life's most binding duties, whereby the bride and groom were ushered
into the intricate pattern of society; and each time a betrothed couple
pledged themselves at the marriage altar, they enhanced the significance
of this emblem. To all who reverenced family life as mankind's most
precious heritage, it was indeed, as the preacher said, the symbol of the
founding of a home with indissoluble ties and affections.

Only in the tales of romance and poetry was marriage to be entered
during the Elizabethan age merely for the dream of love and its satisfaction. This bond was a privilege, a duty, a matter of family policy
even to most young people, who, like their parents, believed an intelligent consideration for each could bring them after marriage the blessing
of love. And far oftener than not, it did bring this gift. True, marriage
was unblushingly accepted by both men and women as a very human
device, blessed by God, for satisfying the insistent demand of strong men
to perpetuate themselves in children about whom there would be no
question of legitimacy. Yet it was also recognized as a means of satisfying woman's instinctive search for someone to sire her children and to
provide a shelter in which she might protect them. Most women still
felt themselves bound to the race, destined to live under the protection
of a mate, and more than anything else, dreamed of a peaceful blossom-
ing for that race. Again and again the Elizabethan wife is referred to as
the vessel of the race, and when idealized as a mother, she is shown with
many children about her.

A few women here and there did see the social codes as iron bars that
shut them out from fulfillment of individual desires, and such women
did feel stirring within them a war of impulses. Increased learning often
brought with it an increased capacity for emotional experience, including
love, and with this expansion of their intellectual and emotional horizon,

they might become critical of those who wooed them, and seek domination by a husband they felt greater than themselves. Then, if they were not lucky in marriage, the only means by which they could endure the loneliness and disappointment of their lot was in heroic acquiescence to the conventional demands made upon them, or in pursuit of social success in groups gathered for the interchange of wit. Rarely did any of them try to break free.

Some of the canny ones concealed the discovery that for them there could be no freedom, bound as they were to the race, and while they shrank from the dangers of motherhood, they exacted heavy payment for their suffering from the lord of the household. Some saw the brevity of happiness based upon emotional experience, yet sipped daintily from the honeyed flowers strewn in their way; they knew full well that the scales holding joy and grief must balance. Born and reared to lean against the protection of father or brother or husband, the great Elizabethan women nevertheless acquired much of worldly wisdom. Even so, when they were deprived by death of the social guardianship upon which their very femininity was based, they were almost helpless in the world of society till another protector came along. In spite of their new freedom of widowhood, therefore, they bowed to the fact that they still lived in a man's world, and all the rights were his for the taking if he was willing and able to pay the price for taking.

As yet, the world has changed little in these fundamental things. A normal woman is still at the mercy of biology, her instincts forcing her to seek a home for herself and the children she hopes to bear. Though science has eased somewhat the dangers and terrors resulting from the mother urge, it has in no way touched the instinctive subjection that possesses most women under the spell of that urge. Seldom did clever Elizabethan women play at love like skilled technicians for the hope of security in the shifting sands of social life. When only girls they were taught that she wins most who has most to give freely. For them this was the practical meaning in the mystic beauty of the marriage ring.

As thoughtful Elizabethans faced the problem of a happy marriage, they learned much that man may learn from them, for they did not bury their knowledge in their hearts. Many of them preached a doctrine in which they united morality with expedience; some derived their information entirely from their own interpretation of the Bible; some insisted on the improvement of women's position by making wives partners of husbands, placing in them full confidence and trust. Many attempted to analyze the mystery of a happy marriage. One may reject much of that analysis, but one must accept one very important part of it: that there may be a mystery in some unions by means of which two individuals can achieve a more nearly perfect state of well-being than is to be found in any other human relationship. To this mystery Elizabethans gave the descriptions of a "high, holy, and blessed state of mutual understanding and comradeship," a "true and holy state of matrimony," and a "marriage ring."

Among the writers and speakers who felt the need of defining and defending matrimony, none met with more general approval among the Puritans than Thomas Becon, who called marriage a bond knitting "together one man and one woman in flesh and body of one will and mind in all honesty, virtue, and godliness" to spend their lives "in the equal partaking of all such things as God shall send them . . ."[1] The ceremony of joining hands and exchanging rings, he said, was indicative of a bond that united two people morally, legally, and physically in a relationship of complete community of life for establishing a family. Although he felt the choice of each other should be based on affection, most Elizabethans believed affection came after as a blessing.

In general the mutual consent of the parties involved was taken for granted as one of the things ascertained before preparations were actually begun for the wedding. For immature people or for those joined in marriage for political reasons, this consent was sometimes obtained after a very slight acquaintance or as a matter of form. To say, however, that most Elizabethan young people obediently followed the dictates of their elders in this great step without any choice of their own is to misrepresent matters shamefully. When modern young men and women insist on the right of free choice, they seldom if ever realize that their marriage contract fixes by law all other accidental relationships which may arise from their union; little do they suspect that this particular characteristic of marriage isolates it from all other contracts devised by man. Young Elizabethans were by no means so blind to the importance of the legal issues involved when they became man and wife.

The religious part of the ceremony was very important to sixteenth-century society as the Church was closely allied to civil authority by means of its power to add both validity and sanctity to the contract. Though the part of the Church has changed little in the Catholic ceremony today, it varies widely among Protestant denominations. Just how much religion still influences thought processes even among the nonreligious is seen in common use of the following quotations: "What therefore God hath joined together, let not man put asunder" (Matt. 19:6). "And I say unto you, Whosoever shall put away his wife, except it be for fornication, and shall marry another, committeth adultery: and whoso marrieth her which is put away doth commit adultery" (Matt. 19:9). Perhaps one does not know where in the Bible such charges are written, still the influence of the words can be measured by the weight they continue to bear in social conduct.

---

[1] *The booke of Matrimony* (1564), fo. DCXVI. This book is not to be confused with Becon's earlier idealization of marriage, the *Golden State of Matrimony* (1542).

When Henry VIII flouted the dictates of the Church by his divorce from Catherine of Aragon, he too used the Bible to defend his course of procedure, and thereby opened the floodgates of discussion on this issue, and others too. Indeed, so great was the shock of Henry's divorce to religious English people that it was no small contributing factor to the forces which combined to shake their belief in the old doctrine of immortality of the soul. The need to cling to something immortal turned them to art and learning and life, and eventually brought them to the point where propagation of self seemed the only living symbol of the indestructibility of that essence of man hitherto called the soul.

Before this time man had put a certain value on woman's chastity because it insured the transmission of his name and his property to rightful heirs. Now those heirs had bound up in them not only the material rewards and gains of his struggles against the ill winds of fortune, but also the very important spiritual satisfaction of his dream of immortality. This mental struggle was still further complicated for him by the prevailing distrust of woman's nature, which the Church, in its attempt as far back as the third century to defend the doctrine of celibacy, had to some extent unavoidably fostered. Now, marriage became so vital a thing in man's spiritual life that it called forth two opposing factions among writers: those skeptics, feigned or real, who condemned women as utterly unworthy of man's trust, and those who praised marriage as the highest source of man's happiness.

A man's general distrust of women before or after marriage might be avoided in isolated instances by his attraction to an individual woman. Unless parents were wise enough to match their children by mutual liking as an element in the marriage bond, the man's distrust of women and the woman's resentment of that distrust might lead to much misery for some young people. Hence the Elizabethan practice, before the parents proceeded very far in the negotiations for uniting families, of bringing the two young people together to discover their reaction to each other. A letter by Stanhope of Harrington in Northamptonshire to Sir Christopher Hatton (whom he succeeded as vice-chamberlain to the Queen) illustrates this custom. He speaks of stopping at his cousin's house not far from Hatton's pretentious manor and, after two or three days' rest, taking his daughter to his brother's house while he went on to Carlisle to conclude arrangements about her matching. There he found Lord Scrope "still desirous" of the union of the two families. He agreed, therefore, "to meet his Lordship again a month hence, in a progress which he intendeth into Lancashire, where the young couple may see one another, and, after a little acquaintance, may resolve accordingly . . ."[2] Nevertheless, conduct books and sermons were so full of advice about

---

[2] Sir Nicholas Harris Nicolas (ed.), *Memoirs of the Life and Times of Sir Christopher Hatton* (1847), p. 77.

choosing mates that young people introduced at such meetings might not make up their minds through inclination only.

The voluminous literature on the debate for and against marriage is suggested as possibly influencing the Queen's wavering stand on matrimony. Although she used whatever arguments were to her liking when she wished a controversial screen to conceal her real motives as she played the cat-and-mouse game with those urging her to marry, it is possible she meant to suggest that her attitude of uncertainty derived somewhat from the third-century ideal of an austere life which rejected propagation of the race with its sensual delights. As Virgin Queen, she did not hesitate to declare that all England was her spouse, and that she had married the nation to whom she gave all her love. Meanwhile, the Church had to continue its old exertions to prevent Christian life from becoming an abstention from sexual life, even in matrimony. The Manichaean doctrine condemning marriage had continued in writings as late as the twelfth century, and these writings were reflected in much of the sixteenth-century argument in praise and dispraise of marriage. Even today *The Catholic Encyclopedia* (III, 481) feels it necessary to remark: "Virginity and marriage are both holy, but in different ways. The conviction that virginity possesses a higher sanctity and clearer spiritual intuitions seems to be an instinct planted deep in the heart of man." But in a later volume (IX, 697) it states: "The assertion that celibacy tends to make the married state seem low or unworthy, is contradicted by the public opinion and practice of every country in which celibacy is held in highest honor. For it is precisely in such places that the marriage relation, and the relation between the sexes generally, are purest." In other words, the example of those living chaste lives in monasteries raises the spiritual level of those living normal lives in the blessed state of matrimony.

The sixteenth-century debates had much to do with this point of view. Dispraise of women was almost always based on the contentions about her supposed frailty, and praise sought to exalt her virtue. In this latter effort both the Puritans and the Anglicans joined forces. Puritan insistence on the purpose of the marriage rite for other causes than continuity of the race or avoidance of promiscuous sexual indulgence may have raised woman's position in the social world, though the Church by its stress on the indissoluble sacrament of marriage had long sought to cause the husband "to copy in respect to the wife the love of Christ for the Church."

For those not too ardent by nature, the Old Testament injunction to "be fruitful and multiply" was not easy to reconcile with Paul's ideal of virginity. Other forces were at work, however, in formulating a pattern of life that might be acceptable to society. The old attempts of the Church to promote celibacy by the condemnation of all unchastity had been somewhat offset by courtly love, which insisted that women might have lovers besides their husbands if they were faithful to these lovers. True, this code was designed for the upper class, but the influence of it was felt even by the underprivileged. At the very time the Church was becoming concerned about marriage as a sacred institution, a man in actual life might offer his daughter to an esteemed gentleman guest for the night as a mark of favor or honor to him, and his act would not prevent him from placing her well in marriage later. Furthermore, the very peasants and workers were not likely to take chastity seriously while careless priests absolved them at confession without any qualms whatsoever. What really brought the idea of virginity into focus was putting the Bible into the hands of the newly formed middle class for their own reading and interpretation. It was this class especially that, with its pride in its new property rights, was inspired to add a feeling of sanctity for *all* property, even the virginity of their women. Undoubtedly, it was partly for this reason that Paul's teaching now burst upon the Elizabethan mind with a force and a significance that turned the current of their thought about womanhood into a new channel. Even so, only gradually did the principle become established that the woman who stained her honor was of no further value to herself or to society. Such a doctrine could not have been advanced, however, had it not been prepared for by the Church teachings of chastity.

Now that chastity had taken on the value of property, Protestantism in spite of its individualism did not give educated women the same chances as they had known under Catholicism to engage in activities outside the home. Woman's sphere became more and more domestic. Though belief that woman had caused the fall of man did not originate with Christ or the Church, and though belief in woman's physical and mental weakness was older than Christianity, these dogmatic statements were advanced by fanatics of both Protestant and Catholic faiths when they wished to idealize celibacy or argue in favor of woman's inferior position in the world. Again and again they presented her as a necessary evil for the propagation of the race or as the source of evil through her fall or as the means by which evil had entered into the world. Regardless of their private misgivings about such teaching, some men who loved and respected their wives might excuse their natural desires by a seeming pious acquiescence to their duty of continuing the race. Others, for their own advantage, might pretend that they believed woman a snare and a temptation to evil. Some even went so far as to agree with an early commentator on Genesis that woman had no soul, and declared marital relations were sinful because woman herself was by nature sinful.

To this sixteenth-century revival of feeling and argument that had been rife when the Church championed celibacy now came the rhetorical expression of those who would preserve chastity to ensure the legitimacy of their progeny and of those who would have wives subject to their husbands according to Paul's teaching. Other writers tried to harmonize the idea of chastity with the sacrament of the marriage bond by intentional or unintentional distortion of the facts. And finally came the writers who seized upon anything that might make a sensation in their part of the debate.

Indeed, any old saw had its value for them. Elizabethan literature is full of wise sayings about women used in earnest or in jest:

Husbands are in heaven whose wives chide not.

Swine, women, and bees cannot be turned.

The love of a woman and a bottle of wine,
Are sweet for a season, and lost for a time.

Women, wind, and fortune are always changing.

Maids want nothing but husbands; and when they
have them, they want everything.

Women, priests, and poultry never have enough.

A ship and a woman are ever repairing.

Honest men marry soon; wise men not at all.

A man of straw is worth a woman of gold.

Women in mischief are wiser than men.

Women and dogs set men by the ears.

Women's jars breed men's wars.

Wife and children are bills of charges.

Wedlock is a padlock.

Age and wedlock bring a man to his nightcap.

Of course many Elizabethan women occupied positions of honor and respect, but unmarried women were likely to be called good on sufferance or till some evil thing could be proved against them. Perhaps the best picture of all women is provided in private or historical records. Yet one must not overlook the conventional expressions about them in sonnets, the laudatory dedications to them in books, etc., and praise and blame of the sex in domestic literature—all of which is valuable for what is behind the words. If the abusive or extravagantly flattering comments on women can be accounted for by the overreligious or oversentimental condition of the authors, what is back of the words may be significant. Why, for example, did John Knox denounce the feebleness of women, recant when forced to do so by Elizabeth in obsequious praise of her virtue, and at the same time write silly notes of undisguised yearning to women who said they admired him for his sanctity and downrightness or his great breadth of vision? Such impulses do not come to an amatory soul in an emotional vacuum. What was the real opinion of this man about women? Was it such as one finds in the sensualist who uses religion as an outlet or a cloak for his overcharged nature? Or were his expressions but a reflection of the many reactions in his age to what a man in his heart thought of women and what certain persistent currents of thought taught him he was supposed to think of her? Where the powerful elements in and out of the Church had led, the laity had followed, and sometimes between them the women had become not a little inferior to men—their lords and masters. This was why marriage was sometimes regarded as but a worldly thing at best.

Yet since it was necessary to propagate families, men must be encouraged to enter matrimony. Hence the countless books extolling marriage and praising women in a manner that but for its somewhat salutary effect upon woman's social and domestic position would be intolerable for its fatuity. Agrippa, writing in the early part of the century, exercised his ingenuity to compose such statements as the following: Woman is different from man physically, but she manifests thereby her superiority to the male; woman's name of Eve, meaning life, shows her affinity to God, and the name of Adam means only earth; woman's creation in the paradise of Eden and Adam's creation outside that paradise show Eve's closer relation to God; when God used merely earth for creating Adam and material already animated by divine spirit for Eve, He established undeniably her rank as superior to that of man. Agrippa then considers woman more beautiful than man since she is subject to neither baldness nor a beard. In the propagation of the race she has the more profound function, as shown in the love between her and her child; more important still, she has been known to procreate without man's cooperation, as in the case of the Virgin Mary. He even defends her copious speech by saying she only ever defeated Christ in an argument, as in the case of the Canaanite woman (Matt. 15: 25–28). With all this in the Preface, what could be added in the essay proper?

Agrippa began his argument in praise of women by shifting the blame for sin in the world from Eve to Adam. Eve was merely deceived by the tempter and Adam actually sinned, because of which his male successors had to be circumcised. By his sin Adam brought death to the human race, and so Christ, who came to save man from death, in His humility assumed the form of the lower sex. All blessing, he said, comes to the race through women, as Christ proves by first appearing to her who did not desert him in his Passion at the cross. Finally, since woman is superior to man in chastity, piety, conjugal love, and generosity, in philosophy, poetry, and invention, being specially famous for her practical services during crises, it is neither natural nor reasonable for woman's subjection to man to continue. Her unfortunate state is due to custom, he says, to education, fortune, and a "certain tyrannical occasion." He closes with the usual "apology," declaring he was moved to write by truth and duty, and though he has not said all he could speak in defense of women, still not to put down as much as he has written would be sacrilege, and he hopes his work will strengthen further words from men in women's praise.[3]

In Anthony Gibson's *A Womans woorth defended against all the men in the world* (1599), the author calls woman "more perfect, excellent, and absolute in all virtuous actions than of any man of what quality whatsoever." He says he speaks with authority, for he has "heard much, seen much, but knows a great deal more." Using as his model Thomas Elyot's *The Defence of Good women* (1545), he dedicates his work to Lady Elizabeth, Countess of Southampton, and "to all honorable ladies and gentlewomen of England," especially the maids of honor to the Queen, Margaret Ratcliffe, Mary Fitton, Anne Russell, etc. His first purpose is to show that the "gifts and graces of women are infinite," and though he insists he has borrowed none of his ideas, he quotes in the conventional manner from the ancients. Then, waxing eloquent, he proclaims, ". . . even as the sun hath more light in his unity than all the stars in number have together, so the very eye of woman contains more graces in it than are to be found in all men's perfections, which . . . could neither be gracious, courteous, or civil, but only by the society of women." This being's beauty is "the model, not only of things that beautify the world, but . . . as . . . the gauge of nature's alliance with the world, and the only mirror of perfect ideas." Her body is the "true temple," and her soul is the very image of God. The house is "not blessed where she wanteth," for by her is the Commonwealth "made immortal, cities peopled, realms strengthened, kings assured, and subjects maintained." By her man lives again in his children, posterity has knowledge of those who have lived before, and the memory of man is continued. By her man learns to respect his family; by her he grows heedful, ripens his lawful actions, and is drawn from the world to live in her company "as in a school of piety, modesty . . . wherein (else) we should but little differ from brute beasts."

Such writing provoked satire like that of Joseph Swetnam's *The Araignment of Lewd, idle, froward, and unconstant women* (1615). Jestingly he alludes to the description by Moses of woman as the "helper unto man," admitting she does help him "to spend and consume" that which he "painfully getteth." Then he divides women into six classes, of which the first two are neither good nor bad, the next two are neither fair nor foul, and the last two are neither rich nor poor. A man finds that if he marries a good woman he spoils her, if a bad one, he supports her in her badness; if fair, he must guard her; if foul, he cannot abide her; if rich he must bear her for her money, and if poor, he must support her with no help from her at all.

[3] Henry Cornelius Agrippa, *A treatise of the nobilitie of woman Kinde* (1529).

Of course he must warn men not to trust their wives with matters of any import, for "every woman hath one especial gossip at least, which she doth love and effect above all the rest, and unto her she runneth with all the secrets she knoweth." He would, therefore, repeat the old man's advice to his son about choosing a wife: "When thou seest a flock of maids together, hoodwink thyself fast, and run against them, and look which thou chasest, let her be thy wife . . . for in thy choice . . . thou must not trust thine own eyes, for they will deceive thee, and be cause of thy woe." Then he enumerates women's lures. One "may seem good whose waist is like a wand," another may have a "spider-fingered hand," and another may stand on her tiptoes most charmingly and read out of a golden book from which she is never separated. Most dangerous of all, however, is the girl who knows how to "stroke a beard," or who, when "she looks [i.e., searches] a head, makes herself afraid of every flea she finds." Such a wench, he says, would make a man a begger "if he were half a king."

Now this writer turns mockingly to "praise" of women and matrimony. As pearls may be found among dust, and diamonds among hard rocks, so good wives may be discovered among maids. "Many are the joys and sweet pleasures of marriage," he says, counting them off on his fingers, "as in our children, being young, they play, prattle, and laugh, and show us many pretty toys to move us to mirth and laughter, and when they are bigger grown, and that age or poverty hath afflicted the parents, then they show us the duty of children in relieving their old aged parents with what they can shift for, and when their parents are dead, they bring them to earth, whence they came." He describes a woman's hard lot, of which he has been "told so often." He wonders how a weak woman can endure the life she is forced into, for "amongst all the creatures that God hath created" there is "none more subject to misery . . . especially those that are fruitful to bear children, for they have scarce a month's rest in a whole year, but are continually overcome with pain, sorrow, and fear, as indeed the danger of childbearing must needs be a great terror to women, which are counted but weaker vessels, in respect of men." He supposes man has no pain that is "one-half so grievous" even though his toothache, gout, colic, "nay, all these at once," come to plague him.

And so the question of whether to marry went the rounds of writers— light, bombastic, satiric, sober. In the dignified analysis of the traits of a lady and a gentleman, found in Richard Brathwait's *The English Gentleman* (1630) and *The English Gentlewoman* (1631), are set down proper relations between man and woman and a code of conduct anticipating the best of modern ideas on the subject. In the first of the two books, Brathwait says, "I find myself strengthened by conference, and that proceeds with best grace and consonance from a faithful mate: I will not touch her with my body whom I dare not make partner of my mind."

As to supporting a woman's good name, he finds man apt "to judge sinisterly of the weaker vessel," and imputes it "either to want of brains . . . or some hard hap" when "making choice of some infirm creature." Jealousy, he says, "publisheth man's shame, more than the occasion of his shame." He believes a wise man "will rather conceive and conceal, than disclose his conceit to others' report." Since the "best reputation" is but "grounded on opinion free from suspicion," it seems to him that charity would "judge the best." For example, he would "rather expound" his "wife's secret parley to some instructions of housewifery, than motives of perverted liberty."

Because marriage was admittedly the best means of fulfilling one's duty to family and posterity, Elizabethans who wished to remain single felt bound to defend themselves. Some complained they could not afford matrimony with its costs and responsibilities, and others clung to the ideal of celibacy. Against the first group Bullinger thundered from the pulpit that they "could afford to keep whores," and such adulterers would never inherit the kingdom of heaven. Anyone of reason knew that God always took care of married people, unless they married "without fear of God," or without respect for "religion, wisdom, integrity of life, or any other virtue . . . ," or without proper consideration of how to live "with sufficient maintenance for their callings and estate." Stubbes referred to these "improvident" people in *The Anatomie of Abuses* as beggars who "filleth the land with such stores of poor people, that in short time . . . the very nation itself is like to grow to great poverty and scarceness, which, God forbid!" Against celibacy the argument was usually threefold: that the average man could live a better life married than single, that the blessings of marriage were too great to forego, and that a man's duty to the state demanded responsible propagation of his kind.

Cardinal Pole in Henry VIII's reign, in spite of the abusive attitude of many church officials toward "frail" womankind, had sought to force marriage upon bachelors by subjecting them to heavy taxes and "humiliating social disabilities" with an "annual income tax of a shilling a pound on all chattels of every bachelor possessing portable goods to the amount of four pounds," these sums to be used for the support of poor families and for dowering virgins for marriage. He had also advocated depriving bachelors of municipal offices and places of honor and trust, and had even recommended the marriage of secular priests.

Many tempers were lost in both Henry's and Elizabeth's reigns over the matter of married priests. During Henry's time an irate neighbor of the vicar of Mandlesham wrote of the churchman bringing home at last "his woman and two children to his vicarage, openly declaring" his marriage. The writer considers such an act "in this country" a monstrous thing, which many "grudge." The vicar, however, declares the king knows he is married, and so no one in the parish dares to do to him what all would like to do and had promised to do. The writer feels this "open crime" should be "reformed," as it is a "bad example to other carnal, evil-disposed priests."[4]

In Elizabeth's time there was some support for marriage of the clergy through the contention they might marry to avoid sin, but this excuse put a clergyman in an embarrassing position. Partial relief from his predicament might be obtained by letting a discreet counselor or committee choose a bride for him, thus making him guiltless of any desire for beauty or wit in a wife. In this way Bishop Joseph Hall, when a parish priest, received a wife said to be chosen for him by his friend, Mr. Gandridge. Even though he lived happily with her for forty-nine years, he always recognized the necessity of marriage in a very condescending manner, and in *The Honor of the Married Clergy*, he spoke of celibacy as "a higher condition of wedlock."

Until recently Richard Hooker was thought to have trusted the selection of his wife to his clever landlady, with whom he lived at the Shuna-mites' House near St. Paul's churchyard. In this way she was supposed to have disposed of her daughter on the unsuspecting man. C. J. Sisson's research[5] into the matter has produced interesting material not only on Hooker's marriage but on the attitude toward the married clergy in Elizabeth's time. Walton reported Hooker's marriage as most unsuitable, saying the girl's father was a London woolen draper fallen into poverty, which induced him and his wife to board and lodge preachers appointed to deliver sermons at St. Paul's. The landlady persuaded Hooker, one of these lodgers, that a wife would cure him of his colds, and arranged thereby his marriage to her daughter Joan, who brought him "neither beauty nor portion," but drew him away from a quiet life at Oxford. Walton's story even tells how Hooker discussed with a pupil and friend "his double share in the miseries of this life."

Sisson's account changes the Walton story considerably. Hooker was married to Joan Churchman on February 13, 1588. Her father was a member of the Merchant Taylors, and a descendant of a fourteenth-century Master and benefactor of the company. His own marriage had been to the daughter of the Master of the company in 1569. By 1581, Joan's father was making his way to high office in the great guild, and was elected its Third Warden. About a year after Joan's marriage to Hooker, her father was made First Warden, and in 1594, he became Master of the Merchant Taylors' Company, which, of course, was "an honor open only to a man of assured means as well as of the highest reputation among his fellows." His "probity and his standing" were further recognized when he was elected City Chamberlain, "an office of

---

[4] Quoted by Lady Cecilie Goff, *A Woman of the Tudor Age* (1930), p. 87, from *Calendars of State Papers*, XIII, No. 236.

[5] *The Judicious Marriage of Mr. Hooker and the Birth of the Laws of Ecclesiastical Polity* (1940).

high financial responsibility and confidence." That he dowered Joan at her marriage to Hooker with £700 although Hooker at the time was only a poor scholar without any rich "livings" certainly proves beyond question that Hooker's marriage was "judicious, and we may believe that it was happy."

Thus Hooker became "a member of the family circle of a great London citizen of wealth and civic rank," and his wife's dowry "provided financial security for himself and his children." He referred to Joan as his "well-beloved wife," and to her father as his "well-beloved father." After Hooker's death in 1600 his wife soon married again and brought her new husband £700 in dowry. The Irish disturbances almost ruined her father and other merchants, however, because they supplied the English army with goods for which they were not paid. Yet in spite of the family's losses, they saw to it that Hooker's daughters by Joan were provided with legacies, "and they made a brother and former master" of Joan's father's company the trustee.

Walton, sharing the common prejudice against marriage for the clergy, might well have chosen to believe his beloved Hooker had been inveigled into matrimony, and like a saint, had borne its hardships with no little grace. Sisson's facts, however, suggest a most interesting situation, in which an Elizabethan father, concerned about the welfare of his daughter, made a wise alliance for her. Shrewd in business and in his judgment of men, Joan's father chose from the clergy a man with attainments that made him acceptable in spite of his poverty. It is possible that he also was strongly in favor of marriage for the clergy, officially approved by the Queen in 1559.

Puritans, of course, were bitterly opposed to those who objected to married men preaching the word of God. William Gouge, a popular minister among them, insisted that the practice of celibacy was unnatural and caused such evils as "fornication, adultery, incest, sodomy, . . . and what not!" In his work, *Of Domesticall Duties* (1622), he proceeded to give further details on the subject. "Many wives have been put from their husbands because their husbands were ministers; and many ministers put from their calling because they had wives," he said. "Many children by this means are basely born; and among them many in infancy are cruelly murdered. Six thousand heads of infants were found in ponds of a religious house; how many more thousands have been from time to time cast into other ponds, or buried in gardens, or other places, or other ways conveyed out of sight?" Marriage not only was a lawful means of "making man and woman husband and wife," but also granted civic privileges to the master of a household—the right to plead causes or give sentence, of being preferred for office, of having the upper hand in meetings, or being exempted from watchings (when a man had children), and of obtaining pre-eminence over an older, unmarried man.

The conciliatory Richard Barckley, in *A Discourse of the Felicite of*

Man or his Summum bonum (1598), placed the benefits of marriage in a philosophical light. Most people looked for the *summum bonum* in pleasures or riches or honor, but pleasure for its own sake was usually voluptuous, and often riches more than anything else alienated man from God. Honor might be bestowed upon an evil man as well as a good, and one might rule while millions served and obeyed. In this way one person could be the felicity of a few and the misery of all, for when all is said and done, honor is but the "vain admiration of common people." Good is really found only in oneself, in the contemplative life. Philosophers declare man the most miserable of all creatures, but man can alleviate his misery by marriage. Man and woman, married, are supposed to bear together prosperity and poverty, their close companionship enhancing the joys of the one and mitigating the sorrows of the other. Actually, however, marriage is a challenge to all one's skill, to all one's powers. Whatever ills cannot be avoided by prudence must be overcome by patience. To achieve the "fountain of happiness," therefore, man must learn to moderate his affections and cleanse his mind of all perturbations.

By this he would not mean for man to shun experience; instead, he should welcome it, reckoning nothing as real injury but loss of his good name. As Plato said, man must learn how to live in his mind, wherein lies the true life. Man's body is "common with that of brute beasts," but his mind makes him resemble the angels and God himself. This is why happiness consists of the effort to enjoy God's benefits and graces, and all actions and labors in this life are but "a shadow, and the way to come by" the life after death. In the labors of this life, therefore, marriage can be good or ill, but man can, if he will, make it good.

The direct sincerity of a letter written by Erasmus to a young man in praise of marriage gave Elizabethans much to quote at suitable times.[6] After enumerating reasons for the "honorable" state of matrimony, he dealt with his subject concretely. In contrast with the bitterness of his criticism of holy people's illegitimate children was his pleasure in describing the friendship between husband and wife. Married people may open their hearts to each other, he says, but with other friends, no matter how close, one must dissemble somewhat. Few friends, like a wife, last till death, and she will be true in adversity to comfort and stay her husband and to share his grief. Marriage also doubles one's alliances and friends and relatives. He appeals to the tenderness in the young man he is advising by saying that when "some little babe shall play" in his hall and "shall resemble" him and his wife, he will find great joy, and especially when "with a mild lisping or amiable stammering" the child calls him "daddy." This child will add unto his wife's love a "bond more strong than adamant, which death itself cannot burst asunder."

---

[6] Desiderius Erasmus, *A ryght frutefull Epystle devysed . . . in laude and prayse of matrymony* (trans. by Richard Tavernour, 1530?).

Erasmus is aware of the nervous fears men have about the fidelity and amiability of their wives, but he calls these fears the "vices of men and not of wedlock." He earnestly believes an evil wife is not a thing of chance but of an evil husband, that a good man can choose a good wife, that wives are falsely blamed, that even a shrew is made so through a husband's fault. Strife comes from not living in a chaste and lawful love [made lawful by marriage] in which "either is so bound to the other that neither would be enfranchised." Such a home is most important to children who are "formed and fashioned in their bringing up" by its environment of willing bondage.

It was almost a century later that the gentle, spell-binding preacher, Jeremy Taylor, felt it necessary to review for his congregation the arguments in favor of marriage, and the causes for the whole controversy about it. In the early days of the Church, he said, celibacy was necessary for the establishment of Christianity, but its purpose having been accomplished, that need no longer existed. Instead, it was now necessary to place the mystery of the holy rite of marriage in the hand of Christ "that all its beauties" might appear. Though the single life might advance some individuals in the Christian state, to others it was a snare and an evil. The Bible never commands celibacy, but does sometimes command marriage. He looks upon marriage as a school with "exercises" in virtue, for though the marriage state "hath its cares, yet the single life hath desires which are more troublesome and dangerous, and often end in sin, while the cares of marriage are but instances of duty and exercises of piety . . ." He is convinced, therefore, that "if single life hath more privacy of devotion, yet marriage hath more necessities and more variety of it, and is an exercise of more graces . . ."

Then, in the simple, personal manner that endeared him to his people, he gave his picture of a husband as holy as a celibate in his own home. He referred to marriage as "the nursery of Heaven," wherein the head of a family might exercise the devotions so dear to his heart. He could spend as much time in prayer as any virgin or widow, he could be chastely (i.e., lawfully) devoted to his wife, both as husband and as father, he could maintain kindly relations with his family and with relatives who might draw heavily upon his store of charity, he could exert himself to unite and make firm the ties of kinship, he could provide hospitality and delicate services for his friends, and finally, he could bless society in the union of hands and hearts in his home.

Yet he also likened the entrance into matrimony to "casting a die of the greatest contingency" and of the "greatest interest in the world, next to the last throw for eternity." Like all shepherds of a flock, he knew the trials of those listening so intently to his words, and he did not minimize their troubles. "Life or death," he said, "felicity or lasting sorrow are in the power of marriage, but a woman ventures most, for she hath no sanctuary to retire to from an evil husband." Though she may "complain to God," she has no appeal in "the causes of unkindness." The man, on the other hand, may "run from many hours of sadness, yet he must return to it again; and, when he sits among his neighbors, he remembers the objection that is in his bosom, and he sighs deeply." Lest such recitals make his audience faint-hearted, he then drew an analogy between the celibate and the husband. The celibate he likened to the fly "in the heart of an apple" which dwelt in "a perpetual sweetness" but sat alone and was confined and died "in singularity." The man in matrimony, like the "useful bee," built a house and gathered "sweetness from every flower," and labored and united "into societies and republics," and sent out colonies, and fed "the world with delicacies." Always, however, he obeyed the king, and kept order and exercised "many virtues." Thus he promoted "the interest of mankind" to that "state of good things to which God hath designed the present constitution of the world."[7]

In spite of parental effort to ease young people's economic problems in marriage, there was often a plea for delay. The mature mind, of course, hesitated then as always over the uncertainty of spiritual or physical contentment when one was to be bound to another for life by the closest of all human ties. Youth, however, would scarcely be able to weigh such heavy odds against future personal happiness. No doubt youth's reluctance, therefore, was due to the fact that it was not ready for the experience. Some, of course, wished first the adventure of travel, though they might not dare to say so. Others wished for a while longer to enjoy freedom from duties they had been trained to expect at marriage. So much talk of celibacy and chastity and so much dispraise of women might also have made very young minds especially reluctant to marry before parental commands gave them no other alternative. To Elizabethans marriage was never thought of, even by Protestants, as a bond that could be dissolved at will.

Henry Smith, a popular and ready speaker before his church audience, always had an especially large attendance at his wedding sermons. In 1591, when he spoke on *A Preparation to Mariage*, he defined matrimony as an institution for "making mothers of virgins," and warned husbands against loving their wives better than God. *The Bishop's Book* explained that the dual nature of marriage was an *outward sign* or contract and an *inward grace*.[8] By the first, *outward sign*, two people consented and promised "each other to company together continually during their lives, without separation, and to communicate each to other the use

[7] Jeremy Taylor, *Works*, Sermon XVII, *The Marriage Ring; or the Mysteriousness and Duties of Marriage* (Vol. IV of 1862 ed.).

[8] *The Bishop's Book* was the popular title for *The Institution of a Christian Man*, 1537, considered by both king and Church as more authoritative than the revision of it by Henry VIII in 1543 under the title of *The Necessary Doctrine and Erudition for any Christian Man*, which was generally referred to as *The King's Book*.

and office of their bodies, and all other faculties and substance." By the second, *inward grace*, the act of procreation was made "lawful," and was the means "whereby the persons conjoined in matrimony" attained everlasting life if they brought up their children in "the true faith and observance of Christ's religion." When Jeremy Taylor turned these definitions into explanations for his audience, he called marriage God's first blessing, which "for many descending ages, not only by the instinct of nature, but by a super-forwardness, God himself inspiring the desire, the world was made most desirous of children, and impatient of barrenness, accounting a single life a curse, and a childless person hated of God." Man's wife, therefore, was his friend, and a "good woman" in her soul was the same (i.e., equal to in honor) as a man. In her body, however, she had the excellency of the one, and the usefulness of the other," thus becoming "amiable in both."

All orthodox Elizabethans would have responded to this language, for they had been taught as soon as they could understand the words that a woman's body was like "the seminary of the Church" to bring forth sons and daughters "unto God." But Jeremy Taylor declared the married person's body was "ministered to by angels," as when (in *Tobit* in the Apocrypha) "Raphael waited upon a young man that he might have a blessed marriage, and that his marriage might repair two sad families, and bless all their relatives." No story was more loved than *Tobit*, and he did well to refer to it. But he had more to say on this delicate subject. "Our Lord was born of a maiden, yet she was veiled under the cover of marriage, and she was married to a widower: for Joseph, the supposed father of our Lord, had children by a former wife." It was fitting, he continued, for Christ to perform his first miracle at a wedding, where all was joy. Marriage, he said firmly, was in the world before sin, and had always been the "greatest and most effective antidote against sin . . . and though sin hath soured marriage, and stuck the man's head with cares, and the woman's bed with sorrows in the production of children: yet these are but throes of life and glory, and she shall be saved in child-bearing, if she be found in faith and righteousness." From the rough utterance of such men as Henry Smith, through the detailed definition of *The Bishop's Book*, to the gentle explanations of Jeremy Taylor, runs the teaching of young people who went to the altar prepared for the new life that was before them.

The combination of mating and parenthood in marriage, as Elizabethans analyzed the institution, made it the chief function of their society because the family was their basic social unit. Accordingly, they insisted that the marriage contract be solemnized in public, and by it they fixed all the relations that might thereafter affect the duties, economic and spiritual, in the lives of the young people. This is why they insisted that the ceremony be ratified by the Church to make it a sacrament to receive the blessing of religion.

When marriage was regarded as more than a means for the sanction of marital intercourse, it naturally caused much discussion of the single standard in sex relations. In general, man was given greater freedom, except by Puritans, and absolute chastity of maid and wife was taken for granted.[9] In this, as in other matters of theory and practice, deviation from the moral code of chastity might be regarded as an individual matter, but only if such defection was kept secret from society. In addition to its provision for children and their rights, therefore, marriage was indeed a lawful means of justifying sexual intercourse and of dominating and restricting extraconnubial relations. The extent to which this was true depended on the fear of social ostracism.

Jeremy Taylor referred to the ideal of the Augustinian marriage, in which husband and wife supposedly took a mutual vow of chastity, as in the case of Joseph and Mary, but Elizabethan Protestants and Catholics alike considered this type of marriage only an ideal. It did, however, stress the consideration for each other's rights. When William Vaughan in *The Golden Grove* (1599) enumerated the four kinds of marriage in order to accentuate the value of people knowing how to govern themselves, he placed the Augustinian marriage first. He called this "marriage of honor" a contract between God and man or the Virgin and the Holy Ghost or Christ and the Church. He listed after it the marriage of love between an honest man and an honest woman for comfort and the propagation of the race, next the "toil" between a man and a woman marrying for riches or beauty, and finally the marriage of grief, as between two wicked people. He spent considerable time on the marriage for beauty because of the discrepancy, no doubt, between the literary use of the Platonic ideal of physical beauty and Elizabethan experience with beauty in daily living.

The closeness which Elizabethans felt in biblical patriarchal life set up in their minds an idealistic conception of the custom of two or more families dwelling under one roof. Few modern people in comfortable circumstances would desire such a home life. And two Elizabethan families might not always be congenial in such circumstances. With this in mind, Bullinger urged parents to avoid bringing discord into the married life of children, especially those living with them. Thus he quoted the biblical admonition that a man must leave his parents for his wife if harmony made such action necessary. The love of man and wife for each other should be "next unto God above all loves," he said. *The Bishop's Book* had also insisted that a man's first care was for his wife, and had quoted Adam's supposed words at the time when he "was by God conjoined in marriage" with Eve. " 'Lo, these bones and flesh of Eve my wife be formed and made of my bones and flesh. And therefore every

---

[9] Alexander Nicholas' *A Discourse of Marriage and Wiving* (1615) reviews Elizabethan ideas about the single standard of morality.

married man hereafter shall endure and cleave unto his wife only, and the husband and wife shall be two in one flesh, and in one body.' "

Nothing could be worse for such a bond than separation. Bullinger likened it to the anguish caused by severing one part of the body from another, and said that only the closeness of the two enabled them to cooperate for the best service. Moreover, if the separation was too long, the devil might busy himself in their affairs. Tigurinus Chelidonius, in *A Most Excellent Hystorie of . . . Christian Princes*, had also described the comforts of the companionship between husband and wife. The 1571 English translation of this popular work speaks of how the wife remembers her husband absent at the wars, and at his return welcomes him home "with many dainty preparations." The children honor both their parents, who "hold them as dear" as their own flesh. Then, like Erasmus and many others, Chelidonius describes the charms of the little ones who "do with their prattlings, in learning to speak, and other toys and fantasies, give . . . much pleasure and contentation of mind," till "it seemeth nature hath given them . . . as things to deceive the time, and to pass over part of this . . . miserable" life.

With so many theories of marriage and its relationships in mind, Elizabethans tried to discover what constituted suitability for marriage. Most writers placed emphasis upon equality in rank, age, and worldly possessions for those to be matched by their parents or for those who, with parental approval, took the initial steps themselves. Of course, there were irresponsible people who contracted themselves as lightly as did Touchstone in Shakespeare's *As You Like It* when he flouted the idea of a church ceremony with Audrey, the simple country wench (III: ii: 40–45). And there were many who, like Jaques, disapproved strongly of a man being "married under a bush, like a beggar," and insisted on the couple going to church and having a good priest tell them what marriage was (III: iii: 84–90). Most of them, like Guazzo, clung to the golden mean for those in the privileged class, urging the young man to choose for his wife one who was well-born and well brought up, young, reasonably rich, indifferently beautiful, of sound health and good wit. Like him, they usually agreed that unhappy marriages were due to inequality of age or condition, or to a marriage forced upon young people by parents or guardians, or to the girl's lack of dowry, which minimized her value in both her own mind and the minds of others.

Many Elizabethan writers also quoted freely from the 1568 translation by N. L.[eigh?] of Erasmus' ideas on the subject.[10] In this supposedly youthful interchange of opinion are a naïveté and worldly wisdom difficult to imagine in the inarticulate speech of inexperienced young

---

[10] *A modest meane to mariage pleasauntly set foorth.* See also Preserved Smith, *A Key to the Colloquies of Erasmus*, Harvard Theological Studies, XIII (1927).

people. The boy tells the girl he thinks they can be happily married, for they have both had good instruction and good examples in their parents, and he believes education is more important than heredity in the development of character. Their parents are friends, he continues, and that is very important for future harmony in their lives; besides this, they have the same manners and rank, and they seem to be alike in disposition. Then he lists the things he expects of his wife: that she love him in sickness and old age as well as in youth, and that she give him children, for he will have no fruitless marriage. At this point he takes considerable time to argue the superior value of a young man capable of procreating children over one of virginal sterility. To all this the girl listens politely, and then tells her suitor that she hopes he has taken much counsel with himself before thinking of entering the state of matrimony, that he must above all obtain the consent of both his parents to this marriage, and while he is doing this, she will pray for them both.

To Erasmus' recommendations, Bartholomew Batty (*The Christian mans Closet*, 1581) added that it was necessary for the young man to consider the girl's whole life as well as the report made of her mother, and, if she had not been trained in housewifery at home, for him to learn something of the friends who had educated her. He also agreed with Aristotle's advice to choose a maid young enough to be tractable for further training in good manners and duties that a husband desired in a wife, and that a maid of eighteen and a man of thirty were well matched in age, though he hastened to add that age alone did not make a man wise or discreet or fit to take a wife. Joseph Swetnam's *The Araignment of Lewd, idle . . . women* urged a man to marry young. If a man must risk all the troubles which come galloping at the heels of a woman, let him do so with least danger at twenty-five and marry a girl not over seventeen, even then only if she is "flexible and bending, obedient and subject to do anything according to the will and pleasure of her husband." Stubbes would have the girl fourteen and the man twenty-four, and came close to the Elizabethan norm in the matter. At the middle of the next century, Thomas Fuller's *The Holy State and the Profane State* (1642) merely urged there be no "disproportion in age," for those marrying old people expecting to bury them did but "hang themselves, in hope that one will come and cut the halter."

When it pleased her to do so, the Queen made much use of her knowledge of current views on marriage,[11] as well as of the tragedy in Mary's union with Philip of Spain. "In truth," she said, "I greatly fear not being loved by my husband, which would be a greater misfortune than the first [old age], for it would be worse than death, and I cannot bear to reflect upon such a possibility." As early as 1559, she said to the Spanish ambassador, who was urging her to marry the Austrian archduke,

[11] Frederick Chamberlain, *The Sayings of Queen Elizabeth* (1923), 64–65, 70.

"It is not fit for a queen and a maiden to summon anyone to her," and in 1561, she begged time of King Erick of Sweden by pleading ". . . for your Majesty knows well how my sex is rushed headlong into everything, and especially so in affairs of this sort." She complained often of being misjudged as to her refusal to marry. "The world, when a woman remains single, assumes that there must be something wrong with her, and that she has some discreditable reason for it." When, in 1565, the French ambassador was pressing her to marry Charles IX of France, who was only sixteen years of age and seventeen years her junior, she said, "I fear that the Queen Mother has not been fully informed of my age, which is such that I am afraid the King and she would reproach themselves, and what discontentment would be my lot, for I should be disagreeable and be neglected by him as the late Queen Mary, my sister, was by the King of Spain . . . and I should rather die than find myself despised and neglected . . ."

Because prenuptial chastity was so very important for Elizabethans, it might, at least in theory, constitute a real treasure for a maid who had no dowry. If, however, a maid was found to be unchaste, this fact might provide an impediment to her marriage in spite of her dowry. Shakespeare presses the theory pretty far in Claudio's rejection of Hero in *Much Ado About Nothing*. Though he was well within his rights when, thinking her unchaste, he spurned her at the altar, still the act was so uncharitable that he had to make heavy atonement for it by taking a maid "sight unseen." Modern minds look upon his treatment of the shy girl as unspeakably brutal, but according to Elizabethan standards his weakness was a tendency to jealousy, hasty judgment, and intemperate action. However, since Shakespeare was making a comedy of this play with the required happy ending, he satisfied his audience that the young man had acquired enough humility to make a good husband for the "restored" Hero. At the same time he did not minimize the importance of chastity in the maid matched to a "very proper gentleman."

Besides unchastity, other impediments to marriage were recognized by Church and State. Canonical law emphasized impotence at the time of marriage, and kinship within the prohibited degrees. Civil law stressed unsoundness of mind, want of full age (the male to be fourteen and the female twelve), and kinship within the prohibited degrees. To these were added impediments listed by preachers and moralists, who might be powerful enough to control the conduct of people sensitive to the beliefs common to their own group. For example, Bullinger had objected to marriage with one of another faith, saying such a union hurt both parents and children, but he would not prevent choosing a mate from people of a foreign land.

The difference between canonical and civil law on impediments thus led to much confusion. Perkins, in his *Christian Oeconomie* of about 1590, drew up what he called impediments causing annulment, and impediments to marriage that did not cause annulment if they were not discovered till after marriage. In the first list he placed marriage to the wrong person through trickery or mistaken identity, a previous marriage of either party, a solemn vow of chastity taken by either person previously, and "cognition." Impediments that might be overruled if not discovered till after marriage were marriage in a forbidden season of the year, prohibition by the Church, precontract, incest or adultery to the fourth degree with any of the betrothed's relatives, murder committed in order to marry, ravishment of another's wife, christening of one's own child, murder of a priest, solemn penance previously undergone, and being a nun. Later, Gouge in *Of Domesticall Duties* added details about the impediment of impotence. He specified such kinds as frigidity, an incurable contagious disease, and castration accidental or present at birth. The Mohammedan practice of castrating Christians taken at sea or in enemy territory was cause for one of the terrors suffered by English parents when their sons traveled abroad. Gouge had this in mind. When he distinguished between impotence and barrenness, he quoted examples of people who might become fruitful after years of impotence, and for that reason he would not place seeming sterility among the impediments.

The most troublesome impediment of all was kinship. *The Bishop's Book* analyzed this problem as follows: after the Flood it was necessary for God to bless matrimony anew and to add in words what was already understood at the first blessing of Adam and Eve, that there should be no marriage between father and daughter, mother and son, brother and sister, and between others "in certain degrees of consanguinity and affinity, which laws of prohibition in marriage, he yet at this second repetition of the same made unto Noah . . . and repeated to Moses" (Lev. 18: 6–13 and ch. 20). For a long time, even before A.D. 506, all Europe had been troubled by impediments to marriage through blood kinship. Later, this hindrance involved kinship by marriage, then spiritual kinship, including the baptizer and baptized, the confirmer and confirmed, the godparents and their children, and the godchildren's relatives. Finally, the whole structure became so involved that Innocent III issued a decree permitting marriage between a husband's and wife's relations beyond the fourth degree, inclusive. It was understood, however, that the godfather was not to marry the mother of the baptized child, and the godmother was not to marry the father of the baptized child. Naturally, this complicated the problem of securing godparents for some children.

As the lists of Perkins and Gouge and writers of other conduct books indicate, impediments besides those set forth by civil and canonical law could be a source of much concern to parents matching their children in marriage. Among these, the following were especially important: forced consent to marriage, a previous marriage not dissolved by death of one of the parties, proof that the contracting individuals were under age, a difference in religious faith, and taking holy orders or a vow of chastity for entering a religious house. Many others were feared also, such as incontinence with a relative of the betrothed, great disparity of years, and misrepresentation of a person's state, as of a pregnant "virgin," and madness, which had to be proved was not of a temporary nature.

The fear of violating the law of consanguinity was greatest, however. Lord Coke once exclaimed in disgust that it was no uncommon thing for a marriage to be annulled by holy church because "the husband had stood godfather for his own cousin." Those who really wished to prevent a wedding might trump up almost any kind of spiritual consanguinity. The scholarly divine, Matthew Parker, knew personally the heartache such legal difficulties might cause, for he had married in 1547 before clerical marriage was legalized by Parliament and Convocation. In 1560, when the Queen asked him to draw up a list of marriage prohibitions, he played safe and included only thirty cases, of which twenty still stand, the other ten not being dispensed with till 1907.[12] Sometimes families of power or influence would secure special dispensations so that marriage might occur among royalty for reasons of state between cousins-german. Among powerful noble families marriage might be permitted with relatives beyond the second degree if not in direct line of ascent or descent. They might also obtain dispensation to wed a heretic if the couple promised to bring up the children in the orthodox faith. The Catholic element in England, though not openly prominent socially or otherwise during the Queen's reign, was very much concerned about the old impediments devised by their faith when civil law did not agree with canonical law in the matter.

Whether impediments to marriage increased adultery may well be pondered. Today the effort to make marriage difficult and divorce easy has scarcely solved this old, old social problem any more than the Elizabethan plan of making both marriage and divorce difficult enough to give pause to hasty action. In Elizabethan times every moral pen produced some sharp criticism over the "perversity and wickedness of men" in adultery. As far back as 1532 Erasmus, who had declared the married life "less spotted and contaminate" than any other state, felt he must accuse lustful men of committing adultery with "their own wives." Half a century later Stubbes was writing bitterly of the prevalence of adultery. The punishment of guilty women by causing them to appear in a white sheet before the congregation only two or three days, and sometimes for not over an hour or two at a time, was, he said, so light a chastisement that it had become a matter of laughter. He would require the guilty pair to suffer death by drinking the "Moyses cup" or to be branded on cheek or forehead to reveal their sin to the world.

Bullinger naturally had much to say about adultery. If a man's goods

---

[12] The full list is repeated in *Time* magazine, August 19, 1940.

were stolen, they could be returned with interest, he said, but if his wife was taken in adultery, he could not be pacified. He complained especially that adultery could alter inheritance, for if a wife secretly had unlawful children, they might inherit her husband's goods. Then she not only defiled herself but produced bastards that removed the family goods from the lawful heirs. For this reason her adultery was worse than a man's. Moreover, she brought grief and shame to her husband who could not know whether he was bringing up his own children; she dishonored her own kindred, but most of all, she dishonored her own lawful children by making people wonder whether they were actually lawful. Eventually her husband, though a virtuous and honest man, became despised and scorned.

Anxiety about matching sons with chaste women was the concern of all classes, not just the moral middle class. At the court of Henry VIII it was said there was scarcely a person in attendance upon the king whose character was not seriously tainted with this vice of adultery, many of them openly ridiculing the marriage vow. J. S. Brewer, in his Introduction to the *Letters and Papers, Foreign and Domestic, of the Reign of Henry VIII, 1524–30* (1876), tells of Sir William Compton, who was cited in the ecclesiastical court for living openly in adultery with Ann Hastings, a married woman, and of George Boleyn, who was executed for complicity in the intrigues of Catherine Howard. It is well known that Cardinal Wolsey left a son and daughter, and that his affectionate concern for the girl was openly shown. Suffolk, who married the king's favorite sister, Mary, was "horribly in love" with her, but he was incapable of returning the singlehearted devotion Mary paid him as long as she lived. Yet when Anne Boleyn at the height of her power over Henry asked him to appoint the sister of her sister Mary's husband to the newly vacant nunnery or Abbey of Wilton, the king denied her request because he had learned that Sister Elinor Carey was "guilty of gross incontinence." Henry never regarded himself as other than a good Catholic, and he may have been truly shocked at the "sister's" conduct, for in a letter to Anne, he says he would not "for all the gold in the world clog her conscience" or his own to make ruler of the house one of "so ungodly demeanor."[13] After Henry's death morals went from bad to worse till England became "famed for the crime of adultery" according to John Strype's *Memorials of Thomas Cranmer, Archbishop of Canterbury* (1694). Now, he says, nobles were putting away their wives by claiming them to be false, because they liked another better or because they hoped to obtain wealth by another marriage. "These adulteries and divorces increased very much," he says, "yea, and marrying again without any divorce at all, it became a great scandal to the Realm and to the

---

[13] Introduction to the *Letters and Papers, Foreign and Domestic, of the Reign of Henry VIII, 1524–30* (1876), IV, ccclxxxvi.

religion professed by it." A reaction was bound to set in, even if Mary's reign had not intervened. By the time, therefore, that Elizabeth came to the throne, divorce was almost impossible for anyone to obtain.

There were times, however, when the Queen granted or withheld favors in regard to divorce without due justice. When, for example, the Archbishop of Canterbury refused to sanction the marriage of Dr. Julio, physician and dependent of her favorite, the Earl of Leicester, because he had chosen another man's wife, Elizabeth had the archbishop sequestered from his see and confined to his house.[14] In the case of the beautiful Penelope Rich, sister of Essex, the Queen took a different course. She preferred to let this mother of two families suffer the agony of her position rather than free her from her legal husband whom she had been forced by her guardian—and perhaps by the Queen, for she was a ward of the Crown—to marry against her will. But Penelope's status at court was unharmed because nearly everyone sympathized with her in her unhappy marriage. She, meanwhile, was so closely bound to conventions and obligations of wedlock that she performed faithfully "the duties of a good wife" to both the fathers of her two sets of children.

Like sickness or health, marriage was an inescapable part of the normal person's experience, yet its hazardous character was never glossed over. With distrust of women and the consequent shallow and unconvincing eulogy of them, with impediments to marriage and the prevalence of adultery, and with the difficulty of matching young people according to suitability in tastes or background, Elizabethans were forced to consider divorce with its upheaval, even though this means of escape from an intolerable marriage was almost completely barred. There were always those who relied on slipping through the bars or over them or under them, but few who dared to try their strength in direct collision with them.

Divorce was an appealing avenue of escape from brutality or unfairness of the bond, but the bars before it were the Augustinian insistence on the indissoluble nature of consummated marriage. Before the Tudors, the Church had been prevailed upon to grant the so-called "imperfect divorce," which provided for "separation from bed and board." Then, during the reigns of Henry VIII and Edward VI, the leading ecclesiastics had drawn up the *Reformatio Legum* to abolish "imperfect divorce" and substitute for it the complete divorce. This new plan permitted the innocent party to remarry in cases of adultery, desertion, or cruelty. Though the plan failed, its principles were carried out in individual cases till 1602, when it was decided that "remarriage after judicial separation was null and void."[15] After 1602, no Elizabethan could legally escape from a

---

[14] Sir Nicholas Harris Nicolas (ed.), *Memoirs of the Life and Times of Sir Christopher Hatton* (1847), p. 52.

[15] Edward Westermarck, *A Short History of Marriage* (1926), pp. 287–92.

marriage except by death. During the whole controversy about divorce, individuals, of course, were the chief victims, though in a measure the issue affected the life and thought of the whole people.

It is not surprising that Henry VIII's divorce should have precipitated a deluge. With no apparent punishment to Henry or his followers for such flagrant outrage against the Holy See, this act and those succeeding it brought a tremendous upheaval in the spiritual nature of the whole nation. Latimer complained of churches being deserted, and Gardiner bewailed the acts of the lower classes as evidence of their having fallen into a state of paganism. The relaxation of religious observance did influence the morals and domestic habits of the people, but the long generations of thinking and feeling could not all be swept away by the innovations of one or two generations. To call the Tudor age depraved is to judge the whole by particular cases and scenes and to emphasize the sensational rather than the actual condition of the somewhat humdrum lives of the masses. In the thinking minds there was consternation for a while, but there was never any feeling of giving up the battle man instinctively wages against what he believes to be evil. Adultery and divorce were the chief points of this attack, and there was need for moral guidance in the struggle.

There were courtiers who plundered the people, there were landlords who evicted their tenants and officials who cheated the government, and there were merchants, usurers, and panders who preyed upon the rich and the poor.[16] Fast days and holidays for a while lost much of their old appeal, and until the pastors were once more trained to lead the people, the churches were in a sad state indeed. Even the diet of the people underwent change, and much to their own hurt, for they discarded vegetables and overloaded their tables and, far too often, their stomachs with various meats and sweets. Tippling houses sprang up like mushrooms, and there were many tabling dens and other vile places where illegal gambling was carried on. "The Clink," which Elizabethans called the "chief resort of stews on the Bankside in Southwark," consisted of "a row of houses under the Bishop of Winchester, painted white with signs on the front: The Boar's Head, The Crane, The Cardinal's Hat, The Swan, The Bell, The Castle, The Crosskeys, The Gun, and The Thatched House by the Waterside." Yes, there was work for reformers and moralists, and there were many who answered the need. Quick to see what the people really desired, the Queen, in spite of all the license she might demand for her own behavior, required more and more decorum in the social life at court and praised the resulting tightening of discipline and the pursuit of better manners in the homes. It was a violent age, but it was not given over to violence. Where before the Church had dominated the lives of people even in their homes, now the Church

---

[16] Hubert Hall, *Society in the Elizabethan Age* (1902), pp. 104–5.

of England and the schools joined forces with the parental teaching in the homes.

It is possible that distorted pictures of Elizabethan life may contribute somewhat to foreign critics' misinterpretation of the literature of this time. Drama naturally takes much that is sensational in an age for plot or atmosphere. With too much dependence on such sources one may easily gain a distorted conception of this complex period. Possibly this method may account in part for Schücking's feeling that in Shakespeare's portrayal of the Elizabethan family there is little closeness in the family bond.[17] He compares their attitude toward marriage with that of Luther, who, he says, meant to praise his wife when he asserted she had never been untrue, and he illustrates this point by Ben Jonson's assertion that his wife was a shrew but honest. The point of Ben's wry remark, of course, is that an Elizabethan husband was expected to forgive more or less every fault in a chaste wife, even the most detested of all, shrewishness. As a realist smarting under a wife's caustic tongue, Ben provides a classic understatement for the henpecked husband. Schücking also assumes Elizabethans tended to doubt all women's chastity; hence Isabella's exclamation questioning her own mother's chastity when she hears her brother ask her to sacrifice her honor to save his life. Schücking merely sees in this remark her doubt that a blood brother could make such a demand of her. To the Elizabethan, however, the effect of the brother's fear of death would be greatly intensified by his asking his sister to save him from the grave even at the sacrifice of her honor. Isabella's exclamation of abhorrence, therefore, was meant merely to call him to his senses, not to show any real doubt in her mother's own character. She knows that in his right mind he could no more ask for the sacrifice of her chastity than she could ever dream of parting with it. Schücking assumes Laertes shows a light attitude toward the marriage bond when he says any drop of blood which did not become inflamed in his body over Ophelia's fate proclaimed his mother a whore. It would be difficult indeed for Shakespeare to use a stronger means of showing the brother's violent grief over his sister's sad death. The *grief* is the point here, not the doubt.

Such misinterpretations, ingeniously defended as they are sometimes, may have been due to Schücking's difficulty with the English language, but more probably to his unfamiliarity with an emotional state that relieves, or expresses, itself by use of paradox or understatement. Such, for example, we find in Prospero's answer to Miranda's question, "Sir, are you not my father?" when he says, "Thy mother was a piece of virtue, and/She said thou wast my daughter" (*The Tempest*, I:ii:55–57). He could not have replied more emphatically, for his answer pays tribute to his wife's chastity and his delight in his child's innocence. Then, to

---

[17] Levin L. Schücking, "The Family in Shakespeare," *Character Problems in Shakespeare's Plays* (1922), p. 220.

appeal to his audience, the dramatist holds up the action of the play while the father tells a long story to show his devotion to this babe left to his tender care.

It was the adherence to their idea of the binding sanctity of marriage which made the question of divorce such a burning issue during the Tudor reign. J. S. Brewer notes that in the play of *Henry VIII*, Shakespeare's only admiration for Anne is in the expression concerning her pretty face. Henry himself was never at ease about the divorce from his first wife, and for ten long years he had many vexatious moments trying to defend himself against the accusations of his conscience and the moralists of his time. The false position in which he placed himself may have been due to love of a woman, but it was also due to need of a legitimate male heir, and he blamed whatever demands were made on him by the political situation for causing him to break his marriage vows. It has even been reported that at times he hinted he might cancel his divorce from Catherine if Francis I abandoned him, and take back Catherine of Aragon to satisfy the Spanish emperor, keeping Anne for his mistress.[18] In spite of all Henry's efforts to quell the controversy about divorce, it waxed strong enough to be a thorn in Elizabeth's side as long as she lived.

The Bishop's Book of 1537, which continued to carry more authority during Elizabeth's reign than Henry's revision of it (*The King's Book* of 1543), quoted Christ when asked about divorce as saying that "sith man and woman conjoined in matrimony be by God's ordinance but one flesh and body, it is not possible that they should afterward be separated or divorced one from the other." The book also gave Christ's answer to why Moses had permitted divorce—". . . to keep the people from 'greater mischief and inconvenience,' but that divorce was not permitted at the beginning, for it is 'clean contrary to the godly institution and natural order and laws of matrimony.'" The book concluded its argument against divorce by saying that to break the "indissoluble ties of matrimony" was to do so "under pain of damnation."

In drama, anything that endangered the bonds of marriage took on real emotional significance. Shakespeare accents the serious element in *The Comedy of Errors* by appealing to the seeming "adulterate" estrangement between husband and wife.

> . . . O! how comes it,
> That thou art thus estranged from thyself?
> Thyself I call it, being strange to me,
> That, undividable, incorporate,
> Am better than thy dear self's better part.

. . . .

[18] Preface to Vol. VI, *Letters and Papers, Foreign and Domestic, of the Reign of Henry VIII, 1524–30*, p. xxv [Du Bellay's report on England and the Pope, Ms. Dupuy, tome 33, f. 52, Paris, paper 1572].

> For know, my love, as easy mayst thou fall
> A drop of water in the breaking gulf
> And take unmingled thence that drop again,
> Without addition or diminishing,
> As take from me thyself and not me too.

Then, turning the situation about, Adriana asks her husband to put himself in her place:

> How dearly would it touch thee to the quick,
> Shouldst thou but hear I were licentious
> And that this body, consecrate to thee,
> By ruffian lust should be contaminate!
> Wouldst thou not spit at me and spurn at me
> And hurl the name of husband in my face
> And tear the stain'd skin off my harlot-brow
> And from my false hand cut the wedding-ring
> And break it with a deep-divorcing vow?

Vehemently, she declares she is so stained:

> I am possess'd with an adulterate blot;
> My blood is mingled with the crime of lust:
> For if we two be one and thou play false,
> I do digest the poison of thy flesh,
> Being strumpeted by thy contagion.
>
> II:ii:121–46

Had Shakespeare's audience not believed in the binding sanctity of marriage, he could never have made Adriana's long speech dramatic enough for contrasting the flow in romantic love with the dangerous eddies in married love.

But there were other disturbances to married happiness besides that of sex attractions outside the bond. For example, there must be no secrets to alienate husband and wife. In *Julius Caesar*, Shakespeare shows Portia's distress of mind when Brutus breaks the harmony of their lives by the first secret he refuses to share with her.

> Within the bond of marriage, tell me, Brutus,
> Is it excepted I should know no secrets
> That appertain to you? Am I yourself
> But, as it were, in sort of limitation,
> To keep with you at meals, comfort your bed,
> And talk to you sometimes? Dwell I but in the suburbs
> Of your good pleasure? If it be no more,
> Portia is Brutus' harlot, not his wife.
>
> II:i:280–87

Nowhere in Shakespeare is the marriage bond more clearly described. It tells dramatically what the Puritan William Whately meant in his wedding sermon, *A Bride-Bush* (1619), when he called marriage a happiness beyond all other earthly blessings. However, Whately emphasized the closeness of the physical union and said its demands must be yielded to readily by husband and wife or they sinned; Shakespeare emphasized the spiritual needs, without which all the other blessings were dust and ashes.

During most of the Elizabethan period, Anglicans and Catholics agreed on a separation for adultery, and divorce if one of the couple before cohabitation became a religious heretic and refused to reform. Most of the Puritans admitted the right of a divorce for adultery, and permission for the innocent one to remarry, though some still clung to the indissoluble ideal of marriage. Objectors to a second marriage feared it might cause trouble for the children; they also argued the guilty parent would have no cause to reform if hope of reconciliation was forever removed. Becon, like Erasmus, Luther, and Calvin, believed in divorce for attempts at poisoning, though Becon said that if the offending party reformed, the marriage bond still held. When the canon law of 1602 forbade remarriage as long as both partners lived, and required security against breaking that law, some unhappy ones forfeited the security. Then the civil law put the actual granting of divorce into the hands of the Church, and permitted the local courts to handle only those cases which before the Reformation had been referred to Rome. The Church granted no divorce but permitted separation for adultery, apostasy, or cruelty, and annulment for an illegally contracted marriage. After 1602, reformers swept away complete divorce and what they considered artificial impediments to marriage. Now the bond of marriage, though easier to acquire, came to be a matter of lifelong responsibility. So confusion was ruled out, but at great cost to certain individuals who, in the uncertainties about the bond, had gambled on more latitude in the marriage and divorce laws.

Until 1602, great care was exercised in making contracts and in trying to foresee any possible impediments to them lest children become the innocent victims of the law. Children of an annulled marriage might become bastards and their parents might remarry without further delay, thus bringing ruin to the very heart of family life. Until 1537, children were made bastards if their parents were found to have married in ignorance of impediments to their union. After 1537, both civil and canon law declared such children legitimate if their parents obtained a divorce when they discovered impediments to the marriage. But after 1602, children could not be legitimized if parents had married in ignorance of impediments, nor could divorced parents remarry to legitimize children begotten out of wedlock. It was this last part of the 1602 law which presumably broke the heart of the father of Penelope Rich's second family of children. Only after nursing her husband, Lord Rich, through a dangerous illness from which he admitted he would never have recovered without her care of him was he willing to grant her a divorce. At that time the Queen refused Penelope and Lord Mountjoy the right to legitimize their children by a marriage after Penelope's divorce. Both parents then hoped that James I, in recognition of their support of his accession to the throne, might agree to the legality of their marriage and permit them to legitimize Mountjoy's children by Penelope. James refused, and under the strain of it all, Mountjoy's weakened physical state was unable to throw off a cold that developed into a fever causing his death.

Elizabeth herself must have suffered great anguish as a child and later when she was called a bastard, for many people believed bastards were doomed to eternal damnation or to the oblivion of limbo. Their hearts, as in the case of Shakespeare's Don John of *Much Ado About Nothing*, were thought incapable of anything but evil. It has been suggested that this prejudice against her in early life may have had a strong influence upon Elizabeth, and may have caused in part her peculiar attitude toward compromise in religious and social matters. So entangled became the debate about marriage and impediments and divorce during her reign that there was danger of finding in almost any marriage some flaw according to canonical law. However, this confusion did not lessen the importance of the bond of matrimony so much as it increased the people's anxiety to secure the legality of their marriage and to protest anticipation of any marital rights before the solemnization of the marriage ceremony. The high value placed on the chastity of marriageable maids, therefore, made its blessing well worth the restraint and preparation exacted of its neophytes. And Shakespeare's appeal was still timely when, in *The Tempest*, the father Prospero repeatedly warns the accepted suitor for his daughter's hand not to break the "virgin knot before all sanctimonious ceremonies may with full and holy rite be ministered" (IV:i:15–23, 50–54).

Love was recognized by all writers and speakers as the foundation of a happy marriage, though many regarded it as the miracle effected through marriage rather than the impelling force before marriage occurred. Still, attraction or inclination was acknowledged as an important factor in securing voluntary consent to a union, and the young people were admonished to choose with the ear as well as the eye, never forgetting their children would inherit the qualities of both parents. They were warned again and again not only against attraction as the chief excuse for marriage but also against the danger of confusing love and lust. This made it necessary to discuss with them the virginity of matrimony, by which was meant a pure physical love that God would bless. The Puritans especially discussed the matter in wedding sermons, conduct books, and in the home. They pointed out that the early teaching of the Church which had placed celibacy above marriage had represented Adam's sin of propagation as interfering with God's plan to make reproduction of man as easy as that of plants and flowers. To these ministers, therefore, insistence on celibacy was to declare physical love impure. Consequently, they leaned over backward to justify its delights. Nevertheless, they were quick to warn against an intemperate indulgence, for down such a road lay the demon of lust, the source of jealousy and all kinds of unstable marital relations. Whatever bore the taint of instability between man and wife was a cursed thing. Not only was it likely to inflame the passions, but it also killed desire, either by satiety or by distrust. Physical love, however, when controlled in the blessed state of matrimony yielded up pleasures that were heavenly. God's own Word sanctioned such joys in Ecclesiastes, when Koheleth commanded the young man to live "joyfully with the wife" of his youth, in Proverbs, when the same command was repeated, and in the Song of Solomon, which was one long paean to physical love. Moreover, Christ himself had sanctioned the physical pleasures when he performed his first miracle to make a wedding merry.

Spenser's *Epithalamion*, of course, is but an idealization of this Puritan attempt to justify physical love in wedlock. There was much more writing by moralists, however, to point out the snares in a love sought for its own sake rather than in one sought first for society and the state and then for personal happiness. *The Man in the Moon . . . or The English Fortune Teller* (1609) is typically scornful of one who is the slave of love. For a man who is "king and commander of all earthly creatures" to become "pale in physiognomy, lean in his limbs, and all for a woman" especially for one who scorns him, is intolerable. And so the writer gives advice to cure the madness of such love. First, one must abandon idleness, "the nurse of wantonness," next, replace solitariness by occupation or discourse, third, take stock of his own good qualities, fourth, minimize the woman's attractions for him, and finally, discover her faults, which should be "set down in . . . table books" and written on the bedchamber walls to bring them ever to mind. The various repetitions of such advice (Vives had applied most of it to girls) denote its popularity. It is noticeable that Congreve found it suitable material for satire in *The Way of the World* (I:iii:68–82). Since so much stress was laid on the functions of marriage, however, it is possible that when young people were snared by love they were not quite so helpless as they might have been otherwise.

It would be difficult for the young people of today to imagine sixteenth-century boys and girls listening to long sermons on marriage and its duties. In these and in conduct books and frequently in advice from their parents, young people were earnestly admonished to love husband or wife next to the Lord, and were told marriage joined their souls and bodies in a mystical union that, blessed by the Lord, made separation utterly impossible. Then followed a long discourse on the wife's obedience and the husband's responsibility to his wife.

Elizabethans tried to present sex as a natural thing in life, though they did not fail to recognize at times its mysterious elements. For the happy union of poetic and prose expressions on marriage none is better, perhaps, than the reflections of Thomas Fuller in *The Holy State and the Profane State* (1642):

Deceive not thyself by over-expecting happiness in the married state. Look not therein for contentment greater than God will give . . . or to be free from all inconveniences. Marriage is not . . . without clouds. Yes, expect both wind and storm sometimes, which, when blown over, the air is clearer and wholesomer for it. Make account of certain cares and troubles which will attend thee. Remember the nightingales, which sing only some months in the spring, but commonly are silent when they have hatched their eggs, as if their mirth were turned to care for their young ones. Yet all the molestations of marriage are abundantly recompensed with other comforts, which God bestoweth on them who make a wise choice . . .

Elizabethans spoke much and wrote more about marriage as an institution designed for economic security for women, especially during the rearing of offspring, for they recognized no marriage but monogamy, whose ties after 1602 were made binding for life. Though much was said of the mutual service of husband and wife, still more was said about a delicate adjustment of the passionate and emotional relationships of man and wife, and the care of their children. Domestic and social life must proceed with as little friction as possible. Toward this end young people must be taught the problems of two people unhappily mated as well as those of people compatible in every way. Always parents must prepare their children for a marriage that meant more than binding together two people: it must be shown as a joining together of fortunes and interests which might affect social groups wider than families, bringing good or ill to the community in which they lived, and to the kingdom itself, of which the family was admittedly the integral unit. This, then, was the Elizabethan marriage ring.

Plans for marriage were never sudden or hurriedly carried out. The Elizabethans sometimes made plans soon after a child's birth, and frequently arranged betrothals at an early age. If these plans were found later to be distasteful to the young people, they were seldom forced to abide by them. Sons were usually given the right of refusal when parents felt they were old enough to make a decision in the matter, and both public opinion and parental love were against forcing a girl into an unwelcome marriage. Few marriages were purely mercenary, for parents sought suitable matching as well as the advantages of good bargaining. Of course there was more freedom of choice among children of the poor who had no property settlements to make.

If a girl was not very attractive her dowry might make her acceptable, and if it did not, she was likely to take gratefully any husband her father could provide for her. To be mistress in her own home was the thing she most desired, for with that would come what love and other advantages she herself could wrest from the hands of fortune. Without marriage she could never prove herself or take her rightful place in society. Most girls were likely to trust their parents' judgments fully in the matching plans, for they knew family pride would induce them to do whatever was possible to enhance their own dignity as well as the family's in choosing for them suitable husbands. Likewise, to match them badly would reflect against the family honor and, in the case of the father, would proclaim him a failure in one of his most important duties in the home.

Because the families of both yeomen and the gentry were interested in land, they frequently matched their children in marriage. A poor squire's daughter, therefore, would not be expected to object to marriage with a rich yeoman's son if the suitor was at all personable. A rich yeoman's son could afford to make a career of law or even seek service in the church, and he might very well be thought a suitable match for a gentle lady. Even trade that brought fortune to a family might provide proud marriages with the gentry, though society was loath to accept men of such origin as gentlemen. When arrangements involved complicated property and social adjustments, negotiations might drag on for months or even years. In families of much pride or power these difficulties might necessitate beginning plans for matching sons and daughters almost as soon as they were out of the cradle.

The betrothal part of the marriage contract, known as handfasting, was in some ways comparable to modern announcements of engagements to marry, yet it might also be as ceremonious as uniting two young people in the "holy state of matrimony." As handfasting might involve legal contracts, it was often referred to as an espousal contract, and consisted of mutual promises of marriage made by two people who might legally exchange such vows. Usually no one but the two people themselves could make the promises, and then they must be formal, just, and right. Exceptions were in political marriages, when handfasting might occur by proxy. Shakespeare exemplifies such an occasion in *III Henry VI*. Warwick, pledging his "constant loyalty" to King Lewis of France, says:

> . . . if our queen and this young prince agree,
> I'll join mine eldest daughter and my joy
> To him forthwith in holy wedlock bands.

III:iii:241–43

The queen does agree, and commands her son to take the hand of Warwick acting for his daughter, and with "faith irrevocable" promise that the "fair

and virtuous" daughter will be his. The prince clasps hands with Warwick, and dutifully answers:

> Yes, I accept her, for she well deserves it;
> And here, to pledge my vow, I give my hand.
>
> III: iii: 249–50

A scene in which both young people are pledged by proxy occurs in
I Henry VI (V:iii:151–62). So many of these scenes occur in Shakespeare's plays one feels they were of no little interest to the audience.

Handfasting was distinguished by "making fast the hands" and the
exchange of a kiss. There were two kinds of handfasting, however: *de
futuro*, which merely promised future marriage with the words "I will,"
and *de praesenti*, which made the promise of marriage in the present
tense with the words "I do." Neither of these rites was "true" marriage,
though often both forms were loosely referred to as marriage. Handfasting might be public or private, though the public celebration was much
more favorably regarded than the private. A conventional marriage, both
before and after the Reformation, required the openly conducted, formal
handfasting.

De futuro espousals set a definite or an indefinite date for the marriage, and this contract might be broken as easily as the modern engagement. This was the contract that was sometimes made by infants too
young for marriage, though such children must be seven full years of
age, except for two or three days, unless they were "prematurely ripe."
Parents could not take the pledges for the children. Children under
seven years could not be legally espoused, though there are reports of
such a "marriage" by a girl of two and a boy of three.[19] It was also irregular to have a child "marriage" which had to be ratified when the couple
came of age, yet this occurred, as in the case of the daughter of Sir Michael
Stanhope of Suffolk, who was "married" at nine years of age to Sir
Thomas Berkeley, who was thirteen. This marriage took place in the
church of Great Bartholomew, London, in the presence of the parents;
afterward the "bride" continued to live with her father, and the boy to
travel with tutors until suitable time had elapsed for the maturing of
the couple.

Such infant handfasting was often due to the desire of conscientious
parents to settle their children's future because the hazards of life were
so great. Frequently this device served to cement an alliance between
families hitherto hostile, or to ensure an existing friendship. For the
most part, parents used espousals as the most effective means they knew
for protecting their estates from possible confiscation by the Crown in

---

[19] Chilton Latham Powell, *English Domestic Relations, 1487–1653* (1917),
pp. 14–15. Powell gives the names of these children reported in the Chester records
as Jane Brerton and John Somerford.

case of their death, and thus preserved the inheritance of their offspring. True, some parents abused this contract by intimidating their children when they came of age (twelve for the girl and fourteen for the boy according to civil law) till they agreed to bind themselves by marriage, but it is doubtful whether more ill than good was the result of infant espousals.

Milton referred to the custom of arranged marriages as "savage humanity," yet he scarcely mended matters in his own case or the girl's when he made his first free choice. It was believed that love rooted in duty (as in arranged marriages between people to whom love became a solemn duty or an expected blessing from God) would have more chance for happiness than an attachment whereby the heart was caught by mere fancy, which often disguised itself as love. Only the disciplined soul or the temperament which yielded gracefully and intelligently to discipline, however, could make a love founded on duty or on the promise of God's blessing or even on personal choice a beautiful or satisfying experience.

There were certain impediments to infant marriages that gave concern. If children seven years of age had lain together, embraced, kissed, and been aware of what they were doing, they were ineligible for the *de futuro* contract. If they were seven years or older and had been pledged by the *de praesenti* espousal, they were not permitted to enter into the *de futuro* espousal. And if the *de futuro* contract was made on conditions that were dishonest or that could not be carried out, the bond was made void. Handfasting by *de futuro* espousals for those who had reached puberty could occur only in the following cases: if one of the couple had not reached puberty; if there was sufficient dowry to maintain them till they were married, and finally, if there was need of this contract to keep peace between countries.

De futuro espousals could be terminated by mutual consent as a rule, but there were still certain impediments which could arise to enable one of the contracting persons to withdraw regardless of the other person's feelings about the matter. Such circumstances were: if one of the two was found guilty of heresy or apostasy or infidelity; if one of the two became afflicted with a serious bodily disfigurement, such as the loss of an eye or a limb; if one of the two was proved previously contracted *de praesenti*; if a long separation occurred between the two contracted people; if one of the two was guilty of enmity or wickedness or gave just or reasonable cause for dissolving the bonds, such as fury or drunkenness. On the other hand, cohabitation might make the contract binding or it might dissolve it: if a woman was espoused against her will yet submitted to cohabitation with her *de futuro* spouse, the contract held; if one of the two committed fornication with another, the contract could be made void; if one of the two made *de futuro* contracts with several persons and cohabited with one of them, that person was bound to the one with whom the act had been performed; if a man carried away by violence a woman to whom he had been espoused *de futuro*, and cohabited with her, he became bound to her; finally, if after a *de futuro* handfasting was made, and there was no cohabitation, but one of the couple lawfully made a *de praesenti* contract, the *de futuro* espousal became void.

Cohabitation made both *de futuro* and *de praesenti* contracts binding, though in general the inheritance of children from the union could not be secured till that union had been solemnized by the Church. Cohabitation after either form of handfasting without solemnization by the Church made the offenders punishable by the Church, although both Church and State recognized them as married. In civil law, however, unless cohabitation was followed by the ceremony of marriage, either party could dispose of property as he or she willed, but after the ceremony, neither could so dispose of goods. If conflict occurred between civil and canonical law, the civil law took precedence. Since the establishment of the marriage bond by means of cohabitation failed to secure financial settlements, particularly in regard to the wife's dowry, the failure to complete the marriage by the proper ceremony before witnesses grew less and less frequent as the Elizabethan age drew to a close.

The *de praesenti* espousal was something less than a marriage, as it gave the woman no dower right, but it was equal to marriage in its indissoluble character. It might be a very simple service or it might be a complete public ceremony, performed before sufficient witnesses and with due observance of all solemnities required by canonical law. Because the *de praesenti* espousal was originally planned to be sanctioned immediately in the marriage ceremony, it never was recognized by the Church as marriage till it received the benediction of the Church. This completion of the *de praesenti* contract might occur at a secret wedding, at a very simple gathering, or in a public wedding in the church.

The purpose of the delay between the *de futuro* and *de praesenti* espousals was to give objectors time to announce impediments to the marriage; the omission of this opportunity might make the couple liable to no little future trouble about the validity of their contract, and at the same time cause society to criticize them severely for their haste. Such criticism could be directed toward the parents or the young people themselves; in either case it would be almost unbearable to those sensitive to public opinion.

Any attempt to marry another after being bound by a *de praesenti* contract was illegal so long as either party lived unless one of them took the vows of celibacy. If such a marriage was achieved, even though it received the benediction of the Church and children were born to the union, it could be made void by proof of the first *de praesenti* contract, and the children bastardized. Naturally there was considerable disagreement over such a tangled state of affairs. Henry VIII held the first *de praesenti* espousal valid over the second only if children were born to the first, but Edward VI repealed his father's ruling. Canonical law further complicated the situation when it ruled that if children were born to a couple whose *de praesenti* contract had not been solemnized, the children could not inherit lands even when the parents afterward had their marriage blessed by the Church. Civil law, however, did not withhold this right of inheritance once the marriage has been properly completed.

It is significant that the chief reason for all this controversy was the Church attitude toward marriage as a holy thing. Although the Church had always considered private espousals valid, it enjoined a public religious ceremony for sanctifying the union. It based its requirement on the Bible (I Timothy 4:5), "For it is sanctified by the word of God and prayer." Not for a moment must it be forgotten that this sanctifying of handfasting contracts provided no little protection for woman. The espousals themselves tried to protect her by making her consent necessary to marriage, and although the *de praesenti* contract could be escaped only by death or by holy orders, and although the *du futuro* contract could be made binding only by the concurrence of the spiritual courts and the consummation of the ties before marriage, still the actual sealing of the ties was at the public church ceremony. By its very nature of being public and religious this made the bond most secure.

The severing of the Church of England from the Church of Rome, in so far as marriage and divorce were concerned, had no great effect upon the conventional moral conduct of the English people in general. Individuals were naturally affected, and the intensity of the consequent discussions of divorce and marriage raised questions where none had existed before. The conflicting rulings of the time, with new laws repealing old ones and still later laws reviving old ones, wrought havoc in individual lives. Though marriage by means of *de praesenti* handfasting was recognized by both Church and State, the Church retained its traditional authority for solemnization of the ceremony.[20] Even the Puritans, who recognized the validity of marriage by magistrates, considered it more "lawful, more convenient, and comfortable" for the marriage to be celebrated in the Church. Not until 1653 was civil marriage by law established by Cromwell.

This confusion of civil and canonical law kept the Church busy during the reign of Elizabeth punishing offenders who, in the eyes of the civil courts, were not guilty at all. Shakespeare shows this confusion in his plays, especially in *Measure for Measure* and *The Tempest*. In the former he leans toward condoning anticipation of marriage rights after either form of handfasting, but in the latter he insists upon strict avoidance of consummation of the union before the solemnization. In *Measure for Measure*, Claudio and Juliet have lived secretly as man and wife after

---

[20] John Cordy Jeaffreson, *Brides and Bridals* (1672), and Henry Swinburne, *A Treatise of Spousals or Matrimonial Contracts* (1686).

a "true" or *de praesenti* handfasting. Claudio declares their marriage lacks only the "denunciation [i.e., formal declaration] of outward order" or solemnization, which they have delayed in order to increase Juliet's dowry in the hands of friends (I:ii:149–156). When Juliet becomes pregnant, however, Claudio discovers he is subject to an old law which the Duke himself admits was "for terror, not to use" (I:iii:26), but which his deputy Angelo will enforce even though it exacts the death penalty. Claudio's resentment would appeal to Shakespeare's audience, for he is being set up as an example for conduct that is common to all the people he knows merely to feed the ambition of Angelo. This injustice is but the beginning of a cruel story of a cruel man who must be made to satisfy the Elizabethan sense of justice by being forced to stand before the pit of suffering he has digged for another.

To do this, Shakespeare shows that the very man who brings Claudio to "justice" for enjoying rights beyond his true espousal contract has himself broken a *de futuro* espousal contract in a manner that is not only cruel but contemptible. For Angelo, who had been bound in honor by the *de futuro* contract to Mariana, deserted her just as soon as she lost her dowry. Worse still, when her beloved brother and protector was lost at sea with the dowry, Angelo had not dried one of her tears with comfort, but had "swallowed his vows whole, pretending in her, discoveries of dishonor" (III:i:221–40). Now Isabella, on the verge of becoming a nun, crosses his path, and his coldly sensual heart, suddenly fired with lust, makes him seek by the grossest treachery to deflower her. Promising to save her brother's life for the sacrifice of her honor, he breaks that promise as soon as he thinks he has had his will with her, and spurns all her entreaties as he orders the immediate execution of her brother. Thus is the coldhearted villainy of the deputy who is to dispense justice contrasted with the natural guilt of his victim.

But since this play is a comedy that must have a happy ending, the deputy is tricked into an assignation with Mariana, his *de futuro* spouse who he thinks is Isabella. Thereby he seals fast the *de futuro* contract by cohabitation. When he learns of the trick and is made to confess his former contract with Mariana, he commits the unforgivable sin of slandering her. His punishment is a hurried solemnization of his marriage with her, after which he is condemned to die for having violated the same law that had made Claudio his victim. All his wealth is to become Mariana's. But she will not have this kind of justice, and pleads so desperately for the life of her husband that she persuades Isabella to join her in her entreaties. She saves Angelo from death in spite of all his "intended" evil, but she thereby achieves the mastery in marriage, which to Elizabethans would be an interesting point. This is a comedy, however, and Mariana's loving submissiveness will not make her husband's life a humiliating one. He is also spared the remorse for Claudio's death, as that youth is saved by the "friar's" trick. Perhaps the last twisted smile is over the untangling of the law, civil and canonical, with the deceit practiced by the Duke as a friar in disguise: he offers no excuse for using a dishonest *means* to achieve the *end* of justice.

The playwrights, of course, were furnished with many dramatic situations through the controversial subject of handfasting. But the private correspondence of the period also presents exciting plots that, if not so romantic, certainly are realistic.[21] For example, John Trueman in July of 1621 writes his "brother-in-the-ministry . . . Good Master Wilson" that a man in Wilson's flock by the name of William Ball, "servant to Master Henry Smith," is intending a violation of a *de praesenti* contract. Already contracted "before sufficient witnesses" to a girl in Trueman's parish by the name of Anne Delves, a servant to "the Right Worshipful Sir Francis Edgeoak," this "same Ball hath a purpose to contract himself to another woman, one Mary Watson, contrary to all truth." Therefore Trueman wishes Wilson to "consider the promises and truly to examine the business" so that "no proceedings" may occur "before the truth may appear from . . . Anne Delves." Then Trueman underscores the next statement. "*. . . for they be man and wife before God and the world although matrimony be not solemnized*," which William Ball had promised Anne to "perfect before St. James' Day" of the very month in which the letter is written. Anne's witnesses will verify Ball's "intentions" to Anne. Needless to say, this letter would end William's philandering with Mary and would march him to the altar with Anne.

When children wished to arrange their own espousals, they must first seek the consent of their parents; if they were under legal age for marriage, this duty was absolutely necessary; otherwise, it was a moral obligation only. In the Church there was some discussion about what constituted the legal age, for not all leaders, among the Puritans in particular, agreed to the ages of twelve for the girl and fourteen for the boy as prescribed by civil law. Bullinger had believed it should be an individual matter, depending on the probable ability of the couple to produce healthy offspring, but Gouge, who stressed the physical duty of love in marriage, insisted that the capability for sexual intercourse should determine the age. Few children entered upon the responsibilities of marriage at the legal age, however, especially among followers of the orthodox faith. Elizabethans wished to delay the actual date of their children's assumption of these duties, regardless of the contracting, till they were certain the young people had reached maturity. Those who could afford the extra expense of additional education often permitted the daughter to marry at as early an age as thirteen, and then gave her special training for her expected career as wife and mother while her husband was sent to Oxford or Cambridge or to travel on the Continent. Yet if a daughter

[21] Quoted by Edgar I. Fripp, *Shakespeare's Haunts near Stratford* (1929), p. 19.

of only twelve vowed marriage to a youth of fourteen in her father's hearing and without his raising any objections, her vows bound her legally in contracting.

There were times when those who had entered into espousal contracts with good faith wished later to withdraw from them honorably and safely, but such a change in plans might present difficulties. If an Elizabethan *de futuro* spouse wished to withdraw from his contract or to contract himself *de praesenti* to another, he had to get a release from the first spouse; that failing, he had to secure a judicial decree. When, for example, Lord Burghley had proposed his granddaughter Elizabeth as a wife for the young Earl of Southampton, the boy's mother (in lieu of the father who had died) agreed to the match, and the *de futuro* espousal was arranged. However, at sixteen, the youth did not wish to complete the contract but desired to adventure in travel with the Earl of Essex whom he greatly admired. The mother listened to his pleas, and did not force him to abide by his contract. To secure his release, she even paid Lord Burghley five thousand crowns from her son's estate. The whole matter was the talk of the early 1590's, and is now referred to as the first "breach of promise suit" in England.

In the church law it was customary to order penance for a breach of promise unless the young couple of a *de futuro* contract hated each other, in which case they were merely admonished. In the old days refusal to complete the *de futuro* contract could bring excommunication, with imprisonment after forty more days of refusal. Release from such confinement could be achieved only through an annulment of the contract or by death of the other person. To be able to extricate an unwilling partner to this contract by a payment of money was a long step forward to the loosening of ties in this particular part of the process of matching in marriage. As the ties of this contract grew lax, however, those of the *de praesenti* contract tightened.

Since a contract became void if its conditions were broken, dishonorable people sought various excuses for dissolving these bonds, particularly if they had power. At the court of Henry VIII, Charles Brandon, later the Suffolk who married Henry's captivating sister Mary, was the most notorious of such offenders. Reared and educated as companion of Henry, he was probably the only one the king ever really loved, and he returned that affection. In many ways he resembled the king, for he had great charm when he wished to display it, and he had great physical attractions. He was first contracted to Anne Browne, daughter of Sir Anthony Browne, Governor of Calais, and grandniece of the Earl of Warwick. He set aside the contract, however, to betroth himself to Margaret of Austria, and then put her aside for the rich widow of Sir John Mortimer of Essex, though she was nearly fifty and he not yet twenty. He succeeded in getting an annulment of this contract on the grounds that the widow was aunt to the discarded Anne Browne, and then married

Anne in a great ceremony at which many relatives and friends were present. At Anne's death he contracted himself to Elizabeth Grey, daughter and heiress of the Viscount de Lisle, but when she refused to complete the contract, Henry gave her title to Brandon. Meanwhile Brandon was making love to Henry's sister, whom he later married only a fortnight after her husband, the old king of France, had died and while she was yet in widow's weeds.

Brandon's son-in-law, father of little Jane Grey, nine-day queen, also violated contracts, for although he was contracted to Lady Katherine Fitzalan, he set her aside in order to marry into the royal family. His *de futuro* spouse, instead of demanding her rights, retired to a life of proud, dignified obscurity. But her family waited for the day of reckoning, and when the uprising occurred which cost Jane her throne, the brother of the discarded Lady Katherine, the Earl of Arundel, betrayed Jane's father to his enemies.

Such acts were sensational material for dramatists, and they seized upon it, especially the common device of a dishonest *de futuro* spouse pretending a previous espousal when he wished to achieve sudden wealth by a different alliance. Middleton's *A Trick to Catch an Old One* makes a somewhat amusing adaptation of the device when he has a courtesan pretend she has been precontracted in order to gain money from her spouse for her lover. With Middleton, Dekker invented a scene for *The Roaring Girl* in which the uxorious husband is approached by his wife who asks for £30 to appease her lover to whom she declares she has been precontracted:

> For o'er the seas he went, and it was said,
> But ruinous lies, that he in France was dead:
> But he's alive, O he's alive!

Such scenes in drama depended for their effectiveness on a very great fear of these situations in real life. It was this dread of anything which might destroy the validity of a marriage that made society frown on secret marriages.

Throughout the Middle Ages and during the Tudor reign, marriages not published beforehand in the church were declared clandestine. In 1200, the Synod of Westminster had ordered "three publications in the church of the intention of the spouses"; in the fourteenth century the Archbishop of Canterbury had ordered the celebration of the marriage ceremony after the publication of the banns on "three separate Lord's days or holidays." The announcements had to be a day apart, not necessarily a week apart. If the two people lived in separate parishes, there had to be announcements for each parish. The archbishop also ordered the marriage ceremony to be conducted in daylight. Yet many of the corrupt clergy continued to encourage secret marriage in spite of these and later strict orders to publish the banns.

The exciting clandestine marriage of Dorothy Devereux, sister of Penelope Rich and of Essex, was carried off in the high-handed manner of a modern cinema "thriller." Her biographers[22] tell how she and Sir Thomas Parrot were able to force their way into a parish church and to be married by a strange minister "whom they had procured." Two men guarded "the church door with their swords and daggers under their cloaks," with the rest of the company of five or six also bearing arms. Two of this company had "that morning repaired" to the vicar of the parish, demanding the key to the church door and the Communion Book, one of them saying he "had been a Preacher a long time" and needed the book to examine certain men "and to swear them." When the vicar had told him the book was locked up in the vestry and could not be obtained and offered instead a Latin testament, the man said "it would not serve . . ." Meanwhile the three men with Dorothy and Parrot approached the church, and the door being open, they entered. The vicar tried to shut the door, but was prevented from doing so. He saw what was afoot, and now tried to prevent the "strange Minister" from marrying the two young people by reading an injunction against the marriage:

. . . no man shall be suffered to marry any person . . . (the banns not being first orderly published) but in the church or chapel where he is Parson, Vicar, or ordinary Curate; neither at any other time than is usual for public and common prayer; neither except he do first show his sufficient license to the Churchwardens of the said church or chapel: and either by his own knowledge, or the knowledge of the said Churchwardens . . . that the parties to be married have thereto the assent of their parents or other governors.

But the impatient group refused to listen to the vicar, and the "strange Minister" said he had authority to do what he intended. With that he showed the vicar "a license under seal, which the Vicar offered to read: but before he had read half of it, Sir Thomas snatched it away from him," and offered the vicar a rial to marry them. Of course the vicar refused, and Sir Thomas ordered the "strange Minister" to proceed with the ceremony. As soon as the man began to read, however, the vicar resisted him and shut the book. At this Sir Thomas "thrust him away, and told him he . . . should answer it for resisting my Lord Bishop's authority." Another of the party then accused the vicar of being "malicious," and the intimidated man after another feeble effort to interfere "held his peace." Still another man, however, tried to "pluck away the book," but

---

[22] Sir Walter Bourchier Devereux, *Lives and Letters of the Devereux, Earls of Essex* (1853), I, 156, and John Strype, *Historical Collections of the Life and Acts of the Right Reverend Father in God, John Aylmer* (1701), 1821 ed., Addition VII, p. 217.

was also told "he should answer for it, and was in danger of a *premunire* for resisting the Bishop's authority." The marriage ceremony then went forward unmolested, although the "strange Minister" was without surplice, and stood in "his cloak, with his riding boots and spurs . . ." When the news of this marriage reached court, there was high disapproval, for Dorothy was a ward of the Crown. The justice of the peace "was commanded to take the examination of the matter, and send it up. And in fine, the Bishop of London underwent much blame . . ."

Perhaps the most spectacular of all clandestine marriages involved William Seymour and the tragic Arabella Stuart. The girl was the closest rival James I had to the throne of England, for she was his first cousin, being the daughter of Charles Stuart, Earl of Lennox, younger brother of James's father. She was so often at Elizabeth's court that gossip in *The Fugger News-Letters*[23] accused her of being the Queen's daughter:

We are told the Queen had with her a young lady who was called by everyone her cousin and next heiress to the English throne after the Queen's death. But now it is said to be evident that she is a daughter of the Queen whom she had by N.N.

This gossip of April 1581 continued, and in March of 1601 rumors were reported that showed intense concern over the succession:

The Queen is said to be inclined to marry her cousin to the Prince of Condé, and he is to be made King. The King of Scots is to be excluded from the succession.

When Arabella, thirty-five and still unmarried, contemplated a union with William Seymour, she was a real threat to James's security even though he was on the throne of England. Seymour, twenty-two, was the son of Catherine Grey, named by Henry VIII as in line for succession; when a maid of honor to the Queen, Catherine had clandestinely married the Earl of Hertford. Elizabeth had promptly declared all of Catherine's children bastards, but many Englishmen refused to accept this harsh sentence. When James heard of the rumored marriage between these two people, he sent for them immediately, but they denied such a thing so stoutly that he dismissed them. Then they did marry secretly, and when this was discovered, the bridegroom was put in the Tower and Arabella in private custody at Lambeth.

Perhaps Arabella had chosen Seymour with the help of the young Countess of Shrewsbury, her dearest and most loyal friend. At any rate, the countess planned the escape of the two lovers and sent Arabella large sums of money and a suit of men's clothing. Arabella pulled the full French hose on over her petticoats, put her arms through the doublet, and placed a peruke over her hair, finishing her disguise with a black

---

[23] The Second Series of these letters, 1568–1605 (ed. Victor Klarwill, 1926).

coat, russet boots with red tops, and a rapier. After she had left the house, she was met by a servant with horses, and mounting, rode away with him into London. There a boat was waiting to carry her and her party down to Lea, where a French ship was to take them to the Continent. Seymour's plans did not work out so well, for he was delayed so long that Arabella finally had to leave without him. Eventually he arrived safe in Ostende, only to learn that Arabella had been captured and sent to the Tower. There she was to spend the rest of her days and to die insane (as reported) or poisoned (as rumored). To the last, however, the countess was loyal and devoted. When called to testify against Arabella, she said she had made a vow, and it was "better to obey God than man," and would not say one word against her friend. Although imprisoned for a while and fined £20,000 she never betrayed Arabella—or herself.

In general, the clandestine marriage was frowned on because it brought danger to all it involved if the parties were important, and insecurity to the couple if they were only ordinary people. Shakespeare's audience would have such things in mind when seeing the play of *Romeo and Juliet*. They would shudder at Romeo daring fate when asking the friar to close his and Juliet's hands with holy words,

> Then love-devouring death do what he dare;
> It is enough I may but call her mine.
>
> III: vi: 6–7

The friar has his qualms also, for he answers sternly, "These violent delights have violent ends . . ." Only because he hopes to unite two families long in bitter feud does he consent to the marriage he even helps to plan. Then, ironically, his very fear of it all causes him to lose his courage at the moment when Juliet's life depends upon the cool, levelheadedness of the church father she has trusted so implicitly. It was the woman who was especially in jeopardy when secretly married, and in this play Shakespeare keeps that fact ever in mind.

Even when preceded by the public promises of young people of marriageable age, a secret marriage might be made only fairly secure by cohabitation or by a secret solemnization. Then, if anything did go wrong with the transaction, it was the woman who was most likely to suffer the greatest injury. In practice, clandestine unions were the exception in spite of all that has been said of young people resorting to them in attempts to escape from unwelcome marriages planned by parents willing to barter their children's happiness for their own wealth or power. Such barter was more likely to be that of guardians than of parents, for natural affection governed parents of this age as much as during any other age. With marriage a life contract, more or less, parental desire for the best possible choice of partner for the child and a proper consummation of the wedding ceremony was bitterly frustrated if such plans were destroyed by a clandestine marriage.

There was also objection to secret contracts and continued long delays after a handfasting between two mature young people. The temptation to enjoy marriage rights during long betrothals was frequently criticized, and young women were warned again and again against granting such favors as well as against entering into any espousal that did not have two or more witnesses present and a written record made of the proceedings, including the consent of parents or responsible relatives. Such cautioning was due to the effort to protect young maids from "invalid promises." Consequently many Elizabethan curates asked most young people coming to them for private espousals whether they had the consent of parents or guardians, and urged upon them the conventional, ceremonious contracts. William Gouge objected to the delay occasioned by a *de futuro* espousal just prior to a young man leaving for his long and uncertain tour on the Continent or for going to the wars. Nor would he have the period between the two espousals too short lest the couple be accused of rushing into their union in a brutish manner. Perkins added to this argument the need of a betrothal period long enough to permit thoughtful preparation for the final step. Not only must the young woman be protected against possible liberties taken with her person during the betrothal period, but her reputation must not be blemished by the slightest scandal.

To review thoroughly all the dangers of a betrothal too long or too short, William Gouge, in the third edition of his book *Of Domesticall Duties* (1634), referred to the Virgin Mary's three-month period of betrothal, and gave six reasons why it should be an example to young women: the orderly step-by-step process which added honor to marriage by putting sacredness before impatient lust; the time provided two young people to observe each other's qualities; the use of this period in wise preparations for marriage and its responsibilities; the time given to ensure the validity of the contract and for publishing the banns; the wise delay which prevented clandestine marriage; and finally, the time for definite preparations for a very solemn occasion. In a certain volume of this edition is a hand drawn with the long index finger pointing to the fourth reason, and in thin, spidery letters of long ago the notation: "A commendable custome: And great pity, that it is so much neglected as it is."

Since the essence of the marriage contract was free consent of both parties, and since the whole service was based on this consent, conscientious parents tried to match their children according to their mutual liking. Brandon's last wife, Catharine Willoughby, had been only fourteen when she was married to her old but still charming libertine husband. He had made her as happy as he could, fettered as he was by his fickle nature, but she must have had her hours of quiet grief even though she always greeted him with a smiling grace. However, after Brandon's death, when her own son was fifteen and she was asked to match him in marriage with Lady Anne Seymour, she wrote a letter full of hesitation and doubt, insisting on the mutual liking of the young people. She wished the "children" to have the chance "to begin their loves themselves, without . . . forcing." Both might consent out of obedience to parents and marry to please them and thereby learn to "mislike" each other for no other reason than feeling they had "lost their free choice." She is sure that would be enough to "break the greatest love." She herself can love the girl like a daughter, but that is not enough; she wishes the children to be let alone "to make up the matter themselves." If they fail to like each other, then neither child's parents can be blamed. So liberal an attitude for the impatient and ambitious Seymours was not to their liking, and they married their daughter to a suitor three weeks later.

But the Seymours were the exception, not the rule, as most Elizabethan parents would have agreed strongly with the duchess in her concern about the happiness of the children. If, however, children forsook their parents before they married and exercised the right of free choice by a union that was not orderly in all other respects, their marriage could be annulled. Delay in beginning annulment proceedings must be short, however. Moralists, of course, complained bitterly of children who married without parental consent or against their parents' wishes. Robert Allott (*Wits theatre of the little World*, 1599) said the Greeks had a commendable custom of whipping children in public who were guilty of such an act, and the Lacedaemonians disinherited such children and put a curse on them. He also quoted the Bible in regard to its curse: "Let no man esteem it light to be cursed of their parents, for in old times the Hebrews' children made more account of their father's blessing than of their grandfather's inheritance." If the public interest in the trouble between a certain Elizabethan father and daughter and her contracted suitor is reported correctly, one may assume that such advice as Allott's did not always fall on deaf ears. However, the commotion caused by the affair indicates that it was unusual.

Sir John Spencer, Lord Mayor of London in 1594, had contracted his daughter to Lord Compton. In 1599, when the marriage was to take place, Compton demanded of the father a dowry of £10,000 and the redeeming of a mortgage on Compton's land of £18,000. John Chamberlain, who reports the affair to Dudley Carleton, says there was so much trouble over the dowry that her father had "beat and misused" the girl, and she was "taken to a proctor and then to Sir Henry Billingsleyes" till the trial about her dowry was settled. Her father was even accused of hiding her away from Lord Compton, who had evidently won the girl's heart, and of pleading a precontract to Sir Arthur Henningham's son to stop proceedings with Compton; for this "contempt to a lord," the father was sent to the Fleet. The affair was settled to the liking of Lord Compton, and the marriage with the girl occurred. In 1601, she bore a son to her lord husband, but her father did "not relent a whit."[24] Perhaps he felt that her dowry of at least £28,000 was too high a price to pay for the lord the girl seemed to have set her heart on.

Among the common people concern about ill-matched unions was due largely to fear of immature minds rashly and foolishly refusing the advice of their elders. But when children took matters into their own hands wisely, parents were more or less reconciled to their act. Drama of the time often chose this motif for its light comedies. Anne Page, for example, in Shakespeare's *Merry Wives of Windsor*, is a gentle girl who dutifully urges her lover to overcome her father's objections to their marriage. To make her role attractive, she is shown unable to follow the wishes of both parents because they have chosen rival suitors for her. Thus she can disappoint both father and mother and marry the man of her choice, but only because she is mature enough to make a wise choice. In the anonymous play, *The Merry Devil of Edmonton*, the heroine is the daughter of a country gentleman who tries to frustrate her elopement. Nevertheless she makes her escape with her wisely chosen lover to a monastery where she is married by a priest who has been accustomed to liberal dealing with the rights of others; for example, he has not hesitated to enjoy a little poaching along with his religious duties. His defection in this marriage offsets the maid's, for she has chosen wisely in spite of her disobedience, and he has escaped punishment for his offences. Together, they are to be accepted in the same lighthearted manner as Anne Page. Bianca, in Shakespeare's *Taming of the Shrew* is the "mild" daughter of a father who, harassed by a shrewish daughter to be married off, does not hesitate to show preference for the gentle sister. When Bianca marries her "tutor" without even asking her father's consent, she is not upbraided because she has unwittingly married a wealthy young man in disguise, and so made a lucky choice. The audience is further disposed in her favor when her father permits old Gremio and the young Tranio to engage in a bidding match for her. The outrageous promises of Tranio cause the father to demand a prenuptial settlement on the spot, and this makes sympathy for Bianca complete. In *As You Like It*, Shakespeare has Rosalind simply tell her father, the banished duke, that she is going to marry Orlando, taking for granted his consent in a forest where almost everything is pleasant enchantment. These examples illustrate a fact that is as old as humanity: nothing succeeds like success, especially if it happens to be the lucky choice of a mate for life.

When the choice was not wise, tragedy was wont to fall in drama as in life. As an immature daughter Juliet consents readily enough to her parents' plans for her marriage to County Paris. When she falls in love with Romeo, she marries this son of her father's worst enemy even though her heart is charged with misgivings about a love that does not follow

---

[24] Norman Egbert McClure (ed.), *The Letters of John Chamberlain* (1939).

an orderly course. Her age puts her well within the limit for legally contracting herself, but for her disobedience in disregarding her parents' wishes she must pay a grievous penalty. In a clearly defined choice with its clearly defined results, the motif might give way to complexities that pleased even as they disturbed. Portia in *The Merchant of Venice* is extremely careful, apparently, about obeying to the letter all the instructions in her father's will concerning the choosing of the caskets. When she falls in love with the handsome Bassanio, she probably does not aid him in making his selection with ears as well as eyes, even though her musicians accompany a singer whose words of *bread*, *head*, and *nourished* can scarcely fail to suggest *lead*. Later, when her husband gives away her gift to him of a betrothal ring because the interest of his best friend seemingly demands it, Portia meets this test without stumbling. Gracefully bowing once more to necessity, she stoops smilingly, and wins—but does not keep—the mastery in marriage. Jessica's disobedience is bound up with a complicated revelation of the Elizabethan reaction to the grotesque. When she robs her father for the sake of her Gentile lover and escapes from her Jewish home in a gay carnival spirit, she is meant to provoke chilled laughter. Next, she buys a monkey with the betrothal ring of her mother to her father, and when Shylock can scarcely believe the account of such unnatural behavior, his reaction to the situation provides just enough of the grotesque to titillate even the most vindictive soul with a kind of astonished horror.

Even under the best conditions, a youth might be unable to choose a mate without too much influence from emotion. If freedom of choice was unencumbered by economic or other conditions, there was still need of parental advice or supervision. For this reason, Puritan ministers, especially, were almost constantly admonishing parents to choose mates for their children and so help them to avoid ungodly marriages. Becon, for example, gave what he considered practical advice to guide parents in this matter. The daughter should be provided with a husband from good honest stock. He should be well brought up, able to make a living, and morally repelled by riots, dicing, cards, etc. The father should make his daughter's dowry liberal, but not to the point of denying himself or his wife or of tempting the young couple to "strut thereby." It was better, he said, to have children ask their parents for aid than for parents to have to ask their children. Bullinger also insisted on parental advice in this matter because he believed that daughters who were fortunate enough to obtain good husbands without it might feel parents had no further authority over them, and this would be a very sad state of affairs. This insistence on parents retaining a position of authority prevailed in all religious households—Catholic, Anglican, and Puritan.

Whether a father maintained a tone of formality or bluff heartiness, he expected obedience in his children, unless, of course, his home was lacking in good management. In the gay comedy by Marston and others of *Eastward Ho,* the obedient daughter is contrasted with the disobedient one and the latter's attitude is due to the disobedience in her mother's attitude. The father calls out heartily to his obedient child:

Come hither, Mildred. Do you see yond' fellow? He is a gentleman, though my prentice, and has somewhat to take to; a youth of good hope, well friended, well parted. Are you mine? You are his.

She is his obedient child, and takes no liberty with her father, answering him in a dutiful manner that delights his soul:

Sir, I am all yours; your body gave me life; your care and love, happiness and life; let your virtue direct it, for to your wisdom I wholly dispose myself.

                                                            I: ii: 163–67

Proud that she can match words with the gentleman he has chosen for her and proud of his own sturdiness that has enabled him to succeed in life without "gentle blood," he contracts Mildred to his apprentice and feels he has accomplished much for her. The ungrateful, disobedient sister, however, will choose for herself, and she is aided and abetted by her vain mother who wishes to place her child in the way of riches and slothful ease. The two have to be humbled for their scornful role of rude and haughty "ladies" and for presuming to take upon their shoulders a responsibility that belonged to the head of the house.

Most of the criticism of "selling children" into matrimony for "filthy lucre's sake" was fittingly directed against guardians. Such people were said to deserve "at the hand of God great plagues and punishments; and before men great ignominy, rebuke, shame, and infamy." From 1540 on, Agrippa's objection to forced marriage was quoted: that love itself "is at no man's commandment," and that forcing children into unhappiness might lead them to perform some evil or, worse still, some crime. During the 'nineties, two plays dealt especially with this idea: *The Yorkshire Tragedy* and George Wilkin's *The Miseries of Enforced Marriage.* In both plays the hero suffers so much from not being permitted to marry the woman of his choice that he murders the wife forced upon him by his uncle guardian. His deserted betrothed commits suicide.

It might be fairly easy and safe for a guardian to line his pockets quickly by marrying his rich wards to fortune hunters not destitute of money themselves. When Penelope Rich, a ward of the Crown, was "bought" as a wife from her uncle guardian, her suitor had paid handsomely for so beautiful a prize. It is possible that the Queen and the girl's stepfather, the Earl of Leicester, also shared in the spoils. At any rate, it is significant that Penelope was received in the best society in and out of court in spite of the fact that she bore to her husband three sons and three daughters, and to her lover, Mountjoy, three sons and two daughters. Moreover, Mountjoy was the friend of her adored brother, Essex, and was as faithful to Penelope as he was handsome and charming; in fact, she was said to be the only woman in his life. When he was home from the wars, she lived with him, but when he was forced to be away, she was a "dutiful wife" to her husband.

Middleton's love of horror piled on horror led him to choose forced marriage for his theme of *Women Beware Women*. The father of Isabella wishes her to marry a very rich young fool, and the girl's aunt wins her confidence when she says it is unjust to force her niece into any match. When Isabella actually sees the fool she is to marry she turns away sick at heart. She explains her desperate plight to her aunt's brother, whom she also trusts, and finds he takes her grief harder than she does herself. But when she discovers his grief is caused by love for her "as man loves his wife," she is so horrified she flees to her aunt and tells her tearfully she must submit to her father's choice. The aunt, seeing through this sudden "obedience" because she knows of her brother's love for the girl, tells Isabella there is no real blood relationship between her and her uncle. She suggests, therefore, that if she marries the fool she may also have the bliss of true love. Then the aunt exclaims impressively, "O my wench, nothing o'erthrows our sex but indiscretion!" Trapped by the argument, the girl takes the road to ruin by deciding to marry the rich fool and at the same time enjoy the love of a man she believes may partly reward her for the sacrifice demanded by filial obedience. Middleton's poetry united successfully in this play for the audience of his time a morbid interest in the mysteries of sex and an emotional reaction to the whole controversy about forced marriage.

Some unscrupulous Elizabethans might benefit not only by marrying their wards to others but even by marrying the young people themselves if death took their own mates. Brandon had gained wealth in this way when, six weeks after his wife's death, he married his ward Catharine Willoughby. That he had paid Henry VIII £2,266 for this ward indicates how wealthy she was. He brought her up in his household with his two daughters and a niece, the daughter of Queen Margaret of Scotland. When he married the girl of fourteen, he was forty-nine. Such discrepancy in years was frowned upon, but it was not uncommon. Lady Anne Stafford at fourteen was married to the aging Duke of Norfolk, and Surrey's young Geraldine was married to an elderly widower. Needless to say, such marriages were usually based on economic or social advantages sought by ambitious parents or avaricious guardians.

A letter by the Earl of Leicester tells John Scudamore of marriage arrangements he has been making for his nephew. If they are to bring any profits, these arrangements must not fail, and he warns Scudamore he must not ask for too much dowry. He reviews the situation. He secured Scudamore's nephew as ward because at the suggestion of Lady Croft he hoped he might marry the boy to his own kinswoman, Sir James Croft's daughter. The two young people "do very well like," but the marriage "doth not take place" because Scudamore demands more money than the father can pay to dower his daughter. Now Leicester has "travailed" much to match his kinswoman with Scudamore's house, and he prays Scudamore will "deal with the said Sir James Croft in such friendly sort, as not only" to cause Leicester himself to give him "thanks," but also to show Scudamore "from time to time the pleasure and friendship" that may be his to bestow. Writing from the court of King James of Scotland, Leicester signs himself in the usual manner as a "loving friend" who is writing to a "very loving friend."

Sometimes a father leaned over backward in declaring that his efforts to marry his child were without any mercenary motives. When the canny Earl of Pembroke, husband of Mary Sidney Pembroke, wrote the equally shrewd Lord Burghley about the arrangements the two men were making for their children's marriage, Pembroke was careful to lay just the right stress on all the points his letter covered. He says Burghley is doubtful whether his granddaughter Bridget, who is but thirteen, would be so bound at her age as Pembroke's son would be. Second, Burghley wishes to know whether she would stay with Pembroke's wife during the son's tour or with Burghley himself. He then speaks of the lawyers they are to engage and the time at which the arrangements may be completed.

As for the girl's age, he believes at twelve she "can by law consent and be bound by marriage." The young people may be kept separated as long as Burghley thinks "good," but he prefers marriage to a contract for them. He also wishes his son's wife to remain after the marriage in his own home that her care may "answer the nearest whereby she shall then be linked" to her mother-in-law. He is "content" with the lawyers chosen. Then comes the delicate part of the transaction. Since he cannot come to Parliament at peril of his health to see Burghley in person, and since his presence is not necessary for the "private business" they intend, he promises he "will make a jointure proportionable" to what Burghley himself will "give in marriage" with his granddaughter. "I seek not by this match to enrich myself or advance my younger children, for whatsoever you give I am content that the young couple presently have, and I will increase the same with as great a yearly allowance as my estate and course of life can spare." He promises to instruct his representative that his absence is to make "no hindrance" to concluding the negotiations. His son will come up at the beginning of Parliament "both to attend her Majesty's pleasure for his intended travel, and to perform what shall be agreed for his proposed marriage." He closes asking Burghley to secure his license to be absent from Parliament, and gives his proxy to the Secretary.

Since the date of Pembroke's letter is September 3, 1597, Lord Burghley must have conveyed the details of it to his son-in-law immediately to secure his consent to the plans, and for an expression of his judgment about the match. Three days later the Earl of Oxford, Bridget's father, answered Burghley:

I return your letters. I am pleased that my Lord and Lady persevere, for Bridget's sake; I always wished her a good husband. I will freely give an opinion on the articles about it. Lord Pembroke, being sickly, desires in his lifetime to see his son bestowed to his liking; his offers are honorable, and his desires reasonable. It is a thing agreeable to your love and care of my daughter. I know no reason for delay. I hope all parties will receive comfort, as the young gentleman has been well brought up and has good parts. I refer all to your wishes.

This proposed marriage never took place, but the letters about it show the procedure followed in arranging family alliances. Oxford's willingness to let his father-in-law manage Bridget's marriage was probably due to the fact that he had remarried after the death of his child's mother, and had had a son by his second marriage. Having been a ward in Burghley's household, and being well acquainted with the manner in which his father-in-law cared for his dependents, Oxford would be only too glad to entrust his child to such capable hands. Furthermore, feeling that Burghley had more or less tricked him into his marriage with his daughter, Anne, Oxford had been an ungracious husband to the mother of Bridget, and was glad to break free from the whole responsibility of the involvement. He had had three daughters by Anne, however, and matching them brilliantly in marriage was a great responsibility for Burghley. He was not successful with Elizabeth's marriage till she was twenty-three, when she was married to William Stanley, sixth Earl of Derby, to whom, in 1607, she bore a son who was to become the Great Earl of Derby. He was more fortunate in the case of Bridget, who at fifteen became the wife of Francis, later second Lord Norris of Rycote and Earl of Berkshire. In 1604, Susan, at seventeen, was married to Philip Herbert, first Earl of Montgomery. Though Burghley died in 1598, his concern for his granddaughters did not lessen with his last years of increasing ill health. He must have felt Oxford's thrust, therefore, in the reference to Lord Pembroke's "being sickly" and desiring "in his lifetime" to bestow his son "to his liking."

One of the purposes of carefully planned marriages among nobles in particular was to strengthen family alliances in an age when enemies might mask as one's best friends. Consequently, at Elizabeth's court a complicated network of related families was the result. The daughter of Sir Francis Walsingham, the Queen's Secretary, married Sir Philip Sidney and, at his death, Robert Devereux, the Queen's last favorite, Essex; after his execution she was married again. Her daughter by Sidney was married to Roger Manners, fifth Earl of Rutland. The mother of Robert Devereux had four children by Sir Walter Devereux, first Earl of Essex. It was rumored, however, that during her husband's absence at the Irish wars she had two children by the Earl of Leicester, uncle of Sir Philip Sidney, and the first and greatest favorite of the Queen. When Sir Walter died, his wife married Leicester, and her son Robert, second Earl of Essex, became Leicester's stepson, and when Leicester died, Essex stepped into his shoes as favorite of the Queen. The other three legitimate children of Sir Walter were Penelope, Dorothy, and Walter. Penelope had been intended for Sir Philip Sidney, but the rich offer of Lord Rich frustrated those plans. In fairness to the Earl of Huntingdon, Leicester's brother-in-law and Penelope's guardian, it must be conceded that Lord Rich was given the beautiful young prize because the Queen, no longer young and beautiful, probably desired it. She no doubt commanded her favorite, Leicester, and her Secretary, now Burghley, for they were also instrumental in making the match.

Sir Philip Sidney's sister Mary was married to the second Earl of Pembroke, and their son would have been a most advantageous match for Burghley's granddaughter Bridget had the plans materialized. Indeed, had Burghley's matching plans for his granddaughters carried, he would have been grandfather-in-law to Southampton and Pembroke as well as father-in-law to the Earl of Oxford, all of whom are attached to the literary prominence of Shakespeare. When one considers the possible objections that could well have been made to the actual marriages above on grounds of at least spiritual consanguinity, one cannot help being amazed at the achievements in marriage in court circles.

After plans for contracting had been arranged, espousals were performed at the bride's home or at the church, which was used more commonly for both secular and sacred matters of public significance. The priest was the official witness, but handfasting was considered more secure if there were two or more witnesses present at the ceremony. The exchange of gifts, especially from man to woman, was an important part of the ritual. Great significance was attached to the gift of a ring, and though it was usually made by the man to the woman, each might present the other with a token. The couple were not pronounced man and wife till after the final ceremony, but they often used these terms in reference to each other or to other couples contracted by the *de futuro* rite.

As the ring of investiture had long been important in law and as the ring set with an amuletic stone or engraved talismanic formula had long served magic lore, so love must have its ring for espousals. With the fashionable revival of things chivalric during the sixteenth century, the magic formula in Latin or French became very popular for rings and also for brooches to fasten garments at the neck, but most of all, for espousal rings. The motto in honor of his beloved which the knight had shown on his shield and pavilion in tourney lists must now be engraved on his espousal ring to his lady. Sometimes the inscriptions were on the outside of the ring, but usually were inside for only the lovers to see or know. They were short, consisting of a word or brief line: "Forever," "With everlasting love," "Love true," etc. In England the tendency to extend the inscription to little poems gave the rings the name poesy rings. Now the inscriptions were embellished with beautiful Roman capitals, as in "I am Yours, Love me Truly," "After Consent, ever Content." They might also point a moral, especially if in Latin, as in "Let Reason Rule," "Know Thyself," or "Keep a Mean."

In Shakespeare's plays the exchange of rings between man and woman usually means a contracting, and the sentimental value of the tokens is often indicated. For example, Gratiano calls attention to "Love me, and leave me not" engraved in the ring Nerissa gives him. Other such verses might be: "Our contract was Heaven's act; In thee, my choice, I do rejoice," or "Despise not me that joys in thee," etc. Some espousal rings were composed of two or more circlets, each complete in itself with its own stone, and all fitted together in close enough contact to form one ring at the wedding ceremony. A poem might be worked out by means of the hoops, as "Love is fixt, I will not range" for the first hoop; "I like my Choice, I will not change" for the second hoop; "Wit, health, and beauty, all do well" for the third; "But constant Love doth far excel" for the fourth; "Love is sure while faith is pure" for the fifth; "Lost all content, if not consent" for the sixth; and "Love, I like thee; Sweet requite me" for the seventh. Such rings were called joint rings or *gimmal* or *geminal* or *gemmal* rings. Eventually they became quite complicated, comprising as many as eight links, each with its own poesy, the first two circlets for the espoused couple, and the others for witnesses to their *de futuro* contract. At the final ceremony, all witnesses came with their hoops, and when the ring was placed on the bride's finger, it was complete, indeed. A ring was always provided if it could be afforded, even at the most secret handfasting, and sometimes if a couple were so poor they could not afford a silver or pewter or brass ring, they might use one made of a rush. Those who had honest intentions seldom used rings that were not durable, however. When two rings were thought better than one, the young people exchanged rings as they exchanged vows. As the half-hypnotized Anne in Shakespeare's *Richard III* takes the ring from Gloucester with the words, "To take is not to give," she implies she is not contracting her heart, but Gloucester exults over having bound her legally to himself by the ring she accepts from him.

Sometimes before the exchange of rings or even afterward, the lover might wear another favor of his lady in a conspicuous place on his hat. Until 1571, this favor consisted of a tiny handkerchief three or four inches square with a tassel at each corner and a button at the center. It was folded in such a way as to expose the button, which might be as fine as a jewel. Later, jewels and brooches replaced the handkerchiefs, unless the lover preferred to wear his lady's glove. It was also customary to wear the lady's garter on the lover's sleeve, and sometimes her ribbon tied to his lovelocks if he wore his hair long behind one or both ears. Wearing such gifts indicated an exchange of *de futuro* vows or the initial steps in a courtship expected to lead to such vows. During courtship it also became customary for a man to make gifts to his lady and to drink her health in public. His gifts must be appropriate to the girl's social position, of course, and they were more acceptable if accompanied by a nosegay wound round with a bit of poesy, the flowers and poetry eventually being called a posy.

Suitable gifts for ladies were handkerchiefs, gloves, scarfs, girdles, a pair of bracelets, buckles, jewelry, and always the posy with such suggestive lines as "If I think my wife [espoused] fair, What need other people care?" or "As God hath made my choice in thee, So move thy heart to comfort me." If the lover was clever, he might work his initials into his verse, as "Abide with P A tience." Among the common people the gifts to the girl often consisted of practical things like lengths of lawn, caps, and even gowns and petticoats. Pretty presents among the poor would be no less acceptable, and then as now many a maid was wooed by gifts that might predispose her in favor of her lover's suit. Among the upper classes the girl might consent to give her picture to her lover, and sometimes such bracelets as those made from her own shining hair. If he received such treasures, he was to gaze fondly at the picture and wear the bracelet. When Benedick of *Much Ado About Nothing* is persuaded by his friends' overheard gossip that Beatrice loves him, he determines at once to "go get her picture," and thereby persuade the girl she does not love in vain (II:ii: 263–64). John Donne, in "The Funeral," refers to the bracelet of hair.

If the *de futuro* espousal was broken, the civil law ordered all tokens bestowed in hope of marriage to be restored to the giver. If the rebellious one had no sufficient cause for breaking the contract, the gifts were supposed to be returned with a twofold restitution. Since rings, bracelets, and jewelry were the usual gifts, their restitution could usually be made without much difficulty.

At the espousal ceremony, the two young people joined hands, the youth giving the maid a ring to be worn on her right hand and sealing his vow with a kiss. When the wedding was completed this ring was to be worn on the left hand. If the girl also gave a ring, she likewise sealed her promise to marry with a kiss. Shakespeare provides many examples of espousals, some of them regularly formal and some most irregular. In *Twelfth Night*, the secrecy and haste of Olivia's espousals to Sebastian are most irregular. When she succeeds without much effort in persuading him to make the *de futuro* vows, she gives the astonished youth a pearl in token of their betrothal, and he is willing enough to consent to meet her later at an appointed hour. At that meeting she appears with a priest and, with no little agitation, asks Sebastian to bind himself to her with the *de praesenti* vow. He may choose the time for having the marriage solemnized, though it must be according to the rite which her birth and rank require for her. Later, the priest affirms the secret ceremony (V:i:159–64).

Shakespeare does not repeat the vows themselves because they were so well known. The Book of Common Prayer, in its form of solemnization of matrimony, comprises the substance of the pre-Reformation espousal ceremony, and the Anglican form begins with the *de futuro* and immediately follows with the *de praesenti* contract. At this ceremony the priest or minister is the official and sacred witness, and the responses of the couple combine the vows of the two espousal contracts. In *All's Well That Ends Well* the king takes the part of the presiding official as he imperiously commands the resentful Bertram to take the hand of the maid, Helena, to exchange the *de futuro* vows. The *de praesenti* contract is to follow that evening, and the solemnization "upon the coming space expecting absent friends." This king commands like a priest that his subject be true to the vow of his betrothal contract and, to show favor to the maiden, plans in her honor the subsequent ceremonies.

In *Two Gentlemen of Verona* the lovers contract themselves secretly with no witness present, exchanging rings and sealing "the bargain with a holy kiss." With Julia's hand clasped in his, Proteus vows "true constancy." Without a witness, Julia cannot prove the contract when her lover flouts it. Before the play can end happily, therefore, the contract has to be acknowledged by Proteus. On the other hand, the preposterous description Petruchio gives of the exchange of vows between him and Kate in *The Taming of the Shrew* amazes those who hear him and leaves the girl shrew so dumbfounded she cannot deny it. He tells how "the kindliest Kate" so hung about his neck, with "kiss on kiss" and "protesting oath on oath" that she won him "to her love" in but "a twink." Then before all the others, he takes her hand and promises to go immediately to Venice to "buy apparel 'gainst the wedding-day." Her astonished father stammers: "I know not what to say," but recovering, cries out joyfully, ". . . give your hands. God send you joy, Petruchio! 'tis a match," and the younger daughter's suitors chime, "Amen, say we: we will be witnesses." Jauntily Petruchio announces: "Father, and my wife, and gentlemen, adieu." As he is leaving for Venice he promises to bring his Kate "rings, and things, and fine array." Lifting her blank face to his, he says gaily, "Kiss me, Kate, we will be married o' Sunday," and leaves before she can say a word.

The handfasting in *The Tempest* occurs before the cave of Prospero, who presides as ruler and priest of magic, but most of all as proud and happy father. The young man has passed successfully all the tests devised for him, and Prospero, clasping the girl's hand in that of the prince, thereby ratifies his "rich gift" to him, saying she "will outstrip all praise,/And make it halt behind her." Then he calls Ariel to assist him in producing a masque to celebrate "a contract of true love." When the happy lovers are "discovered" to the father of the prince, the youth kneels at his parent's feet, begging the blessing of one he had thought drowned, and the blessing is freely bestowed. In answer to his father's question about the girl, the prince tells how "immortal Providence" has made her his when he could not ask his father for his advice, thinking he had lost his father. The dutiful respect of this son wins the father's blessing for the two lovers.

The handfasting in *The Winter's Tale* does not run so smoothly. Here the prince's father has disguised himself to spy upon his impetuous son who, in turn, has assumed the disguise of a shepherd to woo a beautiful maid he thinks is a shepherdess. A sheep-shearing feast is in progress. When the prince fails to buy a gift for his love from a passing peddler, the disguised father pretends to upbraid his son for neglecting his beloved, hoping thereby to learn from the youth's answer whether he is really in love with the charming shepherdess. The prince falls neatly into the trap, answering his father whom he does not recognize that the girl prefers his love to such trifles. He also admits he has given though not delivered his heart and, turning to the girl, softly asks her permission to declare his love before this "ancient sir." The father requests the prince to repeat to him what he has whispered, and the prince responds warmly, "Do, and be witness to't." The disguised king nods toward his companion also in disguise, and asks his son whether he will include him, too. With a quick smile the prince raises his voice so all at the feast can hear, and proudly declares his love. The king and his companion are secretly pleased, for they have found the girl much nobler than her seeming origin would warrant.

Now the shepherd whom the lass calls father asks her whether she can answer her lover in like manner. She modestly admits she cannot, but her thoughts are like his. Hereupon the old shepherd cries:

> . . . Take hands; a bargain;
> And, friends unknown, you shall bear witness to't;
> I give my daughter to him, and will make
> Her portion equal to his.
>
> IV:iv:392–95

At this promise, unfortunately, the prince's romantic pride rushes him headlong into disaster, for he says that when a certain person dies he will inherit more than the old shepherd can even dream of. Then taking the girl's hand, he asks the shepherd to contract him and his love before all the feasters as witnesses. But while the shepherd is in the act of joining the young people's hands, the king steps forth and asks for speech with the prince.

Because his son has dared to forget his duty to his supposedly absent father, the king has been touched to the quick. Looking earnestly into the youth's eyes, he asks, "Have you a father?" and is shocked at the careless answer, "I have, but what of him?" Wishing to give his son every chance to prove himself, the king says sternly, "Knows he of this?" Now the prince is frightened, but he answers hotly, "He neither does nor shall." The king can scarcely believe his ears, but still wishing to be quite fair, he says:

> . . . Methinks a father
> Is at the nuptial of his son a guest
> That best becomes the table. Pray you, once more,
> Is not your father grown incapable
> Of reasonable affairs? is he not stupid
> With age and altering rheums? can he speak? hear?
> Know man from man? dispute his own estate?
> Lies he not bed-rid? and again does nothing
> But what he did being childish?
>
> IV:iv:403–12

Somewhat sobered by these reasons why a father should not be consulted in regard to his son's choice of a wife, the prince answers that his father has his health and "ampler strength/Than most of his age." Thinking his son has now regained a reasonable state of mind, the king urges him to tell his father of this affair lest he do him great "unfilial" wrong. Then, sadly, he states the father's side in the matter:

> . . . Reason my son
> Should choose himself a wife, but as good reason
> The father, all whose joy is nothing else
> But fair posterity, should hold some counsel
> In such a business.
>
> IV:iv:416–29

The prince, however, fears to impart to his father what he has kept secret with such care lest he be separated forever from his beloved. Still the disguised king entreats him to trust his father, who will most certainly find the girl pleasing. Now the prince grows impatient at so much interference from a supposed stranger, and calls for the contracting. At this point, of course, the king throws off his disguise, and in terms as harsh as his pleading has been reasonable and gentle, declares the old shepherd is a traitor who must hang, and the girl a witch whose beauty will be scratched till she is more homely than a common shepherdess. Finally, he warns his son that if he sees the girl again he will be barred from succession to the throne. Thus a handfasting that should have proceeded happily but for the frightened son's undutiful part in it seems doomed to conclude in grief and terror. Again, however, the play is to provide a happy ending, and Shakespeare must fascinate his audience with the rescue of a disobedient son whose rashness has almost plunged him into ruin. The father's harsh treatment must at the same time be not altogether reprehensible.

In *Much Ado About Nothing* the handfasting details are both formal and informal. Use is made of a prince, who performs the courtesy of wooing a maid for his friend, a young count of Florence. The father's brother, overhearing the plans between the two young men, misunderstands them and thinks the prince is to woo for himself. Naturally, he hastens to the father to inform him of the great honor that is soon to be his. The father is amazed by the prospect of such a brilliant match for his daughter, and is all aflutter at the dance he is providing for the entertainment of his guests. He does promise, however, that he will prepare his daughter for the proposal from the prince.

Our next information is that the prince's suit on behalf of the count has been accepted, and the handfasting scene which follows is very simple. The father approaches the suitor with his daughter, and says, "Count, take my daughter, and with her my fortunes: his Grace hath made the match, and all grace say Amen to it!" The girl's best friend and cousin twits the bashful suitor: "Speak, Count, 'tis your cue," to which he answers: "Silence is the perfectest herald of joy; I were but little happy, if I could say how much." Turning to his beloved, he says, "Lady, as you are mine, I am yours: I give myself for you and dote on the exchange." Now the cousin prompts the shy girl: "Speak, cousin; or, if you cannot, stop his mouth with a kiss, and let not him speak neither." This launches a merry jesting in which the answer is lost or never given except, perhaps, in a trembling kiss.

The importance of the play on rings in *The Merchant of Venice* is due almost entirely to the fact that espousal rings are involved. As Portia plights herself in the *de futuro* contract with Bassanio and gives him a ring, she humbly describes herself and her fortune, which she obediently places before her lord. She calls herself an "unlesson'd girl" who is happy that she is "not yet old/But she may learn," and thus commits herself to "be directed/As from her lord, her governor, her king." All that she is and has "is now converted" to her betrothed—her "fair mansion," her servants, and herself. As she gives him the ring, she says he must not lose it or give it away lest it "presage the ruin" of his love, and give her the mastery (III:ii:161–76). Elated by her generosity, Bassanio places the ring on his finger with the rash oath that parting from the ring will be only on pain of death. When later in the play Portia and her maid in disguise persuade their contracted husbands to part with their espousal rings, they prepare for the ring scene in the last act of the play, which adds to the touch of complicated seriousness Elizabethans demanded in their comedy.

In this scene Portia first criticizes severely her maid's espoused lover for parting "so slightly" with his "wife's" first gift. Then turning to her husband, she tells how he would not part with the ring she gave him for the wealth of all the world. Bassanio's aside touches on the grotesque that startles:

> Why, I were best to cut my left hand off,
> And swear I lost the ring defending it.

Portia's "discovery" of his broken promise enables her to feign resentment while she delivers with telling effect a little sermon on erring husbands.

Both this *de futuro* espousal and the ring episode serve to divide the mastery of the bond between husband and wife equally, a most romantic idea to some Elizabethans, simply fantastic to others. In plighting her troth, Portia had sworn complete submission to her spouse according to the Elizabethan teaching, but now, though she has won the mastery in marriage by means of Bassanio's broken promise, she does not take it. Instead, she adopts the sane, intelligent attitude of emotional maturity. No matter how much in love, she knows she must arm herself against the future. So she sees to it that the husbands in the scene are made sufficiently aware of the change in their wives to be embarrassed by it, but not too embarrassed. The friend whose life was saved comes to their defense by taking all the blame upon himself. He has lent his body once to his friend Bassanio; now he is ready to be bound again even to his soul that Bassanio will "never more break faith . . ." Realizing the jest has gone far enough, Portia seizes upon the words of the friend, saying, "Then you shall be his surety." Putting into his hand the *de futuro* espousal ring she had given Bassanio, she says smilingly, "Give him this, and bid him keep it better than the other." Nerissa, her maid, does somewhat the same with her ring, and true Elizabethan laughter and jest follow. Without the importance Elizabethans attached to handfasting and espousal rings, the whole episode would be pointless, and lest this emphasis be slighted, Shakespeare concludes the play with the words of the irrepressible Gratiano chiming his half-rueful witticism:

> Well, while I live I'll fear no other thing
> So sore as keeping safe Nerissa's ring.

All this romantic love in Shakespeare's plays suggests marriages in which the wife is obedient to her husband, who, in turn, is considerate of his wife. In real life such relationships are always rare, but one wonders whether they were not more nearly approximated in an age that made so very much of such attachments in its conduct books, private correspondence, state papers, memoirs, sermons, etc. Such concord is apotheosized by the wife of Colonel Hutchinson as she tells of her husband's character. When he became "possessed with strong and violent affections" for her he would not declare his love till he first told his father. Although the father had made other plans "before he knew of his son's inclinations," he was so "honorably indulgent" that he broke off the negotiations in spite of the fact that they would have been "much more advantageous for his family, and more worthy of his liking." With such a father, her husband naturally had high ideals of integrity. He "would never make any engagement but what his love and honor bound him in;

wherein he was more firm and just than all the promissory oaths and ties in the world could have made him, notwithstanding many powerful temptations of wealth and beauty, and other interests that were laid before him."

His "passion" for her was "ardent" but not "idolatrous." He loved her "better than his life, with inexpressible tenderness and kindness," yet still he considered "honor, religion, and duty" above her, "nor ever suffered intrusion of such a dotage as should blind him from marking her imperfections." These he looked upon with so much indulgence as not to "abate his love and esteem" of her. At the same time he tried to "blot out all these spots" which might make her appear "less worthy of that respect" he paid her. In this way he soon made her "more equal to him" than he found her, and she became a "very faithful mirror, reflecting truly, though but dimly, his own glories." She believed "the greatest excellency" she had "was the power of apprehending and the virtue of loving him." Like his shadow, she "waited on him everywhere till he was taken into that region of light which admits of none . . ." It was not her face he loved, she believed, but her virtue and honor and the Pygmalion images of his own making in her as he polished the rough stone from the quarry till she became a "compliant subject for his own wise government."[25]

Then she tells of her wedding day. When friends of both their families met to conclude the marriage, she fell sick of the smallpox, and was a great trial to him. First, her life was in "almost desperate hazard," and then the disease made her the "most deformed person that could be seen, for a great while" after she was recovered. Yet he seemed "nothing troubled at it," but married her as soon as she was able to leave her chamber, even though the priest and all that saw her were "affrighted" to look upon her. But God "recompensed his justice and constancy" by restoring her to her former state. True, the wife records these impressions of her husband after death has blotted out for her all his imperfections. Still, with due allowance for her bias and her conventional expressions, she does enable one to feel that harmony was achieved by intense effort at adjustment in this marriage.

In England, where the domestic relations were so important, it was natural for both civil and ecclesiastical authority to lay much stress upon the ceremony by which marriage was not only sanctified but also made morally impressive. Gouge called it a kind of public action that "tended much" to the good or hurt of family, Church, and Commonwealth. John Donne, in one of his wedding sermons, called it a "civil contract" in that it must be enacted in public to have "the testimony of men," and a "reli-

[25] Mrs. Lucy Apsley Hutchinson, *Memoirs of the Life of Colonel Hutchinson* (ed. by the Rev. Julius Hutchinson, 1906), pp. 52–53.

gious contract" in that it must have the "benediction of a priest." Without the testimony of men there could be no claim to any benefit of law, and without the benediction of a priest there could be no benefit of Church. No matter how much any couple "may pretend to love and live together, yet all that love and all that life is but regulated adultery," not marriage, he said.

Because of its solemnity, marriage was therefore thought to be best celebrated in the daytime "as a work of light that need not be covertly and closely done," and in a public place where objections might be freely presented and witnesses easily provided. The church was also recognized as the fittest place for it because it was a house of prayer, "where persons and actions are most solemnly blessed." A church official was preferred to a civil magistrate because the ecclesiast stood in "God's room, and by his ministry God joined" together the couple desiring matrimony. Because a secret marriage in home or church was not acceptable to society, such prominent people as Lady Essex and the Earl of Leicester were criticized for their secret marriage soon after the death of the Earl of Essex in Ireland. Therefore the widow's father insisted that she be married in a public ceremony, which occurred at Wanstead on September 21, 1578, before the Earls of Warwick, North, and others. Puritans, of course, always advocated church weddings before a congregation of people, for, as Bullinger had said, such a marriage showed honesty in the act and God's sanction of that act; furthermore, a promise made before many people was more likely to be kept. He also believed marriage ceremonies reminded others of their promises, and were thus good to hear. Finally, the prayer of the whole congregation for the blessing of the couple was always good in itself.

Before the reign of Edward VI, it was customary for the wedding to take place in the porch of the church, but the reformers decided so solemn a tie should be made fast in the church proper. When Queen Mary revived old customs, she included among them marriage in the church porch, and although in Elizabeth's time the Protestants insisted upon weddings in the body of the church, the old fashion of porch weddings continued on through the century. Gradually, however, it lost favor and eventually disappeared.

One of the most troublesome problems concerned with wedding plans was the date of the ceremony. The old prohibition of marriage during the holy seasons of Advent (including the four weeks before Christmas), Septuagesima (including Lent and the three weeks before Lent), and the time from Rogation to Trinity Sunday tended to affect the social morals, according to reformers who removed the restrictions of these periods. Nevertheless, people continued to feel marriage at these times was improper. Marriage had been forbidden during solemn feasts as well as during fasts, and these prohibitions had to be watched carefully. May had once been a favorite month for love and marriage, as seen in the old romances, but through various rulings in the Church, it became associated with ill luck, for the custom of honoring the dead at this time by solemn rites struck a discordant note in the merrymaking of wedding feasts. April and November thus became favorite months for marriage.

During the confusion about marriage regulations in Elizabeth's reign, the time of day for celebrating weddings and even the day of week became as variable as the seasons of the year. Night weddings, though disapproved of, might occur at any hour, but day weddings were most favored between eight in the morning and noon, probably because of the old custom of marrying before noon. If a wedding occurred in the spring, however, it was usually celebrated at dawn. Puritans preferred Sunday morning for their church weddings since a whole congregation could witness the ceremony at that time.

The wedding itself consisted of three steps: delivering the bride by her parents or guardian to the bridegroom, the priest's or minister's sanctioning of the marriage before the congregation, and escorting the bride to her new home. As a rule, there were many festivities attached to an Elizabethan wedding. Whether it occurred among the nobles or the common people, it required as elaborate preparation as the families of the couple could afford. In all this merrymaking, the chief concerns were the wedding feast and the entertainment of the wedding guests. First, however, the house must be prepared for the guests, and aside from the usual cleaning and refurbishing called for, the rooms must be strewn with rosemary and roses. The hall and chambers must be especially made ready in this manner, partly for the sweet odor provided by the flowers and partly for their significance, the rosemary supposedly strengthening the memory, and roses preventing wrangling, sullenness, or strife between the newly married pair. Roses festooned above the tables also reminded the revelers of the old promise that merry companions at a banquet must not reveal anything spoken under the rose.[26]

Delivering the bride to the groom usually involved a procession to the church, and the elaborateness of this procedure as well as the entire wedding varied as much then as now. The guests, and particularly the families to be united by the young people, wore their best apparel, but did not, as a rule, feel impelled to have a special wardrobe for the occasion. The agitated bride of *Much Ado About Nothing* confers nervously with her companions about her dress, collar, and gloves. One of them, anxious to calm her, describes the beauty of an elaborate gown worn by the Duchess of Milan, yet stoutly declares it was only a dressing gown compared with the one the bride has chosen from her best gowns. Somewhat quieted, the bride picks up a pair of gloves given her by her betrothed and enjoys for a moment their "excellent perfume," then con-

[26] Laevinus Lemnius, *Herbal from the Bible, drawen into English by T. Newton* (1587).

tinues her adorning. For such occasions gloves and scarfs were important, as they added the colorful details women love in fancy dress. That the wedding was to occur early in the morning is indicated by the need to rouse a cousin, who was no sluggard, to come to help dress the bride. Shakespeare carefully appealed to sixteenth-century interest in weddings. In *Romeo and Juliet* he has the Capulets concerned about their preparations for a sumptuous banquet, and leaves the gown to Juliet's choice. The parents and nurse and many of the servants have apparently stayed up all night attending to the details of baked meats, cakes, etc., and in the early morning the father rouses the other servants after the second cock's crow, bidding them hurry about their tasks lest anything be amiss when County Paris arrives with his musicians to waken his bride with an *aubade*.

Ordinarily bridesmaids and groomsmen assisted at elaborate weddings, each with set duties for the occasion. The bridesmaids were expected to knot yards of floral rope for hanging on walls of galleries as well as banquet chambers, to see that rushes were strewn from the bride's home to the church, or at least before the entrance to the bride's home, and these covered with flowers, especially roses. Then they were to make little favor bouquets for the guests to carry, to knot the ribbon favors for the bride's gown and stitch them to the bodice, sleeves, and skirt, and finally, to make the garland for the bride's head. This garland might be of fresh or gilded flowers, rosemary, myrtle or bay leaves, or possibly of gilded wheat ears. The two chief bridesmaids dressed the bride, received presents for her, distributed favors to the guests, and arranged the order of the procession, each maid carrying in her hand a chaplet and wearing on her breast a sprig of rosemary or a bouquet of flowers. The bride's hair was carefully combed and sometimes curiously braided, or it was brushed so that it might hang down her back like a veil.

Sometimes the brides wore wedding knives and daggers as part of their costume, but the conventional bride must have three ornaments: the engagement ring, the brooch of innocence on her breast, and the garland she usually carried in her hand till after the ceremony, when she put it on her head and wore it. Sometimes, however, the garland was replaced by a little cap of lace or richly jeweled material. There was much significance attached to the garland, for it suggested that gladness and dignity were a crown to the bride's virtuous course against evil temptations before marriage. In medieval England the bride's right to wear this garland was one of her most treasured privileges. There was even serious discussion about whether gilded or natural flowers should be used for the bridal "crown," Polydore Virgil at Henry VIII's court preferring gilded wheat ears to anything else. In 1607, the preacher Hackett, in a wedding sermon called *A Marriage Present*, urged brides to wear "sweet smelling flowers" with their "native fragrance" instead of those "gilded with the art of man." Most Elizabethan brides did wear flowers, but Herrick's bride in his *Hesperides* wears a garland of gilded rosemary and bay leaves.

The love knots sewed on the bride's dress symbolized the tie that was to bind her to the groom, and the bride usually deliberated long before choosing the colors for these knots. Purple and white or green and white were favorite colors for the garland, with blue, red, peach, orange, tawny, and flame for the love knots, and milk white or russet for the dress. There was not perfect agreement as to the suggestiveness of these colors, however. Gold supposedly indicated avarice, yet perfect yellow was the symbol of joy and honor or of jealousy or of fading love. Green suggested wantonness to some, and fidelity to others. There was more agreement about blue for constancy, flesh for lasciviousness, violet for religious fervor, and red, orange, and peach for good omen. Garters were often blue or perfect yellow. Brides of highest rank usually wore a dress of cloth of gold and chose other colors according to their taste.

The groomsmen had their duties also, for they served as valets to the groom on the wedding morning, trimming his beard and locks, and adorning him with rosettes and streamers of the bride's colors. If there were no pages to escort the bride to church, the groomsmen performed this service; otherwise they walked behind the groom. Their other duties were to direct the ceremonies at the dancing and sports enjoyed by the guests after the marriage ceremony, and to arrange for the seating of friends at the feast, each strictly according to rank.

When the procession was ready to make its way to church, it followed no set order, though in itself it reflected the taste of the bride's family. In general, a rosemary bearer and minstrels came first, followed by the bride, walking between two bachelors, and escorted by her maids as well as knights or pages or groomsmen. Then came her family and friends, though her father was not too far removed because of his part in the ceremony—delivering his daughter to the groom. At the church the bride was usually met by the groom, though sometimes he was not seen till he awaited the bride at the altar. At other times he walked with the bridesmaids. If the bride was led to the altar by pages, she was preceded by her bridesmaids. Unless prevented from doing so, the onlookers might close in after the procession passed by. For such occasions the rabble carried their own "music" and dispelled any semblance of order. This hilarity was likely to occur only at weddings lacking the dignity provided by wealth or power.

To most Elizabethans, a marriage without noise was a poor thing, for noise shut out evil influences and indicated the nature of marriage as one of the crises of life. So there was the blaring of trumpets and the beating of drums and the clashing of cymbals. The drum was the chief instrument, the poorer people making hollow bones serve the purpose and, for cymbals and trumpets, using cleavers, tongs, shovels, saucepan lids, and tin kettles containing pebbles. At church there might be organ music and choirs with fine voices to add to the solemnity of the occasion.

On the return from church the noise of the procession continued its fanfare, however.

Thomas Deloney describes a wedding procession among the industrious middle class in his romantic *History of Jack of Newberry*. His purpose, of course, is to show the fine taste of those in trade as they copied the manners of their betters. The bride is attired in a gown of russet woolen and a kirtle of fine worsted. Her bright yellow hair, curiously combed and plaited, hangs down her back from her garlanded head. Musicians play all the way before the procession. Immediately behind them, and just preceding the bride, is a rosemary bearer, with a "fair bride-cup of silver and gilt . . . wherein was a goodly branch of rosemary gilded very fair, hung with silken ribbons of all colors." The bride was led to church "between two sweet boys [pages], with bridelaces and rosemary tied about their silken sleeves." After her came all the chiefest maidens of the country, some bearing great bridecakes, and some garlands of wheat finely gilded. They were followed by her relatives and friends, and then by the wedding guests.

Suitable gifts for those who could not afford more were chaplets and sweetmeats, the bride and her maids carrying the chaplets to church and wearing them at the ceremony. The guests at such a wedding might carry dishes of food or sweetmeats as they walked in the procession. After the wedding sermon there usually occurred the drinking of wine with sops in it, which were relished by the married couple and the witnesses. The bridecup for this occasion was as fine as the family could provide, unless the church supplied a bowl or cup for this purpose. Sometimes a sprig of rosemary was dipped in the wine before each drank. It was common practice to carry the rosemary of good omen with the bridecup in the wedding procession that each might dip it in the wine later to bring good luck. In poor people's weddings the food gifts carried by the guests were frequently a matter of much satisfaction, for if the ceremony occurred in the early morning, two meals were supposed to be served guests on the wedding day. Sometimes the expenses of weddings were partly defrayed by holding bride-ales at the church, where the bride sold ale for as much as her friends could pay.

In a country wedding the path to church was strewn with rushes and flowers in much the same way as in the city. Along it came the bride and her two bachelor escorts, with the groom led frequently by the bridesmaids carrying their chaplets of gilded rosemary to ensure the couple constancy and love. In some villages the bride and groom were expected to jump over a louping (leaping) stone in the churchyard or a flower garland on their way home; if they refused they had to pay a forfeit, which might be a rough-and-tumble kissing of the bride. Consequently the bride often preferred risking the leap. Since there was much guessing about who was next to marry, charms were consulted for the answer.

At the same time charms were used to determine whether the newly married couple were to be happy. A hilarious game for this purpose consisted of breaking a cake over the bride's head at her return home and reading her future in the scattered pieces.

Elizabethans took much pride in their wedding processions, though the celebrants might become too sportive. The Puritans disapproved of the excessive gaiety, Bullinger saying that in spite of the good nature of the celebration, the "devil hath crept in" there too, and caused it to be "blemished with all manner of lightness." He complained of how "early in the morning the wedding people begin to exceed in superfluous eating and drinking" and as a result "spit until the sermon be done," though some of them are too drunk even to spit. Consequently they "regard neither the preaching nor the prayer." Of course he criticized them for coming to church "with all manner of pomp and pride, and gorgeousness of raiment and jewels." Worse still, they came with "a great noise of harps, lutes, kettles, basins, and drums," after which they troubled the whole church and hindered matters pertaining unto God. He saw them, therefore, as coming into the Lord's house as if it were a house of merchandise "to lay forth their wares and offer to sell themselves unto vice and wickedness." And even as they came so they went forth again "in shameful pomp and vain wantonness."

The noisy processions, however, were pretty much like other abuses of Saint Paul's great interior, which was used for walking, talking, quarreling, and usual street occurrences. In the middle of "Paul's Walk" or "Humphrey's Walk" all kinds of business was transacted between merchants, lovers, and the riff-raff of the street. "At the pillars," in one corner of the Cathedral, stood the lawyers, ready to receive clients; in another were peddlers, crying their wares. The tombs and even the font were used as counters for business. In the churchyard were bookstalls, and if storage space was needed for extra printed matter, including romances, jest books, gay verse, and grave sermons, it might be convenient to use even the vaults. In such a confusion of scenes, a wedding procession was but one more gay little whistle.

Possibly the display of vanities was the most irksome thing of all to the Puritans as they noted the extravagant expenditure of money at weddings. Since all the classes were striving to emulate the vanities of those immediately above them, royalty set a pace that made the race a strenuous one. The Queen's fondness for dress was shared by her successors, and when James I's daughter, the tiny Princess Elizabeth, was married, the train of her cloth of silver dress was valued at £130, and was borne by sixteen bridesmaids who had to be dressed suitably for the occasion. When one considers that the materials for such ceremonies might cost Elizabethans as much as £30 to £50 a yard, one may well imagine the groans of the fathers whose daughters were asked to serve as bridesmaids. No wonder, then, most brides had to be content with a wedding gown chosen from dresses already in their wardrobe, and that the bridesmaids must do likewise.

Nevertheless, the formal Elizabethan wedding was as impressive as it could be made. After the procession had made its way to the altar, where, as a rule, the groom was awaiting the bride, she took her place on his left side. Then the church official (there were no priests after 1584) began the service with the well-known words that take their phrasing from the ceremony used as far back as the twelfth century, their form being perpetuated with but slight change in the first English Prayer Book: "Dearly beloved, we are gathered here in the sight of God, and in the face of this company, to join together this Man and this Woman in holy Matrimony; which is an honorable estate, instituted of God in the time of man's innocency, signifying unto us this mystical union that is betwixt God and his Church." The service would continue with reference to Christ's first miracle at the marriage of Cana, and then would come the question that always brought an anxious pause—can "any man show just cause" why this couple should not be "lawfully joined together, let him now speak, or else hereafter forever hold his peace." Any irregularity in the espousal contracts could be corrected now by asking the couple solemnly whether there was any possible impediment to their union. If their answers were satisfactory, the minister proceeded to confirmation of the *de futuro* and *de praesenti* vows.

His first question, therefore, was asked of the groom: "Wilt thou have this Woman to live with . . . after God's ordinance in the holy estate of Matrimony . . . to love her, comfort her, honor, and keep her in sickness and in health," forsaking all others for so long as both shall live? Upon receiving the *de futuro* promise of "I will," he then asked the bride, "Wilt thou have this Man" to live with according to God's law, to "obey him, and serve him, love, honor, and keep him in sickness and in health," forsaking all others for him so long as both shall live? At her answer of "I will," the minister was given the bride by her father or guardian or nearest relative.

Now the ceremony proceeded to confirm the *de praesenti* vows. If the bride was a maid, she placed her ungloved right hand in her future husband's right palm: if a widow, her right hand was covered with a glove. Holding her hand firmly in his, the groom then repeated after the minister the words: "I take thee to be my wedded Wife, to have and to hold from this day forward, for better and for worse, for richer and for poorer, in sickness and in health, to love and to cherish, till death do us part, according to God's ordinance; and thereto I plight thee my troth." Then loosing hands, the bride took her husband's right hand in her right hand, and repeated after the minister: "I take thee to be my Husband, to have and to hold from this day forward, for better and for worse, for richer and for poorer, in sickness and in health, to love, cherish, and to obey, till death do us part, according to God's ordinance; and thereto I give thee my troth." During this part of the ceremony, the bride may have observed the old Roman custom of holding in her left hand three wheat ears.

The next step, the ring ceremony, was followed by all the participants with close interest. If the popular three-jointed gimmel ring was used, it might be made of three plain circlets or it might be very elaborate. At any rate, the hoops would now be united, and the event would become significant for the lovers and the witnesses. In this ring a hand might be attached to the side of the upper and lower hoops in such a fashion as to close over the heart on the middle hoop. If engraved, each hoop would contain one of three verses to make a poem. Sometimes the heart was a jewel, and sometimes this central hoop was an emerald circlet engraved inside and adorned outside with very small stones. For Puritans, the ring was a plain gold circlet, unless a cheaper metal was used.

Before the outlawing of priests, if the ring had not been previously blessed it was sprinkled with holy water at this part of the ceremony and consecrated with prayers and benedictions. To devout members of the Church, the ring part of the service had always been of great consequence because of the general belief in the ring being endowed by its function with the power to conquer disease and to frustrate devils. Since it was such an essential part of the service, all maids insisted on one no matter how cheap. They must have felt uneasy, however, when a rush ring was given them, for it was frequently used at mock ceremonies, chiefly by men who were attempting to seduce some unsuspecting maid, and in early times it had been commonly used to make legal an illicit union.

Some change occurred in the ring part of the service after the Reformation. If a priest in the old days had blessed a ring before the "churching," the groom at this point in the service gave it to the priest, at the same time putting on the holy man's book gold or silver or a purse of gold in order to indicate the generous provision he intended to make for his wife. The priest then took the ring with his thumb and first two fingers, and pronounced the following words which the groom repeated after him: "With this ring I thee wed, and this gold and silver I thee give, and with my body I thee worship, and with all my worldly chattels I thee endow," holding the ring meanwhile above the wife's left hand. Then, holding it momentarily over the thumb of her left hand, he continued, "In the name of the Father," then over the end of the first finger, "and of the Son," then on the tip of the next finger, "and of the Holy Ghost," and then, pressing it down on the third finger, concluded, "Amen!" Naturally, with the general simplification of the church services, the ring service was shortened. Instead of the priest, therefore, the groom was the one to place the ring on the finger or thumb, saying merely, "With this ring I thee wed, and with all my worldly goods I thee endow: in the name of the Father, and of the Son, and of the Holy Ghost. Amen."

The next step in this part of the ceremony was little changed by the reformers. After placing the ring, the priest had given the benediction: "May you be blessed by the Lord, who made the Universe out of nothing!" Then, with a recital of the Lord's Prayer and a special blessing upon the newly married couple, the priest joined their hands again and said solemnly, "Those whom God hath joined together, let no man put asunder." Now, addressing the congregation, he would pronounce them "Man and Wife, in the name of the Father, and of the Son, and of the Holy Ghost, Amen." Finally came the benediction: "God the Father, God the Son, and God the Holy Ghost, bless, preserve, and keep you; the Lord mercifully with his favor look upon you, and fill you with all spiritual benediction and grace; that ye may so live together in this life, that in the world to come ye may have life everlasting. Amen."

The wedding sermon, of course, took the place of the mass for marriage. But the importance of the mass had been felt so profoundly that its influence was not lost immediately. The gradual change in the old service, therefore, made the substitution of the marriage sermon for it less distressing to the devout. In the old service, the sacred canopy had been held over the couple in the priest's quarter of the church while the couple prostrated themselves at the foot of the altar and the chief of the official clergy pronounced the sacramental benediction that was to purge all taint of the carnal element from the marriage mystery and make it truly symbolical of the Lord's union with the Church. Then, walking at the right of her husband, the bride had followed the ecclesiasts into the church, across the people's quarter, and up the chancel to the foot of the shrine, while the choir had chanted the following verses from the 128th Psalm:

Blessed is everyone that feareth the Lord; that walketh in his ways.
For thou shalt eat the labor of thine hands; happy shalt thou be,
    and it shall be well with thee.
Thy wife shall be as a fruitful vine by the sides of thy house:
    thy children like olive plants round thy table.
Behold that thus shall the man be blessed that feareth the Lord.
The Lord shall bless thee out of Zion; and thou shalt see
    the good of Jerusalem all the days of thy life.
Yea, thou shalt see thy children's children, and peace upon Israel.

Then while the bride and groom had knelt at the altar, the carecloth had been raised over them and held by four ecclesiasts, although the sacramental benediction was withheld from the couple if either of them had been married before.

When the wedding sermon finally supplanted the marriage mass, the couple was required to listen to a dissertation on the duties of wedlock

or to the reading of some passage of Scripture that might "inspire them
with conjugal virtue and strengthen them for conflict with the special difficulties of matrimony." Of all Elizabethan sermons, these were probably
the most popular, especially when an excellent speaker related personal
experience dealing with the perils or trials of marriage and explained
how the young couple should bear with each other in order to avoid discord in their lives. Most of all he was heard attentively when he described
the "innocent arts" they might use "to preserve and to stimulate their
mutual love." These sermons were probably attended by those who
would quote the minister's personal illustrations or "sentences" of advice
or whatever might be useful in quick repartee, for many clever divines
in Elizabeth's time were not averse to diverting those among the congregation who kept their ears pricked for anything that might serve for badinage at dinner or elsewhere in social conversation. Then as now, con-
sciously or under emotional stress, ministers might stoop to the sensational.

But there were serious listeners also and serious speakers intent on
more than notoriety. Those involved in the marriage which was being
solemnized would be most affected, no doubt, for they would realize
they were entering a life contract. Ordinary Elizabethans never looked
upon marriage otherwise because divorce was so difficult and expensive,
requiring an Act of Parliament for each case. Since the only separation
most married people ever expected was death, the minister might well
suggest ways and means by which to become tolerant and faithful and
ready to build married life on one, and only one, foundation. And since
they actually looked forward to making their marriage genuinely happy,
rarely did it end in separation. When that misfortune did occur, it was
usually caused by flaws in the marriage settlements, particularly by the
omission of sufficient provision for a wife's rights to her own property.
If these rights were not stipulated in the contract, her husband was given
full control of his wife's wealth.

Of course, some husbands might be bad managers and run through
all their wife's and their own property that they could put their hands
on; still marriage contracts were usually so drawn up that even in such
a contingency the wife and family would be protected. The minister,
with these things in mind, always stressed the husband's duty of providing for his family. He also emphasized the need of faithfulness for husbands who were required to be absent from home on business, state or
private, and he showed that when temptation lay before susceptible men
it could bring the wife misery. If there were temperamental difficulties,
they had to be faced, not run away from. When the minister spoke of
the husband trusting his wife like a partner, he meant the words literally,
for such was the expected relationship between husband and wife. Thus,
when a husband had to be absent from home, he usually expected his
wife to act as his agent, and gave her full power to do so.

After listening to a long discourse on marriage and its duties, the bridal party was more than eager to enjoy the wine and bread and sweetmeats served before they began the procession toward home. In the old days the priests had blessed the refreshments, and now the ministers observed this custom with the words: "Bless, O Lord, this bread and this drink and this cup, even as thou blessed the five loaves in the desert, and the six water pots at Cana of Galilee, that they who taste of them may be sane, sober, and spotless: Savior of the world, who lives and reigns with God the Father in the unity of the Holy Ghost." Now the bridecup with its sprig of rosemary was passed about, and the groom was given the benediction kiss, after which he bestowed it upon the bride. The old custom was for one of the priest's assistants to kiss the wedding guests, each in succession with due decorum. The kissing of the bride and sometimes of both bride and groom by the guests was a later innovation. The wine and sops consisted of bread or cake broken in small pieces and floating in the wine. This part of the ceremony was to be conducted with the same decorum observed in the rest of the marriage service, whether the bridal party was made up of members of royalty or of the common people.

Because the church nave was used for so many kinds of secular business, a wedding banquet at church might be spread in the people's quarters after the bridal party had made a procession throughout the less sacred part of the church. But whether the feast occurred at home or in the church, the bride's cake was first carried to the church, and afterward distributed among the guests. The church drinking cup (mazer bowl) was of maple or hardwood and ornamented or rimmed with gold or silver. Those who could not afford muscatel used ale, and if any ale was left after the guests had been refreshed, the bride of limited means might sell the surplus for whatever it would bring. It was very easy for friends to see that there was such a surplus if they wished to help the young couple financially.

There were other ways of helping impecunious young couples. Among the poor shires in England the parents extended invitations to all their friends they wished to attend the daughter's wedding. When the couple was proclaimed man and wife at the church ceremony, these friends cast presents into a basin or dish or cup placed upon a table in the church for that purpose. They also aided the poor parents with the wedding feast, for the dishes which they brought for it were carefully determined upon beforehand so that there might be a pleasant variety of food.

The giving of gifts by members of both families was supposed to signify the binding together of the two groups. Then, as now, gifts were often showered upon young married people by friends who felt it a part of their social obligations to the two families involved. Sir Robert Sidney's secretary wrote his master that the gifts at the marriage of Lord Herbert and Anne Russell "were valued at £1,000 in plate and jewels at least." This wedding was attended by Queen Elizabeth who, at the landing stage of the Thames, was carried up the stairs in a litter borne by six knights. The wedding arrangements mostly followed the usual plan, but they were very sumptuous, as the Queen's presence would indicate. Anne's white dress was covered with love knots in various colors. Music beneath her window announced the groom's arrival, and as soon as the wedding service was completed, the young men and maids scrambled for the ribbon favors while the older people drank muscatel from the mazer bowl. As a rule, ribbon favors were not granted till much later in the celebration. Anne and her husband were escorted to their home over sanded streets. The house was festooned with wreaths and flowers. Here in the garden the guests walked and listened to music or looked at the wedding gifts displayed for this purpose, and then all sat down to a sumptuous banquet. After the refreshments came entertainment by a masque.

Gifts must be provided for others besides the married couple. For the bridesmaids fringed grosgrain silk scarfs in bright colors were favored, and gauntleted gloves for the groomsmen. For the guests wedding rings were expected. These were not necessarily engraved inside, but might be provided with simple inscriptions like "A friend to find, No time unkind," "A knot knits love," or "A blessing we do hope to see." Among the rich bride's gifts were candlesticks, fireplace sets, sometimes in silver, gold or silver basins and ewers, cups of various kinds, fancy warming pans of gold or silver, hangings for a room, and all kinds of plate. Poor brides were usually given money or household linens, etc. It was a time for people to be generous and a time to make a display of generosity.

Most bridal parties left the church immediately after the refreshments provided them and proceeded in stately procession to the home or festal house, with musicians playing and the ribbons of the bride's colors fluttering gaily. On the return, however, the bride walked between two married men instead of bachelors. In the country, there was often a race by the young men on horses, the winner receiving a steaming cup of hot pottage or broth, but such hilarity did not belong to the conventional procession of those who cared for dignity. In the city there was much more likely to be closer adherence to formality, but sometimes even here decorum broke down, according to the Puritans, in a scandalous manner.

Since the fundamental purpose of Elizabethan marriage was to provide continuity of the family, much of their ritual was intended to aid in making the union fruitful, to obviate the dangers of sexual intercourse, especially at defloration, and to facilitate the various stages of generation from the first act to the final delivery of the child. Many of these rites were so old as to have lost their origin in the mists of antiquity, and most of them were observed from the moment the bride entered the environs of her home.

The most prominent among these fertility rites was the use of fruit or grain or tiny oaten cakes sprinkled over the newly married pair on their return, and later in the nuptial bed. In Scotland, besides breaking the oaten cake over the heads of the couple as they entered the house, there was the practice of serving the guests whisky. In England, these small cakes were made of eggs, milk, sugar, spice, and the inevitable currants they used for every delicacy. Some of the guests tried to squeeze pieces of these cakes through their wedding rings before throwing them over the bride's head; others ate the cakes with much jesting; still others kept their cakes to place under their pillows to bring pleasant dreams, and some threw theirs to the poor folk thronging the house, crying for "bell money" or a "largess." If any cakes were left, they were piled into a pyramid before the couple at the feast. The present custom of breaking a cake over the bride's head is in memory of the old fertility rite whose purpose was to avert the dangers of defloration and to facilitate the consummation of the union. In medieval times a bride was sometimes forced to submit to embraces of other men, probably because of the superstitious awe with which defloration was regarded.

Other means of supposedly aiding fertility were for a child to accompany the bride to the altar like a little flower girl of today, or for a little boy to bear the ring on a cushion, or for both little girl and little boy to accompany her, one with a flower basket and the other bearing the ring. Untying the knots or laces on the bride's costume was supposed to produce an easy delivery at childbirth. Sometimes, as at Anne Russell's marriage, the guests might dash up to the bride as soon as the service was completed and seek to pluck the knotted ribbons from her dress, but as a rule this free-for-all merriment was delayed till the evening's festivities were at a lull, and the bride and groom were ready to depart for the nuptial couch. Religious families always offered up prayers and sacrifices for the happiness and welfare of the couple when they left the guests.

The wealthy and powerful added to the festivity and splendor expected of them by tilts and tourneys, rich with gorgeous pageantry, and with poets and artists laboring by means of masques to augment the lavish exhibition. But before all this display came the feasting. After Jane Grey's wedding the poor received beef, bread, and ale for three days, and after the wedding of the burghers described in Deloney's fiction, the bridal party feasted on wine and victuals for ten days "to the great relief of the poor that dwelt all about." This remembering of the needy with "crumbs from the table" was expected of all who sought to carry off the whole wedding with general approval. The Puritans objected to the wasteful extravagance of such a custom, and when Gouge drew up his list of things to be avoided at a wedding, he mentioned celebrating feasts on Sundays or in time of mourning, expending more for feasts than a person could afford, gluttony or drunkenness at the feasts, and forgetting to serve food to the poor. Most of all, however, he objected to "poisoning" the company at a wedding feast with "naughty songs."

In 1620, William Bradshaw preached a wedding sermon on *A Marriage Feast* dedicated to Mr. George Wilmer and his wife. He promised to choose a new subject, one that needed discussion, for too often marriage feasts made a "brothel house of a bride-house," with both hosts and guests conducting themselves as if good fellowship or true welcome required "deep carousing and drinking of healths to bride and bridegroom, and every idle fellow's mistress, till the whole company's wits" were drowned in drink. He hastens to say he would not dispense with music and honest mirth, but pleads for Christian sobriety as the feast master and mirth maker, and the observance of a lord of rule instead of a lord of misrule. He believes the devil and his imps have tried to disgrace marriage by making it reproachful, as if it were a day of public penance or execution. Then he describes the "flearing, jeering, and nodding of the head . . . of single . . . and married persons . . . profane swaggerers and those of the damned crew . . . and those that have the reputation of civil honest men, yea, of professors of religion." If the married couple were to measure their worth by the minds, words, and ordinary behavior of the spectators at a wedding, it were better for them to see such people standing in the white sheets of adulterers or carted through the streets like criminals, for they do not belong among the congregation who have come to see young people knit together in the "holy and inviolable knot" of matrimony. No longer should such persons be permitted to attend weddings at all lest they "with their hearts, countenances, and words cast dirt and puddle water in the faces of those about to enter the calling of marriage."

Then he comes to the chief objection among Puritans to uncontrolled mirth with its "beastly and profane" songs, sonnets, and jigs "indicted by some hellish spirit and chanted by those that are the public incendiaries of all filthy lusts; and these are ordinarily made in the scorn and derision of this holy estate to delight and solace the guests withal" as they make marriage a matter of "obsceneness and filthiness." But for God's grace they would make marriage "a very stew and brothel-house." Since all children of God should be married in God's house, they should most certainly have Christ as the chief guest at the wedding. Otherwise it would be better for the day of marriage to be the day of burial than to have it said of husband or wife, "thou wast married and Christ Jesus was not remembered."

Of course Bradshaw refers to the first miracle at the wedding in Cana, and he says that in coming to so humble a feast, the Lord showed it more honor than if He had sent a company of angels to serve the bride and groom. He was no enemy to mirth and delight. If He and His men had been "silent dumps and made dumb shows only one to another," they would never have been invited to so many feasts, whose special use was for "friends to rejoice and make merry together in." The marriage feast of Cana truly gave the lie to the belief in the kingdom of Christ as nothing but "sighing and groaning and fasting and prayer." But those "who would call Christ to a feast of lewdness, ribaldry, and blasphemy . . . would call him to a banquet of carrion, . . . or worse than that would offer Him a bowl of vinegar and gall to drink." Man wants wine, the soul of a feast, he said, and Christ by a miracle made wine. If He could do this to water, He could make husbands good and bad wives good, a miracle indeed.

As Bradshaw's sermon indicates, it is unfair to attribute to the Puritans a belief that any merrymakers should be morbidly conscious of the watchful eye of the Lord. Perkins also approved of the feasting at weddings if it included nothing "dishonest, profane, or of ill report," and if the joy was mixed and moderated enough by reverence for God to keep the laughter and rejoicing from "a mere madness . . . and a riot and excess." Gouge considered feasting a good means of meeting friends who might celebrate the marriage by accompanying the bride to and from the church, all dressed in their best apparel and rejoicing and feasting merrily and honestly. The Independents believed feasting necessary in order to make marriage public, and their representative, Robert Browne, said the wedding guests "must be glad and rejoice together in a joyful and seemly manner." To ignore Puritans in a discussion of the sixteenth-century wedding is to overlook a large part of the society of that time, for in spite of the fact that they lived separately from Anglicans, still they mingled with them in their daily occupations and were an important part of the picture. Together, Anglicans and Puritans were like sun and shadow on an afternoon of a fair day.

For Puritans did not have the Anglican delight in the simple joys of daily living. They were always spurring themselves on to greater mental and spiritual endeavors and felt downright ashamed of any mental lapse they found in themselves. They were good citizens, for they actually tried to be their brother's keeper and to aid their fellows materially and spiritually. They were not so concerned with knowing God's nature as His plan for man. If, by means of a sound moral code, they could improve daily living, they might discover that plan up to a point— then they could be sure of salvation through study of His Word when their study was illumined by education. They could even believe themselves called of God to perform special services in the divine plan, which involved marriage as the possible earthly counterpart to eternal bliss. This is why, therefore, they could endure with proud humility whatever scorn the unenlightened might heap upon them. There was no doubt in their minds that if they desired with all their hearts to see the light, the gift of vision would be theirs by God's grace.

The Puritan joys, then, were sweet meditations and communications with congenial souls about spiritual experience. Of all such souls, husbands and wives could be most congenial. If God gave a man a good wife, He bestowed this gift out of His grace, and she must be regarded as a divine blessing. Because Puritans did not think cause and effect so important for wedded happiness as God's grace, they constantly represented a good husband or a good wife as God's gift. At the same time they admitted God never failed to record the lightest sin as well as the heaviest along with the good deeds, and then, for some reason known only to divine intelligence, forgave or damned a soul before it was born. With this belief in unpredictability, they steeled themselves to meet joy or grief without passion, but also unflinchingly with thanksgiving.

Whether Puritan or Anglican, then, Elizabethans standing at the threshold of married life were sensitive to the mystery of it. They saw about them marriages of seemingly deserved and undeserved punishment and success, or ironical destruction of good with evil or one and not the other in some wedded lives. They felt the heartbeats of despairing and exulting human beings, the tears and the dry sobs and the ecstasy. And they knew that in spite of their most earnest prayers or entreaties, the power to bless or not to bless them lay in the hollow of a mysterious hand. Possibly the hilarity and excitement attendant upon weddings were partly due to the effort to break down the fear in all—the newly married and the guests—the fear of this power that gripped them by the hair.

The usual length of wedding feasts was two or three days, but the festivities might extend over a much longer period of time, during which there must be banquets, dancing, games, outdoor sports, and, in elaborate celebrations, masques and plays. There were no honeymoons, and no time was provided for the young people to be alone together in all this merrymaking; they had all their lives for that. They might spend a little time after the wedding with the bride's family, possibly even a few weeks, but when the bride finally left her parents, she went directly to her new home and was expected to take upon herself its responsibilities. It is quite possible that she, too, wished to enter with all the abandon of which she was capable into the pleasures provided for the celebrants of her marriage.

The first night of the married couple brought the hilarity to its peak. Often at bedtime the bride was expected to untie her garters (if too willing hands did not do this for her), and then the groomsmen pulled them off to fasten them in their hats as a special favor for display. The sack posset of wine, milk, eggs, sugar, and spices was prepared and drunk by all the guests, and it was seen that the bride and groom had their full share of it. Much jollity attended this part of the evening celebration as it was followed by preparing the couple for bed. The bridesmaids undressed the bride in the bridal chamber and put her to bed. Meanwhile, the groom in another room was being undressed, and when this had been accomplished, he was brought to his bride. Sometimes, amid much laughter, the two were sewn between the sheets. At any rate, the wedding guests were expected to crowd into the bridal chamber to wish the young couple joy before the bride's stocking was flung and she was left alone with her husband. In the morning the two were awakened by music played under the window. At more formal weddings the bride and groom held a gay but dignified reception in the bridal chamber for their closest friends, and sometimes a pageant or masque was performed there. And in the morning, they too would expect to hear gay music at the window.

Among some Anglicans too much emphasis was put upon the physical delights of marriage, and Puritans, of course, objected to the consequent lack of decorum. Bullinger spoke sternly of the wedding revelries beginning after the feasting as "vain, mad, and unmannerly . . ." when the bride was brought into the dancing place. Then, he said, there was "such a running, leaping, and flying among them" with "such a lifting up and discovering of the damsel's clothes and of other women's apparel" that one would believe all the dancers "had cast all shame behind them, and were come stark mad out of their wits, and that they were sworn to the devil's dance." The poor bride was forced to "foot it with all dancers, and refuse none, how scabbed, foul, drunk, rude, and shameless soever he be." Moreover, she would hear much wicked talk, "and many an uncomely word." He also observed that all the "noise and rumbling endureth till supper." One reason for Puritan objection to such uncontrolled mirth was their disapproval of whatever loosed too far the reins of moral restraint. Along that way lay instability, and to begin marriage with it was to endanger it forever.

Often wedding dancing was a romping time as the ladies were swung high off the floor and the dancers engaged in many leaping steps. Some tried to be very sedate, but in a group of young and old out to enjoy themselves to the full, dignity had little chance to spread its mantle. The older sisters of the bride, if there were any, must dance barefoot if they did not want to die old maids and then be fit for "nothing more profitable at death than to lead apes in hell." The disdain with which both sexes regarded the unmarried state made it impossible to ignore the daring challenges occurring at a wedding. To most Puritans, and Bullinger in particular, the heightened merrymaking after supper was most uncalled for. To them the evening was "more shameless and drunken than the morning" of most weddings, for piping and dancing began anew. "And though the young couple being weary of the babbling noise and inconvenience come once more toward their rest, yet can they have no quietness" since unmannerly and restless people go to their chamber door to "sing vicious and naughty ballads that the devil may have his whole triumph now to the uttermost."

There were excesses in the best of society, just as they occurred at a wedding feast for the daughter of the highly respected Bridge-Master,

Mr. Nicholls, to a Mr. Coke in July 1562. Among the guests were the Lord Mayor and all the aldermen and many "worshipful men and women," and the wedding sermon was preached by the esteemed divine, Becon. At this time he was in good form and highlighted his discourse with much wise advice. After the ceremony the bridal party and guests returned to the Bridge House, where they enjoyed feasting, music, and dancing till suppertime, when another sumptuous banquet was spread. After that came a masque which lasted till midnight, and then came more meat and drink. On the following day the feasting and dancing continued, but after supper came masquers that caused considerable comments among the guests. One of the masquers wore cloth of gold (permitted only to high nobility), and all were arrayed in gorgeous costumes. Then came a masque of friars, and after that, of nuns, the two finally dancing in pairs and then together. The guests were so delighted at this "novelty" that the masque was repeated on the following evening, the dancers entering so heartily into the jollity of the occasion that "friars and nuns ran into one another's arms, and, after exchanging kisses, danced around a Maypole."[27]

When wedding festivities got out of hand the principal bridesmaids had to exercise their wits to rescue the bride at all from those who pursued her as she retired from the dancing. If the laces and ribbons had not already been pulled from the bride's dress by this time, the groomsmen would start their scramble, for they were expected to wear their "spoil" during the rest of the revelry. If they started the "contest" as the bride was leaving the hall, naturally others might run after the girl as she fled up the stairs to the bridal chamber, and if she lost her slippers in her flight, the winners of them would show their esteem by filling them with wine and drinking to the girl's long life and happiness. Sometimes the bride gave the groomsmen knots and laces and even her slippers, gloves, and garters before she made her departure. Of all these favors, the garters were most prized.

The two chief bridesmaids who prepared the bride for the night often found their task made extremely difficult by guests crowding into the chamber. This might be especially true if the bride had not drunk the sack posset before leaving her guests. In such case she was now forced to drink from a bowl of spiced wine or ale in which floated plum-buns, and naturally the laughing guests wanted to share the drink with her. As the maids undressed her, they took great care to throw away any pins she had worn during the day: these meant bad luck for the bride or a bridesmaid who kept one. When the bride was ready for bed, one of the bridesmaids threw the stocking, and there was a wild scramble for it. The winner in this contest felt the same elation a young girl feels today when she catches the bride's bouquet and is the envy of her companions.

[27] John Cordy Jeaffreson, *Brides and Bridals* (1672), I, 235.

Now the bride was forced to drink again, but this time the benediction posset, and then if there were any knots or laces of her wedding finery left, they were divided among the friends.

The guests did not leave early, especially if the bride and groom were dressed for the nuptial couch that they might sit in state to receive their sometimes clamorous well-wishers. This reception had been common practice in the old days, with one or more priests entering solemnly, with their acolytes swinging lanterns and censers to bless the couch, its occupants, and the truckle bed pulled out from under the main bed for this rite. In *A Midsummer Night's Dream*, Shakespeare romantically substitutes fairies for the priests, and after a song and dance, Oberon blesses "the best bride-bed" so that its issue may ever be fortunate, and without such blots as mole, harelip, scar, or any "mark prodigious" commonly feared in the offspring. In France in 1577, it was ordained that the blessing be given before supper, and in the presence of only the nearest relatives of the couple. Some Elizabethans followed this practice of blessing bride and groom.

After the couple were left for the night, they were not disturbed till awakened by music on the following morning. Often a hunting song was chosen for this purpose. In *A Midsummer Night's Dream*, Shakespeare again adapts custom to action. This time he has the baying of hounds, hunting at dawn, supply the *aubade* as their cries beat on the ears of bride and groom. The bride tells how once she heard the "gallant chiding" of hounds in a wood in Crete make "the groves, the skies, the fountains . . . all one mutual cry." She had never heard "so musical a discord, such sweet thunder" (IV: i: 117–22). Pleased with her appreciation of such "music," the groom tells how he has bred his animals "out of the Spartan kind," and they are "match'd in mouth like bells." Proudly he assures her "A cry more tuneable / Was never Holla'd to, nor cheer'd with horn" (IV: i: 127–29). Many a hunter could appreciate this interlude. Actually, the formality of blessing the bridal couch and waking the bride and groom at morning could be performed with much beauty and solemnity. Again, this part of the celebration could get out of hand and be accompanied by boisterous buffoonery. To Elizabethans, however, it was agitating in any form.

Attendance at the Elizabethan nuptial couch may seem shocking to the present age, but it was often of grave importance to powerful families seeking to strengthen their alliance. When the son of the great Essex was married to Frances Howard before he left for the tour of the Continent to complete his education, King James I and his queen were so concerned about the completion of the union that they remained in the bridal chamber till they were sure the marriage had been consummated. This practice had not been unusual at a marriage uniting two great families, and in this case it raised an almost insurmountable obstacle to the girl bride's later efforts to secure an annulment of her marriage in order to marry the king's favorite. The masque for this ill-fated wedding was prepared by Ben Jonson and Inigo Jones, and was, perhaps, the greatest sensation in the program of events.

When Anne Russell's wedding was graced by the Queen's presence for two days, the masque was its chief attraction also, for Elizabeth delighted in this form of entertainment. Robert Sidney's secretary tells his master in a letter how the eight prominent ladies in it were dressed. Each wore a skirt of cloth of silver, a rich waistcoat embroidered with silks and gold and silver, a mantle of carnation taffeta "cast under the arm," and the hair loose about the shoulders, "curiously knotted and interlaced." When one of them went to the Queen and "wooed her to dance, Her Majesty asked what she was. Affection, she said. Affection! said the Queen. Affection is false!" Nevertheless she graciously consented to dance. In the last years of her reign, Elizabeth was more and more pleased with the masque, so that as a form of entertainment it made considerable progress. James I and his queen also delighted in it.

No wonder, then, the masque at the Howard-Essex wedding in 1606 was so elaborately planned. The theme was Hymen bringing in the bride and Juno the groom, these gods proclaiming that the two mortals were to be sacrificed to nuptial union. Before the sacrifice could be performed, Ben Jonson, standing behind the altar, turned the globe of earth, thereby disturbing eight men masquers representing the four humors and the four affections. They leaped forth to disturb the sacrifice, but Reason, sitting high above them, crowned with burning tapers, came down and silenced the tumult. After the sacrifice was ended, the masquers and Reason confirmed the union of the two young people. So rich was the apparel of the masquers that one witness to the wedding believed "they hired and borrowed all the principal jewels and ropes of pearl, both in court and city," for no imitation jewels or fabrics were used in court masques. At the dancing which followed, Prince Henry performed most gracefully, and the bride and groom were sought in various dances by the many notables present.[28]

When, six years later, in 1613, the princess Elizabeth was married to the Prince Palatine, there were many masques. From February 11 to 16 a succession of spectacles occurred on the Thames, consisting of floating castles, rocks, bowers, forests, etc., but most magnificent of all was the representation of a battle of Lepanto fought in 1571, and still exciting to recall to memory. Besides the ships, galleons, galleys, argosies, etc., there was a castle with its forts, rocks, a beacon, and many Turkish galleys. For the marriage itself, a stately masque of lords and ladies was provided, with ingenious speeches, delicate devices, melodious music, and pleasant dances in the banqueting house. The Inns of Court (the Middle Temple,

[28] Edward F. Rimbault (ed.), *The Miscellaneous Works of Sir Thomas Overbury* (1856), quotes a letter by Mr. Pory to Sir Robert Cotton in 1606, from Bishop Goodman's *Court of James I*.

Lincoln's, the Inner Temple, and Gray's) put on two very impressive masques, for which were chosen the best actors, the best wits, and the most skilled artisans for devising and composing the properties and speeches, music, and costumes. The bride, the bridegroom, the king, queen, and Prince Charles seemed pleased with the result.[29]

The court and its weddings and masques were far, far removed from the preparations of the little country girl for her wedding, and not nearly so full of human interest. As this Elizabethan lass stitched away on the linens that went into her hope chest, and as she planned her trousseau, most of which was made at home, she may have dreamed of gay London weddings, of which rumors might have penetrated to her hamlet. What she could not provide for her chest or for a goodly supply of wearing apparel, she might, if she had sufficient means, buy at the nearest great town, her father or older brother probably making the purchases for her after she had carefully explained her needs. The banquet dishes she could be more sure of if her father was not too poor, and the preparation of these she would talk over with her mother and the maidservants, for even modest homes had their servants. Somehow these weddings always took on gaiety and lavish color since the festivities were planned to last for days or a week or longer.

Elizabethans must celebrate weddings according to their means or according to what they wished others to think they could afford, and though the rich might provide the wedding guests with masques and lavish display, the poorest treasured their bit of pageantry to and from the church. What came after the wedding for entertainment of guests might or might not be planned, but the procession to and from the church service and the linens and apparel and the feasting could not be left to chance. In homes that prepared with honest pride for the marriage of their children, the wedding must not be found wanting in any of the details which society and the church would approve. Much of the celebration afterward would depend on the leaders among the guests. But there must be laughter and gaiety, running feet and excitement, and above all an assurance somehow against the whispering fears or doubts of the worldly-wise.

[29] F. J. Furnivall, in Foreword (pp. 38–39) to William Harrison, *Description of England in Shakspere's Youth* (1877).

Page from *The iiii leues of the trueloue*, printed
by John Day, 1530

CHAPTER VI

FOUNDING AND MAINTAINING THE HOME

My chastity's the jewel of our house
Bequeathed down from many ancestors
Which were the greatest obliquy i' the world
In me to lose.

ALL'S WELL THAT ENDS WELL, IV:ii:46–49

ONCERN for possessions, spiritual and material, gave more and more emphasis to the need for continuity of the family and for whatever might ensure harmony in the home through cooperation of its members—husband and wife, parents and children, masters and servants. This emphasis naturally stimulated the general interest in any marriage that might occur, till John Selden's *Table Talk* complained: "Of all actions of a man's life his marriage does least concern other people; yet of all actions of our life 'tis most meddled with by other people." But this "meddling" seemed necessary to Elizabethan social groups trying to adapt themselves to the strangely new life about them shaken by upheavals in intellectual thought, emotion, and religious belief. In the process of its adaptation social life naturally became very self-conscious, especially when opportunities for sudden wealth and its accompanying innovations in decorum added to the confusion. Consequently, the domestic books dealing with proper conduct as affected by marriage and family relations and duties became so necessary that no home could afford to be without at least one volume of such advice.

Each of these books stressed the importance of good manners for ensuring domestic peace and harmony, and each set down rules of etiquette for practically every member of the household. Like Coverdale's translation in 1546 of Bullinger's *The Christian State of Matrimony*, they followed a more or less set form: they gave some space to a discussion of conditions that might cause disruption in the family, such as divorce or separation, but they were mostly concerned with whatever might dignify marriage and the family relations. All recognized that the husband's government of the household must be "without tyranny," like Christ's care for the Church, and all set down carefully the duties of husband and wife and parents and children. They also discussed problems of housekeeping, proper dress, the education of children, and the directing of servants. Some of the authors, like Erasmus, Snawsell, and Tilney, preferred a semifictional form for their instruction; others attempted a book of organized rules, others published their sermons dealing with such matter, embellished by practical experience, and most of the Puritans supported their statements by biblical references, as in the case of William Gouge's *Of Domesticall Duties* (1622).

If there is any truth in the statement by André Maurois (*The Miracle of England*) that the strength of England today "springs from the kindly, disciplined, trusting, and tenacious character" of its people, then one must give the home credit for achieving this miracle. And the home which still affects modern English life was the very foundation of the Elizabethan commonwealth. Without doubt the closest tie between England and America today is due to this same influence of the home upon American character, much of which is inherited from our English ancestors of the sixteenth and early seventeenth centuries.

In the villages and small towns of Queen Elizabeth's reign, the home, as in medieval times, continued to be practically self-supporting, with each member of the family responsible for definite duties to be performed in it. And, in spite of the differences between rustic and London domestic life, the effort was made, even among the upper classes, to make each person accountable for a part of the home's activities. Of course, travel difficulties prevented the fusion of the nation's social elements, as few country squires went up to London more than once or twice in their lives. What other towns of size existed could not compare in sophistication with that of London, situated at the crossroads of the commerce of the world and the government of the realm. Yet the domestic life of both town and country was alike in that it consisted of both work and play that affected the family as a whole.

The chief pleasures of privileged country people were hunting and the table. Like their city cousins, however, they had their family pride. They learned the genealogies and coats of arms of all their neighbors; they served as magistrates and administered justice and helped to make the local laws. To their sons and heirs they gave whatever advantages they could in the way of education through the local grammar schools or tutors, and then sent them to the university and later to the Inns of Court or abroad for a year or two of travel. When these sons married, they were expected to bring their wives home, where the eldest son would help manage the estate until time for him to take full charge of it. The younger sons went into the army or law or trade.

This country life was not the pastoral idyll Shakespeare describes in *III Henry VI*, with the swain's hours nicely divided for tending flocks, taking rest, contemplating, enjoying sports, and caring for lambing ewes till finally he brings his "white hairs unto a quiet grave" (II: v: 21–54). When the real country home was almost entirely self-supporting in fuel, lights, foods, clothes, linens, and even medicines, it was more or less a beehive of industry. Everything had to be made by hand. Such establishments required stern discipline if they were to be orderly homes with a reasonable degree of harmony pervading the busy activities of household, fields, and farmyard.

In the city of London, even among families whose fathers were often absent from home for uncertain periods of time, the ties of home life never slackened, and parents who took their responsibilities seriously trained their children carefully in the performance of domestic duties. In general the husband was trusted to provide the family with an adequate income, and the wife to disburse that income in so far as it was needed for the support of the household, although she was expected to refer all pecuniary matters of importance to the master of the home. The husband, therefore, when away on business kept in close touch with his family, and his letters to his wife were often filled with minute instructions about the welfare of the children and servants as well as with detailed information to his wife or steward about the management of his estate. When sons were away from home on tour or at school, their connection with home was preserved by frequent letters in which they were expected to report faithfully daily happenings in their lives. This was particularly important in the case of heirs, who were not permitted to shift all the responsibility of making reports to their tutors.

Among those of the recently developed middle class who had come rather suddenly into the small comforts and advantages which their shops and trades provided, life was not so much a struggle for high achievement, except among Puritans, of course, as for festivities and ostentatious display; to them social life was the game of getting on in the world by means of gay, clever use of their wits. London thronged with these people, and it was chiefly the wives and daughters of little shopkeepers who made foreigners feel that England was indeed a paradise for women. Emanuel van Meteren, an Antwerp merchant who spent much time in London and in traveling about the English countryside, observed that unmarried women in England were kept "much more rigorously and strictly" than in the Low Countries, but that English wives were granted unusual freedom. Though they are "entirely in the power of their husbands, their lives only excepted," he said, "yet they are not so strictly kept as in Spain or elsewhere . . . and they have the free management of the house."[1]

Van Meteren was amazed to see housewives in England go to market to buy what they liked best to eat. They were also well dressed and left much of the household management and most of its drudgery to servants. He described them sitting at their doors or windows decked out in fine clothes and watching the passersby. At banquets and feasts they were shown much honor, as they were placed at the head of the table and were served first. Their other activities, he said, consisted of walking, riding, card playing, visiting friends they called gossips, and with them making merry at childbirths, christenings, churchings, and funerals. He says it

[1] William Brenchley Rye, *England as Seen by Foreigners in the days of Elizabeth and James the First, 1592–1610* (1865). Van Meteren's journal, quoted from by Rye, was made during the time he was Dutch consul to England, from 1583 to 1612.

is actually the custom for their husbands to permit such idleness, though they often recommend to their wives the pains, industry, and care of German or Dutch women who do men's work in both the home and the shop instead of having men servants for such tasks. But English men might just as well save their breath, for the women persist in retaining their privileges.

With due allowance for the natural exaggeration that is inevitable in a report judging the whole by a part, one must admit there was more idleness than the serious social groups condoned. The tendency among some of the prosperous middle-class parents to attach too much importance to the rights and frivolities of the privileged class was more or less commensurate with the suddenness by which they had achieved their wealth. Some of them, therefore, did try to better their lot and that of their children by marriage, reasoning that a dowry might marry off daughters without social graces, though a pretty girl with charming manners might marry well on a smaller dowry. So they cheerfully paid the costs for the education and marriage of their children to achieve social advantages thereby, and they read assiduously in conduct books concerning customs and manners of the class they wished to enter or to emulate.

Elizabethan domestic or conduct books, however, like all literature dealing with social etiquette, did not portray life as it actually was but as the authors believed it should be lived. Such material, therefore, measures standards rather than life. The creative literature, then as now, provided serious or satirical or sentimental or romantic sketches of character that sometimes skillfully employed details from life to give the effort some verisimilitude. In all this literature husbands and wives and their complicated relationship in founding and maintaining the home were the subject of many analyses, but in all Elizabethan literature of advice, perhaps the marriage sermon was expected to give most pertinent information on domestic matters. Discounting the personal bias that might distort these homilies, one can gather from them what was expected to appeal to serious members in Elizabethan society. Like Paul's Epistles, written to teach beginners in the Christian faith how to live the Christian life, these Elizabethan sermons also tried to set before the people instruction that would enable them to live like Christians in the sixteenth century home. The fact that these sermons were so well attended voluntarily is significant, especially when one remembers how long they were, and how very repetitious was their subject matter. For a check on these sermons, possibly personal letters are best if they are divorced from the formalities peculiar to the age. However, one must always keep in mind the difference between practice and moral ideas to which the preacher, the literary artist, and even the man in the street may give lip service only.

The preacher usually began his discussion of duties in the home with insistence on the wife's obedience to her husband, and followed this closely

with a warning against the husband's abuse of his power through spurn-
ing or scorning his wife, whom he should love like his own body. She
must love her husband so fully as never to forsake him. A live thing, love
could not stand still; if it did not increase daily, it would surely die. Their
first common duty to each other, therefore, was to cause love to grow
from day to day. Like Bullinger, they agreed that daily prayer and
reading of the Bible were necessary to the cultivation of a healthy love.
Also, like Bullinger, they declared all property distinctions must be
leveled between married people if they would live in harmony: what one
owned, the other owned also, regardless of how much more one of them
possessed before marriage.

Husbands and wives were told to bear with each other's moods, to
answer impatient words kindly, gently, and with loving consideration
for each other and for mutual friends or relatives. They should try to
adapt themselves courteously to each other by an exchange of confidence
with confidence and by refusing to hold resentment. They must never
let the sun set on their wrath: nothing could be more dangerous to future
happiness. They must avoid even the suspicion of evil in associations with
others and in their recreations, and they must avoid all pleasures taking
them from home. When children came, they must be the kind of parents
they wished their children to become, and they must abide in a harmony
that would knit together the entire family. Finally, husbands and wives
must minister to each other in a cleanly, truthful, and friendly way, never
withholding themselves lest they fail in their love for each other and the
home.

After a century of sermons on these themes, the old, old material
could still be turned into sermons by Jeremy Taylor that held his listeners spellbound. To marry for beauty, he said, was to marry for fancy
and to love elsewhere in time. Husband and wife must take great care in
avoiding offenses in conversation, particularly while becoming adjusted to
each other. In the beginning, he said, both were likely to be observant,
jealous, suspicious, easily alarmed; later, they would not need to exercise
so much caution. "After the hearts of the man and wife are endeared . . .
by mutual confidence," he explained, "and an experience longer than arti-
fice and patience can last, there are a great many remembrances, and some
things present, that dash all little unkindnesses in pieces." Nevertheless,
husband and wife even long married should stifle little things as soon as
they jar. "In the frequent little accidents of a family, a man's reason
cannot always be awake; and when his discourses are imperfect, and a
trifling trouble makes him yet more restless, he is soon betrayed to the
violence of passion" unless he subtracts fuel from the sudden flame. It
it important, therefore, ever to remember that "discontents proceeding
from daily little things do breed a secret undiscernible disease which is
more dangerous than a fever proceeding from a discerned notorious sur-
feit." For example, the old Roman practice of forbidding donations be-

tween husband and wife was good in that it taught married people to take great care to avoid the distinction between "mine and thine." As they had "but one person, so should they have but one interest between them."

William Gouge stressed the need of husband and wife governing the family as partners. The husband, he said, added much to a wife's authority by aiding her in it, thereby preventing her from being lightly esteemed or even despised. Among the things in which the husband should take the lead he named the following: conducting the family worship, appointing and settling the ordering of goods, providing convenient house room and other necessities for the family, keeping the children "in awe," and ruling the servants. But the wife should be his partner even here, for she must nourish and instruct the young, adorn the house, order provisions as they were needed, and rule the women servants. Should her husband be sick or away from home, she must conduct the family worship. At other times she must merely gather the family for the worship, and if necessary remind her husband when to read the Bible and when to conduct the catechising of children and servants. By her own respect for her husband's instructions, she would impress upon children and servants a proper regard for the master's teaching. In charitable work or in giving alms to the poor, husband and wife must always act together. By being abroad so frequently, the husband should be able to determine *whom* to aid; by spending so much time in the house, the wife should know *how* to aid. Always they should give mercifully of clothing and food to the deserving.

Robert Crofts promised in *The Lover: or Nuptiall Love* (1638) to teach married people how to gain and retain love. He believed want of love in a husband was stupid, peevish, and unreasonable just as excess of love was weak, dotish, and foolish. There was no pleasure in the world, he assured his readers, like the "sweet society of lovers in the way of marriage," with the husband as head and the wife as heart. Then, indeed, he was her love and joy, and she was his honey, his dove, and his delight. Taking "sweet counsel together," they assisted and comforted each other till they "doubled and redoubled" all their joys. To lose such love was grievous, for it involved "jealousies, contentions, fears, sorrows, strange actions and gestures and looks, bitter words, outrages, and debates." But no love need be lost if care was taken to retain it by pleasant looks, smiles, gentle behavior, compliments, and dancing. Husband and wife should arrange frequent conferences but never insist upon them. He also advocated retaining love by "divers love tricks," such as "tokens, favors, letters, valentines, merry meetings, and love discourse," in which were used compliments, merry jests, and songs, partly premeditated and partly spontaneous. To be all premeditated would make such devices sound forced and insincere. He would even include religious talk, though he admitted that "to many of the blades" who knew nothing of heavenly things such conversation was sure to be "folly, mystical, strange, and very riddles."

Now that he was launched in his effort at making suggestions, Crofts became exuberant. He saw "making honest love" as a sport in which a modest expression "of amorous conceits" suitable to reason and "free from obscenity" as most apt and pleasing and much more "persuasive than any other more grave and solid" conversation. He was sure women esteemed such discourse, and that a good but clever man "might inflame a saint with love and joy." It was impossible to separate two loving people whose marriage was wise and agreeable to their two families, but a marriage based on an evil matching could bring a multitude of sorrows. To prevent discontent after marriage a scold should learn to laugh or be silent, and the husband should maintain his wife in good fashion according to his means, allowing her the same liberties he enjoyed himself. After all, wives were "second selves," and usually it was want of reasonable liberty that made them froward, contentious, jealous, or discontented.

William Whately was known as the "roaring boy of Banbury" because of his strong lungs and lusty sermons. His father had been mayor of Banbury, and his wife was the daughter of a preacher, to whom he dedicated his sermon *A Bride-Bush*. Confidently, even proudly, he attempted to analyze in this sermon the cause for failure in marriages that "with sympathetical understanding and applied intelligence" might have been very happy. He talked of the necessity of a rational sex life, though he insisted on temperance and moderation in it. Nevertheless he said firmly that refusal or incapacity for meeting the obligations of sex should be sufficient grounds for divorce. This statement so shocked the Court of High Commission that it ordered him to retract it, which he did in a preface to another sermon, *A Care-cloth*, saying he hoped he had led no one astray. Then he stated that adultery was the only cause for divorce, but he also warned against an overhasty marriage. However, his first sermon was not soon forgotten for its discussion of the two "principal duties" of marriage which he had called "yielding of the body," and the "benevolence in yielding." The refusing of such benevolence he had called desertion, a loosening of the bonds of marriage, and a frustration of the purpose of marriage.

Although Whately advocated reciprocal consideration in all things in the marriage state, yet he asserted the husband's authority should be conceded by the wife; if she was not sufficiently tractable, there might be times when he had the right to beat her. He also insisted they maintain faith in each other. A wife, for example, must never think her husband unchaste "unless the fault be palpably and notoriously plain." A husband must also believe in his wife's honesty till he had absolute proof against her. Both should conceal each other's little faults from the world and both should keep each other's secrets, as there could be no "quiet and comfortable living in marriage" without the practice of "trustiness" and concealment of private matters.

Apparently Whately was eager to advance harmony in the home by a husband's fair words about his wife. He spoke feelingly against reproving a wife in public, saying she should be only commended before others since "secrecy of reproving . . . doth give a wife assurance that her credit is respected . . ." Moreover, no wife could well "brook distasteful speeches before company," where some might "happen to laugh at her, others to report them again to her shame." The husband's praises of his wife before others should be sincere, however, and not be followed by the reverse when he was alone with her. It was good for a man's wife and servants and children and "all his friends and acquaintances and neighbors and allies" to hear the husband speak well of her whom God had made dear unto him. He might even "after a sort" dote on her. Whately was more than daring to make the last statement, for nothing was more distasteful to Elizabethans than uxoriousness.

Contempt for the "bewitched" husband was expressed again and again in their literature, but Francis Lenton's "Character"[2] of the uxorious man gives a sufficiently effective picture of this Elizabethan attitude. Such a man has "left all the world for a woman, and all women for a thing called a wife." By this "idol . . . he is tied up with a golden calf at home." She is a Delilah, who is his "devotion . . . and his religion." Like Eve, she is the only "edge to his appetite," and he will taste any of her fruits. He is never "his own man, but in thought," for all his actions are either "diverted or writhed by her will," or violated and broken by her supposed wisdom. A man so "tied to his wife's service" can never serve his country and, "tied to her laws," can never be a good churchman. She, on the other hand, is good for nothing but to "multiply her kind . . . and even that only if she so willed." Eventually, caring for "nothing but her, nor anybody at all for him," he lives quietly without company, and dies in his own folly without a funeral. Since to die unmourned and to be buried without ceremony was unthinkable, Lenton contrasts this unlovely type of husband with *A Constant Man*, who is notably temperate in his relations with his wife; who "limits his passions and sets certain bounds to his affections, whose love is without jealousy, but firmly fixed on virtue, and whose wife is happy in him, for he holds to the appointed hour . . ."

In a thousand and one ways Elizabethans were told how to maintain domestic harmony. Henry Smith's sermon, *A Preparation to Mariage* (1591), stressed the "division of offices and affairs." Like "two oars in a boat," the husband and wife should have equal rights and responsibilities. The wife should be "feared and reverenced, and obeyed of her chil-

---

[2] *Characterismi: or, Lenton's Leasures Expressed in Essayes and Characters Never-before written on* (1631).

dren and servants" as entirely as her husband. Though the preacher insisted she must share her lord's privileges and honors, he called her the "underofficer" in their home. Unless the husband was duly considerate of her, the wife became an underofficer indeed in the household economy. Here was the rock on which the household peace might well be shattered, and much was said to avert such misery.

William Perkins described the dangers as well as the means to harmony. A wife might retain certain things as her very own; these things she might lawfully give, even without her husband's knowledge. Such things were hers because "either they were reserved upon the match between them, or else were peculiar unto her by their mutual consent." Such property was usually settled upon the wife at the father's or guardian's demands when the marriage contract was drawn up by lawyers. The goods common to both husband and wife she could not touch, of course, unless her husband was party to the deed. All other property brought by the wife in marriage became the husband's, and descended to the eldest son or, if there were no sons, to the daughters. If there were no children, the property returned to the wife's family by right of succession. If the wife had no property settled on her at her marriage, she was entirely dependent on the bounty of her husband. All the wife's movable property, said Perkins, such as plate, money, cattle, etc., belonged to her husband at her death. However, mutual consent about this movable property could prevent much discord if the wife wished to will any of it to relatives or friends, for such gifts were entirely out of order if the husband did not wish them made. If the husband died first, the wife could enjoy one-third of his estate while she lived, and no more unless it was willed to her. Harmonious relations between husband and wife, therefore, could ease the lot of the widow, for then the husband would have her welfare in mind when he made out his will. Otherwise there might be trouble and downright disaster. Under such a system, if the husband refused to share his goods with a wife who had none of her very own, she was indeed a helpless victim in circumstances controlled by financial arrangements.

Lodowick Bryskett, in *A Discourse of Civill Life* (1606), assumes that friendship between husband and wife is the only means of maintaining harmony in domestic living, though he knows of few relationships of this nature. The author of *Carters Christian Common Wealth; Or, Domesticall Dutyes deciphered* (1627) earnestly advised husbands not to take full advantage of their lordly rights, but to treat their wives tenderly as they would fragile glass that is broken by rough treatment. Any disharmony he lays chiefly at the husband's door. By his "unkind and churlish speeches . . . his unthriftiness abroad . . . his rash furiousness . . ." he causes most of the domestic discord. Since it was the social rule for the unhappy wife to suffer in silence any unkind treatment of her husband, many women did keep to themselves whatever feeling they had about unjust treatment in their homes. Sometimes they exercised all their tact to win justice from an indifferent or unwilling husband, but sometimes they drew up long lists of complaints which they posted to their husbands away from home.

In the latter frame of mind, Mary Windebank writes to her husband, Thomas, who was Clerk of the Privy Seal in 1600. She is disturbed by the Reed family into which her husband's daughter by his first wife is to marry, for she finds them most uncongenial. "Let me remind you," she writes, "of the good agreement that has been between us since Mr. Reed and his wife have been absent." Each time the Reeds have visited them she has suffered trials and unnatural hardships caused by the ensuing slander and disquiet, and she begs him to permit her to go to some of her friends when the Reeds come again, "which will be presently on your coming from Court . . ." She can never forget the wrongs she has received from them, but she hastens to add: "I seek not to withdraw your fatherly kindness from them, and what grief it is to part from you, God knows, but I force myself to it for quietness' sake; I hope at their departure from you we shall come together with as great love as ever." She dreads the time when his daughter is to marry Mr. Reed's son, for then "all the kin" will come for the ceremony. "Use your children as your children," she writes, "and me as your loving wife," but she declares that if he compels her to be present at the marriage, "it will breed strife" between them.

She has other complaints. She is sickly. "Your wheat in the garner is exceeding musty, and makes the bread taste." She wishes her husband to sell some of the grain, and reminds him he will eat no bread made from it while he is home. Furthermore, he has sent all his horses to the park to run, and she had hoped on his return "to ride abroad" to see their friends, "and to take the air." She finds it hard to be so immured. She has not been "on horseback since . . . coming to the country," and is "forced to keep to her chamber." She cannot even go to church, for it would mean to walk a mile and a half each way. Then she comes to the point: has her "care-cloth" of marriage done him any good? She has had little happiness from marriage, for in a postscript she says, "If you will not yield to this reasonable request, it shall be the last breach between us, for my patience has been so tried [by the Reeds] that I can endure it no longer."[3]

The device of some husbands to strengthen their position in the household by making their wives utterly dependent upon them enmeshed them in a web of unhappiness also. They might leave the home as freely as they chose, but they could not leave the troubled hearts of good wives. Thomas Gataker's *A Good Wife Gods Gift: A Mariage Sermon* (1620)

---

[3] *Calendars of State Papers, Domestic Series, 1598–1601*, ed. Mary Anne Everett Green, CCLXXV, No. 3.

uses this theme. Children, like many springs, may flow from the main head, but husband and wife, like two rivers joining, are never swallowed up by the sea. Yet the nearer the bond, the greater the evil that may hurt it. A wicked son may so shame his parents that they will wish to hide their heads, but an evil wife is unendurable. This is why the good wife should be cherished, for she is "better than health." Her price is above pearls, and God is more interested in bestowing her than in giving wealth. As she is the mark of God's special favor, so should she be of her husband's also.

Sometimes, however, God gave in wrath—to give trial, cure, correction, or punishment. Since no marriage on earth could be blessed except by divine mercy, the affections could not be forced at the matching of two people, though there might be such a thing as love at first sight. There was also such a thing as "strange alienation of affections" after matching even when parents had tried to link their children through careful consideration of "all inducements of person, estate, and years." Gataker believed that although a happy marriage was due to God's mercy, a man so blessed was not necessarily deserving but possibly an object of the inscrutable design of the Lord. In such a marriage the woman must remember that she was given to her husband "as to her owner," to live with him, to be guided by him, and never to forsake him. But as each was necessary to the other, the man should not forget that he too was an instrument of God. Acceptance of this type of reasoning, of course, depended entirely upon whether husband and wife were at least conventionally religious.

Naturally, the husband's place in the household was presented in most moral literature as weighed down with responsibilities. His first duty, love of his wife, was discussed in all its important aspects. Many writers, especially Puritans, would have this love first concerned for the wife's spiritual well-being; that is, the husband would seek to train her "in faith, fear, and love of God from the very beginning of their marriage." By gentleness, courtesy, and kindly persuasion he would lead her to respond to him with devotion, lovingly "obeying the ordinance that God hath made between her and her husband." If trouble came to such a union, the husband must look upon it as a means of bringing him and his wife to the joy derived from surviving a severe test of their faith. Becon urged the husband as his wife's spiritual keeper to help and comfort and cherish her, quietly bearing with all her weaknesses, never rigorously dealing with her, but gently and lovingly admonishing her to better amendment and more diligence.

Though he must protect his wife from needing any things necessary for the household, the husband must above all, said Becon, protect her good name. Unto the uttermost of his power he must not suffer her to be "injured, wronged, displeasured, or trodden under foot by her adversaries." This care for a wife's reputation was emphasized again and again by all writers of didactic literature, for Elizabethans knew that no woman could ever be a match for slanderous tongues. As Thomas Fuller was to write later, a woman's good name was like a tree in Mexico, "which is so exceedingly tender, that a man cannot touch any of its branches, but it withers . . ."

The contempt of a worldly-wise Elizabethan woman for a husband who failed to defend his wife's honor was very great. In a time when political intrigue was likely to involve all important families, women relied especially on their husbands for protecting their good name. One plot concerned with the support of Arabella Stuart instead of James as successor to Queen Elizabeth implicated two families in which the husbands were requested to sound out their wives by fair means or foul. One loosed his wife's tongue by "unwonted amiability," and when she discovered his purpose he could not be reconciled to her till after a long period of servile effort toward winning her good favor. The other wife discovered her husband's intent at the start, and so great was her anger that she refused ever again to have anything to do with him. And she kept her word even though her husband was imprisoned and died in poverty twenty years later.[4]

Some writers urged husbands for their own sake to bear with their wives as the weaker vessels lest in their impatience the wives resort to spite of some kind. Certainly no man should ever expect to win a dispute with his wife, and it would be best for him to admit occasionally he had been vanquished. He should also, for his own sake, permit his wife some merrymaking before his eyes; otherwise, she would be likely to resort to it in secret. In *The Golden Grove* of William Vaughan the author advises the husband to be as generous as his means will allow and never to cause his wife to become jealous or suspicious. At the same time, he must never permit her a second bed, even as a temporary arrangement for ragged nerves, lest she seek to make it a permanent practice. Vaughan looked upon women as a somewhat necessary evil with which husbands were honor-bound to live in harmony though the effort would tax the patience of a saint.

Of course the perfect husband to whom writers referred most frequently was Sir Thomas More. They saw in his household discipline all that they idealized in a home, yet he himself declared that he did not think it possible to live with "even the best of wives without some discomfort." A man must expect cares when entering the state of matrimony, he explained, though he hastened to add that men usually made their wives worse by their own fault. All More's biographers praise his tolerant attitude toward his second wife, emphasizing her sharp tongue

---

[4] Violet A. Wilson, *Society Women of Shakespeare's Time* (1925), pp. 126–36.

even as they admit she was an excellent housekeeper. "When any woman in his house or neighborhood was laboring in childbirth," writes Stapleton, Sir Thomas More "would always give himself to prayer and continue until he received tidings of a safe delivery." Yet More himself would be quick to admit that while his hands were folded in supplication his wife's were working busily and efficiently to aid the woman in her distress.

So generally was the husband's duty of providing food, clothing, and shelter accorded his responsibility, and his only, that there is little discussion of the matter. Instead, his other duties of leadership in the household were emphasized and critically analyzed. In matters of discipline he was to be supreme in command unless a capital crime should be committed within his doors. In that case he was responsible for taking the offender to the civil magistrate. In all minor offences, however, he was to punish and admonish according to the character of the offending deed and the condition and state of the person at fault. Should admonitions and corrections fail, he must take the culprit to the proper authorities of Church or State.

Because of the husband's position of authority in the home, his power over his wife became a subject of much discussion during this age. Possibly the husband's authority was partly responsible for Queen Elizabeth's choice of a lonely life as a people's sovereign rather than the married life she was urged to enter. She must have looked with dismay at the humiliating dependence of her sister Mary when she became subject to the will and mood of her husband from Spain. In all seriousness the heads of the Church and State discussed the right of husbands to discipline their wives even to the point of downright beating. Many divines deplored the practice of such chastisement, however, declaring that a man should never use "stripes or strokes" to one who was of his own flesh, but instead should give reproof by word of mouth. Others, not so mild, chanted with a right good will

> A spaniel, a woman, and a walnut tree,
> The more they are beaten, the better they be.

Some objected to the beating of wives because the Scriptures did not approve of such treatment except for children and servants. Jeremy Taylor declared the government of the whole family was disordered if the husband laid hands on the shoulder "which together with the other ought to bear nothing but the cares and the issues of a prudent government." Henry Smith proclaimed from the pulpit that for a man to beat his wife was the "greatest shame" that could be, not so much to her who was beaten as to him who performed the deed. "Every man," he said, "must be ashamed to lay hands on a woman because she cannot match him." Perkins felt that a man with a peevish wife must be pitied, but not excused for becoming impatient with her. A good husband, he said, should cover his wife's infirmities of anger and waywardness by his wisdom and patience. Gouge insisted that a man's love for his wife should enable him to bear with any weakness she might have, and he reminded the husband that since love begets love, he must set the right example to his wife by holding respect for her and by showing a proper regard for her place and person. Thus he must not be too strict in commanding obedience of her; indeed, his command should be as mild as his reproof was rare.

Yet some men of culture and learning did approve of wife beating. In a speech at St. Mary's Church of Oxford a scholarly and witty jurist and poet stated in all sincerity that husbands were granted the right by ancient law and sacred authority to beat their wives, and that when it was necessary they should administer such discipline. William Heale, a member of Exeter College, countered with his *An Apologie for Women*,[5] in which he made the old statement that one mind and one flesh could not be fittingly used in this manner; rather, he urged some cordial should be sought to heal them, not a corrosive to afflict them. The law, he said, permitted a woman to leave her husband if he beat her and to receive from him sufficient maintenance, and she need not return to him till he provided good security not to beat her. He called wife beating inhuman and servile, and concluded with the statement: "God's law supported civil law against it, for man and wife should live together to honor marriage by the unity of their souls."

Some ministers took wife beating for granted and asked wives to submit to it with what grace they could, remembering that they were thereby laying up "no small reward hereafter." Others lamented the "weepings and wailings" made in the streets when "neighbors run together to the house of so unruly a husband as to a bedlam-man who goeth about to overturn all that he hath at home." Some promised husbands reward in heaven if they refrained from beating their wives who deserved such punishment. That the practice was a serious abuse is indicated by the fact that death sometimes occurred from it, and especially by the fact that so much discussion arose concerning it. Throughout the seventeenth century the practice continued, and even a husband of good birth and breeding did not feel guilty of any grievous misdemeanor if he struck his wife.

The literature of the time made frequent reference to wife beating, particularly in ballads, where the cause and effect were often neatly summarized. *Keep a Tongue in Your Head* and *Hold Your Hands, Honest Men* are typical. The first is in two parts, and concludes the first part with:

[5] *An Apologie for Women, or An Opposition to Mr. Dr. G. his assertion. Who held in the Act at Oxforde. Anno. 1608. That it was lawfull for husbands to beate their wives* (1609).

Queen Elizabeth attends a wedding

Ar't asleepe Husband? A Boulster Lecture, by
Richard Brathwait, 1640

In every part
Dame Nature's art
Gives her the start:
With all my heart
I wish she could rule her tongue!

The second part complains:

She can dispute eloquently,
She can sing, play, dance, embroider,
    spin, knit, excel in all housewifery as
    to dairy, servants, but
No venomous snake
Stings like a woman's tongue.

The second ballad has a varied refrain, of which the following are examples:

He has manly beauty;
He is nimble and quick;
He can throw the bar and the stone,
But *he will strike his wife.*

He excels in wrestling, leaping, running,
    cunning, dancing, singing.
He is learned in the arts, has traveled,
    can discourse pleasantly, win all hearts,
    is judicious, understanding, loving,
    is a good soldier with musket and bow,
But *he cannot hold his hands.*

Actually, however, few men or women would have agreed with a statement in Boccaccio as a queen says: ". . . even in a moral sense, we will allow that women are naturally prone and unstable, and therefore a stick may be requisite to correct the evil disposition of some, as well as to support the virtues of others . . ."

The wisest minds, therefore, sought to find the cause of wife beating, and many of them agreed the most common provocation was the wife's shrewishness or the husband's disapproval of his wife's companions. Then they set about advising the husband on how to supplant the wife's friends by being so attentive and confiding that the wife would invariably turn to him instead. Gouge felt that such sympathy was particularly necessary to a woman when she was with child, and declared that "during travail and child-bed" the husband should make every effort to satisfy her "longings," and to provide the necessary companionship and other things required for the ordeal. He also warned the husband against failing to protect his wife at such a time, especially against slanderous tongues or from any danger that might arise, such as the irritation from "children-in-law."

Guazzo believed a husband should judge his wife only after examining his own love, for distrust of wives, he said, came from a weakness of affection. Once suspicion enters, love leaves, but a husband who loves his wife as the other half of himself will not tolerate suspicion. It is fool· ish, he chided, to watch over a woman "with diligence," for anyone should know a dishonest woman cannot be kept in, and an honest one does not deserve such treatment. Relations between husband and wife must be kept delicate lest the beauty of their association be blunted. For this reason he objected to wife beating. Since a wife was truly flesh of her husband's flesh; no man should torment an erring wife, but seek rather to comfort her. How could a husband embrace the body his hands had bruised? How could a woman love a man who had beaten her?

Robert Snawsell's dialogue of *A looking glasse for Maried Folkes* (1610) is directed toward a husband whose wife is obedient and skilled in housewifery and toward one whose wife lacks such virtues. One of the husbands learns from a good wife how to love and honor his own erring wife, and the other husband is reformed by a wife who teaches him how to live prayerfully and amicably. This treatment of the subject also suggests that both married people must grant privileges to each other and then respect those privileges. The husband is cautioned against criticizing his wife and beating her. Like Guazzo, the writer advised the husband to stifle jealousy, one of the chief reasons for dislike of the wife's friends and certainly a frequent cause for wife beating.

Jeremy Taylor would have the husband use his power in a paternal and friendly manner, never despotically. Under a kind husband a wife might well be in perpetual tutelage, he believed, for his power would then be founded on understanding, not on will or force, and he would give advice instead of commands. He referred to Homer's statement that a husband should be "a father and mother to her, and a brother," but he himself thought of the wife as a poor fatherless child who had left her parents for a husband in whom she should find both parents, and one who could give her more than had ever been bestowed on her. He looked upon man's dominion over his wife as similar to that of the soul over the body, "for which it takes a mighty care, and uses it with delicate tenderness, and cares for it in all contingencies, and watches to keep it from all evils, and studies to make for it fair provisions." Though he would not have a man intrude in the nursery and offices of domestic employment, he would have his duties concerning his wife elsewhere cause him to prevail with her "by sweetness and counsel, and charity and compliance." He could not understand how a husband could wrangle with his wife. If it was indecent for husband and wife to embrace in public, how "extremely indecent" was it for them to "brawl in public." He saw the discreet husband as one who made the cares and evils of life as simple and easy as possible for his mate to bear by doubling her joys with his own acts of friendship for her.

In setting a good example for the wife, the husband's first concern, said Jeremy Taylor, was his virtue and felicity. "Above all instances of love, let him preserve toward her an inviolable faith, and an unspotted chastity." Under such a lock he saw deposited "the security of families, the union of affections, and the repairer of accidental breaches." In return for his own fidelity the husband might well expect from his wife "a modesty and retirement" and "a passive nature and colder temper" which, with her "humility and fear," would make her as "pure as the eye of heaven." With such a wife he would have no cause to fear whatever companions she might choose, and the harmony of her discourse with him would echo that of immortal souls.

Other important duties in the husband's leadership were concerned with directing the family worship, for in spite of the Reformation and all its attendant countermovements, religion continued to influence every phase of public and private life even though it did not always dominate the heart. It not only affected all the daily habits, but was especially influential in dress and speech and even the choice of friends. All writing of the period shows these influences: in public announcements and moral literature, in private correspondence, and in the very broadsheets hawked about the streets. It is amazing that religion's hold was so strong when the form of religious service was so frequently altered and debated, and when the shrines were defaced, the priests outlawed, and the clergy that remained far too often lacking in the necessary training for their place in religious life. Even the very language underwent changes in the services. In Henry VIII's time religious faith caused well-known and respected public men to be accused of high treason for refusing to take the Oath of Supremacy, and in Mary's time it caused many people to be burned at the stake for not acknowledging the pope. Still religion retained its hold on life. In Elizabeth's time, friendship between the different groups was still subject to suspicion, and tolerance in religious matters, if it actually was present, was marked chiefly by a seeming indifference.

But in reality there was little indifference, for if religion was not vital to a person, piety was, and who was to draw the line between the two? Everyone naturally talked and wrote of God in all things, and praised Him for whatever fortune brought him, good or bad. If one's fortune was good, it was only for this world; if bad, it prepared the soul for the next world. If disease spared one, it was the will of God; if it swept one's dearest friends into eternity, again it was God's will. If one enjoyed good health, God was merciful; if one enjoyed good friends, they were proof of God's blessed love and kindness. If one saw sin committed, he regarded the offenders as children of night, doomed to suffering and perhaps eternal punishment. If one saw another die loved and respected by mankind, he spoke of the sure salvation of that person's soul. Naturally, then, the head of the household must shepherd his flock and bring it home safe to his Lord.

Family prayers, therefore, were customary in most homes. The loved story of Sir Thomas More's devotion to this family duty was often repeated. Once, while in the midst of the family service, he was summoned to the king, "even two or three times," but refused to leave till the morning worship had been concluded. When urged to come away and attend the king, he answered he must "finish his act of homage to a higher King," and Henry VIII himself would be first to acknowledge the rightness of that response. In great houses chaplains led the exercises. They lectured the households upon their duties, conducted the morning and evening prayers during the week, and preached twice on Sundays. In summer these services occurred at five in the morning, but in winter an hour later. In homes that had no chaplain, the father supervised the worship, kneeling with his family and servants in the great hall or some like suitable place, which might be perfumed at the command of his wife with rosemary or juniper or even frankincense, or freshened with rosewater or just plain vinegar. In the father's absence, the mother took his place at this worship, reciting short prayers or collects, and instructing the children and servants in the family faith.

On Sunday after the evening service at church, the minister often continued with instruction for the home, particularly in the catechism, and during the succeeding week, the parents supplemented this teaching with practical lessons and examples. The mother taught the younger children and the father instructed the older children (unless he was pressed for time and had to leave all the teaching to the mother). Little tots just out of the nursery were carried to church and to family worship, where they soon learned like their older brothers and sisters to answer intelligently the questions put to them on religious matters. Private fasts as well as public feasts might be observed at home, especially in times of disaster, such as during the plague or the massacre of St. Bartholomew's Day, or in times of great national anxiety like that inspired by the Spanish Armada, or during the rejoicing after the Armada's destruction.

On Sunday, the father must take his entire family to church, and he must see that their behavior was proper. On the return from service, Puritan fathers especially were likely to catechize the children old enough to listen to the sermons. Most sermons, therefore, were well attended, but those at St. Paul's Cross and other gathering places of this character were likely to draw great crowds. Since the preachers expected to address large numbers, they had to be licensed during the reigns of Mary and Elizabeth lest they deal with unorthodox matters or let their fancy carry them too far afield in their effort to respond to the eager multitude before them. They also had to be able speakers, with members of the congregation recording their sermons word for word and even school children doing so as part of the lesson material upon which their school-masters were to examine them. In places unable to supply fine speakers, the preacher was required to read printed homilies, and attendance at such churches would have been poor indeed if there had been no fines to pay for nonattendance. It was dangerous to be absent too often without an acceptable excuse regardless of the payment of fines lest the suspicion of recusancy be directed against the offender. Thus fathers in taking the entire household to church were protecting themselves and at the same time watching out for the souls of those for whom they were responsible.

Though there were a good many quietly practicing Catholics, most Elizabethans adhered to the new national Church of which their popular Queen was head. Important as their religious life was, and great as was its hold upon the daily routine, still it did not actually dominate the inner life of the average person except at a time of crisis. Materially and spiritually, Elizabethans were realists, except for Catholics and dissenters, and like their Queen, they followed the secular approach to life. This did not prevent them and Elizabeth, however, from having at the core of their being a pious concern for goodness. Thus the intelligent mind sought the very quintessence of life in spite of the unaccountable mutability it felt pervading all things above and beyond mortal accidents and what seemed to be constant natural change.

For such minds there was no false humanitarianism, no sentimental lamentation about the incompetent person who found no work by which to earn his daily bread but begged or robbed instead. Nor was there sympathy for the stupid poor. But there was much concern about the hazards of fortune. They could see that man is not created equal, but they believed passionately in man's having the freedom to advance as far as he could go, to enlarge the boundaries of his mind as far as it could stretch. It was the father's duty to encourage his sons to take this intelligent, realistic view of the universe, controlled by an inscrutable force whose acts he might question but whose nature he could never even hope to understand. On such subjects the mind was sometimes inclined to dwell when congenial souls consorted together, especially at the evening meal. But the host must be able to lead the discussion according to the tastes and capabilities of the guests, for the welfare and proper entertainment of those within his home was one of the father's important duties. This, too, he must somehow teach to his sons. And, since congenial souls are few and far between, he would try to impress upon these young minds the importance of pious utterance in times of uncertainty about the guests received at the family hearth.

Since the wife assumed the government of the children and household during her husband's absence, it was the convention to name her as "sole executrix" of her husband's will in case of his death and at such a time to give her full government of their children. All moral literature approved of this practice, but it also pointed out the need for a discussion of the evils of suspicion and jealousy in married life. For husbands by their wills to make their widows wealthy was to enable them to marry easily again if they so desired, and most widows did seek a hasty marriage to protect themselves from unscrupulous fortune hunters. To facilitate such a marriage for a wife they loved must have required greater faith in them than husbands had in friends they might choose as guardians of their children. Dramatically, of course, jealousy provides a theme full of tense situations and exciting psychological problems for the audience to respond to, but for moral literature to deal so much with jealousy suggests every effort was being made to strengthen confidence between husband and wife even if confidence must be built on fear of the evils of distrust.

The unknown author of *Tell-Trothes New-yeares Gift*, in 1593, used fantasy to impart homely advice to husbands subject to jealousy. Robin Goodfellow, fresh from hell, meets Tell-Troth near Islington on a frosty morning, and talks about jealousy sending to the nether region most people afflicted with this vice. If a discontented married couple find fault with each other, the husband leaves home when he wishes to be merry, and that causes gossip. And the husband is often more suspicious of his wife than he has cause to be. Bringing home guests for their wives to entertain, men suspect them of being too gracious. If they bring home women for their wives to entertain, they may praise the women so much as to rouse the suspicions of their wives. But the chief cause of jealousy is the bad counsel of busybodies "snooping around," and other causes almost as great are slander from neighbors and the married couple's "hard usage" of each other. This naïve author feels it necessary to make these causes known, for too many married people seem to be ignorant of them. "I swear," he says, "that I had rather see the devils dance the Morris alone in that fiery hellhouse, than a Christian foot it there through want of knowledge of its inventions."

Edmund Tilney, who must have learned a great deal about the disrupting influences in the lives of important people even before he became Master of the Revels at court, wrote *The Flower of Friendshippe* (1568) to give advice in domestic affairs. He felt the early days and weeks of adjustment were so difficult that the husband in particular should make every effort to build on them a firm foundation for a happy marriage. This he could do only if he made his wife "wholly his" by cultivating flowers instead of weeds. Among the noxious plants in married life were the man's addiction to gambling, excess banqueting, and rioting. The flowers of marriage the husband should cultivate were courteous speech, wise counseling, trustworthiness when confided in, careful provision for the house, diligence in caring for his possessions, patience with his wife's importunities, circumspection in honesty, and when children came, zeal in educating them. For one sharp command he should use a hundred loving exhortations. Should he and his wife differ about some trivial thing like the servants' apparel, he should turn the whole thing into sport. If his temper got the best of him, he should "walk it out." Since wise counsel came from hearing and seeing much, he approved of the tour for all young men before they settled down to the founding of a home. By this means the husband would avoid such pitfalls as spoiling his wife with too much indulgence or bringing home for entertainment the wrong kind of guests.

It is possible that Tilney's book may have had something to do with his appointment to the coveted office of Master of the Revels, for its plan followed somewhat that of Castiglione's *The Courtier* and thereby served as a sequel to it. *The Courtier* was in the possession of every person at Elizabeth's court who was interested in proper social decorum, and Tilney's discussion of the duties for husband and wife provided an elaborate picture of marital love and proper domestic decorum. At the beginning of the book, the author and his friend Don Pedro are walking in the fields till noon, when they go to Lady Julia's house to rest. She and her other guests, including "M. Lodovic Vives" and "Master Erasmus," are just ready to sit down to dinner, and she cordially invites the author and his friend to join them. They talk of Boccaccio and Castiglione, and later retire to the garden. It is a beautiful spring day, and as they sit on benches in a "kind of terrestrial paradise" with its camomile and daisy setting, Don Pedro makes a wreath for Lady Julia's brow, crowning her sovereign of the entertainment they are to enjoy, either by stories they are to rehearse or by discussion of a topic they are to choose.

They agree to discuss the duties of the married man, and they ask Don Pedro to give his opinions first. After naming the virtues of matrimony and giving examples of each from the Bible and from the folklore of various nations of olden times, he recounts the means by which a young man may establish love between himself and his wife from the very beginning, and illustrates his narrative by examples of loving husbands who neither chide nor scold. Then he lists the weeds of matrimony, following these with the nine flowers and herbs, which he is asked to deal with fully as to their "planting and preservation." His answers please his audience as he cites many examples of the herbs of matrimony and illustrates his discourse with quotations from the classics.

So much do the company enjoy themselves that they decide to meet again, and they crown Lady Aloisa, the daughter of Lady Julia, queen of the next day's gathering. When the group is assembled once more in the garden after dinner, they listen for a time to sweet music. Then their topic of conversation, gracefully led by Lady Aloisa, deals with the duties of wives. Highly idealistic though all the discussion is, it retained its popularity for a long time among many Elizabethans at court. Just as *The Courtier* would teach them "delightfully" perfect conduct at court, so Tilney's book would teach them an easy way by which to achieve perfect marital love as a foundation for domestic life and how to acquire the proper decorum of gentle ladies and fine gentlemen entertaining friends at home.

By the time satire had rubbed off much of the bloom of such idealism, the "Characters" of Francis Lenton were making laughter for the sophisticated. The author says he will show a good husband how to steer his course in a right line and weigh all his actions in balance. Such wisdom, however, requires him to be a good mathematician, for he must be "always within the compass and never run circles . . . to make himself giddy." Nor must he let sense overrule his reason, but stay "betwixt the two extremes" of prodigality and parsimony. Then he will be "the sole happiness of a good wife, and the torment of a waster." His children will "never have cause to curse him, nor his servants to accuse him for their want of wages." He will not be so "niggardly as to grudge himself or his friend a good meal," but will taste "freely (though temperately)" of what the Lord has lent him, and feel himself "no loser by lending to the needy." His moderate diet will give him longer days, and his care in his calling will free him from idleness which is "the bait of his greatest enemy." He will also educate his children "in a religious way, knowing that grace cannot want goods." Such a man "passeth his pilgrimage with a peaceful conscience, and leaves the world with all good men's applause so that his name dies not with his nature." Even the parson, he adds slyly, is so impressed by his "true and conscionable tithing" that he "preacheth his funeral praise, and perhaps gives him gratis his burial in the chancel." Was there in the flesh such a paragon?

According to accounts of Southampton, the supposedly generous friend of Shakespeare, here was a man not far from the ideal. So romantic was he that he has been suggested as the inspiration for Shakespeare's Romeo or Orlando or even his Florizel and Ferdinand. He was handsome, with a delicate complexion and brilliant blue-gray eyes and a charming smile. In the field of sports he was a veritable Adonis. Intense in his impulsiveness, he might even become violent under stress, though everywhere he was trusted to such an extent that the current anagram for *Southampton* was *Stamp of Honor*. His famous "breach of promise" suit, which his indulgent mother helped him to undergo with honor, first introduced him to the entanglements a man could become involved in through espousal contracts, and gave him due respect for them and for social conventions in general.

After his return from war with his idol Essex who had been successful in his expedition against Cadiz, Southampton enjoyed also the role of conquering hero, and dazzled the eyes of Elizabeth Vernon, a Catholic cousin of Essex. His own eyes were dazzled too, and knowing the difficulty of obtaining the Queen's consent to marry one of her maids of honor, Southampton secretly married his lady before he left for state duties in Paris. Then came news of his wife's being with child and the gossip about her condition. Without even waiting to get leave from the ambassador whom he was serving, he rushed to his wife and made public his marriage to her.[6] A letter of the time written to Colonel Sir William Stanley, "at camp," indicates the character of the gossip that roused Southampton to such haste. Part of it reads as follows: "Lord Southampton has married Mistress Vernon, whom he has got with child. Maids of the Court go scarce twenty weeks with child after they are married, and every man has liberty of conscience to play the knave."[7]

It was partly her desire to prevent this sort of evil talk which caused the Queen to take such severe measures. She was quite as angry as Southampton feared she would be, and although she eventually forgave him for not obtaining her consent to the marriage, she forbade his wife ever to appear at court again. Yet in spite of all the dangers, separations, trials, and afflictions the wife suffered before Queen Elizabeth died, so great was her confidence in her husband that she never swerved from her loyal and tender devotion to him. In all her letters to him she sincerely addressed him as her "dear Lord and only joy." On the whole, he was worthy of her.

A more conventional husband, but no less wise or ardent according to Elizabethan standards, was Sir Robert Sidney. Unfortunately he had to be away from home much of the time, for the Queen turned a deaf ear to his and his friends' protests, and made him Governor of Flushing. His wife, justly famous for her good household management and for her attachment to husband and children, always loved a baby in her arms and was never happy when her husband was not near. In 1597, when Robert was disappointed in obtaining leave to visit his family, he was dismayed to hear his wife was planning to come to him with the children. Excitedly he wrote advising her against bringing the children to a place so ill-suited for them. He begged her at least not to bring the three older ones. He says he knows her delight in them is so great she does not always "care what is best for them" and asks her to find some place where she may leave them in safety, especially since they are old enough to be separated from her. He wishes them left with Lady Huntingdon or Lady Warwick, for he knows "every day more and more it will be fit for them to be out of their father's house." He has no fault to find thus far with their mother's training of them, but he feels the time has come for them to get further training in another household. To bring them to Flushing is unthinkable. They could not have proper care, and their very health might suffer. If she persists and brings the children, she will never have her will again in such matters.

He speaks of the boy who is still permitted to sleep with the maid who dresses him and cares for his wants. He says it is time for him to be taken from such fond coddling, and he suggests a friend with whom she

[6] Charlotte Carmichael Stopes, *The Life of Henry, Third Earl of Southampton, Shakespeare's Patron* (1922).

[7] *Calendars of State Papers . . . 1598–1601*, CCLXVII, No. 111.

might leave him. He knows his suggestions will be "nothing pleasing" to his wife, but he reminds her he has a part in the children too, and must have care of them accordingly. He admits there is no better mother than his wife, though he does fear her "fondness." And he had cause to fear it, for she paid no attention to his warnings and appeared with all seven children. Of course she was forced to take them back to England's milder climate, and to consult the best London doctors for the boy. Her disobedience was a costly experience, for in London she could find no house available till her sister-in-law, the Countess of Pembroke, prepared her vacant town house for the accommodation of the distracted mother and her family. From here the anxious huband and father was kept informed about the recovery of his little son. His own wise understanding of his wife's temperament, however, gave him the necessary forbearance to support her in her distress and not to upbraid her for disregarding his commands.[8]

When choosing a wife, the first thing a young man should consider was whether she was obedient. Unless she possessed this virtue she would fail him as the mother of his children and the manager of his household. As a child he had heard proverbs about a woman's willfulness and the virtue opposing it:

> Every man can tame a shrew but he that has her.
> Silence is the best ornament of a woman.
> A little land well tilled, a little wife well willed.

Bullinger had recognized this difficulty of knowing how to choose. As a person's pastimes determine the capacities of his mind, he said, the maid's dress may proclaim her character, for a clean and neat maid is likely to be a clean and neat wife. But she must also be honest, good-tempered, healthy, well born, congenial, and not poor in worldly possessions if she is to be a fortunate choice. However, among all these requirements, virtue was most important, for riches in land and possessions in the hand of a foolish woman would be like a knife in the hands of a child.

Vives did not think men were likely to manifest good judgment at all when choosing a wife for themselves. That was why it was best, even among the lower classes, for parents or guardians to choose the mates for their children. Men choosing for themselves were likely to be attracted by beauty or riches instead of civil and womanly manners, and they seldom discovered whether a woman was likely to occupy herself virtuously at home or idly and wantonly "spend her time abroad."

Plays frequently presented such ideas. Middleton's *Women Beware Women* makes clever use of the foolish youth choosing a beautiful woman without considering whether she has any practical virtues. The drama-

[8] Arthur Collins (ed.), *Letters and Memorials of State: The Sydney Letters* (1746), II, 42–44.

tist, however, may have taken his fantastic plot from a scandal in Italy connected with the marriage of the Duke Francesco de Medici to the beautiful Venetian Bianca Cappello. Middleton binds up his plot with typical Elizabethan moralizing on the situations he provides. A young factor marries a beautiful young woman he cannot afford to keep at all, much less according to the manner in which she has been living. He dreads to present her to his mother who will criticize him for his rash choice. When his mother does see the bride, she tells her son he will suffer the worst pangs of jealousy for having chosen a wife all men will desire and tempt by offers he is too poor to make. He answers hotly that since he covets no man's wife or sister, no man should covet his beloved. Now he can go to church and "pray handsomely" instead of looking for faces as if "lust went to market still on Sundays."

The mother continues to rebuke her son. He should know all women hope to better their state by marriage and his wife will soon regret her bad choice. The son begs his mother not to teach his wife to rebel when she has shown every disposition to be obedient. He looks at her beautiful face confidently and says she will enter naturally into the simple joys of married bliss, rearing children, and, during her leisure hours, stitching fine embroidery. Thus she will make their poverty rich in love. To all this the wife listens demurely and then dutifully tells her mother-in-law not to fret, for as she has been born again in her husband's love so she finds his home her rightful birthplace.

Almost immediately the young husband is called away on business. His only consolation is that his mother will guard his rich jewel from the covetous eyes of men. He has scarcely departed, however, when his wife contrives to let the duke who rides by gaze upon her face. She is pleased when he smiles, and thinks of how the duke's fifty-five years make him far better than her husband "for wisdom and judgment." But when he gains access to her, she discourses properly on a wife's chastity, to which he answers that even her mother-in-law would favor his suit if he made it worth her while. The bride's beauty is too great for a life of poverty, he says, and begs her not to kiss away a month or two in wedlock only to "weep whole years in want . . ." After the success of his seduction, he laughs over the ease with which his web has caught "love's flesh-fly by the silver wing."

The bride greets her husband at his return coldly, upbraids him for his uxoriousness, and will not have him kiss her. She tells the amazed young man that love between man and wife is "the idlest fondness that ever was invented," and turns from him briskly to prepare for her departure to a banquet the duke is giving her. The greatest blow of all follows when he sees his own mother accompanying the wife. The dove-tailing between creative literature and the didacticism of conduct books and sermons is interesting in Middleton's drama. Indeed, the author must have felt pleased with the speech he put into the mouth of the disillusioned young husband who watches his wife and mother turn from him without one qualm of conscience. At the same time he has been his own worst enemy, for he has violated all the wise precepts on how to choose a wife for a happy marriage.

Young Elizabethans free to choose their own wives knew very well they must "look to't" that the maid be amenable to instruction, but some took this virtue for granted. With all his caution, Sir Thomas More had fallen into this trap when he chose his first wife. He had believed that her age of seventeen years made her young enough to train according to his own tastes, but he discovered that books and music and repeating significant sentences from sermons were all new to her, and boring. She had been brought up in idleness, and had found most of her amusement in play and talk with the servants. More's regimen was so severe she soon refused to abide by it. When he urged her, she would burst into tears, sometimes even throwing herself on the floor and beating her head as if she wished to die. More was wise enough to conceal his vexation, and when she still refused to follow his instruction, he suggested a visit to her parents in the country. This delighted her, and she fell in with his plan. We are indebted to Erasmus for the details of this whole maneuver on the part of the patient husband.[9]

On their arrival, More left his wife with her mother and sisters while he went off with the father to hunt. As soon as they were safe alone, however, he told his story, how instead of the happy companion he had expected in his wife he found her "perpetually in tears and quite intractable." Then he asked his father-in-law for assistance. The answer must have surprised him, for the father said he had given his daughter to More, and if she didn't obey he was to use his rights and "beat her into a better frame of mind." More answered instantly that he knew what his rights were but he preferred a change in his wife effected through her father's authority. The father agreed to do what he could, and after a day or two found an opportunity to speak to his daughter alone. Regarding her sternly he said, "You are a plain child, with no particular charm; and I used often to be afraid I should have difficulty in getting you a husband. After a great deal of trouble I found you one any woman might envy; a man who, if he weren't very kind, would hardly consider you worth having as a servant; and then you rebel against him!"

Of course, this warning was sufficient, and when More returned home with her, his training of her proceeded smoothly. She became a charming companion to him, and More was devoted to her, but she died at the birth of her fourth child. Now More was left with four little children and, solicitous for their welfare, early provided them with a stepmother. Once

[9] Preserved Smith, *A Key to the Colloquies of Erasmus*, "The Discontented Wife" (1927).

more he must train a wife to his tastes, and this time he knew how to manage the affair alone. His merry ways had always made him liked by women, and this trait, together with patience, enabled him to circumvent his second wife's sharp tongue and independent nature. Now he ruled his household with gaiety and charm, and always provided so well for each one that all of them knew he was ever mindful of their welfare. Though he took his duties cheerfully and seriously, he delighted in them, for, as he said, "When I come home, I must commune with my wife, chat with my children, and talk with my servants."

Stapleton tells us how More maintained the proper relations in his family even though such care prevented him from doing other things he sometimes wished very much to do. "All the things I reckon and account among [household] business," he said, ". . . must of necessity be done . . . unless a man will be a stranger in his own house." He believed, however, that a man must always be "merry, jocund, and pleasant" among those whom "either nature hath provided or chance hath made, or he himself hath chosen to be his fellows and the companions of his life." He realized such an attitude required a nice adjustment to all situations, for "with too much gentle behavior and familiarity," he must not mar these relations or "by too much sufferance of his servants make them his masters."

As the conduct books echoed More's attitude concerning a man's domestic responsibilities, they usually stated what would help to lighten them. Robert Crofts felt a man could scarcely meet his obligations unless he chose a woman he could love. Gouge felt a woman's age and piety were most important. If a man was five, ten, or fifteen years older than his wife, the disparity was not too great, he said, because a man's strength and vigor lasted longer than a woman's. He did not approve of old age and youth joined in marriage, for old age became irksome to youth, and then the resulting vexation outweighed all the content that had gone before. Piety was essential because it enabled love to increase and thereby preserve peace in the home. If wives did not have the fear of God in their hearts, they became not the weaker vessels but "the masters of their vassal husbands." With one voice all agreed mastery must be the husband's if peace and harmony were to reign in the household.

But men were not expected to do all the choosing. Women were also advised to have some ideas about the husband they wished to marry. This was true in homes arranging for children to meet their prospective mates before the contract was made, but particularly in homes permitting children to choose their mates for their parents to approve. Patric Hannay's waggish advice (*A Happy Husband, or Directions for a Maide to choose her Mate. As also a Wives Behaviour towards her Husband after Marriage*, 1619) was written in rhyme to make it popular and easy to remember. Since deformed men might have deformed spirits, he recommended suitable stature:

> No stature choose too low, for so in time
> Thy offspring may prove dwarfs; yet do not climb
> To one too tall: for buildings mounted high,
> Their upper rooms seldom well furnish'd be:
> Herein observe the mean, it's best of all,
> Let them not be observ'd for low or tall.

Manners and habits, like appearance, must also follow the golden mean by being not too attractive or too revolting. The maid would be wise, therefore, to learn something of her suitor's parents and whether the young man was given to drink or adultery. If he spent his time well and had a worthy goal he would be a safe risk, but he should not be too scholarly lest he prefer a book to his wife; even as learning polished a strong mind it also could besot a vain one.

Yet Hannay would not have a maid indifferent to books with precepts for guiding her life and tempering her understanding against the fickleness of fortune. For example, she would learn from them that her suitor must not be too talkative or too sullen. While she was appraising men, however, she must prepare herself to meet the biblical qualifications set down in Proverbs (31: 13–28). These he also turned into rhyme:

> . . . the good wife seeks for flax
> And wool, wherewith her hands glad travail takes;
> She's like a ship that bringeth bread from far;
> She rises ere appear the morning star;
> Victuals her household, gives her maidens food,
> Surveys, and buys a field, plants vines, with good
> Gain'd by her hands: what merchandise is best
> She can discern, nor doth she go to rest
> When Phoebus hides his head, and bars his sight,
> But by her lamp, her hands do take delight
> To touch the wheel and spindle; she doth stretch
> Her hands to help the poor, and needy wretch:
> Her words are wisdom, she o'er sees her train,
> That idle none do eat their bread in vain:
> Her children rise and bless her, sweet delight
> Her husband takes still in her happy sight.

The moralists were mostly concerned, however, about choosing the good wife. With his customary brevity, William Perkins, who supported his statements by biblical references, named the duties of such a wife: constant reverence for her husband, obedience to his will and judgment, leaving home only with his permission, and following him wherever he wished her to go. Among her household duties he stressed governing through good works on her own part, appointing work for maids and supervising it, ordering children and servants through both instruction and admonition, and preparing food or supervising its preparation.[10] Gouge listed the wife's duties in the same manner, adding that women would never find the yoke of submission too heavy unless husbands abused their authority. Becon's detailed exhortations were summed up under the four headings most moralists cited: obedience to husband, chastity, industrious performance of all household tasks, and the education and upbringing of children, daughters in particular.

Thomas Becon believed a wife's subjection to her husband was essential "to the maintenance of unity, love, and concord between married folk . . ." By looking to her husband as the head of the home and by trying always to please him, she won his heart to desire nothing more than to be in her company. If the opposite was true, the husband went home like a man "that goeth to battle among his enemies . . ." The wife who was chaste in word, deed, and apparel was a precious pearl. Even her companions were above suspicion. Her words were as pure as her acts, for she knew nothing was more unseemly in woman than unclean talk. It was even better for her to talk but little, for "nothing . . . garnisheth a woman more than silence." Her eyes and her very eyelids would reflect her purity as she moved about with eyes downcast, managing her home so that all things were kept safe in "due order," and all things "conveniently saved or spent." Such labors, besides bringing forth children whom she nourished herself and taught, gave her no time for running about except on urgent business for the family.[11]

When the group in Edmund Tilney's idealistic *The Flower of Friendshippe* discussed the wife's duties, Lady Julia was the leader who chose this subject. As the friends settled themselves comfortably on the benches in the summerhouse with its daisies and camomile, she began by saying they would assume the wife had a husband who was honest in conversation, affection, and especially in love. His wife, then, must be chaste above all things if she would help to keep the marriage a sweet, stable, joyful, and happy state. She would love her husband well enough to forsake family and friends if necessary, but she would never be too easily persuaded her husband loved her entirely lest such overconfidence cause him to hate her. Here she refers not to possessive love so much as to a meek wife's adoration of her honorable husband. A wife's love of an evil husband, however, was even more praiseworthy, for by her affectionate care she might save his soul.

Now Lady Julia turns to the means by which a wife may command her love. First she lists shamefastness as the "only defence that nature hath given to women to keep their reputation, to preserve their chastity, to maintain their honor, and to advance their praise." Then she names obedience, but her daughter, who is queen of the debate, objects, saying

[10] *Christian Oeconomie: Or, a Short Survey of the Right Manner of erecting and ordering a Familie, according to the Scriptures* (1609).
[11] *Worckes. The booke of Matrimony* (1581), fo. DCLXXV–DCLXXVI.

it is just as "meet" for the husband to obey his wife, for "there should be no superiority between them . . . as women have souls as well as men . . ." To this her mother answers calmly, "Man is better for sovereignty because he possesses what is rare in woman: namely, skill and experience, the capacity to comprehend, the wisdom to understand, the strength to execute, the solicitude to prosecute, the patience to suffer, the means to sustain, and above all, the courage to accomplish." Since she has overwhelmed her daughter's objection, she turns to the third help.

This help she calls circumspection, by means of which a woman preserves her good name. It demands constant effort on the woman's part to keep all suspicious persons from even approaching her, and constant employment in looking after her family by conferring with her husband, instructing her children, and pleasing her kindred. The fourth help is housewifery, which must be well performed from the little things to the delicate preparation of her husband's meat (food) when he is ill. The next help is patience, by which she endures all strains. For example, if her husband becomes drunk, she must cajole him into bed, and there reprove him lovingly, for only gentleness can reform a man. She illustrates this help by a favorite example with Elizabethan moralists. A wife, knowing her husband is committing adultery with a poor girl, sends to the girl's home a comfortable bed, pretending its rich trappings came from the girl's sister. The husband, suspecting his wife's care for making him comfortable and daintily served, questioned her about it and, when she admitted the truth, was so overcome by her generosity and kindness he forsook his evil ways entirely.

Such exaggerated writing was not performed with tongue in cheek but with downright seriousness. By this means Tilney supported the queen's effort to improve the morals at court, and Lyly, seeing the advantages it might bring, composed his two books on Euphues, to improve not only manners and morals but also speech. In their weary climb toward the dim goal of perfection, many English women were also close readers of French and Italian conduct books translated or adapted for their use, as in Garin li Brun's instructions for a well-bred lady. Li Brun's wife welcomed everyone to her house, even strangers. Since she could discern folly, she knew how to divert everyone in a pleasing, courtly manner, though she was only polite and never cordial to evil people who came to her home. At the same time she knew how to speak and how to act to make herself loved instead of disliked. She was always cheerful, yet sparing of her gentle, carefully modulated speech, and treated each person according to his mood. With intelligent men she was quiet and laughed but little, and never spoke first on any important topic lest she err. Her dress was in as good taste as her gentle speech, and when she went to church, she was accompanied by a companion whom she honored, walking gently and making little noise.

Another favorite author, Robert of Blois, repeated Li Brun's instructions and made additions. When going to church, women might greet politely those they met, but should not linger to talk with them. Always they must be careful about their eyes, preferably keeping them downcast. They must so dress as not to reveal their persons too freely. When entering a church, they should unveil, but must be very circumspect about it. If they could sing when in company, they should not refuse when asked, but they should never cheapen their gift by singing at the wrong time.

Phillip de Navarre objected to women leaning out of windows to attract attention or merely to see what was going on. At marriage feasts they must avoid speaking too freely; it was better for them to be haughty and scornful or even awkward than too easy. If they guarded well their bodies, they could hold up their heads anywhere, and all their faults would be forgiven. Thus it was not necessary for women to be given as much formal instruction as their brothers. Most women should be taught by their husbands, he believed. Certainly, the husband must teach his wife what people to choose for friends or acquaintances, and if he did not wish her to attend balls, feasts, or weddings he disapproved of, she must devise some excuse to stay at home. A woman must never contradict her husband, and she must never speak in secret to anyone but her husband. If he had cause to reprove her, she must listen in silence and patience. And she must never ask her husband for costly things unless in great need of them.

Giovanni della Casa's *Galateo* advised men as well as women on proper conduct. Dress should be according to one's age, condition, and means, and simple scents should be used instead of heavy perfumes. The subjects chosen for conversation should not be low or frivolous and they should not be too subtle or too delicate for discussion. Certainly they should not cause one or more of the company to blush for shame no matter how amusing they might seem; decent people should try to please decent people. Nothing should ever be said against God or the saints either seriously or in jest. Melancholy stories or talk of pestilence, wounds, illness, etc., should not be used at table during simple or festive meals. It was not good to relate dreams unless they were of unusual interest, and it was bad form to boast of one's own nobility or honors or wealth or judgment. In arguments a person should never mock another or speak ill of another, not even an enemy, and one should never lay down the law or give advice unasked. To monopolize the conversation was as much a breach of good manners as to laugh immoderately at one's own jokes. To talk constantly of children or husband was inexcusable; so were excessive talking or silence. When another person was telling a story, one must not interrupt or show inattention. There were some things a considerate person would never do: rising and walking about while others were seated, yawning or stretching or sleeping in the presence of others, taking out a letter and reading it while others were present, cutting one's nails or humming to oneself or drumming with the fingers while bored in a company of people. To nudge with the elbows was as bad as improper walking or sitting or standing. The custom of wearing tooth-picks on a chain around the neck was unsuitable, though some wore them attached to the girdle. People with bad taste were likely to be indifferent to others, or to embarrass them by staring at them too much or by trying to make themselves conspicuous. Such conduct was as wrong as being too gentle or yielding or flattering to one's superiors.

William Vaughan's *The Golden Grove* showed how well he studied such conduct books. As for the wife, he said she must never contradict her husband or deride him or desert him. Instead, she would cherish and comfort him, and study his moods and manners until she made them the rule of her life. Should he be absent from home a great deal, she would never mistrust or flout him or gibe at him, but would bear with all his coming and going. Nor must she ever speak of his faults to anyone lest she make herself a jest or provide knaves with some means to tempt her to do wrong.

When Jeremy Taylor preached on a wife's duties to her husband, he followed the general pattern of advice, but made his tone more conciliatory. Nowhere, he said, is a man told he must exact obedience from his wife. Rather, he should use "fair inducements and reasonable-ness . . ." When a woman promises to love and honor her husband, she should remember the Lord's explanation of love when he said, "This is love, that ye keep my commandments." In this way he would have a woman obey her husband—in reverence, not in fear. He admits that if she has a fool for a husband she "suffers a calamity," for she obeys in all things except commands that are "impious or refractory" according to her conception of wisdom or piety. By her submission, therefore, a good woman proclaims her opinion of her husband and his right to pre-emi-nence in the home.

In some minds of this period, a wife's chastity and obedience were inseparable. Vives had said a chaste wife's love would embrace father, mother, kin, and all her husband's friends, and after marriage she would be even more unassailable than before lest she blot herself and husband and kin. If she was disobedient to her husband, she was an offence to her own father and mother and kin. Thus she would bear with her husband even if he was evil. She might try to correct him gently, but never in anger. If he struck her or even beat her, she must try to understand his mood and to accord herself with him as long as she could feel she obeyed God's will. This constant reference to God's will was not meant to justify her disobedience when her husband's commands did not please her. Rather, it was a serious admonition seriously taken, for other Elizabethans besides Milton tried to justify God's ways with man. Thus a wife might look upon an evil husband as a cross she must bear with the constant need of choosing what obedience to render to him and what obedience she must render to God by disobeying her husband. Though a wife's obedience might be regarded by some men as purchasable, like that of the biblical husband's handmaid, still the price her husband paid for her was a life fellowship, and for that price she must consider nothing holier than to bear him children and to do his pleasure at his command. This was a duty even her obedience to God did not alter, for marriage had been ordained for the procreation of children. When, therefore, a writer declared the bond between husband and wife was an equal partnership, he might well face strong opposition by those who, like Vives, felt it was a one-sided bond as soon as the question of obedience was raised.

The blessed marriage, said Henry Smith, was the fruitful one of a chaste wife. If she had any defects, as in the case of Jacob's wife, Leah, to bring children to her husband made all amends. By those children she provided a wedding ring that sealed up her marriage. If she and her husband fell out, their little children would "perk up between them like little mediators, and with many pretty little sports make truce when others dare not speak to them." He cautioned newly married people not to be impatient to win the rewards of marriage, however. It took nine years to make a draper, but it took nineteen years to prepare for marriage and domestic concord.

The emphasis upon bearing children as one of the wife's chief duties gave rise to many superstitions. Husbands, if affectionate, were expected to suffer with the toothache during a wife's pregnancy, for most women at this time had trouble with their teeth. Pregnant women and women in childbed were thought to be in danger of being stolen by the fairies to nurse fairy children or to care for human children stolen by the fairies. A piece of bread or iron or the Bible in a bed of labor was supposed to be protection against the fairies. Till the child was christened, it was in danger of being bewitched by the fairies; hence great hastening of the christening ceremony occurred among the superstitious. Since women felt accursed if denied children, dishonest doctors and midwives carried on a flourishing business with gullible women who sought charms or any means whatsoever to bring the blessings of motherhood. In households where an expected heir was born or where the pregnancy of the wife had long been desired, the event was often celebrated with bonfires. Such a practice also strengthened the feeling for marriage as an institution for the legitimate procreation of children.

Even with obedient wives men might still have difficulty in establishing peace in the home, particularly if there were many relatives present, or if the house was so small as to make any kind of privacy almost impossible. Vives had assured women who could live peaceably with their husbands in adversity that they would inherit eternal glory. But he also urged husbands to aid their shrewish wives in gaining control of their sharp tongues by not scolding in return. To prevent disturbance from relatives in the home, Vives suggested that the wife prove her loyalty to her husband and his people by serving her husband's kin even better than her own. Once she gained their love and confidence, she must continue to do everything in her power to keep it, and this was to be a lifelong responsibility.

One of the first things the wife must do, said Vives, was to prevent her relationship with her mother-in-law from becoming that of a resented stepparent and child. He believed that the mother's natural jealous love of her son and the wife's natural objection to her husband's love for any woman but herself could be turned into a real attachment. He could not see why this relationship would be difficult for a wife who felt she and her husband were one through marriage. If she found it so, she must take tender care of her mother-in-law, especially in time of illness, and if by such care she did win the older woman's confidence, her own mother would surely rejoice with her.

In theory, the Elizabethan woman was subservient to husband, father, or brother in a way that present-day women cannot understand. In actual practice, her subservience depended upon the kind of husband and relatives she had and also upon her own temperament and dependence upon others. Shakespeare plays a game with these ideas in *The Taming of the Shrew*. Where does Katharina actually stand in this play? She has puzzled many critics by her speech after she has been subdued by her husband's rigorous training. Does she present a serious description in a rollicking comedy to please Elizabethans who liked that kind of juxtaposition? Or was she providing a comically fantastic application of Elizabethan psychology to the shrew for the intellectual members of the audience? Or was her speech merely a tongue-in-cheek romanticizing on the perfect wife? Or, finally, is the whole play merely a battle of wits to delight those demanding satire?

At first, Katharina is the butt of the comedy, and as such exacts from Petruchio pretty full use of his powers. Later, when she becomes the perfect wife who must be given the opportunity to deliver a lecture on the virtues of the submissive wife, she continues to play an equal part opposite her husband. As such she becomes one of Shakespeare's happily married heroines, and satisfies the conventions of comedy demanding such a conclusion. In his romantic portrayal of the happy wife, Shakespeare will have no struggle for mastery. Katharina as such, therefore, first commands the disobedient wives to stop frowning at their husbands: do they not "blot" their beauty and "confound" their fame as loving women? They will be shunned if they do not bring smiles to their faces: does not the world regard husbands as very lords? When lord-husbands endure the "painful labor both by sea and land" to maintain their wives in snug comfort, they have a right to demand in their wives "love, fair looks, and obedience," which are really "too little payment for so great a debt." Then, with the quick thrust of satire parried by the heavy blow of duty, Katharina drives home the lines that make the play's denouement:

Such duty as the subject owes the prince,
Even such a woman oweth to her husband;

. . . .

I am ashamed that women are so simple
To offer war where they should kneel for peace,
Or seek for rule, supremacy, and sway,
When they are bound to serve, love, and obey.

V:ii:147–65

Shakespeare makes it clear, however, that perfect submissiveness may lead to grief as well as to married bliss. Hermione in *The Winter's Tale* and Hero of *Much Ado About Nothing* are saved from the shipwreck of their fortunes only by the enlightenment of their lords' minds through the intervention of chance and the kind efforts of friends. Paragons of submissiveness need for husbands paragons of wisdom wrought in the crucible of life's suffering if the two are to walk as one. True, Hero merely follows the lead of circumstance and Hermione heroically defends her chastity, but without good fortune and friends both would be lost. Even the Griselda-like Helena of *All's Well That Ends Well* must use her almost masculine wit to fight for her rightful happiness, and still she would never have triumphed in her struggle without the aid of friends. The heroine of this complex plot has forced herself upon her husband and must pay for such an assumption of mastery in winning marriage by much suffering before the play can end "happily." The so-called dark comedies of Shakespeare found not a little of their heavy gloom in the conduct books read as avidly by those who went to the theater as by those who went to church.

In real life the wives of tradesmen enjoyed an independence that was often shocking to the pious. Middle-class women were frequently admitted to guilds on an equal footing with men, and were permitted to engage themselves as shop managers and assistants. Often, too, they were valuable to their husbands in small business ventures, and after the death of a husband, the widow might carry on the business alone. Records of women printers and booksellers preserved in the Stationers Company books prove this fact. Nevertheless, even these women gave more than lip service to the idea of subjection of their sex when father, husband, or brother chose to be master. They had to bow to the fact that man's authority was supported by the Scriptures: "Even as Sarah obeyed Abraham, calling him lord . . ." (I Pet. 3:6), "And the Lord God said, 'It is not good for man to be alone: I will make him an help-meet . . .'" (Gen. 2:18), "For a man ought to cover his head, forasmuch as he is the image and glory of God: but the woman is the glory of man . . ." (I Cor. 11:7). Some writers pointed out the disadvantage of this subjection, but said it was not in any way commensurate with the woman's danger of losing her good name, which obedience to the man having authority over her would avert. Plagued by these two fears, losing favor with her lord or protector and suffering the grief of scandal, an Elizabethan woman would find obedience far less onerous than the risk of losing her good name.

Some authors went to great lengths to illustrate a good wife's submissiveness. Gouge would have it shown in her very facial expression as well as by gentle tones and deeds. If she desired anything of her husband, she must entreat it; if she would move him to perform a bounden duty, she must use persuasion; if she would prevent him from doing evil, she must tell him of the fault, but with humility and reverence, taking great care to observe a "fit" season. If she was met by reproof, she must be patient and silent. In the disposal of her own property given her by her husband, she must consult him, though her intentions might be to supply things needed by the family. All her acts must be subject to her husband's approval—ordering of servants and children, entertaining guests or strangers, going "abroad," or even making vows. To hide away money or possessions from her husband was as disobedient as insisting on an allowance after he refused it, or discharging servants at her own pleasure, or secretly lending horses to vain friends she entertained in her husband's absence. An obedient wife must listen patiently when her husband tried to show her how to make herself pleasing to him. She must always show content with his estate regardless of what it was, and if ill fortune sent him to prison, she must seek permission to accompany him there. Cheerfulness and content must shine in her face as she willingly performed all her duties or accepted her husband's refusal of her requests for pleasure, comfort, or entertainment.

Women themselves wrote their approval of such abject humility expected of obedient wives. For example, Dorothy Leigh's *The Mothers Blessing* (1618) was written for this pious purpose when she wished to give advice to her children lest she, like their father, should die suddenly and leave them adrift in the world. In her apology for her authorship, she said that only her children's welfare caused her to sacrifice her womanly modesty and risk the censure of the world in making public her "scroll." Supported by her belief that her own husband would approve if he but knew, she made this effort to ensure the family reunion in heaven. She urged her sex to be ever willing to give men first place, for sin had entered the world through women. They must, therefore, be constantly on guard against all evil and see that their children frequently called on Christ for aid to cast out sin in themselves. In time she hoped her children would follow her example by writing down for their little ones what they had learned would show them the way to "true happiness."

It is not always easy to tell just where sincerity and convention met in such statements, whether in conduct books, letters, or plays. For example, the grandniece of Anne Boleyn, in pretty much the same vein as Dorothy Leigh, wrote to her husband, Sir Thomas Leighton, who was Captain of Guernsey. She fears her "Most Worthy Husband" has forgotten her, though she craves his pardon for such a thought even though it proceeds from greatest love. She "perceives" he will always keep "that constant course as not to cast off" his poorest friend, his wife, whom he "once thought well of," and which in itself she regards as "none of the smallest" of his "commendations." Now, "so kindly" does she take his "careful inquiry" of her well-doing in his friendly letter that she is moved to tell him how great her love is for him even "though it be fruitless and unaccompanied by such pains" as she has lately felt. It is such, however, as ever to joy in her husband's contentment and to desire his ever-increasing happiness. She hopes her dear husband will accept her "poor acquittals" which her good will can yield for all his "honorable favors" and will persuade himself that he can wish for nothing to be added to his fortune that can want her consent "though it were the favor of her Majesty, which is much for a wife to agree to." Nevertheless, she leaves him to "her good grace," and herself to his "wonted good opinion," and signs herself his "faithful Wife, and well-wishing friend."[12] It is quite possible, of course, that she smiled with no little satisfaction as she read over her graceful phrasing and then sanded her dutiful signature before folding the letter to give the waiting messenger.

A good wife must be humbly faithful in her obedient regard for a philandering husband, but in real life she might have him restored to her quite as dramatically as in the popular plays of the time. For example, it is not known just why Essex reformed so suddenly after the Cadiz voyage in 1596, but from this time on, he was a changed man. Was his wife's loyalty partly responsible? He became "sober, religious, and devoted" to her, "regularly attending prayers and preachings, and using language so replete with moral sentiments, with humility and self-distrust, as greatly to edify the astonished courtiers." Nor did he lapse again, according to his biographer,[13] for "he no longer entered into such intrigues with Court ladies as he had enjoyed before, and which had inflamed the Queen's anger and scandalized his moral friends." So unaccountable was his alteration it has even been questioned as sincere, but for all that, Essex was never again wanting in affection for his wife whom he now acknowledged as of mind and attainments truly suited to him for companionship. Her first attractions had been her great beauty and sweet humility.

The Puritans talked a good deal about the single standard even at court, where in general a husband's fidelity was not so commonly expected as that of his wife. Hence the amazement occasioned by the reformed Essex. To his wife he must have been a proof of God's miraculous power, for she had previously suffered much through him. When her marriage to him had caused her banishment from court, her anxiety

---

[12] Sir Nicholas Harris Nicolas (ed.), *Memoirs of the Life and Times of Sir Christopher Hatton* (1847), p. 228.

[13] Sir Walter Bourchier Devereux, *Lives and Letters of the Devereux, Earls of Essex* (1853).

about her husband's susceptibility to beautiful women had given her many unhappy hours, and their early married life had not been free from storms. However, she was so quick to beg forgiveness and so humble in blaming her fits of temper on her deep affection that she quickly achieved the happiness of reconciliation. Many were the letters she wrote her husband, and all of his she treasured in a little casket she kept always at her bedside.

Essex had lost the Queen's favor, and was seriously ill and in prison when his wife bore him a baby girl. Because the Queen would not let his wife see him, Essex grew worse and worse. Then learning how ill her husband really was, the distracted wife rose from her bed, attired herself in cheapest mourning, and went to court, where she sought aid from first one and then another influential friend. All wondered at her appearance, and all were so touched with pity that the Queen again ordered her away from court. Though she, like Essex, believed Robert Cecil an enemy, she turned to the Secretary in her desperation, and eventually was permitted to see her husband. Humbly, she now wrote Cecil a letter of gratitude for his efforts in her behalf. She said "simple thanks" were a "slender recompense" for his kindness to her, but they came from a mind "desirous to deserve" his "charitable work" and believed the same sincerity on his part would lead him to accept her "beggarly . . . tribute." As she believed pity alone moved him to "honorable mediation" on her behalf, "so no time or fortune" would ever extinguish in her or her lord their "thankful memory and due acknowledgment of so undeserved a benefit" from one who now she is assured "will never be proved" her lord's "malicious enemy." Only respect for his "manifold business" caused her to refrain from troubling him longer with her scribbled lines, but she rested "in thankfullest manner" his "exceedingly beholding friend." Could Essex have humbled himself in this manner he might have saved his head, but then it is doubtful whether Lady Essex could have achieved such willing subjection to another's position of authority without the weight of her experience as an obedient wife to bring her to her knees.

It was the lack of humility in the shrew as well as her shrill voice that made her so objectionable to the Elizabethan male. When she also possessed a ready wit she was an opponent who roused fear as often as chagrin. Henry Parrot's satire on a scold struck a chord in many a husband's memory as to how he had fumed helplessly during a wife's harangue. Parrot calls a shrew a "she-kind of serpent" whose poisonous tongue gives a more "venomed sting . . . than the biting of a scorpion" and cannot be cured. She is the "most untameablest" of all creatures, and "covets more the last word in a scolding than doth a combater the last stroke for victory." When she gets this word, she "loudest lifts it standing at her door . . ." She is not afraid of a justice or constable or even a ducking stool. She is most outraged when called a wasp, or when her husband sings or whistles while she is scolding, and at such times it is best not to come within her reach lest she scratch. If she is held by the hands she "presently begins to cry out murder," and nothing can pacify her but a cup of sack. If she gets enough of it she "thereupon falls straight a-weeping." Now is the time to entreat her with fair words or to flatter her, for she will straightway confess all her imperfections—and blame them on her maid. In her very sleep she calls her husband a rogue, and about all the poor man can do is die a martyr.

Actually a shrew might win her husband's love and certainly his respect if she was loyal to him and had a good as well as a strong mind of her own. But she kept him on tenterhooks and made him feel like another Job. Lady Mary, wife of the Earl of Shrewsbury, made life so difficult for her husband that he had to appeal to Sir Robert Cecil to help him make her obey. If she went uncurbed, he said, her example would be so "perilous" it might "encourage other strong-hearted women to do the like," and he prayed to God to "deliver all good men" from such torment. Yet, as the story runs,[14] when her husband's coat of arms was defaced on an inn in Newark, she told the "rascal" who had done the deed that his own son was also a reprobate and his child yet to be conceived would rue what had been done. Not satisfied with this, she carefully taught a servant to deliver a speech to the culprit, Sir Thomas Stanhope, calling him "more wretched, vile, and miserable than any creature living," and for his wickedness, he would "become more ugly in shape than any creature in the world; and one to whom none of reputation would vouchsafe to send any message." However, she was sending him a message by which she wished him "all the plagues and miseries that may befall any man" to light upon his head to the end that he might live long enough to see all his friends forsake him. She expected no repentance from such a caitiff and looked for him to be "damned perpetually in hell fire." Those not involved in the quarrel might laugh at the explosive shrew's outburst, but they would want none of it shattering the peace in their households.

Consequently, Elizabethan men had a good deal to say in praise of women who knew how to hold their tongues. For such people Nicholas Breton drew his picture of *A Quiet Woman*, whom he praised for speaking few words and keeping "sweet silence." She was a still wind that neither chilled the body nor blew dust into the face. Her tongue was "tied to discretion," and her heart was the harbor of goodness. She was the comfort of calamity, a companion in prosperity, a physician in sickness, and a musician in help. Her ways were a "walk toward heaven," for she was her husband's "down-bed" in which his heart lay at rest. Her servants honored her and her neighbors emulated her thrift and charity.

[14] Violet A. Wilson, *Society Women of Shakespeare's Time* (1925), pp. 178–81.

Such an unmatchable wife was "a turtle in her love, a lamb in her meekness, a saint in her heart, and an angel in her soul."

It was this gentle submissiveness that gave meaning to the letters of the wife of Southampton as she wrote her adoring messages to her husband in the year of 1599. While her "lord" was away from home on state business, she constantly expressed her desire to do only his pleasure. When left in the care of Penelope Rich at the Essex house in the country, she would not leave for trips up to London without her husband's consent. When she wrote for his permission to make these journeys, she always assured him that his will in the matter was the important thing, for one place was like another in his absence, as without him she found "quiet in no place." She did not like to trouble him with such small matters, and if he disapproved he must know what he disliked was most hateful to her also. She insisted that "no earthly power" could make her disobey his commands. Then she ended such letters by promising "never ending to pray to God" to keep him "free from all dangers perfectly well, and soon to bring" him to her, his "endlessly" and "faithful and obedient wife."

When she had first gone to the Essex house, she answered joyfully her husband's letter about the journey and her welfare after the fatigue of travel. "My dear Lord and only joy of my life," she began, "being very weary come to this house with my long journey I was very quickly healed of that pain with the reading your kind letter . . ." which had the same "force that all those dearly esteemed ones . . . have already had," and she "most certainly" knows that those she still is to receive will bring her all the contentment her mind can receive while she is severed from him she does and ever will "most infinitely and truly love." She hopes he will shorten his journey as he promises, for she "most infinitely" longs for him, her "dear and only joy," and she beseeches him to love her forever and everlastingly as she will ever remain his "faithful and obedient wife." Southampton, of course, read into these extravagant repetitions the sincerity and devotion that made them dear and eloquent. Like Perdita, she used for the pattern of her thoughts the purity of his, though she could not speak so well, "nothing like so well."[15]

Such wives took very seriously their duty of caring for their husbands when they were ill. Noble ladies were sometimes even more skillful than middle-class wives in making salves and ointments and in brewing herbs for teas and cooling drinks; certainly they were as faithful in their attendance in the sickroom. Southampton's mother, therefore, was not exceptional in her devoted nursing of her second husband during the long weeks of suffering before his death. In a letter to Robert Cecil at this

[15] Charlotte Carmichael Stopes, *The Life of Henry, Third Earl of Southampton, Shakespeare's Patron* (1922), p. 157. Mrs. Stopes quotes from the *Cecil Papers*, CIX, 31, and gives 1599 as the year in which the wife's letters were written.

time,[16] her husband gratefully refers to her concern, for "never man was more cared for than he is by his "most kind companion that cares not to kill herself to cure" him. He hopes God may reward her, for he cannot "except by the favor of that grace which upon earth is the fountain of . . . grace." Compounding simple remedies at her stills or working over some secret formula, she was tireless in her effort to relieve her husband's distress.

All through the Elizabethan age, capable mothers taught their daughters how to grow and use herbs for illnesses not demanding professional skill. If the remedies were secrets of the family, the mother's instructions were listened to with respect or even awe, and the daughters made a solemn promise to teach them to their own daughters. Some cooling drinks and cordials could be made from herbs and drugs purchased at the apothecary's shop if home-grown medicinal plants were not available. For simple illnesses, mints were used for colic, parsley for toothache, and St.-John's-wort for aching joints. Snails from the gardens were pounded into poultices by the wife who needed them in the sickroom. For serious ailments, the wife would consult an apothecary if one was available, for such men gave advice and sold drugs and even wrote prescriptions. They might also sell charms, such as a snake's head to be worn about the neck if one suffered from quinsy. In most prescriptions a common ingredient was powdered viper's flesh. Rhubarb and senna were used for physics, most housewives keeping on hand a favorite rhubarb syrup for dosing their families when any of them showed signs of illness.

Rich people, though having regular physicians in attendance, leaned heavily on the housewife's nursing and secret remedies. Dressed in black and frequently wearing spectacles, physicians carried a muff when walking abroad to keep their hands soft and white and warm, and to enhance their dignity they carried a cane with a pomander box in the top. If the physician served the general public, he filled his consulting room with bottles and jars of ointment and learned Greek volumes, and perhaps a skull on a shelf or a skeleton in a corner. Common people unable to afford a physician and getting no help from the housewife's remedies might call in herb doctors or wise women, who dosed them with concoctions of wormwood, juniper berries, or the juice of red nettles.

Ironically, the person suffering most was the housewife herself, especially during pregnancy or confinement. If she could afford a midwife who was respected for both her character and skill, the expectant mother might feel well prepared for her ordeal. Otherwise she might fall into the hands of a midwife depending on charms and witchcraft. To circumvent such abuses, the law required midwives to take an oath against any kind of sorcery or incantation during a woman's labor, and against sub-

---

[16] Stopes, *The Life of Henry, Third Earl of Southampton*, p. 90.

stituting any child for the one just born. Yet many simple charms were regularly used in the homes of the superstitious. As soon as labor began, all knots about the patient's clothing were loosened. If her labor was too difficult, the husband might be sent to ring church bells, and a piece of a bellringer's rope might be tied about the laboring woman to ease her pain. When the child was born it might be wrapped in some ancient garment to start it out well in life, and great care would be taken to carry it upstairs and then down. In spite of the dangers and difficulties of childbirth, the good wife must bear many children lest none survive the infectious diseases of the age.

It was necessary that women of all ranks follow the medieval custom of applying with their own hands the poultices and ointments and salves needed in dressing wounds or injuries of even the most menial servants. Physicians and wise women and the superstitious might try to heal diseases they knew nothing about, and the common sense of the housewife was likely to be the chief means of cure in a sickroom. This is why so many ladies nursed their husbands with their own remedies.

But the layman, too, had magic preparations for disease that would not respond to the usual remedies, and tied in with them were likely to be charms and superstitions. Ravens' eggs were thought good for ague, and if not effective, a spider should be swallowed whole in treacle. Epilepsy might be cured by drinking from a murdered man's skull at a spring in the night, and a tumor would disappear if stroked with a dead man's hand. The salamander's skin would prevent sunburn, and eating snakes would restore lost youth. If the eyes were bloodshot, a magic ring pressed against them would effect a cure, and a bloodstone pressed against the neck would staunch the flow of blood from a wound. Moles might be removed by the magic juice of the mandrake.

The king's touch was a supposed cure for many stubborn diseases like epilepsy. Fevers, colds, and rheumatism were the most prevalent diseases, though there were many cases of epilepsy, measles, and syphilis (called the French disease), and some cases of the green sickness. Venereal disease was usually treated by hot salt tub baths, commonly called the salt tub. Shakespeare frequently refers to this treatment.

Because of her practical knowledge, the Elizabethan housewife who hurried to the side of a stricken member of her family was prepared for service, not for the sentimental satisfaction of being close to a loved one. Indeed, she often felt there was no duty more solemn than cheerfully nursing a patient in her home, and if she was not successful, nothing gave her more distress of mind. When Sir Philip Sidney's aunt, the second wife of the Earl of Sussex, was unable to cure her husband, she wrote to Sir Christopher Hatton to thank him heartily for bemoaning her husband's painful sickness, and for comforting her grieved mind. She wishes she might write him that the consultation of physicians or the medicines applied to his feeble body brought him some ease, but "with heart's grief" she must admit his strength is "generally decayed, his pain greatly increased, and his physic hath offered rather torment than remedy." They have decided, therefore, to "forbear medicines" a few days and see what "good office nature is able to work for his ease." She praises her husband's resolute humility in thanking God for visiting him with so much pain, but she humbly beseeches God to "send him shortly to recover." She cannot bear to see the "painful torments of his disease" in spite of the fact that he is all patience in his affliction.

A year later malicious gossip had alienated her husband's affections from the countess before his death. She had been refused permission to nurse her husband in his last illness, and wrote frantically to the Queen. She had not only been prevented from performing a good wife's most important duty at such a time, but had also been greatly injured by gossip about her absence from her husband. "Most Gracious and Most Merciful Queen," she wrote, "I most humbly beseech your Majesty to view these few lines, written with many tears, and even in the bitterness of my soul, with that pitiful regard wherewith God hath viewed your Majesty at all times and in all cases." Then she tried to explain her position, in which she felt "beaten down with many afflictions and calamities hardly to be borne of flesh and blood." The grief that pierces her most deeply is the "sinister suggestion" that she has been undutiful to the Queen and to the honor of her "dear Lord lately deceased." She appeals to God to defend her from the first, for as "searcher of hearts, and revenger of all disloyalties," He alone could know the truth. The second matter requires the Queen's protection, however, for she knows how from time to time the countess was more careful of her lord's health, honor, and well-doing than for her own soul and safety, "refusing all friends and friendships in this world for so dear a Lord," whom she followed "in health and sickness, in wealth and woe, with more care than became a true Christian to owe unto any worldly creature." She accuses her slanderers of long complotting her ruin, and choosing the time when her lord "through anguish and torments was brought to his utmost weakness" when they broke the "perfect bond and love of twenty-eight years' continuance." At the same time they sought to instill into the Queen's ears the countess' want of loyalty, which she would die to preserve. She finds herself, therefore, trodden down by her inferiors, "not only in worldly maintenance," which she little esteems since God has given her more than she deserves, but in the "chiefest point of honor and the highest degree of duty, which bringeth on every side such a sea of sorrows" that, if God would not punish her for it, would tempt her to take her life.

The letter concludes with the countess begging the Queen to protect her from "the malicious speeches and unconscionable extremities" of those taking advantage of her lord's weakness to work her disgrace, and especially not to add to her griefs by royalty's heavy displeasure. She prays God to let her die while she writes the very lines of this letter if she has done anything wittingly to deserve her Majesty's just dislike. In the meantime she will not cease to pray to God for the Queen's life, health, and prosperity, and signs herself "Your Majesty's poor, but true faithful servant, to die at your feet." As this letter indicates, the lady's worst fear was for her reputation, and with good cause.[17]

Any Elizabethan housewife too long away from home was likely to stir the curiosity of gossips or to suffer deeply from the abuse of critics in her own social circle. Often fiery-tongued preachers referred to such women as examples of evil. To be absent from home when the husband was well might be dangerous to a wife's reputation, but to be away during his illness made her guilty of an unforgivable evil. Henry Smith urged women ever to abide at home as if it were a paradise rather than a prison. Thomas Carter believed women went from home chiefly to display their fine clothes, and called them "street wives." No good woman, he said, would ever "spin street thread." Such wives forced their husbands to lay more on their backs than they could put in a purse for a long time after; then the wives would gad from place to place, showing their pride and their husband's folly. Bullinger had insisted that no wife ever cross her doorstep without her husband's permission, and even then not go far from home. Most moralists agreed that a woman exposed herself to unspeakable dangers if she did not stay closely confined at home during her husband's absence or illness. The countess, therefore, had good cause to bemoan her lot when she was separated from her home and husband as the Earl of Sussex lay on his death bed. Indeed, she might well contemplate the sacrificing of her very life.

The demure Virgilia in Shakespeare's *Coriolanus* adopts the idealized convention of the good wife remaining at home while the husband is absent. When a "gossip" comes to invite her to go visiting, Virgilia refuses even though her husband's mother urges her to go forth. The invitation is most proper, for the young wife is asked to visit a mother who is receiving callers after the birth of her child. Virgilia tells her friend she wishes the young mother speedy recovery of her strength and will visit her with her prayers. The gossip good-naturedly scoffs at her, calling her another Penelope who but stays home to spin yarn and fill another Ithaca full of moths. Still failing to change Virgilia's mind, the gossip tries teasing, saying she has news of the warrior husband which she will impart if Virgilia will but go with her. This touches the wife at the tenderest point, as she trembles for the safety of her adored husband. But she will not leave home even to hear news of him. The gossip can no longer bear to keep the faithful wife in suspense, and tells her the wars are to be brief and her lord will soon return. As Virgilia watches her friend and mother-in-law leave the house, she is humbly grateful for the blessed news and also for the strength to refrain from putting

---

[17] Both letters by the countess are given in Nicolas, *Memoirs of the Life and Times of Sir Christopher Hatton.*

her foot over the threshold during her husband's absence from home (I: iii: 76–122).

Of course husbands did not wish their wives to leave home in their absence lest they be indiscreet, even innocently so, for men believed they knew the perils of scandal better than their wives did. Many wives were also tormented by just such fears about their absent husbands, and both preachers and writers of conduct books had much to say on the subject. Should a wife hear evil reports of her husband, she must stop her ears against them, and if on his return she should learn he had been with a mistress, she must remember that to leave a dishonest husband would only please the mistress. A wise wife, therefore, would seek to marry the mistress off to some honest servant. They quoted Vives about a husband not ceasing to love his wife while with his mistress, and even argued that a wife's displeasure might drive the husband to the mistress. Therefore, the wife had but to be patient, and her husband would return to her.

The moralists were right, however, when they said a good Elizabethan housewife, particularly among the upper classes, had little time for "walking abroad." She was indeed kept too busy supervising her servants even though she herself did not perform many actual tasks. True, the chief steward was supposed to take most of the responsibilities off the shoulders of the great lady, but many such women took pride in their housewifery, and did not care to delegate their duties to even the best of stewards. The training and directing of wards as well as maids took much of their time; even among good servants there was danger of undue extravagance unless all the offices were carefully controlled. Possibly the trait of orderliness was more strongly developed at this time, for preachers and writers continued to quote from Gentian Hervet's translation of Xenophon, *Treatise of the Household* (1537). Again and again they admonished the good housewife to see that there was a place for everything and everything was kept in that place. The husband had to go abroad instead of "slugging at home," and therefore the wife must not leave home "to walk about" when she was responsible for maintaining all things well in her household.

Most wives felt the need of economy in household management because of the expense involved in keeping up appearances. This was especially true of the ambitious middle class. Bullinger had advised the saving housewife to demand no more than necessary for her household simply because all unnecessary things were always dear, and "it was easier to save than to get." He had also urged performing all things in their season without delay, leaving to others nothing she could do herself and dispensing with nothing she might be able to use later. Such wives, he had argued, not only enabled their husbands to amass riches honestly, but were rich themselves in their good works and in their giving of their substance to the poor.

Economy for its own sake and for its rewards was drilled into Puritans as a necessity in maintaining a home, but need frequently drove great Anglican or Catholic ladies to display this virtue. The thrifty housewife, if she relied on food from the markets, closely supervised the purchases made for the household, and the middle-class women journeyed to the shops and made the purchases themselves for the accompanying servant or apprentice to carry home. Then the cooking and baking and sewing and mending kept their own hands, besides those of their maids, busy from dawn to dark.

In the country house, hand labor supplied the fuel and lights as well as linens, clothes, medicines, food, and everything needed for the family's welfare. Along with cooking, distilling, preserving, and pickling, the housewife must provision her storerooms with smoked and cured hams and bacon, with fish and other meats pickled or salted down for long keeping, and with large quantities of apples and vegetables for winter use. She must always have large stores of food ready for any emergency, for besides looking after the members of her household, she must be prepared at any time to care for poor travelers and journeymen or visitors and guests who were constantly coming and going through her hospitable doors.

Winter stores had to be planned with especial care. Stored foods like apples and vegetables had to be sorted frequently to ensure them against rot; onions and garlic and herbs were dried and hung from the ceiling of the kitchen or stored in lofts or long garrets under the roof, and in these garrets were also placed trays of dried fruits, such as apples, peeled and cut into thin slices and dried in the ovens when the daily baking was finished. Fruits and vegetables were pickled, and favorite fruits were candied or preserved or made into rich syrups or delicate jellies. When fruit ripened suddenly, the mistress and servants almost melted in the double heat of summer months and the boiling syrup pots.

Yet in such heat were brewed delicate wines: currant, elderberry, and cowslip, and in the great houses, perry (pear cider), mead, and sack. Ale was brewed once a month or oftener in most households, and bread, butter, and cheese were made daily as a rule. Though sack was not a common drink like ale, great quantities of it were made, and in season, vinegars like raspberry and cider. Since there was no tea or coffee or chocolate for a hot morning drink, and since water was seldom wholesome, the wines and other fermented drinks, hot or cold, were an important part of Elizabethan meals.

As if the summer months could not be too crowded, the housewife must see that flowers were grown and picked and made into conserves—rose, violet, and cowslip being the favorites. Flowers were also essential for the perfumes and pomatum essences and for beautifying washes. Great supplies of lavender and rose potpourri must be prepared for linens to keep them sweet and fresh when they were folded away in the presses. Since the great houses might entertain important visitors with whole retinues of servants, their suites of rooms required a great deal of linen to be kept in reserve, delicately scented with rose or lavender.

Yet housewives found time to exchange with trusted friends recipes and secrets about processes for making perfumes, tinctures, juleps, and cordial waters for the sick. In this way each generation increased the number of valuable formulas to be handed down from mother to daughters. Sometimes they made these formulas seem very mysterious by giving careful directions for gathering the ingredients according to the position of moon or stars, and so gave them semimagical qualities. Possibly the mother enjoyed as much as any of her labors the time she spent teaching her daughters about distillation and the preparation of elaborate essences and perfumes and cordials, for they were far more exciting than the ordinary rosewater and lavender waters made for daily use about the house. The girls must also learn how to choose the right flowers for complexion washes or pastes, and how to make the pastilles for burning in rooms to sweeten them. Since pastilles consisted of spiced pastes, they permitted women to exercise considerable ingenuity in concocting new scents for admiring guests to praise. Some women also experimented with new medicines for working magic cures.

Most mixtures in the distillery made use of common flowers and leaves, such as sweet marjoram, lavender, rosemary, roses, pinks, maudlin, thyme, white endive and succory and spinach, saffron, and walnut leaves. All girls must know how to use angelica oil or musk in scents for their gloves and dresses, how to prepare good pot herbs for seasoning, water of fumitory for liver medicine, cold herbs for agues, syrups and treacle and rosewater for medicines or conserves, and tart vinegar made from various fruits in season. Whether they worked alone or with others in the distillery, they whiled away many hours at this fascinating labor.

Rosewater was commonly made by softening or steeping roses in their own juice with a "proper amount" of yeast. After a few days of fermentation, or until the mixture produced a strong, heady smell almost like vinegar, the mass was distilled into well-sealed jars for a warm bath. Then the solution was redistilled until "a perfect spirit" of the rose resulted. This procedure was used for other flowers and herbs, but since it was so tedious, Sir Hugh Platt, in his popular cookery and household book of recipes in the early seventeenth century, *Delightes for Ladies*, suggested a short cut to the distillation. He would have the petals pressed, first their juice distilled and then the petals and then "in one operation more might be achieved than in two or three or four usual ones." He admitted, however, that although this rosewater could be used in syrups, decoctions, and medicines, it was not so pleasing to smell as that made by the longer process.

Sir Hugh's little book, in spite of its early thirteen editions, was so read to pieces that few copies of it remain today. He knew how to meet the demand for new recipes dealing with jams, jellies, and conserves, how to gild pills to make them less objectionable to the patient, how to preserve fruits in vegetable "pitch" (coating), and what was new in cures for little but highly irritating troubles like chilblains and bruises. For bruises he advised an application of hot cloths wet or dry "without intermission" for an hour or until the swelling was gone. For chilblains of hands or feet, he suggested boiling four quarts of oats in a quart of water till dry. Then, after rubbing the hands or feet well with a good pomatum, a person should put them in the oats as hot as he might "suffer them." This was to be repeated three or four times. The oats could be used again several times.

Sir Hugh's recipe for making syrups of roses and other flowers called for a silver basin filled three-fourths full of rain water, to which was added a "convenient" amount of rose leaves or other flower petals. The basin was put in another pan of hot water for three-fourths of an hour. Then the petals were wrung out gently and steeped with other equal amounts of petals till the process had been performed seven times. Now the remaining rose-scented water was made into a syrup, of which the proportions consisted of two spoonfuls of rosewater to one-fourth pound of the best refined sugar or sugar candy. When this syrup was to be used for candying, it must be "hard and glitter like diamonds." Into it could be dipped red roses, gilly flowers, marigolds, etc. Sometimes distilled rosewater needed freshening before it could be used. This was done by putting it through fresh rose petals or broken rose cakes. After three or four hours of softening over a gentle fire without burning, the concoction was ready for redistilling.

When flowers were to be candied, they were dried in the sun or over a fire before being placed in the prepared "glittering" syrup. Or they could be placed in the rosewater and sugar, boiled a little, covered with double refined sugar powder and boiled a little again, then removed from the fire and powdered again with the sugar. Now they were ready to dry in the sun or in a close, warm room for two or three hours. Preserved whole flowers required skill in handling. They must not be quite full blown, and as they were dipped in a cooled syrup of double refined sugar or sugar candy, each of the petals must be carefully opened by a bodkin, and the flowers placed on papers in pewter dishes for drying in the hot sun or close, warm room. With care they might be dried in the oven, but after they were dry such flowers had to be kept in glass jars in a dry cupboard near the fireplace. Sugar plate, so often mentioned as a delicacy at banquets and celebrations, was made by heating any kind of flowers in a mortar with a little hard sugar, then adding rosewater and steeping the mass over a pan of water till it could be worked into a paste.

Most of the small earthen glazed pots used for these preparations were called gally pots. They were much in demand for ointments as well as for preserves, musk sugar, and candied delicacies. Elizabethan delight in strong scents caused them to make much use of musk sugar, but it was so expensive to buy at two shillings a pound that most women made it at home. Placing four to six grains of musk in a piece of fine cloth like sarcenet or fine lawn or cambric, they laid it in a gally pot, covered it with sugar, and shut the jar tight. After the sugar was all used, the musk was good for further supplies of sugar. When flowers were dried in the sun by frequent turnings, they were put up in glasses or gally pots "stopped" with lute, a cement-like clay used for sealing. Then they were stored in warm places like close cupboards opening off the fireplace. Sometimes paper bags were used instead of the gally pots.

The housewife with pretty hands or pride in her appearance was concerned about keeping her hands white. To remove stains acquired in the usual household tasks, she commonly washed her hands in sorrel juice. For removing freckles, she might follow Platt's suggestion about birch sap. In March or April, a hole was made in the birch tree, and a glass receiver was used to catch the running sap, which was patted on the freckles. To whiten the teeth, Platt recommended a quart of honey, a quart of vinegar, and a pint of wine boiled together. This concoction was to be used now and then as the teeth became stained. A simple remedy for a pimpled face was patting the face with a linen cloth dipped in common salt dissolved in lemon juice. But if pimples were hard to remove, Platt had another remedy, which he called "a good skinning salve." Brimstone ground in oil of turpentine should be applied to the pimple for one hour. Then the swelling was to be rubbed with the thick oil of fresh cream from the milk of the previous evening. The skin would then heal, he said, and scale away in a few days and be fair.

Food in season was the common man's fare if he had the comforts of a good table. But the Elizabethan housewife liked to please her guests and perhaps herself with fruits out of season. So pomegranates were covered with a thin wax and tied with strings at top and bottom and hung on nails in a warm, close room. Every three or four days they were turned by means of the string so that they were not touched. With this care they could be kept till Whitsuntide . . . perhaps. Grapes at Easter? Platt had the answer. Put in a basket a grapevine that was to bear, and when the grapes were ripe, cut off the stalk under the basket. Then put the container with its grape-laden vine in a warm place. Such grapes would stay "fresh and fair a long time on the vine." Another device was to dip the end of the long vine in vegetable pitch and fasten an apple at the end of the stalk, renewing it when the old apple was decayed. Vines with such grapes should also be hung on a line in a close, warm room.

More practical was the preservation of dainty biscuits boxed for long keeping and use on short notice. Platt's recipes for jumbolds (fine sweet biscuits) and French biscuits indicate the type of sweet cakes preferred. For jumbolds, a half pound of almonds must be beaten to a paste with grated short cake, two eggs, two ounces of caraway seeds, and the juice of a lemon. Then the paste was rolled into strings and "cast into knots" and baked in an oven. When done they were iced with rosewater and sugar and the white of an egg beaten together, then "gilded" with a feather and placed in the oven till they were iced all over with a white ice. For the French biscuits, one-half peck of flour, very fine, two ounces of coriander seeds, an ounce of anise seeds, the whites of four eggs, and half a pint of ale yeast were mixed with enough blood-warm water to make a stiff paste. This was formed into a roll as big "as one's thigh" and baked in the oven an hour. When it was a day old, it was pared to remove all oven grit, then sliced and sugared over with fine powdered sugar, the slices dried in the oven, and sugared again and boxed.

So fond were Elizabethans of seasoning, that even the butter was made "dainty" by mixing with it as soon as it was made a few drops of extracted oil of sage, cinnamon, nutmeg, mace, etc. A dainty cook always seasoned meats highly, and could easily and ingeniously improve upon suggestions like Platt's. At holiday time seasoning was very important, and typical of indispensable dishes was "soused" young pig, boiled with white wine, bay leaves, ginger, quartered nutmegs, and cloves. It was made ahead of time that it might be on hand for any special occasion, and put down in the broth in which it was cooked. Capons were boiled in clear water and then seasoned with mutton broth, a little white wine, a little whole mace, little bundles of sweet herbs, and a little marrow. These juices were thickened with almonds, cream or egg yolks, and sugar, with a dash of verivace (sour fruit juice) to cut the sweet. Later, the breasts were stuffed with currants and quartered dates. When served they were garnished with lemon sliced and sugared.

Oftentimes the housewife was much concerned about meat for the year round. In cold weather it could be kept reasonably long, but those who raised their own food had ways and means of putting down sufficient quantities to tide them over the off seasons. Salmon, for example, might be kept by seething it first in the usual manner and then putting it into "close vessels" in wine vinegar with a branch of rosemary. Fish of many kinds might be fried in oil, preferably sweetest Seville oil, or that made from rape, and then put down in white wine vinegar till ready to use. Beef was put down in wine vinegar, but the pieces had to be kept reasonably small. Beef was also salted well for ten or twelve days, then seethed, then dried with a cloth, and wrapped in fresh dry cloths. Such beef could then be kept in "close vessels and cupboards" for two or three months before using. Even oysters might be kept for a while by pickling them in white wine vinegar and salt and pepper. They were put into small casks and covered with the "pickle." Platt declared oysters so prepared could be "carried into dry towns or on long voyages." All this preparation for future needs in addition to the daily cooking made the kitchen and distillery a busy place the year round, but probably most of all in the hot months of summer when fruits and flowers were most available, and in the late autumn when animals were slaughtered for winter food.

If soap and candles were made at home, the housewife saved all her cooking fats. In town, soap might be bought by the barrel, and if the extravagant mistress spurned homemade candles, she sold or gave away her household fats to women who came calling for them at the gate. In the country, however, the fats were kept till the candlemaker arrived on his regular visits, and then he made the necessary amount of rush candles for the servants. These yellowish candles with their rush wicks were evil-smelling to sensitive noses, and many a dainty miss turned from them in disdain, longing for the waxen candles with cotton wicks that burned in the parlor and hall. The poor, of course, had only rush candles. When soap was made at home, these same kitchen fats were combined with lye and scented with herbs or rosemary, and if not scented, the soap had its own peculiar odor that the plain housewife described with some pride as "clean." Such soap was not often used in washing clothes or linens. Instead, the family laundry was vat-washed in lye every three months or so, and beaten by maids with wooden bats; this process was hard on the material, but cleansing. London housewives frequently sent out their laundry as Shakespeare indicates in *The Merry Wives of Windsor* when he alludes to the washing, beating, and bleaching given such clothes (III:iii: 140–59).

Since featherbeds were in fairly general use in the latter part of the sixteenth century, the country wife must have her own flock of geese and a goose girl to watch over them. Then came the stripping of the breast feathers and, when the accumulation of cured feathers justified it, the making of pillows, quilts, and mattresses. Such beds must be regularly supplied with clean linen, and with the laundry periods so far apart, the household linens alone would keep the spinning wheel in contant motion. A good housewife always expected her maids to spin or sew when not engaged in some particularly assigned task, and her maids accepted such labor as a matter of course.

Since Elizabethan housewives looked upon their duties as a vocation or even a career, they took pride in their domestic achievements. It is doubtful whether many of them ever objected to their destiny; it is more than likely that most of them experienced great satisfaction from useful accomplishment. Besides having the daily preparation of food and its special preserving and curing for future needs, the fine and coarse needlework, the spinning of wool and flax, and the embroidery of linens, furnishings, and apparel, the good housewife, with her distilling of perfumes and medicines, was also doctor and nurse to neighbors and friends as well as to her own household. Moreover, if her husband was a farmer, she might have to care for sick animals, and if her husband was a county squire, she might have to act for him in any lawsuits that arose. Only the weaklings in such a whirlpool of activities had time or inclination to become enmeshed in corroding distractions of mind or emotions.

The country wife in a large establishment was often called upon to perform heavy labor as well as to assume heavy responsibilities, and was usually the first up in the morning and the last to bed at night. Besides overseeing her maids and engaging in some of the preparation of fruits, herbs, and root vegetables for storage, she must be sure of enough lard for her household needs and enough seeds for the next plantings. She must be responsible for the kitchen garden and the honey bees, she must buy the household necessities or see that they were bought, she must have charge of oven and cellar and see that all supplies were stored under lock and key, she must keep hens, and perhaps geese, pigeons, pheasants, and possibly peacocks, and she must know how her servants should handle hemp and shear the sheep and keep the fleeces or supervise their transformation through spinning, combing, and weaving till they became cloth and then clothing for her family and servants. She might have to supervise the feeding of cattle, calves, hogs, and other animals, and the milking of cows morning and evening. Since few farmers fed their livestock over the winter, she had to know where the grass was first green in spring, for calving cows needing to regain their strength. Though the farm implements were crude, she must see that they were kept in order: scythes for mowing, flails for threshing, and iron-shod wooden plows that worked the soil over and over again, unless, perhaps, a plot was left now and then to lie fallow. Fertilizers were talked of, for example by Tusser and Markham, but seldom used. Yet Sir Hugh Platt's *The Jewel House of Art and Nature* (1594), which deplored the lack of manure in English farming and the lack of winter feed for livestock, would make her wonder whether she might add those tasks to the labors of the farm.

If her husband owned much land and she had to take charge of it, she frequently saw to the leasing of farms, secured markets for the crops harvested under her supervision, and wrote or dictated to her husband long letters about details of management. Sometimes she even wrote business letters as well as the recipes for her book of domestic information she was to hand down to her eldest daughter. If she could not read or write, she might have to delay her letters till the arrival of the "coneyman" who came once or twice a month to buy her rabbits for market, for many a common man's wife depended on such people to write important letters for her. Some yeomen's wives, however, could read and write as well as their husbands, and their daughters at village schools sometimes got a smattering of reading and writing that enabled them later to manage business details in the absence of their husbands. Among the religious wives who could read, time must be found for reading long sermons to their household during the master's absence. In all the multitudinous tasks there was time for the woman's touch when such housewives named their cows and horses and ordered these names entered in the inventories of their wills.

As time wore on, some of the housewife's labors were lightened as weavers of the village or guild took the thread spun at home from flax or wool and wove it into cloth during the fairly regular visits asked of them by certain households. Even so, the housewife must be able to scan all the woven material for possible flaws, and also to keep plenty of wool and linen cloth on hand for sewing. With all clothing made by hand and all households of any pretensions at all dressing the members according to rank, the supervision of such work alone was a great task. On important occasions, gowns might be made by a tailor, but most households, especially in the country, had their wearing apparel made at home. Thus a common country maid was kept busy at milking, brewing ale, washing, scouring, and spinning, but the maid who fashioned materials into garments must be skillful in sewing and willing to accept close criticism as she worked busily with needle and thread. In town where the housewife usually bought materials already woven, she was commonly expected to supervise the making of apparel from them. Good taste in dress was important to a woman engaged in many social activities.

In addition to overseeing all her household tasks, the good wife still managed to find time to rock her babies to sleep, and later to prepare them as young children for entering school with a knowledge of reading and writing, or at least with sound training in morals and manners. That she had left after all these labors the spirit, as well as the ability, to assist her husband when he asked her aid in any of his undertakings makes one wonder how she was ever able to crowd so much into her long working days.

After the charming and beautiful heiress, Margaret Dakins, married Sir Thomas Posthumus Hoby and went north with him to her estate at Hackness, she and her husband led a most sedate country life. In summer she superintended the dyeing of wool, the winding of yarn, the making of wax candles, sweetmeats, preserves, perfumes and sweet waters, etc. In winter she sat spinning with her maids or embroidered while one of them read from some devotional book. At the same time, because of her husband's inability to be a good supervisor, she superintended the activities on her lands, the haymaking, the buying of sheep, the sowing and harvesting of crops, and the paying of workmen's wages. She took care of the tenants with medicines she had brewed and, like a good housewife, dressed burns, set bones, applied cordials and physics and purges, and watched over the moral as well as physical welfare of all her servants. For recreation she fished and bowled, as she did not care for hunting and falconry which more fashionable ladies usually engaged in while at their country homes.

This once lively participant in gay social life settled down into the life of a grave woman, reading each day from the Bible and writing out sermons or spiritual exercises under the guidance of the household chaplain. Her great efficiency made her husband's inadequacy increasingly apparent, and this, added to the reports of his Puritan coldness in entertainment, turned away from him the good will of the people. Naturally his virtuous manner got on the nerves of his jovial neighbors, but his wife, in spite of being more or less forced into her marriage, decided to make the best of it. With the aid of her own Puritan tendencies, therefore, she came to her husband's aid when he was scorned for his sanctimonious behavior. Since she had no children, Margaret gave herself over more and more to her religious interests. When she went up to London she seemed no longer to care for her old pleasure in the gaiety of life, but went instead to the sermons of grave, eminent divines who preached such solemn matter as she read in domestic books of the time. To her mother-in-law, Lady Russell, she became a most satisfactory daughter, achieving almost the impossible in pleasing this sternly critical religious woman who had been both anxious and irritated over the uncertainties of her son's long wooing of the attractive heiress.[18]

With so many details to occupy her mind and hands, no Elizabethan woman would seem to be in danger from scandal, which settles so easily upon an idle, frivolous young woman. But no conscientious Elizabethan housewife ever forgot that she must take every precaution against jeopardizing her reputation. Like Susanna in the Apocrypha, she must be on the alert against lecherous men and capable of defending herself against any villain who might seek to destroy her good name. At the same time she must never fail to keep her air of sweet innocence. Many of these Puritan women especially taught their daughters the moral lesson of the Susanna story, just as it had been taught them, and when Robert Aylett put the story into rhyme in 1622, it became immediately popular.

Aylett sets the saint in an idyllic English scene with her husband superintending the workers in the field while the wife busies herself in the house with her maids. Like the good wife in Proverbs, she had brought her husband prosperity and planted an orchard in which she and her husband retired from the cares of the world. Here also she walked alone meditating and praying and reading the Scriptures. Often, as she supervised the work of her maids she led them in singing David's "sweet lays," and so made her house a "school and academy to instruct the soul." Her being alone in the orchard was her undoing, however, for it gave the elders their chance to try to seduce her, and failing, led them to slander her. But for the young Daniel sent by the Lord to defend her she would have lost her life. Against slander no mortal could defend her, neither husband nor friends; only God could prove her innocence by the means of the spirit-Daniel. As this lesson was taught to Elizabethan girls, they were shown that although their innocence might win them a protector, they could scarcely escape from slander except by the intervention of God himself. Hence the insistence that maids and wives be ever accompanied by one or more companions.

But the Aylett version of this popular tale made another point that good housewives took to heart: a wife was to seek redress through her

---

[18] Violet A. Wilson, *Society Women of Shakespeare's Time*, pp. 23–40.

Plowing. Woodcut, 1569

A harvest scene, from *Chronicles*, by Raphael Holinshed, 1577

husband only when her chastity was threatened. Other injuries she must be wise enough to defend herself against, for she must be a helpmate, not a burden. At the same time, however, she must also concern herself about the welfare of her mate's soul. If ever he grew vain or fell into difficulties, she must be able to quote a suitable proverb in a gentle, sweet voice, or teach him his error by an entertaining tale, or perhaps weave a wise sentence into her conversation with him. Prudent wives with husbands who spent too freely might say at the right time, ". . . stretch out thine arm no farther than thy sleeve will reach," or "Sparing is a rich purse." Many a time they might worry over expenses and express their anxiety in several versions of the saying, "Spend no more than thou wottest how to get it; when thine expenses and receipts be alike, a little loss may overthrow thee." And if that was not strong enough, they might advise gravely, "Spare as thou shouldst never die, and yet as mortal, spare measurably." Perhaps the husband was a procrastinator. Then the wife must find as many ways as possible to say, "Whatsoever thou mayst do tonight, defer it not till tomorrow." She might refer to how often the Bible reminded one to "begin everything in due season," and conclude with "If thou wilt prosper, then look to everything thine own self." If she had a sense of humor, she might know how to add, "everything but what thy wife can do for thee."

With their love of introspection and analysis, Elizabethans enjoyed the character sketch that developed so rapidly at the end of the century. Its brief, didactic material often presented suitable topics for discussion or satiric rejoinders. As writers of such sketches repeatedly identified their subjects with a stratum of Elizabethan home life, and enforced their point by numerous examples of the type under discussion, they frequently wrote vignettes that illuminated the domestic scene. Usually they avoided personal traits lest they detract from the universality of the theme, unless they wished to produce caricature. Even then, the purpose was didactic.

Gervase Markham, who wrote on many subjects connected with domestic life, contributed his sketch of a good wife. After enumerating the usual virtues, he considered the wife as a cook, for in this field he felt himself an authority. She should prepare dishes to satisfy nature, and not to renew appetites, he insisted. Nor should she buy food from markets but grow it in her own yard. In this way she could serve good food, esteemed for its "familiar acquaintance," not for the "strangeness and rarity it bringeth from other countries." A wife who did not know "cookery" or how to sow and gather herbs performed "but half her marriage vow." Her salads, for example, must be both practical and an adornment to the table, both "simple and compound." She must also know how to cut meat as well as how to make cheese, and how to care for poultry. Though he believed distilling herbs for medicine more important than distilling flowers for perfume, he conceded both were valuable to the home, as was also the wife's knowledge of making sauces, wines, ale, etc., and gauging them in casks. In an emergency she should be able to dye wool, but always she should be ready to judge various grades of it as she inspected the woven fabrics at the weaver's or at the shops. Unless she knew such things she was unfit to supervise her household of servants.[19]

Nicholas Breton catalogued epithets to describe the good wife. He spoke of her eye of wariness, her tongue of silence, her hand of labor, and her heart of love. As a companion she was all kindness, as a mistress all passion, as an exercise all patience, and as an example all experience. In the home she was a kitchen physician, a chamber comfort, a hall's care, and a parlor's grace. She was also the dairy's neatness, the brewhouse's wholesomeness, the garner's provision, and the gardener's plantation. Among her personal virtues he noted her musical voice, her meek countenance, her virtuous mind, and her gracious soul. In short, she was a book of housewifery, God's blessing and man's happiness, earth's honor, and heaven's creature.

This fantastic exercise of the writer is a far cry from the emotional outburst of a man who has suffered the death of his wife. The Puritan Philip Stubbes looks back on the virtues of his young wife and, in *A Christall Glas, for Christian Women: . . . of a right vertuous life and Christian death . . .* (1590) pays tribute to her excellent character. In spite of being only fifteen at her marriage, she was commended by all who knew her for her "singular wisdom, and also for her modesty, courtesy, gentleness, affability, and good government." At every spare moment she read the Bible, and was always questioning her husband about his interpretation of passages. She treasured all her time while in his presence, for she learned so very much from him while he was home with her. As a housekeeper she "would suffer no disorder," and as a wife she was so gentle and courteous she never fell out with her neighbors. She became so grave and thoughtful that she would never "without great compulsion go abroad, either to banquet or feast, to gossip or to make merry . . ." Even in London she kept so close to her home "there was not the dearest friend she had in the world that could get her abroad to dinner or supper or any exercise whatsoever."

How much Stubbes mirrors his ideal of a Christian wife and how much is the girl's real character each reader must judge for himself. As she surpassed in the virtue of humility, so she excelled in sobriety, never pampering her body with delicate meats, wines, or strong drink, but refraining from them altogether. She "utterly abhorred" all kinds of pride. She "could never abide to hear any filthy or unclean talk of scurrility, neither swearing nor blaspheming, cursing nor banning, but would reprove them sharply . . ." Her own speech "both glorified God and

---

[19] *The English House-wife. Containing the inward and outward Vertues which ought to be in a complete Woman* (1631).

ministered grace to the hearers . . ." She lived so "constantly and walked so "circumspectly" that no one could accuse her of the "least shadow of dishonesty." As for her loyalty, all her friends thought her the "rarest in the world." She adapted all her moods to his, being merry when he was so, and sad when he was sad. Never did she oppose him in any way, "but by wise counsel and politic advice, with all humility and submission, seek to persuade him."

The husband's long preamble listing his wife's virtues is to prepare for his account of her patient suffering following the birth of her first child. She never complained. Finally, placing her baby in her husband's arms, she asked him to "bring up this child in good letters, in discipline; and above all things," see that he was taught "true religion." It is quite possible Stubbes felt responsible for her angelic nature. Marrying her young, he was able in the short time he had her with him to teach her much about a good wife's virtues and thus fulfill this part of a husband's responsibilities. Undoubtedly he would have agreed with Thomas Gataker that a man's influence upon his wife, whether conscious or unconscious, was very great. If a marriage turned out badly, a man should lay the fault upon himself for turning honey into gall, but if the marriage was good, much of the credit was the husband's.

To the sixteenth-century mind the loyalty derived from chastity was also a key to a wife's perfection, and both the husband and the wife must guard this key if they were to share happy and contented days. Plays dealing with this theme were sure of a responsive audience, and dramatists used it in their plots with all the ingenuity they could summon to their aid. Jonson's *Volpone*, however, substitutes a bitter satirical situation for the usual emotional conflict. Like all good women, the wife regards her chastity as her most precious possession, but for her jealous, avaricious husband, it is a commodity that may also pay dividends. Thus he gives her to Volpone, who he believes is dying, in order to win the Fox's fortune. When the wife, therefore, pleads for protection, she can hardly believe her ears as her husband, who is sure she will be unharmed, commands her to obey the villain's will. Confronted by the problem of being both chaste and obedient, the wife tries every appeal to the one person in the world who should best defend her. She begs him to kill her; she offers to take poison; she is willing to eat burning coals. But she is violently commanded to go in to comfort Volpone. After she is rescued by another, her husband is made a fool in the eyes of all Venice when, wearing the long ears of an ass, he is paraded along the Grand Canal. Moreover, his wife is returned to her father with her dowry trebled. This reward for fighting for her honor gives her thrice as many chances now to achieve happiness in the marriage mart.

Thomas Dekker's popular comedy, *The Shoemakers' Holiday*, uses the fidelity test even though he promises a play of smiles and laughter.

While the wife's husband is away at the wars, she rejects a wealthy suitor and makes a humble living for herself with her needle. Even when told her husband has been killed in battle, she remains faithful to his memory. Finally, the husband returns crippled and broken, but his wife receives him joyfully. Impressed by the devotion of such an unassailable woman, the rejected suitor becomes a benefactor to her and her husband, and the reward for her virtue somewhat atones for the suffering she has endured. Though Puritans would not attend this play, they would approve of the wife's part in the story. They felt that separation between husband and wife put a great strain on both chastity and the happy adjustment constantly demanded by marriage for a true companionship between two people.

They and all Elizabethans felt separation of married people was dangerous to their happiness because it provided gossip with the best sort of material on which to fatten. When separation grew out of financial or religious differences, especially after a couple had been married some years, the arrangements necessary to the decorum to be observed in such a situation often caused great embarrassment. This must have been the case when Rye Fiennes penned his letter to Lord Burghley in April of 1592. He begs the Secretary not to let any of the recusants' suits prevail against him, for his wife now goes daily to prayers with him. On the Sunday before, he says, they received communion together at the Islington Church, and he hopes again to live with her contentedly although it is true that "both in portion and in bed" they live "divided by consent and yet agree." His wife, he says, is willing for him to convert his portion of their inheritance toward discharging his debts and repairing his estate, and he is willing that she dispose of her portion of about £400 a year to maintain herself, two daughters, and the rest of the household, which does not exceed twelve persons. He gives assurance of "the good bringing up" of his only hope, his son, and "will ever defend religion" to his death. He believes his wife is not defective in religion, and he promises he will always defend her reputation, as she does his.[20]

With so much stress on chastity and reputation, Elizabethans were naturally interested in literature providing a psychological analysis of the fallen woman. She was made the subject of many harrowing sermons; she was shown in domestic books as almost too low for grace, and in drama she was the focusing agent in scenes of much melodramatic distress. Doubtless Thomas Heywood's *A Woman Killed with Kindness* was immediately popular. It is still referred to as the last great Elizabethan domestic tragedy, but it is especially interesting for the conditions that would make it appealing to its age. After the villain enjoys his master's wife, he swears her husband will never hear of her fall. But in only a short time the husband hears the whole story. In a noble spirit of for-

[20] *Calendars of State Papers . . . 1591–1594,* CCXLI, No. 120.

giveness he says he will not disclaim his wife or put her away, but will do all in his power to comfort her even though she must never expect to see him or her children again. Accordingly, the wife is sent off to the husband's country estate, where she promptly fades away with grief. On her deathbed the still kind husband comes to her, truly and lovingly forgiving her "as my Redeemer hath forgiven His death," exclaims the ecstatic wife. Then, her heart at rest, she cries out to the man who has "saved" her,

> Pardoned on earth, soul, thou in Heaven art free
> Once more: thy wife dies thus embracing thee.

The paraded subservience to a moral code in this play raises the question once again—who read the other more closely, the moral dramatist or the didactic moralist? Hardin Craig's study of "The Ethics of *King Lear*"[21] maintains that ". . . the renaissance moral philosophy is a greater, worthier, and profounder thing than our current speculations on such subjects usually are," and concludes Elizabethan dramatists had as their instrument "a greater ethical system of which we have grown unconscious." Certainly, the more inclusive one's reading in this age, the stronger the impression of a cohesive pattern of conduct demanded by society for individuals to accept or reject. An individual might fail to reach the standard of perfection at the center of the pattern, but the important thing was his choice; that made or marred his destiny. Heywood's wife in the play made the wrong moral choice that damned her to evil, and her husband saved her from that evil though his idea of kindness cost her her life. Such a price for her salvation was not in her estimation too dear, for she died only to live.

To restore a fallen woman to grace during this age caused no small sensation, according to John Aubrey's account of Venetia Digby in his not-too-trustworthy *Brief Lives* (1898 edition). This woman was born near the end of the century, and lived to be thirty-three years of age. "She was sanguine and tractable," says Aubrey, "and of much suavity (which to abuse was a great pity)." Her "most lovely and sweet-turn'd face" with its delicate dark brown hair, dark brown eyebrows, and "eyelids about which there was much sweetness" attracted the attention of even Ben Jonson. The color of her cheeks was "just that of the damask rose, which is neither too hot nor too pale," and she was not very tall. But she became the mistress of the Earl of Dorset, by whom she had three sons whom he supported with an annuity of £500.

When Sir Kenelm Digby fell in love with her and married her against his mother's wishes, he first secured by suit the annuity the Earl of Dorset had stopped paying at her marriage. Sir Kenelm had boasted that a hand-

---

[21] *Philological Quarterly*, IV (1925), 97–109.

some, discreet man could make a virtuous wife out of a woman from a brothel, and he probably thought he was doing just that with Venetia. He did not reckon on his own feelings of jealousy, however. Once a year the Earl of Dorset entertained the beautiful woman and her husband at his house, and although he was said to look at her with "much desire and passion," he only kissed her hand. She, on her part, carried herself "blamelessly." Then, suddenly, she was dead, and gossips declared she had been poisoned.

Aubrey's account of what followed is typical of gossip at this time. When the wife's head was opened to ascertain the cause of her death, there was found "but little brain," which her husband imputed to drinking viper wine; but "spiteful women say 'twas a viper-husband who was jealous of her." To avoid the scandal caused by her death, her husband retired into Gresham College at London, "where he diverted himself with chemistry, and the professors' good conversation. He wore there a mourning cloak, a high-crowned hat, his beard unshorn, and look'd like a hermit, as signs of sorrow for his beloved wife, to whose memory he erected a sumptuous monument . . ." It is not known how much truth lies in this "biography," but the lesson in the moral preachment is clearly etched—"For the wages of sin is death."

The woman who was "kind, too kind" had no legal redress if her lover refused to marry her, for society was indifferent to her lot after her fall from grace. Even rank did not lighten the burden of her shame if the man who had accepted her favors chose to cast her off. This is why the young Earl of Pembroke, son of Sir Philip Sidney's sister Mary, was not condemned by his social group for his treatment of Mary Fitton, one of the Queen's maids of honor. True, there was much gossip at court about the two young people, of how Mary "would put off her tire and tuck up her clothes, and take a large white cloak and march as though she were a man to meet the Earl out of Court." When misfortune struck her and she was proved pregnant, however, the Earl of Pembroke, "being examined, confessed a fact, but utterly renounced all marriage." For a while gossip had much to say about both being sent to the Tower by Queen Elizabeth, but the rumors were not confirmed, though Mary Fitton was permanently banished from the court to the country.

The heartlessness of the young earl "was come by honestly." Some years before, his father had used such a case among his own kinsmen to "lay up acres" for himself. As lord lieutenant, he had forced such heavy fines from his kinsman, Sir William Darrell, who had seduced another man's wife, that Darrell was compelled to sacrifice all his estates. It was generally believed that Pembroke had not hesitated to line his own pockets with the gains that could have been his for the excessive fines he extorted from Darrell. A corrupt man in power might well find the social laws of morality a useful tool if circumstances shaped themselves to his advantage. At any rate, Pembroke was accused of "conversing like a . . . minister on morality" while he pocketed his gains from the case at law.[22]

The woman in the case had had the sympathy of many influential friends at court, especially when her husband denounced her, employed spies, and suborned witnesses. He was not the kind of man to be dutiful in protecting his wife's reputation; nor could he play the part of a strong man who took matters into his own hands at such a crisis, thereby gaining the respect of his friends and possibly regaining his wife's love. In fact, he had been an amusing but despicable little man to a society that had little but contempt for his kind, whether in court or in the humblest home in the kingdom. Shakespeare appealed to such scorn for the moral coward when, in *The Merry Wives of Windsor*, he caused the weak, suspicious Ford to declare with comical desperation: "My bed shall be abused, my coffers ransacked, my reputation gnawn at . . ." Like all human failings, adultery could be played up to Elizabethans as the cause for derisive laughter as well as for tears and the gnashing of teeth.

Though it was universally condemned, adultery was most severely attacked by the moralists when it endangered the legitimacy of children. The Puritans, of course, urged the pure life for its own sake, but they also sentenced adulterous mothers to more severe punishment than they decreed for their partners in sin. Perkins believed a man should notify the Church authorities when he learned his wife was guilty of adultery, though he was quick to point out that the purpose was chiefly to take notice of the child so conceived "whom afterward the husband might lawfully put off as none of his." Gouge had a good deal to say on the matter of a man not knowing what children he had fathered, and blamed him more than the woman, who was the weaker vessel. Moreover, he believed damaging rumors should be reported immediately to the one slandered, but if there was cause for the reports, every effort should be made to bring the guilty one to a state of repentance. Bullinger flatly blamed women for men's sins of adultery, saying either their scolding or their effort to have pre-eminence drove their husbands out of doors to "strange women."

Some of the ambitious *nouveaux riches* were accused of being "harlots" who resorted to intrigues with men in higher social circles in order to amuse themselves. In *The Anatomie of Abuses*, Stubbes grumbled about women who lay abed till 9:00 or 10:00 of a morning, and took two or three hours to dress. Then they proceeded to dinner consisting of delicate meats and wines. Afterward they walked abroad for a time or talked with gossips. Returning, they went to bed. Others spent most of the day sitting at their doors to show their "braveries, to make known their beauties, to behold passersby," to see fashions, etc. Some walked into town,

[22] Hubert Hall, *Society in the Elizabethan Age* (1902), p. 11.

with baskets in their hands or under their arms, but more for idling abroad than for purchasing necessities for the household. Like most moral writers, he was convinced that idle women were wanton.

Realistic comedies completed his picture. They showed pretty wives loitering abroad on some pretext for shopping, or keeping shop at home and gossiping with idle women or flirting with lovers they met in naughty assignations while their husbands toiled away the hours. Ladies in masks and idle women of the lower classes were berated for attending bear-baitings, executions, hangings, beheadings, and even the theater, where they talked freely with men they met at these places or on the way to or from them. Adultery played an important part in the plays they went to see, especially the murder plays that told in action what they had read with such avid interest in ballads and broadsides. Such was the anonymous *Arden of Feversham*, whose plot closely follows the details of a murder in 1551 described by Holinshed in 1577. The passionate, cruel wife remains faithful to her worthless accomplice in spite of the loss of her family and husband. Both in planning the murder and in her attempts to conceal the deed, she is cool and resourceful. When she is finally overcome with remorse, she tries to expiate her sin, though she maintains the same insensitive composure with which she executed the shocking crime. This play tingled the spines of those interested in horrifying adultery.

A Warning for Fair Women closely follows a similar story of crime narrated by Holinshed and Stow, in which Master George Sanders of London, a merchant near Shooters' Hill, was slain in 1573. The motive for the adulterous wife's crime is the very human longing for a better social position. The moralists' point of inequality in man's and woman's station as the cause for wrecking many marriages is clearly set forth in this horror play of uncertain authorship.

Shakespeare's Cleopatra presents many points set forth by moralists. She is a woman to whom love, even for another woman's husband, is the most important thing in life. In Antony's absence, therefore, she fills her idle hours with lazy, vulgar pastimes, flying into rages with her attendants and displaying amazing skill in the arts of love. With Antony, she sometimes turns her knowledge of provocative technique into sulking or putting him in the wrong, and estimates to a hair's breadth just how far she may pursue this clever device by mood or caprice.

In the first three acts Cleopatra is more or less in control of her passion, but most of all, she is heartless and essentially vulgar. Then suddenly she changes, and is thoughtful. At Actium, she becomes truly feminine in her fright, and her fear increases as she begins to suspect Antony believes she has betrayed him. At the critical point she can think of nothing better for wooing him back to her than to send him word of her own death. When she is actually at the point of death, she becomes most appealing in her forgetfulness of self, for she is all woman giving way to emotions of tenderness and grief and devotion. Perhaps this change from selfishness to tenderness has been prepared for by Antony's bitter censure of her flirting with Caesar's messenger. Certainly her reformation is impressive because it is not so complete as it is sudden. Does she not, lapsing into her old selfishness in trying to save her jewels, betray her cunning self to the canny Octavius? Now she is indeed doomed, but she dies with the name of "husband" on her lips, and so affords a moment of consummate acting as she makes the Elizabethan gesture of a possible last-minute repentance.

As a study of the wanton woman and the disloyal husband, this play does not seek merely to measure the evil itself in these two sinners or to strike a balance between their strong and weak moments. Rather, it seeks to show two souls dominated by a sensual, adulterous passion that brings them to their ruin in death. Yet, although they violate the moral and institutional bonds of public and private Elizabethan life, neither of them is coarsened by adulterous love, for the simple reason that each is a great personality. Their very greatness, however, leads them to sacrifice everything for love. Now, Elizabethans believed that when a husband's or wife's fidelity to the obligations of marriage was sacrificed to love, that sacrifice was intrinsically evil. Antony's love, therefore, is shown to sap his mental and moral strength, and Cleopatra's passion, in spite of its moments of selfless devotion, is hedged about with egoism and coquetry. Because a great poet wrote this play, he could not deny Antony a measure of his own fine imagination or Cleopatra her moments of pure nobility, but even if history had permitted the greatness of these souls to save them, Shakespeare knew the Elizabethan moral judgment would have sent them to their doom.

In "Die Familie bei Shakespeare,"[23] Schücking declares the English wife's supposed quiet submissiveness made poor dramatic material for sixteenth-century plays. Matrimony, he says, cannot provide a whirlwind of passion unless the action is motivated by jealousy, and the vinelike wife must be so soft and yielding and so reserved in the life of the senses that she is quiet in her cold virtue. However, it is Desdemona's "quiet submissiveness" to her husband and her seeming unholy interest in Cassio that put the whirlwind into Othello's passion, although her desire to accompany her husband to the wars and her intimate conversation with her maid reveal the full flow of her love for her lord. Without this revelation there could be no meaning in Othello's anguished "There where I garnered up my heart." To Schücking this cry refers pointedly to his "marriage rights." To the Elizabethan, the words revealed the closeness of a bond in which flesh and spirit met flesh and spirit. Although Schücking admits Elizabethans did not suppress the portrayal of sexual matters,

---

[23] Levin L. Schücking, "Die Familie bei Shakespeare," *Englische Studien* (1927–28), pp. 187–226.

he insists the wife must show only modesty in the enjoyments of these "rights." True, some moralists would give this impression, but the Puritans were frank in their admission of the sweets of married life when those sweets were equally shared. They were most insistent about the modest attitude in the maid's anticipation of the marriage rights, for the ideal of a maid's chastity would preclude any other attitude, yet Shakespeare's Juliet is not ignorant of what to expect. Schücking, however, considers Juliet's ecstatic anticipation of love's rites as immodest and sensual. To Shakespeare as well as to the Puritan Spenser, it was the perfect approach of *natural* chastity to the experience that would unite flesh and spirit.

Schücking denies the Elizabethan wife had the right to share her husband's spiritual life, and points to Portia, wife of Brutus, as an exception influenced by Plutarch's characterization of her. Yet Katharina's speech to the undutiful wives tells frankly what she learned from her husband about the duties of married people: that only as an obedient wife can she requite a loving husband's care, and only by a husband's wise instruction can a wife learn how to share the spiritual life of her lord. This point is so typically Elizabethan it is no wonder Schücking should miss it. In fact, it is seldom adequately stressed on the stage. It is difficult enough to realize children must be taught to respond to love, but it is still more difficult to understand that an adult's heart learns to share experience with another only through instruction. Whether the instruction is one-sided or reciprocal depends on the two individuals. With this relationship in mind Shakespeare gave us Kate and Hotspur and the Macduffs, whom Schücking interprets with difficulty.

He says rightly the relation between Kate and Hotspur is free from uxoriousness. But he says the marriage is happy only because Kate, who wishes to share her husband's worries, cannot overcome his superiority. The point is not that she cannot win the mastery here, but that she can be a loving and contented wife even when her husband refuses to let her share worries which he feels as the family head he must shoulder alone. She simply bows gracefully to his superiority. That she wishes to share his worries indicates she has had a life of sharing with him in other things.

Schücking notes that Lady Macduff violently condemns her renegade husband to her child, yet the husband and wife have been happy because Macduff is so overcome with anguish at the murder of his little ones. Now this scene between mother and son is full of significance, for it proves that in spite of what Lady Macduff says about her husband, she loves him devotedly. It is also noticeable that Macduff's grief over losing his wife is fully as great as that over the murder of his children. Lady Macduff as a loyal wife would never speak disrespectfully of her husband to another. That she does so to the noble Ross and to her son is due to an anxiety that has made ribbons of her nerves. Neither Ross nor her son takes her words in any other way. Ross tries to reason with one beyond the point of reason, and the son tries to calm her by a battle of wits. The man knows the mother's fears for her children and her agony that her husband is not present to help her protect the helpless. The son feels in his childish way the same thing, but he also feels he is his mother's sole protector even as he clings to her for protection. There is no more poignant scene in Shakespeare, and the wild words of the mother come from the depths of love and fear and helplessness in a danger so great it takes all the courage she can summon to speak rationally at all. Yet Schücking draws the conclusion that family relationships in Shakespeare's plays were not expected to be very close except among the bourgeois, for whom the dramatist had a contemptuous coolness.

The loosely constructed story of fortune-telling in the character sketches of *The Man in the Moon* (1609) suggests this closeness even as it describes a wanton wife. The author calls her a husband's affliction, her children's disgrace, and her friends' scandal. He follows this introduction with an account of her "filthiness" under a fair exterior as he prepares his warning against adultery. Finally, he makes the point that if a woman once loses her good name, she will never recover it. If in her youth she has been false to her husband, in her age no one will respect her and she will find her husband rejecting her too. Her children begotten by others may beg or steal, for he will maintain no other man's "gettings." If her husband dies first, no honest man will have her. One of her debased companions may take her "more for lucre than for love," but he will never trust her, knowing she was false to her former husband. The author concludes, however, that a wife's infidelity is usually due to her husband's unfounded jealousy. As such distrust wastes his body and distracts his mind until his is unable to "negotiate" his estates properly, he should learn that the "best way is to think the best" of his wife.

Among the many sermons on adultery were those of John Donne, who was famous for his powerfully devout and dramatic presentation by which he drew a fine attendance. In his popular eighty-fifth sermon he says of jealousy and adultery: "Had Adam and Eve not sinned, there would have been a mutual subjection between them; as there is even in nature between both the other couples: for if man had continued in innocency, yet it is most probably thought that as there would certainly have been marriage, and so children, so also there would have been magistracy, and propriety, and authority, and so a mutual submitting, a mutual assisting one another in all these relations." With deepening conviction he continued: "This contracting of our affections is a burden; it is a submitting of ourselves; all states that made laws and proposed rewards for married men conceived it so." Then, as was customary with many popular divines, he drew upon his own personal experience to explain his words. He told how by becoming a husband he "became subject to that sex which is naturally subject to man," though his subjection was but to love one woman only. "Love, then," he said, "when it is limited by law, is a subjection, but it is a subjection commanded by God. When a married man loves elsewhere he becomes subject to household and foreign jealousies, ill-grounded quarrels, blasphemous protestations, ignoble and unworthy disguises, base satisfactions, clamorous conscience, seared and obdurate and stupefied conscience, and treacherous misuse of a confident friend." There was nothing for a reasonable man to do, therefore, but to follow God's law and love his wife as the mother of his children, and to be the "comforter" of that mother's life.

The details in all this Elizabethan advice concerning the happiness or unhappiness in store for individuals are notable for the moral intensity with which they were regarded. For to Elizabethans, marriage and its ceremonious founding and maintaining of the home were essential acts of dignity and social importance. The husband and wife had common and separate duties they must perform if their lives, always more or less carefully scrutinized by members of their own social group, were to be approved. Responsibility to family or society could not be ignored, and those husbands and wives who would live with honor or with the approbation of their fellow men could never forget or deny their obligations to home, Church, and State.

This is why man's position as head of the household was maintained by a carefully planned moral and economic policy. Woman's subjection and obedience to the requirements of this policy were a matter of necessity if not of choice, though many a woman's wisdom enabled her to reconcile these two factors by weighing nicely, thoughtfully, or piously the advantages and disadvantages of the plan. If marriage was to be a partnership, there must be delegated to one of them the final authority; if it was to be a divine institution, it must have a divinely appointed lord and master; if it was to be a social necessity, both husband and wife must adapt themselves harmoniously to the demands of public and private living; and finally, if the relationship was to be used for preserving their individual selves, they must learn how to function as a unit and without friction in the irksome as well as pleasant details of life bounded by the household. The best minds and hearts, therefore, sought to fuse these elements into an adequate way of life that in spite of its complexity deserves the careful attention of those interested in the stability of home or of a nation founded on homes.

True, the head of the household was entitled to many privileges, but he also carried grave responsibilities. Concern for the welfare of his wife and children was not to be recognized one day and ignored the next. He must help to bring a continual harmony out of the "daily little things" that otherwise might become "more dangerous than a fever." He must always remember that morally he was responsible for the good name of his wife and children, and this responsibility could be carried lightly or only with great labor according to the way he chose a wife, or, if the wife was chosen for him, according to the way he instructed her in preparation for her duties as mistress of his household and mother of his children. Though the law permitted him to beat his wife if she was not responsive to his instruction, still he was liable for the consequences of such treatment as they manifested themselves in his home and in the society he frequented outside his home. Woman's subjection to her lord and master might be easy or difficult, but her religion or intelligence as much as the mores of the times enabled her to adjust herself to the bonds of the marriage relationship. The protection afforded her by marriage and the respectful attitude of society toward a good or discreet wife were rewards sufficient in themselves to make her hesitate to abandon such security for the precarious delight of a personal liberty that might jeopardize both her economic and her social status.

One means of determining the Elizabethan's social status was by the number of servants he kept, for servants in a way indicated gentility. In the homes of the privileged the number was likely to be large, and if so, they made quite an impressive appearance in bright new liveries when the master entertained important personages or when he was accompanied by them on a journey. In the early days of the Tudors the servants wore blue coats with the master's badge in silver on the left arm, but by the end of the century the coats were commonly trimmed with lace, and the color and ornament were determined by the family they served. Numbers of servants and the quality of their apparel, therefore, varied considerably during the age of Queen Elizabeth.

Some masters still harked back to the old days in the number and appearance of their servants. During Henry VIII's reign, little Jane Grey's parents used to go visiting accompanied by thirty to forty retainers fully armed. In 1538, Stephen Gardiner rode forth as Bishop of Winchester with five mules and two carts, all covered with cloths of his colors and arms in Garters embroidered on the cloths. A dozen lackeys followed in gay velvet cheyney cloaks, turned down with large velvet capes, and besides these there were many yeomen and sundry servants and officers. Seven years previously, after he had just been made bishop, he had ridden to Winchester House over London Bridge, past St. Paul's, and down Fleet Street and the Strand to Westminster. Clad in velvet and satin, he rode a mule trapped with velvet and gilded stirrups and bridle, and his gentlemen in costly liveries, bareheaded and wearing gold chains about their necks, rode before and after him. At this time many gentlemen's sons were living with him to learn manners and decorum. One of his lifelong servitors said the bishop's household numbered "seven score and odd," and were "as quiet and well ordered company" as he had ever known.[24] Still, late in the century some Elizabethans sallied forth with

[24] James Arthur Muller, *Stephen Gardiner and the Tudor Reaction* (1926), pp. 44 and 75.

just such fanfare, but since these elaborate excursions were expensive they were reserved for very special occasions.

When Lord Burghley's fortunes were at their best, however, he was said to have eighty men in livery and the best men of England competing to enter his service. Twenty men served at his table, each being handsomely paid, though an ordinary servant's maximum wages were £5 per year. Like most Elizabethans, Burghley dined but twice a day, dinner at 11:00 in the morning, and supper at 6:00 in the evening. Regardless of whether he was at home, his entire household observed these hours, and breakfast was also provided for those who needed or desired it. His entertainment of the Queen and high officials and friends added much to his carefully calculated expenses. When Elizabeth visited him, he could hardly expect to entertain her for less than two to three thousand pounds, and this occurred a dozen times. When she visited Leicester at Kenilworth, the cost of entertaining her was over six thousand pounds. Among the items that ran high in the amusement provided by Leicester were the thirteen bears "worried by ban-dogs." He was said to have died £70,000 in debt to the Crown, but Burghley's careful management prevented any such disaster to his fortune, although his wealth was not so great as those hearing the reading of the will had expected it to be.

Some households were lavish in their hospitality. In 1561, the Earl of Derby paid as much as £2,895 for food alone for his establishment, which consumed fifty-six oxen and over five hundred sheep. In 1579, Sir William Fairfax paid close to £400 for sheep and oxen used at his castle in Yorkshire, and still more in the following year. At Wollaton the hospitality was so lavish that forty strangers coming along dined with the household, and in the Lenten Fair time as many as one hundred twenty lords and ladies with retinues were entertained.[25] Sir William Holles permitted anyone to receive hospitality for three days during Allhallowtide and Candlemas time, with no questions asked. Besides the usual suitable food at such a time, one fat ox and a sheep must be killed daily to feed the guests. At great feasts in these homes elaborate dinners might number sixteen "dishes" in the first course, and fourteen in the second. Even simple meals provided enough dishes to enable the fastidious guests to make a "delicate" selection.

The expenses of such households were a matter of much concern to English nobles. Though with careful management they might keep out of debt, at the same time some of their servants were rolling together little fortunes for themselves at their master's expense. Certainly the extensive scale in the lord's living would be a temptation to many menials. The Earl of Derby living "quietly" in the country at Latham in 1587 had more than a hundred servants to care for his household. His three officers (steward, comptroller, and receiver in general) had three servants each,

---

[25] A. L. Rowse, *The England of Elizabeth* (1951), pp. 254–56, and Martin S. Hume, *The Great Lord Burghley* (1898), p. 49.

and the master had seven gentlemen-in-waiting and a page. In 1590, the earl and his family of five had one hundred forty servants. When he served as ambassador to France in 1584, his retinue consisted of seventy regular attendants and sixty others. All had two liveries each, one of purple and gold lace and the other of black satin and taffeta, and all wore heavy gold chains. So great was the expense of this service abroad that he had to negotiate with Burghley for a loan of £1,000 from an alderman.

In spite of all the private and special hospitality they extended to visiting officials, the great lords in service to the Queen often preferred service at home to going abroad on embassies. Yet in spite of careful management they were fighting debt on one hand and trying to make a suitable impression on the other. After twenty years of service to the Queen, the Earl of Huntingdon died in debt to the Crown for £20,000. Raleigh's services left him "comparatively" poor in spite of special favors in monopolies, etc. Sir Philip Sidney's father sacrificed far more than he gained for all his labors, and he was well known for the excellent management of his resources. An impressive appearance made it next to impossible to break away from the parade of servants so well established by the 1560's. Though the young Earl of Oxford was often referred to as extravagant, he was not accused of making an ostentatious display of respect for his father by returning from the funeral attended by one hundred forty men all in mourning apparel. So strong was the general pride in "great place," however, that most Elizabethans in high office were not averse to their appointments even though they must expect as a result heavy drains upon their financial resources.

All well-regulated households were under strict discipline, but establishments of great lords must be under very strict control if there was to be any order at all. To maintain smooth functioning in all the offices, there were rules similar to those drawn up by John Harrington for the master of a household:

A servant must not be absent from morning or evening meals or prayers without excuse lest he be fined twopence each time.

Any servant late to dinner would be fined twopence.

Any man waiting at table without a trencher in his hand, except for good excuse, would be fined one penny.

The court gate must be kept closed during a meal.

Any man leaving a door open he had found shut would be fined one penny unless he could show good cause.

Any man going to the kitchen without reasonable excuse would be fined one penny, and the cook would be fined one penny also.

Any man provoking another to strike or striking another would be liable to dismissal.

For each oath, a servant would be fined one penny.

For a dirty shirt on Sunday or a missing button, the fine would be six
   pence.

After 8:00 A.M. no bed must be found unmade and no fireplace or candle
   box left unclean, or the fine would be one penny.

The hall must be cleaned in an hour.

All guests' rooms must be tidied within four hours after the departure
   of the guests.

The whole house must be swept and dusted each Friday.[26]

The fines collected by deductions from wages for infraction of the
above rules were bestowed upon the poor. Although the rising hour in
such rules was given as six in winter and five in summer, in most great
households servants rose from five to seven in winter and four to six in
summer. Retiring hours were correspondingly early, for the poor light
given by candles made it necessary for them to engage in most of their
labor during daylight.

The household discipline naturally depended to a great extent upon
the master's force of character, for he was nominally the head of the establishment even though his wife usually controlled the maid servants.
Commands or a box on the ear would keep most servants obedient, but
it was not unusual for both master and mistress to punish servants severely,
especially when they conducted themselves in a childish or impudent
manner. Some Elizabethans, therefore, thrashed maidservants as well as
menservants when they misbehaved. Naturally the treatment of servants
became a subject of discussion for preachers and moralists and all writers
of domestic literature, for servants were no small problem in some of the
homes. Pious authors admonished both masters and mistresses to remember that their own relation to God was that of servant to master, and
to treat their servants fairly and justly.

Since it was customary to expect servants to stay for life in an established household, the relationship between them and their masters was
often familiar and affectionate. Sometimes the relationship took on the
paternal character, and many times, in the homes of country people especially, the servants were looked upon as members of the family and regarded fondly like the children. In such cases, servants in both town and
country houses were chastened gently or severely when they did wrong,
and praised when they were good. More was expected of them than of
children, of course, especially in the way of loyalty. It may be that the
discipline to which they were subject in well-ordered homes and the
humility expected of them made them more attached to their masters than
they would have been had the demands of good service and proper defer-

[26] Henry Thew Stephenson, *The Elizabethan People* (1910), p. 396. Also,
see A. L. Rowse, *The England of Elizabeth,* and Eric St. John Brooks, *Sir Christopher
Hatton* (1946).

ence been at all slack. Most masters and mistresses at the head of a respectful household won their servants' love and fidelity; in return, they tried to the best of their ability to live up to their responsibility for those who served them and lived with them under the same roof.

The author of *The Court of Good Counsell* (1607) presented the usual attitude toward servants in domestic books influenced by Guazzo. He advised the master to win and keep his servant's love and loyalty by using him courteously, aiding him in his troubles, visiting him in his sickness, giving him pleasures that would cost him little but please the servant a great deal, rewarding him when he was deserving, and listening to him when he had good advice to offer. Bad masters might chide servants before strangers, but good masters would not ask for perfection and would know what to overlook when guests were present. Some servants, he warned, might be pleasant to one's face and grimace at one's back; therefore all masters should put up with many faults if a servant was honest and trustworthy and faithful. No servant should be permitted to dishonor God or neighbor, and every servant should perform his duties loyally and ably, looking upon his master as his friend. The master, however, must keep this friendship on the right level, for he must never treat a servant as hail-fellow-well-met lest his familiarity breed contempt.

Guazzo had also advised choosing untrained servants that masters might teach them the ways they wished them to follow, and during their training reprove them when necessary as they themselves would like to be dealt with. Guazzo made the point that the usual faults of drinking and gambling and slandering in servants were due to their feeling the dissimilarity between their lives and that of the master. If masters would but remember that no servitude is voluntary, they would give commands as one who recognized that all men served some master, were accountable to someone directly above them. He disapproved of beating servants, though he considered bad servants to be like bad dogs in their gluttony, in their barking or telling their master's secrets, and in their biting or back-biting.

William Vaughan's *The Golden Grove*, in its general discussion of duties of master and servants, stressed the importance of a master gravely correcting all faults in his servants, keeping them from drinking, swearing, gaming, whoring, etc., preventing them from lying abroad at night, most carefully teaching them the word of God by means of regular catechizing, and finally, being prompt in paying the servants' wages. Servants, on their side, must obey the master without discussion even when they knew more than the master about the task to be performed, in their honest, faithful labors never seeking booty for themselves, never revealing their master's secrets, and always being ready to defend the master's goods even at the risk of their lives. At times, of course, there were such servants, but human nature, being what it was, frequently produced servants that were anything but unselfish in their performance of duties. Verses painted on the kitchen wall of Winchester College smilingly draw a picture of an "emblematic" servant in the 1560's:[27]

> A trusty servant's portrait would you see,
> This emblematic figure well survey.
> The porker's snout—not nice in diet shows;
> The padlock's shut—no secret he'll disclose;
> Patient the ass—his master's wrath will bear;
> Swiftness in errand—the stag's feet declare;
> Loaded his left hand—apt to labour saith;
> The vest—his neatness; open hand—his faith;
> Girt with his sword, his shield upon his arm,
> Himself and master, he'll protect from harm.

Overbury's satirical portrait of the servant shows the man's ability to "marshal dishes at the table, and to carve well," and his discretion in "caring" for his master's credit. Neat in combing his hair and in his "outward" linen, he has wit for bawdy jests and songs, especially when his master's wit is slow. Though his usual inheritance is a chambermaid, he may grasp the opportunity to marry the master's indiscreet daughter and so become his master's retainer, entailing himself and his posterity "upon his heir-maker forever."

Just as he set the pattern for proper relations between parents and children, so Sir Thomas More passed on to Elizabethans the proper decorum to be maintained between master and servants. He took great care of his servants, never letting them waste time in sloth or improper pastimes, which was a common practice among large companies of retainers following great men of the Tudor reign. He refused even to let them play at dice or cards. Some of his servants he put in charge of his garden, each with his own section to care for; others were entertainers for important guests at meals that must be made pleasant by such music as songs or playing on the organ. His wife, of course, supervised the servants performing household tasks. More arranged separate sleeping quarters for men and women servants so that they met rarely. Women entered the men's quarters only in case of such necessity as sickness. Stapleton tells us how every evening before bedtime More called them all together with his family. Then they kneeled and recited three psalms, beginning with the fifty-first, "Have mercy on me, O God . . ." This recitation was followed by "Hail, Holy Queen," with its prayer, and by Psalms 50, 24, 66, 129, and "Out of the Depths" for the dead. On Sundays and feast days the servants joined the family at services in the church, and on the greater feast days of Christmas and Easter, they arose at night to assist at the whole office. If any of his servants committed a fault, More's reproof was as gentle and loving as for his children.

---

[27] Quoted from Christopher Johnson by Elizabeth Godfrey in *Home Life under the Stuarts, 1603–1649* (1903), p. 210.

Servants who were fortunate in master or mistress were treated like the family even in the matter of bequests. The Verney family's mother Margaret mentioned in her will certain maids who faithfully attended her daughters even when the family's altered fortune must have brought some curtailment in the wages of the domestics as the family was forced to modify its generous way of life.[28] That Sir Walter Raleigh was mindful of his servants' fortunes while his own were low is shown by his will of 1618. Here he asks his wife to care for the wives of two servants, but especially for the wife of John Talbot, a faithful attendant of his in the Tower and in the expedition to Guiana, where the servant died. Since Talbot's son was also dead, Raleigh feared that without his aid the woman "might otherwise perish."

Dismissals after long service were frowned on by good masters. Sir Robert Sidney, for example, usually permitted his wife to manage the household servants, but when she wished to dismiss one who had been in their employ for years, he wrote her tactfully yet firmly that the man must not be cast off in his old age. "If he have offended you, he shall ask your forgiveness, and you shall remit the offence to me," he said, and added, "A chamber also I will have him for himself in the house. But it is not my meaning he should keep any family there."

Frequently servants were entrusted with very important family matters, as in the case of Roland White, the faithful and valuable steward of Sir Robert Sidney. White's letters (preserved for us in *The Sydney Letters*)[29] to his master about the home, and especially the children, reveal the confidence placed in him by both parents. White even went so far as to commend his mistress to her husband, saying in one of his letters about the children, "My Lady sees them well taught, and brought up in learning and qualities, fit for their birth and condition." He describes the daughter Mary as "grown so tall and goodly for her years" that her father will scarcely believe it until he sees her; he praises her and William and Katherine as they attended lady visitors at their coaches and brought them up to see their mother "with an excellent behavior and grace," and he compliments young Robert for his wit and courage that caused "all men to wonder at his years" and to say he promised to be a most "singular man." At another time he writes of the precocious boy, "I brought up Mr. Robert when the Knights were at dinner, who played the wag so prettily and boldly that all took pleasure in him, and above the rest my Lord Admiral, who gave him some sweetmeats, and he prated with his Honour beyond measure."

In another letter he praises Mary's dancing the galliard before the Queen on St. Stephen's Day, saying she was the "admirablest dancer of

---

[28] Frances Parthenope Verney and Margaret M. Verney, *Memoirs of the Verney Family during the 17th Century* (1925), I, 220.

[29] Arthur Collins (ed.), *Letters and Memorials of State: The Sydney Letters* (1746).

this time," and was so commended by her Majesty that she was prevailed upon to dance a coranto. He also tells how when William was presented to the Queen while she was returning from chapel, she bent down and kissed him. It was heartwarming for the lonely Sir Robert far from home to read such letters as this as well as the following one in which White tells of the three older children rejoicing in the presents their father sent them and of both Lady Huntingdon and the Queen often speaking of their graceful behavior. White's place of confidence in the family is best shown, perhaps, by the conclusion of a letter dictated by his mistress in which "she commands me to tell you that you are the best husband in the world for your love and care towards her, and her children." That such messages, however, were not uncommon in families whose stewards were men of honor is indicated by Shakespeare in *All's Well That Ends Well*. The countess entrusts her steward to write a difficult letter to her wayward son Bertram. "My greatest grief," she dictates, "though little he do feel it, set down sharply." Then weeping, she excuses herself for losing her composure by saying, "My heart is heavy and mine age is weak" (III: iv: 33–34, 41).

Some servants, of course, were unfortunate in their masters and mistresses. The author complains in *Carters Christian Common Wealth; Or, Domesticall Dutyes deciphered* (1627) that servants were not always given adequate food and clothing. "How can a servant labor faithfully," he asks, "when his body is enfeebled" by lack of nourishing, wholesome food? This condition, he says, is "too common among us, and it is a great reproach unto this our English nation. . . . Worse still, aged servants are too often set adrift because they are too old to labor." Shakespeare takes some space in *As You Like It* to present the grievance of an old servant turned out in this manner. Dismissed by the heir who is also casting out his younger brother, he is shocked to hear the harsh words, "Get you with him, old dog." The old man says, "Is 'old dog' my reward? Most true, I have lost my teeth in your service." Remembering the kind treatment given him by the heir's father, he adds, "God be with my old master! He would not have spoke such a word" (I: i: 87–89). Later, when the younger son does not know where to go or what to do for a living, the old servant tells him he has saved five hundred crowns from his wages, thinking to use the money when too old to work, but now he offers both the money and his service to the youth. "Though I look old," he says, "yet am I strong and lusty," and he promises he will perform all the services expected of a young man, and go "to the last gasp with truth and loyalty." As he leaves his old home with his new master, he looks back on the place where he has served "from seventeen years till now almost fourscore," and tries to soften his grief by thinking nothing can recompense him better than "to die well and not my master's debtor" (II: iii: 47, 70, 76).

It is this pride in loyal service and their stubborn independence that distinguish the good Elizabethan servants, and Shakespeare alludes to these qualities again and again in servants of high and low degree. Gloucester serves the aged Lear partly through pity but also because he takes pride in his loyalty to his king. Kent disguises himself as a menial servant in order to be near Lear and to perform the little necessary tasks so important for the king's comfort. He might have been received with honor abroad, but he chose to remain faithful to the master who had banished him, because his loyalty and self-respect as well as devotion and pity would not let him do otherwise. Faithful household servants, regardless of rank in the plays, manifest this same stubborn loyalty.

Flavius, steward in *Timon of Athens*, bled inwardly for his lord as he watched Timon give away his wealth to fair-weather friends crowding close with outstretched hands. Yet he did what he could to bolster up his master's honor when it had not one leg to stand on, and tried again and again to check Timon's prodigal generosity. When finally his amazed master really understood that his great estates had vanished, Flavius feared his own husbandry might be suspected or his accounts thought to be in error. Consequently he begged his master to call forth the "exactest auditors" and set him to the proof. He had groaned when all the vaults "wept with drunken spilth of wine," and "every room . . . blazed with lights and bray'd with minstrelsy," for he had known that when the means were gone which had bought the praises of the revelers, the very "breath" was gone whereof the praises were made (II:ii:164–70, 178–79).

When Flavius had to dismiss the servants, it was a sad business indeed. "Are we undone? cast off? nothing remaining?" they asked fearfully. Flavius, who had been the proud head servant of a rich and powerful estate, could now say nothing to the others but "I am as poor as you." Still unbelieving, they cried, "Such a house broke! So noble a master fall'n! All gone! and not one friend to come to his rescue?" (IV:ii:2–7). As Flavius told how the friends had gone away "as we do turn our backs from our companion in the grave," he called the friends' "false vows . . . empty purses pick'd," and the master a "beggar to the air." At this moment still other servants entered. When they learned what had happened, one expressed his wish to continue serving Timon whose livery he bore "if only in sorrow," but since he must survive by his labor, he would have to strike out for himself. And so must the others do also. Flavius, agreeing, offered to divide his savings among them, and began giving each his portion, saying, "Let's yet be fellows; let's shake our heads" and say whenever we meet in time to come, "we have seen better days." When some refused their share, Flavius pressed it upon them until the money was distributed. Embracing sadly, the servants parted their "several ways" (IV:ii:8–29).

But Flavius had not given away all his gold. As steward he had upheld his honor by responding to the demands of common humanity toward the servants, but he now had a still greater duty to perform—to follow his master to the death. With the rest of his savings he would "supply" the life of Timon, striving to serve his mind and body with his best will. At the meeting of this servant with his bewildered master, there comes a moment when Timon acknowledges his steward's services—"One honest man . . . but one . . . and he's a steward!" Then come bitter enquiries as to why Flavius has not gone into service elsewhere, "for many so arrive at second masters upon their first lord's neck." When in desperation Flavius cries out, "O let me stay, and comfort you, my master," he is told, "If thou hat'st curses, stay not . . ." Broken and fearful (for what Elizabethan did not quake at curses?), Flavius turns from the man whose mind has clouded over again with black hatred for his kind (IV:iii:464–543).

A servant's loyalty when confronted by the claims of humanity is shown again in the brutal scene from *King Lear* when Gloucester's eyes are put out. Shocked by the mutilation, one of Cornwall's servants orders his master to stay his hand. "I have serv'd you ever since I was a child," he says, "but better service have I never done you than now to bid you hold." Regan, amazed by such interference, turns upon him fiercely, but he says stoutly to her, "If you did wear a beard upon your chin, I'd shake it in this quarrel," for she has so dealt with Gloucester. At this point Cornwall comes to her aid with "My villain!" as he draws his sword. The servant whips out his own sword, crying to his master, "Nay, then, come on, and take the chance of anger." But Regan, snatching her husband's sword, shouts, "A peasant stand up thus?" and rushing up behind him stabs him in the back. Though she kills him she does not prevent his quick, fatal thrust at her husband. The other two servants, who have witnessed the scene with horror, watch the company depart, and then consult how they may take the sightless earl to some place of safety (III:vii:72–105). Such an act, of course, puts their own lives in grave jeopardy. Yet in this play loyalty serves base purposes also, as when Oswald is faithful to the death in his evil labors for his evil mistress Goneril.

In the play of *Romeo and Juliet*, the beginning action was not meant to seem accidental when Capulet's and Montague's servants pitched the family feud into white heat. Because servants were expected to uphold the honor of their families, the prince rightly held the masters of the two houses responsible for the acts of their serving men, and his harsh sentence was a just one. This opening scene must have captivated the Elizabethans who saw it for the first time, and for succeeding times, too, from the moment the first speech was uttered. Those in the pit would cease their uproar quickly and settle down to listen with rapt attention when servants were at swords' points over the honor of their respective houses. This was a bold and clever dramatic stroke that enabled the playwright to plunge into the very heart of the action in his tragic plot.

Where to draw the line between easy, friendly relations between master and servant was most important because the comparative lack of privacy in the home made it necessary to keep servants in their place if there was to be any harmony. This was particularly true of personal servants. At the same time the lack of privacy made it necessary to maintain easy relations lest there develop a strained attitude that in itself would be intolerable. Shakespeare's plays are a fascinating revelation of this harmony in action, as in the give and take between Valentine and Speed (II:i) and Julia and Lucetta (I:ii) in *Two Gentlemen of Verona*, even though the early plays were likely to let realism wait on wit. In later situations of this type, when Shakespeare has acquired more skill, both characters and scenes are more convincing. Portia and Nerissa, for example, very gracefully skirt the edges of familiarity in *The Merchant of Venice*, and Launcelot in all his clowning never imposes upon the good will of Bassanio. It would be so easy for these servants to offend, though they are totally different in character. Nerissa, the well-bred companion of a lady, is notable for her wise "sentences," and Launcelot, the clown, for his ebullient spirits. Yet each attends a superior with the right decorum, for each keeps within the prescribed bounds of service without seeming to exert much effort.

When Justice Shallow, however, gave orders to his servants, he was treated with a saucy impudence that astonished Falstaff, who was himself used to being the victim of such treatment, especially in the prince's company. Therefore he will make much of what he sees at Shallow's house and report it to the prince in such a manner as to keep him in "continual laughter the wearing out of six fashions" (*II Henry IV*, V:i: 71–78). In *The Merry Wives of Windsor*, Falstaff's little page Robin had a quick tongue in his head, and he had no scruples against mocking his master when he might win flattery from the ladies who were amused by his pert manner. Telling Mistress Page he would rather go before her like a little man than follow his master like a dwarf, he preened himself with birdlike satisfaction as she smilingly told him he was a little gallant and would surely become a courtier (III:ii: 1–9). Like all cock-robins, he had no loyalty and only a shallow wit. Asked by the wives to betray his master, he needed no other reward than a new doublet and hose, and pretty pet names to rub his feathers the right way (III:iii: 22–36). In well-managed homes there was no place for pretty little Robins unless they were loyal as well as witty while they entertained master or guests.

Each servant in a stable household had his appointed task and, when well trained and attached to a house of distinction, performed his duties with pride and usually with genuine devotion. The lady's maid in such a home might come from a family of social distinction, who had placed her in service to learn how to be a great lady herself. The women in waiting to an important lady must have gentle blood in their veins in order to qualify for the honor of serving such a mistress. In this same household there might also be several men from families of gentle blood, their duties being commensurate with their social position or as preparation for a master's duties in case fortune brought them such responsibilities.

The maid chosen for personal service must rise early in order to be fully dressed when summoned by her mistress. Before dressing, she must wash her face, hands, and arms, cleanse her teeth, comb her hair, and examine her fingernails to see that they were clean and not too long. When fully dressed, she must inspect herself carefully in a mirror to see that she was neat and fully presentable. After her master had risen, she was to go to her lady, and not leave her till she was fully dressed. If the mistress wished to comb her own hair, the maid brought brush and comb and whatever the lady wished for adornment, such as a lace or band or jewels or cap. Then she held a mirror so the lady might inspect her hair. Next, she brought fresh warm water for washing hands and face, poured the water in a bowl, and placed a fine towel by the bowl. The ablutions over, she removed bowl and towel, and helped the lady to dress.

If this personal maid was sent to the hall on an errand she must conduct herself with great propriety. She accompanied her mistress to morning worship, and throughout the day remained within call unless dismissed and told to go to her own apartment. At table, she did not as a rule sit on a level with her mistress unless ladies and gentlemen of rank sat between her and her mistress. If no gentlemen were present and there was no servant to carve, she might carve meat for her lady. When the meal was finished and her mistress had risen and washed her hands, then the maid rose and washed her hands and followed her mistress from the room. At night she helped her lady remove her clothing, and left her only when dismissed, usually just before the master entered.

In the homes of the middle class, any of the maids taking care of the chambers might be called upon to perform whatever personal service the mistress required. From these maids she might also choose a servant to accompany her on the street when she went shopping, though an older servant or nurse usually filled this need. In addition, if an apprentice from her husband's shop was available, he would escort them in order to afford some real protection in case of need.

Apprentices were sometimes pressed into all kinds of service, from fetching water from the public fountains that supplied fresh water to London or city households, to turning the spit in the kitchen. On mornings, water carriers gathered in great crowds at city fountains to await their turn at a conduit, and then set forth to peddle water to the people who could not afford to send a servant or apprentice for it. The pushing and crowding, therefore, might require an especially strong man for this task unless he slothfully waited till the press was over. In such cases, however, his delay might result in a beating when he reached home with the long awaited water.

Apprentices, of course, were often used as servants to carry torches at night as they accompanied their masters whose business took them forth into the dangerous streets. They went before the little procession, each carrying a torch or lantern and wearing a great club suspended from his neck. Early in the period many strong apprentices were armed with long daggers even in daytime, wearing them on their hips or at their sides. No wonder the warning cry of an approaching mob of rioting blue-coated apprentices had filled pedestrians with such terror that the daggers had to be forbidden. Servants who acted as torchbearers for their masters at night were called link boys. When such a party reached its destination, the link boys extinguished their torches by thrusting them into a metal, trumpet-shaped ornament beside the door, and then stood them up against the stone wall while they went directly into the kitchen if the hospitable host or head servant ordered the household servants to provide them with refreshment. The master, meanwhile, was conducted to the host's private apartments, where he discussed his business if he was not first served with refreshment. It was not pleasant to venture forth at night, and only important business or social matters took Elizabethans from their homes through the dark streets or along the dark and hazardous roads.

In general, households with few servants simply multiplied the tasks of the servants they did have. In small rural homes, for example, a maid of all work was expected to wash, bake, brew, and keep the house in presentable order, from scouring the floor to making the beds. Those who could afford more than one servant were likely to engage them, because many servants indicated prosperity. In great households the gradations among servants were so fine and numerous that all who served were called servants whether they were of the rank of esquire, land steward, private secretary, or merely a menial. Each of these in an orderly home performed only the duties assigned to him and for which he was carefully trained, taking care not to interfere with the tasks of others.

The porter at the lodge gate of a noble's establishment announced the coming of visitors. Usually, arrangements must be made with him for providing or hiring horses when visitors needed fresh mounts to enable them to continue their journey after a short stay with his master. Masters themselves might have nothing to do with the transactions, especially if the servants on both sides were trusted by their superiors. Oftentimes, especially in the early part of the century or in rugged outlying districts, the porter sat at an upper window that he might have full command of the road and be able to prepare the household for the coming of friend or foe. As the age became more peaceful, the porter's duties and their importance declined till he became little more than a formal or informal watchman who notified the other servants that visitors were approaching. But at the great country estates of the rich, he continued to be an important servant, for here, if unfriendly visitors were announced, the master might have time to barricade his doors or to prepare for flight. Sometimes the porter's lodge, therefore, was sufficiently removed from the house to make it a means of defense. In this case the porter was often a rough fellow, whose qualities were little more than loyalty and physical strength. In homes having few occasions to expect troublesome guests, he might be a bluff, friendly fellow whose announcement of visitors would add much to the atmosphere of hospitality.

The marshal and usher and steward might be separate individuals or their duties might be performed by one person. They and the porter might carry staffs of authority; they were usually important members of a large household with several servants under them, those in the first rank taking precedence over their subordinates in both responsibility and rank. The usher and grooms usually took orders from the marshal, who was responsible for fuel supplies in the hall, chambers, and kitchens, and for making the fire in the great hall. All servants, especially butlers, pantlers, and cooks connected with the serving of meals, were accountable to him. He kept tally of the meals served and issued orders for bread and ale, though if the cost of food was questioned, the steward was brought in to give his opinion on the matter.

The marshal must know the ranking of guests and seat them at table accordingly. A king's messenger, for example, might dine with a knight or with even the marshal himself. Poor knights and rich knights varied in rank, though ranking might depend on the town or establishment from which they came. If in doubt about a guest, the marshal must ask his master, and never chance making a mistake. Great personages, of course, were usually dined in private chambers, but the near-great must be shown every respect due to their rank. Great personages also had servants for every office and servants waiting on their superiors in office, and these the marshal must seat according to rank.

In order to avoid confusion among all these servants it was absolutely necessary that each know his duties perfectly, for doubt or fear about what to do would hinder proper service to lord or guests, and that was an unforgivable and unforgettable thing. Tasting, for example, was done only for those of royal blood, and when tasting was performed, it must be according to the procedure adopted by the house thus served. The steward or chamberlain of a prince, therefore, might instruct the servants of his host about all these things lest there be even a slight mistake in the service. Perfection was the aim of high personages; and perfect decorum, which always necessitated much bowing, was a requirement for servants of the great. Sloan's *Book of Courtesy*, written in 1460, gives detailed explanations of the offices of servants in a lord's hall. Most of their services had changed little in their main aspects by the sixteenth century.

When the usher was important enough to have grooms as assistant servants, he might be responsible for the marshal's duties or he might act as personal servant to the master, his duties then in many respects corresponding to those of the servant attending the mistress. The large bed of the master was made by the grooms, but the usher saw that the ladies were supplied with hot water and that the candles on the mantel above the chimney were lighted at the proper time and were replenished when necessary. Ordinarily the usher sat at the door of the great hall or walked about while people were dining, as he was answerable for all who entered the hall as guests and for the proper serving of the meals. If he took over the duties of the master's chamber, he always told the wardrober when to make ready for his master's retiring, and he saw that the night-gown was brought out, a carpet spread by the bed, and cushions placed as his master desired them on the bed. When he had prepared his master for retiring, he then bowed himself out and lay down in an outer chamber, usually on a bed or pallet near the door of his master's room.

In large establishments, the chamberlain was in charge of the master's room. Like the lady's maid, he must keep himself clean and neat at all times and serve his lord cheerfully and courteously with much ceremonious bowing. He saw that his master's linen was clean and warmed at the fire before being put on. He took care also that the fire did not smoke. When his master was ready to rise, the chamberlain placed a cushioned chair before the fire with a cushion for the lord's feet and a cloth to lay over his feet to keep them warm. When, either alone or with the help of other servants under his direction, he had dressed his lord in tunic, doublet, stomacher, short and long hose, and shoes, he trussed the hose as high as the lord wished them, and then placed a kerchief around his master's shoulders to protect his clothes while his hair was combed. His master was then given warm water in which to wash his face and hands. This done, the servant kneeled and asked the lord what robe he wished to wear, and later, having helped him into it, got the girdle and fastened it, and ceremoniously brought his hood or cap or hat and cloak or cape. Before the lord left the chamber, the servant inspected him well, and brushed off all possible lint or dust.

Shakespeare's *The Taming of the Shrew* (Induction, ll. 49–61) travesties a "fine lord" waking in the morning and being attended by numerous servants. The chamber is made sweet with burning scented wood. Music is played to waken the lord, and a servant asks, "What is it your honor will command?" Another servant brings a silver basin of warm water sweet with rose water and floating flowers. Another carries a ewer, and a third, a napkin or towel, saying, "Will't please your lord-ship cool your hands?" Still another servant is ready with an expensive suit, and asks him what he will wear. Finally, another servant tells him how his hounds and horses are. The scene must have provoked roars of laughter among the delighted groundlings and speculative interest among the social climbers.

Sometimes the chamberlain performed the duties of a wardrobe master, but in great houses there was a special servant or servants for this office. It was their duty to keep the master's clothes brushed and aired and to inspect the drapery and bedding of the apartment regularly. If the lord took an afternoon nap, such a servant must have the kerchief and comb, the pillow and its cover, and water and a towel ready for the chamberlain to use when the master rose from sleep. After supper, the wardrobe master must see that the articles for retiring were ready for the chamberlain to use. Then the chamberlain, with much bowing, helped his master to remove his clothes, replacing his outer garments with soft slippers and the dressing gown commonly referred to as the nightgown. This garment was to keep him warm till he removed his underclothing when he went to bed for the night. If the lord wished to read a while, he kept his dressing gown on after he got into bed. Oftentimes the master slept in his tunic, and he usually wore a nightcap. Some masters slept in the nude. When the lord was in bed, the chamberlain bowed, drew the curtains, and prepared to leave for the night. First, however, he must inspect the chamber carefully to see there were no dogs or cats in it and, if there were, to put them out. Now, he was ready to retire himself.

Occasionally the master wished a bath, and usually this was given at night by the chamberlain to keep his lord from taking cold. First, scented sheets fresh from the press were hung about the room to keep out drafts, and after the chamberlain had made sure the door was closed, he arranged sponges in the tub for the master to lean against or to sit on, and to rest his feet on. When he had ceremoniously helped his master to remove his clothes, he wrapped the lord's body loosely with a sheet to keep him warm, and exposed only that part being washed with a soft sponge. After his master was bathed, the servant rinsed him with fresh warm water, scented, and then poured water over him for another good rinsing. Then he dried him with a soft towel, and put him to bed. When bathrooms came into use at the end of the century, the personal servant was no doubt relieved to have his labors greatly lightened. Most people, however, still took their infrequent baths in wooden tubs before the fire with or without the close attendance of servants.

After the lord had left the chamber in the morning, the chamberlain turned to the bed, stripped off the clothes, beat the featherbed, inspected the blankets and sheets to see that they were clean, and if not, got fresh ones. Then he made the bed, covered it with a silk spread or tapestry, and placed a good many cushions about, with a fresh head sheet or cover for the pillow on which his master laid his head. Then he spread the tapestry carpets on the chests, window seats, and cupboards. With the room in order, he replenished the fire and saw that there was plenty of fuel to last another day, or longer. Sir John Russell's *Book of Nurture*, written about 1460, was a standard guide for servants performing these personal services during the sixteenth century.

The chief steward was a very important servant and in some households was more than the overseer of the financial side of housekeeping, for he sometimes took over the duties of marshal, chief usher, chamberlain, wardrobe master, etc. Of course, with so much responsibility, he could do no more than supervise the menial tasks of these offices as they were performed by subordinates. At necessary intervals he interviewed servants under him or called them all together to hold a sort of council about their master's welfare. This was particularly true in regard to servants accountable for the master's meals. Since he kept all accounts, he frequently called together the kitchen clerk, the chief cook, the controller, the surveyor who examined all the dishes brought to the table, and any other servant he felt should be included. Together they planned any changes that had been ordered, or smoothed out any difficulties that had arisen about the lord's or family's diet. The steward was depended on to obtain any dainties ordered by the family members, and sometimes for this alone it was necessary to call a council of the servants involved. Naturally he kept in close touch with the accounts of the controller, who, in efficient households, reported to him regularly concerning the amount of money spent or in hand for household needs.

With all this careful division of labor among well-trained servants, the duties involved in serving a meal were many and complicated. Minor details were superintended by butler, carver, and server. It was the butler's duty to keep special well-sharpened knives provided for chopping loaves of bread, preparing these loaves for the table, and making trenchers when bread was used for this purpose. The lord's bread and that of his family might be cut from new loaves, but all other bread used by the household was one to three days old. When used for trenchers, bread had to be four days old. Lords who owned fine plate never used bread for trenchers unless unusual circumstances required them to do so; such might be a sudden and totally unexpected number of guests that had to be dined. Most of the bread was baked in small, individual loaves that were broken at will by individuals at table. If the loaves were too brown or had oven grit on them, the butler was well reprimanded for his carelessness. In ordinary homes, each person scraped his own little loaf.

The butler must also keep the salt fine, white, and dry. To do this, he must inspect the salt before each meal, and also make sure the top of the container did not touch the salt. He must inspect all the napery used, seeing that it was sweet and clean for every meal, and in sufficient quantity. The tablecloth must be laid with great care, and the napkins neatly folded and properly placed; likewise, the towel on which the lord dried his hands must be neatly folded and ready for use when it was time for the meal to be served. The table knives and spoons must be polished and kept scrupulously clean. Each night the butler looked to the wine to see there was neither ferment nor leak, and was careful never to serve stale wine from lead containers lest the metal cause poisoning. He must also see that the cups and pots were clean inside and out, especially when pewter or other metal was used lest, again, there be poisoning from them. Glasses, of course, must be kept polished for the sake of appearance as well as to observe cleanliness.

When it was time to lay the table, the butler went seriously to work. First, he wiped the table clean and placed on it the silencer and then the tablecloths if the table was too long for one cloth. When more than one cloth was used, as in the case of trestles, he was very particular about the overlapping of cloths, smoothing them down carefully and seeing that they hung at the sides exactly right. If the cloth had to be lapped along the middle to get the edges right, then he must be sure this center fold was smooth and flat. The table properly covered, he must provide fresh napkins for sideboard and cupboards. Then, taking a clean towel, he put it around his neck, grasping one end in the left hand to hold the towel in place over the left arm, on which he put articles with which to set the table. First he must set the salt near the lord's place at table, for the great salt was the most ornamental and the most significant dish on the table. At the lord's place would be arranged knife, plate, spoon, bread, and a neatly folded napkin. When individual loaves of bread were used, the napkin was sometimes folded about the loaf. If guests dined at the lord's table, each was provided with plate, napkin, knife, and spoon, though the service might vary according to rank, the richer plate being used for those of highest rank.

After the lord's table was set, the butler put cloths on the other tables, and laid them with salts, plate or trenchers, knives, spoons, napkins, and sometimes cups or glasses. Usually cups and glasses were kept on the cupboards, and guests were served with drink only when they called for it, the cups being emptied immediately after each person drank, and the dregs given later with the table scraps to the poor waiting at the gates. It was not good manners to drink all the wine in a cup, and good service provided a fresh cup with each drink. When all the tables were laid, the butler arranged the extra plate of silver or gilt or pewter or glass on the sideboard and cupboards, and inspected the pots for ale or wine. Finally the ewers and basins with scented hot and cold water were placed on the ewery board, and now the master and guests might be told that dinner or supper was ready to be served.

Naturally service varied according to the master's social position. In some households the service was much more formal than just described, and in other homes much less formal. But the general pattern followed certain rules without much change. Sometimes, for example, the lord's place was carefully laid and the wrapped bread and great salt arranged before it, but the other places were not laid till all were seated and the lord served. If this procedure was followed, after grace the butler approached his lord with a deep bow, uncovered the bread and set it by the salt, and then provided the guests with knives, spoons, napkins, and bread. Later, during the meal, he saw that bread and wine or ale were supplied whenever desired by anyone at the tables.

Always the butler must be gentle and courteous of speech, clean and neat in dress and grooming, taking care to keep his hands particularly white, with the nails short and clean. A good butler was sure of himself, never fidgeting or stroking his hair or smoothing his clothes or going through the numberless self-conscious movements of underlings who are ill at ease and trying to seem well poised. The careless servant who was untidy or had objectionable habits common to the age, like spitting or belching, was not tolerated in homes of good service. Of all servants, however, the butler must be most immaculate.

As soon as dinner or supper was announced, the ewer took his place in the hall, and the lord approached with his guests. Sometimes the lord washed his hands first in the basin held respectfully for him by the ewer, and dried his hands on the towel held by the ewer, who was accountable for the cleanliness of all napery and the proper state of all candles. Sometimes the lord urged an important guest to precede him in the ceremony. When all hands were washed and the diners seated at table, each according to rank, grace was said. If only the family dined, or if the guests were close friends, a child might be asked to say grace. If an important guest was present, he might be asked to say grace, particularly if he was of the clergy. Sometimes grace was long; sometimes, as in the case of the child's prayer, it might be very short. On formal occasions grace might be long enough to enable the server to hurry to the kitchen to get fruits from the butler and return with them by the time grace was being concluded. Such fruits might be served as appetizers, though the general custom was to conclude the meal with fruit, and to have dishes of tempting seasonal fruit placed on cupboards or sideboards as decorations during the meal. If the fruit was eaten first, the ewer must provide scented water and towels for washing the hands again. Sometimes individual napkins were used at this time, for only the tips of fingers were dipped in the basin as it went from lord to guests and on down the table to those of the lowest rank who had partaken of the fruit.

Most frequently a salad was served first. While the guests at a formal dinner were so engaged, the chief server (frequently referred to as *sewer* in the literature of the period) would ask the surveyor who had examined the dishes to tell him what important or new concoctions had been prepared. Now, at the order of the chief cook, the servers would carry in the dishes in an orderly procession, and place them on the sideboard, from where the surveyor delivered them to the chief server, who, with the aid of the other servers, presented them to his lord and then to the guests and members of the family. On formal occasions all this service was performed with much ceremonious bowing. Aside from serving the meal and superintending the service of those who aided him, the chief server was responsible for all plate and silver used, and when breakable things like delicate glasses were handled, this part of his duties was by no means easy. Sometimes the chief server needed additional help at a banquet and was forced to draw upon domestics of the household; he might, therefore, command the services of a marshal or squire or even a sergeant at arms. After the meal was over, he saw that tables were cleared and trestles removed and placed neatly against the wall.

The carver was very busy while meats were being served. He must be expert in making all cuts quickly and neatly, whether of fish, flesh, or fowl, and he must hold his knife correctly at all times. As a rule he grasped the joint or fowl with the left hand, holding it firmly while he cut the meat, with his right thumb and only two fingers of his right hand resting on the knife. He was expected to keep the knife clean and sharp, wiping it frequently on a napkin, and washing his hands often as he carved. Only careless carvers ever wiped their knives on the tablecloth or ever touched the meat with the right hand.

Besides the many menials and the supervisors in the kitchen there was the kitchen clerk, who was in charge of the meals, directed the dressing of all meats, and measured out the supplies. So valuable were the spices that he took charge of them himself. He even determined the scale of wages for the grooms and yeomen of some households, and ordered the general household clothing. Thus the kitchen clerk was often accountable for some of the important expenditures in home maintenance. The cutler or bladesmith was responsible for sharp edges on the kitchen knives; the pantler supervised the pantry and assisted the butler or assumed all the duties of that office. The cellarer or steward of wines had an important position, for he and the butler must see that the drink for the master and his household was safe and agreeable. The chief cook had charge of the other cooks and the scullions, among whom might be extra help during feasts when the kitchen was likely to be the busiest and noisiest place in the entire household.

Kitchen servants were expected to dine on the remains from the lord's table or to cook simple food for themselves. At feasts they were sure of generous amounts of rich food, but at other times all servants were expected to dine simply, under the watchful eye of the kitchen clerk. Scraps from their table also went to the beggars at the gate, and the almoner saw that "broken meats" from all the tables were gathered at the end of a meal to be given to charity. They were often worth waiting for, as the huge pies with walls several inches thick, molded to resemble a building or an animal, were filled with ham, veal, and large balls of forcemeat. The highly seasoned meat of the latter was even worth fighting for if the beggars were clamorous for food.

The food and the service caused the lord's table to cost him a good deal, far more than the other costs in maintaining his home. If he had other castles or manors or farms, he must have a trusted steward to supervise each, and trusted servants to collect the rents from tenants. If the master's income was derived from other and more lucrative sources, he must have a treasurer to see that collections were made and money paid to his kitchen clerk for victuals used, wages paid to squires, yeomen, grooms, pages, etc. The treasurer must also keep a strict account of the reports made by bailiffs and stewards of the money derived from the master's estates, for there were other servants to be paid also, chief of whom was the master of horse in charge of blacksmiths, yeomen bitmakers, riders, footmen, coachmen, littermen, saddlers, and squires. The master of horse, for example, must provide transportation for the household, purchase adequate mounts, and perhaps improve the breed of his master's horses. Still other servants were the keeper of the park, the farrier who shod the horses, the huntsmen in charge of the hunting dogs, the chandler who trimmed all the candles, the bakers who were kept busy supplying the vast amount of bread used, and all the menials who washed and scoured and swept and dusted and tried in their way to keep the house clean.

In modest homes that could afford several servants, their management was sometimes also a serious problem. In average households the servant problem was somewhat simplified by a division of labor among the overseers and the laborers. In the country, the wife usually supervised the servants in the dairy and at table as well as those engaged in other household tasks. Some husbands, however, did not trust their wives as managers, especially in the towns, and friction might arise. John Lyly's *Euphues and His England* suggested as a remedy that the wife be permitted to carry at her girdle the keys to all household supplies and the husband carry the purse at his girdle. Oftentimes this arrangement was made. In large households, of course, the steward carried the keys to the supply rooms. When the good housewife was expected to supervise and to engage in the tasks she was overseeing, she was kept busy indeed with cooking, spinning, weaving, and sewing. Conscientious women among the gentry also continued to perform such labors, but their sophisticated sisters turned their backs on them. If husband and wife were able to make a showing with numerous servants, just how far the wife or husband supervised them was largely an individual matter.

The country squire usually found it impossible to manage his estate well unless he kept in close touch himself with his overseer, and this often required him to be abroad in the fields most of the day. When necessary, he did not hesitate to bend his own back to a task. Some householders took the care of their servants much to heart, taught them to read, and watched over their moral behavior. This required close supervision on the part of both husband and wife, but it also demanded tact and a genuine interest in those who worked for them. In *The Mothers Blessing*, Dorothy Leigh declared all servants should be taught to read at least the Ten Commandments and if possible persuaded to read from the Bible whenever they had any spare time. No ungodly, profane, or wicked person should be permitted to remain in a household once he was discovered lest he bring a curse upon the other members, she said. She assured householders that if their servants kept the Sabbath holy, they would perform their duties faithfully during the rest of the week. Many masters and mistresses were inclined to agree with her. Some even went so far as to pray for their servants. Dorothy Leigh believed such prayers should be offered twice a day.

In homes that permitted dogs to wander at will through the rooms and to be present at meals when bones were tossed to them by careless masters, cleanliness was impossible. In any age, of course, cleanliness is a relative matter, and certainly it was in the Elizabethan age. When one reads of the requirements for personal cleanliness demanded of servants, one must not forget such rules needed to be impressed strongly upon the ignorant minds of the underprivileged. Thus when the butler or personal servant was commanded to keep his hands and nails clean, it was likely that he could not be trusted to do so except under compulsion. The same is true of rules that a servant must not "claw his head or back as if for a flea," or "stroke his hair as if for a louse," or "pick his nose or let it drip," or "puff his chest," or "pick his ears," or "spit too far," or "laugh too loud," or "let his lips drivel." He might also be commanded not to gape or yawn or pout or lick his dish or breathe too hard or groan near his master or pick his teeth or breathe in another's face. Servants, like children, followed pretty closely the standards of their masters, and since cleanliness was not enforced by any health official, it was not as commonly practiced as in modern times.

Yet cleanliness was not lacking regardless of the historian's picture of Wolsey picking his way daintily among the king's time servers, holding to his nose a pomander of strong, sweet scent that he might escape the unpleasant odors of nobles and servants as he passed by. Clad in the fine livery of a great house, servants might wear clothes made of materials not easily cleaned by washing, and consequently some of their apparel often became extremely odorous. For this reason, no doubt, new liveries were often provided when the master entertained sumptuously. But that there were also changes when liveries were laundered is proved by the fact that some of the chests in the great hall were there for the express purpose of holding clean household liveries.

Since servants dressed according to the requirements laid down for them by their masters, those belonging to the gentry were readily distinguished by the colors of their apparel or by the badges on their left arms. Formerly footmen had worn a bright blue tunic or skirted coat, frogged, and set off by white knee breeches and white stockings; maids had worn a short gown with a large apron, a tippet, and a cap. When sent out on errands, they had tied a hat down over the cap. In the early part of the Queen's reign apprentices wore blue coats in summer and blue gowns in winter, but no man wore his gown below the calf of his leg unless he was over sixty years of age. Since old men's coats might be as long as they liked, they often reached to their shoes. Apprentices' breeches and stockings were commonly of white broadcloth, the stockings sewed up close as if all in one piece. The flat caps of the apprentices distinguished them from other servants at quite a distance, and often they were irked by the contemptuous "Flat cap!" shouted at them as they passed by. After their long daggers were replaced by clubs, they felt free to lay about them with their clubs if such insults hurled at them became intolerable. Except for the dress of the apprentice, the average servant's apparel gradually became a means of advertising the master's generosity or prosperity, and for this reason, the household management had to watch closely the money spent on liveries lest this item become quite a burden on the exchequer. At the same time a servant's livery might be for him the source of considerable pride, especially if it was regarded by servants of another household with undisguised envy.

Securing service with a good master was not easy during the Elizabethan age when employment became a serious problem. This was true of both the apprentice and the domestic servant. A good master had to be paid well to take an apprentice, and these sums varied from £10 to £100. Because unscrupulous masters were likely to use apprentices as servants, these boys and men might be required to perform any kind of household work and to run any kind of errand. With such a master an apprentice learned little about the trade he was supposed to be taught during the seven years of his term. Like all the servants of the household, he was subject to the master's will and if he wished to change masters, he could secure new employment only if he could obtain the good will and recommendation of the old master. Those who found themselves with good masters, therefore, felt themselves fortunate, and loyally stayed with them as long as they were permitted to do so. The same was true of servants primarily responsible to the lady of the household.

All writers of conduct books had as much to say about the wife's as the husband's relation to the servants. They demanded that both learn to rule themselves before undertaking the control of those who labored for them. The wife must be able to speak without bitterness or sharpness, and to treat old, faithful servants kindly, remembering obedience and service were better when obtained by fair means than by fear. She must always think of herself as an example for her maids, and therefore be chaste, sober, and fully aware of everything going on in the management of her home. Such awareness could be hers only when she worked with her servants as she supervised them. Because she was usually close at home, her contact with servants was also likely to be warmer than the master's.

Moral literature dealing with domestic servants and their management varies no more than the advice given for maintaining the right relations between members of the family, particularly those of husband and wife or master and mistress of a household. But the actual conditions were controlled largely by the responsible and irresponsible householders themselves. True, chance might alter the picture by mixing up the human elements without regard for the pattern, and good servants find themselves in evil households and bad servants in good homes. But the influence of the family upon the servants was much stronger when servants became actual members of the family, as so often occurred in Elizabethan establishments. Thus the stress placed upon the need of good and kind household management on the part of husband and wife resulted more often than not in such close ties that the master was frequently his brother-servant's keeper, and the wife, the good angel of her maids.

Picture Post Library

Sheep herding, from Edmund Spenser's Shepherds
Calendar, 1579

CHAPTER VII

CHANGES WROUGHT BY DEATH

It is therefore death alone that can
suddenly make man to know himself.
SIR WALTER RALEIGH (1552?–1618)

o matter how sophisticated, no man can banish fully from his mind the fear of changes wrought by death. For both the bereaved and the marked victim of death are subject to these terrifying thoughts even when beatific visions ease the translation of the pious soul. Elizabethans, torn by doubts in their religious faith, suffered great perturbation when brought face to face with questions of the hereafter. Shakespeare reveals this state of mind in Claudio, young brother of the pious Isabella, as he gives way to the terror which he and all sensitive Elizabethans tried to keep buried deep within themselves. As his fears rise, Claudio laments the uncertainties hurled by death. Looking down on his hands, warm with life, he thinks of the horrid sight they will be "rotting" in the grave, and all the tingling motion of his youthful strength and beauty "become a kneaded clod." First the grave, then the punishments meted out to his delight-loving spirit. Will it be bathed in fiery floods or reside in "thrilling region of thick-ribbed ice," or be imprisoned in "the viewless winds and blown with violence" round the world, or, worse still, be joined to those "that lawless and uncertain thoughts imagine howling!"? The horror is too great. He prefers the "weariest and most loathed worldly life that age, ache, penury and imprisonment" can lay down upon him, for such is paradise to what he fears in death.

When faith in life is stronger than the fear of death, human beings already in the shadow push aside the great horror, assuring themselves that others are to be death's victims, that their own time to die has never quite arrived. For Elizabethans, however, love of life was intensified by realization of the uncertainty of its days. With fear of death casting its dismal cloud across the skies of each fair morning, they faced the fear and its shadow by planning most carefully their own little pageant to the grave. Solemnly, sternly, they considered each detail in the last rites to be rendered for themselves when dead—the ceremonious shroud, "the surly sullen bell," the poor, roughly carved stone, or the impressive monument with its choice Latin inscription, sculptured garlands, and effigy lying in state, marble on marble. What must be, must be, and they braced themselves to meet death with dignity. Some fortified their minds with a stoic philosophy; some accustomed themselves to death's horrors by morbid contemplation of the macabre; some rested uneasily on a faith in eternal happiness or eternal sleep; some went forth to embrace death, singing psalms before they "slept sweetly in the Lord." In each case, the specter of fear was never laid low.

Some, of course, nerved themselves for the struggle by piety. Many sick people raised their fainting spirits by reading Becon's *The Sicke Mans Salve*, published at the beginning of Elizabeth's reign. Of his three folios of advice and encouragement to the religious, this was the most popular, with its promises of rewards for righteous living, for by 1632 it had gone through seventeen editions. In returning health, however, some of these minds could agree with Shakespeare's Lafeu, "Moderate lamentation is the right of the dead, excessive grief the enemy of the living" (*All's Well That Ends Well*, I:i:62). Then, in the presence of death at last, with no hope of return, they met the mystery with mystery.

For example, when the Queen wished to express her sympathy for a bereft mother, she wrote, "We sympathize in your sorrow on the death of your son, and have a grateful memory of his services. Let Christian discretion stay immoderate grief." Yet when she herself faced death she was so overwhelmed before it that her conduct has given rise to many conflicting stories of the struggle. One tells how she refused to go to bed, and spent her last days lying on cushions on the floor. Was she following the superstitious practice of warding off death by lying on feathers? Or was she, who could never reconcile herself to giving in to any defeat, unwilling to acknowledge the greatest defeat of all? Was this why, with some consistency, she could refuse so long to name a successor to the throne even though the good of the country she had always professed as her greatest concern was endangered by her obstinacy? Or must she name no successor prematurely lest rivals prevent James's peaceful succession?

One of the most interesting accounts of her death occurs in a letter by John Chamberlain to Dudley Carleton.[1] He had gained the information from his friend, William Gilbert, physician to the Queen. He says the Queen's disease, according to Gilbert, was "nothing but a settled and unremovable melancholy." She couldn't be made by anyone in attendance "to taste or touch physic," though ten or twelve physicians with her assured her she would easily recover thereby. Her brain was not "distempered" except that "she held an obstinate silence for the most part, and because she had a persuasion that if she once lay down she should never rise, could not be gotten to bed in a whole week till three days before her death . . ." She languished for three weeks, and "died on the same day of the month in which she was born." The Archbishop of Canterbury, the Bishop of London, and the Almoner and Bishop of Chichester had access to her at all times, says Chamberlain, and all "gave good testimony of her faith."

It was like Elizabeth to fight this last battle alone, to let no other mind

---

[1] Norman Egbert McClure (ed.), *The Letters of John Chamberlain* (1939).

peer into the depths of her soul as she faced the enemy she could not conquer. The practical historian, however, will always wonder how far her will or how far her fear was responsible for the thoughts she took with her alone to the grave. According to Professor Neale, her last "royal duty" was to nominate James as her successor, after which she "centered her mind on Heavenly things, rejoicing in the ministrations of her spiritual physician . . . Archbishop Whitgift. And then she turned her face to the wall, sank into a stupor, and . . . passed quietly away."[2] It is hard indeed to think of this Queen, bowed down with the unshakable melancholy that caused her death, centering her mind on heavenly things, even by an act of will. True, at this time it was commonly believed such an act of will could bring salvation. Had the Queen, in her extremity, turned to the last hope and by an act of will forced her mind to dwell on spiritual things? Had fear or reason dictated a forcing of the mind to an act by which she might be saved? Or did death merely brush her with his apathetic wing and let her drift off into the hereafter without thought or willing or terror?

Perhaps those most in love with worldly splendor were most sensitive to the irony of death. Not only must they face the unknown enemy and the possibility of eternal punishment, but at death's door they must give up all they had striven for in worldly accomplishment. It was fitting, therefore, in the macabre Dance of Death to adorn the central figure with the fool's cap and bells. Trained to look at life realistically as well as piously, the worldly mind could listen with rapt attention to Hamlet's soliloquy on longing for death after all the lovely dreams of his life had turned to dust and ashes. In like manner such a mind could sympathetically watch the prince at Ophelia's grave as he turned the skull of Yorick around in his hands and contemplated his mental picture of the once kindly eyes and witty tongue which had filled its caverns. Now, with him, this mind could see the horror of the jest that began life with so much promise and ended it with so much decaying stench.

Though Elizabethans did all they could to veil the horrors of this mocking, tragic, intolerable residue, they could do almost nothing at all to delay the ravages of "this hard-favor'd tyrant, ugly, meagre, lean," this "grim-grinning ghost, earth's worm" (*Venus and Adonis*, ll. 931, 933). The shock of beholding a beautiful or loved face devoured by death's decay could not be softened by any means within their power, and they were driven almost mad at times by anticipation of such dissolution. In *The Life and Death of King John*, Shakespeare had but to look within his own or any English heart to find the words with which Constance, or any Elizabethan mother, would frantically rail about death as she found it stealing upon her son. Tearing her hair, thrusting away the hands that would hold her, not unkindly, she begs death to snatch

[2] J. E. Neale, *Queen Elizabeth* (1934).

her instead from this world. Such a death she calls "amiable" and "lovely." She alludes to its "odoriferous stench" and "sound rottenness." She bids it rise from its "couch of lasting night." She calls it the "hate and terror to prosperity." Yet to save her son from its dread presence, she would kiss its "detestable bones," put her own eyeballs in its "vaulty brows," ring her fingers with its "household worms," stop her very "gasp of breath with fulsome dust," and be like it "a carrion monster" (III:iv: 25–33).

When the horrified people about her exchange glances and say that she is mad, the mother retorts by rapidly calling to mind past events they all know in order to prove that she has suffered no loss of memory and therefore is not mad. Then, as her hearers gaze on her with fearful amazement, she tells them brokenly how grief "fills the room up," how it lies in her son's bed, "walks up and down" with her, "puts on the boy's pretty looks, repeats his words," reminds her of all his "gracious parts, and stuffs out his vacant garments" with the form of grief itself (ll. 93–97). In her anguish she reveals what Elizabethans found most terrifying about death—its putrefaction, its association with night, its bony image, eyeless and monstrous in grinning, and its loathsome transformation of all worldly beauty into wormy dust. Nothing could so climax a terror like this as welcoming it like a bridegroom.

The horror of a newly buried form festering in an ancient family vault could be surpassed only by the dread possibility of being buried alive. Shakespeare froze the tense hearts of his audience with this picture in Juliet's imagination before she drank the potion she feared might be fatal. "How if, when I am laid into the tomb, I wake before the time that Romeo come to redeem me?" she asks herself, and straightway gives the answer. She sees herself either "stifled in the vault, to whose foul mouth no healthsome air breathes in," or driven mad with fright when waking in "an ancient receptacle, where, for these many hundred years," the bones of all her ancestors "are pack'd." She sees "bloody Tybalt . . . festering in his shroud." Recalling tales of night spirits, she cries out in terror in spite of her efforts at self-control. Again she fears she may waken too early, and be so overcome by "loathsome smells" and "shrieks like mandrakes' torn out of the earth" that she, like mortals hearing these shrieks, will lose her wits and "madly play" with her "forefathers' joints" and "pluck the mangled Tybalt from his shroud." Then, in a frenzied rage, she might arm herself with some "kinsman's bone," and "as with a club," dash out her "desperate brains." With a frantic cry she raises the potion to her lips, drinks it, and swoons with terror (IV:iii:30–58). Into this climax are crowded the conflicting, divergent attitudes toward death that caused the subtle influence of their most fearsome thoughts to vibrate every fiber of Elizabethan hearts.[3]

[3] Theodore Spencer, "Death and Elizabethan Tragedy," Chap. II of *Shakespeare and the Nature of Man*, Lowell Lectures (1949).

Yet these people embraced life even as they grappled with death. They could understand the intended dramatic sorrow of Shakespeare's Richard II, therefore, when the doomed man declaimed to his wife how she must learn to think of their former happy state as a dream from which they had awakened to bitter suffering. "I am sworn brother . . . to grim Necessity," he continues, "and he and I will keep a league with death" (V:i:17–24). Well might she leave such a husband at his bidding to enter a religious house, there to "win a new world's crown." It is quite possible that Elizabethan preoccupation with death was the reason why the audience liked to watch people die on the stage. Not all the scenes were given over to the horrors of the grave, however. For example, the anxious prince returning to his dying father, King John, says he is

> . . . the cygnet to this pale faint swan,
> Who chants a doleful hymn to his own death,
> And from the organ-pipe of frailty sings
> His soul and body to their lasting rest.
> *King John*, V: vii: 21–24

With wonder the youth exclaims, " 'Tis strange that death should sing!" This wonder was not unlike that of the Puritan Philip Stubbes, who watched his wife, singing psalms at her death, finally hold up her arms to her vision of the Lord, and die with an ecstatic smile.

In the actual presence of death, the strongest Elizabethans might give way for a time to grief. When Lord Burghley's beloved wife died, the great man was so overcome by his loss that his friends were gravely concerned about him. In vain they wrote him letters of sage advice and gentle sympathy, but one would like to think Sir Walter Raleigh's words helped him to gain some control over his anguish. He tells the Secretary that he would rather be with him now than at any other time if only he might take some of the burden of the sorrow and lay the greatest part on his own heart. His friend has but to request his presence, and he will come. Meantime, he asks him not to overshadow his wisdom with passion, but to "look aright into things as they are." Since death is inevitable to all, we should all take the time of its arrival "in as good part as the knowledge." In this way can the wise man draw "together into sufferance the unknown future to the known present, looking no less with the eyes of the mind than those of the body, the one beholding afar off and the other at hand." In this way also, the true man can participate in immortality and know his destiny to be of God, making his estate and wishes, his fortune and desires all in one.

Burghley's wife, Mildred Cooke, had died in 1589 after forty-two years of genuine companionship with her husband, and the Secretary's personal world was so shattered that he did not see how he could make it into an intelligible pattern again. Raleigh admits, therefore, that Burghley has lost a good wife indeed, but he hastens to remind him that

there was a time when he had not even known her, and now she is no
more his than she was then; he should not grieve, therefore, since he
knows she "hath passed the wearisome journey of this dark world and
hath possession of her inheritance." For her children's sake he must take
care of his own health lest he leave them without a guide, "or by sorrowing . . . dry up" his "own times that ought to establish them."

Sorrows are "dangerous companions," continues Raleigh, "converting
bad into evil and evil into worse and do no other service than multiply
harms." He even calls sorrows the "treasures of weak hearts and of the
foolish," and he asks his friend to remember that the mind which entertains sorrows "is as the earth . . . dust whereon sorrows and adversities
of the world . . . trample and defile." He recalls how often Burghley
has himself had occasion to say to others, especially in his family, that "the
mind of man is that part of God which is in us," and in so far as it is
made "subject to passion, by so much is it farther from Him that gave it
to us." Finally, he says that if he were in his friend's place he would be
patient till he had seen all the evils of this life "and so grieve for all at
once."[4]

Brave words these, reflecting the stoic philosophy that made so much
appeal to Elizabethans—till the blow fell. When Raleigh himself had
to face death and was snatched from its grasp only to find he was just
beyond its reach and slipping ever closer to it, he came to realize the
truth of his own words—that he should be patient and grieve for all evils
at once, for worse still could be in store for him. When committed to the
Tower and declared guilty of treason at one of the most unfair trials
ever conducted in his time, he suffered such agony of soul that he tried
to take his own life. First, however, he set himself the difficult task of
writing his wife. He told her how cut to the heart he was to have the
son of Lord Burghley, who had by this time succeeded to his father's
place, forsake him in his extremity. "I would not have done it him, God
knows," he declared. As Master of the Wards, however, Robert Cecil
would have control of Raleigh's son, and for this reason the father asked
his wife "to have compassion" in her judgment of the man. Then he
wrote of his contemplated suicide.

He asks his wife not to be dismayed that he is to die "in despair of
God's mercies." He assures her that God has not left him, and Satan
not tempted him, but "hope and despair live not together." He admits
it is forbidden that one destroy himself, but he also admits the mercy of
God is immeasurable, though "the cogitations of men comprehend it not."
He says again that he has ever trusted in the Lord and knows his Redeemer liveth. It is not Satan that has tempted him, but "Sorrow, whose
sharp teeth devour his heart," and he exclaims, "O God! thou art mercy
itself. Thou canst not be unmerciful to me!" Near the close, he says, "I

<hr />

[4] Algernon Cecil, *A Life of Robert Cecil* (1915), pp. 98–99.

bless my poor child, and let him know his father was no traitor. Be bold of innocence, for God—to whom I offer life and soul—knows it." Of course he expects his wife to marry again, but he hopes her second choice will be a "politic husband" only, to stand between her and the dangers of the world. "But let my son be beloved," he implores, "for he is part of me and I live in him . . ." Then he asks the Lord to keep his family and give it "comfort in both worlds."[5]

But Raleigh's attempt at suicide failed. Five months later he was told to expect execution, and this time, though helpless before the hand of fate, he could summon his stoic philosophy and compose a letter to his wife that reveals Elizabethan dignity and courage at its best under bitter circumstances. "You shall receive, my dear wife," he writes, "my last words in these last lines. My love I send to you, that you may keep it when I am dead; and my counsel, that you may remember it when I am no more." In this "last Will" he does not wish to present his "dear Bess" with sorrows, but seeks to bury them with him in the dust. Since he believes it is God's will for him never to see her again "in this life," he asks her to bear his destruction gently "and with a heart" like herself. He sends her all the thanks his heart can conceive or his pen express for her "many troubles and cares" taken of him, and for which he can never make payment in this world. By the love which she bore him he asks her not to hide herself many days in grief, for her mourning cannot avail him, "already dust." Besides, she must think of her child.

He reminds his wife that his lands are conveyed to his child, and it distresses him that he cannot provide for her as he had planned with his office of wines and his jewels. "But God hath prevented all my determinations; the great God that worketh all in all. If you can live free from want, care for no more; for the rest is but vanity." He asks that she teach their son to serve and fear God while he is young "that the fear of God may grow in him. Then shall God be a husband unto you, and father unto him; a husband and father that can never be taken from you." He speaks of the money owed him and the "arrearages of the wines" which will pay all his debts, and he begs her for her soul's sake to pay all poor men. This request says much for Raleigh's character.

"When I am gone," he continues, "no doubt you shall be sought unto by many, for the world thinks that I am very rich; but take heed of the pretences of men and their affections; for they last but in honest and worthy men." He can think of no greater misery for her than "to become a prey, and after to be despised." It is not that he would dissuade her from marriage, for that will be best for her, "both in respect of God and the world." He points out that death has cut the two of them asunder, and no longer is he hers or she his; nevertheless, he begs her

[5] Edward Edwards, *The Life and Letters of Sir Walter Raleigh* (1868), Letter CLXIII, written in July 1603.

to love their son for his father's sake. For she must know he is the "child of a true man, and who, in his own respect, despiseth Death, and all his misshapen and ugly forms."

Up to this point, Raleigh has been remarkably well composed, but now the horrors of the grave press down upon his soul, and the rest of his letter reveals his agony. He tries to tell his wife calmly how to dispose of his body, and then, as he attempts to say farewell, his courage falters, and he writes heartbrokenly: "The everlasting, infinite, powerful, and inscrutable God, that Almighty God that is goodness itself, the true life and light, keep you and yours and have mercy on me, and teach me to forgive my persecutors and false accusers; and send us to meet in His glorious kingdom. My true wife, farewell. Bless my boy; pray for me. My true God hold you in his arms." He signs his letter as "Written with the dying hand of sometime thy husband, but now alas! overthrown," and concludes with "Yours that was; but now not my own."[6]

Still death delayed, for the worst of sorrows had not yet fallen on this victim. For more than ten long anxious years he was to endure prison life till released to go on his ill-fated voyage to Guiana. Meanwhile his wife shared his confinement in the Tower, and was untiring but unsuccessful in her efforts to touch the heart of King James I for mitigation of her husband's sentence. When Raleigh finally set out upon his expedition, he took his beloved son Walter with him. Then, while ill with a fever in Guiana, Raleigh let his son go with a small party headed by Keymis, to explore the Orinoco, and to search for a fabulously rich mine. In a fight at a Spanish settlement, the son was killed and all the hopes of the English expedition ruined. When Keymis returned with the news to the father, so bitter were Raleigh's reproaches that Keymis killed himself, and Raleigh's search for El Dorado was brought to a sorry end. He never recovered from his son's death, but in his concern for his wife, he tried to break the woeful news gently: "I was loathe to write," he began, "because I know not how to comfort you; and, God knows, I never knew what sorrow meant till now. All that I can say to you is, that you must obey the will and providence of God . . ." He reminds her of how the queen had borne the death of Prince Henry "with a magnanimous heart," and the Lady Harrington of her only son. "Comfort your heart, dearest Bess, I shall sorrow for us both . . ."

Now the worst grief having fallen, the long awaited execution came to him, and he acquitted himself with the dignity that has made him one of the heroes of his time. But this dignity was clad in despair; with nothing to live for, there was nothing to grieve for. Yet Raleigh, in spite of all his weaknesses, was a great man, a loving and a loved husband, and possibly the most Elizabethan of all Elizabethans. While in the Tower, all passions spent of hope or despair, he wrote his apostrophe to

[6] *Ibid.*, Letter CCXXIII.

death, which, as part of his famous *History of the World*, has done much to give him renown in literature as he won it for a while at court with his extravagant manners and dress and lilting, bitter verse. These words of the apostrophe are important because they speak the thoughts for us which many souls of Raleigh's time would have uttered had they been able to compose them for themselves or for others:

It is therefore death alone that can suddenly make man to know himself. He tells the proud and insolent, that they are but objects, and humbles them at the instant; makes them cry, complain, and repent; yea, even to hate their fore-passed happiness.

He takes the account of the rich, and proves him a beggar; a naked beggar, which hath interest in nothing, but in the gravel that fills his mouth. He holds a glass before the eyes of the most beautiful, and makes them see therein their deformity and rottenness; and they acknowledge it.

O eloquent, just, and mighty death! whom none could advise, thou hast persuaded; what none hath dared, thou hast done; and whom all the world hath flattered, thou hast cast out of the world and despised. Thou hast drawn together all the farstretched greatness, all the pride, cruelty, and ambition of man, and covered it all over with these two narrow words, *Hic jacet.*

Book V, Part I

Elizabethans, believing those about to die were capable of prophesying, kept anxious watch at the bedside when death was felt to be near: a sudden brightening of the spirits might precede some momentous utterance. John of Gaunt's famous apostrophe to England in Shakespeare's *King Richard II* is the beginning of just such a death prophecy, of whose significance he is fully aware as he exclaims, "O but they say that tongues of dying men enforce attention like deep harmony." Then he cries out fervently, "Methinks I am a prophet new inspir'd," and turning his eyes toward his nephew, King Richard, he adds, "And thus expiring do foretell of him." The words that follow are supposed to ring in the ears of the rash, wayward, unkind king when he comes upon evil days, for in dreadful tones Gaunt bids him "Live in thy shame, but die not shame with thee!" and then, with frightening intensity, concludes, "These words hereafter thy tormentors be!" (III.:i:5–6, 31–32, 135–36).

The last words of dying parents were particularly regarded by their children, and writers of conduct books conceded death to be the best time for advising one's offspring concerning matters they should never forget. Gouge admonished parents at such a time to warn their children against the evils which they, dying, would be able to see rising up as snares and temptations to the living. They would also be able to look beyond to the struggle of their own souls seeking the rewards of heaven. He concludes seriously, therefore, by saying, "No means can be thought of to procure God's blessing or with-hold his curse, as the faithful prayers of their children, especially when parents are leaving their children and going to God." Such belief prompted children away from home to make every effort to return to dying parents before it was too late to look into their eyes for the last message they might give in this world, and at the same time perform their filial duty of praying for the soul at the brink of death.

Many parents, no doubt, when stricken by death uttered words of advice they had rehearsed to themselves many times in anticipation of the dread and solemn hour. Doubtless, also, many dying souls were too awed with the change taking place within themselves to be conscious of anything else, if they were conscious at all. But belief of the time was in a parent's awareness of what was taking place and in a parent's effort to rise to the occasion by uttering prophetic words to the awed children about the bed. So the dying King Henry IV says to his heir:

> Come hither Harry; sit thou by my bed;
> And hear, I think, the very latest counsel
> That I shall ever breathe.
> *II Henry IV*, IV: v: 182–84

And Nerissa reminds Portia of the awesome hour when her father lay dying, thus giving to the fantastic casket plot a bit of realism with peculiar interest to Elizabethans:

Your father was ever virtuous; and holy men at their death have good inspirations: therefore the lottery, that he hath devised in these three chests of gold, silver, and lead, whereof who chooses his meaning chooses you, will, no doubt, never be chosen by any rightly but one who shall rightly love.
> *The Merchant of Venice*, I:ii:30–35

When, therefore, the choosing takes place, an obedient Portia must give no sign to any suitor that may help him one jot in making his choice. If the words of "bread" and "head" and "nourished" in the song sung "whilst Bassanio comments on the caskets to himself" were actually meant to suggest to him the word "lead" (III:ii:63–65), then Portia, *if* she has arranged for the song, is guilty of equivocation, which Shakespeare analyzes so well in the porter's speech in *Macbeth* (II:iii:1–31). If she is guilty of breaking the bonds she describes in "the will of a living daughter curbed by the will of a dead father," she sins because her romantic love for Bassanio transcends all compulsion of respect for her promise to the dead, and as such adds a very interesting intensity to the scene. Furthermore, by such an act she would dare to take a hand in resolving the riddle of her destiny, and to Elizabethans who looked upon man's destiny as in God's hands alone, such action would be extravagantly shocking. To interpret this scene, therefore, as a delightful bit of love's harmless prompting is to miss the depth of undertone which adds immeasurably to its meaning.

Part of the fear which Elizabethans felt in the presence of death was due to their belief that good and evil spirits fought a terrific battle over the poor soul about to pass into eternity. Sometimes they believed they actually saw the soul taking part in the struggle between these forces. Such a conflict is described in detail by the Puritan, Philip Stubbes. His girl-wife, ill with childbed fever, had been praying, he reports, looking sweet and lovely, "red as the rose, and most beautiful to behold," when suddenly she frowned as if seeing an ugly thing. With an "angry, stern, and fierce countenance," she cried out, "How now, Satan? . . . Art thou come to tempt the Lord's servant? I tell thee, hell-hound, thou hast no part nor portion in me, nor by the grace of God never shall have . . . Yea, Satan, I was chosen and elected in Christ to everlasting salvation, before the foundations of the world were laid and therefore thou mayest get thee packing, thou damned dog, and go shake thine ears . . ."

Then, with less excitement but with more earnestness, she continued, "Oh, I am a sinner . . . I confess indeed that I am a sinner, and a grievous sinner, both by original sin, and actual sin; and that, I may thank thee for. And therefore, Satan, I bequeath my sin to thee, from whom it first proceeded, and I appeal to the mercy of God in Christ Jesus." After explaining carefully to Satan how Christ's blood had saved her, she then took up the subject of good works, saying, ". . . it is written again, thou deceitful devil, that Christ's righteousness is my righteousness, his works my works, his deserts my deserts, and his precious blood a full satisfaction for all my sins." When she had said enough, she ordered Satan "to get packing," threatening to call Michael to throw him down to hell.

Scarcely had she made this last threat, however, when she "fell suddenly into a sweet smiling laughter because the devil had gone," and in his place she saw "infinite millions of most glorious angels," standing about, ready to defend her, and to carry her soul to God. Then she sang sweet psalms and, after she had finished, asked that Psalm CIII might be sung "before her to the church." At this point, noting the mournful face of her husband, she begged him not to grieve for her, for she was going to "holy saints, to angels, to cherubims and seraphims, yea to God himself." Forthwith she seemed to rejoice as if she had "seen some glorious sight . . ." Lifting up her whole body and stretching forth her arms as if to embrace something, she thanked God for sending Jesus Christ to save her and, commending her spirit into his hands, suddenly she "slept sweetly in the Lord."

Stubbes's account, as indicated in the title, *A Crystall Glas for Christian Women: . . . of a right vertuous life and Christian death . . .* (1590) was to teach the Puritan goal of perfection. In this case, the suffering, which dragged out to six long weeks of fever and delirium, culminated at last in a death that to those watching anxiously at the bedside was a marvel indeed. It also emphasized the importance of recognizing sin, which, according to the Puritans, could be conquered only by Christians who purged it from their souls with great agony and, when successful, with great rejoicing over the victory.

In this prescientific age when anything out of the ordinary was of the miraculous, men lived in a state of wonder and mystery and, at times, fear. Sober scholars, judges, clergymen, and magistrates came to believe in fairies and ghosts as well as witchcraft. One cannot even guess, therefore, how much individual reading about witchcraft, etc., in the Scriptures by ignorant people helped to foster these beliefs and to revive the importance of old medieval charms and newly evolved charms against witchcraft. So great was the fear of witches who by magic means might harm an enemy or friend that, by 1542, sorcery was declared a crime punishable by imprisonment or the pillory or even death, and later acts in 1563 and 1580 increased the harshness of the punishments. By the end of the century, so many frauds resulted from the general belief in magic that in 1604 an act provided the death penalty for anyone convicted twice of seeking the aid of magic or charms or spirits in an effort to find treasure or to induce unlawful love. Charms and amulets were supposed to offset the witch's spell, white magic was used to cure a disease that had been imposed by a sorcerer, and a man's very soul was endangered when he concerned himself with conjurers or exorcists. Although comparatively few references are made in the Bible to the great body of material dealing with magic and witchcraft in its background, especially in the Old Testament, those that remain appealed powerfully to the imaginative mind of the Elizabethans.

We are told that, in 1532, Sir William Neville tried to find some missing spoons by magical powers, and that his "astrologer" led him on to a spirit-raising and to the preparation of a ring of power to gain him the king's favor. About a decade later, Lord Henry Neville, wishing gambling money, tried crystal gazing and image making, and finally landed in prison. In 1562, Arthur and Edmund Pole were accused of invoking spirits against the Queen, and although they denied it, they did admit they had tried by conjuration to determine the date of her death. Even Elizabeth herself called in Dr. Dee several times, especially for finding an auspicious date in 1558 for her coronation.[7] Such interest in the supernatural was certainly not laid to rest when the New Testament was piously interpreted by ignorant minds seeking how to lead the good life.

Since biblical material made both magic and witchcraft theologically justifiable, these "arts" were doubly dangerous to the gullible as manifestations of "the Divil's" power. Nevertheless, here and there, a skeptic

---

[7] Christina Hole, *English Home Life, 1500 to 1800* (1947) provides an interesting account of sixteenth-century witchcraft.

reared his head against the almost universal belief in such practices. In 1584, Reginald Scot's *The Discovery of Witchcraft* represented the evil as a "cozening art" that abused the name of God by profanity and blasphemy, attributing God's power to some "vile wretch," usually an old woman, in whom dwelt, presumably, a "spiritual divil." He declared her "doings" were so "secret, mystical, and strange" that no reliable witness of them had ever been found. He concluded, therefore, witchcraft was "incomprehensible to the wise, learned, or faithful," but appealed to "children, fools, melancholic persons, and papists . . ." For this reason people in their right minds would regard witchcraft as "contrary to nature, probability, and reason" and utterly "void of truth or possibility." But, alas, he counted too much on wisdom in his time or soon after, for James I's *Demonology* "settled" the matter for all his subjects, saying that since Holy Writ declared the existence of witches, they must be detected and put to death lest they cause innocent people to suffer. It is also said he ordered the burning of Scot's book. Now, indeed, belief in the supernatural ran riot.

Because supernatural explanations were made for the simplest things, people sought fortunetellers, magicians, and many kinds of diviners in spite of decrees against magic. Such journeys were made in the greatest secrecy, of course. This attitude did much to foster the morbid fear of death, and the number of strange omens connected with death and dire happenings greatly increased. One of the most frequent was the death-boding cry of the owl or wolf. Shakespeare uses these cries as a matter-of-fact means of suggestion. Tarquin, tossing between desire and dread (*The Rape of Lucrece*), hears the owls' and wolves' cries. Lady Macbeth, while waiting for her husband to murder Duncan, hears a cry whistle through the air and says in a fearful whisper, "It was the owl that shrieked." Other sounds with similar meanings were the croaking of ravens, the shrilling of crickets, the night howling of dogs, the supposed cry of the mandrake when pulled up and its large forked root exposed, the chattering of magpies, the wild neighing of horses, the cries of the fairies, the gibbering of ghosts, and the sound of demoniacal voices lamenting in the air.

But there were other strange signs that took people by the throat and left them gasping with fear—mysterious night fires or lights, dreams of winding sheets or corpse candles or any horrid sights, and hallucinations of ghostly apparitions. Frequent mention of a living being's name by a dying person was thought to augur early death for the named person. Unusual phenomena struck terror to the soul, as with the shaking of the earth, stormy nights, sudden gloom at midday, the appearance of meteors, a bloody-hued moon, the withering of bay trees, and supposed showers of blood. Shakespeare uses many of these superstitions to intensify the horrors of bloody scenes in his plays.

On the night Duncan is murdered by Macbeth, there is a great storm;

chimneys are blown down, and some individuals feel the earth shake. Lamentings are heard in the air; there are also strange screams of death and terrible voices prophesying "dire combustion and confus'd events." The owl clamors the "livelong night," and the king's own horses, gentle, beautiful, and swift, break their stalls and run wild as if to make war on mankind, one lord declaring that with his own eyes he saw them eating each other. The evils in Richard II's reign are prepared for by the withering of bay trees, meteors that "fright the fixed stars of heaven," a bloody moon, fearful whisperings of lean prophets, rich men looking sad through fear of losses, and ruffians dancing and leaping in expectation of what they are to enjoy.

When Shakespeare takes over the superstitions of Plutarch for the Roman scene in his *Julius Caesar*, he makes an intense personal appeal through Calpurnia. Sometimes she is dismissed by critics as merely a woman oppressed by silly fears, but Shakespeare means to show her as a good housewife distraught with her alarming dream and concerned for the welfare of her lord. She tells Caesar that the night watchman is within, and has told her of the frightful things he saw in the night. She reminds Caesar she has never been subject to foolish superstitions, but the watchman has seen strange horrors with his own eyes, and she and her lord have also seen horrid sights, but most of all, she is terrified by the dream she has had of murdered Caesar. When, therefore, Caesar tells Calpurnia that such portents may apply to all alike, she retorts wisely, according to the times, that no comets are seen when mere beggars die. Unless her fears are accepted as both real and natural, Caesar's replies are merely bombast. Shakespeare means him to be both human and great as well as pompous, for unless his death justifies the conflict in the soul of Brutus, who is torn between loyalty to a friend and loyalty to the state, the play loses its power. Furthermore, mighty Caesar does not leave for the Capitol till Calpurnia's dream is given an ironically convincing "fair and fortunate" interpretation by one of the conspirators.

Elizabethans had other superstitions connected with death that seem trivial to our scientific age. Not only was lying on feathers a means of delaying death, but removing a pillow from under the head of a dying person would hasten death. Many looked for a pale flame to appear at the window of the dying person's house, hover for a moment, and then dance away in the direction of the churchyard, the path it followed to be taken by the funeral procession, and the interment to take place where the light paused, burning bright. Since villages were often fifty miles apart and therefore almost completely isolated, it was natural for such superstitions to persist in the minds of the people. But since many of these beliefs were just as prevalent among Londoners, one must conclude that most of them were inspired by doubts and fears about death itself. Partly because of this attitude and partly because of the attitude of the Church toward suicide, one who ran to meet death was held in such horror that in some localities suicides were buried at night, by torchlight, with a sharp stake driven through the heart. In most churchyards, suicides and unbaptized children were buried on the cold north side of the church.

One had to pay a special fee to be honored with burial under the church floor. Of course there was much demand for this favored spot, and to counteract the stench from the shallow graves here, juniper and frankincense were burned, particularly on special occasions when some staid dignitary made his visit to the church. At other times additional layers of rushes were expected to make the place sweet for those who attended the services. But such graves, like those in the churchyard, were not left undisturbed if room was needed for another corpse and a high fee was forthcoming. Yet even the highest fee could not provide Christian burial for the proved suicide.

Self-destruction was a matter of much discussion by intellectual Elizabethans, though they were careful to whom they talked on this subject if their opinions differed from the prevailing religious ones. Although they might express admiration for classical characters who committed suicide and although they might represent virtuous women as gladly sacrificing their lives in order to preserve their chastity, they were reacting in much the same romantic manner by such remarks as when they condoned the deaths of the frustrated lovers, Romeo and Juliet. In real life suicide was severely frowned upon. Thus in the grave-digging clowns' argument over Ophelia's right to Christian burial much folk feeling is shown, and at the burial, the picture of reaction to suicide is completed.

One of the clowns says resentfully, "If this had not been a gentlewoman, she should have been buried out o' Christian burial." The other agrees, adding ". . . the more pity that great folk should have countenance in this world to drown or hang themselves . . ." (*Hamlet*, V:i:26–30). Later, when the girl's brother objects to the shortened rites at the grave, the first priest admits churlishly that since the death was a doubtful one the body should have been "lodg'd" in unsanctified ground "till the last trump," but that "great command" o'erswayed the order. He cannot prevent the girl from being "allow'd her virgin crants" and her "maiden strewements," and her "bringing home of bell and burial," but if he had his way, "shards, flints and pebbles should be thrown on her" (V:i:249–57). The brother still protesting is told shortly it would "profane the services of the dead to sing a requiem," and give "such rest to her as to peace-departed souls." These words drive the brother frantic with grief and indignation, but the king and queen must respect the authority of the Church and take the rebuke without protest. Indeed, they have done well to provide any rites at all at the burial.

The priest's harsh attitude was due to belief in the soul's need of preparation for death. To die suddenly, deprived of the rites of the Church, permitted the black devils hovering about every deathbed to have their own way. If this happened, the devils hurried the miserable soul off to hell even though it had lived as blameless a life as that of Stubbes's child-wife. So great was the fear of leaving this world under such frightful circumstances that even a murderer, in life and in drama, usually gave a victim a chance to pray for his soul. In Shakespeare's *Measure for Measure*, when the duke needs the body of an executed prisoner, he will not take the life of a "creature unprepar'd, unmeet for death" no matter how much the criminal deserves death and no matter how much his body is needed to save a good man's life. With grim humor, therefore, the prisoner stays his execution by refusing to prepare for death, for he knows that no one wishes to be guilty of the "damnable" act of "transporting" him in his sinful state (IV:iii:70–73).

The fact that Hamlet's father had no chance to prepare for death causes the agonized suffering of the king's ghost. As he tells how he was sent to his death unprepared and without extreme unction, he groans "O, horrible! O horrible! most horrible!" Then he adds solemnly to his son, "If thou hast nature in thee, bear it not." He is doomed "for a certain time to walk the night," he says, "to fast in fires" during the day till all the "foul crimes" done in his "day of nature" are "burnt and purg'd away." His sufferings are too great to tell, but if he could reveal the secrets of his "prison house," he could "a tale unfold whose lightest word would harrow up" the soul and freeze the blood and make Hamlet's eyes "like stars, start from their spheres," part the locks of his hair, and make "each particular hair to stand on end, like quills upon the fretful porcupine" (I:v:10–20). Both Catholics and Calvinists had emphasized the medieval tradition of punishment after death, especially for the suicide or the soul dying without repentance. That dramatists played upon this fear is palpably evident, but the important thing for this discussion is that the fear made more than dramatic material.

In the same way ghosts were of great dramatic importance, for few Elizabethans doubted their existence. There were, therefore, certain commonly accepted beliefs about them, and Shakespeare was quick to use such material. For example, ghosts appeared exactly at midnight, dressed in the same clothes and looking the same as when last seen in life. So appears Hamlet's father's ghost in "the dead vast and middle of the night," and "armed at points exactly" as when last seen. Ghosts were also thought to be unable to speak till addressed by the right person in the right manner or till questioned about the subject on which they wished to speak or till called by a particular name. Horatio tells Hamlet how the ghost would not answer him, but "lifted up its head" and made motions "like as it would speak." When Hamlet sees the ghost, he calls it "Hamlet, King, father; royal Dane," and though it does not answer, it beckons him to follow it, addressing him only when private speech is possible between it and Hamlet.

Ghosts were believed to be easily frightened by baying dogs and vexed by malicious spirits and easily driven back to their prison house by the cock's crow. So Hamlet's father's ghost "starts like a guilty thing" when it hears the cock crow. Ghosts were said to have the power of rendering themselves invisible to some and visible to others at the same time, and of coming and going despite walls and locks. In the queen's closet, Hamlet sees the ghost when his mother does not, and is amazed that she cannot see it stealing away. His mother thinks the vision is but some "coinage" of her son's disordered mind, but he proves his sanity by his normal pulse and clear, unimpaired memory (III:iv:139–44). It was common belief that on Christmas Eve ghosts could not bother mortals. Marcellus refers to this superstition when he says on such a night the cock may crow all through the dark hours, and the air will be wholesome as no spirits can stir abroad. On this night, too, fairies and witches lost their evil powers, "so hallow'd and so gracious" was the time (I:i:158–64).

Puck of *A Midsummer Night's Dream* summarizes many of the current superstitions when he describes the "damned spirits all" as wandering here and there, and, at the approach of dawn, "trooping home" to their "wormy beds" in churchyards or crossways or the flood. Superstition would not permit those who died at sea to remain aboard till land was reached, where the corpse might be properly buried. Instead, the body was quickly buried in the waves according to whatever manner its rank and other circumstances permitted lest it bring disaster to the ship and all on board. In the play of *Pericles, Prince of Tyre*, the sailors, fearing the storm will not quiet till the dead queen is put overboard, ask Pericles to part with her. The burial is fully described (III:i:47–53, 59–65).

Whether fear of ghosts or fear of becoming a ghost was greater is not so important, perhaps, as the fact that both fears were very real. Fear of ghosts was due in large part to the belief that evil spirits might assume the likeness of people who had died, so it was said, in order to tempt their loved ones to hell. Hamlet speaks of this belief when he says the spirit he has seen "may be the devil," for the "devil hath the power to assume a pleasing shape," and may do so to tempt a soul in its weak, melancholy state to damnation (II:ii:627–34). Horatio fears the ghost may tempt Hamlet "toward the flood" or to some "dreadful summit of the cliff" overlooking the angry sea, there to assume "some other horrible form" that will deprive him of his reason (I:iv:69–77). In either case, the victim of a ghost-devil was helpless in the grasp of an evil force bent upon both his physical and spiritual destruction.

Now, any person might be subject to ghostly visions. No one, however, unless he believed he was damned ere he was born, need fear becoming a ghost if he repented his sins and was sure of forgiveness before his death. But who could tell when death would strike? Some who would have their cake and eat it, too, delayed repentance till death was at their very door, and thereby lost their souls when death refused to wait for the ceremony of asking forgiveness of sins. Religious souls, there-fore, made full and regular confession of sins and often communed in prayer with their Lord. But those who were careless in the matter might be shocked into proper behavior by dramatic portrayal of desperate last-minute effort at repentance, even by a villain. Such, for example, is Edmund's surprising speech when he says, "I pant for life: some good I mean to do despite mine own nature" (*King Lear*, V:iii:243–44). Angelo, thinking he is to be executed, says he is sorry he has caused so much grief and "so sticks it in my penitent heart that I crave death more willingly than mercy." He means the mercy granting him life. Angelo has reached the point where he prefers salvation through a repentance at death to a life of disgrace before all who know justice demands his death (*Measure for Measure*, V:i:480–81). Undoubtedly he means his repentance to be genuine, for eternal damnation or the terrors of the ghost's travail were an evil to blanch the cheek of the strongest, and at death's door all the courage of skeptic or villain melted like snow before the fires of hell.

In these precarious times, devout Catholics still sought the services of priests for sick or sinful souls, and many were the risks they took in having the holy sacrament performed for dying loved ones. At the shock-ing accident in Blackfriars in 1623, a crowd of people had met secretly in an upper room, where a famous Jesuit priest was preaching when the floor gave way. Beams and joists parted without warning, and took the floor below them as they fell. About ninety-five people perished in the accident, and according to a letter by Chamberlain to Dudley Carleton,[8] sixty people were buried in two pits in the court and garden of the house. For the Catholics tried to remove their dead so that among the living the terror of discovery need not add immeasurably to the anguish of lost loved ones. True to their belief about the efficacy of religious devotion, however, they must have taken some comfort in their assurance that these souls sent to death without warning were listening to God's messenger when cut off from life. To the Catholic's peace of mind, prayer and abso-lution at death were essential, but for Anglicans and Puritans, perhaps, the presence of only friends and relatives gathered prayerfully about the sickbed could bring much comfort during the last hours of one about to die.

Even those who had committed great wrongs they regretted later often faced death with tears and lamentations but with a dignity and courage worthy of admiration. In his portrayal of Wolsey's character, Shakespeare follows the report of the cardinal dying "full of repentance"

[8] McClure, *The Letters of John Chamberlain*. This letter is dated November 15, 1623.

with continual meditations, tears, and sorrows, and giving his honors "to the world again, his blessed part to heaven" before sleeping in peace (*King Henry VIII*, IV:ii:28–30). Part of Wolsey's courage at death was undoubtedly due to his belief that if one died in prayer his soul went directly to heaven. Though evil souls might seek redemption, they could delay too long even when death was still far off. Shakespeare illustrates this belief ironically enough in Hamlet's refusing to kill Claudius, who is trying to pray. Hamlet would rather lose his chance of early avenging his father's death than risk sending Claudius to heaven while he was seemingly "fit and season'd for his passage" (*Hamlet*, III:iii:84–86). Yet at that very moment Claudius knows his soul is damned, for he cannot repent. Not only one's own penitent prayers but those of relatives or friends were believed to be efficacious; hence the conventional close of many Elizabethan letters piously stating the writer was asking God's blessing upon the friend addressed.

Nothing inspired more horror, perhaps, than the death of a damned soul. Shakespeare illustrates the awful event and its effect upon observers in *II Henry VI* as he deals with Cardinal Beaufort. He is shown confessing with terror his evil deeds as the black devil comes for his soul, and the king exclaims:

> O thou eternal Mover of the heavens!
> Look with gentle eye upon this wretch;
> O! beat away the busy meddling fiend
> That lays strong siege upon this wretch's soul
> And from his bosom purge this black despair.

As the pangs of death twist the cardinal's face into a ghastly grin, only the king can bear to look upon the horrid sight with forgiving charity. He says:

> Peace to his soul, if God's good pleasure be!
> Lord Cardinal, if thou think'st on heaven's bliss,
> Hold up thy hand; make signal of thy hope.

But there is no response; the cardinal has waited too long to repent, and the king says sadly, "He dies, and makes no sign. O God, forgive him!" The Earl of Warwick is not so gentle. Gazing down upon the dead face, he declares solemnly, "So bad a death argues a monstrous life." To this the pious king replies:

> Forbear to judge, for we are sinners all.
> Close up his eyes, and draw the curtains close;
> And let us all to meditation.
>
> III:iii:19–32

The living might receive much good at a deathbed, for the blessing of a dying person was believed to be far more powerful than any other benediction. This is one reason why the saintly Queen Katherine of Shakespeare's *Henry VIII* is made to send word to Henry that "in death" she "bless'd" him. Moreover, when dying, people often bestowed material gifts as well as precepts and blessings upon their loved ones. Perhaps most precious of all gifts at this time, however, were secret formulas whispered into the anxious ears of those interested in magic cures or ointments and perfumes which might be of great value to them or to the household. No doubt many Elizabethans planned to reveal when dying some precious secret, partly to ensure the presence at the deathbed of those near and dear to them as well as to reward them, and partly to fulfill a promise to requite those who served them faithfully till death. Shakespeare illustrates the bestowal of such a legacy in *All's Well That Ends Well* by having the heroine's father on his "bed of death" put into the hand of his daughter Helena a prescription which he calls the "dearest issue" and the "darling" of his long years of practice as a physician. He asks her to treasure it as "a triple eye," and to keep it even safer than her other two (II:i:107–12).

Long delayed wills and testaments might also be made at this time, or, if these documents had already been drawn up (as was usually the case), important changes might be suggested by unscrupulous members of the family if they faced no opposition. On the other hand, those who had been unfairly dealt with might hope for restitution of their rights as death, supposedly, clarified the judgment of the dying soul. Should an old will be revised at this time, those who had been disinherited might triumph over the wrong intended when a will had been made under the influence of party hates and feuds. Most important of all, however, for the loving son or daughter, were the last instructions concerning the burial ceremony. To Elizabethans, the last rites performed for the body were the peculiar responsibility of the person designated, either in the will or in the broken sentences uttered on the bed of death. Then, at night, the bellman who acted as watchman announced the death with that of others who had died during the day.

Preparation of the body was a solemn duty and often a labor of love. Burial speedily followed death, and though it sometimes occurred secretly at night, it more normally was accompanied by a ceremonial pageant to the place of interment. After the tragedy in Blackfriars, for example, all the burials that could be made at night were conducted with the greatest haste and secrecy, and many of the bereaved felt compelled to hide any trace of grief. Under normal conditions, those given burial were laid away according to their wealth. The affluent were interred in coffins, the poor in shrouds only. Some were borne to their graves dressed in their best robes and lying in open coffins, and others were wrapped in waxed winding sheets and carefully sealed in coffins of wood or metal.

Shakespeare refers to the shrouding of several people of means. The foreboding Desdemona asks Emilia to shroud her in her wedding sheets (*Othello*, IV:iii:24–25). This juxtaposition of past joy and present grief would touch the romantic hearts of those watching the play. Hamlet describes his father's interment when he asks the ghost why its "canoniz'd bones, hearsed in death" have "burst their cerements" and why the sepulcher in which it was so "quietly inurn'd" had opened its "ponderous marble jaws" (I:iv:47–50). Queen Katherine asks that she be "us'd with honor" when she is dead, "embalmed, then laid forth, and interred like a queen" though Henry has cast her off for Anne Boleyn (IV:ii:167–74). Juliet is told by the friar that she is to be dressed in her "best robes uncover'd on the bier" and borne to the "ancient vault" in which her ancestors have been interred (*Romeo and Juliet*, IV:i:109–13).

Ralph Verney's mother left very careful instructions in her will for her son to follow at her shrouding. Their tone indicates the loving trust she had in this son who had never failed her. She wished to be buried at the family estate of Claydon and in a coffin of lead "next where" his father "purposes to lie himself." The instructions continue: "And let no stranger wind me, and do not let me be stripped, but put a clean smock over me . . . and let my face be hid and do you stay in the room and see me wound and laid in the first coffin, which must be of wood if I do not die of any infectious disease, else I am so far from desiring it that I forbid you to come near me." Just as Ralph had faithfully assumed his father's domestic responsibilities when state duties called the father from home most of the time, so the mother could rely on her son to perform with the same gentle willingness the last personal service needful to her. Indeed, the very words of this mother's strong, unselfish love still live though they were born of death, shrouded in death, and washed by the tears of death.

When the body was to be embalmed, adjusting the winding sheet was a very important part of the ceremony. Sometimes, when the body was sealed in the coffin and not exhibited during the burial ceremonies, its effigy was dressed in fine clothes and covered with flowers and laid on top of the rich drapery over the coffin that was borne impressively to the grave. Often, however, a death mask took the place of this effigy. If the body was laid out for spectators to view, it was clothed in its finest apparel or in a shroud made especially for the occasion. Bits of yew were stuck in the shroud, and the prepared body, covered with flowers, had burning candles placed about it. Then bells were tolled to warn neighbors to pray for the soul of the departed, and all who visited the corpse said a *Pater Noster* or a *De Profundis*. All this, of course, if the person had not died of an infectious disease, such as smallpox, typhoid fever, or the plague. So far as is known, the measures taken for burial in time of plague were similar to those in use when Defoe wrote his descriptions of them in *The Journal of the Plague Year*.

Death by plague would deprive a rich and powerful family of an important means for proud display of their wealth. Still, infectious disease must be accepted without resentment, for it was looked on as an act of God or as the result of some peculiar corruption in the air, or as an indication of some peculiar susceptibility in the sufferer. Death sometimes came from an operation, for the shock of it without antiseptics or anesthetics was sure to be fatal in serious cases. When a physician was called in to treat a person, he usually diagnosed the patient as sanguine, choleric, phlegmatic, or melancholic, and then proceeded to explain that the disease was due to an improper balance in the body humors. The cure, of course, consisted of bringing these humors back into balance. Foods which were believed to have the proper elements for this purpose might be prescribed, or the patient might be given drugs or herbal remedies. The chief methods, however, were bleeding, purges, and emetics. In almost all cases fresh air was carefully shut out. Although doctors knew filth bred disease, they did not insist that much be done to aid sanitation. Fleas and lice and filth and ignorance spread infectious diseases rapidly, especially in the case of smallpox and the plague. It took a brave soul to care for another stricken with either of these diseases or to touch the body in case of death.

Those who had faith in herbs for treating disease believed any illness could be cured if only the right herb for it could be found. Accordingly, there were some strange remedies suggested, and these must have helped many an ailing soul into the deep hereafter. For example, shingles and burns were treated alike with the juice of the house leek mixed in cream. Patients going mad or suffering from paralysis were given a syrup made of the conserve of cowslips or palsy-worts. Scurvy was treated with fresh cuckooflower heads eaten as a salad, and feverish patients were given doses of conserve of violets. One of the commonest complaints, neuralgia, was treated with cloves, cinnamon, nutmegs, and pepper brewed in aqua vitae. For inflamed wounds the patient took a concoction made of royal fern boiled and mixed with wine or ale, and for ague an emetic fusion was mixed with syrup of violets and given the patient. When thorns or splinters caused infection, the swelling was bathed with distilled water of Mayflowers. The fastidious person always carried with him a pomander that he might hold to his nose whenever he came in contact with a foul odor (supposed to cause disease) or a person with a contagious disease. In these pomanders were many herbs and spices. Some people relied on chewing rhubarb or tobacco or lovage, though tobacco was the favorite for those who could afford it, when they came in contact with disease, and some kept fresh onion slices in a sickroom to preserve the health of those attending the afflicted.

Very few sick people left their homes to go to hospitals, for to do so was to leave comfort for hardship. Such places were reserved for those who had no home. The nursing at hospitals was very bad, and the patients were crowded four to six in great beds that were seldom if ever cleaned till the patients died or got well. The nurses were not trained except in cleanliness and moral conduct. At the hospitals only smallpox patients were isolated, and this was accomplished by shutting them off from others by red curtains, as red was supposed to be helpful in fever. Even at home patients with fever were surrounded with red curtains, red bedding, and whatever could be converted into that color. No plague cases were admitted to hospitals unless a city was large enough to have special pesthouses for such highly infectious diseases. If there were no pesthouses, patients were put into small buildings at the edge of town. Because fleas and lice were known to carry disease, during a serious epidemic all stray dogs and cats were killed, but the worst carriers, rats, increased rapidly, and went undisturbed.

Smallpox entered England early in the century as a mild children's disease. Later, adults came down with it, and either died or were left with deep pits and often an ashy skin. Children, who suffered less from it, were frequently exposed to it that they might not become victims to it when grown. Patients at home were kept in warm rooms and with the bed curtain drawn to keep out drafts. Cordials and hot teas were given them to make them sweat. If the temperature ran very high, they were given powdered cinquefoil, mixed with wine, or meadowsweet mixed with a little green wheat, violets in some form, and distilled coltsfoot. These remedies were also used for ague, or any fever diseases, to induce sweating.

Some devoted relatives or friends even nursed patients through the plague, though most people fled from the disease in panic. During the sixteenth century five plague epidemics occurred, though there were probably cases of it in most large cities during all these years. Many preventives were used, chief of which was box in hedges or as specimen shrubs. Sweet herbs were also burned on the hearth, and a light diet was urged which ruled out the wine, beer, and rich meats that people liked. Preventive medicines were also concocted, such as a brew made from the leaves of sage, rue, elder, and bramble, and then mixed with wine and ginger. Teaspoonful doses were taken daily for at least three weeks. Another remedy of this kind consisted of dried ivy-berries, powdered and dissolved in vinegar, the main principle apparently being to fight bitter with bitter. Rue was a milder and much more popular preventive, and was laid along window sills, or hung in coaches if one must leave home during the plague. Special candles were also made with juniper, cloves, and other spices, and red rose leaves were added to the wax, but the poor could not afford such measures. When a home was visited by the plague, slices of onion were laid on plates throughout the house and not removed till ten days after the last case had died or recovered. Since onions, sliced, were supposed to absorb elements of infection, they were also used in poultices to draw out infection. Those who could afford it, however, bought "unicorn horn" (probably rhinoceros horn) in powder at the apothecary's shop and mixed it with angelica root for a medicine to bring on sweats when a patient fell ill with the plague.[9]

After the patient died or recovered, the rushes in his room were burned, his bedding was thrown into a lake or river, and his clothes were aired for three or four months before they were used again. As such methods often caused a new epidemic to break out in a distant area, the fear of contagious diseases was never absent from anxious hearts. With infectious disease such an ever-present concern, no one could be sure of a ceremonious burial. Indeed, one might be hastily wrapped in a shroud and secretly buried at night to escape being carted to a burial trench into which bodies were thrown indiscriminately. Yet each person hoped he might be taken to his grave with all the pomp and dignity his means would allow for his exit from this world.

After a death had occurred from a disease not contagious, the members of a well-ordered home immediately prepared for mourning. The chief rooms and staircase were draped in black cloth, and a black mourning bed was provided for the bereaved wife or husband, who reclined in its funereal depths and received visits from consoling friends. Such beds were common property in a family, and were lent to members requiring their use, black velvet window curtains and carpets accompanying the black canopy and other draperies for the bed. This bed was used only as long as the bereaved person observed strictest mourning. Everything of a widow had to be black, from the bed hangings to the saddle and bridle or the coach she used. Even black night clothes were adopted, as well as black caps, combs, brushes, and slippers. The black coach or trappings of the horse were used for a year or two after the time of death, but the long black veil of the widow, covering her entire head like the veil of a nun, was worn with her other black clothing until she died or remarried.

Since the formal burial usually occurred on the day following the death, preparations for it required haste, especially when it was to be preceded by an ostentatious procession. This pageant, with a band of musicians at its head, passed through the streets from the house of death to the church and thence to the graveyard. A garland of flowers and sweet-smelling herbs was carried before the coffin of a maid by her closest and most honored friend, and this garland of real or imitation flowers, with a glove at the center, was hung up in the church to symbolize her virginity. At first the garland was hung over the maid's customary place in church, but later it was removed to the west wall or chancel. Sometimes the very streets were strewed with flowers for a maid's funeral procession. Some of the ritual of a young woman's burial is summarized by

[9] Hole, *English Home Life, 1500–1800,* pp. 68–73.

Aspatia in *The Maid's Tragedy* (Beaumont and Fletcher) when she bids farewell to the sorrowing women about her and tells them as soon as she is dead to come "and watch one night about her hearse." She wishes each to bring "a mournful story and a tear" to offer when she goes to earth, and each to help with "flattering ivy" to clasp her coffin round. She also wishes her bier borne by virgins "that shall sing . . ." (II:i).

Relatives, retainers, and domestic servants usually formed the procession following the band of musicians, though poor people were sometimes hired as mourners that they might add to the impressiveness of the pageant winding through the streets, pacing slowly while the bell tolled. If the deceased was a guild member, he was provided with an official pall for his coffin, and according to his importance to the guild, either the entire fraternity or merely an official delegation walked reverently and bareheaded in his funeral procession. Great crowds would assemble to watch such a scene, in which the inmates of almshouses and hospitals supported by the guild often helped to swell the number of mourners. The guild pall was generally highly ornamental, and with it went a "hearse," or canopy, to be carried over the coffin unless a horse litter was used, in which case the canopy was fastened to the litter. When Shakespeare refers to a hearse, however, he usually means a coffin borne by pallbearers. The palls, as a rule, were black, except in the case of royalty, for whom purple was used. These palls made a sharp contrast with the white shroud.

For the most part bunches of rosemary or bay or some such evergreens were tied to the sides of the coffin as well as to the pall, although either the bier or the pall might be adorned instead by little crosses or copies of memorial verses fastened to it. Feste's song in *Twelfth Night*, designed to increase the duke's melancholy, refers to "my shroud of white, stuck all with yew," and "not a flower sweet, on my black coffin let there be strewn" (II:iv: 53, 56). Verses pinned to a pall were supposedly written by friends, though actually they were chiefly composed by paid professional writers. The crosses, of course, were largely swept away by the reformers, or fell into decay through indifference to tradition. They had been used to garnish the pall like little prayers supplicating blessings for the deceased; in olden times the bearers of a coffin had set it down at every cross on the way to the church to pray devoutly, on their knees, for the dead. This use of small crosses lingered long in the practices of the devout; it was harder for them to part with them than with any other symbols of the old faith.

The mourners customarily carried branches of rosemary, bay, or other evergreens as emblematic of the immortality of the soul, and laid them on the coffin as it was lowered into the grave. Shakespeare romanticizes over this custom in the play of *Cymbeline* when flowers are strewn on Fidele's grave with the promise that other flowers will be used to sweeten it as long as summer lasts (IV:ii: 218–28). Fidele, deceived by what she believes is the body of her husband, covers his corpse with "wildwood leaves and weeds," saying at the time a "century of prayers" (IV:ii:390–91). Apparently Shakespeare found that the sentimental dirge at the tomb impressed his audience, for he had made extensive adaptation of it in his plot of *Much Ado About Nothing*. Here the chastened Claudio, accompanied by a friend and attendants carrying tapers and musical instruments, appears at the family monument to read from a scroll his vindication of the girl he has slandered and to sing to her memory a "solemn hymn." As the "gentle day dapples the drowsy east with spots of gray," he bids the girl's bones good night, promising to return each year to perform this solemn rite. In the words of his scroll (which he hangs on the tomb as poems of tribute were customarily hung on the pall) and in the dirge, Shakespeare interweaves the Elizabethan Renaissance emphasis on worldly immortality through fame and the Christian emphasis on good deeds through chastity, thus doubly assuring the heroine of being remembered after death (V:iii:3–10, 12–21).

In Juliet's burial Shakespeare makes sensational adaptation of last rites. The friar gives directions for sticking rosemary on the "fair corse," arrayed in its best apparel, and asks that it be borne to the church. Capulet immediately orders the wedding festival arrangements to "turn their office to black funeral": the dance music to become "melancholy bells," the "wedding cheer" to be used for "burial feast," the "solemn" wedding hymns to be changed to "sullen dirges," and the "bridal flowers" to serve for a "buried corse." The dramatist sharpens the horror of this reversal with the macabre when the musicians hired for the wedding console themselves with the fact that they will lose little since they are to "tarry for the mourners, and stay to dinner" (IV:v:146). That night at the tomb, the intended groom somewhat lightens the gruesome scene when, strewing flowers "with tears distill'd," he sings his promise to come each night to repeat the ceremony (V:iii:12–17). Romeo's frantic grief cuts sharply into this sentimentality as he calls the tomb a "detestable maw" and the "tomb of death," which is "gorg'd with the dearest morsel of the earth" (V:iii:45–48). Meanwhile, planning suicide, he forces open "the rotten jaws" of the tomb that he may cram it "with more food." In *Pericles, Prince of Tyre*, Shakespeare makes brutal the conventions observed at death which the wicked wife of Cleon plans to recite to Marina's father about his daughter's burial:

> . . . We wept after her hearse,
> And yet we mourn. Her monument
> Is almost finish'd, and her epitaphs
> In glittering golden characters express
> A general praise to her, and care in us
> At whose expense 'tis done.
>
> IV:iii:41–46

So shocked is her husband by this heartless rehearsal that he calls his wife a harpy with an angel's face who, wishing to betray, seizes her victim with her "eagle talons." The figure of speech would appeal to those who pictured death itself as just such a vile creature.

Heralds came to the funerals of the gentry in their tabards of cape or cloak, blazoned with the deceased person's coat of arms. Their chief concern, aside from gracing the procession with their decorative garb, was to see that the buckram scutcheons were in order and to array the shield, pennon, and crested helmet of a deceased lord. When a man of good family was buried in the church, it was usual to hang his casque, sword, and suit of armor over his tomb, special funeral armor often being made for this purpose. In the play of *Hamlet*, Laertes laments the "obscure burial" of his father, for whom "no trophy, sword, nor hatchments" (the diamond-shaped tablet displaying the armorial bearings of the deceased) were placed "o'er his bones," and "no noble rite nor formal ostentation" was observed at his interment. The disposal of Polonius is one of the most brutal touches in the play.

Heralds' fees for funerals were high, but their services were almost indispensable to those who could command them, for heraldry was about the most outstanding means of revealing one's rank. No wonder, therefore, a knowledge of it was essential in all gentlemen's education. Music also added much to the color of the funeral's spectacle. Sometimes the processions of the gentry were attended with "whole chantries of choice choirmen singing solemnly," and sometimes both heraldry and choirs also enhanced the spectacle of funeral pageants on the Thames. Great crowds witnessing these events added to their ostentation and brought a certain comfort to the afflicted family. It was not an uncommon hope that scenes of this nature would keep alive for a while the memory death would efface. Otherwise, there could be little point to the pageantry, except, of course, the attention it drew to a proud family's proud name. Yet, ironically, what was due a person at death might be considered too great a debt for the living to assume. For example, when the Marquis of Northampton died indigent, he was not buried "for many weeks," so we are told, because "nobody could be found to support the expense" of a sufficiently honorable funeral for a person of his rank. Finally the Queen herself paid for proper interment.

In striking contrast to all the pageantry to the grave were the services held just before the body was placed in the pit or the niche prepared for it. Here there was simply the strewing of flowers over the bier and the recital of a prayer by the church dignitary. The services held in the church, however, might be as elaborate as the processional, and equally representative of Elizabethan taste or affluence or fear of oblivion. So also for the monument. Though yeomen had to be content with slabs as their grave markers, the gentry hired artists to design and construct elaborate tombs for their bones. Indeed, the first art of the English

Renaissance, says Lees-Milne in his study of *Tudor Renaissance* (1951), was expressed in tombs, as exemplified by the monument in Westminster designed by Pietro Torrigiano for Henry VII and his Queen Elizabeth. Bacon called this work "the stateliest and daintiest" in Europe. Beautiful in its delicate simplicity is the tomb of Catherine Parr in the chapel of Sudeley Castle. The queen's figure in white marble lies gracefully on the top of her monument, which is placed under the carved arch of the niche at the right of the altar. On an afternoon when the sun shines through the stained glass windows, it makes Keatsian "gules" on the stone floor, and casts a glow over tomb and altar and the font near the entrance. Seldom has the resting place of the dead revealed with such subdued radiance the personality of one who in life shone with a quiet grace.

Puritans not infrequently objected to expensive monuments and elaborate funerals, saying there was nothing whereby the Church of Rome could reap "more commodity than by prayers for the dead." They called such devotions productions of the "friars' kitchen," and declared there was nothing wherein such mourners' "pompous solemnities . . . appeareth more than in their accompanying their dead to the grave with the sound of bells and cymbals, tapers, torches, prayers, music, church ornaments, solemn processions of the fraternities, and not without contention of orders."[10] They also criticized the less showy ceremonies of the Anglicans, saying their purpose was to "arouse a kind of compassion in the beholders" and so gave "a manner of contentment to their eyes and ears."

Naturally, the "silent and dumb obsequies" of the Puritans, "wanting bells and other noise," could not compete with the orthodox funerals, and drew few observers as their solemn processions made their way along the dirty streets. And yet, when Martin Bucer, the Cambridge Protestant divine of so much importance to the reformed Church under Edward VI died in the year 1551, three sermons were preached over his body, and three thousand people followed him to the grave. And at Amy Robsart's funeral in 1560, the ostentation of the procession was in accord with almost everything supervised by the Earl of Leicester. First came eighty poor men and women mourners, then members of Oxford University (where the earl was held in high esteem), and next a surpliced choir singing beautifully. Color was given the procession by the Rouge Croix and Lancaster heralds in long hooded gowns carrying banners and coats of arms. Eight yeomen, relieved by four alternates, bore the coffin, and were closely followed by the chief mourners. True, it was rumored that by this funeral the earl wished to allay the suspicion regarding his responsibility for his wife's death; still this charge has never been proved true. Much was said at the time about Amy's death leaving the way open for the ambi-

[10] David Person, *Varieties, or, a Surveigh of rare and excellent matters . . . for all sorts of persons* (1635).

tious earl to marry the Queen, but most biographers now find more to praise than to blame in the career of Leicester.

Puritans, Anglicans, and Catholics were much concerned about the sermon to be preached for the soul of the deceased. All followed a general pattern which was adapted to the occasion. A typical sermon for a great man was preached by William Jones at the death of the third Earl of Southampton. Jones called himself the "meanest servant of the Lord," but the earl the "glory of his Country," and his "Ladyship's wonderful joy and honor." Though apologetically, he took occasion to refer to his connection with the family as he paid tribute to the "noble disposition" of the countess who would not despise "the hearty endeavor of the poorest well-wisher" of her "honorable family" to preach this sermon. It had been "no small joy" for him during divers years to come to the earl and "stand in the presence of that mirror of nobility," that he might "hear his wisdom and behold his gracious conversation." Many a storm had he endured for this purpose, both by sea and land, but when he beheld the earl's "gracious countenance," it "dispelled all ill weather." Most willingly would he have spent his days in the service of such a man; indeed, he wished he might have been permitted to sacrifice his life for him that his lady might have continued to enjoy "such a complete ornament and pillar, so wise at home, so valorous abroad."

Then this "servant of the Lord" addressed the countess directly. The preacher's own feeling of personal loss and his sympathy for the bereaved family must have made it hard for him to express himself in the manner that decorum of the time demanded. Moreover, all the listeners expected to hear eulogistic phrases, for the earl was descended from one of the noblest Elizabethan families and had been one of its most illustrious members. "As for yourself, Madam," he began, "who have mightily rent your heart already with fasting and weeping and bitter lamentation: I pray God to give to you patience and comfort." He would have her "take to heart the goodness of the Lord" toward her in the lives of those who remained. He reminded her that she had "two loving and most worthy daughters, married to godly, wise, and virtuous personages," and that she also had "another hopeful young lady." Furthermore, she had a son who gave "great hope" that he would tread "in his noble father's steps, and be heir to his virtues." He would have her think of how "all these things are worthy to be remembered daily, with praises," and he was sure her ladyship did so look upon her blessings. This last statement would be a challenge, for though the countess had "most infinitely" loved her "dear and only Joy," she realized that now she must brace herself to preserve his qualities in his children, and especially in his heir.

After a funeral, refreshments were served at the house of the deceased for those who had been in the procession, and consisted of an elaborate feast of cold foods of all kinds—meats, biscuits, sweets, wine, and ale. Sometimes wills provided definite sums for these feasts, and even stipulated what was to be served. Oftentimes, at the home of a great or wealthy person, many days of feasting, drinking, and even dancing occurred. It is this type of entertainment that Hamlet refers to so bitterly when he complains of the baked meats (food) from his father's funeral feast being used thriftily for the marriage tables of his mother and uncle. The poor had these funeral feasts also, the guests contributing offerings of food as at their weddings.

Funeral meats could increase the expenditures at this time a great deal if meals were served to guests till the Sunday after the funeral or, as in some cases, for a month afterwards. Earlier in the century, a table was sometimes set in the church that the whole parish might share in the bounty after a funeral. Usually, however, people were invited to funerals as to weddings and christenings, and if the will of the deceased stipulated the amount of drink to be served the "public" guests, they had to share with one another when their number exceeded that provided in the will. The amount of ale allotted each person was expected to cost from two- to threepence at this feast. In such an age of ostentation, a lavish table of funeral meats was thought to show regard for the dead as well as to prove the extent of the family's wealth. Thus the entire cost per person at such a banquet might exceed five- or sixpence. Add to this the cost of mourning garments at six or seven shillings a yard, and the total sum can be reckoned as very large indeed.

In the more remote counties of England, the old custom of the wake or the nightly feasting before and after the funeral continued a long time, but besides these real wakes were the festal wakes. William Harrison, in *A Description of England in Shakespeare's Youth*, complained of the "superfluous number of idle wakes" called soul or dirge ales, especially of guilds and fraternities, in spite of the fact that their number had greatly diminished along with the old festal days of the pope's time. And Shakespeare's contemporary, Stubbes, in *The Anatomie of Abuses* (1583), lamented that every town, parish, and village set a day, varying in different localities, called wake-day, for the frank purpose of making great preparations for good cheer. On these days friends and kinsfolk from far and near were invited, and the result was "such gluttony, such drunkenness" as never seen before. Often those giving the feasts spent more for the carousal than during the rest of the year, and as a consequence had to "thripple and pinch, to run into debt and danger," and in some cases even face "utter ruin and decay." The fact that real wakes took on many of the orgiastic qualities of riotous festal wakes is but another indication of the terror inspired by death and the means taken to drown it in drink. At such a time numbers and kinship were comfortable companions before the dark mystery of death.

The money Elizabethans spent on funerals uniquely expressed their love of display, but it also indicated that they dreaded nothing so much as the possibility of future generations not knowing they had lived. The utter blankness of being forgotten was the most tormenting to them of all death's horrors. Hence the pomp and pageantry and costly monuments or even humble markers of the grave. Bishop Gardiner, Lord Chancellor of Queen Mary, left the sum of £1,400 in his will of 1555 to be spent in remembrance of him on a chantry and tomb and funeral. About three decades later, Queen Elizabeth's Lord Chancellor, Sir Christopher Hatton, provided in his will for a splendid funeral and burial in St. Paul's. A hundred poor people were given mourners' caps and gowns in which to lead the funeral procession, and the gentlemen and yeomen in mourning gowns, cloaks, and coats numbered three hundred or more, with Lords of the Council and the Queen's Guard adding at least eighty to the solemn marchers as they progressed slowly and impressively through the streets. Yet even a humble man might have a similar ceremony to accompany him on his final journey. John Whitsun, an alderman, was buried "very honorably," according to John Aubrey, with due acknowledgment of his services as colonel of a trained band. Besides all his relatives in mourning, he had as many old men as his seventy-six years, clad in mourning gowns and hoods, and the mayor and aldermen in mourning, besides the band itself with black ribbons on their pikes and black cloth covering their drums. Special mourners often numbered the deceased person's years, whether they were old men marching for an old colonel or young virgins for a young woman. Heavily draped in their funereal garments, they led the way gravely toward the church.

Hired mourners found their trade well paid, for they often received two or more pounds for marching in the parade, besides being feasted at the funeral banquet. In 1579, Thomas Gresham's funeral costs £800. Two hundred men and women mourners were hired for the occasion, and the cost of their garments as well as the fees of musicians and the sum paid for the banquet made the entire ceremony very expensive. At some elaborate funerals it was not unusual to serve two hundred or more mourners alone at the banquet. Then, of course, there were all the friends and relatives, who, in this time of close family relationships, made a large assembly in themselves.

Important Englishmen dying abroad requested that their hearts be sent home for burial. Infectious diseases and the plague, together with the problem of decomposition of a body during its transit, which often required two or three months, and inadequate facilities for transporting such bodies made it very difficult to send a corpse any distance. A typical disposition of such mortal remains is found in the case of Edward, Lord Windsor of Bradenham, who died in Spa in 1574. He willed his body to be buried in the cathedral at Liége "with a convenient tomb to his memory," but he willed his heart to be enclosed in lead and sent to England, "there to be buried in the Chapel at Bradenham, under his father's tomb in token of a true Englishman."[11]

The monument was just as important as the funeral to most Elizabethans: by the funeral they would impress their own generation, but with the monument they hoped to achieve a certain immortality in the minds of future generations. Lady Russell, who had given her husband so fine a funeral that she never let anyone forget its magnificence, planned an equally elaborate one for herself. Her waiting women were to be accompanied by their pages and gentleman ushers, and besides these mourners there were to be gentlemen, lords, knights, and their necessary servants. Her chief mourner was to have eleven yards of material for her gown, the gentlewomen, four yards apiece, and every earl's daughter ten yards for gown, mantle, train, hood, and tippet. She erected her own monument also with an effigy of herself wearing a viscountess' coronet as she kneeled in prayer, surrounded by the children of her own family kneeling in imitation of their pious mother. To crown this monument, she composed her own inscription in both Latin and Greek.[12]

In churchyards among the yew trees were often placed the mural mounts of lords and ladies, some with their table tops bearing effigies lying at full length, as a knight in armor or a maid in flowing drapery or a pious grouping like Lady Russell's. Some of the epitaphs might be as simple as that which Sir Thomas More had chiseled into the marble of his first wife's tomb: "Dear Jane lies here, the little wife of Thomas More." Again, the inscription might proclaim the honors of the deceased. Such is the epitaph of Bridget Manners as it was composed by her husband, who carefully set forth an account of his wife's noble blood and his own appreciation of it, and had it inscribed on her tomb in Bigby Church in Lincolnshire:

> Here lyeth the Right Honorable the Lady Brigett,
> Daughter of John, Earle of Rutland and Rosse,
>   Baron Hemsley Trushitt and Belvoire
>   Wife of Robert Tyrrwhit of Ketelby esqr.
> Sometime of the Privy Chamber to Queen Elizabeth
>   and in special grace and favor
> Of speech affable, of countenance amiable,
> Nothing proud of her place and fortunes,
>   and usynge her grace
>   Rather to benefit others than herselfe,
> Who having been long visited with sicknesse,
>   the 10th day of July 1604
>   finished this mortall Life
> Leaving behinde her fower children
> William, Robert, Rutland, and Briget.

[11] *Shakespeare's England* (ed. Sidney Lee and C. T. Onions, Oxford edition, 1916), "The Elizabethan Home in Shakespeare's England," by Percy Macquoid.
[12] Violet A. Wilson, *Society Women of Shakespeare's Time* (1925), *passim*.

> In memory of whom as also of himself
> Whenever it shall please God to call him
> from this vale of misery
> Her deare husband Mr. Robert Tyrrwhit
> At his coste erected this monument.[13]

But for his wife's bravery and unselfishness, this husband knew his marriage might have ended in disaster, for Bridget had married without the Queen's consent. Only her willingness to take all blame upon herself reconciled her with Elizabeth, and her husband was always grateful for his "good wife, God's gift."

Frequently Elizabethans spoke to relatives about details for the funeral and the monument even though they had made arrangements for both in their wills. Heirs, no matter how distant their relationship to the deceased, were particularly sensitive to the convention demanding respect for the dead by means of elaborate funerals and monuments. Such, for example, was the splendid monument for Sir Christopher Hatton which his nephew built when he succeeded to the title and estates of this notable Elizabethan. And such also is the well-known tomb of Sir Thomas Lucy of Charlecote, with its effigy in full armor lying prone on the table top, the head on a pillow, with little kneeling figures in the side panels. To ridicule the French and to foster English patriotism, Shakespeare composed an extravagant and ironic parody as he described the ecstatic Dauphin's promises to honor Joan of Arc for her victory at Orleans. By this means, he also satirized all ostentatious obsequies.

> A statelier pyramis to her I'll rear
> Than Rhodope's or Memphis' ever was:
> In memory of her when she is dead,
> Her ashes, in an urn more precious
> Than the rich-jewel'd coffer of Darius,
> Transported shall be at high festivals
> Before the kings and queens of France.
> No longer on Saint Denis will we cry,
> But Joan la Pucelle shall be France's saint.
> *I Henry VI*, I: vi: 21–29

Widows were more than likely to spend lavishly on the funerals and tombs of their deceased husbands, and Vives complained bitterly of this waste. He would have such money used to provide clothing for poor laymen and strangers, or to make some provision for poor widows and fatherless children instead of spending it on wax candles and costly sepulchers. "It is far better," he said, "in the day of thy weeping thou shalt remember them that ever weep, being oppressed with necessity . . ." He also cannily warned widows against "too royal" burial of their husbands

---

[13] Violet A. Wilson, *Queen Elizabeth's Maids of Honour and Ladies of the Privy Chamber* (1922), pp. 197–98.

lest their creditors increase the number of debts in the accounts of the deceased. Yet he would have the widow take great care to "perform the will and bequests of the dead man," so that he might be well spoken of by the people. At the same time he warned her again that men would "curse sumptuous tombs . . . the more spiteously if the money was ill gotten that they were made with."

Vives' advice was no mere mouthing of words for the sake of piety. Even the licentious Duke of Suffolk put some of these precepts into his own will before he went on the expedition of 1544 that he feared might cost him his life. After bequeathing his soul to "Almighty God the Father, the Son and the Holy Ghost," he asked that his body be buried in the College Church of Tatteshall, in the county of Lincoln, and if convenient, "without any pomp or outward pride of the world," with certain masses and dirges "done" for him "by all the priests of the same College and other of my chaplains only, according to the ancient and laudable custom of the Church of England, by the discretion of mine executors . . ." He would have no black gowns or coats for mourners; instead, only his servants and others would be his torch bearers at the time of his burial. And immediately after his death he wished his executors to pay his debts "to all and every person and persons to whom I have done any injuries or wrong." It is certainly to this man's credit that by his will he sought to prevent or to atone for any grief or injury to his family and other families.[14]

During the early part of the sixteenth century, Erasmus satirized wills ordering elaborate funerals, and incidentally provided a model for many of the popular seventeenth-century discussions of holy dying. The satire in his *Colloquies* graphically describes a frightened man on his deathbed. His fear and trembling are due to the will he has made with the aid of corrupt monks who have promised to pray his evil soul into salvation. For their services the monks will make the wife and children martyrs to the cost of saving the man's soul. The wife, thirty-eight, is sincere and virtuous. There are two sons, eighteen and fifteen, and two unmarried daughters. The dying man has acquired his wealth by accepting pay for 30,000 soldiers and hiring only 7,000. He has made his enemies pay him well to save their lives, which as an officer of the army he could achieve, and he has made his friends pay him well to save them from the enemy. All in all, he has "exercised very great skill in arithmetic."

The wife will not consent to enter a nunnery at her husband's death, and he has willed that she must put on the habit of Begbin, an order halfway between the status of the lay rich and the religious. The elder son, refusing to become a monk, must "ride post to Rome" after his father's

[14] Lady Cecilie Goff, *A Woman of the Tudor Age* (1930), pp. 159–60.

funeral, where the pope's dispensation will make him a priest "before his time." After this, for one year the boy must say mass every day in the Lateran Church for his father's soul, "and every Friday creep upon his knees up the holy steps there . . ." The younger son is dedicated to St. Francis, the elder daughter to Ste. Claire, and the younger to Catherina Senensis.

Unless all the members of the family abide by the will they will be disinherited. Even if they abide by it, the bulk of their inheritance will go to the religious institutions they enter. Since they will have at least a living in the monastery or nunnery, it is assumed they will prefer that to beggary. Then Erasmus shows one of the monks guiding the hand of the dying man into writing "Whosoever shall presume to violate this testament, may St. Francis and St. Dominic confound him." The wife and children give the sick man their right hands and swear obedience to his directions.

Now Erasmus describes the elaborate funeral provided for in the will. Nine representatives from five orders will be present with their "choirs of angels," each order carrying its proper cross and singing funeral songs. Besides the kin, there will be thirty torch bearers clad in mourning and accompanied by twelve special mourners sacred to the apostolic order. Behind the bier will come the deceased's horse all in mourning, with his head tied down to his knees as if looking upon the ground for his master. The pall will be hung round with scutcheons, and likewise the garments of the bearers and mourners. The Franciscans and Dominicans will draw lots for first place in the procession, but the parish priest and clerks will go last. The funeral service will be performed by the parish priest, with music "for the greater honor of the deceased."

The body is to be laid at the right hand of the high altar, in a marble tomb some four feet from the ground, with the deceased's image carved at full length on the table top. The image is to be cut from the purest marble and carved with armor from head to toe, with a crest on the helmet, a shield on the left arm, a sword with a gold hilt at the right side, the belt embroidered with gold and pearls, gold spurs on the feet, a leopard lying at the feet, and finally, a worthy epitaph carefully chosen, and beautifully inscribed. The heart is to be laid in the Chapel of St. Francis, and the bowels "interred by the Parish in our Lady's Chapel." One would give much to see the face of Erasmus as he penned this satire.

Opposed to this picture, Erasmus shows how a man should die. Here the husband calls his wife and children to his bedside for last instructions and farewells. The wife is advised to marry again, but to "make such choice of a husband" and to so conduct herself "towards him in the condition of a wife" that either by his own goodness or for her own convenience he will be kind to their children. She is warned against tying herself to any vow, for she must keep herself free for God and children. She is asked to bring up their children in "such a frame and piety of virtue, and take such care of things" that they will not choose a career till "by age and the use of things" they know what is "fittest for them."

Then addressing his children, the dying man urges them to study virtue, to obey their mother, and to observe mutual friendship and affection among themselves. As death comes nearer and the wife bends over him solicitously, he kisses her, prays for the children, makes the sign of the cross, and recommends them to the mercy of Christ. Dismissing all but one child, he asks this one to read to him till time for the others to take turns watching over him. Now Erasmus describes his "holy" dying. When he had passed the night till four in the morning, the whole family assembled, and he had the Psalm read which the Savior recited upon the Cross. Afterward he called for a taper and a cross. Taking the taper he said, "The Lord is my light and my salvation, whom shall I fear?" Kissing the cross, he said, "The Lord is the Defender of my life, of whom shall I be afraid?" By and by, with his hands folded as if in prayer, and with his eyes "lighted up to heaven," he said, "Lord Jesus, receive my spirit." Immediately he closed his eyes as if he were only about to sleep, and so, breathing gently, "he delivered up his spirit as if he had only slumbered." Now, for a moment, Erasmus probably laid down his pen with a gentle sigh of peaceful satisfaction.

Though the evil man seems like a gross exaggeration and the good man a devout idealization, to Elizabethan minds these pictures would suggest people and conditions well known indeed. Such minds would admit that death must be faced, not shunted off from one indefinite time to another till life had run its course. Death, they would insist, must be prepared for individually so that all might be in order when the dread presence cast its shadow. We find this attitude well exemplified in the will of Lady Southampton, mother of the man who became his wife's "dear and only Joy."

All her life the countess did what she could to help her relatives, and in her will of 1607, she showed the same careful consideration for the well-being of others, especially for her third and last husband, who both needed and deserved such devotion. Naturally, her son would receive the family property tied for dowry, and in order to keep up the family dignity through him, she bequeathed to him her best and most showy furniture. At the same time she wished to help her present husband, by whom she had had no children, with what money she could pass on to him, and both her son and friends at court understood and accepted this fact. Of course, when her property was disposed of, some gossips at the time were quick to say ". . . she hath left the best part of her stuff to her son, and the most part to her husband."

After the usual words in the will about "reasonable estate of body and perfect memory," she requested that her body be laid "as near as may be" to the body of her first husband without any "pomp, vain ostentation, idle ceremony, or any superfluous charge" and with "no more blacks to be bestowed" than on the household servants. In this way she would observe the proprieties and prevent waste.

The "best part of her stuff" consisted of ten tapestries telling the story of Cyrus, six describing the months, and two wrought with gold thread, besides all the pictures in "the little gallery at Copthall." In addition to the tapestries and paintings she willed her son a "scarlet bed with gold lace, with all the furniture, stools, chairs, and cushions, and all other things belonging to it"; a "white satin bed embroidered, with stools and cushions, and all other furniture"; all her "chairs, stools, and cushions of green cloth of gold"; two of her "best down beds with bolsters, pillows, and blankets"; four of her "Turkey carpets," one of which was silk; two of her "best and fairest basins and ewers of silver, with four pots of silver belonging to them"; six of her "best and greatest candlesticks of silver, and a ring of gold with a fair tablet [rectangular] diamond in it," besides "sixteen loose diamonds" which she asked her "dear son" to set in a "George of gold," and wear in memory of "his loving mother." (This frame of a figure of St. George was to make a jewel that formed part of the insignia of the Order of the Garter.)

From her treasures she gave her son's wife the "double rope of round pearls" which she herself had been accustomed to wear, her "best tissue kirtle, and 6 pairs" of her finest sheets, with "twelve pillowberes [slips]." To her daughter she left a "jewel of gold set with diamonds, called a Jesus," and this was to be left to her daughter only, not to her descendants if the daughter was deceased when her mother died.

The will also showed her care of the servants. To one of her waiting women she willed a hundred pounds of ready money, and to this same person and her second waiting woman, she willed all her wearing apparel except garments of tissue and those having pearls in them, and all her wearing linen "to be divided betwixt them . . ." To a manservant she willed twenty pounds, and to the rest of the servants, men and women, forty pounds "to be distributed."

All the rest of her "goods and chattels, household stuff and estate" (except a gilt christening cup with cover left to her friend Lord Carew) she willed to her "dear and well-beloved husband," whom she made "sole executor" of her "last will and testament," at the same time "praying him as an argument of love" to her to "be careful" of her page, her sister's son, and "in his discretion" but at her request to "provide for him" that he might be "enabled to live" and to know she had had "a care of him."[15]

In Elizabethan society, the husband's will, however, was considered more important than the wife's. Immediately after a great man's burial an inventory was taken of all his goods and chattels that it might be determined how much of the willed property could actually become the

---

[15] Charlotte Carmichael Stopes, *The Life of Henry, Third Earl of Southampton, Shakespeare's Patron* (1922), pp. 334–36.

inheritance of the legatees. Furthermore, since a good husband must leave his wife and children well provided for, there was intense interest in his social group concerning how well he had met his serious obligation. Even ministers referred to this duty in their public sermons. When, for example, William Whately urged such protection in his sermon of *A Bride-Bush*, he was as conventional as he was earnest in his admonition. "Be therefore mindful," he declaimed solemnly, "that thou art an husband as well as a father, and leavest a mother by thy children, as well as children by thy body; and let thy wife, even after thy death, enjoy such a part of thy substance, as that she need not stand beholding to her children (that in all reason should have them beholding to her) and that she may live as becometh the widow of an husband of such an estate." Though this sermon came nearly twenty years after the shocking will of the second Earl of Pembroke was read at his death, the preacher seems to have had in mind a great injustice similar to that for which the earl was so severely criticized by friends of his wife and family.

Everyone was so surprised when the earl left his wife Mary (sister of Sir Philip Sidney) poorly provided for that the gossips were kept busy chattering about his "bestowing all to the young lord, even his wife's jewels, and leaving her as bare as he could." Two motives might have prompted such a will: first, the husband may have believed his wife would remarry as soon as possible. Though he had no cause to suspect her of undue haste in such a marriage, many Elizabethan husbands labored under this fear. Second, he was deeply concerned about securing his estate for his heirs, through whom he hoped for a certain degree of immortality. He had made every effort to build up a fortune that would enhance the honor of his name, and he did not intend to have that fortune pass on to his son with any diminution whatsoever.

Elizabethan widows, as a rule, were given little time to mourn, especially if they were young. Mother and father, son and daughter, brother and sister, and even a husband might find solace in friends or relatives at the time of bereavement, but as soon as a widow laid the body of her husband in the tomb, she was expected to bury her independence and her grief. Indeed, most widows, as soon as death left them alone, "modestly" put themselves into the hands of their nearest kin, who might proceed with or without haste to launch them into matrimony again. There were exceptions to this convention, however, as when wives of men very popular among the people of their own age married again hastily; then people criticized the lack of respect shown for the dead. If there had been a great attachment between the husband and wife or if the husband was a darling of the people, the widow's marriage would be criticized regardless of when it might occur or to whom she gave her hand. For example, though the widow of Essex waited two years before she married again, her act was frowned upon, and this in spite of the fact that she was left with three sons and two daughters to rear and educate. True, two of the sons died early, but she was still burdened with much responsibility, and needed a person to help her as only a husband could. When a widow's relatives chose to make a good bargain for themselves as well as for her by means of a new marriage contract, the widow might have little to say in the matter, particularly if she voluntarily put herself into the hands of such relatives. To a certain extent, this was the case with Margaret Dakins, the young heiress of Hackness in Yorkshire.

Margaret and her first husband, a handsome young man, had led a rollicking life on the bride's estate in the country. Then adventure called the husband off to the wars, where he met the last adventure, death. Margaret's guardian, the Earl of Huntingdon, once more assumed the task of marrying the attractive heiress. But the situation was complicated by the fact that Lady Russell had determined to marry her indifferent son, Thomas Posthumus Hoby, to the unwilling Margaret. In order to outwit Lady Russell, the Huntingdons kept Margaret a virtual prisoner till her husband's body could be brought home and given decent burial. Yet during this time they permitted their nephew, Thomas Sidney, to see Margaret, and she fell in love with the cultured young man. Lady Russell, suspecting what was going on, arranged an abduction of the young widow through her nephew, Anthony Cooke, but her plan failed because of her son's lack of initiative, and Margaret was married to young Thomas Sidney.

Three years later, Margaret was again widowed. Now young Hoby wanted to marry her, but having fallen out with his mother, did not know just how to proceed with the Huntingdons. Finally, he asked his cousin, Robert Cecil, to ask *his* father, Lord Burghley, to ask *his* sister-in-law, Lady Russell, to ask the Huntingdons. Eventually, the weeping Margaret admitted the bashful young man to her presence, and, of course, liked him less than ever. Amazed that any young woman could fail to welcome marriage with a man of his connections, young Hoby again sought the aid of his powerful relatives, and even of the relatives of Margaret's two former husbands. The Earl of Huntingdon, who was now very ill, urged Margaret to set his mind at rest about her by accepting Hoby's offer, but he died so soon after making his request that Margaret did not feel bound to obey his wishes. Now the heir to the Huntingdon estate, hoping to increase his good fortune resulting from the childless condition of the Huntingdons, laid claim to Margaret's property which had been controlled by the deceased earl, and the young widow was faced with a real difficulty. Because Hoby's powerful relatives could save her fortune for her, she gave way and consented to marry the man she had spurned. In her final decision, therefore, she showed herself to be a sensible young woman of the age, for she took the only course feasible to one in her position even though it required her to marry a man she did not love. She also showed herself to be a young woman with a conscience admired by Elizabethans, for she set herself to the task of making her marriage as happy as possible by becoming a good housewife and a real daughter to the dominating Lady Russell.[16]

As in Margaret's case, the higher the rich widow's social standing, the sooner, as a rule, her remarriage occurred. In any case, however, the rich widow must be quickly matched. Those closest to her and those who were responsible for her financial welfare governed as much as possible the expenditure on funeral and wake unless the will of the deceased placed such matters beyond their control. Then they bargained with suitors for her hand, and if the widow was very rich, she had many suitors of all ages. The old sought her in order to enhance their financial holdings or to increase their power; the young, to acquire the fortune denied them by their older brother's inheritance or to repair an inheritance wasted by their own extravagance or that of their forebears. Some, of course, were but clever fortune hunters. The widow's guardians, according to the deceased husband's will, were to arrange the remarriage, but they were not forbidden to drive a close bargain with the suitors and, for the sake of their own profit, give the prize to the highest bidder. Widows of less wealth, but for the difference in degree, shared a like fate unless, of course, the widow herself was a woman of an unusually strong, independent nature. For even the most unscrupulous guardians had to reckon with the fact that a woman's consent to marriage was necessary to any matching, and the longer she was a widow, the less tractable she might become.

Perhaps out of the practice of cementing family alliances by marriage, particularly among the upper classes, there grew up the many conflicting conventions and laws affecting the widow's inheritance. For example, Lady Norris, at the death of her husband in 1600, was a subject for the busy pen of Dudley Carleton writing to his friend John Chamberlain about a suit against her father-in-law. He reports she would be willing to take £2,000 payable "within the year" for her jointure per annum of £400 that otherwise would be hers for life. If her alternative demand could be met by her father-in-law, her remarriage could be arranged more easily. Carleton says her father is already "hot in pursuit" of a suitable match for her. No doubt he expected to have the £2,000 in his possession soon to bargain with for this matching.

A quaint letter during the reign of Henry VIII tells of the financial embarrassment suffered by Thomas Boleyn, Earl of Wiltshire, through the demands of his daughter-in-law's family. The king has ordered "an augmentation of living" for the widow, and the father-in-law wishes to do "everything that may be to the King's contentation and pleasure" but at the same time is forced to admit his own living of late is "much decayed." However, he will give her yearly fifty marks in addition to the hundred marks she already has per annum, and he promises another two

---

[16] Violet A. Wilson, *Society Women of Shakespeare's Time*, pp. 23–40.

hundred marks a year after his decease. This will give her "one hundred pounds a year to live on when she should have had but one hundred marks," and after his death "she is sure to have CCC marks a year." He urges the Secretary to inform "the King's Highness" that he does this "alonely for the King's pleasure," for in truth when he (Boleyn) married his wife he had but fifty pounds to live on for himself and wife as long as his father lived, and "yet she brought forth every year a child." The letter is full of repetitious assurances that the earl is giving the widow as much as he possibly can bestow on her. His reference to his own early married life makes one wish it were possible to reconstruct as complete and accurate a picture as suggested by this letter so full of personal detail.[17]

Just how much a widow's youth and beauty might count in the marriage mart depended a great deal upon the desires of her suitors; in the case of the rich widow, such charms were often extremely dangerous to her personal happiness. Aware of the hazards that surrounded them, harassed widows yielded more or less readily to the hasty marriages arranged for them by their "protectors." Meanwhile, to offset the charge of being "lusty," they had to conduct themselves with extreme modesty. Yet those who came through the ordeal with a clear reputation did so more through the grace of God than through their own wise or discreet behavior. It was to protect these widows from the human wolves that would rob them of their good name as well as their possessions that Elizabethan society condoned their early marriage. The only stipulation was that the widow must not receive any suitors till her husband's body was buried. For those whose husbands had died abroad, this period of retirement from the social whirl might be longer than one would suppose: two or more months might pass before the body could be transported to its final resting place.

In some instances, especially among the upper classes, the hazards of war and disease might widow a more or less sheltered woman three or four times. Yet for her, happiness in remarriage could be expected with almost as much certainty as for one whose marriage was not interrupted by her husband's untimely death. The mother of the Devereux children, for example, was married soon after their father's death to Robert Dudley, Earl of Leicester, and after his death to Sir Christopher Blount, who was executed because he was a party to the uprising instigated by her own son, Essex. Yet she did not lose her capacity for living. And though she was a warm and affectionate mother, she continued to live a full life even when she had lost all her children, for she was well loved and respected by the poor for her affability and charity. When she was past ninety she persisted in taking her daily morning walk of a mile to her poor neighbors, and lived till she was ninety-four, dying on Christmas Day, 1634.

[17] Sir Henry Ellis (ed.), *Original Letters, Illustrative of English History* (1825), Vol. III, Letter CCLXV.

It is doubtful, however, whether any woman endured more from gossip than this woman, before and after her marriage to Dudley, who was the Queen's favorite, for, womanlike, Elizabeth blamed the lady in this marriage more than she blamed Leicester.

Should the mother of a family die—and mortality from childbirth ran high in this age—the father was expected to find a new mother for his children as soon as possible. Such hasty marriages for men were common to all classes of society, though material possessions were important elements affecting new ties for men as well as for women. In fact, it was a common practice, even among Puritans who were likely to be sensitive to the charge of lustiness, for either man or woman to marry soon after losing a mate in death. The Dutch mother-in-law of Philip Stubbes, the Puritan, was a middle-class woman widowed on September 22, 1563, and she remarried on November 8 of that same year. When she was widowed again some twenty years later, she was licensed to marry within less than two months, yet the moral Stubbes always spoke of her as a woman of "singular good grace and modesty," declaring she was both discreet and wise and chiefly adorned by being "both religious and zealous."[18]

A widow of the lower middle class, unless left with a small shop or estate by which to support herself and family, could do little to make an honorable living. The mother of the great scholar, John Cheke, was the wife of a beadle, but being left poor at her husband's death, she could maintain herself and children only by keeping a wine shop in the town of Cambridge. In spite of her humble position, however, she managed to do very well by her children. Her son John went to college, where he became famous for his knowledge of Greek, and where he formed some important friendships, among which were those with Cecil, later Lord Burghley, and Ascham, his distinguished pupil. One of the widow's daughters married Cecil, who frequented the wine shop during his college days. Though this wife died early, the marriage was not unhappy in spite of the fact that for a time it crushed the parents' high hopes concerning their son's brilliant alliance with an important family. The widow Cheke, however, was no doubt pleased with her disposal of her daughter to Cecil.

Among the upper middle class, a widow with much property needed her family's protection in contracting a new marriage, though at times a headstrong girl might flout such care. Lest she become the victim of a fortune hunter, her family usually took the precaution to see that the new husband offered security for the privilege of taking charge of the widow's property. At the same time the family might seek to profit from the arrangement as did some guardians of rich widows among the nobility. Even such a man as Sir Francis Walsingham, therefore, had been

[18] *A Crystall Glas, for Christian Women: . . . of a right vertuous life and Christian death . . .* (1590).

conventionally bound to prove that his intentions were honest when in 1565 he engaged to marry a widow.

In July of that year he promised to settle upon the widow Ursula lands to the yearly value of one hundred marks, for which he was bound to 2,000 marks. For Dame Ursula's "further advancement," he had to convey to her brother-in-law, John Worsley, "the manor and mansion house of Parkebury . . . to the like uses," and was bound on July 22, 1566, to 1,000 marks for this part of the transaction. At this time he was also required to give security "for £500 in plate to be bequeathed by him to his said wife, upon whom by a still later deed" he settled a manor valued at £100 a year.[19] When a rich widow was protected by such bargaining, she might expect a happy marriage if her family was genuinely concerned about her welfare.

Abuse of such protection of widows might lead to their barter and sale regardless of their birth. If honest measures were not taken to protect rich widows from mere fortune seekers, such women might have good cause to bewail their lot. Besides the matter of money was that of religion, for Protestant and Catholic households alike frowned on intermarriage between members of two faiths. When a rich widow took into her own hands the making of an alliance with a new husband, seldom or never did she engage in such an act unless the barriers of wealth or religion lay between her and the object of her affections. Otherwise she trusted to the integrity and kindly interest of those who were duty-bound to look after her welfare.

The rash action of a widow making her own choice therefore shocked the Verney family in the early part of the seventeenth century. Attractive, generous, kind, and left with a large fortune, she was a prize indeed. Unfortunately, however, her nearest male relative, Sir Ralph, was her nephew and a year her junior. Moreover, he was inexperienced in dealing with such situations. She sent him all her suitors' letters with her comments on them, and she consulted him seriously on matters of her estate. She even wrote him that she would not hear of marriage with the one her mother favored "for all conditions in the world," and confided to him that she believed her mother was influenced by reports of the suitor's great estate. For her part she felt "all the riches in the world without content" were nothing. The suitor's mother also took a hand in the affair, writing the widow that she hoped "the match might go forward." Naturally Sir Ralph was troubled, for the widow's mother was his grandmother, and he knew how she might storm if her wishes were not fulfilled.

The suitor continued sending his flowery messages to the widow, addressing her as his "most honored and virtuous mistress," and swearing that since the hour when he had first seen her his heart had been

[19] Hubert Hall, *Society in the Elizabethan Age* (1902), p. 165.

contemplating her beauties. He asked her pardon for sending her the lines which love commanded to let her know "how insufferable" were his "torments" because of those beauties. He reminded her she had the power to make him the happiest or the "most unfortunatest man upon earth," and he vowed to the "Sacred Heavens" that there was nothing he desired more than to be her happy servant. He begged her to honor him by sending him "gracious lines" from her "fair hands" or to admit him to wait upon her. He was sure she would grant him "these favors" if his "lines" were as pleasing to her as he was pleased to be "perfectly" her "most loyal servant." The widow's confidence in her nephew, shown by her sending such letters to him, should have made Sir Ralph move quickly.

Instead, unsure of himself, Sir Ralph sought advice from Lord Pembroke, the Lord Chamberlain, and was told to consider other suitors for the critical young lady. A family friend and adviser of Pembroke also gave him advice, and still Sir Ralph hesitated and the widow's mother fumed. Then, suddenly, the young woman married a Catholic, and left her Protestant relatives aghast with her "disgraceful conduct." Her mother wrote Sir Ralph the letter he had feared. "Your mother," she said, "writes me about a samite gown. I did remember I did heretofore think of such things, but now I pray tell her she would provide me sackcloth and line it with ashes, then I might mourn for the folly of my disobedient children." Even though the new husband is "without exception" but for his religion, still his religion is "such a cut" that it "hath most killed" her. Had he "never a penny" it would not trouble her at all, though she hears he has £1,000 a year "and so discreet that he will live better of that than some do of two thousand." Still, she must say Sir Ralph has made his house the "common scare of town and country" for letting the widow and her husband fool them all, but she is sure some of the household knew it all along. She also upbraids her grandson for his pious "what God wills must be," for she knows "God is not the author of any ill." Then she writes bitterly, "I have not youth and time to revenge, so I will betake me to my beads and desire I may live to forgive and forget the injuries done me."[20]

Perhaps the young widow dared to marry a Catholic because she hoped her love for him might cause him to turn Protestant, but if so her hopes were not to be realized, for he was soon killed at war. Now she wrote Sir Ralph that she was "overrun with miseries and troubles, but the greatest misfortune that could ever happen . . . in this world was the death of the gallantest man that ever" she had known. Her comfort was that he had had time "to prepare himself for a better world," which she was confident he would enjoy. She also wrote that though she had

[20] Frances Parthenope Verney and Margaret M. Verney (compilers), *Memoirs of the Verney Family during the 17th Century* (1925), I: 166–77.

not had good fortune, she still had been able to bring her mind to her fortune, and that was the greatest happiness she could now enjoy. Yet in another year she was married again, this time to a Protestant, much to her family's relief and no doubt to her own peace of mind also.

Even though her first marriage legally freed a woman from parental authority, to flout that authority when she became a widow was a serious matter according to social customs. If she did not leave the arrangements for a new marriage entirely in the hands of her protectors, she must at least secure their good will in the alliance. Such an attitude was "fit and convenient" because of the children's duty to honor their parents according to God's law, said William Perkins. Most Elizabethans agreed with him in regard to the son as well as the daughter who lost a mate. When, for example, the son of Sir W. Clark married at forty-five a widow of thirty-two without first gaining parental consent, his father threatened him with disinheritance and vowed the couple should never again come within his doors. He relented later, saying the marriage in itself was not objectionable to him. The son, alas, did not live long to enjoy his father's favor. This fact, of course, did not make it any easier for Dame Ursula as a widow, though she soon remarried and, if she was wise, dismissed the old hurts from her mind.

A widow's children usually complicated her problem of remarriage a great deal, especially if a widower with children presented himself as an acceptable suitor. Writers of conduct books expressed themselves fully on this subject. Vives, whose opinions were borrowed as freely in this matter as in others, justified the marriage of a young widow on the grounds that she needed someone to care for her property and to control her servants and to keep her household in order. Of course he agreed with Paul that the new husband would serve as a means of keeping her from lustful living, but he objected to second marriages when two sets of children were involved. A widow would not have the liberty with the other children that she had with her own. Her love of her own children might make her second husband jealous of her first husband and cause the stepfather to regard her children indifferently or with dislike. But what troubled many a timid mind was that if one of the husband's children should sicken, the widow might be accused of being a witch, and if she forbade giving it food at such a time, she would be called cruel, or if she gave it food and it died, she would be called a poisoner. In spite of such fears and admonitions, however, families of two sets of children often lived together amicably, and the family structure was frequently as patriarchal as that in the Bible.

If the widow had children old enough to comprehend their mother's problems when she contemplated remarriage, they might help or hinder her in her plans. When, for example, the Countess of Southampton was first widowed, her only son and heir approved so heartily of her acceptance of the proposal of Sir Thomas Heneage that he was chief master of the ceremonies at the elaborate wedding which followed. When, however, after the death of this second husband she contemplated a third marriage, the son raised troublesome objections. There were probably several reasons for his disapproval. First, the rank of her choice, Sir William Harvey, was inferior to that of Sir Thomas Heneage. Second, she had entered into her plans without consulting her son, probably because he himself had just secretly married one of the Queen's maids in waiting, and thereby offended his mother and put himself in disgrace with the Queen. Finally, and possibly most important of all, there may have been financial arrangements necessary for the union that were embarrassing to the newly wedded youth. At any rate, so great was the feeling aroused between mother and son that outsiders had to come to their assistance before harmony was once more established between them.[21]

The young earl's concern about his mother's marriage to a man of lower rank was not purely selfish, for widows who married in this manner were severely criticized, though the fine character of the countess' third husband mollified this criticism of her. An extreme case of a woman demeaning herself by an ill-advised marriage was that of Lady Jane Grey's mother. She disgusted the whole court when she married within a fortnight after her husband's death his groom of the chambers, a red-haired youth fifteen years her junior. The haste of the marriage and the disparity in years would have been overlooked but for the fact that she married a man beneath her in rank—indeed, a man of middle-class origin. Such mismatching was so condemned by all classes of people that a discreet widow before remarriage and in arrangements for the new alliance took great care to keep up all her old connections with society and to maintain dignified relations with all her servants.

Vives had given very explicit advice in regard to the widow and her servants. First, widows must not shut their doors to the world lest they be given an ill name with their servants. Next, they must not array any servant in "over gorgeous apparel" lest the servant suspect his mistress of liking his body or looking on him as "apt for pleasure." Special favors to a servant were likely to make him arrogant or "high minded" through knowing "he was loved of his mistress: which love, though it be well hid, yet many times it appeareth when he despiseth his fellows, as they were his bondsmen." Shakespeare's careful attention to all these details is shown in his portrayal of Malvolio's stupid vanity, the revenge taken on him by disgruntled servants, and Olivia's delicious amazement at her steward's conduct in the skylarking comedy of *Twelfth Night*.

Vives would also have the menservants in a widow's household diminished in number, and the widow's close companion some aged kinswoman upon whose virtue and wisdom she might rely. He considered it better still for her to dwell with her mother-in-law's kin, for this would

<hr />

[21] Stopes, *The Life of Henry, Third Earl of Southampton*, pp. 133–35.

make her seem to love her husband's blood better than her own, and add a further safeguard to her chastity. Though suspicion of a widow's virtue appears in all Elizabethan literature, and its classical models, it is the subject of close analysis in most moral writing of the sixteenth century. When, therefore, Becon exclaimed, "How light, vain, trifling, unhonest, unhousewifely young widows have been in all ages, are also at this present day, experience doth sufficiently declare," he did not preach to deaf ears. Indeed, the Pauline admonition that young widows should marry again soon to avoid the "danger of everlasting damnation" was on the tip of all tongues. Guazzo had also warned that widows were exposed to such harsh judgments they must be extremely circumspect in talk, countenance, apparel, and behavior, and he had strongly recommended that they live retired lives. "Even the wisest and honestest" widows "serve for a mark for ill tongues to shoot at," his English translator had written, "and it seemeth the more they cover their face and their eyes with their masks, the more busily men labor to discover in them some faults."

Vives provided a detailed account of a widow's proper conduct. "A good woman feels that with the loss of her husband goes part of herself," he began, and therefore mourning is "right and natural" provided her grief is "neither too much nor too little." Her mourning is proper because her husband was the defender of her chastity, keeper of her body, father and tutor of her children, provider of the wealth of the household, and governor of all in that household. Shakespeare's queen to Edward IV in *Richard III* briefly summarizes all these misfortunes with "The loss of such a lord includes all harms." For this reason, explains Vives, lack of mourning proclaims a widow's feeling of release from her husband's bondage and domination. But a woman is foolish indeed to welcome such freedom from one who was her "best earthly guide and mentor."

After her first grief is past, however, she should "begin to study for consolation," which should consist of the Christian belief in "immortality of the soul and in reunion after death of friend and friend." Death, said Vives, does not merely separate body and soul: when a husband dies he is not utterly dead, "but liveth both with life of his soul, which is the very life," and in his wife's remembrance. Just as her friends live with her, whether absent or dead, if she keeps a lively image of them imprinted on her heart by thinking of them daily, so her husband will wax fresh in her mind. But if she forgets him, he dies for her indeed. He would not have the image of the husband remembered with weeping, however, but with reverence. This she can do by taking "a solemn oath to swear by her husband's soul" whom she will seek to please from now on as "a spirit purified, and a divine thing." Thus a widow should take her husband for her "keeper and spy, not only of her deeds, but also of her conscience." Then she can manage her household to please him and bring up his children in the same manner, feeling that she is making him happy by leaving a wife so well able to carry her responsibilities. The husband's soul will never have cause to "be angry with her and to take vengeance on her ungraciousness" if she follows this pattern of living, but she must cease her weeping, lest she give the impression of believing her husband "clean dead, and not absent." It is a pity, says Vives, that widows are not properly instructed by their spiritual advisers at funeral feasts instead of being told to be of good cheer for they will not long lack a new husband. Such promises he accounts for by saying they come from those who "be well wet with drink."

After her husband's death, the widow should not care for "trimming and arraying her body in order to make it beautiful" as in the past when she sought to please her husband. Such "trimming," said Vives, would make her seem to be "seeking a bargain." She should refuse at this time any offers of men for a second marriage, for "what body would not abhor her, that [soon] after her first husband's death, showeth herself to long for another . . . ?" Now she must go covered with a long black veil, accompanied always by her good, grave companion, and directing her steps to a quiet church where she will be seen by few people and where she will not be disturbed at prayer. If she feels the need of spiritual advice, she must avoid priest and friar and seek out a wise, aged man "past the lust of the world," and counting nothing dearer than truth and virtue. Such a man would possess no desires of the flesh and would covet no worldly wealth to be gained by flattery. Always the widow must avoid gatherings of men and people, remembering that no matter where she goes or what she does she must now guard her chastity even more carefully than when she was a wife.

To maintain this virtuous life, the widow must pray "more intensely and oftener, fast longer, and be much at mass and preaching, and read more effectually" as she devotes herself to spiritual things, says Vives. He believes the best marriage for a widow is Christ, whom she would do better to please than even her husband. This is especially true since now that she has her freedom, her real self, formerly inhibited by marriage, may seek to assert itself. Now as never before, therefore, she must walk most warily, even fearfully. Now the influence of her husband can no longer augment her virtues and minimize her weaknesses; now she alone is responsible for herself. Christ as her incorruptible champion would rejoice in an obedient, earnest widow seeking the spiritual life, and that is why she would do best of all to be married to her Savior. With such precepts in mind, Shakespeare has the Duchess of Gloucester in the play of *Richard II* ask John of Gaunt to whom she can complain about the death of her husband, whose murder has never been avenged. Quick as a flash the duke answers, "To God, the widow's champion and defence" (I:ii:43).

Up to this point in his advice, Vives has been concerned with young women. Now he turns to widows "well worn with age" and "past the pleasures of the body," and admonishes them to devote themselves to holiness. Before her husband's death such a woman should be unknown to the world, but after his death she should become famed for her virtue and acts of charity. He was more concerned about her health than were most writers of conduct books, saying he would have her labor more in mind than in body, praying more, thinking more of God, fasting less, and wearying herself less with long walks to church. Although she must give all possible aid to those needing her ministrations, she must also give her aged body proper care so that she may live long to give wise counsel and to set a good example. Later, Becon agreed to all this program, but with less consideration for old age. Instead, he emphasized the need of widows busying themselves by prayer, attending sermons, visiting the sick and needy, and even washing the feet of saints. It was such stress on the importance of good works that must be performed by widows which probably kept the mother of Essex making her morning pilgrimages to her poor neighbors till she was past ninety.

The pious, modest widow was presented as a model for all widows in one of the first books printed in England. In 1487, William Caxton translated and printed Le Grande's *Boke of Good Maners*, in which the author wrote much of widows, saying they must possess "great humility" and "great devotion" and spend their time in going on pilgrimages and performing "other good deeds." So much was the widow's humility or modesty stressed during the sixteenth century that widows sought to be known for this trait no matter what their station in life might be. Lady Russell, for example, in spite of all her independence and forthrightness of speech, was always careful of her modesty. When she besought her nephew, Sir Robert Cecil, to help the widowed Earl of Kent, she insisted that he keep her part in the matter secret because of her widowhood.

Much of this concern about modesty, of course, grew out of the widow's fear of slander, especially in regard to her remarriage. Richard Flecknoe's character sketch of *A Very Widow* describes widows as shaking off husbands "as fast . . . as pellets out of pop-guns," and once discharged, all their care is to charge again. She makes her mourning dress "as curious as if she rather counted a new husband than mourned for the old"; and her glass and women have more ado with putting on her veil and peak than "with putting on her masking clothes." With the widow of Ephesus in mind, probably, he scoffs at her grief as she makes lamentable moan before company and squeezes out a tear, but when alone with her women laughs with them over "Who is the properest man?" or "Who would make the best husband?" He accuses her of counting herself widowed "not for her bosom but for her bed," which she seeks to have "warm still when her husband is scarcely cold." Then she so soon forgets her first husband as never to make mention of him "but only as a spur to the latter . . ." In fact, she has but married "for a good dowry," and when she has that, she cares not how soon she is "rid of her next husband."

There were many miniature character sketches of the widow in the early seventeenth century, summarized neatly in Fuller's staircase-attempt.[22] Commiserating with women as the weaker vessels, he proceeds to feeble women, old women, and widows. Now he descends the steps rapidly, naming poor widows, barren widows, widows whose children have died, and widows with children in a foreign land, "their condition most comfortless." Francis Lenton cynically wrote of "A Country Widow":[23] a "broken rib of Adam turned loose into the world again," she is in search of a new bonesetter and polishes herself for "a more fair impression." She has been "somewhat mortified in the memory of the deceased," but she has gathered up the few crumbs he left her of his estate, and pretends she has been willed "a brace of hundreds" more than the whole estate is worth, including all her husband's debts and legacies which she can hardly afford to pay. Nevertheless she "carries herself smooth, demure," and with just the right touch of ease and aloofness in her manner to attract a suitor. If she is young, the sooner caught the better, if past her prime, she is "libidinous, subtile, and dangerous" and likely to prove herself a "pig in a poke." If she is wealthy, her only value is that she is "her own woman," and not subject to her avaricious parents. Having tasted of mandrakes, she likes the fruit so well she "longs to graft more imps on that stalk." For this purpose she is trimmed up for the next fair, where she may be bargained for, though her husband will have to make the best of his ill bargain.

Overbury presented both sides of the widow's character in the "ordinary" and the "virtuous" types.[24] The former, he said, was like the "heralds' hearse-cloth" in that she served "too many funerals" and with very little "altering the color." She weeps, but though "the end of her husband begins in tears," the end of her tears "begins in a husband." She goes to cunning women to learn how "many husbands she shall have, and never marries without the consent of six midwives." Her greatest pride is in the multitude of her suitors, and she uses them to advantage, for one serves to draw on another, and with the last she "shoots out another, as boys do pellets in eldern guns." If she lives long enough to be married thrice, she "seldom fails to cozen her second husband's creditors," and finally, like a too ripe apple, falls of herself.

The virtuous widow, however, is like the palm tree that does not thrive by "the supplanting of her husband." Since she married "that she might have children," for their sake she marries no more. Like the purest gold used only for princes' medals, she receives but one man's impression. She cannot be bought by "large jointures or titles of honor," for she feels

---

[22] Thomas Fuller, *The Holy State and the Profane State* (1642), Book I, Chap. 1.

[23] Francis Lenton, *Characterismi: or, Lenton's Leasures Expressed in Essayes and Characters Neverbefore written on* (1631).

[24] Quoted from Edward F. Rimbault's edition of *The Miscellaneous Works of Sir Thomas Overbury* (1856).

it would be a sin to change her name. She thinks she has "travel'd all the world in one man; the rest of her time therefore she directs to heaven." True, she is a bit superstitious, for she feels her husband's ghost will walk if she does not perform his will. "She gives much to pious uses, without any hope of merit by them," and as diamond dust polishes diamonds, so she is "wrought into works of charity with the dust or ashes of her husband." She lives out her long life only because she is "necessary for earth," and therefore "God calls her not to heaven till she be very aged." In the frailty of her last years she stands "like an ancient pyramid, which the less it grows to man's eye, the nearer it reaches to heaven." Her chastity in late life "is more grave and reverend" and serves as a mirror for young dames to dress themselves by. No calamity can touch her after the death of her husband; all else is but trifles. She buries her husband "in the worthiest monument that can be . . . in her own heart." Of all precious beings in this world, therefore, she is "most reverenced."

Most of these sketches condemned fortune hunters along with widows, and rejoiced when a widow inveigled such a man into a marriage that appealed to his cupidity only to prove herself to be very poor. In the literature of plays, popular sermons, and conduct books, only one thing was worse than marrying a rich widow for her dowry, and that was to marry a widow past her prime but still appealing to the elemental nature of man. Shakespeare has Edward IV roundly condemned in *Richard III* for his marriage to a widow so described by her enemies. The king, overcome by the love provoked by the widow, has broken his marriage contract with the sister of the King of France, and has married a woman beneath him in rank and burdened with several sons. The Duke of Buckingham rants about the scandal (III:vii:177–94) which has caused factions to develop at court. True, Buckingham's tirade is for the purpose of proving that the heir from this marriage is illegitimate in order to prepare the way for Richard to ascend the throne. And Buckingham's harangue is successful. But the point here is that his success is due to the feeling about the widow. That she could even unintentionally make a king's eye wanton and cause him to break a marriage contract proved her an evil thing in theory if not in fact in the minds of those at court as well as among the common people. Such an attitude could be used to advantage by the unscrupulous.

Bartholomew Batty, a self-avowed altruistic writer in *The Christian mans Closet,* attacked the practice of marrying a rich widow for her dowry by composing a dialogue which he believed was "most pleasant to read and most profitable to practise." His chief complaint is that widows are not so tractable as maids and look rather to be obeyed because of their acquaintance with love matters and because of their wealth, which is usually greater than that of maids. Men should be wise enough to avoid slavery to dowry.

Plays and court sketches in prose or verse usually adopted the cynical

A deathbed scene

Ioan. Stradanus inunt.

The sick chamber

tone when referring to marriage with any kind of widow. Shakespeare's crazed Timon of Athens, while digging among roots, holds up one of them as if it were gold and says with a leer, ". . . this it is that will make the wappen'd widow wed again" (IV:iii:38). Such comments in time made it not unusual for men to hold their noses at the very mention of "stale widows." In his play of *The Widow*, Middleton makes greed for the widow's gold stronger than loathing. One of the characters lists the cures for the ills of man, and names the rich widow for the gentleman without land. A little later he says, "Why, dost think if I had kept my lands still, I should ever have looked after a rich widow? Alas! I should have married some poor maid . . ." When the widow of the play is finally tricked into marriage with a fortune hunter in spite of her efforts to outwit the wily ones at their dishonest game, she gives the delighted audience cause for roars of laughter.

George Chapman carried the abuse of the widow to a bitterly cynical conclusion in his play of *The Widow's Tears*. It is quite possible he wrote from real as well as vicarious experience, though perhaps he, like many other Elizabethan writers, was only trying to surpass the old story of the widow of Ephesus.[25] Chapman first shows the wife of his play swearing eternal fidelity to her husband, but also inducing him to make a will that in the event of his death will place his son's fortunes in her control. This causes the younger brother, through jealous fear for the paternal estate, to prevail upon the husband to put the wife to trial.

The husband, therefore, is supposedly murdered, and the wife, grieving by his body, is persuaded by a charming soldier to agree to a substitution of her husband's corpse for a stolen corpse placed in the custody of the soldier. The sudden love of the wife for this soldier persists even when he confesses to her that he was the "murderer" of her husband. Thus the younger brother's doubt about the wife is justified, and when he sees his sister-in-law in the arms of the soldier (who is her husband in disguise), his cynical amusement finds expression in words that show he has no faith in any widow's purity or constancy, but considers them all shamefully lustful. He may well feel, therefore, that a widow's tears are but the cause for laughter, that her weeping is in truth but laughing in her sleeve.

The later domestic books were seldom as kind to widows as Vives was; usually they tolerated them as a necessary evil. *A Discourse of marriage and wiving* (1615) by Alexander Niccholes, like Chapman's play, condemned all widows as a matter of principle. To marry a widow, he said, was to thank death if she was good and to upbraid death if she was evil. Marriage with a widow meant to take a woman half-worn, to become involved in trouble over her estate, to take one for whom marriage meant

---

[25] The playwright's personal attitude toward the widow is discussed in the *Athenaeum* of March 23, 1901.

ease and lust more than affection and love, and to cause the dead husband to accuse by her tongue and be flattered by comparison with her next husband. After the death of the first husband, widows learned how to dispose of the second, and so were in league with death, for they could "harden their own hearts like iron to break others" that were but "earth." He liked them worse when they were married, therefore, but disliked them "utterly" when they married again "so soon." Because he felt this way about them, he could not understand how any man could love a person who would undoubtedly forget him as soon as he was dead. He looked upon widow-wives as but "summer swallows for the time of felicity," that would "hang about one's neck" as if they had "never arms for others' embracing, or as though extreme affection without control could not but thus manifest itself and break out." Worse still, if the second husband died, she would be "churched again," and tell her third husband all about the one just dead.

Then this writer turned to younger brothers and poor knights who sometimes benefited by the birth and title of widows. He declared they would do far better to choose a maid without a dowry: a widow would make them "pay for the jewel that another hath stolen." He admitted a widow might have a fairer face than a man's, but he was sure her heart was more deformed than the devil's. To marry such a woman was to build upon a broken foundation. It was a pity that the laws of man and God did not forbid marriage between youths and old widows, for "no policy on earth" commended them. Man and wife, he said, should be two in one, but heat and cold, youth and age in one could be nothing but "repugnant." He could but believe, therefore, that widows married so often because they thought "variety of men" would make "old pleasures new delights again."

When the ballads took up the hue and cry against the widow, no doubt they gave many an Elizabethan a chuckle and left the widow to face the attack with whatever grace was at her command. The ballads were often written in two parts, and illustrated satirically a popular proverb or a catch phrase of the day. Such a ballad, based on the proverb, "Strike while the iron is hot," and sung to the popular tune of *Dulcina*, advised young men to marry widows "while there is store." Two of the stanzas indicate how the proverb was applied to marriage with wealthy widows:

> Wealthy widows now are plenty,
>   where you come in any place,
> For one man there's women twenty,
>   this time lasts for but a space:
>   She will be wrought,
>   though it be for naught,
> But wealth which their husbands first got,
>   Let Young-men poor
>   make haste therefore,
> 'Tis good to strike while the Iron's hot.

Now is the wooing time or never,
    Widows now will love Young-men,
Death them from their mates did sever,
    now they long to match again,
        they will not stand
        for House or Land,
Although thou be'st not worth a groat,
        set forth thyself,
        thou shalt have Pelf,
If thou wilt strike while the Iron's hot.[26]

In the second part, sung to the same tune, the following stanzas show how the young man is urged to heed the command in the proverb:

If a poor Young-man be matched
    with a Widow stored with gold,
And thereby be much enriched,
    though he's young and she is old,
        'Twill be no shame
        unto his Name,
If he have what his Friends have not,
        but every Friend
        will him commend
For striking while the iron is hot.

Young men all who hear this ditty,
    in your memories keep it well,
Chiefly you in London city,
    where so many widows dwell,
        the season now
        doth well allow
Your practice, therefore lose it not,
        fall to't apace,
        while you have space,
And strike the iron while 'tis hot.[27]

Another ballad laments the plight of maids who, because they cannot compete with the rich widows, are left without husbands. This ballad's first stanza declares how easily a man may marry, so great is the competition between widows and maids desiring husbands.

A young man need never take thought how to wive,
For widows and maids for husbands do strive,
Here's scant men enough for them all left alive,
They flock to the Church, like Bees to the Hive.
        Oh this is a wiving age.
        Oh this . . . etc.

[26] Hyder E. Rollins, *A Pepysian Garland* (1922).
[27] *Roxburghe Ballads*, by Martin Parker (*ca.* 1625).

The second part of the ballad continues in the same strain to the same
tune of *The Golden Age*, though the plight of the unfortunate maid is
the chief theme:

> My song unto Virgins is chiefly directed,
> Who now in this age are little respected,
> Though widows be chosen and maids rejected,
> They will be esteemed, though now they're neglected.
>   Yet not in this wiving age.
>   Yet not . . . etc.

Still another ballad carries on a dialogue of a woman remarried, a
widow, and a young wife, and is sung to the tune of *The Wiving Age*.
In a way it answers the ballad above, for it presents a widow who is wise
enough to avoid the pitfalls of remarriage. The first part is a dialogue
between the widow and a woman remarried.

> Oh, woe is me, Gossip, that e'er I was born,
> I married a Boy that now holds me in scorn,
> He comes among whores both evening and morn,
>   Oh, this is a cozening Age,
>   Oh, this . . . etc.

The second part, sung to the same tune, introduces the young wife. She,
too, has been unfortunate in marriage, her husband having won her by
"fables" of his wealth, but after their marriage presenting her instead
with poverty and five children, "four girls and a son." The widow retorts
with some spirit:

> Your speeches will make me still willing to tarry,
> Sith Widows and Bachelors both do miscarry;
> Yet 'tis said in London, that when we do bury
> Our Husbands, next month we are ready to marry:
>   Oh, this is a lying Age,
>   Oh, this . . . etc.

> Nay more, to abash us, the Poets o' the times,
> Do blazon us forth in their Ballads and Rhymes,
> With bitter invective satirical lines,
> As though we had done some notorious crimes,
>   Oh, this is a scandalous Age,
>   Oh, this . . . etc.

Then, with more lines to the effect that she wishes she could get such poets
in her "clutches" to teach them a lesson, she tosses her head and sings a
stanza in which she dares such knaves to "say their worst," for she is sure
they are merely envious men who would marry a widow at once if they
only had the chance.

Because there was so much disparagement of the widow in plays, sermons, conduct books, character sketches, and ballads, one wonders how much of this literature reflects the actual attitude of the age and how much of it was merely designed to be entertaining or to propagandize moral beliefs. Just as we tend to judge our own age by pictures of society in sermons, the printed word, stage plays, and the films, possibly we preserve from the past similar sources of "information" largely because we attach importance to what they seem to tell us of life long ago. When private records bear out these sources, we feel still more confident that we know something about the lives of our ancestors. With due allowance for exaggeration in all these sources, we cannot help wondering why the Elizabethan widow was shown favor by society only as she won it by some Herculean effort from the unwilling regard of those about her. True, the age reflects the influence of Paul in regard to widows as well as the whole moral pattern his teaching set before readers of the Scriptures. But the feeling toward widows seemed to be an instinctive one more than an attitude implanted even by constant moral preachment. Gossip in official letters or in private letters about important personages, for example, shows general distrust of the widow. What, then, of the unprotected widow in private life? If she was so insignificant as to escape the morbidly speculative interest in her every word or speech, was she, nevertheless, aware of the unfriendly, suspicious, and abusive attitude she might arouse if she thoughtlessly deviated from the pattern of perfect decorum?

Of course, much of the upheaval in sixteenth-century thought and feeling about womanhood was caused by the Protestant tendency to discard everything connected with worship of the Virgin Mary. When, therefore, the old worship of virginity and the chivalric ideal of woman on a pedestal were so powerfully affected by decline in Mariolatry, widows naturally suffered far more than did maids or wives. The widow's supposed knowledge of married life's pleasures put men on the defensive in any relationship they might have with such women, and strangely enough, most men assumed that the knowledge they resisted was actually far greater than it was. Perhaps this was because society, though it no longer worshiped virginity itself, still held fast to the conventional attitude toward a maid's or a wife's chastity. In these women the preservation of chastity was more important than the preservation of life. The widow, not sheltered by this fetish, stood alone unless her family immured her against the dangers that threatened. Those without this family protection could survive only by the grace of their acquired experience or by sheer good fortune. If they escaped the dangers of slander, they presented a challenge to both their protected sisters and the protectors of their sisters. Their own sex disliked them for their supposed worldly wisdom, and the opposite sex distrusted them because of the supposed power in that worldly wisdom.

Widows, therefore, no matter how innocent their motives, were not given the benefit of the doubt in anything that invited suspicion regarding their conduct. The old war of the sexes, which from as far back as the memory of man had always revolved more or less about the widow, now made her more than ever the target at which to hurl the bitterest invectives against the "weaker" sex. Furthermore, when the people read in the Bible or in conduct books Paul's advice concerning the duties and position of the widow, they were strengthened in their antipathy to women who had lost husbands. And this strong admiration for Paul's Epistles was largely due to Colet's and More's interpretation of them, with the precepts they emphasized in regard to the government of the home by the man as head of the household.

True, long before Paul, the Old Testament had taken a definite stand against the widow. In the precepts for the priests as set forth in the book of Leviticus, the widow is classed with poor company when the law states: "A widow, or one divorced, or a profane woman, or a harlot, these he shall not take: but a virgin of his own people shall he take to wife" (21:14). Ezekiel's ordinances for priests find among women who had lost their husbands only the widows of priests worthy of marriage (44:22). With the Bible in their hands, the common people could have found many convenient quotations to support their contentions about the supposed unstable character of the widow. Perhaps they referred to Paul so frequently because he was more detailed than any other biblical authority in his instructions concerning the widow, but even more likely because his statements as to why widows should marry were so agreeable to the male sex and to women dominated by the male sex. In his words they found the quintessence of their prejudices, and pious widows as well as maids and wives quoted his words: "But I say to the unmarried and to widows, it is good if they abide even as I," which was quickly followed by: "But if they have not continency, let them marry: for it is better to marry than to burn" (I Cor. 7:8–9).

In an epistle to Timothy, Paul set forth specific rules of conduct for old and young widows, and as he gave the rules, he gave reasons for their stringency. Of course Elizabethans interpreted these rules with the idea of literal adaptation of them to their own time instead of considering them in relation to the time of Paul.

Now she that is a widow indeed, and desolate, trusteth in God, and continueth in supplications and prayers night and day. But she that liveth in pleasure is dead while she liveth. . . . Let not a widow be taken into the number [i.e., into the congregation] under three score years old, having been the wife of one man, well reported for good works; if she have brought up children, if she have lodged strangers, if she have washed the saints' feet, if she have relieved the afflicted, if she have diligently followed every good work. But the younger widows refuse: for when they have begun to wax wanton against Christ, they will marry; having damnation, because they have cast off their first faith. And withal they learn to be idle, wandering about from house to house; and not only idle, but tattlers also and busybodies, speaking things which they ought not. I will therefore that the younger women marry, bear children, guide the house, give none occasion to speak reproachfully. For some are already turned aside after Satan. If any man or woman that believeth have widows, let them relieve them, and let not the church be charged; that it may relieve them that are widows indeed.

Here is shown the source for most of the rules for a widow's proper conduct as set up by Vives and his followers. And here also is shown the weak and foolish and even evil nature of the unstable widow as opposed to that of the saintly widow loaded down with years as well as with good works. It is significant that distrust overshadows the picture—that unless a widow be old indeed, she is to be married, or to be taken in charge by her own people.

But there are other factors involved in the distrust of widows. Enough has been said about the influence of women sovereigns during this age to make it unnecessary here to do more than refer to the effect of Elizabeth's reign upon women's status in the economic life. Never, perhaps, had woman been so close to her coveted position of economic freedom and equality with the male sex. But this economic freedom was enjoyed in general by widows only, for the rich maid was likely to have relatives that guarded her possessions carefully, and the dutiful wife gave into her husband's hands full control of her wealth when she exchanged vows with him at the marriage ceremony. The widow, especially when left with a fortune, was thereby possessed of a tangible independence, but only, of course, if she grasped the full significance of her freedom and had the strength of character to keep up the fight to maintain her freedom. There is a real point, therefore, in Petruchio's fantastic promises to Katharina's father in the play of *The Taming of the Shrew* when he says he will even provide for the girl's widowhood with all his "lands and leases whatsoever." The last thing this healthy, ebullient youth can think of happening to him is to die or to lose the upper hand in his conquest of the lady. His speech defies fate, destiny, all the uncertainties of life. As he elaborates on his promises, the audience must have responded with much sly laughter and some rather grim smiles.

How, then, might the rich widow's power be curbed before she had ever realized it? Certainly nothing could be so effective or so speedy in its conclusion as the device of rushing her into another marriage. Just how far the Pauline argument was adopted for this purpose cannot be estimated, but that it was a very convenient doctrine to preach at certain times cannot be denied. For what young, healthy widow could look with equanimity upon the existence described in the life of "widows indeed"? If that was the alternative to hasty remarriage, better far to chance another matching, and that as quickly as arrangements for the contracting and the final ceremony of marriage could be arranged. If, however, the widow was bold (but her first virtue must be modesty) and strong (in spite of her weaker-vessel-God-given-nature), she might stand her ground. And for what? A fine funeral and a finer monument in marble or bronze?

Because the rich widow's position was open to so many attacks and because she would have to fight against an unfriendly group if she tried to achieve independence by her wealth, she was placed in an almost intolerable situation. But the wise and loving husband prepared for just such an eventuality by a carefully drawn will, and even before marriage her own family often prepared for such an emergency by carefully planned jointures and agreements to keep her a contented member of an intricately related group. Among the husband's important duties, then, was provision for his wife in case of his death, and this provision was to enable her to maintain her social status and to bring up any children of their union according to the position in life he had established for them. At the same time he must secure the paternal estate for the eldest son.

If, however, the husband could leave his wife provided for in such a manner as to enable her to attract wealthy or powerful suitors who, in turn, might enhance the holdings of his heir should they themselves be without heirs, he might play a game by means of his will that would be worth all the effort it would cost him. Meanwhile, the wife's own family had to be assured that she was protected against mere fortune hunters when she was provided with a dowry that would enable her to make another honorable marriage. For these reasons the wills of husbands were often very complicated but also minutely explicit, and the marriage agreements entered into by both parties for the future of the bride were equally complicated and explicit. As a result, young widows frequently returned to their parents or guardians as soon as arrangements could be made after the funeral. Sometimes, however, they were content to remain with their deceased husband's parents, or whether content or not, were required to do so. In either case arrangements for another marriage would be considered as soon as the two families could come to some agreement about it. If, for some reason, a widow stayed on with her children in the home her husband had provided, she was expected to keep in close touch with her own family and that of her husband. All this, of course, pertained to rich or powerful families. In the case of widows left with little to care for them or their children, the family of either side helped them or not according to the cordiality of relations in existence, but for the most part, parents felt responsible for their children married or unmarried as long as they lived. Any outward changes that occurred in family relations, therefore, were chiefly economic.

Some husbands, of course, made every effort to keep intact their power as head of the household. Though they planned for eventualities, they also expected death to pass lightly over them and take someone else. Furthermore, they did not intend to instruct their wives along lines that might make them look upon the advantages of an independent widowhood till they would come to desire the opportunity for enjoying a little power of their own. The wife must be kept sufficiently asleep, as it were, not real-

izing the freedom that widowhood could bring, if the old, old game game
of alliances through marriage was to go on safely enough to satisfy all
families involved. Into the minds of such wives the Pauline doctrine
might be subtly instilled so that they would look upon the widow's plight
as the greatest calamity that could befall them. If by chance they were
widowed, such women might truly keep their gaze bent demurely upon
the ground, actually and unfeignedly unaware of the new economic freedom that might be theirs for the grasping. Then, indeed, they could be
easily guided into another hasty marriage, and once more the family
would be united instead of broken or disintegrated by death. Certainly
the whole suspicious attitude toward the widow, with the epithet "lusty,"
might hurry a delicate, sensitive woman into the shelter of marriage more
effectively than the fear of fortune hunters.

On the other hand, if a woman was sufficiently strong-minded, she
might try to use her new freedom to her own advantage, even to the point
of disregarding the wishes of her deceased husband not made binding by
his will. Instead of being married off by parents or guardian to a suitor
not to her liking, she might choose one more acceptable to her own tastes,
even though she might endanger the interests thereby of her deceased
husband's heir. Or she might refuse another marriage altogether. It
took more than a strong will, however, for an Elizabethan widow to
stand alone. Unless the widow could think for herself, she might be
convinced that she was in an unenviable position, or if suspicion could be
directed at her in such a manner as to leave her still marriageable but not
too marriageable, her family's concern about her stubbornness might be
dispelled, and a new alliance formed that would satisfy all those who
had some interest in her holdings. The Pauline teaching could be a for-
midable weapon for those waging war against a redoubtable widow, but
in the case of the pliant widow, it might be used persuasively, gently, to
move her either way—to marry or not to marry.

A strong economic reason for the abusive attitude toward rich widows
was the scarcity of men caused by wars and the inability of maids with
small dowries to compete with the wealthy widow. As the whole inheritance system left most younger brothers with but two alternatives if they
did not wish to go to war—a rich marriage or losing caste by entering
trade—it was seldom indeed that such a youth failed to join the group
of suitors about a rich widow. Maids in real life as well as in ballads
might well complain that they had little chance in marriage when men
were out to win their fortunes in the quickest and easiest way possible.
Among middle-class widows in particular many a woman felt the barbs of
both rejected suitors and disgruntled maids with small dowries. It took
a great deal of hardihood on their part to be a target for arrows sharpened
by wit or poisoned by ingeniously fabricated scandal. Women of such
courage might well pause before they roused the ire of envious ones,
weighing well in their minds the question of whether the prize was worth
the price that must be paid for it.

When a widow did exercise her rights, she was so great a novelty that she was inevitably accused of taking undue advantage of every person within her power. The women themselves were as severe as the men in condemning her. Certainly no widow's abuse of her advantages could ever have justified the cruel slander which satirists directed against her in their plays, or which other writers accused her of in their bawdy stories and ballads. Yet among many Elizabethans, delight in the sensational and sensual made such literature popular and helped to strengthen the prejudice against the widow. The scorn or cynicism of these men and women who thoughtlessly criticized widows kept the prejudice alive in the undercurrent of thought. Most Elizabethan widows who married again (and perhaps again) asked that their bodies be buried by the side of the first husband, even though their married life with another husband may have been far happier. What was it that called forth this earnest request? Convention was back of it, but what was back of convention? Perhaps it was the desire to unite in this way the founders of a broken household, to re-establish in the only way they knew how the order of things changed by death. Or perhaps the request was due to mere disillusionment—to a realization that life is hard no matter how one may look at it. The widow may have felt she would have done better to follow her first husband, not only to the grave, but into it. For the disease of melancholy had swept in with its brooding darkness, and the answers to life's riddle were no longer clear.

Possibly the "widow indeed" found a romantic pleasure in such thoughts as inspired Crashaw to write his *Epitaph* on a husband and wife buried together. But some widows, at least, saw between the lines of sweet phrases a grinning, mocking mask. In either case, the poem suggests an answer to the widow's dilemma in the sixteenth century.

> To those whom death again did wed
> This grave's the second marriage-bed
> For though the hand of fate could force
> 'Twixt soul and body a divorce,
> It could not sever man and wife,
> Because they both lived but one life.
>
> . . .
>
> They, sweet turtles, folded lie
> In the last knot that love can tie.
> For though they lie as they were dead,
> Their pillow stone, their sheets of lead,
>
> . . .
>
> Let them sleep, let them sleep on,
> Till the stormy night be gone,
> And the eternal morrow dawn;
> Then the curtains will be drawn,
> And they awake into the light
> Whose day shall never die in night.

Unless a man's life was closely bound up in his home with few contacts outside—and that was unlikely, even in the rural districts and not at all in towns and cities—he might find the changes wrought by his wife's death not impossible to meet. Had he lived many years with his wife and had she become very dear to him, he might find it most difficult to face the stretch of loneliness before him, but in time he would gather his forces together and bury himself in his work. If he was still young, with most of his life before him, he would marry soon, especially if he had children to be mothered. A new wife to train to his way of life (if she could be so trained), some minor changes in housekeeping to please the new mistress, and then once more the home would swing into its daily round. For if he had used good judgment in his choice of a stepmother for his children or of a mother for his future children, and if his financial arrangements had been satisfactory and economic problems did not trouble him too much, then in time home would be home again, with its duties and contentments, its responsibilities and cares, its pleasures and, perhaps, its rewards.

Among those who most feared the changes wrought by death was the young wife, who had cause to feel her soul caught and held in a grip of terror when her husband died. Her little world had indeed fallen about her. Children might console her, but they also weighed down her shoulders with the responsibility she felt for their future. When, after the interment of her husband's body she entered her home again, she might find the household of relatives and friends and servants willing and anxious to share her grief, but since human emotions are of necessity short, she knew she must soon take up her burden alone unless she could put herself trustingly into the hands of her nearest kin. When she could do this with full confidence, she might well expect changes in her life to follow swiftly. A new husband, a new household of servants to manage, possibly new children to mother and to adjust to her own children, new relatives to win by a careful graciousness on her part—all these she must be prepared for with what good will and Christian charity she could summon to her aid.

But if her love for her husband had been so great that the thought of another was repugnant? Then she would be told kindly or brutally of the future trials she would have to meet as a widow. If she was rich and intelligent, she would learn that men feared the power in a rich widow's hands, that some even envied that power, and that out of their envy grew hate. She would learn that men believed widows incapable of talking over financial matters impersonally, that one reason for their distrust was due to woman's tendency in a crisis to fall back upon her womanhood—even to trade upon it—and to refuse to meet an issue straight, like a man. If she was exceptionally intelligent, she would learn that man and woman could never meet as equals, but most widows would be only instinctively aware of this fact without knowing the cause for it. This was why so often they used the weapon of sex to fight their battles. But a wise widow did not, as a rule, try to fight her way against the current of opinion held by friends and family unless love for her husband gave her unusual strength of soul. That such a gentle creature as the wife of Essex could hold out two years against another marriage, urged by her family and frowned on by the wavering common people who had idolized her husband, speaks much for her devotion to him. In her place most widows would have followed the dictates of those who felt responsible for guiding them through the crisis of bereavement.

Now, if a widow thought of the perplexities she had faced as a young bride, how small and trifling were they likely to seem in comparison with those she must brace herself to meet presently. Changes wrought by death might try the souls of men, but they brought havoc into the lives of women born and reared to the belief that a wife's whole life was centered in the home. But life about her was geared to mutability. Stoically, if not heroically, she must bury the past, or seem to do so, and meet the present and its future with grace and ease and a smiling composure. To do this her whole life had been more or less conditioned: to meet each crisis as it came, sternly or gracefully. So she brings serenity to her features, she lifts her head and veils her eyes in an obedient smile, and once more she is ready to step into the new-old role demanded of her. She is ready to take the vows of love and obedience "till death do us part."

Henry E. Huntington Library

The bellman, from *The Belman of London*, by Thomas Dekker, 1608

CHAPTER VIII

ELIZABETHANS AT HOME

The man that hath no music in himself,
Nor is not mov'd with concord of sweet sounds,
Is fit for treasons, stratagems, and spoils;
The motions of his spirit are dull as night,
And his affections dark as Erebus;
Let no such man be trusted.

THE MERCHANT OF VENICE, V:i:83–88

AITH in home and faith in music—music that set in motion the smallest orb in the whole wide world till it sang its own song attuned to the "quiring" of angels—these were the two faiths by which most thoughtful Elizabethans sought to order their private lives. If music bound round the universe to make of it one harmonious whole, then man must let music creep into his ears till he, like the stillness of night or the very smallest activities of day, was touched by its immortal sounds. Although these faiths in home and music did not fully arm Elizabethans against the usual frailties of human beings, they did produce a manner of living to inspire any age. This was particularly true of those who, though they felt the urge to better their lot by the acquisition of worldly goods, still recognized the fact that life need not make man a prisoner to his accumulated wealth. To them life was a great storehouse of worldly and spiritual goods, and the wise ones sought a temperate balance of the two.

But not all were wise. Poised at the lips of a scarlet trumpet flower nodding above the motionless shadow of the enemy, a hummingbird thrusts its bill deep into the nectar it finds there, stored seemingly for its own particular use. With the same assurance an Elizabethan often drew upon the sweets of the world made known to him by discovery of new lands and new inventions and new learning, and felt himself the special recipient of this garnered wealth. Just as the bird holds its position in mid-air by means of its rapidly whirring wings until the swifter motion of the beast stills those wings forever, so by use of their intelligence or wit, some Elizabethans struggled to maintain a measure of stability while gathering treasure from their storehouses till, vain of their achievement, they ventured too far and lost all. But even for them the heart of their world, whether stable or uncertain, was the home in which they had their being. Here they centered their hopes, their affections, and their ambitions. Here they built their treasure house in which to display the evidence of their achievements, and here were the hearths at which their children played, assuring them of the continuation of their name and its proud significance.

Every age is more or less transitional and formative, but such was particularly true of the sixteenth century. Much of its distinctive energy, of course, came from the past, but it also impregnated future generations with elements that are still potent. Many of our ideas and movements originated among our Elizabethan ancestors. They, like us, were attempting to solve problems that are always present in a new era. They, despite their remarkable integrating powers, were often reckless in their nonconformity, and this spiritual instability revealed itself even in the family life, in the privacy of their luxurious surroundings, in the performance of their family social obligations, but most of all, in the extraordinary prodigality of their feasts and clothes.

Many an Elizabethan stood bewildered before the mysterious questions of existence and significance. Many a man then trembled as the life he had known crumbled at his feet, destroying forever the security of place and position to which he had been accustomed. Despair or cupidity often caused such men to channel their energy anew in exploration of the unknown. They sent "scientific" expeditions to the very "edge" of the earth. These projected journeys across the deep were fearful speculations. They bent their efforts toward opening great deposits in the earth for their enrichment and power, they carried on destructive wars with their neighbors whom they considered the aggressors, and when time and opportunity met, they turned their attention to the discovery of strange new materials with which to house and clothe themselves sumptuously and with unparalleled comfort.

A sudden influx of wealth from fair and unfair ravages upon the world's El Dorados enabled some to gratify their expanding taste for luxury and splendor: hence the fabulous sums spent for gorgeous clothing, fantastic and colorful, with rich ornaments weighing down the stiffness of their costly silks and velvets, and perhaps the still more fabulous sums spent on elaborate ceremonies and feasts, to which they invited great companies of people. These fortunate ones built palatial homes, laid out gardens of intricate design with displays of rare plants and animals, and crowded color into their lives that they might dispel for a while the anxiety that came to cloud their thoughtful moments. Those with little or no riches at all, meanwhile, taxed their ingenuity to the utmost to follow the example of their ostentatious "betters."

Some, according to their taste, made use of whatever means they could to accent the voluptuous. Their very speech took on this quality, though among the cultivated it achieved, by a careful design of figure and antithesis and sentence structure, a beauty of form in spite of its sonorous bombast. But in the speech of the man in the street ran a current of vivid slang that has no counterpart unless in American slang today. Such expressions raced through their ballads and pamphlets and began a style of epithet and scornful abuse that sounds strangely familiar to readers of contemporary political news.

Although every period has its own extravagance and dissipation and vice, there is a peculiar quality in the weakness of people who feel the ground slipping from beneath their feet. The Elizabethans were no exception. Often they showed the tendency to drown fear in pleasure, to cast aside restraint for license, and license for wantonness. At such times the home was bound to be profoundly affected by the chaos around it. Thoughtful parents, sometimes in panic, asked how they could encourage intellectual freedom and at the same time help their children to remain untouched by immoral excess. They questioned whether it was even possible to teach their children to love the beautiful and still limit their delight in exuberant extravagance that too often prevailed in the new spirit of beauty. Elizabethans, when confronted by such problems, usually sought safety for themselves and their children in compromise.

Even at its best, however, compromise usually fell short of its aim. In Elizabethan efforts to achieve this mean, often in the same person there would exist the pattern of high, chivalrous conduct or paternal concern for the family, suddenly and painfully distorted by a hot passion or a cold, calculating greed. Such a person's temper or ambition ran too full, titillated by a restless energy that in its search for the new, the exotic, or the vigorous, depended too much upon wealth or power as a means of achievement. No wonder the literature of the age is full of conflicting thought and feeling—lilting in its lyric, passionate in its poetry, gorgeous in the pageantry of its masque, keen in its ballad satire, heavy in its didacticism of conduct books and sermons, searchingly skeptical in its private letters, but most of all, intense in its Shakespearean drama portraying misunderstandings between parents and children, husband and wife, brother and brother.

For always at the center of the social disorder which threatened at times to overwhelm these people stood the home. Some of its members might affect the popular melancholy pose, others might show a morbid interest in the horrors of death, some might seek frantically to recapture magical beauty and intense passion, and still others might pursue material pleasure in a reckless life of the senses. Yet always, in the whirlpool of these conflicting forces, was the steadying influence of the home, saving man from utter dissipation of his faculties. And where the home was, there was music also.

To music, Shakespeare paid high tribute. Nothing, he said, was so "stockish, hard, and full of rage" but that music in time would change its nature. Toward one not yet susceptible to its harmonizing influence, he urged caution. Thus in the play of *Julius Caesar*, he has the emperor doubt the loyalty of Cassius because this lean conspirator "hears no music." In *Measure for Measure*, Mariana, whose heart is heavy with grief, listens to her servant's song because she believes music has the power to "make bad good." Benedick in *Much Ado About Nothing* marvels that the strings of a musical instrument can "hale souls out of men's bodies," and the grief-stricken weakling, Richard II, orders music stopped because, he says brokenly, it "mads" him. Yet Brutus, whose nature is noble, depends on the power of music to quiet his troubled mind, and cannot bear to chide his weary servant who falls asleep over his instrument. Just as the child Montaigne was wakened of mornings with gentle music that he might be more susceptible to the instruction of the day, so the heroine in the play of *Cymbeline* is awakened by a morning serenade to make her more susceptible to her suitor's wooing. Shakespeare's audience probably liked to hear their beliefs about the power of music woven into the very structure of his plots. When songs, jigging tunes, serenades, or madrigals were forced into plays for their own sake, they merely touched the ear. Thoughtful Elizabethans liked to see music proved a touchstone of man's soul.

Most airs were accompanied by the music of the lute and were usually preferred to plain songs. The lute, an instrument of eight strings arranged and tuned in pairs, somewhat resembled the mandolin. When the strings were unfretted, they required retuning at every change of key. Since lute strings were expensive, a gift of them was a dainty present. Other instruments might accompany airs, but in the home the lute was so sweet and intimate in tone that it was highly favored, especially when the singer's voice was that of a young girl or boy. For more formal occasions, the madrigal was sung, as it was a continuous part song with interwoven themes for three or more voices. Such music was in much demand at banquets or where good voices got together to "harmonize." After dinner or supper in the hall or in the garden, there was likely to be a group who entertained themselves and others by this means if professional singers did not perform instead.

From 1560 on, pious homes of Puritans depended much upon the singing of psalms for their enjoyment of music, and this custom continued until long past the end of the sixteenth century. In the gardens, however, the singing was bound to be more informal, and there sweet voices sang to their hearts' content with or without accompaniment, unless the household was a very pious one. For formal entertainment of guests in the gardens of the cultivated Elizabethans, there might be instrumental music in the banquet house, either for its own sake or for those who wished to dance, and if the household had its own band of musicians, they were an important part of the establishment.

Strolling musicians were not in high repute, partly because the group often played upon similar instruments, monotonously; in this case they were referred to somewhat contemptuously as a *consort*. Sometimes a consort included one or two or even more unlike instruments to give variety to the music, though such a combination was frequently called *broken music*. One such group playing before the Queen consisted of a lute, a bandore, a cittern, a bass viol, and a flute. Occasionally a group of musicians might be called a *noise* regardless of the quality of sound they produced. Because musicians were easily obtainable singly or in groups, it was customary, even in taverns, to demand music at meals or to while away the weary hours. Fine inns, of course, had lute, bandore, and sometimes the virginal to entertain their guests. Since few households were so poor that among the servants no singers or musicians could be found to entertain master or mistress, music was a favorite means of relaxation for husband or wife. Indeed, as the mistress sat busily sewing with her maids, she often called upon one of them to entertain their group by singing or playing on some instrument, particularly the lute, which served double duty as instrument and decoration in the house. In Puritan homes, of course, the maid or the entire group would probably sing psalms.

Musical instruments were frequently used as house decorations. This was true of the virginal in particular, for it was an expensive instrument and was therefore a coveted possession. Those who could play on it were very proud of their accomplishment. The lute was easily mastered as it required only plucking of the strings, but the virginal had keys that had to be struck; they caused small quills to twang the strings, which produced high notes that, in spite of their small volume, were very pleasing to the keen Elizabethan ear. Queen Elizabeth played the virginal well enough to win the praise of foreign visitors who happened to hear her. They were also impressed with the sweet tones of the instrument, which had strings of gold or silver. Other music that might entertain royal visitors, or those of distinction waiting in great houses for an audience, came from an organ in an outer court. Again, there might be music suitable for an occasion from cornets, flutes, fifes, trumpets, viols, sackbuts, violins, harps, and boys' voices.

Even in modest homes, lovers of music might acquire several instruments for members of the family to play—viols, flutes, citterns, and even, in rare instances, the virginal or harpsichord. Music on these instruments would be played by note, and in a family possessing many instruments, there was sure to be a collection of books of music. But even more important than the musical instruments was the musical voice, of which there were many. Each village, for example, had its own choir as well as a team of bell ringers that was likely to be the chief pride of the community. In the home, when guests were dined, they were expected to contribute to the madrigal singing between courses or at the end of the meal. Then the mistress of the house would bring out the music books, and each guest received the part he could sing. He was expected to read the music at sight. It was not written in scores for such occasions, but in parts for the voices that were to make harmony in the madrigal, and there might be as many as eight different parts.

When a modest householder wished a lute, he ordered one from a craftsman, who would inquire about the size, the kinds of wood he was to use, and the ornaments he was to add. If a real music lover was ordering an instrument for himself, he might arrange for intricate decoration, such as carving in the geometrical roses or sound holes that could become very artistic under the skilled fingers of the craftsman. As a rule the lute was a large instrument, and always it was pear-shaped with a long neck. A particularly prized possession might have the back made of small strips of wood glued together in an artistic manner. If the person wished an instrument with a somewhat more brilliant tone, he would be likely to order a cittern, which was made with a flat back and was played by plucking its strings with a small piece of ivory or metal held between the thumb and index finger. The pandora, somewhat like the cittern, had a deeper pitch, and its strings might be of steel instead of gut. For the intimate music in the home, the stringed instruments, of course, were in high favor.

The recorder, a forerunner of the flute, was popular for its variety in pitch—somewhat regulated by its size—and for the ease with which it could be carried about. It was an open pipe with a number of finger holes, and the larger ones were fitted with one or more keys to lower the pitch. Such an instrument was made of ebony or some similar type of hardwood. Viols came in different sizes also, and were called by different names, the treble and bass viols occurring most often in lists referring to this type of instrument. The treble viol was very popular because it blended well with other instruments. It was very much like the violin, particularly in the easy way it fitted into the crook of the bent arm. Its upper strings could produce clear, penetrating notes, and the lower strings, notes of deep, almost tragic intensity. The bass viol was pitched far lower than the treble viol and was a larger instrument, up to four feet in length, held between the knees as the musician sat while playing it.

If a family had a harpsichord or virginal, it was quite likely to have girls to play such an instrument and to demonstrate they were very accomplished young ladies. Indeed, the virginal has been said to be so named because it was meant for young girls to play. Since it was usually played on a long table, it was kept in a case, which was often quite decorative with hand painting. The instrument and its case were usually referred to as a set. The girl stood while performing on it, even when legs were added to the case and the virginal took on the appearance of a piano or of the harpsichord, which became the forerunner of the grand piano. The harpsichord's strings were also plucked by quills, with two or three or even four strings to a note, but its greater number of strings and its more complicated mechanism gave it a shape that the Germans called *Flügel* because it looked somewhat like the wing of a bird. Its bass strings were longer than those of the virginal and had to be strung in a harplike frame, and as the instrument developed, its keyboards increased in number to as many as three. The upper row or rows of keys acted upon one string each, and the keys of the lower row on two strings each. Though the touch of the fingers might control the tone a little, the material of which the jacks were made was far more effective in this matter. Since the harpsichord was such a prized instrument, its case or exterior was beautifully decorated by the best of skilled painters, and as a handsome piece of furniture it might well become a household god like the virginal.

All through the Tudor age, however, singing voices of fine quality were always in such demand that England became famous for its choirs of sweet singers. Such voices in Henry VIII's choir were said to sound like angels in glorious harmony. His love for vocal and instrumental music led him to write ballads and masses which he set to music and played on recorders, flutes, virginals, and the organ. He also introduced the first Italian masque at court because of its emphasis on music, and he whiled away many hours inventing musical instruments with which to delight his own ears as well as to satisfy his inventive and artistic powers. But Henry loved fine voices so much that the demand for them in England became urgent and remained so during the century. Fathers of sons gifted with beautiful voices might profit from having their sons actually impressed into service in nobles' bands of entertainers when important lords and ladies were to be received as guests at the great houses.

Yet some fathers had cause to be shocked at the practice, especially when a gentleman's son was kidnapped on his way to school in 1600, and was not released till after two days of anxious negotiating on the part of the father. Such high-handed methods were possible only because the Master of the Children of the Chapel had secured a patent which was used to impress boys to play at Blackfriars Theatre. The son with a fine singing voice, therefore, might cause some parents grave fears, although his gift might arouse the cupidity of others. If, after the voice changed, the boy could not continue to sing his way into favor and fortune, he might become a page, and eventually a servant of considerable importance. Or he might be retained in a company of actors, with whom he could make a good living for himself provided he had a good head on his shoulders. To Puritans, of course, such a career was unthinkable.

During cold, unpleasant weather all entertainment for the household took place in the great hall or long gallery. Battledore or shuttlecock (somewhat like badminton) whiled away many long hours, as did "troll madame," in which the ball was rolled (trolled) along a board with holes at the ends. However, if the master of the house had a band of musicians, they were likely to be kept busy at this time of year playing for dancing by old and young between supper and bedtime. At these dances the young men at home dressed very simply in doublets with sleeves puffed at the elbow, the trunks paned, the hose cross-gartered, and the soft collar of fine lawn lace-edged. The maids were also simply dressed with tight bodices, full sleeves, and very full skirts. These in-

formal dances were lively enough to require an ease and freedom of movement that formal dress would make difficult.

Elizabethans enjoyed several kinds of dances, from the stately, slow
steps of the pavan to the galliard and lavolta, so popular among the upper
classes. The common people, of course, enjoyed romping dances, especially the morris dances performed, as a rule, by professionals. In the
simplest form of the galliard the pattern consisted of five steps, a beating
of the feet together, and a leap into the air, all done briskly in triple time.
Its five steps also gave it the name of cinquepace, and its leap was called
the cabriole or caper. Eventually this dance became full of "tricks and
turns," as its new steps and modifications were called. The waltzlike
lavolta performed by two persons could be danced somewhat like the
galliard with high leaping. When the man lifted his partner high into
the air to rousing tympanic effects, there was much gay laughter. Such
romping was severely criticized by foreigners and staid Englishmen, especially Puritans, but the Queen was enchanted by it. Other lively jigging
dances were the coranto and the Spanish canary.

When professionals danced the morris, they provided such intricate
steps and wore costumes so elaborate as to delight the common people
beyond measure. This tended to make the sophisticated regard them
with contempt. Shakespeare also provides good-natured ridicule of the
country dancers' delight in the footing of the "Saltiers" at the sheep-shearing festival in *The Winter's Tale*. The dramatist describes them clad in
goatskins, the men pretending to be satyrs as they pranced about, and one
of them exercising such skill at leaping that he can jump twelve and a
half feet "by the squire [foot rule]." Such dancing in imitation of the
elaborate steps in masques and anti-masques at the great houses was as
amusing, supposedly, as the performance of rude mechanicals putting
on a play.

Since the country lout has always been the butt of the city man's mirth,
the rural dancing provoked indulgent smiles from city cousins witnessing
such frolics. Yet they themselves were not above the criticism of others,
especially when they indulged in the freedom provided by the masque,
whether performed in the great hall or in gay carnival along the streets.
Shylock, for example, well illustrates the moral soul that beheld such
merrymaking with disgust, referring to the "vile squeaking" of the "wry-
neck'd fife" and the Christian "fools with their varnish'd faces." He asks
his daughter, therefore, to stop his "house's ears" lest some "sound of
shallow foppery" enter the casements of his decent "sober house."

No matter how much the older Elizabethans might enjoy dancing,
they could not keep pace with the young; as they watched the lively
dances of their children and friends, therefore, they found a great deal
of pleasure in smoking. Like many other fads, smoking was first introduced to society by court gallants who had hired "professors" to teach
them to "drink" tobacco. By such instruction, they learned to blow smoke

into shapes of bells, rings, and long tubes. Then snuff taking became as popular as smoking, partly because it was not so expensive. Of course, there was much disapproval of the "filthy extravagance" of using tobacco, one father going so far as to state in his will that if ever one of the heir's sisters or brothers found him smoking, his inheritance was to be revoked. Batty's *The Christian mans Closet* considered smoking cause enough to disinherit a son, and a year after James I came to the throne, he published his *Counterblast* against the use of tobacco.

There were a good many people who, like James, believed tobacco was bad for the body and soul. In 1601, a book entitled *Work for Chimney Sweepers* declared that tobacco dried up the natural moisture of the body and caused sterility, rheums, and "infinite maladies." Among the last were included vomits, many stools, great gnawings, cold extremities, cramps, convulsions, sweats, bad color, defects in feeling, sense, and understanding, loss of sight, giddiness, and in some cases a hasty death. Worst of all, however, it was thought to cause melancholy, which became so corrosive that it inflamed the brain, making it hard and dry and sapping all its moisture necessary for life and health. Six months later this work was answered by *A Defence of Tobacco*, which declared smoking was not unprofitable as a physic; moreover, it left the throat and nostrils so clean it could not hurt the brain.

All this discussion naturally interested the women, and since fine ladies at court could afford such extravagance as smoking, they made it a delicate pastime by using pipes with long stems and silver bowls. These they smoked "abroad" as well as at home, and often urged their lovers to smoke by offering them with "their own fair hands" such pipes of tobacco. Some doctors began to prescribe smoking as a cure-all, and almost immediately grocers as well as apothecaries began to carry tobacco in stock. Tobacco shops sprang up and increased so rapidly in number that soon there were seven thousand of them in London alone. For the poor, however, smoking was a real luxury to be enjoyed sparingly or not at all. Still, tobacco came to mean a great deal to the Elizabethan who found it a means of withdrawing quietly to his own apartments or to the garden or banquet house where he might indulge in a pipe with his own thoughts. The young people who had used tobacco as a fad soon found it to be more rewarding in solitude than in company. But youth seeks company, and when other diversions proved to be more entertaining than the pipe, they left it with comparative ease and went on to more exciting adventures.

Their elders, meanwhile, found recreation in the banquet house and the quiet retreats of arbored walks, and settled themselves to card playing, which, now that they had the pipe, was much more diverting than before. Even the poor played cards or dominoes or checkers (which they called draughts), but they were usually denied the excitement of gambling with cards, which was considered one of the chief English vices. The English gambled at every opportunity, and then made more opportunities for gambling. The element of chance in cards especially appealed to them in such games as primero, played for high stakes, and backgammon in its various adaptations, such as tables and tick-tack. Dice also attracted them in such games as one-and-thirty, novum, and tray-trip. Players interested in testing their own skill at checkmating their opponent usually played chess and took great pride in possessing beautifully carved chessmen. When young people played cards, they nearly always played for gain, though if they were too poor to do so, they enjoyed the competitive element of matching wits at cards only when the weather did not permit games outdoors to test their strength or physical fitness.

For such a purpose tennis was in high favor by those who could afford the fragile leather balls stuffed with hair. Chamberlain writes Carleton on November 8, 1598, that John Vernon of Hodnut, Shropshire, lost 18,000 crowns at tennis in Paris. Such great losses from the game were incurred in gambling, of course, as Henry V's acknowledgment of the "tun of treasure" in tennis balls sent him by the Dauphin, indicates:

> His present and your pains we thank you for.
> When we have match'd our rackets to these balls,
> We will, in France, by God's grace, play a set
> Shall strike his father's crown into the hazard.

I: ii: 260–63

Nevertheless, as this present also indicates, the fragile balls did not last long in the game, and a large amount of them would be a very fine present. That the Dauphin accompanied his gift with a stinging rebuff made France the aggressor in the ensuing war, and Henry's punning, two-edged wager to strike the French crown into the "hazard" returned bombastic insult for arrogant insult.

Besides tennis there were other competitive sports for young men, such as wrestling, leaping, and running. Many games long popular among children were played by young men and women who had the leisure and the inclination for such pastimes. They included run-sheep-run, prisoner's base, hide-and-seek, blind man's buff, fox and geese, etc. City dwellers in modest homes with gardens restricted in size sometimes tried to adapt games to their home surroundings, but when they wished strenuous exercise, they went out to open spaces that would accommodate them. Here they played some type of ball game (football, arm ball, handball), or tested their skill at archery, throwing javelins or stones, or just running and leaping. Some of these games, like football, might involve large groups of people, even whole villages.

In winter, when the moor north of London was frozen over, the common people skated. Tying bones to their feet and under their heels, they pushed themselves along with a little piked staff. This sort of skating was not limited to Londoners only, but could be enjoyed wherever sufficient ice occurred. On the rare occasions when rivers froze over, ice

The archer, from the frontispiece of *The Arte of Archerie*, 1634

The title page from *The famous game of Chesse-play*, 1614

Whipping vagabonds, from Harmon's *Caveat*, 1573

If on your man you light
The first draught shall you play,
If not tis mine by right
At first to lead the way

games were freely indulged in by those who could withstand the cold. In the raw days of early spring, spinning tops was often enjoyed by men as much as by boys. In fact, many parishes kept a huge top to be whipped by the unemployed that they might keep themselves warm by the exercise, and also keep out of mischief. A long whip was used to keep the top spinning.

Under the Tudors archery was always a sport, but since it was compulsory, it was not likely to be enjoyed so much for its own sake. From seven on, a boy had to be trained by his father till he could handle the bow and arrows adequately and so meet the demands of the law of 1541. According to this law, each man over seventeen was to keep in his possession a bow and arrows with which to meet the enemy in case of sudden attack. By 1588, however, most Londoners were equipped with firearms, though rural areas continued to use the longbow. In order to keep the practice of archery from declining, most parishes were provided with butts and marks which were erected at public expense and located in a convenient open place. While interest in this sport was fed by concern about foreign invasion, public-spirited citizens often contributed valuable prizes to winners in contests. Along with such displays of skill went pageants and festive celebrations. Elizabeth encouraged this sport by becoming a fair marksman with the bow and arrow as she hunted deer, and caused the ladies to try to match their skill with hers. Though she must of necessity be surpassed by no one, still she tried to keep the love of the game high, even after she was convinced that archery was to be replaced by firearms and that there was much evasion of the archery laws.

When the village green was not occupied with dancers or people engaged in games or sports during leisure hours, it might be used for bowling by the common people. In the fine gardens attached to great houses there were delightful bowling alleys where both men and women enjoyed the sport, and such luxuries probably increased the common man's interest in it. Ninepins was a popular game everywhere, and so were tipcat (a boys' game of sticks that could be dangerous when boisterously played) and stool-ball, a sixteenth-century game of cricket, also played by women. The simplicity of many of these games is illustrated by tipcat, which required merely a stick or bat and another stick pointed at both ends. After the pointed stick was either thrown into the air or batted in such a way as to make it spring up, it had to be kept moving through the air to a distance by means of the batting stick. Common people got as much exhilaration from this game as the rich did from tennis, which with its expensive courts and stringed rackets and fragile, expensive balls limited it to nobles and kings or the very rich.

There was often no little resentment by the poor against the nobles who indulged their passion for hunting to the extent of enclosing fields once cultivated by the poor for farm products, and who even went so far as to enclose whole parishes that they might have room for chasing the deer. Coursing was also a popular sport for those who could afford it, but devastating to the crops if the hares decided to take to cultivated land and the hounds hotly pursued them there. Since this sport required greyhounds that ran by keeping the prey in sight instead of following the scent, the hunters, too, in their excitement might do much damage to the poor man's fields. When country gentlemen got their exercise by riding at the quintain with lances and poles instead of chasing game over the countryside, the poor must have sighed with relief. However, this sport was usually a part of holiday festivities to which the tenantry were invited by the masters. Then, indulgently, the gentry could watch the clumsy performers, who might include anyone able to sit a horse and foolish enough to believe he could avoid the resounding whacks of the sandbag or dummy figure with its shield and sword on the turning cross-piece. Toward it they spurred their horses and leveled their lances, and provided laughter for all. Men afoot sometimes played the game of hurling darts at the quintain. So popular was this means of amusement that it continued to liven festivities on country estates long after Elizabethans were no more.

Strenuous sports belonged to cool weather as a rule. Such, for example, were the football contests held around Shrovetide or in the fall when the husky lads and men of a village came forth to do or die. It was a rough game with no set rules; a person merely had to be able to stay on his feet and kick the ball. Consequently many hard knocks were given and received, and the contestants usually scored according to their endurance against mud and blows and general rough tumbling and running after the ball. At home once more they might also tax the patience and skill of the good housewife who must heal their bruises and sometimes set broken bones.

Whitsuntide, with its usually fine weather and spirit of hilarity, found crowds of people leaving their homes to gather at various towns and villages to engage in sports and contests or merely to watch the performers. Now, under the supervision of an elected king or queen, the contests were eagerly followed, for coursing matches were likely to be held, and hurling or hockey matches included all able-bodied people wishing to take part. Of course there would be wrestling, cudgel-playing, running, and leaping contests, and throwing the hammer, but most important of all would be the morris dancers without whom no celebration for the common people would be complete. The church must have an ample supply of ale by means of which it raised funds for the needs of the parish. But in the country, the sheep-shearing festival, if the yield had been good, was filled with the highest carnival gaiety, partly because it was a gathering at home where hospitality was warm and hearty.

In midsummer the middle-class young people of towns and villages spent much time walking about the streets unless forbidden by their par-

ents. Girls in the stricter and better families were expected to take their
exercise in their gardens, and were not permitted the pleasure of going
along the streets idly. Holidays and Sundays, however, were devoted to
no little strolling about, even some of the older people going to see plays
out of church hours or to baitings or to enjoy the sports, rough or otherwise, which moralists so heartily condemned. William Prynne's *A Briefe
Answer to Some Materiall Passages, in a late Treatise of the Sabbath-day*
(1636) mocked bitterly those who strutted about in their finery on Sunday, attending plays after the noonday meal, indulging in excessive drinking, or engaging in such sports as casting stones, running, shooting, tossing the "light and windy ball," wrestling, or fencing. He complained
that if they did not go "abroad," they spent their time just as badly at
home either at cards or sitting before their doors backbiting or quarreling.
The young he accused of making illicit love at dances, and he referred
especially to their abuse of the "joyful feast of John the Baptist," when
bonfires were lighted at night and in all the towns the young people
danced through the streets with wreaths in their hands. He scorned their
superstitious throwing of these wreaths into the flames while they spoke
"solemn prayers" to drive away all their ills. Most Puritan criticism fell
as heavily on one innocent amusement as another.

Londoners, of course, were criticized most of all for spending so much
time on the streets. But when one considers the spectacles Queen Elizabeth gave her people here as well as in the country when she went on
progress, one can understand why Elizabethans flocked to see these parades. Mayors of cities followed Elizabeth's example by staging pageants
when they were elected to office. Hadn't Elizabeth always delighted in
opening Parliament by throwing a red velvet cloak over her rich attire
and placing her crown on her bright hair before she stepped into the coach
or litter that was to carry her through the streets? On such occasions her
solemn maids of honor, in single file, rode behind her on their gor-
geously caparisoned horses, their beautiful gowns sparkling with colorful
adornment that must always accentuate but never surpass that of the
Queen. As the procession passed fine dwellings decked with gay banners,
the householders and their crowding friends greeted it joyously.

Whenever a tilt-yard show was to occur, the common people thronged
to see the pageant connected with it. Fortunate indeed were those who
could watch it from windows instead of being jostled by the milling
crowds. Knights with a sense of humor might vie with one another in
taking off popular characters from the old mystery plays or from marvelous travel tales. One, for example, might attach golden hair to his
helmet and hang apples on his armor to represent Eve, or another might
dress like a savage from Africa or the New World, with strange emblems
of moon or star on his forehead. Small wonder the Puritans objected to
the spirit and extravagance of these parades calling the people from the
sober pattern of domestic life, especially when the exhibits included ex-

pensive floats representing some event of biblical or lay history or even a military victory of the Christians over the Turks.

They had more cause to object to the extravagance of the tilt itself, with the knights' rich livery and impressively caparisoned horses. One of Sir Christopher Hatton's suits for this purpose was white with gilt bands of ornament and strings of roses and knots; another was russet with gold bands and lozenged designs between the bands, and a breast-plate of brilliant decorations. Each knight was expected to use a predominant color for his suit and for his horse's outfit. Such splendor fired the hearts of some eligible young men who wished by this means to prove their valor, but it also attracted the interest of maids who loved display and longed for an opportunity to leave the guardianship of their homes for possibly the less strict guardianship of great court ladies willing or unwilling to chaperone them through this part of their social training.

Like her father, Elizabeth loved the tilt, and in 1562 she revised the old medieval rules of combat. The lists must be sixty paces long and forty wide, running east and west, with a gate at each end. The knights were to be known as challengers and defendants, and their pledges or hostages were to remain in the royal box till redeemed by their champions. The challenger usually arrived at the east gate, where he was asked why he had come and by what name he was called. His answer, according to form, gave his name and the cause for his coming "armed and mounted to perform." Then he gave the name of the defendant whom he challenged in order to "acquit" his pledge, whom he named. To identify the challenger, the constable opened the knight's visor, and then signified he recognized him. Now the defendant came to the west gate, and was duly identified. Both men's lances were then measured by the constable, who swore them to their oaths, the challenger reiterating the truth of his challenge and "swearing" by the "Holy Evangelists." Both knights gave their pledge that they had no unlawful weapons like enchantments, and both declared they trusted in God alone.

Now the heralds cleared the lists and asked the spectators not to take sides. As the knights took their proper position, the constable came forward and cried out three times, "Let them go!" shouting on the third, "Let them go and do their best!" Riding full tilt at each other, the knights did not give up till they or their horses or their spears were spent, endeavoring to prove all the while, according to Castiglione's ideal in *The Courtier*, that "the beauty of chivalry" rested indeed in "the noblest persons." Moreover, Henry VIII had set up a challenging standard for the knight: often he had ridden seven courses at single tilting and later engaged in the violent charge of all jousters with their opponents. Though the common man must content himself with the parade, he might dream of the glories of this tilt-yard performance, and with no compunction at all he would declare to anyone who might listen which knights were best and which would be victorious. If he was young and ambitious and aggressive, he might, with fortune's help, become a witness someday to such a thrilling sight, if not a participant in it.

In spite of the fact that those Elizabethans who did not have the spacious rooms and gardens and playgrounds of the rich were often compelled to seek their amusement and relaxation outside of the family circle, it is amazing to find so much rollicking entertainment in most sixteenth-century homes. Not only did they feel dependent on the home for their pleasures; they wished to make their homes the center of their merrymaking.

On New Year's Eve people ushered in the year by drinking one another's health. In villages, bands of young men sang wassail along the street, and then visited the farmers to ask a blessing on basket and bin, on larder, dairy, beehives, stock, stacks, and haymows. In the towns and cities, those who ventured abroad in the dark streets found the doors of their friends' homes open to them at midnight for general rejoicing, but on the morrow their own homes were first in their minds and hearts. Here was feasting, with guests adding to the number at table, and all quarrels and even debts put aside for a week. One means of increasing the merriment was to provide special wooden trenchers with witty epigrams carved on the under side, each verse adapted to the individual or some incident in his life that could bring laughter. As soon as guests were seated, therefore, they turned up their trenchers to see what was written thereon. Gifts were exchanged as they are today at Christmas, and consisted of anything from capons, wine, and food delicacies to gloves, clothes, and furniture. At court, the members gave Elizabeth what they could afford, and more, usually in the form of money or jewelry. She in turn gave silver plate, the pieces ranging in weight from fifty to a hundred ounces, and she entertained these people at great feasts consuming tons of butter, eggs, cheese, game, etc.

But throughout all the holiday entertainment, home was the setting and the impetus to all the most enjoyable festivities. It was also a time when those away from home must be remembered. The Earl of Shrewsbury in a letter to his son Gilbert indicates the thoughts and feelings roused in him by New Year's. He has received a letter from his son, and now he will write the first letter of this day in answer to it, wishing him to observe "this New Year and many years after to God's glory and fear of Him" that he may live in the credit of his ancestors. To do so will make him "faithful, loyal, and serviceable to the Queen's Majesty," who to himself "under God is the King of Kings and the Lord of Lords." Now he turns to more personal matters. His own gift to his son is a promise to supply all his needful wants, and so long as he sees that "carefulness, duty, and love" of the son for him remain as they have been, he promises that his purse and all he has will be as free to him as to himself. He excuses himself for his brief letter by saying time is so short and so many are coming to him with gifts that he cannot write more but he sends his thanks for the son's gift of a perfumed doublet. He closes by praying God to bless his son on this New Year's Day of 1574, and signs himself "Your loving father."[1]

The time of St. Agnes' Eve, January 20–21, was likely to be cold and dreary, but it meant much to a maid who had marked the night for dreams of her future husband. The conditions for this joy were not easy to meet in homes that provided little or no privacy. First, the maid must pray alone. If she was a wealthy man's daughter, she might go alone to the family chapel, but if she was of the common class and was well cared for, it was difficult for her to go to a church alone. Then the maid must go supperless to bed, and on the way thither look neither to right nor left, and never behind her. She must utter no word to a soul about her, and this was next to impossible since she was expected to sleep with a sister or servant. Having reached her bed without violating any of the conditions, and having fallen asleep praying, she might well dream of the man she was to marry. Today, with homes commonly providing more privacy than even rich Elizabethans could hope for, such a superstition has lost about all its romantic appeal.

Elizabethan maids looked forward to St. Valentine's Day because of the excitement of being squired to some festivity by a man drawn by lot. Did they cheat at drawing lots? Did they know for whom their gifts were made? For these girls must reward their escorts suitably: the poor maid might give a ribbon or a posy, but the rich girl, a jeweled "trifle." Wives presented their husbands with some of their handiwork, such as embroidered bands, and poets wrote sonnets to their ladies, but more often, perhaps, to the ladies whose lovers paid handsomely for their verses.

Shrove Tuesday was often celebrated energetically at the boys' schools, where tossing the pancake was a hilarious occasion; but at home the family might also enter into the spirit of the day, when all ate as many pancakes as possible against the self-denial of Lent to begin on the morrow. All the eggs and fats and grease drippings could now be consumed in poor homes that were usually sparing of these tasty bits, for the religious household was to forego all rich foods till Easter Sunday. Preparation for the forty lean days of Lent, therefore, usually consisted of as much feasting as possible on Shrove Tuesday in schools and homes of both rich and poor. Finally, on Good Friday, no one would partake of fish or flesh but set his thoughts on the feast for the following Sunday with its paschal eggs, veal, lamb, wild fowl, salmon, and March hares. The effect of the whole family's acting as a unit in the Lenten season gave these days a particular importance.

When spring and May Day arrived, even the best homes reflected

---

[1] Maud Stepney Rawson: *Bess of Hardwick and Her Circle* (1910), p. 109.

a spirit of revolt against the musty routine of everything connected with
winter. Now the rooms could be freshened with clean rushes and May
flowers, and who but the young people should gather the flowers growing in meadows and spring woods. There was all the excitement of the
Maypole and of choosing the May queen, there were morris dancers in
towns and villages that could afford to attract such performers, and in
London and large towns there were feasting and revelry in all the gathering places out of doors. It was carnival time again, and such high carnival as had not been enjoyed since Christmas. Besides the usual contests
of skill, there was everywhere the joy of music and laughter and dancing.

Before dawn eager souls were astir, as the morning dew must be
gathered for beauty lotions and the girls must bathe their faces in this
dew to make them charm-proof against blight. Then the Maypole must
be brought home by twenty to forty oxen, their horns tipped with flowers,
and the people would crowd about, dancing along as the beasts dragged
their trophy to the village green. The pole itself must be covered with
flowers and herbs and bound round with ribbons, or painted, and when
set up, must have handkerchiefs flying at the top. Soft greens must be
strewn under the pole to make pleasant dancing, arbors must be set up
near the pole, and the homes as well as the town hall must be decked with
birch boughs and green tree branches. Now came the procession with the
gorgeous lord and lady of May, riding in the midst of playing minstrels.
Then the dancing would begin.

Attired in their best and most colorful garments, they romped
through the old country dances and the new ones. Rarely did their celebration end before the time of evensong. The best performer was the
one who could lift his lady highest off the ground, or who could cross his
legs twice in a pirouette before he touched the ground. Among the morris
dancers, who numbered as many as the community could afford, were
the Negro, the Moor, the hobbyhorse, the dragon, Friar Tuck, Little
John, and Maid Marian, all producing pantomime of remarkable execution, but of these the hobbyhorse was by far the most popular. It was
formed by a man inside a frame fitted with the head and tail of a horse,
and with trappings reaching to the ground, thus hiding the feet as the
man pranced and curvetted about. Like all performers, he had bells tied
to his costume, often at the legs. Since these bells were of different sizes
and tones, they were known as the fore bell, the second bell, and the
treble, mean, tenor, bass, and double bells. They contributed immeasurably to the dance.

Foreigners from the sunny countries of southern Europe could not
understand why the English celebrated the coming of spring with so
much hilarity. They could not realize that as they threw wide their windows on a sunny May day they were simply intoxicated by the warm
spring air. Nor could the moralists feel their extravagant joy. These
sober ones could only complain of how old men and wives as well as

young men and maids ran to the woods, groves, and hills to spend the night before May Day in pleasant dalliance, and then rushed forth in the dawn to gather dew. Such critics could no more understand the thrill of the defeated dragon hissing and flapping his great wings in the May Day procession as a sign of spring's triumph over cruel winter than they could comprehend why staid merchants would turn over as much as ten pounds of their hard-won profits for a slip from a foreign rose, phenomenal for its coloring and numerous petals. Perhaps only a Shakespeare could make clear why the common people and the privileged classes turned to fields and woods and gardens for most of their entertainment outside the home. Because he did understand the pull of his countrymen's heartstrings, he had Duke Theseus, who in *A Midsummer Night's Dream* is the soul of proper decorum, say briefly to the furious father finding his daughter asleep with her lover in the wood, "No doubt they rose up early to observe the rite of May" (IV:i:136–37).

Midsummer Eve, or St. John's Eve, came on the twenty-third or twenty-fourth of June, when the days were long and sultry. Its origin was the Vigil of St. John the Baptist, and although observed in London with rich pageantry and merrymaking that mingled sacred and legendary and traditional observance, its ceremony of feasting and gorgeous display in pageantry was known all over Europe from Scotland to Spain. Expanded by civic pride, it was finally regulated in London by city ordinance; even then, however, it became so burdensome financially that it had to be suppressed, although eventually many of its rites survived in the November pageant of the Lord Mayor's show. Since, as in Hallowe'en, the vigil was important, Midsummer Eve abounded with many superstitious practices. For example, on this night souls of those who were to die during the year were thought to leave their bodies and wander sadly to their final resting place. If sleepless watchers could prevent the journey, death might be cheated of some of its victims. The old pagan custom of midnight fires to celebrate the passing of the sun god through the highest point of the zodiac at the summer solstice was so adapted by Christians in the celebration of this eve that they too set fires on lonely hilltops and in crowded city streets. Daring individuals, as Prynne had complained in his *Treatise of the Sabbath-day*, would leap over these fires "to cleanse" their souls, not realizing the pagan influence in their act of "passing through fire."

There was much danger from these fires in the cities because of the very few conduits and individual wells. Each house, therefore, must keep a tub of water before its door, although many of the people in the homes were away, walking the lighted streets and making merry till dawn. Cutpurses and rogues taking advantage of the excitement and the individuals who might use this night to settle private grudges must be guarded against by enlarging the standing watch. In this addition of men to keep the peace in the streets and at the gates, there was much going to and fro, and finally the "marching watch" or Midsummer Watch was organized. During the reign of Henry VIII, who loved all this merry display, the marching watch became a splendid cavalcade of armed control. It was reviewed by the important members of government as it paraded before awestruck throngs, and was supposed to display the community's power and pomp as well as to restrain evildoers.

Sometimes in the pageants there were huge paste figures, stuffed out with brown paper and tow and armed at all points, and made to move as if marching. They alone would have enticed people from their homes, for they provoked joyous shouts at their approach. Since the parade took place at dusk, it was lighted with torches, called cressets. Town or city officials of London, wearing their richest parade garments, and accompanied by torch bearers and trumpeters, also graced the march. Sometimes in addition to their polished armor, the aldermen and attendants of high officials like the mayor would wear particolored red and white dress, with red on the right and white on the left, and again they would be all in white with a band of red. Thus they flaunted the city colors. In small towns and villages the people danced out the night on the village green or paraded about their fields with torches. In cities, the hours were not likely to run so long. Scotch farmers kept up the custom of this torch procession about their cornfields till late in the seventeenth century.

In London, the parade was most spectacular under the Tudors, and the peak of its entertainment lasted from eleven at night till two in the morning. The huge, armed giant-like figures, bowing and turning their heads amusingly, marched with archers, musicians, naked boys dyed black like devils, goading Pluto sitting under a canopy on a serpent spitting fire, and other spectacular pageantry with prophets, the Virgin, St. George and the dragon, a company of morris dancers, companies of armed men properly interspersed to keep the peace, and many musicians, the whole parade being climaxed by the imprisoned John the Baptist and then Herod at table with Herodias' daughter, a tumbler, and an executioner.[2] Such lavish display with its great expenditure of money caused the celebration to languish till Elizabeth revived it in 1585. Then birch boughs were brought to the city and sold for decorating the homes and other buildings, and the streets became a veritable bower.

Elizabeth excused her desire to outdo all previous midsummer watches by saying the parade would provide much work for the unemployed, who by now were one of her worst problems. Everyone, therefore, went willingly to work to revive old customs, to make new ones, and to surpass anything ever shown before in this parade. Every parish church, fraternity, and company took part in the effort. Lamps and cres-

[2] R. Liddesdale Palmer, *English Social History in the Making, the Tudor Revolution, 1485–1603* (1934), p. 125.

A picnic for a noble hunting party, from *The Noble
Art of Venerie*, by George Turberville, 1575

A fishing scene on a rich man's estate

sets were put in order, and fuel was collected for the bonfires. Bunting, buckram, silk, and canvas were sewn and draped over wagons and stages. The people, of course, prepared their homes for the celebration also, but watched with eager eyes when, after sunset, the bonfires were lighted in the streets. In spite of the precedence now taken by firearms over the English bow, marching men with weapons were divided accordingly. Those with the arquebus had flask, touchbox, match, powder, and a crested steel cap fastened under the chin. Those with bows had sheaves of arrows covered with red leather, swords, daggers, and red Scotch caps. Their coats of leather or quilted material had metal plates on the outside. The pikemen and halberdiers had corselets for back and chest, metal plates arming the hip and upper thigh, and their headpieces. The corporals, who held the marching line in order and kept the people back and prevented rioting, were dressed in comely hat, scarf, doublet, and fair hose, but no armor, though they carried sword, dagger, and partisan (a long-handled spear). By this display of military force, the wise Queen would quiet the people's fears, and perhaps her own, of the threatened Spanish invasion. For this reason the marching must be perfect in performance.

On the day before the event, therefore, all marching bands met at Moorfields at seven in the morning to parade and to be inspected by the officers. Old soldiers acted as instructors and kept the recruits at drill all day, teaching them how to wear their armor and how to march. The men with muskets had to be especially trained lest they blow up themselves and others. Finally they were dismissed with instructions to meet at five o'clock on the evening of the great day outside the Guildhall. But even then, before they were permitted to join the march, they had to be put through a hasty drill.

Meanwhile, the cressets or lights were a big problem too, for they had to be distributed along one side of the entire marching route, with one man to bear the light and one to bear his "cresset light stuff." The Guildhall and its companies had to bear the expense of all the cressets, and the beadle of each hall attended to the lights of his company. The whole watch had to be carefully organized by dividing it into "battles" (battalions) which were interspersed with pageants, and the cresset men had to be spaced equally along the entire route, the beadles seeing that no light was lacking all the night. When the companies of marchers were actually assembled in their proper marching order, they passed out Northgate of St. Paul's Churchyard into Cheap Street, led by Guildhall cresset men.

But this great spectacle was to involve every self-respecting household of the city, for the standing watch or police force had to be augmented lest the disorderly element take advantage of the occasion to plunder at will. Therefore each householder who had not shared in the expense of the marching watch now contributed what he could to the standing watch. If a servant could be spared, he was armed with corselet and halberd, and dressed according to instructions before he set out for his appointed place where the constables took charge. Each constable was attended by a page properly appareled and bearing his weapons as well as a cresset and drum or fife. In order to dignify their position and also their attitude toward it, the constables were required to swear to keep "well and truly" their town till the next "sun-rising." They must also swear not to enter any house without license or "cause reasonable." For all casualties of "fire, crying children," etc., they were to give due warning to "all the parties" required by each case, and they were to make search "of all manner of affrays, bloodsheds, outcries, and of all other things that be suspected." As they marched, the constables went three abreast, each with page, and posted themselves among the men along the marching route.

At such a time as this the Lord Mayor, with his three parties of escorts, was at his most imposing magnificence, and outside his house the band was carefully arranged. First came two cresset lights, then a company of morris dancers with twelve hobbyhorses in four ranks of three, and two sword players with large swords to make way through the crowds. Now came two more cresset lights, with two drums, a fife, and an ensign, forty-eight constables and their pages, three in a rank, and in their midst two drums, a fife, and an ensign. In the next group, one bearer of a cresset light marched in front, and one at the side of the pageant, followed by a sword player. Then came twenty-four grave personages wearing black velvet coats and hats, heavy gold chains, and gilt swords in velvet scabbards. They made a sharp contrast with the hobbyhorses as they rode solemnly on their small nags, three in a rank, with four trumpeters and choir children of the city. The sword player accompanying them was in fair armor, and was mounted on a great horse. Now, at last, came the Lord Mayor himself on a fair courser, with two spare horses, footmen, and staff torch-bearers, accompanied by a fife, a drum, an ensign, and thirty men in light armor, each man bearing a partisan, and in the middle of their marching ten ranks, a fife, a drum, and an ensign. It took six experienced soldiers to keep this band in order.

The hobbyhorses, more than the Lord Mayor, delighted the gaping crowd, however, for they were of pretty painted buckram or linen, and the boys "riding" them were armed with headpieces of pasteboard with strange designs, silvered over, and on their backs some device painted on linen or buckram. Each boy carried a little sword with an iron foil, and tried to obey instructions to prance his horse or stage a fight from time to time, six against six, in true form, but not hurting one another.

Other important personages besides the Lord Mayor were his two sheriffs, who were richly clothed and armored in red, white, and gold, with great plumes on their headpieces that stood up or fell down their backs. They attracted no little attention by making their horses rear and plunge. The leader of the watch was also an important figure in his jerkin of velvet or doublet of silk, his velvet hat, a silk scarf, a sword, a dagger, and a halberd. He rode a handsome horse, and was accompanied by two cressets and their bag-bearers of "cresset stuff."

It was all a splendid array that proclaimed what might be accomplished by an enthusiastic concerted effort, and it must have been as important as the Queen had hoped in giving the people confidence in the military power of their country. Yet with all this breath-taking spectacle for celebrating St. John's Eve, what intensified its effect after the marching was the individual's plans for the rest of the night—plans wrapped about with the hush and expectancy of the supernatural.

For more than branches of birch decorated the homes of the common people. Great care had been taken to collect rose and rue and fern seeds to provide their magic invisibility. During the late hours toward morning maids set up two fern fronds in a dish. If, at sunrise, the fronds leaned together, they knew their lovers were true, but if apart, they knew their love was doomed to disappointment. Above some doors were also placed branches of broom, fennel, St.-John's-wort, orpin, white lilies, and garlands of flowers to keep away evil spirits. And the house was kept fairly illumined by lamps of glass with oil burning in them that they might keep away evil ones unknown to the watch. But the solemn members of the household would sit with friends in porches of the parish churches, keeping one another awake and watching fearfully for the wraiths of those doomed to die. The "I saw it" or "I knew it" or "Do you remember" introducing mysteries of the past years were not the least of the melancholy delights which they derived from their vigils.

Wealthy households, on the other hand, were likely to be cheerful, and they set out decorative cressets, containing hundreds of lamps alight all at once. They also set out tables with sweetmeats and drink for the entertainment of friends who might stop by, or whom they asked to visit them after the march. Indeed, the people's preparations at home for the festive night had scarcely been surpassed even by the practice marching of the day before on Moorfields, and now that the celebrating was almost over, the Queen must have felt that this could be called the most brilliant St. John's Eve ever known in England. In their homes the people and their guests talked of the costumes and lights and pageantry, and said over and over again that the celebration had left nothing to be desired in the way of splendor and excitement. It had indeed provided the Queen and her people with that emotional outlet for the spirits checked or weighed down by the fear of the enemy just when they could respond most rapturously—on a night when nature itself was warm and lush and at the peak of its seductive attractiveness.

Michaelmas Day on September 29 was more closely connected with the home, however. In September the geese were at their best for feasts, and all homes that could afford a goose turned it on the spit before the fire. Now if ever the goose hung high, and the family sat down with eager appetites to a rich dinner with cakes and pies and puddings. There was the beautiful Michael, prince of all the angels, to thank for this day of good things, and as they enjoyed the bounty of their table, possibly they talked of some picture they had seen of this being, carrying his lance proudly against the dragon of evil.

But the goose was the main feature of still another feast, this one of St. Martin, who, while preaching, had been disturbed by a goose and had ordered it killed. The day of November 11, therefore, must be graced by a table as bounteous as that on Michaelmas Day. When gathering in the grain harvested in the fall, the drivers of the carts vied with one another to see who might receive the goose for not overturning his load of grain, and the lucky ones shared their goose prizes with high good nature amid the general merrymaking. Another celebration at this time of year was St. Catherine's Day, which, coming at apple harvest, provided this communal feast with beer and cider and much hilarity. November was always ushered in with much good cheer—the night of all the witches, the last night of October, having been transformed by the Church to All-hallow Eve, and celebrated by gay dancing around the communal fire. On November 1, All Saints' Day, came the drinking of healths and the feasting that continued, in a way, the revels of the night before. It was observed like St. Martin's Day on November 11, and was sometimes so called. In the country the pleasures of a well-laden table took the place of some of the city man's outdoor entertainments, but at times villagers had both.

Bull- and bear-baitings were attractions that villagers talked of long before they actually saw them, for news of these London entertainments had been carried to even the smallest hamlets. In 1588, much of England was still a wilderness of heath, turf, and marsh, its ten thousand parishes consisting of tiny rural communities with only about a hundred people to a village. In all England the population did not exceed five million people, and London was the only city of any size. Still, to a villager, the Elizabethan town that duplicated what it could of London's ways was very impressive, and when such towns could have their own baitings and the gambling that went with them, many villagers yearned to see these exciting events. Finally, at the wakes held annually to celebrate the dedication of a parish church, part of the entertainment consisted of the fight between a bear and mastiffs. When these fights became an important source of revenue to their promoters, every parish of any consequence obtained a bear and bear-warden to provide such excitement for the festivities which brought people from their homes, especially in fair weather, to towns and villages. Even private dedications calling for a celebration yielded to the demand for such contests, as some bears were actually loved like heroes for their stamina in beating off the fierce dogs trained to attack them.

Cock fighting also became popular because of the chances it provided for gambling and the near frenzy it aroused when the birds engaged in a fierce struggle. In the country the trained cocks were carried from one great house to another or from one successful contest to the next. Though there were laws against it, the people were so in love with the sport that they had their cock fights in spite of the restrictions. In London these fights were most frequently held on round straw-covered tables in an arena near Smithfield, with a charge of only a penny for admission as the people had to stand while watching the contest. The fierceness of the cocks was stimulated by brandy, and the eager watchers were influenced by ale as well as by the fight to bet heavily on their favorites. So much talk about these fights went the rounds that even children shared the excitement, and evolved their own sport called throwing a cockstele. Tying a cock to a stake, they threw a cockstele or stick at it till they knocked it down and killed it.

The parish wake was anticipated with delight by all the villagers, not only for its exciting sports and contests, but also for its miniature fairs and feasting. These fairs were intended to give all the people a chance to make the celebration an event of importance, for carts had to be decorated before they were loaded with the fresh rushes for the church floor, and musicians and dancers were to lead the cart procession. Then booths and stalls were to be set up close by, and sometimes they might be located in the very churchyard. If ale was to be sold to provide something needed for the church, he who could drink the most cups of it without getting drunk was the hero of the wake. Did the patron saint of the church in whose honor the wake originated smile or frown at this remembrance of himself? With none of these questions bothering them, the villagers entered the drinking contest with such a right good will that their efforts were highly conducive to the carnival spirit of the gathering. And in the booths were sweets and rich foods, as well as the usual items at fairtime, till feasting and drinking whirled the day to a dizzy conclusion.

Feasting was so heartily enjoyed, especially in the country, because it was hedged in by so many days of work that became monotonously dull. If the country gentleman took seriously the problem of managing his estates, he found his time well occupied with the multitudinous demands of his productive acres and the repairs of houses and outbuildings as well as overseeing the work of laborers and tenants. In such a life leisure hours for feasts at table were likely to become important in themselves. Some of the landowners and land workers found their world sadly altered during the Tudor years when the debasement of coinage in Henry VIII's reign and the influx of silver from the New World led to inflation. Somehow country landlords had to find more and more money if their fortune was tied up in land. Those who could not cope with the problem of high prices and the maintenance of a household demanding thirty to forty servants took chambers in London with only one or two servants and left their estates in the hands of stewards. When at the dissolution of monasteries the lands were sold to the highest bidder, the farms became actual merchandise, and there followed in quick succession rack-renting (extortionate rents) and the enclosure movement by which produce farms were converted into sheep-raising establishments, and common land was appropriated and fenced. The important changes which followed led to a reorganization of English rural social life.

At first the formation of fields by enclosing the old medieval strips of land by ditches and hedges was regarded with consternation but no revolt. But when farming land was converted into pastures, and dwellings of the tenants were pulled down, or when the common land of a community was enclosed, then there was trouble indeed. In some cases the villages became sheepfolds as whole hamlets were depopulated, and the evicted people who could not meet the exorbitant rents demanded by the new masters were left to make their living as they could. Those who could not find work in cities (when the only thing they knew was labor on the soil) became far too often vagabonds on the road or cutpurses in towns. Even though statutes tried to limit the owner's sheep to two thousand and to require him to keep as much land tilled as in former years, still the poor suffered. As late as 1596, Queen Elizabeth herself had to order country gentlemen to return to their country homes and to remain there "as well for the comfort and relief of their neighbors as for the service of her Majesty in these doubtful times," yet in spite of these orders the number of country gentlemen in London did not diminish.

Not all the results of the enclosure movement were evil, however. True, there was much complaint over common land or open heath or forest being converted into deer parks for owners of fine mansions; still in comparison with the land which enclosed the sheep, the park areas were very small. The Queen herself had nearly two hundred parks of many acres for deer and large coney warrens, but still there were vast tracts of virgin forest or brushwood with tall trees. The new masters, and the old, now saved money by better tillage of the soil and felt they were in no way taking an unfair advantage when they established their deer parks. Animals and fields now received better care, and consequently yielded more wealth to their owners. Money from the fine wool paid for new, comfortable farmhouses and Tudor mansions set in beautiful locations, and the order that the gentlemen live on their estates eventually resulted in their doing so and evolving a squirearchy of landlord, farmer, and laborer that was to last for over three hundred years. When masters of such estates took seriously their duties to their tenants, the conditions were far from unfavorable to the laboring class. Even so, the man of modest means and the dependents of little or no means looked forward to holidays or Sundays for a change in their monotonous living.

Meanwhile some rich country gentlemen and their wives found keen delight in the sports of hunting and fishing, and especially in the luxury of falconry. In this last sport women took far more part than in the more common pastimes of hunting. For this expensive sport, a young female hawk called a falcon (the males were called tercels) when well trained was considered a fit present for a king. The eyas or young hawks might be taken from the nest and trained, but a haggard or full-grown hawk might be caught and trained. This feat was accomplished by the simple process of keeping it awake till it was tamed, and then by careful, tireless training, teaching it how to serve its master perfectly while he hunted according to the rules of falconry. As a result, the falconer's office in some of the old manor houses descended from one generation to another, for patience and skill and love of the birds must be the chief virtue of this servant.

Even the dress of the falconer was important, for it must indicate his rank. A noble's falconer, therefore, wore a slight ruff above the open collar of his shirt, and tassels on his gloves where the long gauntlet cuff ended in a point. His soft-crowned hat with its plumes and slashed felt brim was very gay. A long coat, girdled at the waist, ended just above his knees, showing the puffed trunk hose, below which the cross-gartered nether hose were tied with bows at the knees. Buckled sandals completed his costume. The hood for most falcons, like the dress of their master, was a distinctive feature of the office with its silk-tasseled top and ties; it must fit the bird's head perfectly, for it adorned the most important pet of the household.

A wild hawk's eyes were seeled by a fine thread pulled through the tough, insensitive skin of the lower eyelid and passed over the head and through the lower eyelid of the other eye. As the hawk progressed in its training, the eyes were gradually freed. When not following the game, a trained hawk was hooded with its richly ornamented silk or leather hood. Jesses or cords were fastened to a leather strap on the leg of the bird, and bound the hawk to the wrist of the owner. Tiny bells, a pair on each leg, aided in tracking the hawk if she hunted out of sight. After the game was started from cover by dogs, the hawk was released to fly to a high pitch above the game. When its prey was caught, the bird was rewarded with the head. When not hunting, the hawk was kept in her cage or yard called the mew, but owners of fine falcons became so attached to them that they often carried them about wherever they went. It is not unusual, therefore, to see portraits of Elizabethan lords or ladies with a hooded hawk resting like an emblem of aristocracy on the owner's wrist or even sitting on a dining table. Such birds, however, were falcons, never the more common kestrel, sparrow hawk, or goshawk.

Wealthy Elizabethans also enjoyed hunting in the forest. If the game was dangerous, like the wild boar or wolf, the husband was likely to stalk it alone, but his wife might accompany him if he rode out for the fox, hare, or deer. Her main responsibilities in the chase would be the festivities before and after the hunt. This meant feasting in the wood and at home, and for this part of the entertainment of guests, the mistress must make ample provision or be sure that her steward could be trusted to do it for her. Up and away before daybreak, the hunters had a feast far out in the woods where their prey would not be likely to hear them. Then the hounds would be set free, and the hunt would begin.

In the south of sixteenth-century England, hedges were being planted around the fields and pastures and along the highways, but in the less developed areas, there was much unenclosed country over which the hunt could take its course. Birds haunted the marshes and provided a fowlers' paradise. Lakes and rivers teemed with fish, and many households had their own ponds stocked with roach or tench. Salmon still provided good fishing in the clear water of the Thames, and there were many unrestricted areas in which citizens from town or where dwellers in the country might fish. If a landlord owned the fishing rights on his estate, he often permitted his tenants to enjoy them also. However, the fish and game laws were not strictly enforced until well on into the seventeenth century. Though poor people might not hunt the deer, they could enjoy coursing the hares and rabbits. They might also hunt wild birds, and their method was to make a dummy horse of wood or canvas behind which they could stalk their prey. Squires and yeomen hunted hares with hounds, and sometimes foxes, badgers, and otters.

A host fond of hunting deer or fox or hare sought hounds with well-matched voices as well as skill in tracking the prey. These animals would be the admiration of his heart, and perhaps of his guests also. Writers of the age frequently refer to such dogs as "matched in mouth like bells" when their voices were in full cry. Shakespeare naturally admired such dogs, and Gervase Markham, who was general informer in all matters regarding animals for Elizabethan households, tells in *Country Contentments, or the Husbandman's Recreations* (1631) how to choose suitable hounds for this harmony. There must be some large dogs, he says, "with deep, solemn mouths . . . to bear the bass in the consort; then a double number of roaring and loud-ringing mouths, which must bear the counter-tenor; then some plain, sweet mouths which must bear the mean or middle part; and so with these three parts of music . . . make the cry perfect . . ."

Costumes for the nobility at the hunt were elaborate, Henry VIII having set a standard which Elizabeth followed. Henry usually preferred green for such an occasion, but Elizabeth might appear in any color. At one time she and all her ladies were dressed in white satin, and her archers in green with scarlet boots, yellow caps, and gilded bows. As the hunt was directed past the booth of the Queen and her party, a nymph sang her a sweet song as she presented a crossbow with which Elizabeth

Ready for the hunt, from *The Noble Art
of Venerie*, by George Turberville, 1575

Hunting with falcons, from *The booke of
Falconrie*, by George Turberville, 1575

was to shoot the deer. Musicians under the bower played sweet music to delight the waiting Queen. It might be added that although the Queen was a good shot, a concealed archer would bring down the prey if she missed, and no one would know she had failed.

Whenever there was entertainment at a great house, the poor looked forward to having full stomachs again, and during the hunting parties the feasts were likely to be most bountiful. But at other times also, in town and country, Elizabethans fed the crowds flocking to their gates on festive occasions. True, some of them did not give willingly to charity even when they believed such giving might be an effective means of buying salvation, but they gave because society expected it of them. Poor prisoners depended on the food left in baskets hung outside the prison walls, and those who unquestionably believed charity meant salvation did not neglect regular food offerings on days not marked by feasts. Fondness for food no doubt made feast days still numerous in spite of the loss of so many of them after the English ruler became head of the Church. Thus the long, lean days of ordinary food were not without end for those who willingly or unwillingly, in or out of prison, depended for their living upon alms. With the feasting, therefore, came the clamoring of the poor and the noisy merriment of the fortunate.

As a matter of fact, the general love of noise and revelry among the common people impressed foreign travelers, who frequently spoke of it as being due to an immoderate use of ale as the prevalent drink. They agreed the English had very good ale, but that it was also strong and, hence, intoxicating. Under its influence some daring spirits would go up into a belfry to ring bells for hours together through sheer love of the noise and exercise. Some of the drinking was due to the many church ales, but a great deal of it was done at home, for the preparation of ale and wine by the mistress and her servants was taken for granted as a part of the necessary provision in every well-managed household.

Christmas, of course, was celebrated with much drinking and feasting, and the carnival spirit was enhanced by the Lord of Misrule, a temporary leader of the festivities at great houses, the universities, the Inns of Court, and various villages. Even mayors of cities and sheriffs had their lords of misrule, and when the common people took part in the general merrymaking, they were likely to turn it into an uproar. Although a Master of the Revels provided entertainment for the court, Henry VIII appointed a Lord of Misrule annually to devise disguisings, masques, and mummeries during the Christmas season. Dressed elaborately in velvet and cloth of gold, the Lord of Misrule made an impressive entrance as the drums rolled and the trumpets blared, and he was followed by his courtiers, fools, hobbyhorses, prisoners, gibbet, stocks, and whatever might add to the masques for his "kingship." Then came grotesque masques in which the disguised persons entered with torch-bearers and musicians, bestowing gifts on the host and principal guests. A spokesman or presenter explained the meaning of each masque, and after its performance, the company usually danced gracefully a while before mingling with the guests and inviting them to join in the general dance to follow. Elizabeth preferred a simple version of this kind of entertainment in which the chief appeal depended on gaily dressed per-formers, torchbearers, and musicians, but her father had favored the spec-tacular effects of pageantry. As the masque was but an episode in Christ-mas revels, it was usually followed at Greenwich by a tourney of hobby-horses and a "state" visit to London where the Lord of Misrule was to entertain the Mayor.

At the universities, the Lord of Misrule was a Master of Arts who supervised all the revelries and was in charge of the Latin plays given by the students, but at the Inns of Court at London he was a splendid personage attended by his lord keeper and treasurer and guard of honor. He even had two chaplains who preceded him on Sunday in the Temple Church, gravely saluting him as they ascended the pulpit just as the Queen's chaplains saluted her in the Chapel Royal. His term of office was even longer than that of most such "lords," for instead of the usual month, he ruled his fellows from Allhallow Eve to Candlemas on Feb-ruary 2, when the judges and sergeants-at-law were feasted. On Satur-day evenings after supper, the gowned benchers of the Inner Temple danced their solemn revels with a song or carol begun by a Brother of the House, and then the young gentlemen danced while the benchers watched.

Before Elizabeth ascended the throne, the Middle Temple had ob-served more elaborate ceremony at Christmas than that used in the Inner Temple, but later abandoned its expensive entertainment. Then, by 1561, the Inner Temple was providing more feasting and richer masques than ever staged before. During this year their presentation of *Gorboduc* was followed by such sumptuous entertainment to their crowding guests that there was scarcely room for dancing. Reports of the Inn's revels were carried far and wide, and soon the spirit of emulation ran high in many communities, though the resulting revelries outside the Inns were characterized by high spirits rather than by the solemnity of pageantry. Naturally the great houses with important guests to entertain were af-fected by the Inner Temple's example, but on the whole they reserved this time of year for the feasting and merriment in a household of family, relatives, and servants.

Small towns and villages, however, must also have their "lord," who was usually one of the wild lads of the community, elected by the people for his daring spirit. After he had been solemnly crowned king, he would choose assistants and a bodyguard of twenty to sixty or a hundred souls as boisterous as himself. These he invested with fantastic liveries of green or yellow or other light colors and decked with scarfs, ribbons, gold rings and odds and ends of donated ornaments. Then, like the morris dancers, they tied bells on their legs, carried rich handkerchiefs in their hands, and with their hobbyhorses, dragons, and musicians, struck up a dance. On a Sunday the "lord" and his men might interrupt the services by approaching the church with drummers, pipers, and whatever means they had for making noise. As the door swung wide, the "lord" would be borne into the church on a litter of state, followed by his hobbyhorses and dragons managed by his faithful followers. Clad in his gay colors and wearing a tinsel crown, he banished at once any solemnity still lingering from the service. While the people gasped and shivered and laughed at his daring, he would ride in his odd procession down the nave and up to the chancel, where with a sudden halt he would order "proper" obeisance from the rector before he and his company danced their way out, then round and round the outside. Here they feasted in bowers and arbors set up in the churchyard, and here, too, were sold badges of the "lord," and other holiday gifts of cheese, custards, cakes, tarts, cream, meat, and always the inevitable ale. Now indeed everyone was in the right mood to prepare for the Christmas festivities in town or village, but especially in the home.

All houses and great halls were joyously decked with ivy, bay, and laurel, even the conduits and signs over the inns, or whatever might be festooned with red berries and green leaves. This was the one time of year when all class distinctions were supposed to be leveled, and lord, lady, and rustic met in the same hall, played the same games, and romped as equals. Though the holiday period was to extend till the twelfth night after Christmas, the lower classes, in compensation for the heavy toil of other days, liked it to continue as long as possible.

On Christmas Eve the church bells were rung with a right good will, and all the young people who had been engaged in the labor of rolling the Yule log now felt free to gather in the great hall of the household to which they were attached as laborers or servants. Otherwise, they might have a Yule log in their own home and celebrate this evening with close friends and relatives. The poor, with their great wooden bowls, went from house to house begging ale, and for the most part were so well supplied with it that they were merry too.

The Yule log was one more means by which the holiday season triumphed over all evil spirits. Because of its importance it was chosen with great care, and was as large as the fireplace would accommodate; frequently the root of a large tree served this purpose. Into the great hall of the manor it was rolled with many willing hands. Huge candles on the mantel and large sideboards and cupboards gave light, and when the log was in the center of the room, each member of the household was invited to come forward and sit on it while singing a song, such as that to ward off any evil preventing the log's burning:

> Wash your hands or else the fire
> Will not tend to your desire:
> Unwash'd hands, ye maidens, know,
> Dead the fire though ye blow.

This revelry was followed by drinking to a merry Christmas and a happy New Year.

Now, with merry tumult the great log was rolled into the fireplace, and the material for kindling it was arranged about it. When all was ready, a brand, said to be saved from last year's Yule log, was used to ignite the fire. As the flames began to play up the chimney, the festivities began, and the whole household of family, friends, and domestics feasted on Yule dough, Yule cake, and bowls of frumenty. Music and carols enlivened the feast. No wonder the poor came in large numbers to get their share of drink and cake.

On the following nights, except Christmas, there would be dancing and bowling and masking and children's games, but for those who preferred a quiet entertainment, there would be card games with and without dice, since restraints against gambling were removed for this gay season. In modest homes and cottages of villagers, mumming took the place of masking.

Christmas Day usually began with waits singing carols and then with services in the church or, for the rich, in their own chapel. For those who wished breakfast, this meal among the fortunate consisted of brawn with mustard, and some drink like malmsey. Dinner, of course, was the main event of the day, and in some homes it might be delayed till about three in the afternoon and last till nearly midnight. In the great houses the dinner consisted of several courses, each of which was preceded by music. The high point of this feast was the boar's head, not only because of pleasure in its meat but also because of its symbolism. The boar had long been revered for having taught man how to plow the fields by its habit of rooting in the ground with its tusks. Then, too, the danger of hunting the wild boar made its flesh prized as a delicacy, especially in the fall when it was at its best. The boar was hunted with spears or driven into nets, where hunters and dogs dispatched it. Its weak point, the ear, must be found by a dog, but as the dog held on, the tusks or teeth of the boar sometimes killed both dog and hunter. For this reason the boar hunt was often carried on by several men and many dogs, and if we may judge the hunt by pictures of it, as many as seventy-five to a hundred dogs were used in the contest. Most households serving the boar's head, therefore, used a domesticated beast.

The boar's head was served on a large platter, accompanied by gay

songs and, in the great house, by music from the minstrels' gallery. At
court, the bearer of the boar's head was ushered in by the Master of the
Revels, and then came choristers and minstrels, singing and playing. In
some homes the eldest son would bring in the boar's head. If this custom
was followed, the family and guests would rise and greet the proud bearer
with a song, one of the most popular, with its many stanzas, beginning
thus:

> Caput apri defero,
> Reddens laudes domino.
> The boar's head in hand bring I,
> Bedecked with bays and rosemary;
> I pray you all sing merrily,
> Quot estis in convivio . . .

Sometimes the chief cook in the great house was given the honor of bringing in the boar's head. He might be preceded by a man who carried in
his hand the bloody sword with which the boar had been slain. Then
all the guests' eyes rested with delight on the head, garlanded with rosemary and laurel, and bearing in its mouth a lemon, suggesting plenty.

Other festive dishes included various kinds of roasted beasts and
fowls, and great pies. Some pies are reported as being nine feet in circumference and weighing one hundred sixty-five pounds. They had to be
wheeled in on carts built for the purpose, and served from these carts.
It has been estimated that at least two bushels of flour were used in these
pies, twenty-four pounds of butter, and such a combination of meats, perhaps, as geese, rabbits, ducks, and pigeons.[3] If a fowl was the dish of pride,
it was likely to be a peacock or pheasant, roasted whole, with its feathers
replaced in all their glory, or baked in a crust with only the gilded bill
protruding, and the colorful tail feathers propped up in all their splendor.

An honored lady was usually the bearer of the peacock, and after she
had brought it in, knights might take what was known as the peacock
vow. One by one they would advance and lay the right hand on the back
of the bird and make a pledge to defend women, to be the first to strike
a blow at the enemy, etc. Each would make an effort, of course, to surpass the bravery and gallantry of the others in his vow.[4] In some homes
the eldest daughter would bring in the dish of fowl. In this case the bird
might be a pheasant or goose. She, too, might be greeted with song as
was the son who brought in the boar's head. Of course, the boar's head
was most prized, for Henry VIII had made it so during his reign, and
Elizabeth continued the practice.

In modest homes, after the Christmas dinner came games, some with
music and dancing. A game like shoe-the-mare consisted of chasing the
girl to be shod till she was caught, and then, as she struggled in the midst

---

[3] Alfred Carl Hotter, *1001 Christmas Facts and Fancies* (1937), p. 110.
[4] *Ibid.*, p. 112.

of the hilarious group, attempting to shoe her. In hot cockles, a blind-folded person tried to guess who touched him, causing the same excited laughter as in blindman's buff. These simple games were full of fun and high spirits as grown-ups and children, domestics and householders mingled together in running to and fro. In great houses there were likely to be masques during and after the meal, but they were not the elaborate masques of the other holidays of the Christmas season.

Expecting to be feasted and given largess, the Christmas mummers performed in the great hall of the manor house before family, relatives, guests, and servants. Then they went on to the farmhouses of the common people to present their play of St. George and the dragon and the Saracen. In most communities they appeared on Christmas Eve. The characters in this mumming were chosen with much consideration of the candidates, and the costumes must be the delight of all who were to gaze upon them. Besides the main performers there must be the merry men to accompany St. George, the doctor to cure the "wounds," and Father Christmas with his holly bough, the youth with the wassail bowl, and the pretty little girl to carry mistletoe. The plots for mumming were frequently taken from some old legend, Father Christmas being an important character of such sources. Allegorical representations of goodness and plenty and feasting were often interwoven fancifully in some dialogue dealing with the Christmas spirit, and mirthfully adapted to the talent of those taking part in the mumming. Frequently the mummers went the rounds of every house in a village, and by the time they had been hospitably received at each, were probably in far better spirits than voice.

The masques in the great houses grew increasingly sumptuous as the Queen's taste for this kind of entertainment mounted toward the end of the century. Though Christmas Day was not an occasion for such performances, four of the twelve holidays were often celebrated lavishly: St. Stephen's Day on December 26, to commemorate the death of the first Christian martyr; St. John's Innocents, on December 27, to represent the death of this saint who, though plunged into burning oil, did not die, but was swept uninjured into heaven; New Year's Day; and Twelfth Night on the twelfth day after Christmas, when the Magi visited the Christ child with their gifts. Elizabeth's first masque had occurred on Twelfth Night of 1558, and the performers had been solemn dignitaries of the Church in their gorgeous silk, velvet, and satin robes. But by the next year the nature of the masque was greatly changed. On New Year's Day the chief characters in the entertainment were six "barbarians" in red cloth of gold and Venetian commoners in white damask acting as torchbearers. On Twelfth Night occurred a double masque of six Venetian patriarchs in green with purple headdress, and six Italian women in white and crimson. They were accompanied by torchbearers and a drum and fife. Though the elaborate costumes were still the high point of interest and were to remain so during the rest of her reign, the tone of the masque had already lost much of its heavy seriousness. Undoubtedly the Queen's delight in masques led to their fantastically ornate development in London, where the rivalry among the Inns of Court plays and pageantry was climaxed in the masque given by the Middle Temple in 1597.

Meanwhile, out in the country, where at the Queen's order in 1589 the tenants were to receive cheer and comfort from the presence of their young masters returning from the Inns, the farmers had learned to get along without the young heirs at Christmastime. In fact, the farmers had developed their own way of celebrating Twelfth Night, the last night, supposedly, of the holiday season. Now they lighted huge bonfires in the grain fields, around which they danced with an agility not a little increased by the ale and cider they drank so freely. Then came one of the most curious moments in their celebration. At the house the women had prepared an enormous cake, which was now carried in great triumph to the stable. Here it was set on the horn of the biggest ox, whose nose was tickled with a straw until the animal tossed his head and flung off the cake. Amid the scrambling for the pieces, only the strong and lusty were likely to engage, for it was a rough-and-tumble game. After all the pieces had been gathered and eaten, the revelers returned to the house, where the rest of the night was spent in song and jollity, and with not a little additional good cheer from the housewife's store of cider or ale or both.

Perhaps they would cease their hilarity now and then to tell old folk tales, and if so not the least of these would refer to the night of the sacred birth. It was commonly believed that at the moment of the birth of the Christ child there came a universal pause in nature, pervaded by a profound silence, and followed by the adoration of the animals. Then the bees awoke from their winter sleep to "utter in marvelous canticles" their songs which only those "free from stain of mortal sin could hear." Meanwhile, "a language was put to the sound of birds and animals" which none but the pure in heart could comprehend. The cock crowed "Christus natus est," the raven croaked "Quando," the rook cawed "Hac nocte," the ox mooed "Ubi," the sheep answered "Bethlehem," and the ass brayed "Eamus." The "let us go" of the braying ass invariably touched a chord of sentiment in the hearts of these rustics.

At other homes this festive night might be celebrated in a very different manner. Since Epiphany was called the Little Christmas because of the Magi's gifts to the Christ child on this night, some people now exchanged gifts with their friends instead of on Christmas or New Year's. In such homes a great cake was baked and decorated with many candles. Within the cake had been placed a bean and a pea. If a man found the bean in his piece of cake, he was made the king, and if a woman found the pea, she was made the queen. Eventually the king and queen were "discovered," and the two were seated on an impressive throne from which they supervised the festivities for the rest of the evening. First, however, the king must be raised on the shoulders of four men that he might mark a cross on the rafters to keep away evil spirits. Among the revels of the evening were mock trials, the enacting of scenes from English history, and much dancing and singing. At midnight the Christmas greens were all taken down and burned in the fireplace to indicate that the holidays were come to an end.

Although the real wassailing occurred on New Year's, the wassail cup had been introduced at the holiday season with much ceremony. After the fanfare announcing Christmas dinner in a noble's home, servants entered with torches or candles of wax, and the musicians and trumpeters followed. Then the steward, treasurer, and controller marched in, followed by all the servers, carvers, and ushers in grave procession with the cup twined with green garlands. By the time the procession returned with the bowl to the end of the hall, the gentlemen of the household had taken their stand at the other end of the room. Now the steward would cry joyously, "Wassail," and the gentlemen would answer with a wassail song or carol. In most homes the chief servant went for the wassail cup, and on his return was greeted joyously by the family and guests with "Wassail, wassail, wassail." At the homes of the rich where the poor had come with empty wooden bowls, the servants would fill the bowls with ale, and the people would march away singing:

> Wassail! wassail! over the town,
> Our toast it is white, our ale it is brown:
> Our bowl it is made of the maple tree
> We be good fellows all, and we drink
> now to thee.

At such homes the holiday masques grew in favor with the Queen's increasing delight in them. Perhaps Elizabeth came to feel that the country people did not need their masters to help them celebrate the holiday season, but more than likely she was too delighted with the clever masques devised by the young men at the Inns of Court to dispense with their holiday spectacles. So rich and "glorious" were their costumes at the 1597 celebration that only Elizabeth's gorgeous apparel surpassed theirs as she sat in state on a high throne provided for her as their chief guest. Eventually the masque was adopted by lords of great houses whenever it was necessary for them to entertain distinguished guests at banquets. Shakespeare's plays provide many interesting adaptations of such entertainment. Though the humble people might not know much, if anything at all, about these fantasies, they were likely to receive extra employment at these places during festive times. They might hear rumors, however, of how the lord and lady and their guests watched a performance in the great hall, where fine tapestries of exotic scenes provided background for the action, and costumes beyond description in color and rich texture were paraded by the actors. When the modest home, however, had its mumming, the costumes depended on the ingenuity of clever women with needle and thread and scraps and odds and ends of material brought to them by members of the community. As for the poor, their interest was in food and drink, and, like Lazarus, they could always gather up crumbs from the tables of the rich.

One reason why the ruling in regard to young heirs visiting their estates at Christmas was not strictly enforced was that at this time the roads were almost impassable. Indeed, any such visit home to the country in winter would be more a labor of love for the tenants than fear of the law. It was bad enough to fight the dust in summer and the swarms of gnats from undrained marshes as riders forced their steaming horses along the country roads. In winter there were snow and rains, frequently floods, and always seas of mud into which their horses might sink out of sight without any warning whatsoever. If a rider was not pressed for time, he might use one horse for an entire trip, but if he must hurry, he would hire post horses that could be exchanged at inns along the way. On the highways there was likely to be no little travel in spite of the difficulties, but the other roads were too dangerous for much traffic. Officials like circuit judges and justices of the peace must attend to their duties, which called for regular journeys, and goods must be transported somehow in carriers' carts or by pack-horse trains. As far as possible they all followed the highways, as did students going to and from the universities.

All of these travelers helped to swell the numbers entertained at the inns, where they were made as comfortable as possible. Good food, dressed to their taste and served with music if they could afford it, and beds with clean linen, from which they might be roused in the morning by hired music or merely a knocking at the door, were expected and usually found at all reputable inns. Large hostelries could accommodate two to three hundred people, and were beehives of industry and hospitality when at their best. During fairs they were crowded beyond measure, for most fairs were held in fine weather when all who could attend them left home for this pleasure. But comparatively few of the visitors at fairs ever stayed at inns, for even with the prospect of good entertainment at inn or fair, most people were reluctant to leave home for this purpose if the journey required one or more nights away from their hearths. People at inns, therefore, were away from home because of business of one kind or another.

In lonely districts highwaymen and footpads were sure to be lurking, and it was best to keep to the main roads in spite of dust and flies or quagmires and deep holes. Even then one must go heavily armed and accompanied by friends or servants. Popular stories of the supposedly Robin Hood character of robbers in general may have prevented the law from taking drastic measures against all of them when caught, but few if any of them deserved this consideration. That there were nobles' sons among them was likely, for older brothers of noble rank were not infrequently known to plead lenience for erring younger relatives caught red-handed and jailed for such unlawful conduct. If these culprits could plead the injustice of being discharged soldiers who could no longer stand the rigors of such a life, or if they could show they had been dispossessed of their estates or wealth, or if they could convince their responsible family members that they were merely following the call of adventure, they might be rescued from the toils of the law and later appear as men in good social standing. Shakespeare's account of Prince Hal's experience with Falstaff's men engaged in their questionable lark appeals to a general feeling of romantic tolerance toward highwaymen (*I Henry IV*, scenes ii and iv of Act II). Moreover, the connivance between robbers and dishonest innkeepers, who informed the thieves concealed in lofts and cellars about guests who had money, made it difficult for the watch to apprehend such criminals. Even drovers felt it necessary to pay some of these rascals tribute to protect them and their flocks from the depredations of other members of the gang.

The danger from robbers, therefore, was great. Since no roads had signs to mark the way, a person might easily get lost if he ventured from the main roads and become the victim of robbers who were always in search of such unfortunates. As a rule, however, these thieves were more intent on money than on murder. Only they really knew the roads, which farmers themselves traveled very little and then only in midday and good weather. When poor people traveled in the country, they went in carriers' carts or on foot, and only fine fairs indeed could induce them to make such journeys. Naturally, such travel was not for women.

Country people also knew the dangers of serving as guides, and usually refused to take any such risks. When floods filled the rivers and streams, what few bridges existed might be washed out or made unsafe, and then wide detours would take the traveler straight into the arms of highwaymen. If ferries were in operation, they were likely to be unsafe and certainly very uncomfortable to one who was no longer full of the spirit of adventure; hence, the choice of detours. On these detours, even men born and bred in the country could easily become lost, for they went so seldom far from home. City people, therefore, were not at all likely to try the hazards of travel in winter unless driven by dire necessity, and young men from the country attending the Inns of Court would not take the journey home if they could be excused at all. If one's errand or duties required him to travel, he left in the morning fortified with a good breakfast unless he knew he might stop at an inn when he had ridden two or three hours.

For the traveler with a long journey to go, the table might groan under food, but it would all be cold: chines of beef or breast of mutton, roasted the day before, eggs, custard, cold meat pies, jellies, butter, or some cold fowl and game. There was no time for ovens to heat or for smoky fireplaces to get under way before breakfast; besides, both were needed for the day's baking. No wonder those who did have a hearty breakfast washed it down with strong drink, and no wonder those who could adjust themselves to their first meal at eleven or twelve dispensed with breakfast altogether.

As only the traveler or weakling was expected to have breakfast before morning worship or between six and seven before entering upon the duties of the day, this meal was usually served in the privacy of one's chamber. This did not apply to town or country or city laborer, however, for he must leave home with food in his stomach. Possibly one reason for the loss of interest in breakfast among the leisured or pampered class was that the meal in Elizabethan times was no longer hearty and had none of the attractive drinks that were eventually to bring it back into favor. Hot milk or some light brewed ale or mead or just hot barley water, which young ladies were supposed to sip at breakfast, would scarcely be worth the effort of early rising unless, of course, people wished to brace themselves for the walk to church on a cold winter day. Men might have strong drink, but unless they had strong stomachs, they usually breakfasted on butter and eggs and possibly yesterday's cold bread. Children, however, usually had eggs and milk and butter before they left for school.

By 1557, only the farming class and laborers were likely to have more than two meals a day. For others, dinner was served at eleven or twelve, and supper at five or six. Merchants and businessmen usually dined at twelve and six or seven, but laborers, especially during the long summer days, had supper as late as seven or eight o'clock. The upper class revived the old Norman custom of sitting long at table, and when dinners lasted from two to three hours, some officials had scarcely time before the evening meal to do more than attend prayers. Of course, the early supper hour gave the privileged class a great deal of leisure before bedtime, and they spent much of it in their gardens. Since the last course of supper was served here in pleasant weather, its sweetmeats became associated with evening recreation during warm weather. Now they might talk with their guests about some new imports which they were trying to adapt to English soil or climate, such as nasturtiums from the Indies, tomatoes from Spain, or tiger lilies from Constantinople.

Reducing the number of meals did not lighten the labor involved in preparing them, however, for cooking, like ornate architecture or elaborate dress or anything else that might impress one's acquaintances with a display of wealth, became a very important advertisement of a man's financial status. Now Elizabethans spent so much time at table that they needed more servants to prepare enormous quantities of food, especially meats, than they required for any other household task. Among the rich, elaborate cooking with eccentric flavoring was popular, and with increased prosperity, luxuries and extravagance in food became more and more general. At a dinner expected to last two or three hours, for example, several joints might be served, several kinds of fish, and several kinds of game, venison, etc., besides salads, vegetables, sweetmeats, fruits, and several kinds of wine and other drink. No one was ever expected to partake of all the dishes but to eat and drink moderately by making a selection from the variety so bounteously offered.

When the rich merchant or gentleman dined alone with his family, he had about three dishes at supper, such as roast mutton, boiled rabbit, or fowl, served with vegetables and bread, and always some drink, such as ale or claret. If he had guests—and a rich or ambitious man could scarcely afford not to have guests frequently—four to six dishes were served at a simple meal. Salad usually came before the meats, and fruit last. Servants in such a household needed close supervision lest they depend too much on the leavings from the master's bountiful table instead of dining on the plainer food they were expected to prepare for themselves. Only the competent housewife was likely to prevent the waste that could occur from such an extravagant use of expensive food.

The common people were compelled to live chiefly on "white meats," consisting of milk, butter, cheese, and bread, though soups and thick broths also formed a large part of their diet. Often, no doubt, they longed for the "brown meats" of the fortunate households in which beef, mutton, game, and pork abounded, but the diet of the common people was much better balanced, for they used proportionately more vegetables than the rich ever had at their meals. Vegetables were considered common food unless artfully cooked or chosen from imported articles difficult to obtain. Since during Lent even the pampered were expected to deny themselves, then, and on fish days, Elizabethans supposedly dined off salt fish, ling, turbot, fresh whitings, sprats, or eels. If fresh fish came from their own ponds, they suffered no hardship, but the poor man got only the fish he could buy at market. Other luxuries denied at this time were strong drinks, beer and wine being used instead. Seldom did the common man, therefore, indulge in the strong drinks that began to appear in England during the last of the century.

As English drinks were sweeter than those of other countries, they helped to increase the enormous quantities of sugar which were consumed. The whole nation had one great sweet tooth. Currants were used in such large amounts in cakes and puddings, sauces and custards that foreigners thought the English must use them to fatten hogs. Sugar and drink were combined in the usual diet of the fashionable in town or country, and if the table was well laden, these supplemented some form of fowl or hunted game like venison, hares roasted and boiled, and even rabbits. These meats were also served in pies with powdered ginger or cinnamon, cloves or saffron, and stiffened with eggs. The crust might be dotted with currants or minced dates. A choice dish consisted of a capon, the meat being cut from the still-warm bird, then parboiled till the flesh fell apart; this was dried and then cut into as small pieces as possible and cooked in a sauce prepared from two quarts of milk and two quarts of cream and half a pound of rye flour. When the whole concoction was thoroughly cooked, half a pound of beaten sugar was added, and a saucer of rosewater for flavoring. When very thick, the mixture was removed from the fire and chilled before serving.

The English habit of cooking boiled food till it was sodden had to be offset by the use of sugar and spice to make it palatable even for them. If boiled meat was put into a pastry, however, it seldom went begging, hot or cold. Of all table fowls, none was more popular than the goose at certain seasons, either when fattened upon the wheat stubble after harvest or when made sweet by keeping the birds on green pasturage. Yet some of those living in the country might not enjoy this luxury, for farmers of modest means sent their fat geese to market for the good price paid by prosperous city dwellers for such coveted birds.

A common man in the country, therefore, did not always spread a a liberal table. Farmers used barley and rye for bread, for example, more often than wheat, not only because it was cheaper but because it was more hearty. Some farmers were so poor they made bread of beans and oats, and some even used acorns for bread in lean years. Ordinary dinners in the country consisted of bread, bacon or fish, peas or some other vegetable, milk, butter, eggs, and home-brewed cider or ale. If farmers in such comfortable circumstances carried a lunch to the field, they might have in addition to their beer or ale an apple pasty or bread and butter and cheese, and also a jug of buttermilk. Those who could afford meat from their flocks dined occasionally on mutton or beef or veal or lamb or pork. Souse (pickled pork) and brawn (pressed pork) were holiday delicacies for both farmers and city laborers, although the latter enjoyed such treats chiefly at Christmas. The thrifty farmer, of course, sent his best butter and cheese to the cities, there to compete with the inferior imports from the Dutch, who were frequently referred to with contempt as "butter-boxes." Ironically enough, city laborers rather than the farmers themselves were likely to enjoy the best of the farmers' bacon, eggs, butter, fowls, and rabbits.

Besides brawn, another favorite dish among the common people was frumenty. Many a homesick boy at school, even from well-to-do homes, longed for these delicacies, and sometimes mothers managed to get brawn to their sons for the Christmas holidays if a servant could be sent safely with the present. Brawn was more than just pressed pork; it was the pressed meat of a boar that had been fed on oats and peas for a year or two. The flesh was first boiled till tender, and then soaked in ale or pickled in a container that had a lid pressed down tight upon it. Being a winter dish, it was soon associated with Christmas in most households. Frumenty was made of new wheat boiled till soft and big, drained, and put into new milk and eggs. The mixture was then colored a deep yellow with saffron, and stirred over the fire till it thickened. It was served with honey and sugar.

Bread, important at all tables, was made from various grains. Manchet was a fine white wheat bread, used by the rich, and cheat, also a wheat bread, was used by the less wealthy, or by the economical household. It was cheaper because only the coarsest bran was removed from it, and its grayish yellow color made it less attractive to the eye. Raveled bread contained more bran than wheat, and was still cheaper in price. Brown bread was made of whole wheat, unsifted. If a little rye was added to this unsifted flour, the bread was called meslin. All bread had to be chipped before eaten in order to remove oven grit or burn. In well-managed households this chipping was done before the bread was brought to the table, though the humble householder usually chipped his own bread at table. For such a person, bread and wine were frequently a meal in themselves.

The home-brewed wines and other drinks of the English were seldom so strong as the imported wines and beverages the rich learned to drink so immoderately at the close of the century. Elizabethan wines were made chiefly from grapes, currants, ginger, oranges, elderberries, and cowslips. Mead, made from honey, was much stronger than their other drinks, and remained popular, especially with the men, in spite of the new and imported beverages. The general drink, however, was ale, made from barley. At the church ales held on Christmas, Easter, and Whitsunday, the church wardens provided the malt, and parishioners the rest. Not only was the ale drunk at these festivals, but it was bought to supplement the home supply, and those who bought most liked to think themselves most godly. As a result there was as much buying as households could afford, and with so much on hand, the consumption of ale at home naturally increased. Even tipplers salved their conscience by reminding themselves that money spent for church ale went to buy such things as cups for celebrating the sacrament of the Lord's Supper, etc. Ales continued in favor in spite of the 1607 law to suppress them for their abuses.

At table, drinks were served in earthern pots, garnished with silver or pewter, or in silver jugs, bowls, cups, goblets, or glasses, the finest service in the latter part of the century consisting of Venetian glasses. Since it was customary to call for a cup as one wished to drink and then to return the cup to servant or child serving at table, the number of cups on the sideboard or cupboard might be numerous. Although a person did not often drink more than once or twice at an ordinary meal, he must have a fresh cup for each drink, and he must never drain the cup if he used good manners. The dregs from feasts or ordinary meals provided more drink for those at the gates as the common drinking bowl or jug went out of fashion. By the end of the century even modest homes were using light, cheap, but very breakable glasses instead of the old heavy ones made of fern and burned stone. Breakage by careless housewives or servants was often criticized harshly by moralists who deplored such waste.

Elizabethans took great pride in their table service, not only because it enabled them to display beautiful possessions and carefully trained servants, but because they frankly enjoyed food and drink. In fine homes much silver plate continued in use in spite of the new expensive glassware coming into fashion. The massive sideboards, therefore, continued to hold both useful and ornamental objects, such as silver basins and ewers and beautiful vases of all kinds made of gold, silver, crystal, ivory, and myrrh wood from Africa or Arabia. Earthenware from Malacca, varnished red, was very popular. Decanters and phials of every kind would be arranged with the cups and glasses on the cupboards and small tables of polished wood, whose tops were protected by imported or homemade scarfs. Great platters and plates were also a means of ostentation.

Ordinary homes duplicated what they could of this display in their tin, horn, shell, or earthenware pieces. According to William Harrison, by 1588 in homes that could afford better, wooden bowls and platters had been discarded for pewter vessels, and wooden spoons for tin or silver or pewter, and the great salt, still the most ornamental table decoration, was of silver. His contemporary, Robert Greene, in *The Thirde and Last Part of Cony-Catching* (1592), describes an ordinary shopkeeper's home built "end-on to the street," as was customary, the shop on the ground floor and the living room and children's and maids' and master's bedrooms on the next floor, with sleeping quarters for the apprentices in the attic, over the master's room. In one incident, wishing to entertain a guest hospitably at supper, the wife sets out all her plate on the cupboard for show, and beautifies her house with cushions, carpets, stools, and other articles enabling her to display her needlework. Since the guest arrives a little early, the husband entertains him by showing him the shop, and while they are dining, there is drinking "twice or thrice" to the health of the guest and relatives, presumably, from whom he has just come. Alas, the "guest" is only a very clever thief and impersonator, and in the night steals what he can from the sleeping household. Much of his loot is taken from a chest at the foot of the master's bed, and consists of "very good linen, a fair gilt salt, two silver French bowls for wine, two silver drinking pots, a stone jug covered with silver, and a dozen silver spoons." Of course he also takes what he can from the shop itself. By the time Greene was writing this pamphlet, even the farmers as well as humble town folk had acquired some pieces of pewter or silver, such as spoons or small, plain cylindrical salts or bowls, but still kept for daily use wooden trenchers often with mottoes carved on them, and wooden or horn bowls and beakers.

The wealthy did not commonly use their rich plate either, but for everyday use they clung to pewter, which was by no means cheap. Sometimes they rented pewter by the year, but owned as much as they could afford of fine display pieces made of silver and gold plate, cut glass, and china. Of these the great salts and ewers and basins used at meals were most decorative. The beauty of the basin was usually centered in a raised boss, enameled with the arms of the owner, and on this base rested the ewer. These pieces were often gifts covered with gilt, and then they were used only on special occasions. Such, for example, was Lord North's show basin and ewer kept for the use of the Queen when she visited his house. Gossips liked to talk about its weight of fifty-seven ounces "paid for by the weight of five shillings and six pence per ounce."

Fynes Moryson, in *An Itinerary* (1617), speaks of the better sort of gentlemen and merchants having cups of silver and gold plate valued up to £200, and so much of it that in a whole day's feasting, or longer, they seldom had to use the same plate twice. This might be true of the drinking vessels, certainly, although Moryson points out that Venetian glass was preferred to cups of silver, for by this time "houses of any reasonable condition drink in silver." The French and Italians, whom the English imitated in such matters as well as in dress and manners, used as much fine glass as possible instead of pots or bowls or cups of silver, continued Moryson, but the less refined Germans still drank from pewter or stone pots because they had no plate. To keep the wine cool, the English used great tubs of wood or copper that must be filled with fresh cold water before a meal.

During the latter part of the century, cups and other pieces of crystal, agate, china, and beautiful stone mounted on gold or silver were considered greater rarities than old heavy plate, and were used for lighter, artistic gifts. The Queen, however, when returning a present, usually chose gilt plate and tried to match it in value with the gift she received. The Earl of Leicester presented her with a porringer of bloodstone, the four feet and two handles garnished with gold, made to look like snakes, and Lady Sidney gave the Queen a salt of blue stone, lapis lazuli, with pillars slightly garnished with gold. At banquets and for decorative purposes, large standing cups were used, and they frequently served as most acceptable gifts. At this time the great salts stood over a foot high, though there were many small, highly finished salts used for lesser gifts, as in the case of Lady Sidney's gift. When the great standing cups in wealthy homes were supplanted by small cups and bowls, some householders indulged exotic tastes in having cups of carved cocoanuts, ostrich eggs, nautilus shells, and rock crystal.

During the middle of the century, the German stoneware jug had been popular for common use. Then, for about a decade, it was mounted with neckband, feet, and a cover of elaborately engraved and chased silver. As the bowl died out, the tankard came in, but its shape was slight till 1600, and it was never adapted in pewter for the poorer people till after 1610. As styles changed rapidly in tableware, the confusion in pieces set out for display by hosts who could not or dared not part with gifts of old heavy plate must have made very trying the achievement of any artistic order among the old and the newer, lighter, more graceful pieces.

For this reason some felt it was better to make gifts of money, and such presents were highly favored by the Queen. Many ladies gave her silken purses with some twenty pieces of gold, and hoped thereby to make a favorable impression on her. In 1578, she is reported having received over £900 in such gifts. She also counted on gifts of clothing to replenish her wardrobe at New Year's, and accepted with pleasure richly embroidered and bejeweled sleeves, variously colored pieces of cloth of gold for gowns, and satins, velvets, and fine laces. Lesser presents consisted of bolts of cambric, and even such things as a great pie of quinces and a pot of green ginger. Like gifts might be exchanged by great ladies too, but the most expensive and most beautiful must of necessity be bestowed upon the Queen. Practical as they might be, however, no gifts appealed so much to the taste of those who liked display pieces as did plate and decorative pieces for the table. Such gifts were not only in good taste but were also welcomed by those who had the collector's instinct or desire to pass on to successors whatever articles might provide an impressive listing in the will.

Some prominent English prelates and nobles were noted for their taste in plate, and were also generous in their gifts of it. At his death in 1598, Lord Burghley, though not so rich as believed, left to his heirs plate to the value of £15,000 in English money. Archbishop Parker made superb gifts to colleges, and many of these fine specimens are still in existence. At the Inns of Court, where were many sons of the nobility and the gentry, the table service was good, with silver cups used instead of glasses, perhaps to save breakage as well as to please the taste of the time.

Elizabethan men did not remove their hats at table except while drinking a toast, and no one was seated at table till all had washed their hands. Thus the ewer and basin were very important before and after meals and sometimes after each course, because forks were not used, except by the ultrafashionable, till the early seventeenth century. Forks for special purposes had been known in England since the middle of the fifteenth century. They were of Italian origin, long, slight, two-pronged, of steel with beautiful handles, and often accompanied by a matching knife in a highly ornamental case. Their owners took them along when they dined with friends. By 1588, gifts of a crystal knife, fork, and spoon and of a coral fork are recorded, but most Elizabethans used only spoons, knives, and their fingers when dining. When the carver presented hot and cold meats to those at table, he offered them on the flat of a knife, some of which were four inches wide, but often each person cut off his own meat with his own knife. Coryate's *Crudities* of 1611 expressed his delight in the Italian use of the fork. He could not "by any means endure" to have his dish "touched with fingers, seeing all men's fingers are not alike clean."

He told how the Italians held a knife in one hand "to cut meat out of the dish," fastening "their fork they held in their other hand upon the same dish." If one of them "sitting in the company of any others at a meal, should unadvisedly touch the dish of meat with his fingers," he would give offense to the whole company by "having transgressed the laws of good manners." But Coryate's manners were considered "affected," and provoked smiles of amusement or irritation from his readers.

Among the many books with rules about the proper serving of a meal, most agreed that the first dish at a formal meal should be for show only and, whether bird, beast, fish, or fowl, should indicate considerable ingenuity on the part of the cook. This, like the boar's head at Christmas, would be brought in with much ceremony (each occasion having its own ceremony), and placed in the center of the table as a decoration. If there were several tables, or long ones, several "decorative dishes" would be brought in. Sometimes dishes were made for show only; then they were usually of pastry or sugar and water, hardened to look like snow, and sometimes they were elaborate enough to form animals in a scene, or a castle and its environs, or mythological settings, or fortifications. The last was very popular, for its realistic details could be achieved easily in sugarwork, with drummers, trumpeters, and soldiers in true outline. Mythological scenes made much of mermaids, dolphins, fish, etc. Among the animals affording most delight for their own sake in sugarwork were unicorns, lions, bears, horses, camels, bulls, rams, dogs, tigers, elephants, antelopes, and apes. Birds were also favored with artists of this craft, and they made good displays in themselves or in scenes with other things. Favorites were eagles, falcons, cranes, quails, larks, sparrows, pigeons, cocks, and owls. Even reptiles were displayed in sugarwork, the most common being snakes, frogs, and toads.

As a rule, dinner consisted of only two courses, for each of which the dishes were placed on the table at one time in order to provide guests with a wide selection and to make a lavish display. In the first course there might be manchet as well as other varieties of bread, besides meats and vegetables. The second course or "banquet" provided sweetmeats and ripe fruits in season, such as cherries, plums, pomegranates, quinces, or figs. Wine, red, white, or black, was served during the meal. If a common drinking cup was still used, it might be a large ebony wine bowl or a covered drinking cup or a cup of some foreign wood bound with a silver edge. But by the end of the century individual cups or glasses were so much in use that the common cup was rare.

Of course the most important part of a formal dinner consisted of its many meats, such as cocks cooked with lettuce, ox tongues cooked with endive, and mutton and veal, accompanied by mustard and parsley in small dishes. Soup or broth, rice, and more bread would be served with the meats, and then followed fish, such as pike roasted with vinegar and capers, a turbot cooked with the juice of pointed sorrel, fresh sole or pike fried, fresh and salted tunny fish roasted, fresh small sea fish, and boiled lobster and crabs. Little dishes containing pounded mustard, garlic, and pepper would garnish the fish. Next might be served the fowl and small game, such as roasted chickens, partridges, thrushes, ducklings, wood pigeons, and rabbits and hares and veal, with a sauce of vinegar and oil, and pickled fruit like citron, or a garnish of olives. Since game was plentiful, it was used in great quantities on feast days. After the fowl and small meats came stag, deer, and the boar, followed by pears, apples, and many kinds of cheese, English, Dutch, and German.

The banquet, or second course, was spread on tables in the garden if the weather permitted or in the pleasant banquet house. If the weather was rough, the family and guests made what conversation they could while the table was cleared and hands were washed in rosewater. Or the company might be entertained with music or a masque or a short dialogue, much of it improvised by the clever speakers. The second course would consist of tarts, winecakes, cupcakes, or fried cakes which had been made of a rich concoction fried in oil and then spread with honey. Other sweets would consist of such delicacies as preserves, jellies, marmalades, and always the popular suckets, comfits, and, at special feasts, marchpane. These would be followed by dates, pomegranates, quinces, and sugar-coated coriander seeds. If this last course was not served out of doors, it was usually followed, especially in pious homes, by a prayer and then the washing of hands in scented water.

When guests were invited in the common man's home, the children usually sat at table with their elders unless they helped to serve the meal. Children, however, always sat at the "board's end." The eldest son in a pious home might be asked to read from the Scriptures before the meal, and even to say grace. After a simple meal of three or four dishes, before the board would be removed from its trestles, the entire company might engage in singing. Then a small child might say such a grace as the following:

> O Lord our God, we yield thee praise
> For this thy gracious store
> Praying that we may have the grace
> To keep thy laws and lore.
> And when this life shall flit away;
> Grant us to live with thee for aye.

An older child might use a prayer a little more difficult:

> O Lord, which giv'st thy creatures for our food,
> Herbs, beasts, birds, fish, and other gifts of thine,
> Bless thee thy gifts, that they may do us good,
> And we may live, to praise thy name divine.
> And when the time is come this life to end:
> Vouchsafe our souls to heaven may ascend.

Before rising, however, the host might ask another child to recite a wise sentence, with the response: "For one pleasure, a thousand sorrows," or "The best smell is bread, the best savor salt, the best love that of children." Then the company would wash their hands and, after leaving the table, draw near the fire on cool days to talk. Here, however, the children would be seen and not heard if they were allowed to remain in the room. Their part at table, of course, was due entirely to the Elizabethan practice of teaching the young good manners and proper religious observance.

Even everyday meals were served with due decorum in well-managed homes, and the table was carefully set. But the best of linens, plate, glass, etc., was always reserved for special occasions in most homes. If different ranks were not represented at table, one basin was frequently used for a small company, two or three washing their hands at the same time, but if guests of various ranks were present, there must be one basin for each rank, and music between courses. Sir Francis Drake, for example, liked to live up to his rank even at sea, and besides observing the usual decorum, he had his meals served with the sound of trumpets and other instruments.

Since Elizabethans used almost every opportunity that offered for feasting, such occasions in the home, besides christenings, weddings, and wakes, were birthdays and visits by important people. Loud was the rejoicing among the poor when they learned a great house, lavish in its hospitality, was to provide such entertainment, and no doubt the retainers also welcomed the prospect of feasting on dainties. When important promotions occurred to men of high place in Church or State offices, banquets at which they feasted their friends meant plenty for the poor who clamored for the broken meats, as well as possible employment for those whose spirit was not yet broken by poverty. As far back as 1466, when George Neville was made Archbishop of York, he reportedly served a banquet consisting among other items of 3,000 geese and 4,000 each of ducks, rabbits, pigeons, and woodcocks. At the enthronement of William Warham as Archbishop of Canterbury in 1504, the feast was no less extravagant.

Henry VIII, who liked his meals served in many courses, had also set a pattern for the rich and powerful lords to follow. He had required fresh scented tablecloths and napkins for every course, and the table decorations were most sumptuous. His great silver and gilt salts were handsome pieces, running from twelve to eighteen inches high, his tall silver-gilt cups were intricately engraved with scenes, particularly the hunt, his spoons contained many complete sets of apostle spoons, his knives had beautifully carved handles of bone or ivory, and his porringers, ewers, and basins were ornately massive. For the showpieces of his table he had exotic birds dressed in their spread plumage, and boars' heads reminding him of the hunter's skill as they were paraded before his appraising eyes. Among the dishes he liked most were great pies, especially potato pies, a fine delicacy at his time and in Elizabeth's too; venison cooked in sour cream; roasted turkeys, also a delicacy; roasted capons, swans, and many kinds of wild fowl, cooked with and without vegetables and sauces; and much ale and wine.

Elizabethans, therefore, often stretched their purses to meet the demands made upon them when they must entertain notables, or when they gave private feasts or banquets, which resulted in a lavish display of large quantities of food of every description, especially the exotic. For example, a feast of this kind must include yams (called potatoes), Irish potatoes (called Virginians, and not yet developed in size beyond an inch or two in diameter), and artichokes. They boiled fowls with leeks and mushrooms, smothered dried ox tongues in a sweet sauce colored with saffron, and used on some meats a highly spiced sauce made with white wine. There were vegetables in season, the ones most favored being green peas, cucumbers, lettuce, radishes, spinach, and small French turnips. They often garnished fish with olives or marrow on toast or smothered it in a black sauce or a high Dutch sauce, very tart. Salads were exotic, with buds from violets and other flowers and the green leaves from rosemary, sage, borage, endive, and lettuce, covered by strange new dressings with ingredients known only to the housewife or special cook. Sometimes sauces were colored by saffron and flavored by musk and expensive ambergris, and were used on meats or salads or tarts. Accordingly, they were sweetened by sugar or made sour by rose or fruit vinegar. At the banquet, chief among the delights were quince pies, almond and cherry tarts, and many kinds of comfits.

Besides the beer and ale used at regular meals, the host provided a great variety of wines—sack, alicant, claret, muscadine, Rhenish, and charneco—to name a few of the fifty-odd varieties, of which at least thirty were quite strong. Sack was a general name used for Spanish and Canary wines, and was popular with all classes, though its cost somewhat limited it to special occasions for modest homes. When Falstaff paid his bills for sack, he laid down five shillings and eightpence for two gallons of this drink, according to Shakespeare. Another popular drink, called bastard, was a sweet Spanish wine commonly sold in taverns. Alicant, a red Spanish wine, and charneco, a sweet Portuguese wine, were favorites of the period, and, in the west country, pommage or cider. To all their wines, Elizabethans commonly added sugar, spices, and ambergris when they wished something exotic.

For all manner of cakes and sugar meats they used the general name of comfits. Gingerbread was one of the most popular among all cakes, though the Elizabethans consumed large quantities of Naples biscuits and marchpane, the latter a great delicacy still in favor for its rich contents of almonds, pistachio nuts, sugar, flour, and various kinds of essences. At feasts this delightful sweet was often highly ornamented and sometimes gilded after it was molded into such forms as apples, pears, plums, grapes, and flowers like the periwinkle. It was even made to look like fish, crabs, and lobsters. When the dainty sugar plate was molded into fantastic shapes, it was usually made of gum dragon laid in rosewater two days, then thickened by orange juice and powdered sugar and hard beating. Sugar sops, another favorite, was a sugary dish of steeped slices of bread, sweetened and highly flavored. Eringo, the candied root of the sea holly, was used like kissing comfits to sweeten the breath. There was much demand for kissing comfits because the large consumption of sugar made the teeth decay early and become offensively black. Queen Elizabeth, who was inordinately fond of sweets, carried some kind of confection with her wherever she went, and consequently suffered much from aching, decayed, blackened teeth.

Besides the expense of providing large quantities of rare and costly foods at feasts, there was still further strain on the purse caused by the need of additional servants in the kitchen. Here, under the numerous cooks, was required almost a small army of boy scullions and kitchen wenches. It has been said that Henry VIII often used over four hundred servants at such times, the helpers being distributed among the offices of scullery, pantry, scalding house, buttery, wafery, and bake house for the preparation of the feast, and among the servers, cupbearers, food tasters, etc., for the serving of the food. When the household was back to normal, the gentry often managed to get along with three or four men house servants to serve at table, and three or four maids for upstairs work, in addition to the servants needed in the kitchen.

Of course these kitchen servants varied according to the amount of entertaining provided by the master at his table. If he was not convivial or was not attempting to make a show of his wealth or trying to gain favor by inviting guests he wished to impress by his home, he might reduce his kitchen staff sharply as soon as special feasts were over. In the country, guests remained longer than in the city, but this expense was somewhat offset by the host's being able to supply the table with produce from his own estates. Furthermore, servants in the country cost less than in town. City households were likely to be burdened with feasting that followed whatever public celebration might occur, for visitors would come to town to enjoy the pageants and general merrymaking. When, therefore, the Lord Mayor of London or of any large town was sworn into office or when the feast of St. George was held, the private householders, as well as the city officials, might feel the cares of openhearted hospitality.

As might be expected, moralists complained not a little that "hospitality, the chiefest point of humanity" which a household could show to friends, strangers, and wayfaring men, should consist so often of "gluttonous diversities." They were also quick to point out that much of the money wasted in this way might "clothe the naked and give alms to the poor." Vaughan (*The Golden Grove*) listed five causes for the extravagance which he declared brought "decay" into English life. He placed ambition first, since it made men of large revenues wear expensive attire and maintain such costly retinues that they were forced to leave home and take chambers in London. Hatred he named second, as it made gentlemen fall out with their neighbors, thereby enriching lawyers. The third, covetousness, set men to hoarding their goods in order to increase their incomes, to raise their rents lest their yeomen keep better hospitality than themselves, and to convert so much tillage to the more profitable raising of cattle and sheep as to cause laws to be made for restoring lands to tillage. Fourth, he said the building of stately homes consumed too much income to enable their owners to leave anything to the poor. His fifth and chief objection was to the extravagant hospitality of the Elizabethan table, for it caused the preparation of many kinds of exotic meat (food) instead of wholesome food. Of course there was much truth in his five "causes" for decay; as to food, the common man was often far better nourished than his envied cousin who picked daintily at the many dishes before him at table.

Most Elizabethan table conversation put equal stress on morals and manners, as did Francis Hawkins in *The School of Virtue*, based on conduct books of the fifteenth and sixteenth centuries. George Washington, like many early Americans, used this book. Some of the conduct books contained literary allusions, witty jests and stories, polite phrases, and whatever would provide guests and hosts with cheer at table. Sometimes they also included recipes for making sauces and for preparing meats and drinks, for at some tables this information might provide housewives with topics of conversation that would be of great interest to them. For men or mixed company, the conversation would be more general, and might even run along philosophical lines. A book designed for almost any type of table conversation was Thomas Twyne's *The Schoolmaster or Teacher of Table Philosophy*, with its discussion as early as 1576 on the "nature and the quality of the meats and drinks" and its merry questions to provoke mirth "touching them their condition and manners with whom we meet at the table." Other conduct books provided anthologies of compliments, similes, and anecdotes, and still others served as "guides" to polite discourse which would season table talk when it was grave and serious with "conceits of wit and pleasant invention, as ingenious epigrams, emblems, anagrams, merry tales, witty questions and answers, mistakings," and the like, all of which Henry Peacham urged in his later book, *The Compleat Gentleman* (1622).

Such writers usually followed Guazzo's popular work in the translated form of Pettie's *The Civile Conversation*, and invariably included his main precepts: guests should not number less than three or more than nine if they were to be entertained intimately in the home; at table one should not be too talkative or too silent; no man should do all the talking; the discourse should be for recreation, not for business; conversation should combine pleasure and intellectual profit but should not be too liberal or too contentious, and finally, table talk should not be too difficult for women to understand if ladies were present.

During Queen Elizabeth's reign, table manners underwent considerable change. When she was a child, grace was usually chanted before and after meals by a priest and choir serving the royal household. Nobles had their own singers in the minstrels' gallery to perform such services on important occasions. At this time it was considered impolite for anyone at table to talk unless addressed by master or mistress. Instead, the chaplain read aloud during much of the meal from the Gospels or from the Martyrology. Occasionally a minstrel was invited to sing a ballad or to tell a story. Travelers and Venetian ambassadors, especially, complained that the English bolted their food in silence and ate little bread because it was too dear. England was culturally far behind the Italians at this time, but its young men were traveling abroad with the express purpose of reporting to the Crown what they found worthy in foreign culture for the English to imitate, and this helped to bring about a change in table manners as well as in other ways of living. But there were other influences also contributing to the general improvement.

The substitution of English heroic traits and English idiom by Sir Thomas North in his popular translation of Plutarch's *Lives* was not purely accidental, for in this work there was a patriotic effort made to impress on English minds a vivid appreciation of classical culture. Nor was Sir Thomas Hoby's translation of Castiglione's *The Courtier* made merely to while away the hours; instead he was filled with the desire to make English lords and ladies shine at court with more splendor than graced the decorum of even Italian and French nobility. Lyly's books on *Euphues* were designed primarily to improve the manners of his readers as well as his own financial and social position at court, and Spenser's *Faerie Queene* was at heart a poet's attempt to show his age the courteous conduct of an ideal gentleman. These men, like Sir Thomas More, did much to advance English culture without making it slavishly imitative. But More by the example of his home life helped most, perhaps, to start the great change in table manners and in other matters of the decorum of the household, for he made a graceful compromise between the severe formality and the frivolous gaiety toward which the reaction was inclined to swing.

After the reading at table of a chapter from the Scriptures (a daughter performing this service, intoning in the ecclesiastical fashion of the period), came words used in most religious houses, "And do thou, O Lord, have mercy on us." More suited the reading to his guests, however, and always indicated how long it was to last by making some sign to the reader, who glanced his way from time to time. Often he interrupted the reading to ask an interpretation of such and such a passage. This permitted an intimate, friendly discussion to occur at a time when such discussions were highly valued by people who did not yet have the Bible as their own. If some learned guest was present, the discussion would be more formal, but always, after it ended, More would suggest some lighter topic, and all would enter heartily into this form of amusement.

During this cheerful part of the table entertainment, More's fool, Henry Patenson, would join; after More became Lord Chancellor, however, he could not indulge so often in levity, and therefore gave his fool to his father. Always, in spite of the formality which More felt he must maintain as Lord Chancellor, he provided some delightful interchange of wit when he entertained important guests at his home. During all Elizabeth's reign, the ceremony of saying grace and the general pattern of decorum observed at the More table prevailed in households that were concerned with gracious living. Nevertheless, the lighter element in conversation rapidly gained importance till it became necessary for one to be a charming guest and able to talk on any subject that might arise in table conversation if one was to be an Elizabethan with acceptable or superior table manners.

As More proved, it was necessary to begin such training while children were young and impressionable. Thus Thomas Twyne designed his book to meet the needs of parents by including many illustrative stories dealing with teaching children according to their gifts and inclinations. At the same time he made his book appeal to adult readers by presenting his instruction for them in a complete and orderly manner.

First, a guest must observe at table the "estimation and calling" of everyone who was present so that when he had occasion to speak he would not be likely to pour forth his own secrets even though he might be under the influence of too much wine. Next, he must make his talk profitable with "delightsome questions," never being at all crabbed in asking them. Suitable ones according to Twyne were: Which is more nourishing, bread made of barley or wheat? Why does stale bread seem whiter and fairer than new? Why is unsalted bread heavier than salted? Other questions he suggested dealt with air, meat, hunger, thirst, indigestion, wine, eggs, fish, grains, herbs, honey, oil, etc. He hastened to say none of them should tax or disturb the brain, but should provide light, merry, honest mirth, and if any awkward silence occurred, it must be broken by the use of wit and quips and questions. He also recommended pleasant tales or histories for refreshing the mind, and he warned that quips must never be sarcastic, but kindly, and always free from any reference to bodily mutilation. In this respect he was far in advance of many of his contemporaries.

Next, Twyne urged people at table to reveal their knowledge of a subject without any ostentation and without obtruding in the conversation, and he cautioned the host to be very careful not to ask questions that might cause a man to confess his ignorance before people or to be drawn into making ill-advised statements. Among the safe subjects for table talk he listed the following: travelers' experiences, dangers encountered by soldiers and any other men, entertainment provided ambassadors when abroad, especially when they were honored by princes, and escapes from pirates by means of one's wit or valor. Other acceptable subjects he related to individual interests: a hunter discussing forests, the chase, deer, etc.; holy men, the rewards to the virtuous, religious ceremonies, and the like. A subject that could never be discussed without reflecting very bad taste was one's own good fortune because most people envied the good fortune of another. Old men should be particularly careful not to "ramble on," as might be their inclination, lest they make too many people weary by their "tiresome discourse."

Then Twyne proceeded to give jests about a sentence or two in length which he considered suitable for table talk about kings, princes, knights, soldiers, squires, armor bearers, novices, physicians, lawyers, usurers, buyers, merchants, husbandmen in the country, thieves, merry jesters and their devices, women, maids, boys, the lame and the halt, sisters, blind folk, fools, the possessed, popes, cardinals, bishops, artificers, archdeacons, canons, priests, abbots, priors, monks, preaching friars and other friars—his list, like that of Chaucer's pilgrims, giving a fairly good cross-section of Elizabethan society. As an example of a widow's faithlessness, he quoted a story popular with Elizabethans: "There was a woman which oftentimes would say unto her husband that if he should die, she would never marry more. But when he was dead, and she talked as touching marrying another, even by his coffin's lid, her maid rebuked her, saying that her master was warm yet: 'If he be warm quoth the mistress, I will blow upon him till he be cold.'" No matter what topic was chosen for table talk, each guest must be able to contribute his story, but his was best which had never been heard before and also had a merry jest to provoke laughter.

The mumming and disguising, used in the early part of the century for entertainment between courses at banquets, developed into the elaborate masques of the late sixteenth and early seventeenth centuries and were used more frequently at the great houses and at court for table entertainment, especially after the banquet. But when drinking and dancing became the main feature in the reign of James I, the dignity and charm of Queen Elizabeth's more decorous forms of amusement were lost. The influence of the court upon the people's domestic life is hard to estimate, but it must have been considerable upon those who tried to improve their condition by following the example of important people in the social class above theirs.

It is doubtful whether any sovereign was ever more sensitive to the reactions of the common people than was Elizabeth. When she was entertained on her progresses, therefore, her host was wise if he managed to include some of the country people in the elaborate program he arranged for his Queen's amusement. In this way she kept close to her people, feeling that she knew how they lived and what they thought and what they admired, especially in their Queen. No one understood all this better than the Earl of Leicester, and when in 1575 he provided a week's series of sports and frolics, he planned each day with great attention to the smallest detail, with the country people bringing the last day to a fitting climax. Fortunately, an account of the festivities is preserved in a letter by Laneham, a man of the burgher class, to a mercer friend of his in London. It shows how a man of low origin but quick wit who had attached himself to a great lord could, in his prosperity, look down upon those near the foot of the social ladder. For this reason, his lively description includes details that a person born among the gentry would scarcely notice.[5]

Most lords expecting the Queen's visit fretted over the expense involved, for they must provide "thoughtful" gifts to erase from her mind the fatigue of her journey besides arranging a day-by-day program of events. The gifts might include rich jewels daintily concealed in nosegays, gowns and accessories like fans and embroidered jackets, spoons and salts of silver, and even musical instruments like the virginal waiting for her in her apartments. To Leicester such gifts would be only another detail by which to show his taste and consideration.

Elizabeth arrived at Kenilworth on Saturday, and on the next day attended preaching at the parish church. In the afternoon there was music for dancing among the lords and ladies at the palace. On Monday the July day was so hot that the Queen did not leave her room till 5:00 in the evening. Then she rode to a deer hunt, and shot the animal as it fled into a lake. The party returned by torchlight from the wood. On the next day came more music and dancing, and the Queen went to stand on a bridge over a pool, from which issued a barge with "delectable" music. On Wednesday, another deer hunt was provided, and this time when the animal fled into the lake, the hunters only wounded it. Cutting off its ears "for ransom," they let it go free.

On Thursday, there was bear-baiting with the thirteen bears for which, according to Laneham, the Earl of Leicester had paid so handsome a sum. The very fierce bandogs (part mastiff, but lighter and better fighters than full mastiffs) performed so well that the Queen described the sport as "very pleasant." The common people, who also must watch the contest, were simply frantic with excitement, for the bears with their pink eyes leered at the dogs which nimbly and quickly took advantage of the beasts. The bears were experienced enough to avoid the dogs, but if bitten would try to get away, biting, clawing, roaring, tossing, tumbling, and winding themselves free. Finally, when loose, they would shake

[5] Robert Laneham, *A Letter of 1575* (ed. F. J. Furnivall, 1907).

their ears two or three times and make everyone roar with laughter as they looked "so comical with their faces covered with blood and saliva."

Thursday night was enlivened by fireworks and guns, which gave to both eye and ear two hours of "grace and delight." Then an Italian tumbler performed such feats of agility, forward, backward, and sideways, up with turnings, and in circles, that Robert Laneham declared he could not believe his eyes. However, he remembered how Mandeville had told of two-headed men who could "reason and talk with two tongues and with two persons at once, and sing like birds" while they nimbly performed in a manner requiring joints and bones as lithe and pliant as sinews. With those feats in mind to compare with the tumbler's, he could more readily believe the tumbler was real also.

Friday and Saturday were too windy and rainy for open shows. The storms tempered the heat, however, and Sunday surpassed all the days that had gone before. In the morning there was worship at the parish church, and again in the afternoon at Kenilworth to celebrate the memory of St. Kenelin for whom the castle had been named. The high point of the day's entertainment was a solemn bridal procession to the tiltyard, followed by the popular sport of riding at the quintain. Laneham carefully describes this quintain as consisting of a thick plank of wood set fast in the highway where the bride and groom were to pass. Young countrymen with poles were to tilt on horseback at the bag of sand fastened to the crossbar on the plank. The one that broke the most poles would be declared to show the most activity, and would be crowned with the victor's garland. When the bridal procession came marching toward the tiltyard, all watched it with keen interest.

As the procession entered the yard, it was in proper form. Lusty lads and bold bachelors came first with blue buckram and bridelaces (or ribbons) on a branch of green broom tied to their left arms; they marched two and two. Each carried a spear in the right hand, and some wore hats and some caps. Laneham called them a motley group, for some wore coats, some were in jerkins, some in doublet and hose, some had boots and spurs, some had boots and no spurs, and some had neither. One even wore sandals, and another had pads fastened to his feet with cords. Yet with the Queen to see them, they carried themselves as well as they could.

Following them were sixteen riding men, well clad, and then the groom. He was "bravely attired" in his father's tawny worsted jacket, and he wore a straw hat with a crown like a steeple. On his hands were harvest gloves as a sign of good husbandry, and on his back a pen and inkhorn to show he was bookish. He walked with a limp, however, for one leg in his youth had been broken in football. A new muffler or kerchief was tied to his girdle to "keep it from being lost," scoffed Laneham, and also to show he was not only aware of the importance of handkerchiefs, but that he was well loved by his mother, who had lent him hers.

Next came the gay, prancing morris men—six dancers, a Maid Marian, and a fool. They were followed by three virgins Laneham described smartly as "pretty as a breast of bacon," since they were very old—at least thirty-five. The three special spice cakes they carried had been made from a bushel of wheat from Leicester's bakehouse, and as they walked along before the bride "with set faces," they kept their lips "demurely pressed into a simpering smile." Now the sophisticated Laneham searched for another simile, and compared them to "a mare cropping a thistle." Close upon their heels appeared an "unwieldy, misshapen lout, freckle-faced, red-headed, clean-dressed in doublet and hose," but "so bashful because of his new clothes" that he was "loath to advance." His task was to bear the bridecup in a barrel of sugarplums. The decorator of this barrel evidently considered it a work of art, for it was adorned with a branch of broom, "gaily gilded like rosemary," and streaming bride laces of red and yellow buckram, which was a fine linen. As he carried the barrel proudly aloft so that its ribbons might flutter in the wind, his poor freckled face became covered with flies swarming after the sweetmeats. Patiently he beat away the insects, "killing them by the score," and marched along "in good order."

Now came the bride, riding (as in the country) between two ancient parishioners, good, honest townspeople. Her steed was a fat stallion, which carried itself well in spite of the heat, though it was ill-smelling and made the bride so, too. Laneham estimated her age at thirty-five also, and described her as "brown as a bay, ugly, foul, and ill-favored, but proud as could be that she was to dance before the Queen." Immediately after her came her bridesmaids, two by two, dozens of them, who seemed for favor, fashion, and cleanliness, as "meet for such a bride as a wooden ladle for a porridge pot."

As the procession entered the tiltyard, many were the martial acts performed before the eyes of the Queen. Just where Elizabeth was stationed Laneham does not say, but one may be sure she was reasonably safe from the dust, though not so far away as to be remote to the people whom she delighted by her royal presence. No matter how amusing their country ways might seem to some of her courtiers, her own courteous manner never embarrassed the people as the superiority of Laneham and others might. Thus the bridal party put on their pageant with natural delight, confident they were pleasing good Queen Bess and her brilliant following.

The bridegroom had first chance at the quintain. He broke his spear, but his mare stumbled, and he had all he could do to stay in the saddle, for he had no stirrups. He recovered himself, but broke his girdle and lost his pen and inkwell, which he was ready to weep for, but he did not lose his muffler, or handkerchief, which, Laneham felt, cheered him somewhat. At this point the writer's pen runs along merrily: ". . . yet durst he be bolder to blow his nose and wipe his face with the flappet of his father's jacket than with his mother's muffler," and adds derisively, ". . . 'tis a goodly matter when youth is mannerly brought up in fatherly love and motherly awe."

After the bridegroom's effort the rest of his band tried their luck, but soon with no order at all, some running their horses into the crowd of people watching the spectacle, and some missing the quintain and being hit on their heads by the swinging board or bag of sand. Later, some of the riders jousted with their opponents, "their countenances stern, their looks grim, their attempts courageous, their adventures desperate, their courage dangerous," and sometimes both horse and man toppled to the ground. "One would have laughed to see it," wrote Laneham, "even had he been told his wife was dying."

Meanwhile, in the castle of Kenilworth, preparations were under way as the servants and entertainers jostled one another preparing for the banquet and masque that were to show how a queen *should* be honored. We are told that over three hundred rich dishes were proudly shown in the display procession before the company was formally served. Apparently the two-hour masque which followed the sumptuous meal was well received, though Laneham failed to describe it. Instead, he remarked with satisfaction on the gorgeous apparel and set down with great care the details of the costume worn by a minstrel who took his fancy as he sang his song, accompanied by his harp.

This man was about forty-five years old, and in good voice. His hair was cut round, and smoothed down with capon's grease; his beard "smugly shaven." His cape of Kendal green, gathered at the neck with its narrow gorget, was fastened with a white clasp close to the chin, and every ruff on his shirt stood up "like a wafer." From a lappet in his bosom was drawn his handkerchief, edged with blue lace and marked with a true lover's knot, for he was still a bachelor. His girdle was red, and Sheffield knives hung at his side. The long side sleeves of his gown were slit from shoulder to hand, lined with white cotton, and hung down to his mid-leg. Thus they permitted the black worsted sleeves of his doublet to be seen with their wool and silk cuffs, laced at the wrist with blue threaded points, and finished with a welt toward the hand. Nether stocks of red and pumps blacked with soot and shined, for they were not new, completed his costume. These pumps also had a fashionable crosscut slashing at the toes, which Laneham said must have "eased his corns." The man's harp hung on a red ribbon around his neck, and his tuning hammer (to tune the pins of the harp) was tied to a green lace. Under the gorget of his gown at the throat was a fair silver chain, which minstrels of Middlesex used when traveling in the summer from fairs to fine houses; and from it hung a scutcheon resplendent with color and metal, which showed against his breast its ancient arms of Islington.

Laneham, like most Elizabethans, took a certain pleasure in meeting the challenge to measure a man's worldly success by his dress. Perhaps clothes have never meant so much to people as during this age; consequently the rapidly changing styles and the straining of the lower classes to approximate some of the extravagances of the rich resulted in a clothes-consciousness from which scarcely anyone could break free. Almost like a disease grew the coveting of rich new apparel. Although many sober people were disturbed over this infatuation for dress, they also became more or less the victims of fashion.

After Queen Elizabeth's death, old established families tried to maintain the dignity of what they called sober apparel, but in spite of them the taste of the time turned to lighter and lighter colors and richer and richer materials till Fynes Moryson accused the English of becoming "more light than the lightest French and more sumptuous than the proudest Persians." He lamented the fact that people wearing old clothes which were good in everything but style were mocked by others as "proud and obstinate fools" till they were forced to join the real fools of extravagance. Thus they decked themselves out in beaver hats, "shirts and bands of finest linens, gilded daggers and swords, garters and shoe roses of silk with gold or silver lace, the seams of their stockings wrought with silk or gold, their cloaks in summer of silk, in winter at least lined with velvet or cloth of gold or silver," and all so overlaid with gold or silk lace that the "rich stuffs" could hardly be seen. Elizabeth's commanders of war had used light colors, "richly laced and embroidered," but gentlemen at court had looked on reds and yellows as less comely than their dark colors, though at times they wore white.

During Elizabeth's reign one of the best dressed men was the Earl of Oxford, whose clothes during the four years before he reached his majority are reported as costing him £600. Even when he wore black satin doublet, velvet breeches, silk stockings, silver-buckled garters, flat-footed shoes of soft leather, a velvet cap with a pheasant feather on its side, and a rapier in a silver-studded belt, he was elegantly clad. The Earl of Leicester loved fine clothes so much that he is said to have paid £500 for seven colorful doublets and two cloaks. Lord Burghley, however, in spite of his prominence, always dressed soberly in gray or black.

Moryson also complained of the English imitating the French in wearing scabbards and sheaths of velvet or embroidered linen on their rapiers and daggers. Until 1580, every gentleman over eighteen wore a weapon—a sword, rapier, or dagger, and at times both rapier and dagger. Even the laborer had his sword and buckler, or bow, except when actually at work; parsons carried daggers and apprentices carried knives. But so many weapons encouraged duels, and the 1580 law restricted the long sword to three feet, the dagger to twelve inches, and apprentices' weapons to clubs. But if weapons were restricted, colors were not, and neither were jewels. Gradually, as the colors grew lighter and the materials richer, the chains and plain gold rings gave way to jewels and diamond rings. Few men were wearing chains at all by 1603, and the fine ladies used rich chains of pearl or light chains from France. All jewels were real, the counterfeit being considered disgraceful.

Masks, busks (stays), muffs, fans, periwigs, and bodkins were first devised by courtesans in Italy, and got to England for "gallant" wear about 1572. The English were making pins and fine knives by 1562, and Spanish needles by 1565. By 1573, the old wooden setting sticks for ruffs were replaced by steel ones, and almost immediately ruffs became very beautiful, for delicate laces could be set with the new steel sticks. Now love of clothes caused inventive minds to produce many new devices for adorning the person that would have made Henry VIII envious, for when he was young and handsome he was very much concerned about his appearance. He would have been amazed at the velvet and silk masks at his daughter's court, the long waists achieved by corsets, the frilly muffs and fans, the pins and periwigs, the love kerchiefs and silk garters, the shoe buckles and roses, the many, many beautiful buttons that so far surpassed the crystal ones he had thought so fine, and the richly embroidered waistcoats and gowns. He would have been surprised too at the smart blue gowns and caps worn by the apprentices.

Indeed, so eager were all classes to dress themselves and their servants well because the Queen's taste encouraged such extravagance that all articles of adornment were constantly increasing in numbers and undergoing change. Though the laws still stipulated that people must dress according to their station in life, there was much complaint that even "players and cutpurses" dressed like gentlemen. In spite of this flouting of the law the general feeling was that dress should proclaim one's place in the social structure of the time.

Emanuel van Meteran, traveling in England in 1575, was impressed by the elegance of the light and costly garments of the people. They were always wanting novelties, he said, and changed their fashions each year. He observed they wore their best apparel, even when riding abroad, as no one else did anywhere in the world. Their light clothes, he felt, enabled them to change more frequently and perhaps caused them to wear less clothing than used by people in the Low Countries. He found the English clever, handsome, and well-made, but like all islanders, tender. The women, who were especially fair, protected their faces against the sun with hats and veils, and their hands with gloves, even if they were only peasants. Once only married women had worn hats and daughters had gone without hood, mantle, or veil, but now ladies of distinction covered their faces with velvet or silken masks or vizards, and feathers. They also carried silver-handled fans and small mirrors attached to their girdles or on chains about the neck.

Hats, of course, changed styles rapidly "to the astonishment of many." In about 1570, all citizens' wives were required to wear white woolen caps instead of the white three-cornered miniver caps, with their peaks rising to three and four inches. The bonnets of aldermen's wives had been somewhat like these, only larger and showier. By 1575, hats had become flat and turban-like, or flat like a pancake with a feather hanging down over the shoulder. They were worn over jeweled hair and, in cold weather, over light caps. Ten years later hats had changed so much that any style was in vogue if it flattered the lady's individual beauty.

The bright lights at court so enhanced the delicate coloring of the women's faces and the richness of their apparel that visiting ambassadors often compared them to a choir of angels. When the German merchant Kiechel was traveling in England in 1585, he said the women were the prettiest "by nature" he had ever seen, for they did not paint or bedaub their faces as in Italy and other places. But their dress style was "somewhat awkward" because of the splendid materials used for their three cloth gowns or petticoats worn one over the other. In 1592, Frederick, Duke of Württemberg,[6] was amazed at the "exceeding fine" dress of the English women, who wore velvets in the very streets and never went without hats even when he was sure they had not a crust of bread at home.

Moryson criticized the general extravagance of the 1590's in English dress, though he felt the merchants' wives in spite of their "proud and expensive" clothes were decently clad. All their gowns, he said, were made of some light stuff, gathered at the back, girdled, and provided with guards or trimming on the skirt. Their aprons were of silk or fine lawn or linen, and they wore their silk caps a little raised from the forehead. If their "state" decreed otherwise, however, they wore beaver hats. None went without a light chain or necklace of pearl.

Among all classes, rich or poor, the general rule was to scant the undergarments and to spend money on those that would be seen. Shirts were men's inmost garment, and smocks were women's. These were commonly used as night clothes if people did not sleep in the nude. Not until 1640 did real night clothes evolve, and these were long-sleeved, straight robes with a V-shaped neck that was gathered close by a cord. Elizabethan men's shirts were of white linen or silk, had high necks and long sleeves, and were about three feet long. Fine shirts were elaborately embroidered on the front, on the neck band, and on the sleeve bands with gold or silver or colored silk thread. If not embroidered, they were ornamented with cut work or drawn work or edged with bobbin lace. Women's smocks were thirty to forty inches long and were made somewhat like a man's shirt. The slit front opening and the neck and sleeve bands might be trimmed with lace or embroidered with black, gold, silver, or colored silk, but there was always a lace edging on the neck band, too. If she used her smock for a night garment, the Elizabethan woman on rising put on

[6] William Brenchley Rye, *England as Seen by Foreigners in the Days of Elizabeth and James the First, 1592–1610* (1865).

a sleeveless circular cape to hide part of the smock; this was called a thin night mantle. Both men and women wore the same kind of slippers in the house; the only difference might be size. Such slippers covered only the front part of the foot and were made of wool, silk, or leather, and were often embroidered.

A woman might wear several petticoats at one time, though two or three were the usual number. They were slipped on over the head and tied by a draw string or fastened to the bodice by points. They were worn over the smock. Sometimes they were lined. Gold or silver lace was used so extravagantly for fine petticoats that it almost covered them. Since they were about two and a half yards in circumference, petticoats trimmed with lace took a great deal of time as well as material for the making. Yet when a woman had put on her petticoats she was only at the beginning of her dressing for the day.

Stockings usually came over the foot and up to, or over, the knee. In men's apparel they were called nether stocks or nether hose. Poor people wore nether hose of cloth, but after 1561, no fastidious dresser wore hose that were not knit. Gallants, like fine ladies, wore silk hose. The garters were often extravagantly ornamented, their wide sashes of taffeta or sarcenet edged and fringed with gold, or of cypress edged with bone lace or spangled and adorned with roses, and tied in large bows. For the plain wear of the common man, garters were simply bands of worsted tape (caddis) usually tied just below the knee. After knee breeches were introduced, cross garters went out of fashion, except for old men who continued to wear them till well on into the next century. Women's hose were of silk if they could afford such extravagance; otherwise, they wore knit stockings unless they were too poverty-stricken to possess anything but cloth hose. Their garters were often extremely intricate in design. Made of satin, cloth of gold or silver, gold tissue, velvet, or whatever seemed beautiful and satisfactory for tying, their garters were embroidered and edged with delicate lace and ornamented with spangles and roses. As a favor to be worn by an admirer or lover, such a garter might be well worth the effort so frequently demanded of young men when ladies granted it as a reward for chivalrous deeds. As gifts they were acceptable to ladies themselves when New Year's Day brought several pairs from men or women friends. No wonder the best shops kept a lavish assortment of them on display at all times.

The upper hose (or trunks) worn by men were called by several names according to their style. During the 'eighties and 'nineties, the popular Venetians were close-fitting, and bombasted, pleated, or bell-shaped. At first they reached below the knee, but later were short. Wide breeches, called Galligascons or Venetian galligascons or gallyslops, were fitted at the hips and full at the knee. Slops were wide or bagging breeches of knee length or shorter, and some of them were clumsy in appearance. Such were the Switzer and German slops that were paned (with loose panels) and ornamented with a very full lining of contrasting color to hang between the panes in loose puffs. Swaggering slops in favor at the end of the century were made of rich velvet, silk, or cloth of silver or gold and expensively trimmed with lace or gold embroidery. French slops or breeches were merely round trunk hose. All the trunk hose reached from the waist to just above or just below the knees, and were padded with hair, rags, bran, bombast, or whatever would make them round as pumpkins. They were pleated and paned with rich linings of contrasting colors and were sometimes embroidered in rich designs. When James I came to the throne these trunk hose were discarded by the fashionable for full Venetians, but poor people continued wearing trunk hose for another generation, stuffing them with rags or sawdust till they must have been very uncomfortable, as they made it difficult for the wearer to bend. The fastidious rich, however, dispensed with this bombast, though they kept their trunk hose full enough to permit them to hang in folds. At about this time Spanish breeches also became popular, for they were quite comfortable, being loose and tubular and not confined at the knee. All trunk hose were attached to the doublet by tagged laces called points, and no lord or fine gentleman could do this lacing for himself. When the trunk hose were unlaced, they were said to be untrussed.

The trunk hose, lengthened to just below the knee in tubular continuations of rolls in contrasting color or material, were called canons. They had the advantage of dispensing with garters, for the nether stocks could be tucked under them or merely rolled over their edge. All these breeches except the loosely fitting Venetians had the codpiece. This baglike appendage was sometimes padded into various shapes and sizes and even ornamented with silk bows or gold pins or pocket bags. In time the full Venetians were succeeded by "little breeches" that were still full by means of pleats, but were tapered toward the knee, where about three inches above the knee they were fitted into a band and finished by a circle of points with dangling aglets. The garters for the nether stocks were wide silk bands or ribbons tied in soft bows below the knee.

By the end of Elizabeth's reign the waistcoat had become very popular, perhaps because fashionable ladies also wore it. Originally it was designed for men to wear under the doublet, but when women adopted it, it became very showy with its rich embroidery. All kinds of material were used for it, from flannel and velvet to silk and taffeta and damask. Essex was very fond of his waistcoat made of bright red woolen material, and wore it on the day of his execution. Sometimes there were sleeves but not when it was worn under the doublet and quilted for extra warmth or beauty. It was put on over the head and fitted snugly to the figure, thus adding as much to personal comfort on cold, damp days as the modern sweater.

The doublet was also close-fitting, and its detachable sleeves were frequently of contrasting material and color, yet this garment must always be in harmony with the rest of the costume. When women took to wearing doublets, they fastened their petticoats to them just as men laced their breeches to them with points. This trussing consisted of running tagged points of breeches or petticoats through eyelets in the doublet, and tying the two ends of each point in a bowknot. Points were used to lace in sleeves of men's and women's garments, and men also used points to tie in the codpiece. Even when hooks and eyes came in for joining men's trunk hose and doublet, still points were used on the outside for ornamentation, the laces consisting of fine silk and the tags of engraved gold or silver.

Doublets must not be confused with the jackets of this time, which were also form-fitting and worn with or without sleeves. Usually jackets were put on under the doublet, but they might also be used as outer garments, especially by lackeys. Frequently they were quite ornamental when so used, being made of silk, guarded, and trimmed with lace or embroidered. When women adopted this article of clothing, they usually wore it outside and made it as beautiful as possible.

As doublets could provide the wearer with rich color and trimming, men possessed more of them than changes in hose. The doublet's sleeves, made of contrasting material, might be of crimson satin, for example, completely covered with embroidery in Venice gold or white, trimmed with white delicate lace, and lined with black velvet. Or their material of brocade, velvet, satin, taffeta, or a silk and woolen fabric called rash, might be slashed and pinked to show the contrasting lining, and the garment trimmed with fine lace. Doublets were likely to be expensive, the cost depending on the materials used. The buttons, for example, were jewels in themselves, and ranged in number from fourteen to thirty-four. When hooks and eyes came into use, lace and embroidery sufficed for the button ornamentation. Should a man wear a woolen cloak, his doublet would be of silk or satin, and his breeches of velvet, the colors of this costume being chosen with great care to achieve perfect harmony.

On the whole, men's costumes were form-fitting, but women's were not. A very peculiar and popular style of doublet in the 'nineties consisted of the stiff peascod front that came down to a long point. Its popularity was due to its tendency to make the waist look long, and this was why women adopted it for a bodice and then proceeded to cover it with lavish ornamentation. One fad, which caused doublets of white canvas to be stuffed out to make a man's body look twice its natural size, resulted, perhaps, in the worst of all distortions in his apparel. Doublets worn over the armor might have attached pleated skirts (called bases) that reached from the waist to the knee. Military men either replaced this type of doublet with a short coat (called a jerkin) or wore the jerkin over the doublet. This garment had a collar and it usually had sleeves. Officers had it made of silk, satin, velvet, or like rich materials on one side and trimmed with lace, embroidery, or pinking and slashing. On the reverse side for practical wear was soft buff leather. The jerkin continued in use long after Elizabeth's time, for it was very practical. Even gentlemen attendants used it instead of the expensive doublet.

When men had to outfit themselves with a new suit, they must expect to pay for several garments—doublet, hose, coat, jerkin, and mandilion or cloak—all of harmonizing or matching material. It is amazing how many yards of silk or velvet or rich woolen mixtures went into such an ensemble. One of the Queen's courtiers might count on buying sixteen to twenty yards of satin or velvet besides that much in a contrasting color for rich lining of a suit. Then he must buy yards and yards of lace and ribbon and as many buttons as he could afford. When the mandilion was first used by gentlemen and soldiers, it was a short, loose coat with hanging sleeves, worn with one sleeve hanging over the chest and one over the back, and usually was made with bright silk and silver or gold lace to make it gay. Eventually it became a garment for grooms and lackeys.

A practical coat for soldiers and travelers and men out on business in bad weather was the gaberdine, worn over the cloak. Long, loose, with long sleeves and a belt, it was made to provide protection and warmth, and was sometimes lined throughout with fur. The rich used fine material for this garment, but the poor used russet, a coarse homespun wool. Soldiers' coats were usually of buff leather, and servants' coats for a long time were blue. A coat usually reached to the knees.

In the early part of the sixteenth century, men had worn Spanish capes with hoods. These cloaks came to the knee also, and their circular edge was ornamented with lace or guards of velvet or silk. Later came the French cloaks, long, circular or semicircular garments. For lovers of clothes, these cloaks were provided with shoulder capes, which were often used separately. They were made of rich silks or woolen, trimmed with bugles (beads), pearls, jewels, and so beautifully lined that either side could be used. These shoulder capes were so draped as to reveal the owner's rich suit beneath. Finally came cloaks for every occasion—morning, afternoon, or evening—cloaks with or without sleeves and hoods and with all kinds of linings, cloaks of all lengths from the waist down, cloaks entirely of fur and called pilches, cloaks that were loose, wide-sleeved, reaching to, or halfway to, the knee, and called cassocks. They were elaborately made of rich materials, embroidered, and lavishly trimmed. The cloaks of scarlet and other rich colors contrasted sharply with the blue of apprentices and servants and the dull browns and blacks and blues or natural colors of the homespun cloth used by the poor, not because they liked such dull colors but because their economic status demanded them.

Shoes were of many styles and materials, and were made of velvet, satin, and leather for wear indoors and out, and styled for comfort or appearance. Pumps were most favored, and were used by both men and women—ladies, gentlemen, and servants. They covered all the foot but had no heel and were used chiefly indoors, unless an affected person chose to wear them outside. Made of one sole and close-fitting as well as low, they were comfortable and quiet. For making these shoes, various materials were used, consisting of light leather or cloth, fine silks or satins or velvets, and most of all, tuft-taffeta. They had no ties. If one had to go outside, he put on pattens if he was a servant or common man, and pantofles if he was rich. Pattens had wooden soles to raise the foot off the ground, and were attached to the ankle by two straps. Pantofles, also called mules or high slippers, protected delicate shoes in the house or street. They were made of leather or velvet or silk over the front of the instep and were richly lined, but their soles were of cork that rose toward the heel. They stayed in favor till well on into the next century, and when made of rich materials, were lace-trimmed, spangled, embroidered, pinked, and slashed.

Chopines, favored by those who cared more for fashion than comfort, were an exaggerated form of the pantofle. Chopines were leather shoes fitted to a column sometimes fantastically high, and were held to the foot by means of a piece of pinked or decorated leather over the toe or by two pieces of leather or silk fastened with ties over the ankle. They somewhat resembled today's open-toed, open-heeled sandal. The high column of cork was painted or covered with leather or silk, and jeweled and embroidered for the fastidious wearer. Only women, of course, wore such shoes, and if they chose those with very high heels, they could not walk without the aid of an admirer's arm. If overshoes were needed for real protection against the weather, both men and women wore galoshes.

Dancing shoes had flexible soles and were held in place by small ties concealed by roses of metal lace with spangles and eyes. Sometimes the ties of women's shoes were ribbons, and their colors might be chosen to compliment a lover. In this case, the ribbons were tell-tales, and the happy lover might beg them as a favor to wear in his hat or over his ear. As ribbons grew in width and length because of the fad of intricate knotting in the ties, over a yard of ribbon might be used for each of the lady's shoes. Yet the men's dancing shoes also had their roses and spangles and pinking and slashing, and were trimmed with buckles, rosettes of ribbons and lace, and jewels.

A man's dress shoes were made of various materials; if of cloth, he could pull them on, but if made of leather, they might require a shoehorn, some of which had handles reaching to the knee. Dressy leather shoes had cork soles and were decorated with ties, etc. Foppish young men preferred velvet or soft perfumed leather shoes in which they went mincing along the streets, turning up their noses at the rude shoes of rough leather they called start-ups, made for rustics. Brogues were heavy shoes made of untanned leather, and only tough feet could wear them at all. Buskins were heavy or light. If worn by the common or working man, they had thick soles and came halfway up the leg with straps at the ankle to make them secure. If worn by the rich, they were made of light leather and were highly ornamented with laces and pinking or slashing. The common man had to polish his shoes with soot-blacking or preserve them for long wear by rubbing them with oil or grease, but fine gentlemen scorned such "liquored" shoes, and would not tolerate their use by servants in their part of the house.

When going on a long journey, the gentleman wore riding boots that came up to, or over, the knee, but which could be folded down to knee or calf when off the horse for comfort in walking. It was never easy to pull off boots. Usually gentlemen wore boot hose or foot leggings to protect their boots and nether stocks from the stain of travel. For such leggings, the rich used fine linen or wool, lined with velvet, making them both attractive and serviceable. Gallants wore boot hose with showy ruffles at the top of wide boots, and arranged the ruffles carefully when they dismounted. The common man who could not afford boots wore only thick, heavy boot hose of coarse wool, laced or tied at the ankles to make them less clumsy.

In general, Elizabethan headgear consisted of hats for men (though women liked hats too), caps for women, and hoods for both men and women. Children, especially little ones, wore the biggin, a close-fitting cap that covered well the top and back of the head. Soldiers and sailors used the round, brimless Monmouth cap, with its tapering crown, but the flat hats of the apprentices had brims. If a gentleman wished a Monmouth type of hat, he simply had it made of velvet or some other fine material, trimmed to suit his taste. The two most popular fur caps were the miniver, tricornered in shape and made of ermine and spotted weasel fur, and the lettice cap of soft gray or white fur, with three corners like a pope's hat. This latter cap was very different from the lettuce cap (also called lettice cap), which was actually made of lettuce and was supposed to be able to induce sleep. For old men a favorite hat was made with a slight brim that was turned up and fastened with buttons of their choosing.

Since men wore their hats or caps in the house and on the street, as women did their caps, both felt the need of caps at night. Men's nightcaps were tied under the chin by ribbons or laces, and women wore coifs, made in many ways of many materials. Most common was their coif of fine white linen, embroidered and edged with lace. It fitted the head somewhat like a biggin and, if not tied under the chin with ribbons, was pinned to the hair. Women also wore kerchiefs and pastes, the latter made of a folded material that encircled the head in such a fashion as to frame the face and not conceal the hair.

Brimmed hats had crowns varying in height and covering only the top of the head. Such was the popular Milan bonnet. From 1570 on, the high-crowned hats were worn by both men and women, though most women preferred the little cockleshell caps, and hoods. Hats were usually of velvet or silk made over buckram frames, as in the case of the popular

Caointank, which was high, conical, and pointed or flat on top. Various kinds of trimming were added, such as hatbands, plumes, and a large jewel placed against the upturned brim. If turned up on each side, a cable hatband was used. Women who wore hats favored those made of beaver fur, for they came in many colors, were trimmed and lined with satin and taffeta, and were attractive whether much ornamented or merely graced by a plume. Taffeta hats, of course, were for dressy wear, and were pinked, jeweled, and embroidered. For common wear, felt hats were used. They were practical for traveling, and still could be made very modish, chiefly by hatbands. An especially attractive band for this purpose was made of cypress or ribbon or even pearls and gold and silver twisted into the cable or put on plain. Other trimming consisted of buttons, pinking, and fine feathers.

Common people most often used a very coarse woolen hat that soon wore shiny. Consequently, they had to rub or thrum the felt to make its nap stand up, and their hats became known as thrummed hats. In the country during summer, the rustics wore straw hats shaped somewhat like beehives. At other times, here and in town, the common people wore their coarse hats, caps, or hoods.

All during the sixteenth century the hood was worn by some of the men and by many of the women. For a time the French hood was highly favored by the women till they discarded it for the hat. The common people, however, did not part with it so soon, and some type of hood remained in favor with many of the women in various parts of the country till the present century. The French hood was made of softly pleated velvet or silk, and was worn over the back of the head as far forward as the ears. This left the hair to frame the face with curls, or in lieu of this method of softening the face, various types of decorative bands were used.

When ribbons were not used to keep the hair in place under the hood, cauls and creppins were worn. The caul was usually a close-fitting hair-net of gold or hair threads decorated with pearls and lined with taffeta, cloth of gold, or some smooth fabric. The creppin was a caul of velvet, cobweb lawn, or a network of gold or silver thread. Ornamental borders were also worn with hoods to enhance their beauty. These were called "billiments," and consisted of circlets of pearls, precious stones, and velvets or silks edged with lace or pleated cypress. Frontlets were devised to shade the eyes, and the bongrace was one of these. It was a projecting brim or shade, and was worn with caps and bonnets as well as with hoods. It was made of linen, cypress, network, and lace. Today an adaptation of the hood with its bongrace makes one understand a little better how women of the sixteenth century faced the weather with some degree of comfort and not a little charm in their appearance.

If a lady was dressed informally, she usually put on over her petti-coats a kirtle or loose-bodied gown that looked very much like a wrapper as it hung from her neck and shoulders to the ground. It had close sleeves and no waist, but over a shapely figure might be very attractive. Men also wore similar gowns, especially if they were old men or members of such groups as lawyers, the clergy, or civil officials. Old men and staid citizens wore these gowns with ease because the lines were flowing, and the garment opened in front like a modern coat. But they were dear, for they took six to twelve yards of material, and if they were richly guarded, embroidered, trimmed with lace, pinked, or jagged, they could be very expensive indeed. They came in several styles known as the Dutch or round gown without a train, the Flanders gown with a fitted bodice and stiff collar, and the French gown with full skirt, rolls or wings at the sleeves, and hanging sleeves, all very decorative with pinking.

Less costly and more comfortable for lounging, especially at night, were the nightgowns or dressing gowns. These were of ankle length and came with sleeves and a shawl collar. They were used by both men and women, for they were warmer than other gowns, less elaborate, and could be used outdoors as well as indoors, some of them even having a hood. Their materials varied from silk to wool, and sometimes they were embroidered and trimmed with fur or, if much warmth was desired, lined throughout with fur. Falling open from neck to toe, they had many buttons, and sometimes very rich linings. Their colors, like their materials, ranged from brilliant to sober.

While the partlet was in fashion, it was worn over the bodice, first as a jacket and later as a detachable covering for neck and chest. Men wore partlets during the reign of Henry VIII because then their doublets were cut low, and matched their partlets and sleeves. Women's partlets were more elaborate than men's and also matched their sleeves. They were made of fine materials and closely embroidered. After 1580 they lost favor and, by the 'nineties, were completely out of style.

When corsets became a necessary part of woman's dress, they were put on before the bodice and were sometimes referred to as the under-bodice. Their stays or busks were made of whalebone or wood and were often richly carved and ornamented. These busks were inserted in casings and tied by laces or busk points. In some extreme cases the underbodice was made entirely of wood or even of iron. Sometimes a lady's busk points were given as a favor to a man; then they were worn proudly, tied to his wrist.

Kirtles, worn over petticoats or over both petticoats and farthingales, consisted of a separate bodice (known as a pair of boards) and a skirt. They might serve as an outside dress, though a gown or cloak was commonly worn over them. Since they were open from neck to toe as a rule, they provided for two or more matching accessories to the lady's costume, the stomacher and the forepart. When men wore stomachers under their doublets, this garment was richly ornamented with embroidery and jewels. The lady's stomacher, worn over the breast and upper abdomen, was stiffened with busks. It was also made of very rich material and ornamented to show through the lacings of the gown. The forepart was a triangular accessory pinned to the sides of the Spanish kirtle below the waist, and it was as richly ornamented as the stomacher, which it matched in every detail of decoration. The many materials of which kirtles were made ran from heavy to light and delicate and from warm woolens to sheer lawns and silks. Their stomachers and foreparts alone surpassed them in decoration.

The type of kirtle known as the Catherine-wheel farthingale was closed in front, and had to be slipped on over its supporting framework. By the latter part of the Queen's reign it had grown so wide that it extended out around the hips till it was as wide as the hem of the extremely wide skirt. Though very popular, it lacked the grace of the Spanish farthingale, which was stiffened by hoops of wood or wire or whalebone to make the skirt stand out like a bell, and to make the waist look small. A distorting fashion was the French roll that was round and stiffened by wire and stuffed with cotton. Placed about the hips, it was covered by a closed, pleated skirt. Sometimes only half a roll was used across the back, and sometimes an embroidered frill like a ruff was used to head the skirt covering the French roll, and folded down like a flat ruffle at the waist. A woman so attired had to endure both the weight and the restrictions of such clothing.

No part of the dress received more carefully planned decoration than the sleeves of both men and women's apparel. Pinking, slashing, scissoring, and jagging were used to cut holes in the outer fabric to permit the contrasting color of the lining to show through. Pinking made the smallest holes, rounded or straight slits ranging from one-sixteenth to three-fourths of an inch in length. Many rich effects were gained by this cutting in suits and gowns, the latter having sometimes as many as 9,000 pinks. Any kind of garment might be pinked, but nowhere was it so effective as in the sleeves. Bone lace that trimmed sleeves was made with bone bobbins and pins on cushions; gold, silver, and linen thread were used. Black and white and silk thread were used for openwork lace to adorn accessories, but drawn work on sleeves had the material cut away after the lace was made.

As a rule sleeves were detachable, and since there was so much work on them they made most acceptable gifts to both men and women, but especially to women. Men wore on their sleeves jewels given them by fair ladies, and even wore in their hats or caps sleeves of their ladies given as favors. Many sleeves were padded. Trunk sleeves, tapered from shoulder to wrist, had their width held out by wires or reed or whalebone, and still others were filled out by an undersleeve called a farthingale because of its wire, etc. Among the many other kinds of sleeves were the down sleeve, long to the wrist; the side sleeve, open from the shoulder; and the colorful foresleeve, embroidered and button-trimmed, its underpart attached at the shoulder and covered to the elbow by an upper sleeve of the same material as in the gown. This particular sleeve stayed in fashion during the entire century. The long, hanging sleeves were for decoration only, some of them reaching to the very hem of the ladies' gowns, some to mid-thigh. Wings, or rolls of stiffened buckram, covered by material of the garment, concealed the juncture of outer sleeves and bodice, where they were buttoned or tied by laces with points; a ruffle, band, or flare, often lined with a bright-colored silk, finished the sleeve at the hand.

The neckwear underwent much change during the Elizabethan period. When the ruff was at its most complicated form, the fingers pinning it in place often had difficulty fastening the ruff in straight, and this part of dressing could be most trying on the nerves. The neckband was worn before the ruff came into style near the middle of the century. It was at first an upright collar of holland, lawn, cambric, or linen on shirt or bodice, an inch or two wide, and plain or edged with a narrow ruffle, or embroidered. Later, about 1580, came the falling band (or robat) that was simply a turned-down collar, which, as it grew wider, was fastened to the shirt or smock by pins, fitted by darts or clocks, and tied in front by strings. Then came the ruff-band or ruff, stiff and multipleated. As the band widened, so did the ruff, though both band and ruff were worn at the same time by well-dressed men and women. By the end of the century the multipleated ruffs of three "falls" were the fashion.

Of course the ruff could not be pinned to the same edge to which the band was attached. Therefore the picadel or rebata was used for this purpose after it had been pinned to the neck of doublet or gown. Originally the picadel was merely a border of scallops or bobs about the top of the collar, but later it was a wired or stiffened frame to support lace or thin lawn. When it was used to support the band and collar, it made them stand up straight from the neck, and in extreme styles gave the appearance of an elongated neck. The rebata was first used as an open ruff on its wire frame, and was worn by virgins only. Later, when it was worn by all ladies, the frame was fastened to the gown and the delicate lace it supported was so bent as to frame the face in a most flattering manner. Naturally this part of a woman's adorning took much pinning, as did the high, straight collars.

Since cuffs matched ruffs or bands, the two were known as sets. If the ruff was tiered, the cuffs were tiered also. At court, men and women needed several sets, and ladies kept theirs in bandboxes. So valuable was this part of the costume that when ladies went traveling they had a servant specially in charge of bandboxes, for ruffs and cuffs were made of very fine material, often edged with delicate lace or decorated with embroidery and gold and silver threads. When in 1564 starch supplanted the little sticks of bone or wood used in the wire framework, this starch was colored, yellow being very popular for a time, but white remaining longest in favor. So wide were ruffs at one time that special spoons with long handles had to be used to eat with at table.

The rail was adapted to the needs of rich and poor. Sometimes it was a flattering part of fine ladies' neckwear, worn over the back of the head like a veil, and bowed out with wire at the shoulders. Much delicate work went into its making, consisting of beautiful lace, drawnwork, or elaborate use of gold thread on very fine linen or network. When used as a shoulder shawl, it was made of less delicate material and trimmed with decorated ruffles. Then, folded crosswise, it fitted comfortably about neck and shoulders. The rail was used only as a shawl by the lower classes and was made of far coarser material than cypress or lawn. If worn as a cape at night it was made long enough to hang below the shoulders. As a rule it was used like a kerchief over the neck and shoulders.

Other articles of neckwear were the tippet, wimple, and scarf. The tippet was a strip of material, usually decorative, and worn sometimes like a muffler. It was also used as a band of fur or velvet on the sleeve just above the elbow, and widows trimmed their mourning hoods with it. The wimple was tied on of mornings, and consisted of a square of linen so folded as to envelop the head, chin, sides of face, and neck; it was not so flattering to old faces as to young. A scarf was frequently worn across the face as protection from the sun, especially when a lady was riding. Often women gave their scarfs to men, who wore these favors diagonally across the chest and knotted at the waist. Such scarfs were made of silk, lawn, and cypress. Cypress was very flattering to the face, for its delicate black transparency provided the same dainty concealment of passing youth that women have always sought behind veils.

Aprons were used as ornaments by women from 1550 to 1640, and were a part of all fashionable costumes, even for royalty. They were made of the finest cambric, silk, lawn, etc., and trimmed with lace. Sometimes they were made entirely of lace. Women of the lower classes wore this accessory also, and when they could adorn themselves with aprons embroidered or lace-trimmed, they were proud indeed.

Until about 1580, women used the cassock as an outer cloak, but after that time they discarded it for something more elaborate. It continued to be used by old men and rustics, however. When fashionable women had worn it, it was made of black velvet or black damask, with both the hood and garment embroidered or guarded with velvet. Capes for ladies reached to the waist, and were faced with velvet or rich silk. When they went out of fashion, they were succeeded by coats over caped dresses. Cloaks of fine ladies, especially at court, were very rich, made of such materials as changeable blue taffeta and lined with wool of straw color or pinked carnation taffeta, and trimmed with gold lace and buttons. Ladies also wore shoulder cloaks of such colors as carnation satin, furred with mink or lined with perfumed leather, ash satin, or striped satin, and trimmed with Venetian gold or silver lace and set with small buttons.

They tried many color combinations, but always chose lighter and lighter colors as time went on.

When riding, women wore what was called a safeguard. This was a skirt with a short coat or cloak to protect the lady's elaborate costume from dust and from possible contact with the sweating horse. Such a garment took seven to eight yards of material, usually velvet, and three to four yards of lining. Other materials were used also, such as taffeta, plush, coarse and fine woolens, satin, and even fine lawn. These garments of the rich were elaborately trimmed with lace. Such a riding habit called for a scarf and plumed hat and expensive gloves.

Fine gloves were scented, the Spanish being in high favor with both men and women: they never lost their scent because they had been dipped five times. For cold weather, fur-lined gloves might be used, but regardless of the time of year or type of glove, ornamentation was its chief feature. Consequently, gloves were gladly received as gifts, especially if one attended many weddings or bethothals, when the groom was expected to present gloves as favors to those helping with the ceremony. Sometimes in excited gatherings both gloves and caps would be flung into the air, though a man might restrain himself if he wore his lady's glove in his hat. That they might have suitable gloves for every occasion, the wealthy had several pairs, all chosen with great care. It would be hard indeed to find a well-dressed Elizabethan man or woman without gloves expressing the wearer's own individual taste.

Accessories for men and women were so numerous that they must have added no little weight to the already heavy, stiff clothing. Both men and women used jeweled buckles for their hats and shoes, ornamental clasps, rings, and bracelets, and many, many buttons, some bright with enamel, some set with precious stones like pearls or diamonds, some of heavy gold acorn shapes, and some of silk or hair or self material. The pomander was also in almost universal use, for it was supposedly a protection against contagious diseases, especially the plague. The rich carried their pomanders in very ornamental hollow perforated metal balls, but at night kept them in tight "pouncet" boxes lest they lose their scent. The metal balls had hinged sections opening out like an orange when the top was unscrewed. Onyx was frequently used for the pouncet boxes, though ornamented gold and silver were also favored by those who could afford them. Some of the balls were made of gold and jewels, and hung from chains about men's necks and from women's girdles. Common people usually bought cheap hollow balls from peddlers, who were supplied with such kinds made of base metal. The pomander itself could be easily made by sticking an orange full of cloves, but each lady had her favorite way of concocting scents for this accessory.

Many articles were suspended from women's girdles along with the pomander. Such included fans, mirrors, purses, muffs, scissors, etc. The fans were made chiefly of ostrich feathers, with handles of gold or ivory or both, carefully designed by a goldsmith to hold a tiny mirror of steel or crystal on the side. These fans might have five straight, uncurled feathers in a group of curled tips, with the handle designed to look like two winding snakes, or made in one piece, chased and ornamented to please the owner. Some fans had white feathers and others had feathers of various colors that harmonized with the costume. They dangled from the girdle by a gold chain or silk cord or ribbon, and were often precious with jewels like diamonds, carbuncles, and pearls. Small mirrors were placed in brooches as well as fans, or were worn on a beautiful chain or ribbon attached to the girdle. If a woman gave her mirror to an admirer, he wore it like a jewel in his hat. Purses were made in the form of pouches from tooled leather and handsome materials embroidered with silk. If they did not hang from the man's or woman's girdle, they were carried in the sleeve or muff. As a rule, however, most women carried muffs only for show. Some were of fur or very expensive embroidered silks, and some were lined with plush. They could hang from the girdle because they were small. Even children wore girdles from which were suspended accessories they needed, particularly the handkerchief. Men and women always carried their large, showy, and expensive handkerchiefs in their hands.

If a woman could afford to have a girdle designed by a goldsmith, she chose a handsome chain; otherwise, she wore a ribbon or silk cord about her waist. Men's girdles were of silver or gold or velvet, though for common wear they used embossed leather, especially when dressed for outdoors. To their girdles were attached their hangers for sword, rapier, or dagger. These hangers were made of two straps and a pad or plate to which was buckled the scabbard. Embroidered hangers were suitable gifts for ladies to present to men, and fine hangers were often chosen as gifts for male guests at a wedding. If a man did not go armed, he was attended by an armed servant. Most men, of course, preferred to carry their own sword.

As the purse was so often worn at the girdle, it was very easy to steal unless a guard was present for protection. Purses were drawn at the top by strings and adorned with tassels; thus they were conspicuous, and a temptation to light fingers. When great ladies mingled with the people in a public gathering, they expected their masks to protect their faces and to conceal their identity, and their guards to protect them and their purses. Such precaution became more and more necessary during the Queen's reign. After her coach was surrounded by rogues in 1581, stringent laws were passed to try to bring crime under control. Now, for the first time many good people learned of the crime schools for boys. At such places a pocket of coins was hung about with hawks' bells and a bell put over the top. When a boy could remove the top bell without a sound he was ready to be sent onto the street as a pickpocket or cutpurse. The common people frequently referred to these young criminals as "nyppers" or "foysters."

Watches were also the object of thieves, but only the rich could afford to carry them, and they were usually accompanied by adequate guards. Watches were large, extremely thick, and their outer surface was pierced with elaborate openwork to enable the wearer to hear the little bell inside strike the hour. These oval or round or octagonal time-pieces were called " 'larum bells," and gallants who possessed them often wound them in public in an affected manner. Such men also wore many rings on their fingers. There was one type of ring, however, that served for more than adornment; it was the seal ring with intricate designs cut in its agate. These rings could be sent with servants carrying messages, for they would vouch for any requests. There are many instances in Shakespeare's plays in which rings are given to persons bearing messages to ensure their safe delivery.

Among the many other kinds of jewelry were brooches, medals, amulets, lockets, beads, necklaces, earrings, earpicks, and toothpicks. Both men and women used brooches, which were set with jewels and worn on a chain or as a buckle, clasp, or breastpin. There were many elaborate designs for brooches, such as hearts, squares, and ovals, with a large precious stone at the center, bordered with pearls or diamonds. Medals were of metal, shaped like a disk, and inscribed with a figure or verse to serve as a charm. Amulets, sometimes called "periapts," were also worn as charms against evil, and were of all kinds from plain metal to elaborate jewels. Lockets, frequently referred to as "talents," were used to carry locks of hair, and were favorite gifts between lovers. Beads were very popular; made of glass, amber, metal, or wood, they could be purchased by rich or poor. Fine ladies especially liked "bugles" or black glass beads which they sometimes alternated with pearls to twine in their hair.

Usually the "carcanet" referred to gold or jeweled necklaces, though sometimes it might indicate a bracelet or hair ornament. The Earl of Leicester presented the Queen with a carcanet he called a gold "collar." It was a jewel on a chain set with two emeralds and four rubies and "garnished" with small rubies and diamonds. Both men and women wore earrings of precious stones. Toward the end of the century men also wore ear strings for a while. This fad consisted of a black string drawn through the pierced lobe of the left ear; some of the strings hung down to the shoulder. Earpicks were at times beautiful ornaments. The Queen had one of enameled gold, set with rubies, sapphires, and seed pearls. She also had gold toothpicks presented to her in a set of six for a New Year's gift in 1574. Such "tools" were worn on chains, but it is doubtful whether they were used often. Just as the fan was designed to whisk away flies, it was far more often used by pretty ladies in flirtatious games which they played with much skill.

Color was a matter of no little concern to fine ladies choosing their costumes at the end of the century. No longer were they satisfied with a black or dark red (murrey) velvet kirtle unless they brightened it with the dress accessories of sleeves, stomachers, etc., in light colors such as peach and pearl. They also contrasted light colors with blackwork, in which the all-over pattern in fine black silk threads of slender stems and leaves in continuous scrolling was very beautiful. Men as well as ladies liked tapestry designs and colors combined with rich materials in brilliant solid color, and set off by openwork bobbin lace of gold and silver threads. Even common people might use bobbin lace of linen thread if they could make their own lace.

There were many kinds of red, and each had its own symbolic meaning. Blood red signified power or cruelty or vengeance or joy. Scarlet, reserved for royalty and state officials, was supposed to keep one warm in winter and cool in summer. This is why scarlet was used in sickrooms of feverish patients. Gallants wore maiden's blush, and the common people wore russet red. Flame red was a color for lovers, murrey (dark red) for those who were constant in love, and also for servants' livery, perhaps to assure faithful service. Gallants preferred horseflesh red (bay) to any other color, even maiden's blush, and sober minds chose a red-violet called gingerline. The Queen was very fond of peachflower, a deep, fresh pink, and used it in many of her dresses. Naturally courtiers adopted it too, especially for their shirts and hose.

Yellow, of course, suggested the sun and warmth and fruitfulness and, sometimes, arrogance. Some shade of yellow frequently occurred in costumes for the purpose of contrast. The Queen most often used straw yellow for this purpose. Orange-tawny was in high favor during the Tudor reigns. Henry VIII had serving men dressed in tawny coats when he entertained the French king in 1533, and Elizabeth's pages had jerkins of this color. Its lion-skin color suggested pride, but when deepened with red, it might also suggest love or jealousy, or power, courage, and grandeur. Men used it frequently for hose and footwear, and women for cloaks and kirtles and accessories.

Blue and green were often in use, especially the bright sky-blue for servants' apparel. Azure blue in fine materials was worn by the rich to indicate honor and wisdom and power. The many shades of green told tales of spring, hope, and happiness, and were associated with youth. Green gowns and green sleeves were linked with gay or charming ladies, but green ties or laces were the insignia of lovers. Most women avoided yellowish green as it indicated faint hope, and sea green as it suggested a changing, deceitful nature, but popinjay, a bright blue-green, sang of high hope.

Brown and gray in their many shades were used by both rich and poor, though brown stood for autumn and despair, and gray for winter and barrenness. Nobles liked maidenhair brown and often achieved artistic harmony in costumes of it combined with silver. Both russet (reddish brown) and ash gray denoted steadfastness. The rich used russet satin, and the poor, homespun materials in russet. Although silver and ash supposedly indicated fear, passion, jealousy, or suspicion, and although ash indicated fraud, poverty, and vileness, these two colors were frequently combined with various shades of brown in cheap woolens as well as in beautiful satins and silks. Not all colors, therefore, were chosen for their meaning. Many a lass and many a wife chose her colors according to how much they might flatter eyes or complexion. White, of course, was representative of purity, chastity, faith, truth, and sincerity, just as black bespoke darkness, constancy, woe, death, sadness, and grief. Yet black velvet and satin lined with white or cream satin or silk were in frequent use till lighter colors were so generally adopted. The bride was most concerned about the colors to use for favors at her wedding, and many were the combinations achieved, but most garters were of gold and the bridelace was white, with the knots according to the whim or fancy of the bride.

All bridelace was made with bobbins; it was tied to the wedding cup, nosegays of flowers, and to the left arms of the groom's attendants. Purl lace was very narrow, and its silver, gold, or silk threads were woven into tiny scalloped loops to decorate ruffs, cuffs, and edges of gowns. Fringe was the common name for lace, often gold, made with looms, but parchment gold lace was fashioned over inked patterns on parchment; it was used on hats and handkerchiefs and coats and doublets. For the fastidious, lace must finish all edgings and ornament both men's and women's accessories.

Guards, when applied as bands or borders for decoration, were also used by both men and women. Bonnets were "guarded" with silk; great coats had wide guards of coarse russet wool or velvet, and white kersey hose were frequently edged with yellow guards. This ornamentation was first used for royalty, but by 1600, it was commonly used on clothing of servants. When it adorned rich costumes, however, it was beautifully embroidered with gold or silk or silver thread.

Those who could indulge their taste in fine clothes were as fastidious in selecting materials as colors and trimmings. Woolen and silk fabrics must be very fine for such people, and they had many kinds from which to choose. As the common people were able to dress in better style, they used materials once designed primarily for the rich, and clothes of still finer texture were then contrived for the wealthy. Of course some fabrics continued in favor with the rich for one reason or another even when common people were able to adopt them. Illustrations have helped to give a fair idea of how people dressed, but unless the materials are known for such clothing, one can have no adequate impression of the beauty or ugliness characterizing the apparel of rich and poor.

The dress of merchants varied a good deal, some of them taking as much pleasure as their wives in showy apparel. Then, as the laws for restricting fabrics to various classes became less and less sternly enforced, it was increasingly difficult to judge a man's estate by his apparel, except in the case of such people as apprentices, laborers, and public officials. When the clothing of the apprentices was not stipulated by law, they might be dressed according to the taste or status of their masters. In 1582, they were forbidden ruffles, cuffs, and loose collars. Their ruffs were limited to one and one-half yards of material, and if they wore doublets, the material for these must consist of canvas, rough fustian, sackcloth, or English leather. Winter cloaks for them were faced with cloth, and their shoes were of plain English leather. They wore no jewels, and eventually their plain woolen caps were replaced with the despised flat caps. City laborers, like farmers, wore coarse, homemade garments, as did their wives, whose kirtles, however, might be of some light stuff, girdled up over their petticoats to form a roll under the waist and about the hips. Their aprons were long and narrow, and their heads were covered with linen and with big hats of felt or straw according to the season. The workingman's coat reached to the knees, and was girdled at the waist. His hat, with its narrow brim, had a tallish crown. At public meetings, aldermen wore scarlet gowns, and if their wives accompanied them, they too were resplendent in their black velvet skirts and gowns, guarded with scarlet. These brilliant contrasts pleased the admiring mob, and they flocked to public ceremonies promising any parade of colorful apparel.

On Sunday, little children of the common people were dressed carefully if their parents were self-respecting people who took the entire family to church. All their garments were similar in style and material to those worn by their parents. A little boy, however, wore dresses until three or four years of age, and sometimes older. If his parents were rich, he might wear a heavily embroidered kirtle and skirt, with rows of braid around the skirt and up and down the kirtle. As an infant he would be likely to wear a taffeta coat with satin sleeves, a petticoat and bib, and a coral on a gold chain. Little girls, like their mothers and sisters, were often dressed in gowns hanging loose at the back. They might be elaborately dressed, however, in all the rich garments of a fashionable lady, though for practical purposes their kirtles would be closed. Sometimes children's clothes were protected till they were ready to go out with their parents by smocks put on over all their fine apparel; these were called dust smocks. All day long little children were cautioned to take care of their clothes and to conduct themselves like little men or women, which meant for them to act a difficult part if they were encased in clothing as stiff and uncomfortable as that of adults.

When stylish ladies dressed for the plays held of afternoons, they went abroad in gay colors, wearing their best gowns as often as not, shoes or pumps of silk or velvet or cheveril (a very soft flexible kid), and highly scented gloves. Of course, by the end of the century, they expected to be carried through the streets in a chair or to travel down the Thames in boats with luxuriously cushioned seats. When farthingales became popular, the stylish ladies were round and stiff and rigid as if made of metal. The wires and bones in their dresses accentuated straight lines and sharp angles. A flannel petticoat for such attire in 1596 was trimmed with yards and yards of "billiment" lace. How women carried the weight of such clothes, with all their heavy jewelry, and accessories swinging from the girdle—fans, mirrors, pomanders, smelling bottles, cosmetics, and other articles—as well as a book or two in the capacious pockets of their skirts, is painful even to think of. Walking in their cork-soled pantofles with heels three inches high and, over these, chopines to keep out the dust and dirt, no wonder they looked to Stubbes like young goats tripping along gingerly on their toes. Men who wore pantofles suffered from swelling legs, yet they, like women, were willing to be slaves of fashion.

Although the Queen used cosmetics with a lavish hand, applying paint to face, neck, and breast till it was a thick covering for her aging skin, woman's right to beautify herself by such means was a favorite topic for anyone in any social stratum. Ben Jonson satirized women painting in *The Silent Woman*. "I love a good dressing before any beauty o' the world," says True Wit (I:i). "O, a woman is then like a delicate garden; nor is there one kind in it; she may vary every hour; take often counsel of her glass, and choose the best. If she have good ears, show them: practise any art to mend the breath, cleanse teeth, repair eyebrows; paint and profess it." All this, however, she must do in private. "Many things that seem foul in the doing, do please done. A lady should, indeed, study her face, when we think she sleeps; nor, when the doors are shut, should men be enquiring; all is sacred within them." And why so sacred he explains by adding, "Is it for us to see their perukes put on, their false teeth, their complexion, their eyebrows, their nails . . . no more should servants approach their mistresses, but when they are complete and finished."

Vives, as one would expect, had objected strongly to the use of cosmetics. He could see no use for them at all. If a woman painted to please herself, he wrote, "it is a vain thing," and if to delight men, "it is an ungracious thing." He compared paint to a visor, which once off made one loathed as much as liked when on. He pointed out the disgusting sight of a face when paint melted "by the occasion of sweat or heat," and the danger of it "both by the reason of the ceruse [white lead] and quick silver . . ." used in it. He felt that if paint was necessary to win a husband it would be better not to marry at all, for the ruddy lips and white faces and necks achieved through paint were "like a fire unto young men, and a foment of lechery." He wondered, therefore, that women did not try to make themselves less beautiful than they were by nature since beauty brought so much grief.

Not only Vives but the pious Bullinger objected to any devices for making women unnaturally beautiful or attractive. In his sermons Bullinger frequently expressed his disapproval of jewelry, velvets, silks, perfumes, and all vanities in women's dress. Riches, he said, were given noble women not to wear in gold or silver ornaments, or in velvet and silk gowns, but to share with the poor and destitute. For this reason all women should dress soberly that their beauty might honestly shine forth in raiment of shamefastness, chastity, grave sobriety, and few words.

That pious women should echo these precepts to their daughters was natural, and to them Thomas Carter especially wrote against painting in his *Christian Commonwealth*: "Oh woe to that soul on whose face God shall with anger look, denying to know it because it is not as he made it! no marvel . . . that nothing under heaven will satisfy your pride, when the works of God's own hands in yourselves will not content you, but that you will alter that!" In fashionable women's boudoirs, of course, such sentiments scarcely arched an eyebrow. Nevertheless, the complaints of Vives against painting the face and dyeing the hair had set in motion long criticisms by Elizabethan writers who were disturbed by such vanities.

On the other hand, many writers provided books with information on how to enhance natural beauties. Their hints and suggestions might be but one chapter in a work about domestic matters like candying and distilling and preserving, but it was sure to give enough material about personal adornment, secret distillations, perfumes, toilet waters, sweet powders, and dainty ointments to make the book enticing to its feminine readers. And such books sold well, so well that Philip Stubbes complained of the excessive use of sweet powders and musk, fragrant pomanders and perfumes, saying that their odor permeated the entire house, and the beds in which such women lay and the places where they sat as well as their clothes, and the things they used or even merely touched carried the scent a week or a month or longer. Furthermore, he added, these women also carried nosegays in their hands and posies or flowers to smell, and two or three nosegays stuck in their breasts.[7]

Stubbes's objection to dyeing the hair was even more forthright than his disapproval of time wasted in dressing the hair and the unnatural effects sought by it. He described how the women curled it, frizzed it, laid it on wreaths and borders from one ear to the other, and, lest it fall down, propped it up with forks, wires, and . . . well, he couldn't imagine what else. Then they laid on the edges of it "great wreaths of gold and silver, curiously wrought and cunningly applied to the temples of their heads." Women had started to frizz and crimp their hair during the 1580's, and as the "puffed" effect grew in favor, wire frames were devised to support the curled locks from ear to ear in a crown. If the hair was

[7] *The Anatomie of Abuses* (1583), pp. 77–78 of the 1877 ed.

not pulled down over the ears, it was combed back to show the ears, and sometimes the curls were built up to look like a bird's nest. As a rule, however, the arrangement was in imitation of wreaths of flowers and settings for precious stones in a gold or silver framework. Since the elaborate arrangements required so much hair, wigs and added curls had to be bought from children and peasant women. Then a suitable hat must be worn to surmount the framework of hair, and for this purpose a large velvet hat was perched on the front or side of the head, and almost invariably a long feather was fastened in its hatband.

While combing their hair, women used combing cloths to protect their clothing, which may have taken hours to arrange in an artistic ensemble. During the additional hours rich women must now spend with their hair before completing their toilette, they often made much use of some of the articles suspended from their girdles—scissors, pincers, a penknife, a knife to close letters, and a seal, a bodkin, and perhaps an earpick. At night a lady might wish to comb out her hair with or without her maid's assistance. After all the snarls were removed with her fine ivory comb, she usually had a forecloth fastened round her head to help the headache brought on by the heavy, hot hairdressing during the day. Or the forecloth might be used to prevent wrinkles from coming to mar the high, broad brow made higher and broader by plucking low-growing hair. As these services were performed, the lady tried to keep herself comfortably warm on cool evenings by wrapping close her dressing gown. She might also look very handsome in this gown if it was made of silk grosgrain lined with velvet and trimmed with silver or gold cloud-lace and ribbon-edged seams.

When the hair had to be washed, the Elizabethan lady put on a protective covering that must keep her clothes from getting wet. It was a serious matter for her to find water stains on unwashable materials, especially if her warm gown was made of silk or velvet. Much perfume made sweet the rinse water, and dainty, scented soaps were used in washing the hair. Every lady, of course, had her favorite recipe for making her own scented toilet preparations; after 1597, some of these came from John Gerard's *Herbal*, which abounded with interesting formulas by this famous herbalist. If the lady herself did not go to the distillery, she left such matters in the hands of a trusted servant and confidante.

Though the common housewife might dress her own hair, no great lady could perform the miracle of arranging her hair. She and her maids might make many of her clothes, unless she left such matters entirely to her trusted maids or bought her best dresses at a tailor's, and she might distill washes for both her hair and complexion, but the intricate designs in plaiting and curling and winding of her hair with jewels and ornaments required the skillful hands of an artist. Thomas Carter said he prided himself on defending women unjustly accused, but he found all women guilty in the matter of silly fashions. It would seem that "hell were emptied of all her devices, toys, tricks, and fashions, and that women had got them all." Everything God had made "under heaven, the whole earth and the sea, with all the creatures therein" failed to satisfy women's pride. The very "entrails of the earth" were daily "torn and rent" to seek adornment for them, "the bottomless sea and the poor fishes" were robbed daily to find them pearls to bedeck themselves with, and the hard rocks were "digged to find . . . a variety of precious stones . . ." Indeed, all of God's creatures, "both beasts, birds, and worms" were used "to furnish up" women's pride, and still they could not be satisfied but must cause the devil himself "to find more new fashions . . ." So the devil went to hell to bring back to women "beauty to paint themselves withal," for only there could ever be found what would please them.

Next, Carter proceeds to show how unchristian women are making the Commonwealth by other evils besides extravagant adorning. Now, alas, women can no longer walk from place to place, but have grown so proud they must be carried in chairs or coaches. He compares them to the ladies of long ago whom the Hebrew prophet accused of going about "mincing and tinkling" with their feet, only the feet of Elizabethan ladies will not even bear them. He hastens to add that of course kings and princes are honorably carried in coaches drawn with horses, but "it is unfit that courtesans should be coached, which should rather be carted." Strong language this, but he has more to say about light colors that are worn by these ladies. Once pure white linen would serve, but first one color then another has become the fad. ". . . blue was, and now yellow is, and primrose and straw color, and I know not what, but black will be next, assure yourselves," for as pride has exceeded all else, so will their punishments that are to come excel all that have gone before.

If stylish ladies heard or read these words, they were probably provoked to much laughter. They might also be reminded of the wrathful warnings of *Purchas, his Pilgrim*[8] in which the writer proclaimed that if wickedness herself could "take a habit and visibly appear to human eyes," her vanity could not surpass that of ladies with their "colors, wires, tires, faces, fashions," and their debates over "where to be naked, where to be clothed," and where to apply "spots, paintings, powderings, frowses, frizzlings," and what ruffs or cuffs to use from all "the restless rabble" of their apparel. Then they would laugh again, recalling how in this same work woman was declared to be the first and worst sinner, with "more eager, vehement, violent, unbridled passions than man." A poor successor, they would call him, to such a man as Hakluyt who published things worth reading about foreign lands and people. Let Purchas keep his Pilgrims to himself!

But Puritans would find Purchas worth quoting. The women's fad

---

[8] Samuel Purchas, *Purchas, his Pilgrim. Microcosmus, or the histories of Man* (1619).

of adopting men's articles of dress gave moralists much cause for complaint, and soon ballads as well as sermons were accusing men of being effeminate, and women of being mannish, frivolous, and indifferent to home and its duties. Some went so far as to say outright that women were refusing to have children lest their sport and pleasure be interfered with. Women were urged, therefore, to emulate their grandmothers, who in the Queen's girlhood had not painted their faces, cut short their hair, smoked pipes, danced to excess, gambled at cards, sworn great oaths, ridden astride, worn short skirts, visited public theaters, or fallen in love with popular actors. No doubt many women smiled wisely over this idealizing of the past. Had they not heard their own mothers or grandmothers tell what the times of Vives were like? And had not Vives himself complained of women dressing extravagantly and painting their faces thick with paste? The moralists' complaints of women dressing like men show the daring of feminine styles, which, pressed for something new, turned to masculine attire. But more still, they reveal the old, old war of the sexes.

It is of further interest that in many respects men's apparel was more extravagant than women's. Their clothing was considerably richer in material, and consequently very expensive. Even military dress must be rich, with tassels on the armor, the ruff rising above the military collar, the peascod doublet slashed to show rich linings, and the trunk hose padded and embroidered. As far back as 1560, Edward More had declared men's extravagant dress was influenced by the weaker sex when he answered Edward Gosynhill's abusive *Schoolhouse of Women* by a merry rhyming, *A Lytle and bryefe treatyse, called the defence of women, and especially of Englyshe women, made agaynst the Scholehowse of women.* More had referred to the styles of men's hairdress, and showed men combing and stroking their beards, washing and plaiting them in divers ways and binding them with bands. Then he had asked whether it was any marvel that a woman should dress her hair now and then. Though he admitted he could not defend the farthingale, he called attention to the fact that men had invented them, and that in itself was excuse enough for women to wear them.

At no other time, perhaps, was an inordinate love of apparel to disguise or to distort so amazingly the human body. Gigantic ruffs made the heads of both men and women look strangely small and insignificant; bombasted breeches gave men a disproportionate shortness like that of women in farthingales, and this stubby appearance was exaggerated in men by the bombasted peascod doublet and in women by the V-shaped stomacher. Both styles must have made stooping next to impossible, and both were undoubtedly designed to conceal stoutness. It was natural for them to disappear in time, though one is surprised they lasted a decade or longer. Then Elizabethans turned to whatever might suggest youthful lines and agility.

While it lasted, however, this extraordinary dress gave moralists much to criticize. William Harrison[9] said that except "it were a dog in a doublet, you shall not see any so disguised, as my countrymen of England." Such men made their tailors miserable, and in their fittings they themselves were likely to sweat till they dropped from exhaustion. He was even more outraged by men's treatment of their hair, which was clipped or curled or grown like a woman's or cut off above or under the ears as "round as a wooden dish." In 1598, Hentzner[10] described the hair as cut close on the middle of the head and long on the sides. Most often, men's hair came to the shoulders, though the "ear-locks" were quite fashionable during the 'nineties. The hair, cut short in back, was allowed to grow in front and on the sides of the head to form these love locks, hanging down on either side of the face till they rested in a curl on the shoulders.

Beards, like the hair, were of all styles, and they too might be dyed any color to match the costume—straw-color, purple-in-grain, French crown color, or perfect yellow—and cut in any way to suit the contours of the face. Some beards, said William Harrison, were shaved from the chin like a Turk's; some were cut short; some were round like a bush, and some were allowed to grow long. The barber cut beards to make the face what he willed. "If a man have a lean and straight face, a marquis . . . cut will make it broad and large; if it be platter-like, a long, slender beard will make it seem narrower; if he be weasel-beaked, then much hair left on the cheeks will make the owner look like a big . . . hen, and so grim as a goose . . ." Many old men, he said, wore no beards at all.[11] Since fashionable men painted their faces quite as often and quite as carefully as the women painted theirs, and dyed their hair and beards as fancy or costume dictated, naturally they introduced many styles in dress that women copied and moralists deplored. A man in love, for example, was often most fastidious, brushing his hat and hair of mornings, shaving his beard, applying cosmetics, combing out his shoulder curls, and rubbing himself with civet.

Much of this passion for dress originated in Henry VIII's reign when nobles dressed for banquets, tourneys, jousts, processions, and pageants in gorgeous materials heavy with embroidery and stiff with jewels flashing against the somber hues of their garments. In Elizabeth's time lighter materials and colors were the chief differences in fine dress. When Raleigh was acclaimed the most lavishly attired courtier to pay homage to Elizabeth, he was merely accentuating the splendor of the Tudor dress as he paraded before his approving queen. At one time he appeared dressed as follows: his ruff and falling band and matching cuffs were of

[9] William Harrison, *Description of England in Shakspere's Youth*, ed. F. J. Furnivall (1877).

[10] Paul Hentzner, *A Journey into England in the Year of 1598* (trans. by Richard Bently, 1757).

[11] *Description of England in Shakspere's Youth*, p. 169.

fine lawn and exquisite lace. Twelve jeweled buttons gleamed on his doublet, which was pinked to show its beautiful lining. Likewise, his trunk hose, slightly padded, were slit to expose a lining of the same color as his nether hose. He wore sword and earrings, slipper shoes with fur collars and pearls, and over his shoulders he had thrown a splendid cloak. Of course he wore many jewels and rings. Perhaps, however, he excited the greatest sensation when he appeared one day clad in silver armor adorned with diamonds and precious stones. Essex, whose disdain for Raleigh was heightened by this gorgeous display, rewarded his rival with sneers and sharp criticism, and those who were loyal to Essex joined their sneers with his even as they gazed yearningly at the splendors of the favorite.

In his last days Essex grew so sober as to discard almost all the vanities of dress, though at his execution he presented himself attired in a gown of embroidered velvet, a black velvet suit, and his prized scarlet woolen waistcoat. When he was the Queen's favorite, however, he frequently went to her without really knowing how he was dressed, for most of his garments were put on while he gave audience to the many friends and suitors crowding his chamber as soon as he wakened in the morning. His biographer, Walter Bourchier Devereux, tells how he "gave his legs, arms, and breast to his ordinary servants to button and dress him, with little heed; and his head and face to the barber, his eyes to his letters, and ears to his petitioners; and many times all at once." Only in his bath was he "somewhat delicate." No wonder, therefore, he was repelled by the grandeur of "the upstart" Raleigh.

According to Hentzner, Elizabeth's presence chamber in 1598 was hung with very rich tapestry, but the floor was strewn with "hay" (rushes). One wonders at this contrast, for both court furnishings and dress were sumptuous at this time. Elizabeth was close to seventy on this occasion, but she was dressed as usual to proclaim the ideal of her virginity that had become for her subjects a symbol of her power. Her gown of white silk was bordered with pearls of the size of beans, and over it was draped a mantle of black silk, shot with threads of silver. A marchioness bore the end of her very long train, and instead of a chain, the Queen wore an oblong collar of gold and jewels. In her ears were pearls with very rich drops that shone against her red false hair. Like all unmarried English virgins, she had her bosom uncovered, and she wore a necklace of exceedingly fine jewels. Of course, she wore gloves. Most of her ladies in waiting were also in white, but in spite of the rich material of their gowns, they studiously avoided any competition with the splendid attire of the Queen.

With all their love of elaborate dress, Elizabethan women loved comfort when they could achieve it. For such times they wore their loose gowns hanging from the neck with many, many folds and long, close sleeves. Elizabeth herself had over a hundred of these dresses. One

reason for their almost universal use was that they concealed any alteration of the figure, and for this reason they were also subject to much
malign comment. No doubt many a woman encased in the splendors of
silks and satins looked forward with longing to slipping into these loose
gowns she could wear in the dubious privacy of her chambers.

Though fine dress for men and women had many similarities, there
were wide differences between men's and women's dress among the poor,
especially the self-respecting poor. Here the hose and girdled overgar-
ment coming to the knees proclaimed the man at some distance as he
worked in the field or walked along with his wife who was clad in a
coarse gown of ankle length. If country women were able at all to afford
good clothes, they brightened their dark gowns with a fancy white and
colored apron. Sometimes they appeared in light-colored gowns with
bands of dark material and aprons of white. Their plain bodices were
laced up the back. Under their gowns were their smocks, gathered into
neck bands, and made with long, full sleeves finished with narrow wrist-
bands. Their square-toed shoes were of black leather, their hose and caps
of linen, and their hair was concealed entirely under their headgear.
Maids at work in a household kept their sleeves rolled up to the elbow.
They also wore neckerchiefs and a square of linen tied about their hair
to keep it clean. Their simple aprons were of a long piece of linen, narrower at the waist, where strings were attached to tie it about the waist
in such a way as to permit the corners at the side to fall in rippling folds.

Small-town merchants' wives usually wore dresses of gray cloth with
bands of black on their full skirts, which were gathered to the bodice and
finished by a narrow belt that was often of a contrasting color like white.
The full sleeves were gathered into the armhole and cuff at the wrist,
and the cuffs were turned back and bound with a cord of some color. A
neckerchief might be drawn down under the arms and tied at the back
by its corners. Not all the hair was concealed as with poor women; instead, a white cap, gathered about a band, exposed some of the hair
curled at the forehead. From her belt hung a purse or pouch for small
articles needed frequently, like a needle case, thread, and scissors.
Though she might covet the handsome footgear of fashionable ladies,
she would have to wear something sensible, like high leather shoes without heels or possibly leather shoes low in the instep and provided with a
wide ribbon or band or wide tie to keep them snug over the arch.

Wives of wealthy merchants, of course, would do their best to dress
like fine ladies, wearing light colors, rich materials, and handsome accessories. Much of the embroidery they would be likely to have done by
their maids unless they wished to try some original designs of their own.
They might use pansies, little roses, knots, and pomegranates in the
designs with borders of mulberries, and all worked in colored silks or
gold or silver thread. If their fancy did not turn to flowers, they might
try beasts and fowls or fish and insects. Of course they would have de-

tachable ruffs and cuffs and sleeves, and much jewelry. In time wives of the London citizens and of Englishmen throughout the kingdom were wearing all the jewelry they could obtain, and it was in high favor as gifts. Carcanets of gold or silver inset with stones, rings, bodkins for the hair, pins, brooches, earrings, etc., were most common. Ornaments made with ingenuity often displayed in elaborate settings such figures as cats, dolphins, dogs, and insects, beautifully mounted for the wealthy and surrounded by precious stones. For those of limited wealth silverwork or semiprecious stones simply mounted would have to suffice.

Costly dress called for chairs or carriages. After Queen Elizabeth had had several coaches built for herself, it was not long before all the great ladies rode up and down the streets of London and even out into the country in coaches of their own. One of Elizabeth's was lined with red leather, one was upholstered with black velvet embossed with gold, and all were richly gilded and adorned with ostrich plumes. Some ladies were not content with one coach, and they drew the scorn of men like Drayton, who felt their painted faces at coach windows were indicative of an indecent age. As a matter of fact, the extravagant coach linings and upholstery might well draw the barbs of poets and moralists, for velvet "laced with gold" was commonly demanded, or some "sweet cloth" laced with scarlet or lace and silver.

Normally, four horses were used to draw these heavy coaches, and for a journey into the country, there must be two coachmen, two footmen, and two spare horses. Yet it was expensive when a woman rode horseback through the streets, for she must keep two or three good saddle horses for this purpose, and she must be accompanied by two gentlewomen and six to eight gentlemen on horses. For a journey, there must be carts to carry the baggage, and that meant more horses, drivers, and laundresses, chambermaids, and grooms. Fine ladies in the time of Queen Elizabeth were a luxury indeed for wealthy men who did not share their taste for extravagant show.

Usually a lady took her clothes and best household furnishings with her when she went to stay for a while at her husband's country estate. To move a whole family back and forth from the country was so difficult that it was avoided whenever possible. On long journeys few women rode in carriages, however, but on their best saddle horses. The square, heavy body of a coach swung about on rough roads like a ship at sea, for it was supported by leather straps fastened to upright posts that were attached to the axles. Consequently its occupant was often sick from the jolting, and such rough travel was forced on children only in extreme emergency. Though doors on the coach soon replaced the leather curtains at its sides for privacy, such a means of transportation was favored only in the city or on short journeys into the country by one unable to travel horseback. If too ill or weak to go by horse and still forced to make a long journey, one might be carried in a horse litter or a chair on slings. Four men were required for the chair, but if the journey was long, eight were used in relays.

The carts for moving a lady's possessions might be loaded down with one or two prized chairs, expensive beds and mattresses, fine cushions, carpets, and silver warming pans, the choicest plate and glass, and clothes. She might have twenty or more gowns, half a dozen beautiful ones, half a dozen very good ones, and half a dozen for wear in the country. Those she did not wear would be kept folded away in chests. Of course, her jewelry would go also, and the servant responsible for its safe transportation must have felt the burden as well as the honor of the confidence placed in him. A rich woman's jewelry might include a pearl necklace or chain, in itself worth several thousand pounds, and she might have with her considerable money, for while merely shopping in the city she would often carry as much as £200 to £2,000. As the lady customarily went about with so much money, it is no wonder her husband or other men in her class might be considered a fine prize by those who were willing to run great and dangerous risks to rob him of his gold.

Whenever possible, Londoners who had to leave their homes traveled up and down the Thames rather than through the dirty streets of the town. The magnificent royal barges and splendidly decorated boats of the nobles made a fine sight. Rich merchants also had their own fine wherries. Though London watermen arrogantly demanded good tips, they were likely to provide comfortably upholstered boats for those who depended on hiring them for transportation. On clear, warm days boat travel was full of entertainment, for then innumerable barges were out to give the people pleasure trips, and the gardens of the great houses on the river were beautiful in the sun. When special events were scheduled, like boat racing, swimming matches, or water pageants, and when the weather was pleasant, one could hire a boat and enjoy the river with its gay costumes and excited, laughing, singing people. If the tide was not just right, however, when the boat approached the great bridge with its overhanging dwellings and goodly shops, it would land its passengers (unless they were particularly daring), and pick them up again lower down. Only very adventurous souls were willing to "shoot the rapids" where the river entered the nineteen arches that converted its peaceful waters into dangerous cataracts.

Aside from this delight in life on the streets and thoroughfares, there was real pleasure experienced by Elizabethans in their homes. Here the husband found content at the end of his day's labor, and here the anxiety about elaborate feasts and fine clothes might be forgotten or at least pushed aside while the master of the home was with his family. After the evening prayers and the withdrawal of the children by the mother or servants, the father might take a little time to read or to write letters.

There was much letter writing in this age, although its transportation, unless urgent, was a tedious matter.

Slow carts at stated intervals carried mail between towns, but for rapid delivery of his letters, a writer depended on his own servant or a fast mail that, for a special fee, carried letters by horses kept at inns for just such relay service. Naturally, if a master had his own trusted man to carry his letters, he preferred this means. When it was necessary for husband and wife to be separated for even a brief period of time, they found much comfort in the almost daily letters which they wrote to each other. Such correspondence would require one or more servants to travel the roads daily. Sealing wax and paper for letters had to be bought, though the ink might be made at home of gum, copperas, and gall. Since paper was expensive all during the age, no envelopes were used; instead, the sheets were folded and sealed down with the address on the outside. The fine, neat handwriting of some Elizabethans crowded many expressions of concern for each other's welfare and many endearments into one page of paper, though the elaborate ceremony necessary for correct correspondence prevented getting many ideas into small compass.

With guests in the house the supper hour would lengthen while the host led the conversation all Elizabethans delighted in after meals. When the children had been taken off to bed and the guests had retired to their chambers, in which the beds must all be warmed on cold nights, the housewife would probably think of some last instructions to give a servant before she too retired for the night. Now the master, if not pressed to write some letters, might choose a book to read, and perhaps take it to bed with him if he felt restless and wakeful. During the latter part of the century, Elizabethan libraries had added more and more books to their shelves if the master was a lover of books either for their contents or for their decorative appearance.

Although most books still sold at high prices, the effort to acquire knowledge and social graces appropriate to a cultivated mind increased enormously the sale of cheap as well as expensive editions of books and pamphlets on manners and morals and general information. Cheap editions of expensive encyclopedias of facts relating to everything about the home and garden and farm, and even the world itself, were great favorites with the common people. A herbal, for example, could be found in almost every middle-class home, rubbing the covers of cheap adaptations of manuals like Erasmus' *De Civilitate* or Castiglione's *The Courtier* or Guazzo's *The Civile Conversation*. To learn to act like a gentleman and to give his children the advantages he had missed led many a father to buy the proper books for their instruction. Eventually, therefore, the refining influences of these books became noticeable in the speech and conduct of many middle-class families.

Because of their concern for the whole problem of morals and manners, Puritans carried on their business transactions with the same fervent desire to achieve respectability as they conducted their private lives to win the blessings of the good life after death. Naturally their library shelves would include, besides the usual manuals, books of pious sentences, prayers, sermons, adaptations of the psalms for singing in the home, and many pious pamphlets crowding close to their worn Bible. If the after-supper talk had dealt with some interpretation of the Lord's Prayer, or one of the Ten Commandments, or something in Paul's teaching, or some difficult passage in his Geneva Bible, the master would most certainly choose a book now that would both clarify his mind on the subject and assure him that what he had said was well founded on some analysis by an honored churchman, like Bullinger or Perkins.

If, however, the talk had grown quite animated when first one and then another of the guests had expressed his opinion of the harmful effect of certain popular songs from plays or of secular verse, he might ponder how to combat the evils of coarse levity sung and shouted in the streets. Feeling responsible for the moral superiority of both society and his children, he might then talk with his wife. Although the master knew his good wife would follow where he led, he also knew that she might unwittingly suggest a direction in which to go.

But the master might be the head of a pious Anglican household, and if so he would have the Bishops' Bible and printed copies of sermons preached at St. Paul's Cross. He might also have Foxe's *The Book of Martyrs* and St. Augustine's *The City of God*, but he would certainly have histories of England and the world. Almanacs and books on needlework, lace patterns, and cook books would crowd romances and anthologies of verse like *England's Parnassus* of 1600 with excerpts from the "choicest flowers" of the modern poets, or *England's Helicon* with selections from the most important writers of the century. Such a home would also have many songbooks providing music to some of the favorite lyrics as well as the new songs and their music. These books might be either expensive or cheap according to the owner's means. Next to them might be moral ballads like Martin Parker's, and moral stories like those in William Averell's *A Diall for daintie darlings*. Lyly's books on *Euphues* would have their place, and North's translation of Plutarch's *Lives* would be well worn.

For a time all social classes above the underworld became interested in people of low life, and the literature about the slums fed and intensified this interest. Consequently such books written to teach that evil brings its own reward found their way into most moral households, and Greene's and Dekker's gulls and coneys and repentant authors became household chitchat. Plays and ballads dealing with like material and especially with the causes for women falling from virtue were thoughtfully or thoughtlessly bought and placed in home libraries. The home of modest means bought cheap copies of such books, and the ambitious owner of an imposing home bought expensive editions for display in his sumptuously furnished library. Since Elizabethans did not read for the pleasure of reading but rather for information or consolation, their books were often a good indication of their taste in reading.

As a rule, Elizabethans were provided with too many distractions to read much. The home was such a beehive of industry or entertaining or providing for the morrow that reading hours were snatched at odd moments. Yet women's capacious skirt pockets always carried a book or two for such reading pleasure, but few women and not many men could find time or opportunity to sit long and quietly with a book. That few copies of first editions have survived indicates, perhaps, that these books were read to pieces. This loss occurs more often, however, among fine anthologies of lyrics and airs and songs for the lute than in any other type of literature if one rules out religious material. It was music that made life go round for these people, and it was music in one form or another that took most room on the shelves of their libraries.

In spite of the fact that Elizabethans lived at such a quick tempo, they did not direct their music toward a frenzied or distracting mode of entertainment. At home, especially, they sought an expansion of the soul by means of a cultivated living in spite of what, to us, may seem like flagrant vulgarities in their way of life. The tinkling notes of an instrument, accompanied, perhaps, by the voice of a child or servant, was their relief from the tension caused by some exciting or dangerous or merely monotonous enterprise. Even among the poor the love of music was not stifled.

Consequently, this was a vocal age. In both town and country the householders were apprised of the peddler's coming by his lusty voice shouting his wares in song. In the narrow, dirty streets of London each singing voice strove to be heard above the wheels grinding over cobblestones or the loud cries of carters urging their beasts forward through the slow, congested line of moving wheels, lumbering carts, plodding horses, and padding feet. Along the main roads they came into the city, past the archery fields to the north and past the theaters to the south.

But none among the throng would be more eager than a father returning home after a long absence from his family. He might picture his wife directing the servants in special tasks for the feast in honor of his coming. He might wonder whether the youngest children had grown much, and whether their manners were still natural in their perfection. And he might plan how he would tell them about the success of his journey in spite of its disappointments and dangers and unexpected turns in fortune.

If he was of a philosophical or romantic turn of mind, he might let his thoughts wander as he waited on the slowly moving traffic which he could neither hurry nor circumvent as long as his way toward home forced him to follow the usual mode of entry and dispersal controlled by the city gates. He might, therefore, reflect briefly on the intricacies of the pattern into which his life had been woven by the establishment of his home, and how in preparation for his life as a householder he had been told by his father that marriage was a privilege as well as a duty, but most of all a matter of family policy. These words had never been forgotten, but had risen from time to time demanding attention. Now, at last, they might begin to unravel their meaning for him.

The time was drawing close when he must prepare his first-born son to enter a pattern of society that he realized was far more intricate than that in his own youth. He could still use many of the old words of his father, but now with a conviction born of understanding, of experience. True, his marriage had met the primary urge of man and woman—his, of course, the perpetuation of his own self; and his wife's, the security of a husband's protection for her and her children. But it had meant more than that, and he must make it seem more to his son.

He must be ready to show the pattern of the family as more than a dreary round of duties and responsibilities. That it involved obligations which lasted as long as a father of children lived, he could not deny. That it required a father's best efforts to teach his children to be *willing* to be obedient, he most certainly believed. That the ties between parents and children could never be severed so long as either lived, he was sure was the foundation upon which the whole social structure of his country was built. Did not the Government itself count on family loyalty as indispensable to the health of the nation? Did not the Church look to the family and its perpetuation of family relationships as the very means of its existence? Did not the Church remind him and all who listened to the services day after day and year after year that these family bonds were strong only when love and beauty energized their cohesive strength? That in themselves these bonds were good and right and productive of power?

It was clearer now what he must say to his son—that personal happiness depended on collective happiness, and that both were born and bred and flowered in the home: that the home made living purposive. But he must be sure his son understood what purposive living meant to an Elizabethan. There was such a thing as living for one's own time as well as for those to come after. He had tried to help his son understand why good manners would always have value, and that it was necessary to know how to recognize a person for what he was in order to treat him kindly, with understanding. Only in the center of the family group could this instruction be given. Otherwise the individual might seem to stand alone, for what the family was, he was, and he could never quite sever the bonds uniting them. Family policy could make those bonds cruel, stifling, or lovingly tenuous and strong as steel. Out of the family's daily living grew the bonds. If the father could control them firmly and gently, he could make of those he must guide almost what he willed. And what they became, their children would be.

Back of all he had been trying to impress upon his son about the old rule of conduct was the greater rule: one must endeavor not only to adapt himself intelligently to intercourse with his fellows but also to hold fast to his own soul. It had not been easy to make clear the reason why a knowledge of people was so essential in a world of men who were infinitely different in purpose and ability and desire. But living could not be purposive without intelligent social contact, fellowship, communion; and such social experience must be taught in the home. He had tried to show that the ugly traits, sometimes frightfully ugly traits, of human beings must be recognized and admitted, but at the same time his son must hold fast to a belief in the good element that somehow would break through all evil.

Yet in all this advice which he had tried so carefully to give to his son, how much of it was mere words to him? Listening to advice, good or bad, and testing it or flouting it by trial and error was the way to learn. Now he must help his son to believe that the principles he had set forth were worth testing. In so far as he had been able, he had put his own precepts into action. With his wife's help he had made home a refuge of harmonious living, and without too much preaching he had tried to show that as the homes of the nation sought daily to achieve peaceful relations within themselves, so the principle of purposive living might become more than a pleasant dream. Had he prepared adequately for what he felt must still be spoken to his son? He had cause to believe so, and the words of the Preacher, Koheleth, might comfort him as he approached nearer his home. Long, long ago this wise man had written: "To everything there is a season, and a time to every purpose under the heaven."

It was this need for order and for a self-knowledge which recognized the compulsive purpose of order, this awareness of self in relation to others and a recognition of the reflection of one's own self in others, he must yet discuss with his son. Thus he might become aware of the mystery which bounded life and made each day a challenge. He must remind his son that human reason was fallible, and that he must open his ears to harmonies from a higher intelligence, an intelligence that used such shifting little forces as men for tools to work out its design. This was why he must hold fast to the precious gift of grace by which he might choose between good and evil. This was why he must make the most of his education and teach his children to make the most of theirs. Only by this means could he acquire the self-control that could free his soul from a passion that might otherwise sweep both knowledge and freedom of will into chaos. He must, then, make room in his mind and teach his children to make room in their minds for the unknowable, whose music might yet creep into mortal ears.

Bibliography

This bibliography does not include the plays or familiar literature of the age. To add such titles would make the list endless. All references to Shakespeare are to *Complete Works of Shakespeare*, edited by Hardin Craig (New York: Scott, Foresman and Company, 1951).

Agrippa, Henry Cornelius. *The Commendation of Matrimony*. Translated by David Clapham. London, 1545.
———— *A treatise of the nobilitie of woman Kinde* (1529). Translated by David Clapham. London, 1542.
Alberti, Leon Baptista. *The Art of Love: Or, Love discovered in an hundred severall kindes*. London, 1598.
Allott, Robert. *Wits theatre of the little World*. London, 1599.
Anderson, Ruth Leila. *Elizabethan Psychology and Shakespeare's Plays*. University of Iowa Studies, Vol. III (1927), No. 4.
Aubrey, John. *Brief Lives chiefly of Contemporary set down by John Aubrey between the Years 1669 and 1696*. Andrew Clark (ed.). Oxford, 1898.
Averell, William. *Foure notable histories, applyed to foure worthy examples: As, 1. A Diall for daintie darlings. 2. A spectacle for negligent Parents. 3. A glasse for disobedient Sonnes. 4. And a myrrour for virtuous Maydes. Whereunto is added a Dialogue, expressing the corruptions of this age*. London, 1590.
Aylett, Robert. *Susanna: Or, The Arraignment of the Two Unjust Elders*. London, 1622.
Aylmer, John. *An Harborowe for faithfull and trewe Subjects, agaynst the late blowne Blaste concerninge the government of women*. Strassburg, 1559.
Ayrault, Pierre. *A Discourse for Parents Honour and Authoritie* (1599). Translated by John Budden in 1614. London, 1616.
Bacon, Francis. *Essays and New Atlantis*. G. S. Haight (ed.). New York, 1942.
Baldwin, T. W. *William Shakspere's Small Latine & Lesse Greeke*. 2 vols. Urbana: University of Illinois Press, 1944.
Bansley, Charles. *A treatyse shewing and declaring the pryde and abuse of women now a dayes*. London, 1550(?).
Barckley, Richard. *A Discourse of the Felicitie of Man: Or, His Summum bonum*. London, 1598.
Barton, Lucy. *Historic Costume for the Stage*. Boston: Walter H. Baker Co., 1935.
Baskervill, Charles Read. *The Elizabethan Jig*. Chicago: University of Chicago Press, 1929.
Batty, Bartholomew. *The Christian mans Closet*. Translated by W. Lowth. London, 1581.

Becon, Thomas. *Worckes.* Edinburgh, 1584. See especially *The booke of Matrimony* and *Catechisme* (London, 1581) and *The Sicke Mans Salve* (London, 1559).

Bercher [Barker], William. *The Nobylytie off Women.* London, 1559.

Bishop's Book, The. See *Institution of a Christian Man, The.*

Bodley, Sir Thomas. *The Life of Sir Thomas Bodley, Written by Himself, Together with the First Draft of the Statutes of the Public Library at Oxon* (1545–1613). J. C. Dana and H. W. Kent (eds.). Chicago: McClurg and Co., 1904.

Boyd, M. C. *Elizabethan Music and Musical Criticism.* Philadelphia: University of Pennsylvania Press, 1940.

Bradford, Gamaliel. *Elizabethan Women.* New York: Houghton Mifflin Co., 1936.

Bradshaw, William. *A Marriage Feast: A Sermone on the Former Part of the Second Chapter of the Evangelist John.* London, 1620.

Brathwait, Richard. *The English Gentleman.* London, 1630.

———— *The English Gentleman and the English Gentlewoman: Both In one Volume couched.* London, 1641.

———— *The English Gentlewoman, drawne out to the full Body.* London, 1631.

Brinsley, John. *A Looking-Glasse for Good Women.* London, 1645.

Brooke, Iris, and James Laver. *English Costume from the Fourteenth through the Nineteenth Century.* New York: The Macmillan Co., 1937.

Brooks, Eric St. John. *Sir Christopher Hatton.* London: Jonathan Cape, 1946.

Brown, David. *What Shakespeare Learned at School.* Bucknell University Studies, Vol. I (Spring, 1940).

Bryskett, Lodowick. *A Discourse of Civill Life.* London, 1606.

Bullinger, Henry. *The Christian State of Matrimony.* Translated by Miles Coverdale. London, 1546.

Bundy, Murray W. "Shakespeare and Elizabethan Psychology," *Journal of English and Germanic Philology,* XXIII (1924), 516–49.

Bunny, Edmund. *Of Divorce for Adulterie, and Marrying againe.* Oxford, 1610.

Byrne, M. St. Claire. *Elizabethan Life in Town and Country.* London: Methuen and Co., 1925.

———— *The Elizabethan Home, Discovered in Two Dialogues by Claudius Hollyband and Peter Erondell* (rev. ed.). London: Methuen and Co., 1949.

Calendars of State Papers, Domestic Series, 1591–1594. Mary Anne Everett Green (ed.). London, 1867.

Calendars of State Papers, Domestic Series, 1595–1597]. Mary Anne Everett Green (ed.). London, 1869.

Calendars of State Papers, Domestic Series, 1598–1601. Mary Anne Everett Green (ed.). London, 1869.

Candee, Helen Churchill. *The Tapestry Book.* New York: Tudor Publishing Co., 1935.

Carter, Thomas. *Carters Christian Common Wealth: Or, Domesticall Dutyes deciphered.* London, 1627.

Caxton, William. *Le Grande's Boke of Good Maners*. Translated from the French. London, 1487.

Cecil, Algernon. *A Life of Robert Cecil*. London: J. Murray, 1915.

Cescinsky, Herbert. *English Furniture from Gothic to Sheraton*. Garden City, New York: Garden City Publishing Co., 1937.

Chamberlain, Frederick. *The Sayings of Queen Elizabeth*. New York: Dodd, Mead & Company, 1923.

Chambers, R. W. (ed.). *A General Rule to teche every man that is willynge for to lerne, to serve a lorde or mayster in avery thyng to his plesure*. From a fifteenth-century manuscript in the British Museum. Introduction and notes by Chambers, 1914.

Chambrun, Clara Longworth de. *Shakespeare, Actor-Poet*. New York: D. Appleton and Co., 1927.

Charles, C. J. *Elizabethan Interiors* (3d ed.). New York: F. Greenfield, n.d.

Chelidonius, Tigurinus. *A Most Excellent Hystorie of the institution of Christian Princes*. Translated from Latin into French by Bouaistuan, and from French into English by James Chillester. London, 1571.

Cheyney, Edward P. *A History of England from the Defeat of the Armada to the Death of Elizabeth*. 2 vols. New York: Longmans, Green & Co., 1914–26.

Chuse, Anne R. *Costume Design*. Pelham, New York: Bridgman Publishing Co., 1930.

Chute, Marchette. *Shakespeare of London*. New York: E. P. Dutton and Co., 1949.

Cleaver, Robert. *A Godlie Forme of Household Government*. London, 1598.

Collins, Arthur (ed.). *Letters and Memorials of State: The Sydney Letters*. 2 vols. London, 1746.

Court of good Councell, The. An adaptation of Stefano Guazzo's *The Civile Conversation*. London, 1607.

Craig, Hardin. *The Enchanted Glass*. New York, 1936.

——— "Shakespeare's Depiction of the Passions," *Philological Quarterly*, IV (1925), 289–301.

——— "The Ethics of *King Lear*," *Philological Quarterly*, IV (1925), 97–109.

Crane, Thomas F. *Italian Social Customs of the Sixteenth Century*. New Haven: Yale University Press, 1920.

Crane, W. G. *Wit and Rhetoric in the Renaissance*. New York: Columbia University Press, 1937.

Creizenach, Wilhelm. *The English Drama in the Age of Shakespeare*. Philadelphia: J. B. Lippincott Co., 1916.

Crofts, Robert. *The Lover: or Nuptiall Love*. London, 1638.

Curtis, Mary I. *England of Song and Story*. Boston: Allyn and Bacon, 1931.

Davey, Richard. *The Nine Days Queen, Lady Jane Grey and her Times*. London: Methuen and Co., 1909.

Davies, John. *Works*. A. B. Grosart (ed.). 2 vols. Chertsey Worthies Library, 1878. See especially *A Select Second Husband for Sir Thomas Overburie's Wife, now a Matchless Widow* (1616).

Davis, William Stearns. *Life on a Medieval Barony*. New York: Harper & Bros., 1923.

Devereux, Sir Walter Bourchier. *Lives and Letters of the Devereux, Earls of Essex*. London, 1853.

Ditchfield, Peter Hammpson. *The England of Shakespeare*. New York: E. P. Dutton and Co., 1917.

Donne, John. *Works*. London, 1839. See especially Vol. 4 and Sermon LXXXII.

Dowden, Edward. *Essays Modern and Elizabethan*. New York: J. M. Dent and Sons, 1910.

Draper, John William. "Desdemona: A Compound of Two Cultures," *Revue de Littérature Comparée*, XIII (1933), 337–51.

—— *The Humors and Shakespeare's Characters*. A selected list of Elizabethan treatises, etc., on humors. Durham, N.C.: Duke University Press, 1945.

Dunne, E. Catherine. *The Concept of Ingratitude in Renaissance English Moral Philosophy* (dissertation). Washington, D.C.: The Catholic University Press, 1946.

Dutton, Ralph, and Angus Holden. *English Country Houses Open to the Public*. Boston: Houghton Mifflin Co., 1934.

Edwards, Edward. *The Life and Letters of Sir Walter Raleigh*. London, 1868.

Einstein, Lewis. *Tudor Ideals*. New York: Harcourt, Brace and Co., 1921.

Ellis, Sir Henry (ed.). *Original Letters Illustrative of English History*. London, 1825.

Elyot, Sir Thomas. *The Boke named the Governour*. London, 1530.

—— *The Defence of Good women*. London, 1545.

—— *The education or bringinge up of children, translated oute of Plutarch by syr Thomas Eliot knyght*. London, 1530(?).

Elze, Karl. *William Shakespeare*. Translated by L. Dora Schmitz. London: G. Bell and Sons, 1901.

Erasmus, Desiderius. *The Censure and judgement of Erasmus: Whyther dyvorsemente stondeth with the lawe of God*. Translated by N. Lesse. London, 1550(?).

—— *De Civilitate Morum Puerilium*. Translated by Robert Whytyngton. London, 1532.

—— *A modest meane to Mariage, pleasauntly set foorth by that famous Clarke Erasmus Roterodamus, and translated into Englishe by N. L.[eigh]*. London, 1568.

—— *A ryght frutefull Epystle devysed by the most excellent Clerke Erasmus in laude and prayse of matrymony translated in to Englyshe by Richard Tavernour*. London, 1530(?).

Fairchild, Arthur H. R. "Shakespeare and the Arts of Design," *University of Missouri Studies*, January 1937.

Farnham, Willard. *The Medieval Heritage of Elizabethan Tragedy*. Berkeley: University of California Press, 1936.

—— "The Mirror for Magistrates and Elizabethan Tragedy," *The Journal of English Philology*, XXV (1926), 66–78.

Fenner, Dudley. *The artes of Logike and Rethorike*. Middleburg, 1584.

Fergussen, James. *History of the Modern Styles of Architecture* (3d ed.). Vol. II. New York: Dodd, Mead & Company, 1891.

Fisher, M. F. K. *Serve It Forth.* New York: Harper & Bros., 1937.

Ford, Harold. *Shakespeare: His Ethical Teaching.* London: Smith, 1922.

Fripp, Edgar I. *Shakespeare, Man and Artist.* 2 vols. London: Oxford University Press, 1938.

———— *Shakespeare's Haunts near Stratford.* London: Oxford University Press, 1929.

———— *Shakespeare's Stratford.* London: Oxford University Press, 1928.

Fugger News-Letters, The. Translated by L. S. R. Byrne; Victor Klarwill (ed.). Second Series, 1568–1605. New York: G. P. Putnam's Sons, 1926.

Fuller, Thomas. *The Holy State and the Profane State.* London, 1642. (See also the 1938 edition; M. G. Walten, ed.)

Gardiner, S. R. *History of England from the Accession of James I to the Outbreak of the Civil War, 1603–42.* New York, 1894–96.

Garner, T., and A. Stratton. *The Domestic Architecture of England during the Tudor Period.* London: P. T. Batsford [1908–11?].

Gataker, Thomas. *A Good Wife Gods Gift: A Mariage Sermon.* London, 1620.

Gerard, John. *The Autobiography of an Elizabethan.* Translated from the Latin by Philip Caraman. Introduction by Graham Greene. London and New York: Longmans, Green & Co., 1951.

Gibbon, Charles. *A Work worth the Reading. Wherein is Contayned, five profitable and pithy Questions, very expedient, aswell for Parents to perceive howe to bestowe their Children in Marriage.* London, 1591.

Gibson, Anthony. *A Womans Woorth, defended against all the men in the world.* London, 1599.

Gilbert, Sir Humphrey. *Queene Elizabeths Achademy: A Booke of Precedence.* Frederick J. Furnivall (ed.). London, 1869.

Godfrey, Elizabeth. *Home Life under the Stuarts, 1603–1649.* New York: E. P. Dutton and Co., 1903.

Goff, Lady Cecilie. *A Woman of the Tudor Age.* London: J. Murray, 1930.

Gordon, George Byron. *Rambles in Old London.* London: Macrae Smith and Co., 1924.

Gosson, Stephen. *The Schoole of Abuse.* London, 1579.

Gosynhill, Edward. *The prayse of all women, called Mulierum Pean.* London, 1560(?).

———— *Schoolhouse of Women.* London, 1560.

Gotch, J. Alfred. *Early Renaissance Architecture in England.* London: B. T. Batsford, 1901.

———— *The Growth of the English House.* London: B. T. Batsford, 1909.

———— *Old English Houses.* London: Methuen and Co., 1925.

Gouge, William. *Of Domesticall Duties* (3d ed.). First printed in 1622. London, 1634.

Graves, Thornton S. "The Adventures of Hamlet's Ghost," *Philological Quarterly,* IV (April 1925), 139–50.

Gray, Henry David. "The Evolution of Shakespeare's Heroines," *Journal of English and Germanic Philology,* XII (1913), 122–37.

Guazzo, Stefano. *Civile Conversazione.* Translated by George Pettie as *The Civile Conversation.* London, 1581.

Hall, Hubert. *Society in the Elizabethan Age.* New York: E. P. Dutton and Co., 1902.

Hall, Joseph. *Works.* London, 1634.

Hannay, Patrick. *A Happy Husband: Or, Directions for a Maide to choose her Mate. As also a Wives Behaviour towards her Husband after Marriage.* London, 1619.

Harbage, Alfred. *Shakespeare's Audience.* New York: Columbia University Press, 1941.

Hard, Frederick. "Sir Henry Wotton: Renaissance Gentleman," *The Pacific Spectator,* VII, No. 4 (Autumn, 1953), 364–79.

Harrison, G. B. *The Elizabethan Journals,* revised and reprinted in one volume. New York: The Macmillan Co., 1939.

———— *England in Shakespeare's Day.* New York: Harcourt, Brace and Co., 1928.

———— *A Jacobean Journal, 1603–1606.* New York: The Macmillan Co., 1941.

———— *Shakespeare under Elizabeth.* New York: Henry Holt and Co., 1933.

Harrison, William. *Description of England in Shakspere's Youth,* edited from the first two editions of Holinshed's *Chronicle* by F. J. Furnivall. London, 1877.

Heale, William. *An Apologie for Women: Or, An Opposition to Mr. Dr. G. his assertion, Who held in the Act at Oxforde, Anno. 1608, That it was lawfull for husbands to beate their wives.* Oxford, 1609.

Hearnshaw, F. J. C. (ed.). *Social and Political Ideas of Some Great Thinkers of the Renaissance and Reformation.* London: G. G. Harrap and Co., 1925. See especially A. W. Reed, "Sir Thomas More."

Henderson, Helen W. *A Loiterer in London.* New York: George H. Doran Co., 1924.

Hentzner, Paul. *A Journey into England in the Year of 1598.* Translated by Richard Bently. Strawberry Hill, 1757.

Herford, Charles Harold. *The Normality of Shakespeare Illustrated in His Treatment of Love and Marriage.* Oxford: The English Association, Pamphlet No. 47, September 1920.

———— *Shakespeare's Treatment of Love and Marriage and Other Essays.* London: T. F. Unwin, 1921.

Hervey, Thomas K. *The Book of Christmas.* London, 1888.

Heywiidm, John. *A dialogue concernynge two maner of marryages.* London, 1561.

———— *A dialogue conteinyng the nomber in effect of all the proverbes in the englishe tongue, compact in a matter concernyng two maner of mariages.* London, 1546.

Heywood, Thomas. *Ar't asleepe Husband?* London, 1640.

———— *A Curtaine Lecture.* London, 1637.

———— *How a man may choose a good wife.* London, 1608.

Hole, Christina. *English Home Life, 1500–1800.* London: B. T. Batsford, 1947.

Homilies: Certaine Sermons appointed by the Queenes Majestie, to be declared and read in Churches for the better understanding of the Simple People. London, 1582.

Hornbeak, K. G. *The Complete Letter-Writer in English, 1568–1800.* Northampton, Mass.: *Smith College Studies in Modern Languages,* Vol. XV, No. 3–4 (April–July), 1934.

Hotson, Leslie (ed.). *Queen Elizabeth's Entertainment at Mitcham: Poet, Painter, and Musician.* Foreword by Hotson, who attributes the work to Lyly. Yale Elizabethan Club. New Haven: Yale University Press, 1953.

Hotter, Alfred Carl. *1001 Christmas Facts and Fancies.* London: De la Mare Co., 1937.

Houghton, Walter E., Jr. *The Formation of Thomas Fuller's Holy and Profane States.* Cambridge, Mass., 1938. Harvard Studies in English, No. 19.

Howard, Clare. *English Travellers of the Renaissance.* New York: John Lane Co., 1914.

Hulley, Lincoln. *Shakespeare's Dream of Fair Women.* De Land, Fla.: O. E. Painter Printing Co., 1914.

Hume, Martin S. *The Great Lord Burghley.* New York, 1898.

Humphrey, Lawrence. *Of Nobilitye.* London, 1563.

Hutchinson, Mrs. Lucy Apsley. *Memoirs of the Life of Colonel Hutchinson.* The Rev. Julius Hutchinson (ed.). New York: E. P. Dutton and Co., 1906.

I. G. *An Apologie for Womenkind.* London, 1605.

Institution of a Christian Man, The. Popularly known as *The Bishop's Book.* London: Thomas Barthelet, 1537.

Jeaffreson, John Cordy. *Brides and Bridals* (1672). 2 vols. London, 1872.

Jeayes, I. H. (ed.). *Letters of Philip Gawdy of West Harling, Norfolk, and of London to Various Members of his Family, 1579–1616.* London: J. B. Nichols, 1906.

Jones, Sir Henry. *Essays on Literature and Education.* H. J. W. Hetherington (ed.). London: Hodder, 1924.

Judges, A. V. (ed.). *The Elizabethan Underworld* (tracts and ballads). London: G. Routledge and Sons, Ltd., 1930.

Knappen, Marshall. *Tudor Puritanism.* Chicago: University of Chicago Press, 1939.

———— (ed.). *Two Elizabethan Puritan Diaries.* Chicago: The American Society of Church History, 1933.

Knox, John. *The First Blast of the Trumpet against the monstrous regiment of Women.* Geneva, 1558.

Laneham, Robert. *A Letter of 1575.* Frederick J. Furnivall (ed.). London: Chatto and Windus, 1907.

Latham, Grace. "On Volumnia," *Transactions of the New Shakespeare Society,* Series I, Part I (1887–92), pp. 69–90.

Lawrence, Margaret. *The School of Femininity.* New York: Frederick A. Stokes Co., 1936.

Leach, Arthur F. "The Refoundation of Canterbury Cathedral and Grammar School, 1541," in *Educational Charters and Documents 598–1909.* Cambridge: The University Press, 1911.

Lee, Sidney, and C. T. Onions (eds.). *Shakespeare's England.* 2 vols. Oxford: Clarendon Press, 1916.

Lee, Sidney L. "Elizabethan England and the Jews," *Transactions of the New Shakespeare Society,* Series I, Part II (1887–92), pp. 143–66.

Leeming, Joseph. *The Costume Book.* New York: Frederick A. Stokes Co., 1938.

Lees-Milne, James. *Tudor Renaissance.* London: B. T. Batsford, 1951.

Leigh, Dorothy. *The Mothers Blessing.* London, 1618.

Lemnius, Laevinus. *Herbal for the Bible, drawen into English by T. Newton.* London: E. Bollefant, 1587.

Lenton, Francis. *Characterismi: Or, Lenton's Leasures Expressed in Essayes and Characters Neverbefore written on.* London, 1631.

Letters and Papers, Foreign and Domestic, of the Reign of Henry VIII, 1524–30. Arranged and catalogued by J. S. Brewer. London, 1876. British Museum.

Ling, Nicholas. *Politeuphuia. Wits Common Wealth.* London, 1598.

Lyly, John. *Works.* R. W. Bond (ed.). Oxford: The Clarendon Press, 1902. See also Leslie Hotson.

McClure, Norman Egbert (ed.). *The Letters of John Chamberlain.* 2 vols. Philadelphia: American Philosophical Society, 1939.

MacKenzie, Agnes Mure. *The Women in Shakespeare's Plays.* Garden City, New York: Doubleday, Page and Co., 1924.

Macquoid, Percy. "The Elizabethan Home," in *Shakespeare's England.* Vol. II. Sidney Lee and C. T. Onions (eds.). Oxford: Clarendon Press, 1916.

Madden, D. H. *The Diary of Master William Silence: A Study of Shakespeare and of Elizabethan Sport* (2d ed.). London: Longmans, Green & Co., 1927.

Man in the Moon . . . or The English Fortune Teller, The [by "W.M.," 1609]. J. O. Halliwell (ed.). London, 1849.

Markham, Gervase. *Certaine excellent and new invented Knots and Mazes.* London, 1623.

———— *Cheape and Good Husbandry . . . for beasts and Fowles.* London, 1631.

———— *The Countrie Housewifes garden.* London, 1618.

———— *Country Contentments, or The English Huswife.* London, 1623.

———— *Country Contentments, or the Husbandmans Recreations.* London, 1631.

———— *The English House-wife. Containing the inward and outward Vertues which ought to be in a compleate Woman.* London, 1631.

———— *The whole art of husbandry.* London, 1631.

Mathew, A. H., and A. Calthrop. *A Life of Sir Tobie Matthew, Bacon's Alter Ego.* London: E. Mathews, 1907.

Matthew, David. *Sir Tobie Matthew.* London: Max Parrish, 1950.

Millet, Fred B. *English Courtesy Literature before 1557.* Departments of History and Political and Economic Science, Bulletin 30. Kingston, Ontario: Queen's University, 1919.

More, Edward. *A Lytle and bryefe treatyse, called the defence of women, and especially of Englyshe women, made agaynst the Scholehowse of women.* London, 1560.

More, Paul Elmer. "Sir Henry Wotton," *Shelburne Essays*. New York: G. P. Putnam's Sons, 1908.

Morse, H. K. *Elizabethan Pageantry, A Pictorial Survey of Costume, 1560–1620*. Special Spring Number of *The Studio*. London: The Studio Ltd., 1934.

Moryson, Fynes. *An Itinerary*. London, 1617.

Moulton, R. G. "Some Canons of Character-Interpretation," *Transactions of the New Shakespeare Society*, Series 1, Part I (1877), pp. 123–39.

Mulcaster, Richard. *Positions wherin those primitive circumstances be examined, which are necessarie for the training up of children, either for skill in their booke, or health in their bodie*. London, 1581.

Muller, James Arthur. *Stephen Gardiner and the Tudor Reaction*. New York: The Macmillan Co., 1926.

Murphy, Gwendolen (ed.). *A Cabinet of Characters*. London: H. Milford, 1925.

Nash, Joseph. *The Mansions of England in the Olden Time*. Charles Holme (ed.). Introduction by C. Harrison Townsend. London: The Studio Ltd., 1906.

Neale, J. E. *Queen Elizabeth*. New York: Harcourt, Brace and Co., 1934.

Niccholes, Alexander. *A Discourse of marriage and wiving, and of The greatest Mystery therein contained: How to choose a good Wife from a bad*. London, 1615.

Nichols, John. *The Progresses and Public Processions of Queen Elizabeth*. 3 vols. London, 1825.

———— *The Progresses, Processions, and Festivities of King James I*. London, 1828.

Nicolas, Sir Nicholas Harris (ed.). *Memoirs of the Life and Times of Sir Christopher Hatton*. London: R. Bentley, 1847.

Norris, Herbert. *Costume and Fashions*, Vols. II, VIII. New York: E. P. Dutton and Co., 1938.

Oppenheimer, Sade. "The Elizabethan Citizen and His Wife" (master's thesis). Stanford, Calif.: Stanford University, 1911.

Overbury, Sir Thomas. *Miscellaneous Works*. E. F. Rimbault (ed.). London, 1856.

Palmer, R. Liddesdale. *English Social History in the Making, the Tudor Revolution, 1485–1603*. London: I. Nicholson and Watson, 1934.

Parker, Martin. *A Book of Roxburghe Ballads*, John Payne Collier esq. (ed.). London: Longman, Brown, Green, and Longmans, 1847.

Parkinson, John. *Earthly Paradise* (Elizabethan gardens) (1629). London: Methuen and Co., 1904.

Parry, Edward Abbott. *The Overbury Mystery*. London: T. F. Unwin, 1925.

Passionate Morrice, The (evils of dancing). London, 1593.

Peacham, Henry. *The Compleat Gentleman*. London, 1622.

Perkins, William. *Christian Oeconomie: Or, A Short Survey of the Right Manner of erecting and ordering a Familie, according to the Scriptures*. London, 1609.

Person, David. *Varieties: Or, A Surveigh of rare and excellent matters . . . for all sorts of persons*. London, 1635.

Platt, Sir Hugh. *Delightes for Ladies* (1608). Introduction by G. E. Fussell and Kathleen Rosemary Fussell. London: Crosby Lockwood and Son, Ltd., 1948.

——— *The Jewel House of Art and Nature.* London, 1594.

Plimpton, George Arthur. *The Education of Shakespeare.* London: Oxford University Press, 1933.

Plutarch. *A President for Parentes: Teaching the vertuous training up of Children and holesome information of yongmen.* Translated by Ed. Grant. London: Henry Bynneman, 1571.

Powell, Chilton Latham. *English Domestic Relations, 1487–1653.* New York: Columbia University Press, 1917.

Prynne, William. *A Briefe Answer to Some Materiall Passages, in a late Treatise of the Sabbath-day.* London, 1636.

Purchas, Samuel. *Purchas, his Pilgrim. Microcosmus: Or, The histories of Man; Relating the wonders of his Generation, vanities in his Degeneration, Necessity of his Regeneration.* London, 1619.

——— *Purchas, his Pilgrimage: Or, Relations of the World and the Religions observed in all Ages.* London, 1616.

Quiller-Couch, Sir Arthur Thomas. *Paternity in Shakespeare.* London: H. Milford, 1934.

Raleigh, Sir Walter. *Sir Walter Raleigh's Instructions to His Son and to Posterity* (1632). London: Peter Davies, 1927.

Rawson, Maud Stepney. *Bess of Hardwick and Her Circle.* London: Hutchinson and Co., 1910.

Rea, John D. "Jacques on the Microcosm," *Philological Quarterly,* IV (October 1925), 345–47.

Richardson, C. J., J. D. Harding, Joseph Nash, and H. Shaw. *Old English Mansions.* Special Spring Number of *The Studio.* London: The Studio Ltd., 1915.

Rickert, Edith (ed.). *The Babees Book: Medieval Manners for the Young.* From the texts of Frederick J. Furnivall. London: Chatto and Windus, 1923.

Rimbault, Edward F. (ed.). *The Miscellaneous Works of Sir Thomas Overbury.* London, 1856.

Roberts, Michael. *Elizabethan Prose.* The Life and Letter Series, No. 78. London: Jonathan Cape, 1936.

Robie, Virginia. *Historic Styles of Furniture.* Boston: Houghton Mifflin Co., 1916.

Rogers, Daniel. *Matrimoniall Honour.* London, 1642.

Rollins, Hyder E. *A Pepysian Garland.* Cambridge: Harvard University Press, 1922.

Roper, William. *The Mirrour of Vertue . . . or the Life of Syr Thomas More, Knight, sometime Lo. Chancellour of England.* Paris, 1626.

Rossetti, William M. *Fifty Courtesies for the Table.* E.E.T.S., pub. for the Italian and English. London, 1869.

Routh, E. M. G. *Sir Thomas More and his Friends.* London: H. Milford, 1934.

Rowlands, Samuel. *The Bride* (1617). Boston: The Merrymount Press, printed for C. E. Goodspeed, 1905.

Rowse, A. L. *The England of Elizabeth.* New York: The Macmillan Co., 1951.

Roxburghe Ballads. See Martin Parker.

Rye, William Brenchley. *England as Seen by Foreigners in the Days of Elizabeth and James the First, 1592–1610.* London, 1865.

Salter, Thomas. *A Mirrhor mete for all Mothers, Matrones, and Maidens, intituled the Mirrhor of Modestie* (1579), in John Payne Collier (ed.), *Illustrations of Old English Literature,* Vol. I. London, 1866.

Salzman, L. F. *England in Tudor Times.* London: B. T. Batsford, 1926.

Santayana, S. G. *Two Renaissance Educators: Alberti and Piccolomini.* Boston: Meador Publishing Co., 1930.

Schelling, Felix E. *Elizabethan Drama, 1558–1642.* Boston: Houghton Mifflin Co., 1908.

———— *Elizabethan Playwrights.* New York: Harper, 1925.

———— *English Literature During the Lifetime of Shakespeare.* New York: Henry Holt & Co., 1910.

Schücking, Levin L. *Character Problems in Shakespeare's Plays.* New York: Henry Holt and Co., 1922.

———— "Die Familie bei Shakespeare," *Englische Studien,* 1927–28, pp. 187–226.

Seibel, George. *The Religion of Shakespeare.* London: Watts and Co., 1924.

Seybolt, Robert Francis. *Renaissance Student Life.* The *Paedologia* of Petrus Mosellanus, translated from the Latin. Urbana: University of Illinois Press, 1927.

Shakespeare's England, see Sidney Lee and C. T. Onions.

Sharp, Frank Chapman. *Shakespeare's Portrayal of the Moral Life.* New York: Charles Scribner's Sons, 1902.

Sisson, C. J. *The Judicious Marriage of Mr. Hooker and the Birth of the Laws of Ecclesiastical Polity.* Cambridge: The University Press, 1940.

Smith, Henry. *A Preparation to Mariage.* London, 1591.

———— *The Wedding Garment.* London, 1590.

———— *Works.* Thomas Fuller (ed.). Edinburgh, 1866.

Smith, Logan Pearsall (ed.). *The Life and Letters of Sir Henry Wotton.* 2 vols. Oxford: Clarendon Press, 1907.

Smith, Preserved. *A Key to the Colloquies of Erasmus.* Harvard Theological Studies, XIII. Cambridge: Harvard University Press, 1927.

Snawsell, Robert. *A looking glasse for Maried Folkes.* London, 1610.

Somerville, H. *Madness in Shakespeare's Tragedy.* London: The Richards Press, Ltd., 1929.

Spedding, James A. *The Letters and the Life of Francis Bacon.* 7 vols. London, 1861–74.

Spencer, Theodore. *Shakespeare and the Nature of Man.* Lowell Lectures. New York: The Macmillan Co., 1949.

Stapleton, Thomas. *The Life and Illustrious Martyrdom of Sir Thomas More.* Translated by Philip E. Hallett from the 1588 Latin edition. London: Burns, Oates, & Washbourne, Ltd., 1928.

Steele, Mary Susan. *Plays and Masques at Court.* New Haven: Yale University Press, 1928.

Steinbicker, S. T. D. *Poor Relief in the Sixteenth Century*. Washington, D.C.: The Catholic University Press, 1937. Chaps. II, IX.

Stephens, John. *Satyrical Essayes, Characters and Others*. London, 1615.

Stephenson, Henry Thew. *The Elizabethan People*. New York: Henry Holt and Co., 1910.

Stevenson, Robert Louis. *Familiar Studies of Men and Books*. London, 1882. Chapter on John Knox.

Stopes, Charlotte Carmichael. *The Life of Henry, Third Earl of South-ampton, Shakespeare's Patron*. Cambridge: The University Press, 1922.

———— *Shakespeare's Environment* (2d ed.). London: J. Bell and Sons, 1918. See especially "Sixteenth Century Women Students."

Stow, John. *Annales . . . continued by Edmund Howes*. London, 1631.

———— *A Survey of London, 1598*. C. L. Kingsford (ed.). 2 vols. Oxford: Clarendon Press, 1908.

Stoye, John Walter. *English Travellers Abroad, 1604–1667*. London: Jonathan Cape, 1952.

Strype, John. *Historical Collections of the Life and Acts of the Right Reverend Father in God, John Aylmer* (1701). Oxford, 1821.

———— *Memorials of Thomas Cranmer, Archbishop of Canterbury* (1694). Edition with notes. London, 1853.

Stubbes, Philip. *The Anatomie of Abuses* (1583). Frederick J. Furnivall (ed.). London, 1877–79.

———— *A Christall Glas, for Christian Women: . . . of a right vertuous life and Christian death . . .* London, 1590.

———— *A Perfect Pathway to Felicity* (1610). In Furnivall edition of *The Anatomie of Abuses* (1877–79), Part I.

Studies in Shakespeare. Arthur D. Matthews and Clark M. Emery (eds.). Coral Gables, Fla.: University of Miami Press, 1953. See especially "The Problem of Ophelia," by J. Max Patrick.

Swetnam, Joseph. *The Araignment of Lewde, idle, froward, and unconstant women with a commendation of wise, vertuous, and honest women Plesant for married Men, and hurtfull to none*. London, 1615.

Swinburne, Henry. *A Treatise of Spousals or Matrimonial Contracts*. London, 1686.

Taylor, Henry Osborne. *Thought and Expression in the Sixteenth Century*. New York: The Macmillan Co., 1920.

Taylor, Jeremy. *Works*. London, 1862. Vol. IV. See especially "The Marriage Ring; or the Mysteriousness and Duties of Marriage" (*ca.* 1650).

Tell-Trothes New-yeares Gift. (News from hell about evils of jealousy.) London, 1593.

Tilley, M. P. *A Dictionary of the Proverbs in England in the 16th and 17th Centuries*. Ann Arbor: University of Michigan Press, 1950.

Tillyard, E. M. W. *The Elizabethan World Picture*. New York: The Macmillan Co., 1944.

Tilney, Edmund. *A brief and pleasant discourse of duties in Mariage, called the Flower of Friendshippe*. London, 1568.

Turberville, George. *The Noble Arte of Venerie or Hunting*. London, 1575.

Tusser, Thomas. *Good Points of Husbandry*. Dorothy Hartley (ed.). London: London Country Life, Ltd., 1931. The 1557 original facsimile on pp. 25–48.

Tuvil, Daniel. *Asylum veneris, or a sanctuary for Ladies.* London, 1616.

Twyne, Thomas. *The Schoolemaster or Teacher of table philosophie.* London, 1576.

Vaughan, William. *The Golden Grove.* London, 1599 or 1600.

Verney, Frances Parthenope, and Margaret M. Verney (compilers). *Memoirs of the Verney Family during the 17th Century.* New York: Longmans, Green and Co., 1925.

Vives, Juan Luis (Joannes Ludovicus). *The Instruction of a Christian Woman* (1523). Translated by Richard Hyrde in 1540, republished in 1541.

——— "The Office and Duetie of an Husband" (1550). Sir Edgerton Brydges (ed.). Translated by Thomas Paynell, 1553. *Censura Literaria,* IX, 25–31, 1809.

——— *Tudor School-Boy Life: Dialogues* (1539). Introduction by Foster Watson. London: J. M. Dent and Co., 1908.

Ward, H. Snowden, and Catherine Weed Ward. *Shakespeare's Town and Times.* London, 1896.

Westermarck, Edward. *A Short History of Marriage.* New York: The Macmillan Co., 1926.

W.M. *The Man in the Moon.* See *Man in the Moon, The.*

Whately, William. *A Bride-Bush: or, A Direction for Married Persons. Plainely Describing the Duties Common to both, and peculiar to each of them.* London, 1619.

Wheatley, Henry B. "London and the Life of the Town," in *Shakespeare's England.* Sidney Lee and C. T. Onions (eds.). Vol. II. Oxford: Clarendon Press, 1916.

Whiffen, Marcus. *An Introduction to Elizabethan and Jacobean Architecture.* London: Art Technics, Ltd., 1952.

Whitforde, Richard. *A werke for housholders or for them yt have the gydynge or governaunce of any company.* London, 1530.

Williams, Franklin B. *Elizabethan England.* Museum Extension Publications, Illustrative Set, No. 1. Boston: Museum of Fine Arts, 1942.

Wilson, F. P. *The Plague Pamphlets of Thomas Dekker.* Oxford: Clarendon Press, 1925.

Wilson, Violet A. *Queen Elizabeth's Maids of Honour and Ladies of the Privy Chamber.* London: John Lane, The Bodley Head, 1922.

——— *Society Women of Shakespeare's Time.* New York: E. P. Dutton and Co., 1925.

Wragge, Sybil (ed.). *The Age Revealed.* London and New York: Thomas Nelson and Sons, Ltd., 1929.

Wright, Louis B. *Middle-Class Culture in Elizabethan England.* Chapel Hill: University of North Carolina Press, 1935.

Xenophon. *Treatise of the Household.* Translated by Gentian Hervet. London, 1537.

Yates, Frances A. *John Florio: The Life of an Italian in Shakespeare's England.* Cambridge: The University Press, 1934.

INDEX

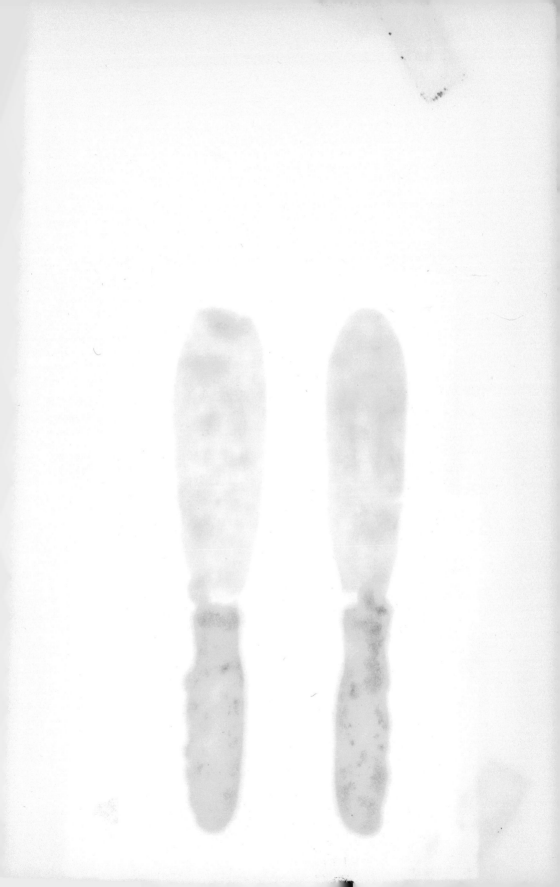

DATE DUE

DEC 1 2 2008	